D1565469

ACTING THE RIGHT PART

ACTING

POLITICAL THEATER AND POPULAR DRAM

THE RIGHT PART

CONTEMPORARY CHINA

Xiaomei Chen

University of Hawai'i Press | Honolulu

© 2002 University of Hawai'i Press
All rights reserved
Printed in the United States of America
07 06 05 04 03 02   6 5 4 3 2 1

Library of Congress Cataloging-in-Publication Data
Chen, Xiaomei.
    Acting the right part : political theater and popular
drama in contemporary China / Xiaomei Chen.
        p.   cm.
    Includes bibliographical references and index.
    ISBN 0–8248–2287–0 (alk. paper) —
ISBN 0–8248–2483–0 (paper : alk. paper)
    1. Chinese drama—20th century—History and
criticism.   I. Title: Political theater and popular
drama in contemporary China.   II. Title.

PL2393.C524   2002
895.1'25209—dc21   2001037790

University of Hawai'i Press books are printed on acid-free
paper and meet the guidelines for permanence and dura-
bility of the Council on Library Resources.

Designed by April Leidig-Higgins
Printed by The Maple-Vail Book Manufacturing Group

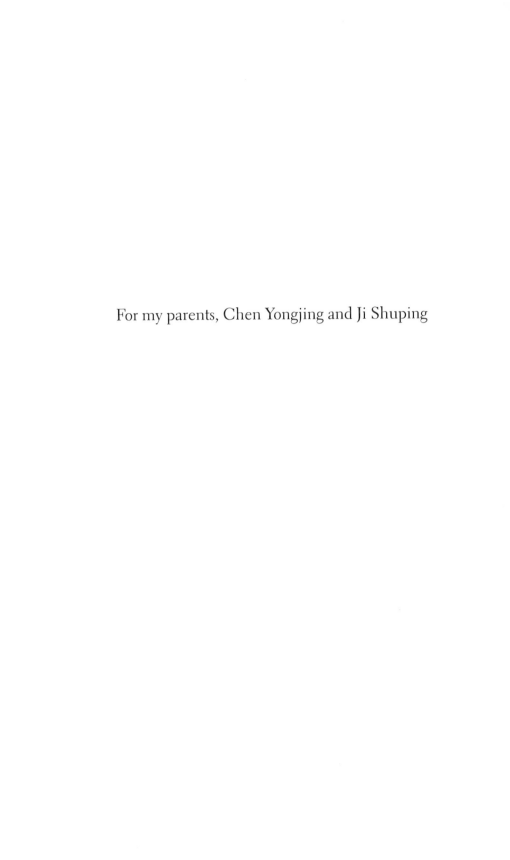

For my parents, Chen Yongjing and Ji Shuping

CONTENTS

ACKNOWLEDGMENTS

Acknowledgments are difficult to write for a book project ten years in the making. Inevitably I will omit the names of people who have in one way or the other helped me in most generous ways.

This study was first supported by an Andrew W. Mellon Fellowship from the Stanford Humanities Center for the 1990–1991 academic year, which allowed me an opportunity to use the Hoover Library to conduct my initial research on contemporary Chinese drama. A seed grant from Ohio State University and a special research assignment grant from the College of Humanities provided an uninterrupted period of writing for two quarters, during which I was able to complete two chapters on model theater. An Andrew W. Mellon Fellowship for Area Studies awarded by the Library of Congress for part of 1998 allowed me finally to revise the manuscript. A Pacific Cultural Foundation Fellowship in 1994 and a grant-in-aid from the College of Humanities at Ohio State in 1997 provided me with funds to travel and do research in China. Finally, the College of Humanities graciously granted me a subvention to cover the cost of color illustrations for this publication.

I am very grateful to my friends and colleagues for their nurturing spirit and for continued support from my two departments, the Department of East Asian Languages and Literatures and the Department of Comparative Studies at the Ohio State University. In particular, I would like to thank

Kirk Denton, who never fails to render his friendship, support, and help when most needed, and whose dedication to the field is an inspiration. I am also fortunate to be able to work with Julia Andrews, whose exemplary work on modern Chinese art encouraged my interest in interdisciplinary studies of modern China. Our collaborative work on the Interdisciplinary Symposia on "Visual Culture as Memory in Modern China" in 1999 has left an imprint on the final revision of the Introduction and the chapters on model theater, in which I connected theatrical performance with other aspects of visual culture. I would like to thank Patricia Sieber for her conversations and for providing valuable suggestions for the Introduction; Jiwei Ci for critiquing earlier drafts on model theater; Karen Winstead and Barbara Mittler for commenting on the earlier versions of the manuscript; and my colleagues and friends from the Department of Comparative Studies, whose group discussion on the Introduction speeded its completion.

I would also like to thank those scholars who encouraged and supported my research, among them Paul Pickowicz, Dai Jinhua, Michelle Yeh, Jeffrey Wasserstrom, Michel Hockx, Edward Gunn, Leo Ou-fan Lee, Mayfair Yang, Barbara Mittler, Lydia Liu, Hu Ying, Meng Yue, Wen-hsin Yeh, Kuiyi Shen, Lindsay Jones, Thomas Kasulis, Chris Zacher, Julia Watson, Jennifer Terry, Galal Walker, Shelly Quinn, James Marshall Unger, William Tyler, Sabra Webber, and David Horn. I thank my former teachers at Indiana University, Sumie Jones for her caring spirit and for remaining my mentor many years after graduate school, and Eugene Ouyang, for reading through the manuscript and for his continuing faith in my work. I am also grateful to graduate students in my seminars (Chinese 879 and 764) for being sounding boards for the earlier drafts of my chapters. Parts of this study were presented in talks at the University of California at Berkeley, National Normal University in Taipei, University of California at Santa Barbara, University of Westminster, State University of New York at Buffalo, and the University of California at San Diego, and I would like to express my gratitude to those audiences for their comments and critiques. I thank two anonymous readers whose suggestions were helpful in revising this book, executive editor Patricia Crosby for her professionalism and efficiency, copy editor Barbara Folsom for her patience and skills, and managing editors Masako Ikeda and Cheri Dunn for their patient help throughout the process.

Earlier versions of parts of this book were published in the following places: "The Making of a Revolutionary Stage: Chinese Model Theater and Western Influences," in *East of West: Cross-Cultural Performance and the Staging of Difference,* ed. Claire Sponsler and Xiaomei Chen (New York: Palgrave, 2000), 125–140; "Can Tiananmen Theater Go Global? A Case of Cultural Studies from a Non-Western Perspective," in *Poetrica,* ed. Kawamoto Koji and Sumie Jones, 52 (1999): 19–33; "Audience, Applause, and Counter-Theater: Border-Crossing in 'Social Problem Plays' in Post-Mao China," *New Literary History* 29.1 (winter 1998): 101–120; "Feminism, Countervoices, and the Utterance of Women as Dramatic Other in Post-Mao Theater," *Canadian Review of Comparative Literature* 24.4 (1997): 819–828; "A Stage of Their Own: the Problematics of Women's Theater in Post-Maoist China," the *Journal of Asian Studies* 56.1 (February 1997): 3–25, and "Time, Money, and Work: The Flow of Transnational Cultural Capital in the Making of Neo-American Nationalism in Chinese American Women Writers' Autobiographies," *Journal of American Studies* (Seoul) 29.2 (winter 1997): 414–421.

Special thanks go to Gerd Kaminski and the Ludwig Boltzmann Institute for Research on China and Southeast Asia for their permission to reprint two children's paintings, and to Harriet Evans and the University of Westminster Chinese Poster Collections for their permission to use two posters. I am also grateful to Lin Kehuan, the president of China Youth Art Theater, who granted me permission to use the stage photos of the theater's performance as illustrations. Due to the complexity of copyright issues, I was not able to use stage photos of other theaters in China. Not being able to include their performance photos does not in any way suggest a lack of respect for their work. On the contrary, I hope this book does justice to the significance of all the theaters in China that inspired it in the first place.

I would also like to thank my parents for inspiring my interest in Chinese drama and theater at an early age and for believing in my work. It is most unfortunate that my father did not live to see the publication of this book, although he listened patiently about how I conceived and wrote it. I am grateful to my mother, brother, and sister, especially during the last three months, when we moved through the difficult period of losing our father, for sharing their thoughts on how to celebrate his life dedicated to the development of modern Chinese drama.

Last but not least, I thank Mark Halperin for reading and critiquing the entire manuscript. I am grateful for his confidence, devotion, and good cheer.

Prologue

Written fourteen years after I became part of the Chinese diaspora in America, this book is intimately related to my memories of growing up in a family of celebrated theatrical artists in Beijing. In my early childhood, theater was a form of "child's play," a taste of paradise granted me each Saturday night, when I was placed on a small stool next to the stage lights, at the corner of what seemed the immeasurably vast stage of the China Youth Art Theater (Zhongguo qingnian yishu juyuan). From behind the curtains, I watched with curiosity and wonder as my mother played the role of Almaviva, the countess in *The Marriage of Figaro (Feijialou de hunyin)*, performed for the first time in 1962. Well known in the Western theater repertoire, this play was originally written by Pierre-Augustin Caron de Beaumarchais, and on the occasion of its premiere in 1784, it met with ecstatic applause from all sections of the house not occupied by the aristocracy. My parents later told me that, although pronounced foreign and bourgeois by Marxist doctrinaires, *The Marriage of Figaro* was nevertheless a remarkable and thoroughly revolutionary piece of theater for its time. In the historical context of the coming French Revolution, it can be imagined what alarm and fright the spectacle of the servant Figaro daring to mock his master gave the aristocratic members of the audience. I was also told that the performance of this French play on the Chinese stage was intended to illustrate a revolutionary truth taught by Chairman Mao Zedong —to wit, that those of the most exalted class strata were the most foolish among us, whereas society's humblest were the most intelligent.

I also watched my mother in the Chinese play *Young Folk in a Remote Region* (*Yuanfang qingnian*; premiered in 1963) playing the role of Amina, a beautiful Moslem girl who devotes herself to constructing the socialist motherland in the Xinjiang Uighur Autonomous Region. It was beyond my powers at the time to discern that these two culturally different plays both re-created two extraordinary revolutionary dramas taking place on the larger stage of the outside world. Unexpectedly, the antiroyalist French play could be viewed as pertaining somehow to the Chinese ethnic-minority play about thousands of ex-slaves in feudal pre-1949 Xinjiang enjoying for the first time the fruits of a socialist revolution.[1] The slaves were depicted as masters of a new Chinese nation—as happy citizens in a predominantly Han state that generously and lovingly "parented" its fifty-five-plus ethnic minority groups, as seen in the harmonious Uighur community (Fig. 1). I later learned that Wu Yuxiao, a Han Chinese, wrote the play after living in Xinjiang, where he gained firsthand experience in the life-style of minority groups. The play premiered in Beijing in December 1963 and enjoyed a successful run of seventy-six performances in the first season, an impressive record in comparison to the other ten plays that opened the same year.[2] Ten premieres in the single year of 1963 also marked a record high in the history of the China Youth Art Theater. The theater thrived at that time, with approximately two hundred professional employees. Such state sponsorship, which provided an unparalleled opportunity for developing the dramatic arts in the 1950s and 1960s, disappeared in post-Maoist China.

At age ten I was awaiting my mother's return from her year-long tour in Xinjiang, where, in addition to playing her acclaimed role in *Young Folk in a Remote Region*, she coached the Moslem amateur actors and actresses in stage acting. I remember how, in the breezy September evenings, I felt reluctant to go to bed, sitting instead on a stool in the courtyard, counting the stars in the sky and guessing which ones were twinkling over the faraway land where my mother was. I was not then aware that this play,

FIGURE 1. *Young Folk in a Remote Region*, premiered by the China Youth Art Theater in 1963.

written and performed by Han people, the majority ethnic group, was already being introduced in the vast areas inhabited by diverse ethnic and religious groups as an exemplar of popular theater.[3] In contrast to the traditional theater of indigenous cultures, this new and modern dramatic genre was being explored as a means both of teaching Mandarin, the major Han dialect, and the way of life of the Han people. Ultimately, it became a convenient medium through which still other ethnic and religious groups might express their experience under socialist China in Han terms. Nor was I then in a position to foretell the powerful role played by theater in contemporary political culture in creating a Chinese national identity centered around Han culture and paving the way for various ethnic identities to assume their place in a socialist "melting pot."

In more than one sense, Chinese theater exemplifies Ronald Harwood's description of theater as "by its nature giv[ing] rise to the most vehement enthusiasms and hostilities."[4] I received an early impression of this function when I made my own theater debut, at age four, playing the part of little Yingzi (Xiao Yingzi), a Korean girl in *Iron Transportation Troops* (*Gangtie yunshubing*). This 1958 production[5] portrayed the Chinese volunteer soldiers who were fighting on the side of the North Korean Communist army against South Korean troops and their US military advisors

FIGURE 2. *Iron Transportation Troops*, premiered by the China Youth Art Theater in 1954.

in the Korean War of 1951. During my few minutes on stage I was carried in the arms of a Korean woman, who gave Chinese soldiers an account of how I had become blind after picking up a "toy" (which turned out to be an explosive device) dropped by a US bomber. "Why did American devils deliberately target and hurt children?" the Korean woman indignantly asked (Fig. 2).[6] The Chinese soldiers compared the miserable lot of Korean children with the felicity of Chinese children in Beijing, from whom they had just received letters and gifts in celebration of National Day (October 1). On the eve of this day the children had been asking what their "dear uncles"[7] would be doing in war-stricken Korea the next morning, during the hours they themselves would be taking part in the annual Tiananmen Square parade. Intent on answering this question in deeds rather than mere words, the Chinese soldiers vowed to avenge, more fearlessly than ever, the injuries inflicted on innocent Korean people by US imperialism. Despite my awareness that I was only participating in a type of child's play, as well as a theatrical play, this early exposure to nation-

FIGURE 3. A *Doll's House*, performed by the China Youth Art Theater in 1956.

alist sentiments in the China Youth Art Theater made a lasting impression on me, as did the internationalist and anticolonialist initiatives being played out on the global stage outside the theater during my formative years in the People's Republic of China (PRC) in the 1950s and 1960s.

My childhood world of play was also influenced by the renown of my father, who was equally well known in the theater for organizing, directing, and training his illustrious team of stage designers.[8] Theatrical histories cite his achievements in designing the stage settings and costumes for lustrous productions of Gogol's *The Inspector General (Qinchai dachen)* premiered in 1952,[9] Chekhov's *Uncle Vanya (Wanniya jiujiu)* in 1954,[10] Ibsen's *A Doll's House (Nuola)* in 1956,[11] and Schiller's *Love and Intrigue (Yinmou yu aiqing)* in 1959.[12] In effect, I grew up absorbing the stories of my parents' shared glory: my mother's acclaimed roles as Nora in *A Doll's House* (Fig. 3) and as Yelena (standing in the middle) in *Uncle Vanya* (Fig. 4) were more than complemented by my father's prize-winning stage designs for these two plays. In the long history of Chinese theater, which saw the proliferation of numerous Nora-like characters thanks to the far-reaching influence of Ibsen after 1919, my mother's Nora was cited as

FIGURE 4. *Uncle Vanya*, performed by the China Youth Art Theater in 1954.

the first to grace the PRC stage after 1949. I was amazed to see exhibited in Norway six 18 × 24-inch photos of this 1956 production of *A Doll's House*, featuring my mother in the foreground and my father's stage design in the background. Years after this performance, my mother was invited to Oslo by the National Theater of Norway and the Norwegian Drama Festival in Commemoration of the Centennial Birth of Ibsen in 1996, in recognition of the "brilliant Nora" she had created on the Chinese stage. As their distinguished guest, on September 13, she visited Ibsen's residence in his native village of Skien. My seventy-two-year-old mother was surprised that her performance of forty years before should have had such wide-ranging impact, although Chinese theater historians apparently remained unaware of it. These photos of the Chinese production of *A Doll's House*, selected for permanent display from many similar photos of productions representing other diverse cultures and languages, were meant to illustrate the extension of Ibsen's influence to a socialist country with a very different ideological and cultural heritage.

This account reflects a distinctive moment in the Chinese theater's golden age of the 1950s. The history of The China Youth Art Theater reveals that the socialist stage in the PRC before the Cultural Revolution

FIGURE 5. *How Steel Is Made*, premiered by the China Youth Art Theater in 1950.

produced many bright theater stars and luminous performances in plays from the Western repertoire. From 1952 to 1962 the China Youth Art Theater performed eleven other plays from foreign countries, such as the USSR, Czechoslovakia, India,[13] Japan, and Argentina, solidifying its reputation for producing world-class foreign plays. Many theatergoers remember the 1950 premiere of a Russian play *How Steel Is Made (Gangtie shi zhenyang liancheng de)*, which promoted the image of Pavel Korchaghin (Bao'er Kechajin), a Soviet national hero, as a role model for many young people in Beijing. Based on an autobiographical novel of the same title *(Kak zakalyalas' stal')* by Nikolay Alekseyevich Ostrovsky, the play represented the life story of Pavel, who, in spite of paralysis and blindness, still pursued his revolutionary career with an optimistic spirit. As a crucial step in his earlier career, Pavel had to break up with his first love from the bourgeoisie (Fig. 5). The play was such a success in Beijing that Jin Shan, the actor who played Pavel, was frequently invited by young people to give lectures on Pavel's life stories and on his performing experience as Pavel. During one performance, the audience waited for three hours, without complaint, for his eventual appearance after his car broke down during his return from a lecture tour in Tianjin. The performance did not end until one o'clock in the morning, when many audience members had to walk home after the buses had stopped running.[14]

Unfortunately, this cosmopolitan tradition was aborted in 1963 with Mao Zedong's call "to never forget class struggle," which resulted that year in the openings of ten plays, six of which[15] had in common the theme of "class struggle" as it supposedly was manifested in socialist China.[16] Chinese audiences would have to wait almost twenty years to see the China Youth Art Theater put on another foreign play, Brecht's *The Life of Galileo (Jialilue zhuan)* in 1979. This was followed, in 1980, by *Guess Who's Coming to Dinner? (Caiyicai, shuilai chi wancan)*, adapted from an American movie[17] and the first American play ever produced in the PRC after Nixon's visit to China in 1972. Chinese theater had traveled a long way since 1958, when I had appeared in *Iron Transportation Troops* as the young victim of American imperialist soldiers.

For me as a child, theater was the window through which I came to view Beijing, the city, and China, the motherland. Through this window I also gradually grasped how Beijing functioned as a central stage for the performance of historical events and for imagining successive revolutions. Situated on East Chang'an Street, which leads westward toward Tiananmen Square, the building housing the China Youth Art Theater was itself a geopolitical landmark not far from other national monuments clustered in and around the square. Previously a movie theater whose screenings gave Chinese audiences a glimpse into Hollywood culture and its influence on the West, the site was remodeled in 1951 to serve as a platform for socialist drama, in itself a milestone in the young republic's political and cultural life. As the designated "national theater *(guojia juyuan)*," the only one under the direct jurisdiction of the PRC's Ministry of Culture,[18] the administrators of the China Youth Art Theater, in the years to come, tried especially hard to see to it that its repertoire would reflect China's past and present national history.

First established in 1941 as Yan'an Youth Art Theater in the liberated area of the Chinese Communist Party (CCP) during World War II, the company was renamed China Youth Art Theater on April 16, 1949, in Beijing, as part of the events celebrating the republic's founding. Liao Chengzhi, the first president of the theater, declared his "two-fists policy" in 1950, with which he hoped to combine the strength of two groups of dramatists—those from the KMT (Nationalist Party) areas such as Nanjing, Shanghai, and Chongqing, and those from the liberated areas— in their efforts to establish a first-rate national theater true to its name. Figure 6 demonstrates the atmosphere of a staff meeting when Liao delivered his speech. A survey of the company's repertoire over fifty years (1949–1999) testifies to a tenacious preservation of the plays from the time span extending from the May Fourth movement (1915–1925)[19] to the PRC period.[20] Its nearly two hundred multi-act plays and seventy one-act

FIGURE 6. Members of the China Youth Art Theater listening to a speech delivered by Liao Chengzhi, the first president of the theater, in 1950. It was held in the auditorium of the theater compound in Dongdan Street, now part of the Oriental Plaza.

plays[21] show a team of dedicated artists fully realizing its mission as China's national theater, whose history was intricately interwoven with the history of a new nation/state. The theater's intimate identification with the nation/state and its mass audiences reached its zenith during the socialist era of the 1950s and early 1960s. Figure 7 records the crowd waiting for the 1950 premiere of Lao She's *Fang Zhenzhu*, a play depicting the title heroine's struggles as a folk performer in Beijing before liberation. Considering the accomplishments of such a national institution, one must deplore the destruction of its building in 1994 to make room for an "Oriental Plaza," a shopping mall cosponsored by a Hong Kong entrepreneur. In a post-socialist era when economic growth and materialist pursuit turned audiences away from theater, a previously prestigious national theater, deprived of its venue, was forced to turn to popular-media ventures like television drama. Thus do we arrive at the current, sad chapter of the China Youth Art Theater's story, to which I will return at the end of my Introduction.

To this day I continue to think back to the many times when, after school, I would get off the bus on East Chang'an Street and make a little

FIGURE 7. The audience crowd in front of Youth Palace (Qingnian gong), the original name of the theater along East Chang'an Street where the China Youth Art Theater performed for decades before it was torn down in 1994.

detour so I could glimpse the "picture" windows of the China Youth Art Theater, that is, the displayed photographs of dramatic performances. Amid the brilliant golden colors of October, I would marvel at the building's handsome decor and lose myself in contemplation of posters heralding new plays to be staged on National Day, when my long anticipation would be rewarded with the opportunity to venture once more into the theater and sample the new, thrilling offerings. The plays put on by the China Youth Art Theater and by other theaters in Beijing provided me with a formal and informal ideological tutelage from which I learned who I was and what was expected of me as a young citizen. Although most of the people in the audience were adults (an unfortunate circumstance from a child's perspective), enthusiastically applauding along with them the heroic actions on stage cemented my identity as a member of the young republic, fortunate to have been born and raised in the brilliant sunshine of the socialist motherland.

I grew up with dramatic characters who depicted the handsome heroes

FIGURE 8. *Red Storm*, premiered by the China Youth Art Theater in 1958.

and beautiful heroines in worker, peasant, and soldier plays *(gong-nong-bing xiju)*, a core repertoire of the China Youth Art Theater.[22] The worker play *Red Storm (Hongse fengbao)* left me with a particularly deep impression of its spectacular staging of the Beijing-Hankou railway workers strike on February 7, 1923. Premiered in 1958 to commemorate the thirty-fifth anniversary of the event, Jin Shan wrote the script in two weeks, then directed and played the lawyer Shi Yang, an underground CCP leader of the worker's union later murdered by the authorities.[23] Figure 8 records one famous scene where a charismatic Shi Yang, in a soliloquy of more than one hundred sentences, defends the accused workers with passion, grace, and elegance. I was told that this speech established a "Jin Shan style of acting" and was repeatedly imitated by drama instructors in their teaching and by applicants to drama school in their auditions. Some people watched the performance night after night: they quietly came in and sat down in the last row in the middle of the performance, just in time to savor this speech. A charming Shi Yang helped me relate to a group of passionate railway workers depicted on stage, whose simplicity, honesty, and devotion to their cause inspired me to try to grow up just like them.

I also treasure a memory of watching peasant plays such as *Li Shuang-shuang*, in which the title heroine represented the best and brightest women in rural China. I enjoyed the same story from other genres: a 1960 fiction

FIGURE 9. *Li Shuangshuang,* premiered by the China Youth Art Theater in 1963.

entitled A *Brief Biography of Li Shuangshuang (Li Shuangshuang xiao-zhuan)* written by Li Zhun; a 1962 "picture book" *(Lianhuanhua)* for children; and the popular 1962 film by Beijing Film Studio that had won a "one-hundred-flower" award. Situated in the general background of the Great Leap Forward of 1958, these works depict Li Shuangshuang as a witty, selfless, and courageous woman who dares to criticize selfish fellow villagers despite her husband's efforts to stop her from alienating too many people. In my younger years, Li Shuangshuang seemed to be a perfect role model who could reconcile the demand to serve the public and her commitment to her husband. Such a complex relationship inspired some of the best dramatic scenes, marked by quarrels, compromises, separations, and homecomings. Figure 9 shows one such moment, when the couple breaks into laughter after a tearful fight. The story has a happy ending, as Li wins her husband's love and respect both as a model member of the People's Commune and as a devoted wife. Yu Daiqin, who played the role of Li Shuangshuang after having lived with peasants for months, won national acclaim for her performance as a lively, beautiful, and, most important, believable peasant woman, who was accepted by her peers when the play toured the countryside after its Beijing premiere. My teenage

FIGURE 10. *The Leopard Bay Battle,* premiered by the China Youth Art Theater in 1964.

attachment to Li Shuangshuang helped me later in the countryside, when I expected to live a peasant's life as she had.

Among the soldier plays performed by the China Youth Art Theater, I remember especially well the dramatic success of *The Leopard Bay Battle (Baoziwan zhandou),* premiered in 1964.[24] The play depicts Ding Yong, a brave CCP commander who leads his soldiers in another "battle" for self-reliance to defeat the KMT blockade. Figure 10 illustrates the moment when Ding shows his soldiers a new spinning wheel to make cloth for their army uniforms. I well remember the outstanding performance of cast members such as Lei Ping, who actually participated in these events in Yan'an during the war. Her practiced spinning and weaving on stage and her flamboyant personality as a woman soldier impressed me with the idea of art imitating life, which helped me to appreciate socialist theater in its salad days. Knowing her personally as a family friend and a caring "aunt," I loved her stage characters and admired her pursuit of a revolutionary acting career during the war.

Deeply engraved in my memory also were those confusing times during the early days of the Chinese Cultural Revolution (1966–1976) when I saw my father, for the first time after he had been taken into custody by the Red Guards, waiting in line in the theater's cafeteria for lunch along with several dozens of counterrevolutionaries rounded up for having promoted "poisonous" plays advocating Western and bourgeois ideologies. I remember my mother periodically putting together a bundle of daily necessities to be sent to my father, who, on a piece of paper passed on to my mother, seldom forgot to ask for more of Chairman Mao's works, so that he could study them even harder in order to reform himself into an artist once again acceptable by the people. I remember, in particular, how my mother took me and my brother to the Great Wall, finally fulfilling one promise for which she had never had time before the Cultural Revolution, when she was devoting all her time and energies to dramatic performances for the masses. After we returned from my first exciting train trip to the outskirts of Beijing, however, she instructed me how to cook and how to open the drawer where money and food-ration coupons were kept, so that I could take care of myself and my brother should she not come home from work the next day. As one of the most famous actresses instrumental in promoting Western drama, she expected to be taken into custody by the Red Guards any day. I remember even more vividly how, after the Cultural Revolution ended, my mother and father once again enthusiastically threw themselves into reviving dramatic productions without wasting any time to settle personal scores. Regardless of whether she was playing the protagonist in an anti–Gang of Four play, or a minor role in a French play celebrating the uprising of the People's Communes, my mother took her roles seriously and left behind on the Chinese stage, with her tears, laughter, and sweat, vivid and lively characters to be remembered by many audiences, some of whom had been her fans long before the Cultural Revolution. Together with their colleagues, my parents participated in the rebuilding of the theater, which regained its vitality in its subsequent productions of Western drama, experimental theater, and socialist-realist plays, some of which I will discuss in Chapters 4 and 5. The China Youth Art Theater even initiated the first women's theater, as seen in Bai Fengxi's women trilogy, which I will examine in Chapter 6.

Such remembrance of things past sparked my academic interest when I pursued a Ph.D. degree in comparative literature at Indiana University, where I buried myself in reading plays and dramatic histories from different cultures across diverse historical periods. It was then, inspired by brilliant teachers, that I confirmed my mission to introduce the "Chinese cousin" to the global family of modern drama. This mission drew from my personal commitment to an entire generation of Chinese dramatists and artists who dedicated their lives to the development of modern drama. Yet, for reasons to be discussed in the following Introduction, no monument has ever been erected in Chinese cultural history and the collective memory that traces their sleepless nights and long journeys across the country in the painful process of dramatic creation and production. No comprehensive study has ever portrayed those unfortunate and unknown players who paid, some with their lives, for extraordinary dramatic careers they had pursued over many decades. Most recently, my mother related to me that in the late 1990s many funerals were held, one after another, to bid farewell to many ex-stars who once shone on the Chinese stage and yet are hardly remembered today by many, especially the younger generation whose entertainment has little to do with drama. When my mother described to me, with tears in her eyes, how few people even bothered to attend those sad valedictory occasions for these almost forgotten artists, I felt a strong urge—if not a call to duty—to preserve their stories, hitherto untold. With deep respect for and emotional attachment to those "aunts and uncles" who watched me grow up, and to well-known and unknown people whom I do not know personally but know of their contributions to modern drama, I dedicate this study. To the memories of their tremendous courage, endurance, and persistence—and above all else, their artistic talents—I dedicate this book.

1

Introduction

WHY NOT MODERN CHINESE DRAMA?

This study is intended as a cultural history of Chinese theater (both *geming yangbanxi*, or revolutionary model theater, and *huaju*, hereafter understood to refer to modern Chinese drama) in contemporary China from 1966 to the early 1990s. Modern Chinese drama was introduced to the Chinese stage at the turn of the twentieth century in imitation of the plays in the Western Ibsenesque tradition.[1] *"Hua"* simply means "spoken language" and *"ju,"* "drama," but many May Fourth intellectuals promoted this dialogue-centered modern Chinese drama as a potent alternative to traditional operatic theater, which was performed with singing, dancing, and acrobats. To begin this cultural history, I shall focus first on one particular period—that of the Cultural Revolution and of the post-Maoist years (1976–present), a time characterized by intriguing continuities and discontinuities with the PRC era of the first seventeen years (1949–1966) and the preceding Republican period (1911–1949).

To my knowledge, there are very few book-length critical studies in English that deal exclusively with modern Chinese drama from its inception.[2] Moreover, in Chinese most of the scholarly works on the subject either are historical surveys or else focus on a single playwright. It is my strategy therefore to situate this study of contemporary Chinese drama, first, in the context of modern Chinese literary and cultural history, and second, in the context of comparative drama and theater, cultural studies, and the critical issues relevant to discussing other national theaters. With both general readers and specialists in mind, I here explore the marginality of modern Chinese drama in relation to other genres, other periods, and other cultures. After a detour to examine the origin of modern Chinese drama at the turn of the century, I reflect on the problematics of canonicity and literary history in a cross-cultural context, especially as they relate to the history of East–West comparative theater.[3] I then go on to delineate what I consider the critical issues for modern Chinese drama in current investigations into national identity, mass culture, ethnic studies, and the political nature of cultural discourse. Treating Chinese theater as a dynamic genre that both constitutes and reflects culture, and reproducing and interrogating the knowledge and social order that derive from it, I look upon contemporary Chinese drama as one of several subcultures within a distinct culture while refraining from ascribing hegemony to any single one of these subcultures.

Surviving at the Margins: A Stepchild of an Unhappy Family Romance

The marginality of modern Chinese drama studies strikes one as so obvious that it might not seem to need much documentation. Students of modern Chinese literature, for instance, are familiar with C. T. Hsia's claim that fiction should be valued as "the most fruitful and important branch of modern Chinese literature," whose pattern should be further tested against "the Communist idea of the modern Chinese literary tradition."[4] Modern Chinese drama, owing to its emphasis on audience and mass participation, was deemed too propagandist to count as serious literature. Recent scholarship on Chinese film radically redeems visual culture on the silver screen, thereby making available resources for the study of performance as visual text. As a result of dedicated efforts to bring Chinese studies into the wider arena of a world audience through insightful, close readings of Chinese film, however, some Hollywood-like, exotic films about forbidden love affairs, patricide, and concubines in rural China— for example, *Judou* in 1990 and *Raise the Red Lantern (Dahong denglong gaogao gua)* in 1991—could perhaps partially explain the increasing presence of Chinese film in Western movie houses and in scholarly discourse. Compared to the way in which Chinese film has been laid open to the global gaze, modern Chinese drama (although initially formed from Western dramatic influences) has remained for the most part a native phenomenon addressing a local audience and a peculiar social and cultural institution that both patronizes and censors public performance. Despite steady attempts to engage the attention of the larger world, with which it has become increasingly familiar, modern Chinese drama, because it is by nature a staged performance, has not been able to shed its identity as a nonprofit, domestic commodity in the international market.

Furthermore, differing as it does from other genres such as ballet and opera by virtue of its heavy dependence on spoken language and indigenous culture, the content of modern Chinese drama is necessarily confined mostly to specific localities within the boundaries of China. In truth, one can often detect a conscious refusal on the part of Chinese dramatists to see their material universalized and applied to a global stage.[5] Also still relevant today is the complicating factor alluded to by Hong Shen in 1935 with regard to the collective nature of dramatic art. In his study of modern Chinese drama's first ten years (1917–1927), Hong Shen pointed out that the challenge of drama required the talents of a poet and a fiction writer, and much more. The finished script, which delineates the culmination of the poet's and the fiction writer's creative work, represents only one-third of the dramatist's accomplishment. An even greater test of that accomplishment resides in the collaborative efforts with other artists to attain the other essential elements: directing, stage and costume designing, acting, and revising the script in response to perceptions of audience expectations and the dramatic criticism of ongoing performances. The ephemeral nature of all these components, moreover, would also ensure their precariousness insofar as the ability to record and preserve them for students of culture in future generations.[6] Thus the localized and temporal aspects of Chinese drama (unlike films, which can be replayed to study their textual and visual implications) present unique difficulties for the student and scholar wishing to pursue sustained, innovative research into the genre.

A final, equally important impediment that must be addressed is the pronouncement that the PRC period produced no works of "literary excellence," a dismissal generally accepted by students of modern Chinese literature and culture. Recently, some scholars have asserted that the exclusion of literary works of the earlier PRC period (1949–1976) from current anthologies of modern Chinese literature is unjustified and, among other things, necessarily distorts a historical treatment of the subject.[7] Even more problematic is the fact that, for the rare PRC literary studies included in surveys of the post-Maoist period, the few years immediately following 1976 have been the least scrutinized and anthologized. And on the rare occasions when this early post-Maoist period was considered, crime fiction, love stories, and obscure poetry garnered the attention, while drama was ignored, despite being well supported by local audiences and followed closely by critics of the time.[8]

This present study, therefore, is intended to help redress the threefold marginalization by (1) focusing on the cultural and social function of modern Chinese drama; (2) discussing it as a "cross-breed" of multiple traditions that paradoxically carried out the legacy promoted during the "seventeen years" of the PRC (1949–1966), a period of marginalization whose literary output deserves to be the subject of literary and cultural studies; and (3) treating it as a significant voice rescued from an even more marginalized era in literary studies—that of Cultural Revolutionary China and early post-Maoist China.

Compared with that of its European counterpart, the marginal position of modern Chinese drama was also related to an episode in the history of comparative literature, the enchantment with traditional Chinese operatic theater (xiqu) as an "exotic" other.[9] A familiar example is that of the neoclassicists' enduring fascination with such Chinese Yuan drama as The Orphan of Zhao (Zhaoshi gu'er), attributed to Ji Junxiang and first performed in China around the late thirteenth century. The reincarnation of Ji's Yuan drama in French, English, German, Italian, and Russian versions during the eighteenth and nineteenth centuries testifies to the attraction of Asian theater. One thus detects some limited scholarship on East–West comparative drama that manifests Orientalist interests.[10] The absence of scholarly work on modern Chinese drama, except for a few studies on its Western influences,[11] may be attributed to its seeming more familiar and therefore less interesting to Westerners compared with traditional culture, which seemed more remote and, hence, captivating. An abetting factor was that the field of sinology on premodern literature also exhibited a bias

—in this case toward traditional and classical poetry—with the result that drama was the subject least likely to receive scholarly scrutiny. Both the comparatists' favoring of and the sinologists' disinterest in traditional theater, as evinced by their respective discourses, pose challenging, perhaps contrary questions about power relations between East and West, performance and written texts, and tradition and its modern exegesis.

Exhibiting an equally problematic position, scholars from China tend to vaunt the superiority of traditional Chinese theater over its Western counterpart. In his study on Chinese–Western comparative drama, Lan Fan elaborates the several characteristics of Chinese theater that he believes render it more spiritual and "aesthetic" than Western theater. He asserts, for instance, that the emphasis in Western theater is on dramatic form, which exploits plot structure to snare the audience's attention, whereas in Chinese operatic theater a "sense of aesthetic beauty" is cultivated in order to "touch the soul of the audience."[12] As to audience reception, Lan contends that, in the West, audience preoccupation centers around whether the characters on stage are positive or negative figures, whereas in China, audiences are more likely to be concerned with how realistically and artistically the actors project the emotions of the dramatic characters, whatever their moral cast.[13] Referring to the theatrical space in dramatic art, Lan concludes that Western drama is an art *in* space and Chinese theater, an art *of* space.[14]

Paradoxically, Lan's essentialist analysis, which is based on binary oppositions between East and West, highlights at least one advantage of traditional Chinese theater: it can point to a tradition, which thus serves as a basis for comparison with other traditions. Modern Chinese drama, on the other hand, cannot lay claim to such an asset, having always been sustained by its existence at the margins of "great" cultures. Imported from the modern West at the turn of the century, it was discounted either for not being "Chinese" in origin or for being too "modern" to relate to a China with its own long-established cultural traditions. For traditionalists and Chinese-cultural essentialists alike, modern Chinese drama did not represent a plausible pathway for reviving traditional theater. Zhao Taimou epitomized the earliest expression of this attitude when, around 1926 during the Republican period, he argued against those who advocated a wholesale supplanting of "old theater" (*jiuxi*) with "new theater" (*xinxi*). The pro–old-theater group to which he belonged was divided into two camps: those who were for reforming the established theater and those who would have liked to see it preserved unaltered. The two factions, however, were united by the conviction that the import from the West, modern Chinese drama, could never fill the place of the existing art derived from the indigenous culture. Modern Chinese drama, moreover, held no appeal for the audiences that operatic theater still drew, according to these traditionalists.[15]

Despite being rebuffed as a foreign product, modern Chinese drama could not garner the respect of Chinese modernists either, because it failed to reflect European themes and strategies faithfully. It inspired not only a supposedly "correct understanding" of the nature of drama as performed and received in its original setting—that of the West—but at the same time was symptomatic of the frustration of first-generation Chinese dramatists, who had constantly to justify their efforts to introduce modern drama while attempting to maintain a delicate balance between its political and its artistic orientations. One of the earliest expressions of this concern is discernible in Yu Shangyuan's call for a "national drama movement" (guoju yundong) in the mid-1920s. Yu declared that Chinese dramatists' imitation of the Ibsenesque drama was wrongheaded, issuing as it did from a misunderstanding of the Western "master's" artistic essence. Instead of plumbing the depths of the human heart to reveal the interrelationships of art and life, as Ibsen had done, Chinese dramatists, according to Yu, tended to regard dramatic art as a means of rectifying a faulty heart and thus improving one's life. But as life grew increasingly complex, the Ibsenesque "social problems" ceased to exist, and consequently "real" drama, such as it was, departed from the Chinese stage. In Yu's opinion, modern Chinese drama's failure to achieve acceptance was attributable to this deviation from the "genuine art" of Ibsen.[16]

The urge to cultivate "authentic" Western tastes proved so persistent that it led directly, in contemporary times, to Xiao Qian's demand for an authentic production of Ibsen's Peer Gynt (Pi'er jinte, 1984–1985) that would replicate its original Norwegian terms.[17] Caught between the two opposing views throughout its history, modern drama forfeited any sense of belonging: it was perceived as neither modern nor traditional, neither Chinese nor Western. Thus one could say that modern Chinese drama became the neglected "stepchild" of an unhappy family romance, whose foreign genes caused its adoptive parents to feel frustrated and unfulfilled because they had not obtained the ideal child they wanted.

The neglect of modern Chinese drama presents an interesting parallel with the marginal status of European medieval drama, explored by Clifford C. Flanigan in his definitive article, "Comparative Literature and the

Study of Medieval Drama" (1986). Some of the reasons for that glaring omission in the field of comparative literature, Flanigan argued, resulted from the belief that "medieval drama fails as literature in that it lacks the marks of that institution as it was invented in the eighteenth and nineteenth centuries" under the strong influence of national consciousness and Kantian aesthetics.[18] The so-called didactic nature of medieval drama was seen by historicists and formalists alike as being inconsistent with the disinterestedness and universality that Europeans believed typified the " 'higher' realms of 'art.' "[19] Accordingly, French literary scholars canonized merely a few of the more "literary" medieval plays while dismissing other texts for their incompatibility with neoclassical or modernist standards.[20] In a contrary vein, German scholars singled out the passed-over dramatic texts for canonical status precisely because they were not regarded as literary but rather as "popular, even 'völkisch,' " and therefore lent themselves to overt political interpretations—as, in this case, expressing the kind of German national consciousness exalted under National Socialism. Why the study of medieval drama in Germany was subsequently quite neglected in the two decades after World War II may thus be easily understood.[21] The foregoing examples underscore the problematic history of medieval drama, which was either disregarded for being non-literary or was acclaimed for its very lack of literary values and its great political and national significance—an unfortunate fate not unlike that of modern Chinese drama. In Flanigan's view, the neglect of the medieval drama by comparatists implicates "not the deficient qualities of that drama, but the deficient qualities of the discourse, as well as the related discourse on national literature."[22] This conclusion may be borrowed to characterize the marginal position of modern Chinese drama within both the narrower field of sinology and the broader inquiry of comparative literary and cultural studies.

Of course, at the core underlying biases against modern Chinese drama are the age-old diametrically opposed ways of seeing drama as either purely artistic practice or strictly ideological activity. Thus the audience-oriented properties of modern Chinese drama, and hence its potential appeal for a mass culture, have drawn the appreciative notice of literary historians, who applauded it for helping to raise people's political consciousness in times of national crisis, such as the War of Resistance to Japan (1937–1945). However, in different contexts these very same attributes were construed as negative, and modern Chinese drama was then castigated as a literary creation whose overly ideological basis rendered it inhospitable to artistic values.[23] Chen Baichen and Dong Jian, for example, argue that dramatic literature during the the War of Resistance to Japan occupied a distinctive place at the forefront of literary production, surpassing poetic and fictional works, although the latter had seen a fuller development than dramatic works in the 1920s and 1930s. In the very same chapter, however, the authors criticize these plays, whose artistic depth they claim was adversely affected by the hasty way they were created in response to a national crisis.

China's modern drama, whose marginal status has been reinforced by contradictory considerations of the political and aesthetic cultures, has continued to be vulnerable to the same currents in its most recent history, the early post-Maoist period. At a time when many "masterpieces" in fiction, poetry, and—later on—film were hailed as "real literature," many dramatic works of substance were once again repudiated for being the least aesthetic genre in China's literary output. Zhang Zhong and others, for instance, although crediting theater for serving from 1978 to 1980 as a "powerful weapon" against the Gang of Four and thereby forging a mutually gratifying tie with its audience of that period, in almost the same breath fault its supposed reliance on one-dimensional characters and stereotypes, which they see as responsible for the dearth in drama of "monumental works."[24] Other drama critics lamented the "crisis of drama" (xiju weiji) in 1984, when the fewest plays were staged since 1976. This reduced yield of a stagnant theater, another critic claimed, could not possibly meet the new criteria for artistic works and the changing requirements of audiences, especially of the younger generation, which had been gradually turning away from politically oriented theater.[25] One should not forget, however, that 1979—the year that marked a renaissance of the drama—was once viewed by such critics as Dai Jinhua as crucial in the political and cultural history of early post-Maoist China. In 1979 Deng Xiaoping espoused the late Mao's principle of "seeking truth from facts" (shishi qiushi) to challenge the legitimacy of the Cultural Revolution, thus precipitating a naive but singularly sincere surge of democracy, a flood of "wounded literature," and a "dramatic art that addressed the politically forbidden area with unprecedented courage and insight."[26] All these developments required extraordinary daring from members of literary and artistic circles, whose freedom of expression was still hampered by traditional discourse and outmoded socialist-realist perspectives, Dai argued. As might be predicted from the foregoing, many of the plays (known as "anti–Gang of Four plays") issuing from this period were later given short shrift and deemed too political for canonization.

For my part, I have chosen to focus on these early post-Maoist texts precisely because I regard them—and many audiences' warm receptions of them—as invaluable cultural keys to understanding a specific historical moment when drama played an indispensable role in constructing a new national discourse. As will be seen in Chapter 5, "Performing Tiananmen," audience participation at the critical moment was capable of subverting some of the ideologically correct themes of anti–Gang of Four plays, in the process challenging the early post-Maoist regime that had previously endorsed the plays. Looking beyond the rhetorical eloquence of the theatrical event, one may detect clues in the guise of randomness, contingencies, and inversions that underline the deviations on stage from the written texts. Audience response in theater challenges or reinforces script, resists documentation, eludes political repercussion, and may sidestep the barbs of writing such as theater reviews, critical debate, and other forms of official censorship. It transgresses the boundaries separating individuals from their public role that the mainstream culture has seen fit to observe. These acts of what I call "border crossing" in theater encapsulated the specific cultural living conditions of Chinese dramatists and audiences, whose play writing and theater going in themselves constituted a playing out of dramatic roles and situations in their confined social and political circumstances.

Representing Cultural Revolution: Model Theater, Visual Art, and Popular Culture

The first part of this introduction addressed the question: Why not study modern Chinese drama in order to provide a historical context for studying contemporary theater? In the following section, I pose a parallel question: Why study the revolutionary model theater, promoted during "the Great Proletarian Cultural Revolution"? Like modern drama and the performing arts, the Cultural Revolutionary theater as a literary and cultural topic has occupied a peripheral place in Chinese and Western scholarship.[27] This neglect is understandable, as any serious study of model theater would affect the way in which the Cultural Revolution itself is remembered. PRC official culture would erase it as an essential part of the unprecedented "ten-year disaster." It is this sort of willful amnesia that led to the sealing off of forbidden areas of national and local libraries for classified documents issued by former leaders of the CCP during and after the Cultural Revolution.

Recent studies by scholars in China, in spite of their advertised challenges to this state of affairs, only seem to ratify the official view; that is, they call for a shift from focusing on political events and the power struggle within the party hierarchy to examining the problematic mentality of the masses who carried out the Cultural Revolution. It was the negative national characteristics of the Chinese people and of traditional Chinese culture, for these scholars, that touched off and intensified the massive violence, betrayal, cruelty, and indifference that characterized the Cultural Revolution. Other aspects of their inquiry, which emphasize the discursive strategy of political power, the traditional concept of "loyalty to the king" *(zhongjun)*, and the national spirit of the Chinese, succeed in assuring that the Cultural Revolution will be remembered as a chaotic event, without agency and in which no subjects are to be held responsible. These views expunge the connection between earth-shaking events as they occur in history and the mystified participants and collaborators, who cede their authority as witnesses to and owners of that history. Some scholars, for instance, judiciously point out that the Cultural Revolution is selectively remembered in the memoirs of former Red Guards, whose narcissistic gaze effectively incriminated others as the criminals. In the process of explaining why they have "no regret for their lost youth" *(qingchun wuhui)* and "no regrets about the Red Guard experience" *(hongweibing wuhui)*, they relegate the past to the past, present themselves as having sacrificed their adolescence on the altar of duty, and construct themselves as glorious and charismatic while portraying others as ignorant and reprehensible.[28] Relaying this perspective from the vantage point of the present, they enjoy assuming the guise of innocent idealists in order to deny their own role as partial agents of the Cultural Revolution.

Writing Cultural Revolution in the Diaspora

It must be noted, however, that while scholarship on the Cultural Revolution was being marginalized within China, a select group of Chinese writers living in the West explored this historical period in the book markets and movie industries abroad as a means of representing China to the West.[29] Increasingly, American and other international best-seller lists host Cultural Revolution memoirs—written in English and geared to the interests of English-speaking audiences—that proffer horror stories of Maoist China, in which the Orient is seen seeking salvation from the Occident. In many of them, one perceives a common pattern of the narrator portraying herself as the heroine while relegating others to the role of persecutor. Almost all of these works read like stories of survival, culminating in the obligatory happy ending in America or Europe.[30] Predictably, the memoirs found great favor in America, where the authors' cheerful view of their adoptive country through the lens of a miserable Asian other proved to be a financially rewarding formula, as attested by the profitable sale of best-sellers.

A case in point is Nien Cheng's *Life and Death in Shanghai* (1986), an early exponent of the genre that set the tone for those that followed. It begins with the author's manipulation of two time frames, that of a horrific past in 1960s Cultural Revolutionary China and a peaceful present in North America, where she has "ample time again and again to recall scenes and conversations in a continuing effort to assess their significance." She claims that she has set down "as nearly as possible a faithful account" of her experience,[31] and this assertion is buttressed by the tone of calm reflection, in which she introduces herself as a privileged Chinese woman in postliberation Shanghai living in a luxurious house with her own maid and servant. Cheng lingers over this part of the story, evidently enjoying her reminiscences of the good life, during which she was the only agent in Shanghai working for the Shell Oil Company after 1949.[32] However, it is this job that causes her and her colleagues to be branded "running dogs of the imperialist West" during the Cultural Revolution and to be thrown into prison. After having lost her only daughter to the ravages of the Red Guards and wasted six and a half years in prison, Cheng is aghast when she looks in the mirror and sees a colorless face and eyes "overbright from the need to be constantly on the alert."[33]

Succor comes in the form of Western Christianity and its gracious God, which allow her "to see the distant green hills on the horizon." The memoir ends inevitably with a happy life for the author in America, where the "Jewish survivors of the Holocaust, persecuted dissidents from repressive regimes, boat people from Vietnam, and political refugees from tyranny" make her feel at home.[34] It was while paying a visit to some friendly, curious Americans in a handsome California house adorned with Asian treasures that she was encouraged to tell the horrendous story of her life in China. Inspired by these Americans, she "felt a compulsion to speak out and let those who have the good fortune to live in freedom know what" it was like "during those dark days in Maoist China."[35]

Cheng's book, in light of Sidonie Smith and Julia Watson's pioneering anthology of writings on women's autobiography, can be explored as expressing the "colonial subject" in women's autobiographies as a significant cultural and ideological site where gender, class, race, and nation "intersect and dissect one another" in cross-cultural contexts.[36] *Life and Death in Shanghai* can therefore be fruitfully analyzed as an inquiry into the Chinese woman as an "autobiographical speaker," or as an agent of "a conflicted history, inhabiting and transforming a complex social and cultural world" in the postcolonial era.[37] One could also view Cheng's English writing as harboring problematic and contradictory I-narrators: a privileged Shanghai woman, an imprisoned dissident, a loyal Confucian widow, a heartbroken mother, a pious Christian disciple, and a spirited China basher in the diaspora. My problem with Cheng's version of the Cultural Revolution does not lie so much in her basic experience during the period as in her lack of critical reflection on her own subjective positions in a complex historical context. It is puzzling to read, for instance, how Cheng, as a privileged woman representing a Western business in the early 1950s,[38] gave no thought to China's Communist politics, only to undergo a sudden conversion into a martyr at the height of the "white terror" of 1966. Her open defense of Liu Shaoqi, the then imprisoned former president of the PRC, sounds unconvincing when many ardent Communists were shying away from political involvement.

Whereas in Nien Cheng's story the narrator is presented as asexual, Anchee Min's *Red Azalea* (1994) evokes a China whose politically demonic system apparently kindles a steamy homosexual encounter. Appearing eight years after *Life and Death in Shanghai*, *Red Azalea* had something new to offer Western readers in the way of Cultural Revolution horror stories. The homosexual experience depicted in *Red Azalea*, however, has less to do with alternative life-styles than with reduced choices in a land that forbade heterosexual love. It is important to note that Anchee Min (the I-narrator in *Red Azalea*) falls in love with Yan Sheng, her lesbian partner on the farm, only after Little Green, another farm worker, is captured hiding with her heterosexual lover. When her lover is convicted of rape, Little Green goes mad and drowns herself in the river. Only after realizing that heterosexual love is precluded does Min begin to acknowledge her heretofore suppressed sexual desires: "The body and the restlessness worked hand in glove. They were screaming in me, breaking me in two."[39] So intense was the monster of desire that she "chased mosquitoes every night," pinching them to death, playing with their long legs, and watching their insertion into her skin, feeling their bite.[40] As an apparent aftermath to this experience, Min decides to seduce Yan, who is still maintaining the facade of a typical Maoist woman uninterested in sex. At the same time, she feels guilty for driving Little Green mad since, as the party secretary and commander of the company, she was responsible for capturing her and her lover on the spot. Banned heterosexual love is thus the instigator of the lesbian episode with Yan (they end by sleeping together under a mosquito net), but the prisonlike farm environment during the Cultural Revolution eventually drives the lesbian couple apart. Yan renounces Min's love in order to facilitate her resolve to leave the farm, "escape from hell," and forge a better life in the city. As Min puts it, when Yan "was not allowed to have a man to love," she "had to pretend to be a man for her."

This brief exposition may still give some sense of *Red Azalea*'s appeal to a cross-cultural readership, which depicts a Cultural Revolutionary China as politically horrific, culturally alien, and erotic. This combination elicited a warmer reception in the West than any of the book's predecessors, with reviews touting it as "intensely moving and erotic" and "the most memorable."[41] While not doubting Min's account of her basic experience in the countryside, I question her selective use of memories of the Cultural Revolution for different audiences. The author, in a 1997 speech to a Christian women's group at a YWCA in Columbus, Ohio, omitted any mention of the sexy lesbian affair that made the book a smash, dwelling instead on the ways in which hatred of Americans was bred into her while she was growing up in China, and on her odyssey toward personal fulfillment in America.[42] This points up the irony in the author's intentional or unintentional expenditure of cultural and symbolic capital: namely, whereas the book's sales benefited from an erotic lesbian tale that Americans could comfortably enjoy while simultaneously discounting it as an exotic experience of an other, the author, in her speech, honed in on a different exotic tale, to ensure that certain audiences would not be offended by the erotic content.

Of course, gender politics and eroticism are not the exclusive province of Chinese women memoirists. Guanlong Gao in fact outdid his female competitors with his erotic memories of childhood, *The Attic: The Memoir of a Chinese Landlord's Son* (1996). In it he discloses that before the age of seven he shared his mother's bed every night and was transported into a state of excitement by the sensations aroused by fondling her breasts and pressing against her body from behind.[43] The setting of these graphic, Oedipal reminiscences in an attic in Shanghai evokes the circumstances under which Anne Frank and many other Jews tried to survive the Holocaust. With its novel, provocative version of growing up in Cultural Revolutionary China, *The Attic* outstripped earlier Cultural Revolution memoirs, which consisted of stories about Red Guards' ransacking and general mayhem.

Unlike these three texts, which were originally written in English, *Scarlet Memorial*, published in 1996, was an English translation; but, more important, it constituted a more sensational manifestation of exoticizing China. Its author, Zheng Yi, tells of cannibalism among the Zhuang ethnic minority in Guangxi Province during the Cultural Revolution, when many people were murdered and their bodies cut into pieces and eaten by rival factions of the Red Guards. Personal interviews and investigations would seem to support the author's assertion that the book consists of factual, "authentic" tales. In determining how much credence to give such a claim, one might consider that Zheng Yi is also known among the Han majority for his erotic fiction, and that as far as the present work is concerned, he was the sole arbiter as to whom he interviewed, what questions he asked, and which materials he selected for inclusion in his book.

Given the complex racial diversities in China, it is not surprising that Zheng paid more attention to the historical roots of cannibalism, such as witchcraft and other folk customs among the Zhuang people, than to the immediate ideological context of the Chinese Cultural Revolution.[44] That his work was criticized in China as possibly reflecting a Han chauvinistic view is also unsurprising, since upholding the reputations and rights of minority groups is an important part of official PRC rhetoric. The officials responsible for carrying out the ruling ideology, moreover, are supposed to recognize and weed out discrimination against ethnic groups. Such rhetoric in favor of the welfare of minorities would surely be a cause for celebration on the part of Native Americans, African Americans, Asian Americans, Latino/Latina Americans, and other ethnic groups were it ever similarly institutionalized in the United States. However, once translated and promoted in the West as a "banned" book from China, Zheng's work found favor as another proof of China's much publicized dismal record on human rights, although it did not seem to occur to China's critics that human rights include the rights of ethnic minority peoples anywhere in the world, not just in China. Thus the question posed by a Peking University student to President Clinton in June 1998—whether racial conflicts with African Americans and other ethnic groups did not present a problem of human rights in the United States—was a valid one, especially in light of Clinton's public debate with the president of the PRC, Jiang Zemin, on China's Tibetan policy. This student made another telling point when he asked Clinton how much he knew about Chinese culture, and whether perhaps his knowledge was not based on the spate of Western-bound best-sellers about the Cultural Revolution.

In view of the complicated issues of race, gender, nation, and state raised by Zheng's book, its subtitle, "Tales of Cannibalism in Modern China," is certainly misleading. It suggests that cannibalism occurred not just in Guangxi Province but elsewhere in China, and not just among Zhuang people but also among other groups; it could lead readers with almost no knowledge of Chinese history to believe that the practice persists in China today. Nor have we evaluated the impact of the process of translation: the subjectivity of the translator—another implicit "I-narrator"— surely plays a significant part in the international "joint-business venture"[45] of representing China, especially in an already exoticized minority tale such as this, whose sensational aspects are duly magnified through consumption by Westerners innocent of China's culture and history.

All the works under discussion seek to certify the authenticity of the autobiographers and/or the disguised I-narrator. Yet is it conceivable that this self has "faithfully" reflected the self that lived through the Cultural Revolution all those years ago? Or are we dealing with a modified self, one that has been so re-created as to strike us almost as a free agent, detached from the principal events of the Cultural Revolution and nearly always innocent compared with its vicious and evil perpetrators? Is it plausible that the transformations of the Cultural Revolution could have been achieved in a country peopled by helpless victims and passive observers who were never, not even early on, captivated enough by the events to participate in them?

A brief account of my own actions during those times is relevant here. Around 1966, a proud young citizen of the PRC at the age of twelve, I responded with enthusiasm to the initial events of the Cultural Revolution, despite being precluded from joining the Red Guards by the ideological incorrectness of my family background. Rather than anger, I felt sorrow at being excluded from this paramilitary youth organization, and I would wistfully make my own band out of red cloth and follow the Red Guards on their raids against the "bad elements" in my neighborhood. After my father's denunciation as an enemy of the people for his affiliation before 1949 with a theater attached to the KMT government, I pleaded with him, in the timid tones of an adoring Chinese daughter, to make a clean breast of all his sins against the Chinese people and to repudiate the stage and costume designs that had served to promote Western, decadent, and bourgeois plays. I remember how guilty I felt afterward for not being harder on my father. Writing in my diary, I speculated as to whether I could be more severe and critical if I were confronting class enemies who were unrelated to me. Many were the chilly late November nights I waited in the Beijing train station to be first in line to obtain a standby ticket so I could travel by train anywhere outside Beijing and spread the revolutionary spirit to the rest of the country. At this early stage of the revolution, my rejection by the Red Guards and my politically undesirable lineage merely spurred me to exert myself all the more to prove that I was as militant as anybody else in rooting out our common class enemies. I cannot know to what extent other people's reactions resembled my own, but I am convinced of the necessity for each of us to acknowledge the inescapable fact that many of us were players in this national drama and to relate honestly the particulars of our participation, with the goal of arriving at some understanding of and tolerance for the way we lived our lives at that particular point in history.

In Ronald Harwood's play *Taking Sides*, Major Arnold's characterization of the Austrians' post-Nazi mentality might just as well apply to a Chinese audience: "To think, a million of these people came out to welcome Adolf [Hitler] on the day he entered the city [of Vienna], a million of them," and now look at them—they say they were "all at home hiding Jews in their attics"; "The point is they're all full of shit."[46] One wonders whether the issues of accountability raised by this play do not constitute a political allegory for all traumatized peoples emerging from tumultuous eras, whatever their political stance, who, in vying to cleanse their pasts, completely exonerate themselves and fix the blame on predictable targets. One is moved, furthermore, to try to imagine what kind of documents would result if millions of Red Guards who ardently saluted their "great helmsman" Chairman Mao in Tiananmen Square at the peak of the Cultural Revolution were somehow granted a knowledge of English and the privilege of living among and writing "autobiographical" accounts or "factual reports based on personal experience" for readers from other cultures.

Remembering Model Theater and Revolutionary Posters

I have questioned the subject positions of writers in representing the Cultural Revolution in the diaspora and raised the issue of accountability for participation in the Cultural Revolution. I do not mean to argue, however, that Cultural Revolution memoirs do not have their own value if discussed in the complicated, local context of the period. Indeed, I want to draw attention to several accounts of the tremendous effects of model theater, the posters that represented such theater, and the mass performance related to it. Taking Anchee Min's *Red Azalea* as a point of departure, I intend to discuss the interrelationship of model theater, revolutionary posters, and mass performance of the period as a dynamic and dialogic process in which visual culture, model theater, and other performance activities can be seen as integral parts of the political drama of the period. In this way, I hope to reveal various aspects of visual culture and examine it as an extended stage of the model theater, which did not cease when the curtain went down.

As is well known, from 1966 to 1967, when schools, libraries, and all other cultural institutions were closed in China, the purveyors of the Maoist official ideology started to promote what were known as the eight revolutionary model works, which consisted of five Peking operas (*jingju*, also known as Beijing opera), two modern ballets, and one symphonic work.[47] The majority of the people were compelled to see these plays for the sake of their political education; sometimes performances preceded or came at the end of political meetings. Since the Cultural Revolution aimed to eliminate the "four olds" (thought, culture, customs, and habit), the masses were encouraged to imitate the protagonists of the model theater by watching and even performing model theatrical pieces themselves in order to become better revolutionaries.

For those who remember model theater, Anchee Min's beginning paragraph sounds particularly familiar: "I was raised on the teachings of Mao and on the operas of Madam Mao, Comrade Jiang [Q]ing. I became a leader of the Little Red Guards in elementary school. This was during the Cultural Revolution when red was my color."[48] Min, of course, was not alone. Her neighbor downstairs "liked to chat, quarrel and sing Comrade Jiang [Q]ing, Madam Mao's operas."[49] Like many people around her, Min became an opera fan, singing opera everywhere, on the radio and in school, during her meals and even in her sleep. She was so obsessed with opera that she identified Yan Sheng, her company leader in the countryside, as the protagonist in the opera. In singing the opera, she sings "the song of Yan," "the heroine in real life"; she wanted to "reach her, to become her," and to "worship" her.[50] At the end of a long day's hard work—in which she persisted by singing Mao's quotation song to fight off sleep—Min was elated to see Yan, her "sun," appearing in the distance, wishing that she herself could be recognized as the same kind of strong-willed person as Yan. Her tears welled up when she saw Yan "pacing in the sun."[51] Gazing at Yan, Min sat back, "enjoying her happiness, sharing her pain," when Yan conducted the young farmers in singing the model opera *The Red Lantern* at the study meeting. The reference to Yan as the "sun" reminds one of the numerous posters of the Cultural Revolutionary period that depicted Mao as the red sun rising from the east, dispensing brilliant sunshine to nurture all living creatures on the earth.

Whereas model theater permeated people's lives, posters reinforced, recalled, talked back, and also constructed personal and collective identities during the Cultural Revolution. Where the model theater stopped on the radio, in the movie theaters, and within the four walls of the theater, the images of its revolutionary heroes and heroines printed on posters continued their gaze at their beholders, exhorting them to further revolutionary actions. Min depicted the dynamics between opera and poster: "I grew up with the operas. They became my cells. I decorated the porch with posters of my favorite opera heroines. I sang the operas wherever I went. My mother heard me singing in my dreams; she said that I was preserved by the operas."[52] Min's narrative helps to explain the popularity of a poster entitled *Acting Revolutionary Opera and Becoming Revolutionary People (Yan geming xi, zuo geming ren)*; (Plate 1) by Liu Chengqi. Displayed in the National Art Exhibition (Quanguo meishu zuopin zhanlanhui) to celebrate the twenty-fifth anniversary of the founding of the PRC in 1974, Liu's *nianhua*-style painting was later printed as a poster in private and public space, as often happened to many pieces.[53] It portrays a female worker, a member of the workers' "propaganda team to spread Mao Zhedong Thought" *(Mao Zedong Sixiang xuanchuandui*, hereafter refered to as *xuanchuandui)*, as indicated on a musical instrument case (most likely an accordion). She is helping to arrange the hair of a little girl who belongs to an elementary-school *xuanchuandui*, as suggested by the characters on the drum. Both of them are dressing to perform the same role of Li Tiemei, the heroine of the Peking opera *The Red Lantern (Hongdeng ji)*, the little girl wearing Li's red, flower-printed jacket and her "big sister" wearing Tiemei's green striped pants. This frozen moment nevertheless suggests the fluidity of time, as one imagines that before long both "sisters" will have appeared as identical images of Li. Both of them, however, have already done their hair as Li and will use the red lantern prop, which is placed on the lefthand dresser when they alternate as Li on stage. This spirit of sisterhood backstage indeed reflects the central theme of the model opera. Just as the character Li is determined to carry out her father's last wish to deliver secret codes to revolutionary soldiers fighting against the Japanese during the war period, so the little "sister" will carry on the task of performing model theater undertaken by the big "sister" when she grows up. In the act of learning to perform the model opera that depicted a revolutionary past, the younger generation was also expected to learn from their real-life role models such as this female worker, the so-called backbone of socialist China.

Model theater can also be found in *New Creations (Chuxin)* by He Shu-shui in his *nianhua*-style painting,[54] another selected piece for the same 1974 National Art Exhibition (Plate 2). Reflecting the central aim of the Cultural Revolution to eliminate old cultures, this piece portrays a group of workers and artists gazing at the new porcelain products they have just created. A new design on a lamp cover depicts happy children singing and dancing to express their love for Tiananmen and for their great leader, Chairman Mao, a scene most probably staged by a children's *xuanchuadui*. Next to it, one detects a design on a vase of a much celebrated scene from *The Red Detachment of Women (Hongse niangzijun)*, a revolutionary modern ballet. In this scene, known as *Changqing Points the Way (Chang-qing zhilu)*, Hong Changqing, the CCP representative, guides Wu Qing-hua, a slave just escaped from her oppressor, in her effort to join the Red Army during the war. This and other familiar images in the numerous posters made from the stills of model theatrical pieces could be found on many other objects, such as thermoses, postcards, stamps, and other gift items and necessities of daily life. In the poster entitled *Martial Songs Raised Our Spirit While Carrying Our Guns for the People (Zhange gu douzhi, kangqiang wei renmin)* by Gu Qing (Plate 3), for instance, a woman of the militia shares with her friends a poster of the film *The Red Detachment of Women*, which prints the same signature scene of *Chang-qing Points the Way*. The movie screen behind them and the movie pro-jector standing next to the little boy suggest the happy occasion of a festive movie night that attracts villagers from miles away, a similar event I used to look forward to when working in the countryside during the Cultural

FIGURE 11. Anonymous, *Changqing Points the Way*. From *Oil Paintings of The Red Detachment of Women* (Shanghai People's Press, 1972).

Revolution. The poster within a poster illustrates the popularity of the model theater and the posters that promoted it.

I still remember the excitement I felt when, as a sixteen-year-old in the northeast wilderness in Heilongjiang Province, I received from my mother the birthday gift of a photo album with stills from the revolutionary model ballet *The Red Detachment of Women*. My mother knew of my desire to possess them before I went to the northeast, but I could not afford it because of its exquisite, expensive design and high-quality paper. I was especially struck by the photos (which had become very popular posters) of Wu Qinghua, the female revolutionary heroine whose long, straight legs and graceful body had resisted a vicious landlord. The example I chose for this introduction, however, reveals another aspect of the visual culture of the time. Entitled *Changqing Points the Way* (Fig. 11), it is an oil-painted version of the same image as that on the vase in He Shushui's *nianhua*-style painting of *New Creations* and on the poster in Gu Qing's *Martial Songs Raised Our Spirit*. As one can see more clearly in this oil painting, next to the dynamic and heroic image of Hong stands a beautiful Wu Qinghua, poised, balanced, supple, angular, and elegant. Her red costume embraces the "red" culture of the period; it also crosses the boundary of the revolutionary culture of the time, with its flowing and soft silk materials not commonly seen in everyday clothing.

For audiences in China in that period, however, these embodiments of youth, beauty, grace, passion, and energy on posters and other art works were among one of the rare decorations to be seen in public spaces and private homes. As such they could be gazed on with the same intensity as images of Rita Hayworth and Marilyn Monroe, accompanied by portraits of an attractive Chairman Mao. The combination of these two kinds of images, keeping each other solitary company, enticed countless masses of both men and women to join the Cultural Revolution. By means of this not-so-subtle exploitation of the erotic—rendered all the more powerful because other expressions of a romantic and sexual nature had been officially banned—patriotism was aroused, a crusade was launched, and a revolutionary dynasty was established. And a national discourse took root in both the conscious and unconscious of men and women alike.

Today, looking back, I am aware that my treasuring of these images was not unrelated to their voluptuous appeal, disguised though it was by the focus on an ideologically correct story and the endowment of the womanly body with a "manly spirit." Thus the androgynous nature of model theater accounted, to some extent, for the appeal of the posters of the period. The posters conveyed their political messages through the written word in captions and titles, while model theater did the same through script, lyrics, and dialogue. However, in both forms the visual representation, comprised of body language, color, and light, might sometimes provide cues for other interpretations not necessarily endorsed by mainstream culture. The two forms also differed in that the shapely body of a female lead could be accentuated by elegant movement in model theater, especially in revolutionary ballet, whereas in posters, the female figure might be dressed in baggy clothing to hide its curves and, in any case, was fixed—a special feature of the art object—without benefit of the flow of movement, a property of performing art.

In the context of the comparison between different genres of visual art, moreover, it is perhaps interesting to mention in passing that the appearance of the oil paintings of Wu Qinghua and Hong Changqing indicated conscious attempts on the part of Chinese artists to integrate different art media in creating a new and revolutionary culture. As proclaimed in the preface to the collection of oil paintings of *The Red Detachment of Women* from which the above-mentioned picture was taken, forty paintings of the main scenes and characters from the ballet (ranging from 89 cm × 93 cm in size, as in Wu's picture, to 233 cm × 127 cm, as in *Changqing Points the Way*)[55] were completed within a short period of three months from June to September 1970, the result of the collective efforts by a group of painters determined to use this Western-imported media to re-present the revolutionary model ballet (itself a Western medium). They were finally presented as gifts to an exhibition in Shanghai commemorating the thirtieth anniversity of the publication of Mao Zedong's "Talks at the Yan'an Forum on Literature and Art," thus providing useful models for worker/peasant/soldier amateur artists to imitate revolutionary art on canvas.[56] Whereas model theater on canvas celebrated the canonical text of the great CCP leader in 1970, He Shushui's *nianhua* painting of *New Creation* expressed a similar passion to represent the familiar scene of *Changqing Points the Way* through a different art genre, thus qualifying his painting for the National Art Exhibition to commemorate the founding of the nation. *New Creation*, together with 109 other pieces, was hailed as "one of the most popular pieces welcomed by workers, peasants, and soldiers."[57] Here, art collection and museum culture carved out a niche of their own, constructing an image of the new revolutionary culture in their very act of reproducing the same scene from the performing art.

The canvas also reflected other crucial activities that took place during the Cultural Revolution as reflected in products of visual culture. Tang Jixiang's *Red Frontline (Hongse de zendi)*, another piece selected for the 1974 National Art Exhibition, portrays a worker getting "picture books" ready for the little Red Guards from an elementary school (Plate 4). The young amateur actors and actresses frequently performed *The Red Lantern*, as the stage prop of a red lantern on top of a bookshelf testifies. When the model theater performance was over in the school, images of the protagonists and their heroic actions remained in the reading room. The picture books include *The Red Lantern*, held in the worker's hand, and *Raid on the White Tiger Regiment (Qixi Baihutuan)*, another model Peking opera that depicted the heroic deeds of Chinese volunteer soldiers during the Korean war. Together with posters, these picture books functioned as another important aspect of visual culture that provided role models for young people as well as old. Children's picture books could also further their understanding of model theater characters and improve the performance of the *xuanchuandui*, a frequent school event, as indicated by the red flag of the *xuanchuandui* and various musical instruments in the upper right corner.

The practice of children watching or playing model theater was also vividly recorded in a teenage girl's painting clearly entitled *Model Opera for Children* (Fig. 12). In it, a group of young children are watching *Taking Tiger Mountain by Strategy (Zhiqu Weihushan)*, with the image of

FIGURE 12. Chen Xiaoli (fourteen years old), Hebei Province: "Model Opera for Children." From Gerd Kaminski, *Pandabären Statt Parolen* (Panda bears instead of [political] slogans). No. 24 of the Reports of the Ludwig Boltzmann Institute for Research on China and Southeast Asia, p. 107. Archive of the Italian-Chinese Friendship Society.

Yang Zirong, the protagonist, in the middle of the playground. To the right side of the picture, four girls are preparing to enact three other scenes from model operas. A teacher is applying makeup to a little girl who wears a sheepskin jacket, a sign of the role of Chang Bao in the same opera, who disguises herself as a boy to escape from a bandit's persecution. Inspired by Yang Zirong, she joined the revolutionary army in order to liberate the rest of China. Two other girls, each dressed in the garb of Tiemei and her grandma, with a red lantern at their feet, are ready to perform the celebrated scene of "Listening to Grandma's Story of the Red Lantern," where Tiemei learns about her family history. Another girl next to her, holding a storefront sign for a teahouse, suggests the role of Sister A Qing. She is a protagonist in a model Peking opera entitled *Shajiabang*, who, as an underground CCP member, risks her life to protect and take care of eighteen wounded soldiers. The red flag in the upper right corner, which bears the characters "Little Red Guard *Xuanchuandui*," drives home the message that model theater and *xuanchuandui* formed important parts of children's play, sport, and theater.

The practice of *xuanchuandui* indeed dates back to before the Cultural Revolution, when professional artists followed Mao's directions and went to the factories and the countryside in the remote areas of China to perform for workers, peasants, and soldiers. *Xuanchuandui* reached its heyday when amateurs joined professionals in performing model theater and other ensembles as part of the mass movement to learn from the revolutionary spirit of its dramatic characters. Peasant artist Shi Huifang's *nianhua*-style painting, entitled *An Evening at the Production Brigade (Dadui de yewan)*, vividly depicts a village *xuanchuandui* staging a show for its local peasants (Fig. 13). The amateur actor and actress in center stage are apparently performing a piece denouncing ex-landlords. They still harbored hopes of returning to the old society before 1949, as is shown in their effort to keep accounts of how much money the poor peasants owed them. Among those in the left corner waiting to perform the next piece, one can detect a woman with the costume and makeup of Xi'er, the protagonist of *The White-Haired Girl (Baimao nü)*, a revolutionary modern ballet. Xi'er's story forcefully demonstrates how miserable the old society was: as a daughter of a poor peasant who could not afford to pay his debts, Xi'er flees into the mountains to escape persecution. Her hair turns white from lack of salt. This portrayal of Xi'er's bitter past life onstage within the picture frame invites one simultaneously to gaze at the heroine from model theater, the play reenacted by members of the *xuanchuadui*, and the audience around them, with whom the beholders of this art work could identify.

These visual images suggest the degree to which model-theater characters were appropriated as models, not only to construct the individual's relation to society and its revolutionary idealism, but also to structure the everyday life experience of those participating in *xuanchuadui*. I still remember the excitement I found in my own childhood experience of performance. After being rejected several times for membership in *xuanchuandui* due to my undesirable family background, I went home and organized my own troupe with the children who lived in my courtyard, where more than a dozen families working in the China Youth Art Theater resided. Ranging in age from six to thirteen, we presented a curious lineup of all sizes and shapes. What we had in common was the fact that at least one of our parents (who had been performing artists) was undergoing investigation. Without our realizing it, our performances, in addition to join-

FIGURE 13. Shi Huifang, *An Evening at the Production Brigade* (People's Art Press, 1975).

ing in with the activities that supported the mass movement, probably expressed our personal desire to carry on the artistic tradition of our parents. To demonstrate our pride and passionate commitment to the movement, we made our own team flag by embroidering gold thread on a piece of red cloth. Joining the street theater of the Cultural Revolution, we were able to attract crowds to watch our ensemble, and no one ever questioned us about our family backgrounds or whether we were politically qualified to perform. Our popular performances undoubtedly benefited from the skills we had picked up and the abilities we had inherited from our families. At this time I had an intense desire to be on the stage, just like my mother, who at the time could not act because she was charged as being one of the *"sanming"* (three famous groups of actors and actresses, directors, and writers) and *"sangao"* (three "high" groups of professionals who were distinguished by their salaries, living standards, and symbols of royalty)— all remnants of the bourgeois culture and thus opposed to the interests of the common people. Walking on the street with my homemade *xuanchuandui*, therefore, I felt relief and pride: I had my own team without having to be a Red Guard. It was not without a certain sense of being "celebrities" that we performed for the public, but as we had not been formally trained in the performing arts, we were not burdened, like our parents, with the professional artist's fear of being criticized by the masses. I was

FIGURE 14. Zhang Duanying (f), fourteen years old, 1975, Shanxi Province: "Cultural Program," from Gerd Kaminski, *Pandabären Statt Parolen*, p. 106. Archive of Austrian Association for Research on China.

delighted to play the actress, and yet I did not have to be labeled as performing the wrong kind of art. The experience may have helped later when I auditioned successfully for the *xuanchuandui* in my middle school. Figure 14, another children's painting, vividly portrays similar experiences in other parts of the country.

Because no serious learning took place in Chinese schools during the Cultural Revolution, I devoted most of my two years of middle school to the performing arts and consequently became almost a professional at it. We would perform in the street, on various stages in squares after public gatherings, and in rural areas not far from Beijing before local peasants and fellow students who had come to help with the autumn harvest. *The New Ensembles from the Cultural Club (Wenhuashi de xin jiemu)*, (Fig. 15) by Wang Liping, another peasant artist, might easily be retitled *The New Ensembles from a Beijing Middle School* Xuanchuandui, recording our own performance for the local peasants.

Every time a new quotation of Chairman Mao regarding the Cultural Revolution was released, I would stay up all night with my teammates, writing scripts, adapting old songs to new lyrics, and producing new dances

FIGURE 15. Wang Liping, *The New Ensembles from the Cultural Club* (People's Art Press, 1975).

and skits for it. We competed with other teams in these activities, anxious to be the first to give expression to the new idea in street parades and celebrations. Intent on being the best, we worked hard and played just as hard. In hindsight, I view my *xuanchuandui* days as one of the most exciting times of my adolescence, when fun and duty intertwined so well as to render perfectly natural my role of little player in the larger scheme of political theater. There was a tremendous sense of thrill and freedom in riding a bicycle to wherever my performing duty called me. For the first time in my life, I even had enough pocket money for snacks and cookies before and after performing.

In 1968, a remark of Chairman Mao's radically changed the course of my adolescence and those of my peers. He proclaimed the countryside an enormous arena where educated youth from the city could fully tap their talents while being reeducated by local peasants. Joining the national movement of repairing to the countryside, my class of 1969 went to Beidahuang, the northeast wilderness bordering the Soviet Union, then regarded as a threat to the Chinese nation. The twin glories of defending the border while casting my lot with the peasants to reclaim the fertile land of the frontier appealed to me. Although I was one year younger than the minimum age posted for these exploits and thus did not have to volunteer, I insisted on going. Before I left home, my sister, who had never had a chance to see me perform, asked me to do a *xuanchuandai* skit. I chose a dance called "A Red Army Soldier Misses Chairman Mao" *(Hongjun zhanshi xiangnian Mao Zhuxi)*, which expressed a Red Army soldier's longing for Mao Zedong during wartime. I performed the story of the protagonist who, during a trying period, beheld the twinkling northern star in the dark sky, which reminded her of the oil lamplight shining from Mao's office in the Jingguangshan soviet area. Recalling the journey in which she had followed Mao from victory to victory, she was able to muster her spirit and march on. My sister praised my solo act and was glad to see me in high spirits, wearing my green *xuanchuandui* uniform with its red band on which was embroidered my team's name in gold thread. I was ready to join my teammates in the Beijing train station and looked forward to our journey together to the wilderness to spread our performing tradition. Although I felt sad to be leaving my family, friends, and school, I was excited by the prospect of a new life in a faraway land where we would be adapting our performances to the local audiences. I wished to continue the work my parents had done in Xinjiang and Henan of serving the ordinary people.

At the Beijing train station, I was tearless as I waved to my family and friends. My mind was occupied with the tasks facing us: keeping up the morale of our schoolmates; helping the train attendants serve food and hot water and clean tables and floors; and pitching in as "little helpers" in whatever other ways needed. As members of *xuanchuandui*, we were supposed to do "good deeds" for the people around us and to spread Mao Zedong thought by our own good examples. We had even brought a medicine box in case of emergency. I hoped that, depending on the space available, we might also be able to perform, or at least conduct a few singing sessions when the time was right.

As soon as the train moved out of the station, however, something I had never anticipated happened. People around me began to sob loudly and I could not help but feel sad. My greatest despair, however, came with the sudden realization that my *xuanchuandui* had ceased to exist! We were not seated together, and I was not able to find our team leader, even after a frantic search for her. Finally, I was told that now that we were leaving Beijing, our middle school had lost its function as an organization. We were *bingtuan zhanshi*, or soldiers of the military farm—that is, adults waiting for orders from our work unit supervisors. In the face of this profound disappointment, I tried to maintain the spirit of optimism with which I had set out and to persist in my original plan of serving the people around me. I hoped that somehow the members of my *xuanchuandui* would find their way to each other soon. It was not that I wanted special privileges, but rather that I felt willing and able to endure any hardship as long as a *xuanchuandui* of some sort existed.

When, during my first day in the northeast wilderness, I learned that all of our team members had been assigned to different villages hundreds of miles apart, I was devastated. In a region where transportation meant ox carts and tractors, we might not see each other for a long time, let alone perform together. I remember being totally confused and heartbroken when a truck dropped a dozen of us off in the middle of the wilderness, in front of a pile of lumber with which we were to build our own lodging. Luckily we had been preceded by fifty educated youths of our age from Tianjin, Shanghai, and Harbin who had settled there in the past year. Otherwise we would have been obliged to cut down trees and clear the ground before building. Although I was not yet deterred by the hard labor, I was really frightened to realize that, for the first time in my life, I was alone, without my team and without my family. Up till then, my team, which had defined my very existence, had seemed more important to me than my family. Now, for the first time since leaving Beijing, I missed my family terribly.

I now felt vulnerable, seeing part of my childhood dream shattered. I still worked hard in the fields, but deep in my heart I longed for the real spotlight. It did not have to be on a formal stage, I argued inwardly; I would have been glad to perform in the open fields, as my parents had for local peasants. Many times while tilling the land or harvesting wheat or soybeans, I would gaze off toward the horizon at the dirt road stretching to faraway places and hope to see a truck that had been dispatched from farm headquarters to recruit "new blood" for its own *xuanchuandui*, whose mediocre performance had not impressed me.

In those days, I wanted to visit Beijing, but even more than that I fantasized about being recruited by a performing troupe. Yet when a rare opportunity presented itself two years later, I shied away from trying out for serious parts in the headquarters' *xuanchuandui*. I was more comfortable adhering to my commoner status on the farm, dancing in holiday celebrations and feeling no pressure to occupy center stage. Shi Huifang's *An Evening at the Production Brigade* captured the fun and commitment of those evenings when we performed in our own work unit, where there was no real separation between audience and performers. We all worked in the same field during the day and in the evenings sometimes gathered together as families and friends. On the day I started back to Beijing in 1973, I felt despondent at leaving my friends behind. I felt no need now to look for my "teammates" from my *xuanchuandui* (as I had on leaving Beijing): they were all right there, standing next to me and around me, saying goodbye and wishing me the best in a new start in life.

I hope this digression into my *xuanchuadui* experience will once again proclaim my own responsibility in having participated in, if not always enjoyed, many activities in the visual and performance culture of the Cultural Revolution. For my part, positioned as I have been between two continents, first, as a native participant in the unfolding of the Cultural Revolution and, second, as a cultural critic in American academia sensitive to the intricate postsocialist politics stemming from the new power relationships, I have found it particularly challenging to explain to my students and friends the frequent *xuanchuandui* scenes from Chinese films. In many of them, Red Guard *xuanchuandui* waving Mao's little red quotation book and dancing loyalty dances are instant indicators that the Cultural Revolution has just started. Usually they are followed by brutal beatings at mass criticism meetings and the breaking up of traditional families where fathers, sons, mothers, and daughters denounce each other as enemies of the people. While not denying that these events did occur, I want to point out that these are not complete pictures. As Wang Ban points out in his insightful study, a sublime pleasure existed in the mass participation of political theater: "The Cultural Revolution had created a life that was aesthetically driven, ritualistic, and theatrical."[58] To a large extent, many of us were there; we were players and even supporters of the Cultural Revolution.

Indeed, in spite of some problematic representations of the Cultural Revolution in the Chinese film market, other films simultaneously questioned the individual's role during the revolution. Whereas the film *To Live* presents innocent, ignorant townspeople living close to outlying rural areas as hapless victims, another film, *Farewell My Concubine (Bawang beiji)*,[59] hints at an alternative reading of viewing survivors of the Cultural Revolution as having collaborated, to some extent, in their own persecution. We are shown Duan Xiaolou, a famous actor known for playing the king of Chu in the Peking opera *Farewell My Concubine*, being publicly humiliated and tortured as a remnant of the "old society" along with Cheng Dieyi, his costar, who was acclaimed for playing the female role of the concubine Yu.[60] When being beaten by the Red Guards, Duan buys a reprieve by exposing Cheng as a traitor during the Japanese invasion and as the former homosexual partner of a counterrevolutionary executed by the PRC government. Cheng avenges this betrayal by revealing that Juxian, Duan's wife, was a prostitute before 1949 and an instrument of evil who brought about the ruin of many people. However, it is Juxian who commits suicide so she will not have to inform against others and not have to share Duan's and Cheng's fate of surviving the Cultural Revolution with their memories of betrayal.[61] Fittingly, both principals are skillful actors experienced at assuming varied gender identities and political and ideological colorations, thus highlighting the theatricality of the Cultural Revolution, during which many felt compelled to play a role in order to survive. As some of the film's other settings suggest, this propensity to act while under duress was also propelled by historical events during the Republican period, the war period, and the Maoist and post-Maoist periods.

In the film's denouement, when Cheng and Duan, finally reunited on-stage after the Cultural Revolution, enact the scene from *Farewell My Concubine* in which Yu commits suicide rather than witness the king of Chu's military defeat, Cheng horrifies everyone by using a real sword. This invocation of Juxian's suicide by Cheng can be read as a repudiation of his own act of betrayal during the Cultural Revolution while conveying the crushing guilt he bore as a survivor. In refusing to continue to live the life of a coward, Cheng, by implication, celebrates the steadfast loyalty of the female characters, both onstage (Yu) and offstage (Juxian), and signals that it was their courage which forced him to stop acting in real life, even after the "disastrous"[62] Cultural Revolution was over. Killing himself in real life also guaranteed Cheng would remain faithful to his beloved dramatic role, the loyal concubine Yu. The theater doorkeeper's remarks, which castigate the Gang of Four for keeping the two actors apart from each other and away from the stage for twenty-one years, strike one as particularly ironic, as they are uttered at the very time when Cheng is dramatically assuming responsibility for his conduct.

Jan Wong's interview on February 12, 2000, with Chen Kaige, the director of *Farewell My Concubine*, supports this reading of guilt and responsibility. Chen confessed that this film "about love and betrayal during the Cultural Revolution" was his tribute to his father. At the age of fourteen, Chen denounced his father to win the acceptance of the Red Guards. When he shoved his father, whom the Red Guards had forced to kneel, his father's eyes "really scared [him]. There was no anger there. It was something else, like, 'I feel sorry for you.' " Chen was shocked, a few years later, when his father begged permission to be allowed out of jail to see his son off to the countryside. Chen cried as he watched his father run after the train, realizing how much his father loved him. "After the Cultural Revolution, nobody wanted to take responsibility for their crimes. But everybody, including myself, should take responsibility."[63]

With this brief look at the complexities entailed in representing the Cultural Revolution, I have hoped to raise fundamental questions about the connections between memory, gender, and nation during a specific historical period. The study of the Cultural Revolution must be grounded in its own historical contexts. That is why Chapters 2 and 3 discuss the Cultural Revolutionary model theater, focusing on the dynamic relationship between theater and revolution. Chosen during the Cultural Revolution as the exclusive artistic vehicle to promote proletarian art and eliminate all other literature and art, model theater paradoxically resorted to a "feudal" form of traditional opera and the "Western decadent" arts of ballet and symphony. More important, model theater set the stage for many of the theatrical events in early post-Maoist China, as we shall see in Chapters 4 and 5. Furthermore, as I have shown in these two chapters, the formation of a new culture by model theater cannot be fully appreciated without a close scrutiny of the gender politics involved, which resulted in female protagonists who were portrayed solely as revolutionary warriors and party leaders. This feminization of revolutionary theater was a complicating factor in the overall picture of "official feminism," which had already been receiving attention from scholars in China studies. However, although it seems to represent a divergence from the written texts, the masculinized image of revolutionary women in model theater, by virtue of its theatrical *re*-presentation, is fundamentally feminine in terms of body politics.

Acting between Roles: Race, Nation/State, and Revolution in Political Theaters

To further demonstrate the importance of modern drama studies, this section branches out to extraliterary events: the intricate relationships between theater and revolution. As I have pointed out, the Cultural Revolution itself can be explored as a theatrical event that involved interaction between symbolic script and intended audience on the more comprehensive stage of the political arena. From the reverse angle, one might treat model theater as an integral part of the political theaters that relate to and are central to understanding a culture's past and present. After the highly theatrical incidents of the 1989 Tiananmen student demonstrations riveted the attention of the outside world, a corpus of critical discourse grew up in the West examining the historical roots of political theater in Tiananmen Square since the beginning of the twentieth century. In the crucial acts of this "street theater," several scholars found historical continuities and discontinuities between Imperial China, Republican China, Maoist China, and post-Maoist China that revolved around such events as the demonstration on May 4, 1919, to protest the terms of the Treaty of Versailles; the demonstration on December 9, 1935, that set off the resistance movement against the Japanese invasion; the mass memorial accorded the former prime min-ister Zhou Enlai on April 5, 1976; and, finally, the student demonstrations of 1989.

Literary critics, anthropologists, and historians have sought interpretive clues to the phenomenon of Tiananmen as political drama by looking at the traditions of Chinese operatic theater. For David Strand, the 1989 Tiananmen demonstration was a public, ritual event characterized by a singular rhetorical construction that framed current politics into a morality play, Peking opera style.[64] Anthropologist Frank N. Pieke, studying what he calls the ordinary and extraordinary 1989 Tiananmen events in the context of protest traditions in modern China, believes that dramatization and ritualization were the two common strategies used there: it "started," he points out, "as a dramatized event, but ended as an abortive rite of passage."[65] Whereas the students were social actors who focused on eliciting certain responses from their intended audience,[66] the government blocked its own access to a social role when it cold-bloodedly refused to give the moral dialogue of the hunger strikers a hearing and thereby was branded an amoral and irresponsible actor in the drama.[67]

Joseph Esherick and Jeffrey N. Wasserstrom define the street theater of the 1989 student demonstrations, which they studied in depth, as "untitled, improvisational" political theater, "with constantly changing casts" who "worked from familiar 'scripts' which gave a common sense of how to behave during a given action, where and when to march, how to express their demands, and so forth."[68] They cite key interludes of the demonstrations such as the hunger strike and the erection of the Goddess of Democracy as particularly powerful pieces of theater and identify the best actors.[69] One of the most effective actors was the student leader Wu'er Kaixi, who wore hospital pajamas during his nationally televised meeting with Li

Peng, the state premier the authors describe as both an indifferent audience and the worst actor on the national and international stage, who was unsuitable to his expected role of showing sympathy to his people.[70]

By challenging Esherick and Wasserstrom's study, such cultural geographers as Linda Hershkovitz and cultural performance critics as Richard Schechner further enrich our understanding of the subject. Hershkovitz argues that although Esherick and Wasserstrom see Tiananmen as an important setting for political theater, they tend to "highlight the symbolic provenance of the performance, while largely ignoring the significance of the stage."[71] In her study of the politics of space, Hershkovitz delineates "two distinct but intertwined spatial traditions": (1) Tiananmen Square and its historical monuments, which attested to the dominant political power of the Chinese state; and (2) the square's symbolic geography as shaped by political dissidents, who throughout history appropriated the orthodox tradition the square represents.[72] Hershkovitz's study on the political geography of Tiananmen Square provides the important dimension of space, which we can discuss as text, as theater,[73] and as an ongoing dialectic whose social meanings and cultural significance are constantly being produced and metamorphosed.[74] Although written from a political-geographical standpoint, this study confirms Wu Hong's earlier architectural account of the history of Tiananmen Square, in which the square is seen as a focal point for political identity and collective memory.[75]

For Richard Schechner, who also questions Esherick and Wasserstrom's conception of Tiananmen as a struggle between official ritual and student theater, the relationship between theater and ritual should be a "dialectical and braided" one.[76] Before the tanks entered, Schechner contends, the confrontation was not so much one between rigid ritual and rebellious theater as between two groups of authors (or authorities), each of whom preferred to be the one to draft the script of China's future and each of whom "drew on both theater and ritual."[77] Schechner's brief narrative on theatricalizing media highlights yet another previously unexplored area of Tiananmen studies, but there are many more areas to be plumbed before we can obtain an all-inclusive understanding of the complex dynamics of the Tiananmen stage, whose image has continued to be intensely gazed upon and re-created by global and local audiences long after the theatrical events themselves ended.

The perspective of cross-cultural politics helps to shed light on another aspect of the subject: the process of scripting domestic and international stage roles centering in and around Tiananmen. President Clinton's visit to China in June 1998, for instance, was reported on the American television channels CNN, ABC, and NBC, which made sure to display for their dramatic background near-perfect shots of those parts of Tiananmen Square where the bloodshed occurred in 1989. American anchormen and women debated as to whether Clinton's saluting of the People's Liberation Army during the welcoming ceremony in Tiananmen Square constituted an insult to the massacred of 1989. In my view, however, these provocative dialogues were concocted not so much to instruct Chinese people about democracy as to boost domestic TV ratings and stimulate controversy among Republicans and Democrats with competing political agendas. The Clinton bashing at home, fed by the soap-opera fare of a sensational sex scandal and secret phone tapping, gained dramatic momentum when scripted in the context of China bashing and with the addition of characters such as the Chinese American fund-raisers for the Democratic Party and alleged high-spending contributors from China assuming bit roles or more important parts. The much publicized "open debate" between Clinton and PRC President Jiang Zemin struck me as the ultimate in performances on the international stage on the part of two politicians skilled in addressing their target audiences at home and abroad. Both had obviously rehearsed their "talking points"—to which they referred intermittently—in order to make the best possible case on sensitive issues such as human rights and Tibet. The event, which took place around Tiananmen Square and was transmitted on American television, then engendered further debate among reporters, who, wondering whether Clinton had been as courageous and bold as some Democrats were claiming, zestfully took up the question of whether the "open debate" had not in fact already been scripted behind the scenes long before the public performance as a result of compromises previously reached between the respective negotiation teams.

It is therefore likely that, rather than saying anything meaningful about China, these kinds of Tiananmen stories reflect discursive strategies directed at China as political theater. As a corrective to this situation, Tiananmen studies should be approached from the native Chinese perspective, so that all the discursive tactics within the dynamics of Chinese political theater may be brought to light. In this regard, Wen Fu's study, *A Witness History of Tiananmen*, presents an instructive case for what it contains that Western scholars have ignored. For example, it foregrounds the imperialist history of Tiananmen, detailing how in 1900 the Eight Allied Armies (*Baguo Lianjun*) from Japan, Great Britain, the United

States, Russia, France, Germany, Italy, and Austria occupied Beijing, burned down the imperial Summer Palace, and looted numerous national treasures and historical archives of the Forbidden City adjacent to Tiananmen. The armies massacred innocent citizens, sometimes entire households, and mass-raped Chinese women. Then, after "turning Beijing into a graveyard," the Eight Allied Armies held their own military parades in Tiananmen Square, on August 28, 1900, to commemorate their victory. Although the United States was one of the last nations to join the Allied Armies, its troops raced to edge out the other foreign armies in attacking the gate of Tiananmen so as to have the best pick of the national treasures inside the Forbidden City.[78] Imprinted in the memories of many relatives of the massacred, these witnesses' accounts of Tiananmen were given no place in American television coverage of Tiananmen events on July 1, 1997, when Beijing citizens celebrated Hong Kong's epoch-making return to China after a hundred years of British imperialist rule. Instead, American TV anchors lamented the loss of one of Britain's last colonies while watching a solemn Prince Charles and other British dignitaries participating in the farewell ceremony in Hong Kong. If this American news coverage of Hong Kong's return to China can be construed as part of America's post–Cold War discursive strategy toward China, the accounts of Tiananmen that revolve around the imperialist humiliation of the Chinese people function, in an equally forceful way, as part of the Chinese Communist Party's strategy toward America in the two nations' new power struggle at the end of the millennium. In both political theaters, it so happens that Tiananmen Square was chosen to be the central stage for history writing and mythmaking.

Wen Fu also collected oral histories from major actors in the key events that took place in and around Tiananmen and from the ordinary people who worked behind the scenes preparing for those events. In the process he recorded this kind of telling anecdote. On October 1, 1949, at the beginning of the first national parade to commemorate the founding of the People's Republic of China, 54 cannons were used to fire a twenty-eight-gun salute. Although the salute was conventionally known as having come from 54 cannons, 108 cannons were used that day to shorten the interval time between the filling and firing of the projectiles. The number 54 was interpreted to symbolize 54 ethnic minority groups then identified. The number 28 referred to the twenty-eight-year history of the Chinese Communist Party since its founding in 1921—an idea that purportedly came from Mao Zedong himself, who had had a CCP document drafted to explain to other political parties why the twenty-eight-gun salute was selected instead of the twenty-one-gun salute used in other countries.[79] In the early days of the People's Republic of China, Mao and other CCP leaders customarily consulted with other political parties about state affairs, even on such a small matter as this one—in sharp contrast to the late 1950s, when Mao was suppressing many of his former allies during the anti-rightist movement. Had oral histories of Tiananmen events not been preserved, anecdotes like this one would have been lost, and along with them the origin of certain cultural rituals.

Detailed analyses of highly theatrical events during the Cultural Revolution have not been included in the recent studies of Tiananmen as a site for cultural performance.[80] However, Maoist discourse continuously referred to the Cultural Revolution, depicting it in the official media as a great, living, historical drama enacted by the proletariat and its supporting classes. (In the aftermath, of course, the Cultural Revolution was characterized as a national tragedy directed and enforced by a few antirevolutionary clowns.) Mao's reviews of Red Guards in Tiananmen Square were in themselves highly theatrical performances. From August 18 to November 26, 1966, Mao performed the spectacle eight times of receiving 12 million Red Guards who paraded in front of him to show their loyalty; later on, the guards traveled throughout the land so that they might spread the Maoist cult by recalling these dramatic events in fervent speeches.[81] Mao assuredly broke all world records for such military reviews and national parades: 12 million people represented 1.6 percent of China's total population in the 1960s.[82] On National Day of October 1, 1966, alone, Mao received 1.5 million Red Guards in Tiananmen Square. This also marked the last time that Liu Shaoqi, then president of the People's Republic of China, appeared on the same rostrum with Mao. Two years later, Liu was expelled from the Chinese Communist Party after having been denounced as a "traitor" (*pantu*), "spy" (*tewu*), and a "conspirator" (*neijian*), the archenemy of Mao and the Chinese people. The script for this Tiananmen drama, which had been determined by party politics, was intuitively understood by the public, for whom the disappearance of a CCP dignitary such as Liu signaled the likelihood of his imminent purging from the party and the concomitant reappearance of someone else who might, at this juncture, be rehabilitated or even promoted within the party hierarchy. Lin Biao, who was Mao's choice to succeed Liu Shaoqi as inscribed in the charter adopted at the ninth national congress of the party in 1969, suffered a fate similar to that of his predecessor. In 1971, when Mao and other

CCP leaders joined Beijing citizens to celebrate International Labor Day, Lin Biao, already alienated from Mao, did not linger long enough in Tiananmen Square to have his formal picture taken with Mao and the assembled party chiefs. To forestall the suspicion on the part of millions of Chinese people that there was friction between the two because they would not see a photograph of them together in the next day's newspapers, Premier Zhou Enlai decided to print the only picture of the occasion that was available, despite its inferior quality. The occasion would never be repeated, for on September 13, 1971, Lin Biao died in an airplane crash in Mongolia after allegedly staging an unsuccessful coup d'état against Mao, and Mao never appeared again in Tiananmen Square as a vigorous, dynamic national leader. Such events, which typify the interplay between Tiananmen stories and inside stories of the CCP, afford enlightening angles from which to consider print culture as discursive strategies in the PRC, especially during, although not limited to, the period of the Cultural Revolution. On many occasions such as these, people read between the lines and take seriously visual images such as photographs of major state leaders; their absence might indicate impending political changes. These nonverbal means of expression could furthermore help elucidate state censorship and control at all levels and in all media, and are an invaluable aid in preserving the part of Tiananmen history not usually contained in the official history books issued by the CCP.

The dramatic intensity and theatricality of the performances engaged in by the main actors of the Cultural Revolution cannot be overemphasized. In his famous eight reviews of the Red Guards, Mao would appear just as the sun was beginning to rise in the east, at exactly five o'clock in the morning, accompanied by the solemn music "The East Is Red." Attired in a green army uniform, he would stand in the middle of the Tiananmen Square rostrum and wave to millions of Red Guards. Walking dramatically, first to the eastern end of the rostrum and then the western end, he would respond to the enthusiastic displays of his audience by repeatedly calling out: "Long live the Red Guards!" and "Long live the great Cultural Revolution!" For Mao, the public performances in which he acted as the audience for the surrounding masses reaffirmed his absolute power as the director of a grand theater, and the parading Red Guards were a dramatized model of military units-cum-political organizations, whom he used in the guise of rebels to bring down such archenemies as Liu Shaoqi and Deng Xiaoping. Mao, on the other hand, was himself a spectacle for the masses, a veritable one-man show. Both sides partook of the playing and watching of the play, although at this early stage of the Cultural Revolution Mao was the show's chief designer, drawing to his side millions who were at one and the same time supporters of and passionate participants in his revolutionary drama. Numerous posters of the time depicting Mao as the glorious leader in front of enthusiastic mass audiences, and other posters depicting the political rituals of the period, as Harriet Evans and Stephanie Donald have argued, provide "a major visual text central to the processes of constructing meaning and practice" during the Cultural Revolution.[83] Once again, visual culture has left behind a body of valuable and lasting images for the study of the theatricality of the political life during the Cultural Revolution, in the same way that other posters have illuminated us about the cultural practice of revolutionary model theater.

Mao engaged in another spectacular performance at this time: he swam across the Yangtze River to promote an image of himself as a robust, vital national leader at age sixty-eight. The photo of Mao—and the posters based on that photo—dressed in swimming pajamas, was efficiently distributed far and wide by the print media and was accompanied in the newspapers by the caption, in large type: "Even great storms are not to be feared. It was amid great storms that human societies developed." Constantly reminded of the benefits of "learning swimming, crossing the Yangtze River, and following Chairman Mao in revolutionary wind and waves," as the popular saying put it, millions of people followed his energetic example. Men and women, both young and old and from all walks of life, joined in, precipitating a national surge of swimming contests. Aged twelve at the time, I eagerly followed suit and swimming became my only sport. This was the only period in my otherwise inactive youth when sport culture meant anything to me: I might have been excluded from the Red Guards and denied the honor of being received by Mao in Tiananmen Square, but I felt that here was something I could enjoy, and had the right to enjoy, along with any other adolescent. Swimming offered me a limited public space in which my private body could not be rejected, either physically or symbolically, by the collective body. Thus I became a proud actress, playing my own part in the national drama of the ongoing revolution, which, to a child, often signified the spontaneous joy surrounding festival- or carnival-like holidays from school and from other daily routines. Above all else, swimming allowed me to delve into the "swimming pool" of the mainstream political culture and shed the fear of being an outsider. Never again in my life would I lose myself in play as I did then, rather than remaining content to be the observer on the sidelines. A poster from that period entitled "Swimming across the Ten-thousand-mile Yangtze River" vividly portrays the theatrical spectacle of the mass movement to imitate Mao's heroic act, with children and teenagers swimming with balloons and an enthusiastic audience cheering them on in the background. The photo of Mao waving at revolutionary masses became the central part of the backdrop of the "stage."[84]

Recent scholarship on Tiananmen has centered on the rendering of political events as theatrical acts, but in Chapter 5 of this study I emphasize the *interplay* between real-life Tiananmen drama and its staged representation, focusing particularly on a special form of street theater in early post-Maoist China, which I call "the theater of the street." This theater presented, on a small stage, the dramatic events of the street theater of the April Fifth movement of 1976 (siwu yundong), which saw the first public display of anger against the Maoist regime in the PRC period. As a type of distilled "theater of the street," it drew from the larger street theater in many other crucial political moments, with cultural performers establishing for themselves how to act and what to express in their stage lines. From the perspective of theater of the street, the seemingly uninteresting and "jargon-ridden" texts of "anti–Gang of Four plays" will yield insights into the dialectical relationship between theater and revolution, and modern Chinese drama could perhaps reveal more than has operatic theater about the rhetoric and performing strategies gleaned from Cultural Revolutionary and post–Cultural Revolutionary experiences. Indeed, it is impossible to take the full measure of the discourse on Tiananmen without giving serious attention to this unique incarnation of street theater.

Studies of street theater can, moreover, have arresting comparative and cross-cultural implications when considered in different national and cultural contexts. In spite of the vast differences in culture, ideology, and history of the two countries, recent scholarship on the theater of Nazi Germany has revealed surprising similarities with the national drama of China. Programmed to think in terms of politically oriented art and theater, both the Chinese and the German intelligentsia were enlisted as architects of and leading actors in the rebirth of a national culture by creating theater in general and a new national theater in particular; in that capacity they scripted such political theater as rallies, speeches, and parades, and were responsible for theatrical productions. Moreover, as I demonstrate in Chapter 3, Chinese intellectuals and artists were relied upon to formulate various imagined communities for utopian China. Like their German counterparts, they were both "divisive and critical intellectuals," in that they complied with the persecution of their brethren while also functioning as inventors of the Volksgemeinschaft.[85] The theater of both nations had in common a vision of the politicization of theater, the acceptance of the "Volksgemeinschaft as not only a fact of life, but also the highest form of life,"[86] and an idealized view of that folk community as engendering a revolutionary spirit that would effect what Adolf Hitler called the "nationalization of the masses."[87] Goebbels' declaration that any healthy storm trooper should have the same values as those held by a "conscious artist"[88] could be read as the simple obverse of Mao's motto that urged conscientious artists to "move their feet over to the side of the workers, peasants, and soldiers" so as to serve their interests and become identified with their life and struggles.[89]

One cannot, in other words, become a conscientious artist unless, and until, one has learned to appreciate and appropriate as one's own the ideals of the common people. The poster of the Cultural Revolution, entitled "Art comes from a life of struggle; the working people are the master," depicted this dual persona in an artist. In it, a painter dressed in peasant attire eagerly paints on a wall images of a golden harvest in a prosperous village, with two peasant-like women painting a similar picture as the background.[90] The central image of the male artist embodies the dual process of revolutionary art and its creator. He can be seen as a peasant painter who has acquired artistic skills through truthfully portraying his own life, or as a "conscientious artist" who lives and dresses as a peasant in order to faithfully represent their life. If, as mentioned before, the revolutionary masses need to imitate professional artists' performance of model theater, which was based in the first place on the life experience of the proletariat, so the peasant painters, as seen in this image, have already taken over the common people's persona and acquired the professional skills of the professional. Once again, posters and performing arts together have taught us a significant lesson in the political process and cultural productions of the period.

Furthermore, Robert A. Pois' analysis of the political culture of Nazi Germany, as informed by Martin Esslin's theory of drama, provides another basis of comparison, evoking as it does the political theater of the Cultural Revolution. First, Esslin's definition of drama as "action-oriented" is used by Pois to examine the Nazi rallies and party leaders' political addresses that took place around 1933 and were particularly efficacious in attracting enthusiastic young people.[91] Himself a masterful manipulator of high drama, Hitler would enter his center stage accompanied by the rousing music of the Badernweiler march, and his speech would be preceded by a performance of Beethoven's Egmont Overture, whose patriotic theme memorializes the struggle of the Dutch people against their Spanish enemy.[92] In his speech, which usually focused on Germany's "rebirth," Hitler would speak of the anticipated emergence of "a new German man"[93] in a manner not unlike that of Mao during the Cultural Revolution when he spoke of China's rebirth as a proletariat state purer than any other socialist states.

Second, Nazi political theater exhibited the characteristic of drama, as described by Martin Esslin, of unfolding the action in an "eternal present" that is considered sacred because of "the natural truths expressed in the name of the folk-community,"[94] a feature reflected in the Maoist view that literature and art must serve the divine course of the Communist revolution and the interest of the masses. Maoist and Nazi political leaders, but especially Mao and Hitler, manifested a "kind of 'giving and getting' play" evocative of an interaction between mother and child that suggests the third characteristic Esslin designated for drama.[95] Thus Mao and the CCP were described, in political and literary discourse, as caring for their people with a mother's love, a sentiment evoked in the 1950s and 1960s by the popular lyrics of "When I Sing a Song for the Party" (Chang zhi shange gei dang ting): "When I sing a song for the party, I compare my party to my mother. Mother only gave birth to my body, but it is the brilliant sunshine of the party that warms my heart and soul."[96] Both the looming Maoist image of the mother and the towering Nazi image of the Führer could be sensed behind the dramatic characters who strode the Chinese and German stages and left their profound mark on the world's larger political stage and on everyday life.

Interestingly, both Mao and Hitler were interested in the particulars of theater production, and both believed with a passion that great consequences ensued from the way a country managed its theater. Mao's ambivalent relationship to theater was expressed in his attack on the Peking opera Hai Rui Dismissed from Office (Hairui baguan, 1960), an event that triggered the Cultural Revolution, for Mao believed that this opera was intended to criticize his unjustifiable discharging of Peng Dehuai, the then minister of defense, from his top party and military positions after he had spoken out against Mao's policies. The overriding concern Mao had about theater was that, in the hands of enemies like antirevolutionaries, plays could become "bombshells" leveled at the Communist Party and its socialist regime.[97] His support for model theater, on the other hand, was motivated by the intention to prove that proletarian art was possible and, in fact, very desirable. Hitler's concern in regard to German theater, according to Glen W. Gadberry, was influenced by his fear that it was being contaminated by Jewish culture, as the Jews were especially adept at role playing in their "host" countries as a means both of survival and of gaining entry to the theater. Thus Hitler considered acting "an ideal craft for a race without artistic talent."[98]

This brings us to the issue of ethnic diversity, and it was in this area that there was a distinct difference between Maoist and Nazi theater. As I explain in Chapters 2 and 3, model theater, and by extension the radical ideology of the Cultural Revolution it represented, distinguished negative and positive characters along class lines and according to their family relationship to the Communist revolution before 1949. Nazi theater, on the other hand, differentiated dramatic characters along racial lines: German people, as pointed out by Robert A. Pois, were taught to identify themselves "as unified 'Volk' tied together by traditions sanctioned by blood," whereas Jews were designated by Hitler as "cultural destroyers" who inevitably lacked the "real greatness" of artists.[99] After all traces of Jewish influence had been expunged from every aspect of the German theater, Nazi Germany was in a position to achieve what it had sought: an idealized, heroic, political twentieth-century theater passionately in tune with a "mythically 'better' German past" and a racially purer German nation.[100] The comparison between Chinese and German theater would not be complete without our acknowledging the fine line that exists between class and racial discrimination. This is exemplified by Chinese class theory, which in its extreme form during the Cultural Revolution also resorted to sanctioning by blood ties, and by the findings of recent studies of Nazi culture that point up the ways in which class discrimination worked in close association with the discrimination that led to racial elimination.[101]

According to Ron Engle, the German political theater's central theme of struggling to achieve racial purity is reflected in Friedrich Forster's *All against One—One for All (Alle gegen einen—einer für alle)*, a typical drama of the Nazi period. In this play a Germanic tragic hero's efforts to free his country symbolize Hilter's struggle to liberate the German people.[102] Similarly, in several dramatic works by Eberhard Wolfgang Möller, the playwright who was the most effective proponent of these views, a Volk desperately seeks "a strong military Führer to combat the evil alien who is a Jew, a greedy capitalist, a traitorous politician, or some combination of the three."[103] While new plays were being written in Germany expounding the themes that honored the birth of the new nation, old repertoires from both native and foreign soil were also plundered for any plays that lent themselves to glorifying the existing regime. In the very few years during which Friedrich Schiller's dramas were singled out by Goebbels as embodying blueprints for the Fatherland and a united people,[104] *Thomas Paine* by Hanns Johst (1937) became one of the most produced plays in Germany because of its dramatization of an American hero's struggle for freedom and its exaltation of a patriot who inspired his people with his "national spirit of unity for its fatherland."[105] From the foregoing it appears that both Germany and China, in trying to effect the rebirth of their corresponding nations, looked to theater as a forceful tool for restoring lost purity, whether in racial or class terms. Despite differences in motive and historical background, Cultural Revolutionary model works, like Nazi theater, evinced the unusual "paradox of an essentially elitist movement being able to articulate itself in egalitarian terms."[106] A related paradox is that countries with movements benefiting from the unstinting participation of intellectuals forged a political agenda that was profoundly anti-intellectual, mass-centered, and antimodern in approach and content.

The creating of a national theater out of elements dictated by the political theater is by no means a process unique to Germany and China. Jonathan M. Weiss' recent study on Quebec theater, for instance, traces just such a development as he follows the formation of a contemporary French-speaking Quebec national theater in English-speaking Canada.[107] Preconditioned by the political theater that accompanied Quebec's Quiet Revolution of the early 1960s, and further inspired by the national aspiration for separatism and a number of pivotal political events,[108] the national theater acquired a distinct cultural and intellectual identity that closely reflected the rise of Quebec nationalism.[109] This artistic and political declaration of independence from English Canada, Weiss shows, "encouraged a cultural intimacy that allowed theater to become, in many instances, popular entertainment. . . ."[110]

In the case of China, the germinating elements of its modern theater can be detected in 1866, when residents from Britain and other foreign countries living in Shanghai built a theater named the Lyceum (transliterated as *Lanxin xiyuan* in Chinese) in order to perform Western plays for their own entertainment.[111] Modern drama, however, appeared somewhat later, around the turn of the century. In June 1907 a group of Chinese students in Tokyo performed *The Black Slave Cries Out to Heaven (Heinu yutianlu)*, a dramatic adaptation of Harriet Beecher Stowe's *Uncle Tom's Cabin* that seems to embody the anomalous development of modern Chinese drama.[112] While stirred by the American founding fathers' conception of equality and exploiting it to counter the Confucian tradition, the first generation of Chinese dramatists was simultaneously attracted to the work for its stinging critique of black slavery and the subsequent liberal criticism it generated that exposed the hypocrisy underlying the United States' founding principles.

Furthermore, the 1901 Chinese translation of Stowe's novel by Lin Shu, on which the adaptation was based, was prompted by Lin Shu's indignation over the reportedly cruel treatment overseas of Chinese coolies by the American "white race." This same "white race" oppressed both the "black race" and the "yellow race," according to Lin Shu, who informed his audience that the racial discrimination and oppression abroad had kindled his impassioned determination to bring the play to the attention of the Chinese people.[113] Thus ethnic conflict, cultural and national identity, and resistance to foreign oppression were issues that came to the fore in modern Chinese drama from its inception and that would subsequently be elaborated upon during the War of Resistance to Japan, when the Japanese, who were of the same "yellow race" and yet an ethnic "other," fulfilled the role of enemy of the Chinese nation in both onstage and offstage dramas. This was in fact a time of national crisis when the drama achieved unprecedented popularity and was seen as a more effective genre than fiction or poetry for mobilizing war efforts and stoking national sentiments against the Japanese invaders.

As the foregoing indicates, it was ironically in Japan, where Western spoken drama was experimented with in the Meiji period (1868–1912), that the first Chinese dramas were performed. In 1906, Ouyang Yuqian, Lu Jingruo, and other Chinese students established a drama club in Tokyo known as the Spring Willow Society (Chunliu she). While applying their knowledge of Western dramatic conventions, the students also drew from the political orientation of the reformers of Japanese theater to shape the early content of Chinese drama. Preoccupied especially by political events surrounding the 1911 Republican Revolution that was intended to overthrow the Qing dynasty, several early Chinese dramas initially depicted the experience of Asian ethnic others such as Japan and Korea to express their similar political concerns. Set in the period of the Meiji Reformation of Japan, *Blood-Stained Straw Cape (Xuesuo yi)*, pro-

duced by the Evolution Troupe (Jinghua tuan) in Nanjing in 1911, dramatized the struggle of Japanese parliamentarians against imperial monar-
chists, which for Chinese audiences would have been a clear allusion to
Chinese revolutionaries' efforts to end imperial rule in China.[114] A similar
response would have been elicited by *The Storms of East Asia (Dongya
fengyun)*, premiered in 1911 by the Evolution Troupe in the same season.
This play recounted the life of An Chung Keun, a Korean national hero
who in 1909 assassinated Itoh Hirobumi, the Resident-General of Korea
from Japan responsible for planning Japanese colonialism.[115]

These plays aptly represent the trend in early drama of utilizing prototypes from ethnic and national "others" to help construct Chinese national characteristics. The process was made complex by the travel of
many Chinese dramatists to the West, where they were influenced by the
Western dramatic canon and such contemporary American playwrights as
Eugene O'Neill. This continuing exchange between Eastern and Western
theaters became one of the most significant factors in the canon formation of modern Chinese drama, and in early Chinese drama it can be dis-
cerned in terms of such cross-cutting categories as nation (China versus
Japan versus America), race (Afro-American versus Chinese Japanese
versus Chinese American), and class (coolies versus their social and economic "superiors" either in China or in America).

John Conteh-Morgan, in his study on the literary drama in Francophone Africa, provides a similar account of the intimate relationship between the origin of modern drama and ethnic and racial conflict. According to Conteh-Morgan, the first seeds of French-speaking drama were
sewn at the turn of the century when Roman Catholic schools helped
their students in colonial Africa enact biblical stories in the context of
their religious education.[116] Some historians of Chinese drama have
argued that a parallel embryonic modern drama arose in China in the
latter part of the nineteenth century when Western-sponsored missionary
schools in urban centers such as Beijing, Shanghai, Tianjin, and Guangzhou promoted students' amateur dramatizations of biblical stories and
other Western plays to enhance their religious instruction and instruction
in the English language.[117] These theatrical experiences were forerunners
of the Chinese-language plays that sprang up at a later point on campuses
and at other elite sites in major cities. An important distinction to be
made at this point is related to the fact that China was only semicolonized
by foreign powers and therefore the anti-Western imperialist theme
was downplayed in the early Chinese plays. On the other hand, the first

African play written in French in 1933 dealt with the confrontation between a Frenchman asserting his colonialist privileges and a native chief defending his territory.[118] Conteh-Morgan notes that in molding the Francophone African drama, the oral and epic traditions were particularly inspirational to Francophone playwrights, who rediscovered in them native heroic figures and events they could use to foster a national consciousness in the wake of French colonial domination.[119] The relevance of heroic history to drama remained vital in postcolonial Africa owing to the urgent task of nation building, which made heightened ethnic loyalties and cultural integration desirable.[120] Chinese audiences were made familiar with this proud, independent history of postcolonial Africa via the performance on the Maoist stage in 1965 of *War Drums on the Equator* (*Chidao zhangu*) by Li Huang and others, which portrayed the efforts of African people to eradicate burgeoning US imperialism from the continent.[121] Playwrights and cast members created this play to dutifully promote Mao's campaign to build Chinese nationalism, in which, as Frank Dikötter points out, he combined his concepts of class and race into a blueprint for the "colored people's" common struggle against "white imperialism."[122]

The Maoist emphasis on race and class culminated in a new PRC subgenre called the "ethnic minority play" (*shaoshu minzu xiju*). Literary historians have determined that, although China is a multiethnic nation with more than fifty national minority groups, ethnic theaters did not exist before 1949 except for the sprinkling of folk dramas to be found among Tibetan, Bai, Zhuang, Dai, Tong, and Buyi minority groups. It was the evolution of the People's Republic of China as a strong and unified nation, they maintain, that led to the flourishing of ethnic theaters throughout the country.[123] However, love-interest themes and mythical tales to explain ethnic origins were not fully developed as drama until after 1949, when the state government began to sponsor professional theaters to work with and promote ethnic traditions. The theaters were undoubtedly imbued with the PRC conviction that ethnic groups before 1949 were oppressed and exploited, whereas in socialist China ethnic groups would live peacefully together. *The Marriage of the Hezhe People* (*Hezheren de hunli*), premiered in 1962, for instance, recalled the three hundred-year history of the Hezhe people who inhabited northeastern China and their wretched existence during the Qing dynasty and Japanese occupation, which underwent a dramatic transformation in the PRC period.[124] The subject of both the Tibetan and the modern Chinese ver-

FIGURE 16. *Princess Wencheng,* premiered by the China Youth Art Theater in 1960.

sions of the play *Princess Wencheng* (*Wencheng Gongzhu;* Fig. 16) is the interracial marriage of Princess Wencheng of the Tang dynasty and a Tibetan chieftain, and the communal attempts at bringing economic prosperity and cultural development to the remote regions of Tibet. That the play was given a much publicized, special performance for Premier Zhou Enlai signifies its perceived importance in the PRC for promoting ethnic harmonies.[125]

Forging a national identity centered around the values and heritage of the majority Han people was made possible in contemporary Chinese theater precisely because it was done by having recourse to the voices and characters of ethnic others, either in or outside Chinese territories. The practice extended to post-Maoist China when, according to historians of the drama, the Chinese stage was provided with increasingly vivid, realistic characters from disparate ethnic groups who felt encouraged by the newly liberating influence of the Dengist government to pursue their private ambitions.[126] Thus, in the case of the Han-centered new regime, as before, legitimacy was sought through formation of a seemingly multiethnic voice.

In Chapter 8, I consider some formalistic aspects of Chinese theater, showing how the introduction of theatrical canons from ethnic and national others in Europe and America shaped the contour of what was known in the 1980s as experimental theater. These other traditions, however, could not have taken hold on the Chinese stage without assuming much of the coloration of the cultural and social conditions in contemporary China. Indeed, the tension between a globally oriented theater heavily indebted to foreign influences and a locally centered theater that produced plays with a strong regional flavor became the dynamic, dialectical foundation of the recently formed Chinese canon. The ongoing critical debates on how best to explore the images and styles of the other on the Chinese stage have been inextricably interwoven with issues of form and content, especially in China today, when, in my view, the discourse on aesthetics cannot remain culturally relevant without also being political and personal.

In Chapters 6 and 7 I address the relationship between the personal and the political in the course of exploring women's theater. These chapters are informed by Sue-Ellen Case's pioneering study of feminist theater, which challenges the patriarchal history of Western drama, taking its cue from Aristotle's *Poetics*, that traditional history had always regarded women as inferior and therefore confined them to the role of audience.[127] From the beginning, Case argues, the "aesthetic prescriptive" formula that has governed the Western criteria for canonicity was integrated into gender politics and thus never ideologically separate, so that women, as a consequence of their poor showing in representational politics, were excluded from the theatrical experience. Case's feminist approach, it seems to me, dictates her conclusion that a patriarchal tradition which usurps the mainstream necessarily casts women as "outsiders" vis-à-vis the political system.[128]

In surveying the work by women playwrights in post-Maoist China, I look beyond this Western discourse as I investigate the double role of women playwrights who were simultaneously supporters of official feminism and advocates of a women's theater with a degree of political power. Adopting a personal approach for the purpose of dissecting the political complexities of that period, I interviewed women playwrights and recovered in the process the subjective voices and the collective identities they had attempted to convey. Although I concluded that, owing to the particular cultural and ideological circumstances of contemporary China, women's theater could never be a genuinely countercultural force, I saw that it nevertheless had managed to effectively challenge and resist the mainstream, patriarchal culture through limited political interventions during a period of political transformation in the 1980s.

To update my study of post-Maoist drama at the point of its completion and eight years after it was first undertaken, I returned in 1998 to a China marked by rapid economic development. I was pleasantly surprised to encounter a spring theater season acclaimed by critics for its vigorous dramatic output after many years of stagnation and decline. It was particularly refreshing to interview Lin Zhaohua, one of the most successful contemporary Chinese directors, whose experimental theater had changed the dramatic landscape in the early 1980s. In a departure from the way in which he sought to finance his earlier attempts at "avant-garde" plays— for example, *Bus Stop (Chezhan)* in 1983, *The Alarm Signal (Juedui xinhao)* in 1982, and *Wildman (Yeren)* in 1985[129]—Lin Zhaohua had felt it necessary to borrow 200,000 Chinese yuan (an equivalent of US$24,490) to produce his latest independent play, *Three Sisters Waiting for Godot (San zimei dengdai geduo)* in 1998; this was a daring act that would once have been unthinkable in China, where the state government had been responsible for all theater payrolls and production costs since 1949 until not long ago.

When I asked Lin why he was assuming the financial risk for putting on a new play while he was still vice president of the Beijing People's Art Theater (Beijing renmin yishu juyuan), which had provided him with all the resources he needed, he stressed that sponsoring the production himself would mean that he could more easily hew to his own artistic standards without having to worry about state and city censorship. Convinced that the artistic merit of his play could not be measured in monetary terms, he had felt from the beginning of the project that he was prepared to lose money on it. Yet although the playwright was unanimously praised for his single-minded pursuit of his art, the play *Three Sisters Waiting for Godot* received considerably less than wholehearted praise. If Anton Chekhov's *The Three Sisters* and Samuel Beckett's *Waiting for Godot* are difficult works to produce in their own right, it can be imagined what a daunting task Lin set himself by combining in one play these two masterpieces from different centuries and cultures. In Lin's play, three Russian daughters of a deceased general sit together toward the back of the stage, talking, weeping, and looking forward to the day when they will move from their old home to Moscow and lead an entirely different, happy life, while toward the front of the stage two French tramps wait by a dying tree for the arrival of a Mr. Godot. In response to the criticism that his dull, plotless, and incomprehensible play accomplished little but drive audiences away from the theater, Lin maintained that it was not the artist's job to cater to audiences' existing tastes; his mission was to create an innovative play that would find its own, new generation of audiences capable of appreciating a higher, more sophisticated level of art. Lin professed himself pleasantly surprised to see only two dozen audience members walk out in the middle of each performance—he had expected half of the audience to be gone before the play was over, as had happened at the performances of his earlier experimental play, *Wildman*.

From my interviews with audiences after the performance, it became clear to me that there was a multiplicity of reactions to Lin's play, with only a minority of audience members appreciating the play in the precise way that would have pleased him; many in this minority were university students and members of the intellectual elite who were able to take the play on its own terms. Two university students who were active in their own campus' theatrical events were grateful for the opportunity to enjoy "real theater," even though they considered the ticket price of 50 Chinese yuan too steep. They also understood the sense of pain, isolation, and loneliness expressed by the three Russian sisters, relating it to their own experience in China. A young artist saw in the still and serene three sisters a kind of "sculptural beauty" that reminded him of his own artworks. Others approached the play from a socialist-realist angle: they interpreted the play's thematic concerns as having to do with not giving up hope after setbacks in one's personal life. A small portion of the audience came automatically, without a care to what play was being presented, to show their continuing support for the Beijing People's Art Theater, which retains the reputation of producing regional, Beijing-flavored plays. It was also clear to me, however, that many of the traditional audience for drama, the common people and Beijing citizens for whom socialist works had been created in drama's golden age, would never return to a theater whose elitist and artistic programs were now deliberately devoid of any reference to them.

This fundamental change in the nature of modern Chinese drama was ironically accompanied by the news—carried on the front page of the *People's Daily* on April 14, 1998—that after forty years' delay, the first and only National Grand Theater (Guojia da juyuan) would finally rise on the western side of the Grand Hall of the People in Tiananmen Square, taking its place among the national monuments erected to promote art and culture. Thus would be fulfilled Premier Zhou Enlai's vision of forty years before when he supervised the designing of the building during celebrations surrounding the tenth anniversary of the funding of the PRC. Insufficient funds had caused the project to be canceled at the last minute in favor of other constructions considered more vital, such as that of the Grand Hall of the People. In the intervening years Chinese architects helped train foreign architects who built their own national grand theaters in North Korea and elsewhere. They also watched as many world-renowned theater complexes and structures came into being, such as Lincoln Center in New York in 1965, the Kennedy Art Center in Washington, D.C., in 1971, and the Sydney Opera House in 1973. After all the years of waiting, said the *People's Daily*, the Chinese people would finally be able to celebrate the ground breaking for an outstanding national theater capable of reflecting China's image in the world as a mighty, affluent socialist country.

However, my parents and their friends from the China Youth Art Theater received the news about the National Grand Theater with mixed emotions. In the late 1950s they had been overjoyed at the prospect of a theater they saw as becoming their new "home," where they might found a national modern drama for the Chinese people. Forty years later, with many retirements having taken effect in recent years and their old theater building torn down in 1994 to make room for a shopping center, they had to make do with a China Youth Art Theater fallen on hard times, with no place to rehearse and to perform, and, most important, no means of attracting and interacting with the kinds of audiences who, back in the 1950s and 1960s, camped outside the theater overnight so they could be the first to purchase tickets the next morning.

Over the years many talented young actors and actresses recruited by and trained in the theater gradually left to become movie stars, including Jiang Wen, who won over many Western audiences with his films *Red Sorghum (Hong gaoliang)* and *The Small Town of Furong (Furongzhen)*. Seeing no impending rescue from its limbo-like existence, the China Youth Art Theater had no choice but to rent and remodel an old club (with only four hundred seats) in a back alley of a residential area far from the commercial and cultural center of Beijing. Besides requiring an investment of 700,000 yuan to remodel the club, the theater had to pay an annual rent of 300,000 yuan under a four-year lease. No longer fully supported by the Ministry of Culture—which now earmarks only one-quarter of its annual budget—the China Youth Art Theater had to cast about for innovative ways to achieve financial independence. Luckily, the very pool of talented actors and actresses it trained turned out to be its best assets, since film and television stations were willing to pay high fees to "borrow" them.

More depressing to me, however, than the small, dark space in which the China Youth Art Theater functioned was the performance I attended, in April 1998, of A *Girl from a Green House (Huafang guniang)*. The play might charitably be described as a bewildering piece of theater with unclear thematic concerns and unimaginative production. The female protagonist appeared to be a pure, naive girl who lived in a "green house," oblivious to what was happening in the real world. One might interpret her leaving home to counter her husband's cunning schemes to borrow money for the purchase of their apartment as a protest against the excessively commercialized, materialistic Chinese society of the late 1990s, and/or one might see her subsequent return to the apartment as the sanctioning of a patriarchal society that shuts women up in a "green house" guarded by men. For many audience members, however, the play simply did not make any sense, according to my interviews with some of them after the show.

Walking out of the theater, I could not help but think of the play as reflecting some bitter truths about this national theater. Isolated from a new era that prizes modernity and economic success, the China Youth Art Theater takes pride in being the naive, simple "girl from a green house," uncontaminated by the pollution of the urban environment and uncorrupted by the surrounding materialistic society. The saddest aspect of this state of affairs, however, is that whereas a young woman could perhaps survive living alone in her own space (although the play seems to suggest otherwise), a national theater can never endure without taking the plunge into the real world and carving out a meaningful place for itself in a society increasingly alienated from dramatic art and the mass audience. It is in this sense that we can best appreciate the irony of constructing the physical space for a National Grand Theater in a historical period when the substance of such a theater has been emptied out, when the project that is hailed for its resplendence and promise has in fact been revived forty years too late to salvage the idea of a national theater worthy of the name.

In the end, for the sake of financial survival, the China Youth Art Theater did venture into the realm of popular culture. In 1998 it sold to the China Central Television Station a fifteen-part dramatic series, *Long Journey into Endless Night (Heiye manman lu changchang)*, to be aired on fifteen consecutive days, depicting the struggles of four unemployed female workers after their state-owned enterprise went bankrupt. The high ratings for the series indicated that it had struck a responsive chord among many audience members made anxious by the CCP policy of eliminating inefficient state-owned companies and government agencies at the expense of the millions of ordinary people left unemployed. Many of these kinds of workers had once been lauded in socialist plays produced by the China Youth Art Theater before the Cultural Revolution as "model factory workers" and as new, joyous masters of the PRC. Perhaps, without intending it, the China Youth Art Theater had located its own audience by reviving its former promise of producing "socialist-realist" plays that deal with the lives of the common people. However, with the bonanza of 300,000 yuan, it could continue to maintain its newly renovated theater, where that promise was no longer necessarily heeded. Thus in this ambiguous fashion did a proud national theater finally succumb to the commercialization it had so long resisted.

The China Youth Art Theater's subsequent enterprise did not, however, meet with financial success. Bertolt Brecht's *The Threepenny Opera (Sanjiao qian geju)* premiered on May 25, 1998, but, despite sold-out performances for the following twenty-one consecutive shows, no profit was made from the ticket sales. The play was directed by Chen Yong, the world-acclaimed woman director of more than fifty plays for the China Youth Art Theater, including Brecht's *The Life of Galileo* and *The Caucasian Chalk Circle*. Enthusiastic theater critics and audiences welcomed, in their own words, "the return of a magic director, actor, and actress and authentic dramatic art commensurate with the name and reputation of the China Youth Art Theater." The play might have had a long run had the theater been able to afford the continuing expenses for each additional performance: 240 yuan for each leading actor and actress, and 100 yuan for each stage technician, dancer, and orchestra musician, for a total cost of more than 10,000 yuan per performance. My interview with Chen Yong and some of the other theater artists struck a nostalgic note as we acknowledged the difficulty of working in "nondramatic times," when a national theater must discover ways of competing with Western ballets, foreign orchestras, and international drama companies in addition to domestic entertainments such as soap operas, television dramas, films, rock and roll, VCD, and MTV.

This introduction would not be complete if I did not mention the various dramatic roles I myself played in the process of conceptualizing and writing this study. My formative years as a native PRC citizen allowed me to constantly redefine, negotiate, and ultimately question my critical perspectives and the impact of the knowledge I acquired during my aca-demic training as a comparatist and cultural critic in North America. My performatory role as an associate professor of Chinese literature and comparative literature at Ohio State University at both the graduate and undergraduate levels drew my attention to the particularities of audiences: their performances in cross-cultural contexts and the relevance of my teaching to their life experience. Finding myself in an academic environ-ment where undergraduate students are obliged to take such courses as Modern Chinese Drama in English Translation to fulfill the "non-Western literary requirement" of their general education curriculum compelled me to address the following questions. How do I help them relate to some-thing as foreign as Chinese drama? What do I expect them to learn about Chinese drama that might have a bearing on their lives and careers, which usually have little to do with either theater or China? In my own classroom performance, how do I articulate a voice predetermined by Chinese cul-ture without conveying either Sinocentric or Eurocentric biases? These and other related questions consciously and subconsciously impinged on the writing of this study and the critical and cross-cultural issues that preoccupied me.

Throughout, as I have suggested in this introduction, my multiple posi-tions and experiences in China filter through. In my discussion of Cul-tural Revolutionary theater both on and off stage, my voice may sometimes emerge as a teenager and as "one of them" who watched, improvised, played along, and at various points performed the "great drama of the Cul-tural Revolution." Although innocent and uninformed, I was not entirely guilt-free, belonging as I did to that large company of cast members who generated, adapted to, and dressed up for their roles in the cultural per-formance. Now and then my study also betrays my own voice as the daughter of a theater's celebrated actress and stage designer, who always strove to serve ordinary people in spite of their elite backgrounds, and whose perspectives and perceptions no doubt directly and indirectly color my understanding of theater. In Chapters 4 and 5 on social problem plays and Chapters 6 and 7 on women's theater, I drew on my personal involve-ment as I watched the plays I discuss during that early post-Maoist period when to engage in performance on and off stage was both politically pro-vocative and emotionally gratifying. Although I benefited from my two-fold role as local audience and cultural performer, it was inevitable that I should later interrogate that role from my vantage point of theoretically informed cultural critic in North American academe. Above all else, I am painfully aware of my multiple subjectivities—the "I-narrators"—that dictated much of the telling of my stories about modern Chinese drama. The most prominent of these voices is undoubtedly the one growing out of my North American experience as a member of an ethnic minority eager to introduce her native drama to English-speaking audiences while acutely aware of having been affected by the very discursive strategies that made the writing of this study possible. Space limitations unfortunately do not permit more attention to the performing aspects of theater. My study seeks to break new ground for the research on the post-1966 period of the PRC theater up to early 1990s in regard to both practice and text, which is still lacking.[130] By exploring the cultural, ideological, and political background that gave rise to particular theatrical events, I seek to study theater within the more general context of cultural performance.

2

Operatic Revolutions

TRADITION, MEMORY, AND WOMEN
IN MODEL THEATER

Over three decades have passed since the heyday of the Chinese Cultural
Revolution. Memories of some of the main players of model theater,
though, remain strong. Qian Haoliang, who played Li Yuhe in the revolutionary model Peking opera *The Red Lantern*, hoped very much that audiences from the 1960s and 1970s would have forgotten his association with
Jiang Qing, and his performance and promotion of model theater. He
wished to erase from the memory of his audience the fact that Jiang Qing
changed his name from Qian Haoliang to Hao Liang in 1968, as "qian" in
Chinese might suggest "money," or "bourgeois materialist pursuit."
Thanks to his star status in the model theater, he even became a representative of the Ninth Chinese Communist Party Congress in April 1969 and
the vice minister of the Ministry of Culture in 1975.[1] After the trial of the

Gang of Four, the post-Maoist regime detained him for a five-and-half-year investigation as having been a key player in Cultural Revolutionary politics. His biggest wish was to "live the remainder of his life in peace," according to one journalist from the *Beijing Youth Daily* who visited him on March 6, 1993.[2] When he appeared on stage to portray characters from the traditional repertoire, however, audiences urged him to perform "Poor Children Learn to Work at an Early Age" *(Qiongren de haizi zao dang jia)*, from *The Red Lantern*, before letting him exit. The fascination with model theater persisted in Beijing universities. In March 1996, 613 students reportedly showed up during the first session of a new course entitled "Peking Opera Art," an amazing number considering the fact that Peking opera and modern drama had been declining for years.[3] After viewing excerpts from *The Red Lantern* and two other traditional operas on video, many students stated that they had already become "lovers" of Peking opera. They expressed their gratitude to their teachers who opened to them a new world of art and showed up at classes early to be sure of finding a seat in the overcrowded classrooms. After learning the dramatic art, some even performed for campus entertainment a skit from *Shajiabang*, another model Peking opera.[4] In an era of modern consumer culture, traditional operatic art, along with a tinge of revolutionary idealism as expressed in model theater, still retained its appeal in contemporary China.

This phenomenon has led me to inquire into the cultural and ideological dynamics of Cultural Revolutionary theater, which shaped—and was shaped by—the political contingencies of China in the 1960s and 1970s. As a powerful cultural memory, model theater reveals much about the way a people and a nation envisioned the self, imagined the other, and, in turn, as a result of coming to an understanding of the other, reconstructed the self. To some extent, the study of model theater evokes Edgerly Firchow's point, expressed in *The Death of the German Cousin*, that "literature does not only mirror national stereotypes; it shapes them, changes them, and makes them respectable."[5] And indeed, in many different ways, model theater did not simply reflect the cultural and ideological dynamics of the period that gave rise to it; it significantly contributed to the ways in which China imagined itself in the public arena of national and international drama. Accordingly, in this study I am chiefly concerned with elucidating the "theatricality" of political life in contemporary China as a basis for understanding modern Chinese theater; for a remarkable feature of contemporary China's cultural scene is the extent to which theater is political and politics is theatrical. One quick way to recognize the latter point is to recognize contemporary life as a stage on which is enacted an on-going political drama that has all the actors scrambling to perform the "right" parts in order to ensure their political survival.

To illustrate this cultural phenomenon, I analyze the model theater promoted during the Cultural Revolution as a theatrical means of evoking the Maoist memory of a past revolution and, with its re-creation on stage, as a means to continue the revolution in post-1949 China. I also take issue with the conventional view that model theater was a unique result of the Cultural Revolution. Theatrical reform did not start with the Cultural Revolution, nor was it a mere concern for the revolutionary agenda of the PRC period. Its themes can indeed be traced back to the late Qing period. A historical overview will also help us to explain the representation of revolutionary women on the Chinese stage. In particular, I would like to demonstrate the dramatic process by which women characters in this model theater were transformed from oppressed women into revolutionary warriors and party leaders. Portrayed strikingly as lacking families or any attraction for the opposite sex, these women were deprived of womanhood, motherhood, and the intimacies of family life. Chinese women's touted equality with men, popularized in posters and other means of visual culture, emerged as an ideological myth. During this period of "Cultural Revolutionary feminism," radicals used the issue of women's exploitation to consolidate political and state power. The "worker-peasant-soldier model women"—represented on stage so that they would be imitated in real life —were reduced to the status of "revolutionary masses," whose only raison d'être was to celebrate the party and Chairman Mao.

One of the most important subjects of model theater was the enactment of a past revolution, which, as we have seen, was intended to spur the Chinese people to a continued revolution, the Great Proletarian Cultural Revolution. Paradoxically, this continued revolution sought to eliminate the very group of top Communist Party leaders who had made the 1949 revolution possible.[6] Of the eight revolutionary model works officially promoted between spring and summer of 1967 (known as the first group), seven were direct representations of the revolutionary war experience, dramatized in three different artistic genres, such as Peking opera, ballet, and symphonic music. The subject of the Peking opera *Shajiabang* is an armed struggle during the anti-Japanese war, in which Guo Jianguang, a political instructor of the New Fourth Army, and seventeen wounded soldiers defeat KMT troops who collaborated with Japanese invaders.[7] Such a military theme repeats itself in the revolutionary symphonic work (*geming jiaoxiang yinyue*) *Shajiabang*, another model work that represents the victory of proletarian art in the realm of Western classic music. The revolutionary modern ballet (*geming xiandai wuju*) *The Red Detachment of Women* presents a group of poor women in their armed struggle against KMT soldiers.[8] In the Peking opera *Taking Tiger Mountain by Strategy*, Yang Zirong, a People's Liberation Army scout, ventures into enemy headquarters disguised as a bandit to liberate the poor people from the northeast mountain area during the Civil War period.[9] The Peking opera *Raid on the White Tiger Regiment* depicts the Korean War (1950–1953), during which Yan Weicai, leader of a scout platoon of the Chinese People's Volunteers, overthrows the invincible South Korean White Tiger Regiment advised by the American military.[10] The other two model works, although not primarily war stories, are wartime narratives. In the Peking opera *The Red Lantern*, for example, set in the War of Resistance to Japan, an important facet of the plot concerns Li Yuhe and his family's successful transmission of secret codes to Communist guerrillas. Similarly, in the modern revolutionary ballet *The White-Haired Girl*, also set in the same war, Xi'er finds herself rescued by the revolutionary army on its way to the battlefield to repel Japanese invaders. The Peking opera *On the Docks* (*Haigang*), the only one of the eight model works set in peaceful socialist China, evokes the war heroes of pre–PRC China, as well as armed struggles against imperialists and revisionists in Third World countries, as inspirations to continue Chinese socialist revolution.

Following the success of the first eight model works, Jiang Qing crowned another ten revolutionary model works. Different rounds of revisions had begun in 1970, known as the second group of model theatrical pieces. Although the first group remained much more influential, five model works among the second group became better known than the rest, both in terms of their artistic achievements and their popularity in the media. Added to the first eight model works, these five were occasionally mentioned as the "thirteen model works," although Jiang Qing once claimed that she had guided the productions of a total of eighteen model works.[11] Almost all of them emphasized the war experience and memory. The five better-known pieces in the second group include the Peking opera *Azalean Mountain* (*Dujuanshan*), which depicts Ke Xiang, a female Communist Party secretary who reforms a peasant army into a revolutionary unit in its struggle against a local despot and nationalist troops. The ballet performance of *Song of Nimeng Mountain* (*Nimeng song*) dramatizes a peasant woman who risks her life to nurse a wounded Communist soldier back to health by feeding him with her own milk at the expense of her husband's misunderstanding.[12] The piano concerto (gangqin xiezou qu) *Yellow River (Huanghe)* expresses the national spirit of the Chinese people in their resistance against Japanese invaders, while the piano accompaniment (gangqin banchang) of *The Red Lantern* repeats the wartime story in its Peking opera version. The Peking opera *Song of the Dragon River (Longjiang song)* turns out to be the only one of the five better-known pieces that depicts the rural life of the 1960s, when the past sufferings of the local peasants before liberation constantly justify their continuing sacrifice to the socialist state.

The five other lesser-known model works of the second group shared a similar preoccupation with war experience and memory. They include the Peking operas *Hongyun Hills (Hongyungang),* adapted from the ballet version of *Song of Nimeng Mountain,*[13] and *The Red Detachment of Women,* adapted from the ballet of the same title.[14] Similarly, the Peking opera *Fighting in the Plain (Pingyuan zuozhan)* depicts guerrilla fighters' heroic battles during the War of Resistance to Japan. Its plot was based on several popular works created before the Cultural Revolution, such as the novel and film *The Railroad Guerrilla (Tiedao youji dui),* a film *The Guerrillas in the Plain (Pingyuan youji dui),* and a novel *An Armed Working Team behind the Enemy's Lines (Dihou wugong dui).* It also adapted ideas from *Land Mine War (Dilei zhan)* and *Tunnel War (Didao zhan),* two of the very few surviving films still shown during the Cultural Revolution, after the majority of the films produced before and after the PRC founding had been condemned as counterrevolutionary "poisonous weeds." By the same token, the Peking opera *Boulder Bay (Panshiwan)* dramatizes how the soldiers and local residents along the coastal areas of Guangdong Province defeated the agents and spies sent by the KMT.[15] Although set in 1962, the opera constantly evokes the memory of the Civil War to warn the Chinese audience of the imminent danger lying across the Taiwan Straits. Also set in 1960s China, the modern ballet *Son and Daughter of the Grassland (Caoyuan ernü)* represents the story of two youngsters risking their lives to save the sheep herds of a people's commune during a blizzard. Even though it was set in a peacetime, the praise of the two youngsters as worthy successors to the revolutionary cause, to which many had sacrificed their lives before 1949, evokes the violent past. It continues the theme of *The Red Lantern,* which carried the title *Successor to the Revolution (Geming ziyou houlairen)* in its precursor texts.[16] A wartime story thus finds its own "worthy successor" in a tale of contemporary times in which the wishes of the dead are carried out by two ethnic Mongolian youngsters, thus further validating the revolutionary past supposedly shared by different minority groups in China.

The Chinese state at this time derived many benefits from reenacting a past revolution on stage. The plays and ballets served to divert the attention of the populace from their severe poverty, an intractable problem that defied economic solution and that the government tried to conceal and dismiss from public scrutiny. Served up as spiritual sustenance, the model theater charged the masses with the revolutionary energy required to defend the fruits of a hard-won revolution. Thus theater functioned as a shelter from the chaos and civil war that prevailed at the peak of the Cultural Revolution. However, by depicting the new class of proletarian men and women as happy and powerful masters of the new China, theater could also intensify the tension between the various social and ethnic groups. To some audiences whose lives were tinted in dreary monochrome hues, colorful theatrical representations could only highlight the gap between the promise and the reality of the Maoist project.

To explain how he had achieved the national revolution from which the People's Republic was born in 1949, Mao had once alluded to poverty as the source of revolutionary energy: "The ruthless economic exploitation and political oppression of the peasants by the landlord class forced them into numerous uprisings against its rule. . . . It was the class struggle of the peasants, the peasant uprisings and peasant wars that constituted the real motive force of historical development in Chinese feudal society." This statement frequently appeared in the official reviews of the model theater, which was said to have dramatized the miserable lives of poor people before 1949. Yet in post-1949 China, the majority of the people, especially those in the countryside, were still poverty-stricken. They were poor before 1949, after 1949, and perhaps poorer still during the Cultural Revolution, when a civil war disrupted normal agricultural activities. That this mass poverty did not lead to another revolution was a function of the severing of the link between revolution and an appropriate ideology—a sine qua non for the successful progression from poverty to revolution by virtue of the Maoist ideology.

This disruption of the essential sequence was exemplified in the model theater. Through the cultural practice of "recalling the bitter past in order to appreciate the happy present" (yi ku si tian), the roots of poverty were conveniently traced to the old society, which "forced a human being to turn into a ghost." Glorified by contrast, the new society presumably "changed a ghost back into a human being again." In the model ballet *The White-Haired Girl*, for example, the poor peasant girl Xi'er survives in a mountain cave as a wild person. After being rescued from her ghostly existence by the arrival of the Communist army, she joins the revolution so that she can follow Chairman Mao's example and liberate other poor sisters like herself.

Chinese audiences attending this ballet were supposed to compare Xi'er's ghostly life with contemporary life in socialist China, which was supposedly infinitely better. Official press articles documented such reactions from members of the audience. Li Shanyuan, a "model peasant"[17] from Lugouqiao People's Commune, for instance, was quoted as saying: "When I saw [Yang Bailao] beaten to death and the vicious way [Huang Shiren's] family treated [Xi'er], I thought: That isn't make-believe; this is [exactly] what poor peasants had to put up with in the old society."[18] What took place here was the replacement of the theatrical convention, suspension of disbelief, with a suspension of political belief. As Li's additional comments indicate, the testimony from survivors of the old China served to perpetuate both past and present class distinctions: "This ballet teaches us not to forget the crimes of the landlord class, not to forget class hatred; it teaches us that it was not easy for us people to win mastery over our land and we must keep the state power firmly in our own hands."[19] Many statements were also obtained from female audience members who claimed they had been subjected to similar exploitation in the old society, or had known someone who had gone through the same kind of experience. It thus appeared that the female agency onstage was speaking for the local communities offstage, whose bitter stories, stimulated by the staged events, then served to reinforce the legitimacy of the official ideology.[20]

Members of the cast made similar statements, which were printed in the official press. Ling Kuei-ming (Ling Guiming), who in *The White-Haired Girl* danced the part of Wang Dachun, the Communist soldier who saved Xi'er from a life in the wild mountains, gave his own account of the bitterness of the old society. Born into a poor peasant family, Ling said, "I could never have attended a primary school, to say nothing of going to a school of dancing."[21] In the old society, in order to avoid the oppression and exploitation of the landlord, Ling claimed that his family went to Shanghai to escape poverty in the countryside. Unable to feed his family, his father had to send Ling's elder brother to an orphanage. Onstage Ling recalled his family tragedy, which enabled him to express true outrage in his performance.[22] Theater therefore helped write modern Chinese history, which, as Jiwei Ci points out, "serves as a record of debts, the debts owed by the ruled to the rulers," with the expectation on the part of ruling ideology that each and every reading of past bitterness will "renew and redouble the memory of debts and the readiness to act as debtors."[23] In this context, theater also served as a suitable stage where the representation of past bitterness and debts might justify a present revolution. A revolution rehearsed night after night onstage within theater could also, however, keep at bay any potential rebellion against the ruling state outside of the theater. The two dramas fundamentally conflicted with each other, but at the same time paradoxically reinforced each other's demands.

The history of *The White-Haired Girl* presents a number of interesting additional ironies. The ballet version of the work was adapted from an earlier folk opera *(geju)* premiered in Yan'an, the capital of the Communist liberated area, in April 1945, at the Seventh Chinese Communist Party Congress. It received a warm reception from Mao Zedong, Zhou Enlai, Zhu De, and other party representatives, and Mao supposedly even suggested that the vicious landlord be executed at the conclusion.[24] According to He Jingzhi, the main scriptwriter, the opera was based on popular folklore about a "white-haired goddess" forced by a despotic landlord to repair to the wild mountains. Because she was a "white-haired girl," local people mistook her for a goddess and worshipped her, and she lived on the offerings given her.[25]

With its central theme of the life-and-death struggle between the rich and the poor, the folk opera was enthusiastically received in the liberated areas during the 1940s revolutionary war period. Troops often performed it at mass meetings in order to raise the peasants' class consciousness and turn them against such class enemies as Huang Shiren. Party officials frequently attributed its success to the implementation of the principles laid down in Mao Zedong's "Talks at the Yan'an Forum on Literature and Art" in 1942, in which Mao demanded that literature and art serve the interests of the people and the Chinese revolution. Indeed, as the following report indicates, the popularity of the folk opera *The White-Haired Girl* seemed unprecedented: wherever the "red flags fluttered" in the newly liberated area, the opera would be performed and loud cries to avenge Xi'er would be heard everywhere.[26]

Yet this piece of revolutionary theater paradoxically met with criticism during the Cultural Revolution as a "counterrevolutionary" work, which presumably had been influenced by Liu Shaoqi's bourgeois approach to literature and art. The critics accused the folk opera of portraying "middle-of-the-road-characters (*zhongjian renwu*), who were neither positive (pro-letarian heroes) nor negative (bourgeois or counterrevolutionary). Yang Bailao, they maintained, took his own life (after having been forced to sell his daughter Xi'er to Huang Shiren) without rebelling or even raising any protest against the injustices he suffered, which distorted the heroic image of the revolutionary peasant. In contrast, leftist radicals argued, the ballet version of *The White-Haired Girl* promoted during the Cultural Revolution more accurately depicted the historical truth; it portrayed Yang as filled with the spirit of revolt and beaten to death by Huang Shiren after a valiant struggle. The ballet revision also contributed a revolutionary Xi'er —unlike the Xi'er in the original folk opera, who had been characterized as so naive that she failed to view Huang Shiren as her enemy after having been raped by him and giving birth to his child. These elements were de-nounced as attempts deliberately to obfuscate the class conflicts between the poor peasants and their oppressors. To emphasize the correct political stance of the ballet, a new epilogue showed Xi'er and other villagers join-ing the revolutionary army to demonstrate their infinite gratitude to their party and their love for Mao, a sentiment echoed in the theme: "Mao Zedong is the Sun, / The Sun is the Communist Party."[27] One of the main achievements of the new ballet, attributed to Jiang Qing, was said to be its emphasis on armed struggle, a key issue that divided Mao's revolu-tionaries from Liu Shaoqi's counterrevolutionaries in the party's history.

Ironically, when Jiang Qing was denounced as an archenemy of the people, party officials reversed the verdict on the folk opera. Now its past condemnation was frequently cited as part of the effort by the members of the Gang of Four to subvert Mao's correct approach to literature and art. Jiang Qing's promotion of model theater—of which *The White-Haired Girl* was a prime example—offered a classic instance of using theater for anti-party activities, an accusation previously leveled at the opponents of the Gang of Four.[28] Perhaps no other case reveals such an intimate and ironic relationship between theater and politics, between the fate of a revolution and the metamorphosis of that revolution's repercussions in theatrical representations.

The divergent representations of revolution in theater reconstructed the past histories of the party and of modern China. During the Cultural Rev-olution, revised plays of model theater carried out this task. These differ-ing representations served to illustrate the correctness and invincibility of

Mao Zedong Thought, the beacon of the Chinese Cultural Revolution and of world revolution in the past, and to consolidate the power of Mao, and Mao alone, in the present. Along with the much acclaimed publication of the *revised* edition of Mao's *Collected Works* and the *revised* edition of the party's history book—which deleted from the earlier editions the undesirable names and events now considered counterrevolutionary—the *revised* model theatrical works heralded a new age by rejecting the old. Of course, *The White-Haired Girl* is far from being the only work whose history is closely associated with the rewriting of China's political history. The history of almost every other piece of model theater exhibits similar revisions and diametrically opposed interpretations as a consequence of changing political conditions and shifting ideologies.

The richness of model theater as a powerful cultural memory, however, transcends its place at the center of political discourse. Moving beyond political analysis, recent scholarship has explored the complexities and paradoxes of early versions of model theatrical works to highlight the convergence of diverse discourses already embedded in the texts. In an exemplary study, Meng Yue demonstrates how the evolution of the different versions of *The White-Haired Girl* constitutes a typical process in which the discourses of "new culture" *(xin wenhua)*, "popular and folk cultures" *(tongsu wenhua)*, and "newly established political authority" *(xin de zheng-zhi quanwei)* are woven into one text that interweaves the traditional cultural values with those of the modern and contemporary.[29] According to Meng, the folktale of the white-haired goddess was first collected by the men of letters in the Yan'an liberated area as part of their efforts to learn about and adapt material from the regional and popular cultures while creating their own new, revolutionary culture. At the same time, many of these writers drew heavily from May Fourth culture, which in turn absorbed Western artistic influences, such as the European operatic tradition. The most immediate impact, of course, came from the political culture and ideological circumstances of the liberated areas, where land-reform and thought-reform movements dictated much of the content of literary production.[30] As a result of these concurrent influences, the folk opera *The White-Haired Girl* is a multilayered text that combines elements of old and new cultures, foreign and indigenous cultures, and urban and rural cultures found in the mid-1940s.[31]

Meng's detailed analysis of the folk opera version demonstrates that, although the political concern with how a new society turns a ghost back into a human being supposedly touched the hearts of many people, traditional aesthetic and ethical principles played at least equally important roles. A father's sudden death on New Year's eve, the desolate girl abducted from her fiancé just before the wedding, the lovers' hopeless separation followed by their tearful reunion, and the revenge taken on a vicious man in the end—all these motifs are familiar narrative structures in popular culture and folklore.[32] Long before Marxist class analysis had branded the rich landlord Huang Shiren as an archenemy of poor people, the ethics of popular culture had already tagged him as a sworn foe.[33] Similarly, when Dachun, Xi'er's fiancé, returns to his home village, he is recognized first as the local boy whom everyone trusts before his new political status as a Communist soldier is accepted. In both instances, political legitimacy rests on such nonpolitical foundations as ethical principles and community practices.[34]

Meng further argues that the film version of The White-Haired Girl (1950) translates the familiar tale of "the sorrows and joys of partings and reunions" (bei huan li he) into a popular love story. Although it incorporated such cinematic techniques as the close-up to accentuate Xi'er and Dachun's passion and the agony of their separation, it was still the traditional love story that legitimized the political discourse of class oppression and struggle contained in the film.[35] It is important to note that the film version eliminated the scene in which Xi'er fantasizes about marrying Huang Shiren after becoming pregnant with his child. Meng believes the change, intended to emphasize Xi'er's loyalty to Dachun, both strengthens the love story and advances the Communist ideology of class distinctions, which prohibited love affairs across class lines. The prominence given to romantic emotions also considerably helped to transform the film version into a popular urban text.[36]

The 1966 ballet version of The White-Haired Girl showed drastic revisions, as much of the traditional narrative structure and the popular love story were omitted in order to emphasize the class-struggle theme. Both Yang Bailao and Xi'er are portrayed as having a highly developed political consciousness and waging a fearless, heroic struggle on behalf of the exploited class to which they belong. This overt political text, Meng rightly remarks, points up the conflicts and contradictions between the political and apolitical discourses, which in previous versions had been brilliantly blended. Even in this ballet version, however, the tearful reunion of Dachun and Xi'er retains much of the overflowing emotion exhibited in the earlier versions, thus providing audiences with some opportunity to interpret an official text along nonofficial, and perhaps antiofficial, lines.[37]

With its interpretation of model theater as an embodiment not only of the political context but also of the conflicts and convergence of various cultural, ethical, and literary traditions, Meng's study suggests a new way of taking seriously the study of revolutionary literature in contemporary China. In fact, the similar trajectory that she pursues in *The White-Haired Girl* can be traced in other works of model theater. The revolutionary modern ballet *The Red Detachment of Women*, for instance, was adapted from the film version of the same title, which premiered in 1961.[38] As the winner of four national film awards (for best movie, best director, best actress, and best supporting actor), the film version had great appeal among Chinese audiences from all walks of life.[39] It did so despite the reduction to a minimum of the love story between Hong Changqing, the male party representative of the women's military unit, and Wu Qunhua, as a result of the political atmosphere created by the Great Leap Forward movement.[40] The subplot of the slave girl he rescues from the clutches of the local despot was reduced to a minimum.

In a 1962 essay, however, the scriptwriter Liang Xin provided intriguing information about this aspect of the film. It appears that after the film's premiere he received a letter from an audience member who congratulated him for not having fallen into the "old trap" of telling a conventional love story, which would have burdened Hong with too many roles, making him simultaneously a military commander, a mentor, a comrade-in-arms, and a lover.[41] On his part, Liang actually disagreed and rather regretted that, because of the political pressure to express proletarian rather than romantic feelings, he could not fully develop the love story present in the original script version.[42] Yet if one compares the portions of the original script cited in Liang's essay with the finished film version, one can see that, even after a few explicit lines were excised, the romantic story would still have been clear to anyone familiar with the characteristically subtle ways of expressing love in Chinese culture. In my view, the finished film, capitalizing on cinematic techniques that emphasize facial expressions and body language, stimulates the audience's imagination and leaves much room for it to fill in the gaps. In fact, Zhu Xijuan, who played the role of Wu Qunhua, admitted that she saw Qunhua (and played her accordingly) as having already fallen in love with Hong Changqing, since, in her view, Qunhua's capacity to love was at least as great as her capacity to hate her class enemies.[43]

There may be some question about the explicitness of the love story between the main characters in the film, but there is none at all about the love between a pair of less important characters: Honglian, another woman soldier, breaks away from her arranged marriage to a woodcut figure, the image of her husband long dead even before the marriage. She joins the Red Army with her lover, happily marries him, and gives birth to a baby girl right on the battlefield. The couple's wish that their daughter become a little Red Army soldier draws an optimistic picture of revolutionary women who, once freed from their oppressive domestic life, could embrace both a public career as soldiers and a private life as loving wives and mothers.

Even such an idealized vision of love and revolution disappeared in the ballet version of *The Red Detachment of Women*, which received much play during the Cultural Revolution. To the Chinese audience familiar with what Hans Robert Jauss characterizes as "the horizons of literary expectations"[44] acquired from the film version, the potential love story between the male and female protagonists still loomed large. Furthermore, the film and ballet art forms (both of which, not incidentally, had been imported from the West) were equally capable of replacing what had been verbally omitted through visual images and body movements. Instead of the close-up and other techniques employed by cinema to convey emotions, the ballet had the duet, which permitted body contact between a male and a female dancer and made sexual attraction quite palpable.

Recent literary history gives credit to Zhou Enlai, not Jiang Qing, as the first state leader to come up with the idea of using the Western form of ballet to create theatrical works to represent the revolutionary experience for the masses before the Cultural Revolution. It is said that in 1963, after watching *The Hunchback of Notre Dame (Bali shengmuyuan)*, performed by the ballet troupe of the Beijing Ballet School (Beijing wudao xuexiao shiyan baleiwutuan), Zhou congratulated teachers and students for their outstanding achievements in mastering Western ballet. Indeed, Zhou's interest in theater did not merely arise from his concern with revolutionary art in a Maoist state. From 1914 to 1917 in the Republican period, Zhou actively participated in the new spoken drama movement in Nankai School in Tianjin, alternating as actor, stage designer, critic, and editor of the school newspaper.[45] At a time when women were not allowed to act on stage in modern drama, Zhou played the part of the female protagonist in the play entitled *A Silver Dollar (Yiyuan qian)*, which, after its premiere in Tianjin, was performed for the Beijing Youth Association (Beijing qingnianhui) in the summer of 1915.[46] On this occasion, Zhou urged the ballet artists not just to re-create characters of prince and fairy, but to experiment with representing revolutionary events such as the Paris Commune and the Russian October Revolution. These Western stories might gain an easier success than Chinese ones, as ballet, after all, might prove too alien to depict Chinese lives and struggles. Enlightened, but not limited, by Zhou's directives, students and teachers from the ballet school decided to choose *The Red Detachment of Women* as their first attempt.

In February 1964, members from the ballet troupe of the Beijing Ballet School traveled to the former soviet area in Hainan. They visited retired women soldiers, learned about the local customs and cultures, served as soldiers in an army unit, and interviewed Liang Xin, the scriptwriter of the film *The Red Detachment of Women*. Before returning to Beijing, they had already planned the dramatic plot for six acts and several major dance scenes. Their first production proved a resounding success, a unique combination of Chinese folk dance, folk music, and Peking opera. After its dress rehearsal in Tianqiao Theater on September 25, 1964, Zhou reportedly was so touched by the ballet that he had tears in his eyes and apologized to the cast for having been too conservative in his earlier suggestion of first experimenting with a foreign story. Although Jiang Qing was invited, along with Liao Chengzhi and Zhou Yang, to attend this dress rehearsal, she did not participate in any discussion of the ballet's production until after Mao Zedong and other state leaders such as Liu Shaoqi, Zhu De, and Peng Zhen watched it on October 8, 1964. Mao praised the ballet as having "headed toward the right directions, succeeded in its revolution, and [having been] artistically satisfactory."

After its public performance, *The Red Detachment of Women* received enthusiastic endorsement from experts, critics, and audiences as a huge success of the first generation of Chinese ballet dancers who created a truly Chinese style of ballet.[47] Jiang Qing's later suggestions to improve the ballet, such as changing aspects of stage designs and adding a scene in which Hong Changqing holds a meeting to discuss battle strategy, were tried out but eventually not incorporated into the work.[48] Never before did a ballet attempt to depict a meeting, although excessive meetings were an important aspect of contemporary Chinese life. Both her own claim that she helped to create this model ballet and the post-Maoist critique of her as masterminding model theater in order to suppress other forms of art were on shaky historical ground. As in the cases of other model works, the lasting appeal of *The Red Detachment of Women* was the outcome of artists' years of experimentation in combining a Western genre with aspects of Chinese dance, music, and opera. The ballet indeed represented one of the best artistic achievements of the PRC stage, which drew largely from the literary and artistic developments of the Republican period and traditional culture.

Ballet also came to serve the interests of proletarian art in creating *The White-Haired Girl*. The cast from the Shanghai Dance School (Shanghai wudao xuexiao) was inspired by the success of *The Red Detachment of Women* and of the Peking opera reform that used a traditional form for modern themes. After the writing team was formed in 1964, they observed the directive of Ke Chingshi, First Secretary of the Shanghai Municipal Party Committee, to incorporate a Chinese-style folk-song chorus into the ballet in order to appeal to the common people. Eager to create their own version of revolutionary ballet, after a one-act premiere in May 1964, the cast solicited criticism from Shanghai workers, some of whom failed to understand the scene in which Yang Bailao tries to commit suicide. The cast members realized that it was not just the ballet "body language" that one worker had failed to understand; he was also puzzled why Yang Bailao should choose to die. "When I was insulted and abused by a landlord, I rebelled and killed two of those bad eggs. That was why I escaped from the countryside to Shanghai before liberation. Yang Bailao should fight back. He cannot simply kill himself." The worker's words helped the cast members to realize the importance of the theme of "class struggle" for which *The White-Haired Girl* was later celebrated as a model theatrical work. As a result of a series of revisions, Yang fights back three times until he is finally beaten to death by Huang Shiren.

To guarantee the success of the ballet in all artistic aspects, the CCP Shanghai Municipal Party Committee invited celebrated directors, scriptwriters, stage designers, musicians, and a symphony conductor to join the production crews. When the eight-act *The White-Haired Girl* was finally performed at the Sixth Shanghai Spring Festival (Shanghai zhichun) in 1965, it was a notable success. In addition to its use of vocal accompaniment to the ballet and folk musical instruments such as *banhu*, it also borrowed from Sichuan opera *(chuanju)* the idea of "face change" *(bian-lian)*: Xi'er's hair color changed from black to gray, then to white, to indicate the passage of time and her sufferings in the mountain cave.[49] All these successful attempts developed a Chinese style of ballet without the direct involvement of any political leader. Zhou Enlai first saw the ballet on July 19, 1965, with Chen Yi, when both of them were accompanying foreign state guests in Shanghai. Zhou remarked after the performance,

FIGURE 17. Anonymous, *Let Socialist New Arts Occupy All Stages.*

"Shanghai is a lovely place, full of innovative energies." He reportedly attended sixteen performances. Jiang Qing, on the other hand, did not see a performance until April 24, 1967, after the Cultural Revolution started. She went with Mao, who reportedly commented, *"The White-Haired Girl is good."* Nevertheless, in a poster entitled *Let Socialist New Arts Occupy All Stages (Rang shehui zhiyi xin wenyi zhanling yiqie wutai)*, Jiang Qing is portrayed as the sole leader pointing out the correct directions for producing proletarian arts by following the examples of the model works she had already created in the background (Fig. 17). Despite such a depiction of Jiang as the promoter of the model theater, *The Red Detachment of Women* and *The White-Haired Girl* were the products of a collective experiment of combining Chinese tradition with Western forms, achieved through the creative energies of many artists of different genres.

Ironically, this supposedly highly political, and hence anti-Western, version of the model theater depended for its success on media, genres, and techniques imported from the West. To denigrate model theater from an artistic standpoint, therefore, would have been to denigrate the aesthetic traditions of the West, to which model theater had always been presented as diametrically opposed. Yet the impact of the West becomes even more apparent in the context of the popularization of model theatrical works during the peak of the Cultural Revolution. Aided by film adaptations of the stage productions that had their limitation in reaching a broader audience, model works were made available to the masses in many other cities and in the countryside, thus transforming them into an even more popular cultural form than before. In short, the media of the West played as large a role in promoting and developing model theater as did the incorporated folklore and popular traditions. It could never have achieved its effects without an infusion of Western influence and traditions. Even during the height of the Cultural Revolution, when the West was the apparent enemy in Maoist ideology, it had infiltrated China in forms such as ballet, film, musical recordings, and symphony, and had already been shrewdly coopted even when surface appearances hid its presence.

One finds the best example of this phenomenon in the creation of the revolutionary symphonic music of *Shajiabang*. Established in 1956, the Central Symphony (Zhongyang yuetuan) held successful concerts playing classical musical pieces by Bach, Haydn, Mozart, Beethoven, Schubert, Liszt, Berlioz, Tchaikovsky, Dvořák, and Shostakovich, along with classic Chinese works by Chinese composers such as Huang Zi, Nie Er, Xian Xinghai, He Luding, Li Huanzhi, Ding Shande, Huo Wei, Ma Sichong, and Shi Yongkang.[50] In the 1960s, when critical debates on how to assimilate Western culture and Chinese traditions before 1949 intensified and intellectuals shied away from Western culture and ideology, the Central Symphony could not find a niche for its artistic productions because of its traditional strength in Western music. According to Dai Jiafang, Jiang Qing's visit to the symphony on November 18, 1964, however, seems to have steered the symphony in a new direction. During this visit, Jiang lectured to the effect that Western symphony consists of nothing but mere form, with different movements linked together without coherent connections between them. Not only did the Chinese fail to understand it; laboring people of the "white race" could not appreciate it either. Many of the bourgeoisie merely pretended to like it in the attempt to show their sophistication and good taste, Jiang claimed. Encouraging Chinese musicians to "revolutionize foreign symphonies," Jiang invited them to attend the dress rehearsal of the Peking opera *Shajiabang*. Inspired by the opera's new experiments, Li Delun, the principal conductor of the Central Symphony, came up with the idea of a symphony accompaniment to *Shajiabang*. After training themselves in the musical techniques of Peking opera, Li and his composers experimented with the fourth act of *Shajiabang* by revising individual passages from the opera into a chorus accompanied by orchestra instruments. Using tenors, mixed chorus, and counterpoint to depict the spirit of the eighteen wounded soldiers who persevere in their war efforts under difficult circumstances, the symphony offered a kind of artistic charm different from that of the Peking opera, some critics claimed.

After many experiments and collective works by the symphony musicians, the one-act experiment led to a successful performance of *Shajiabang* in its entirety (eight acts), premiered in Beijing in 1965, before the October First national day to celebrate the founding of the PRC. In the spring of 1966, Li Delun and his musicians, while working in the countryside to participate in the Socialist Education movement, studied the official report of the forum attended by cultural workers from the People's Liberation Army (PLA), presided over by Jiang Qing with Lin Biao's endorsement.[51] They were surprised to hear that in this party document almost all works of literature and art produced after 1949 fell into the category of "antisocialist poisonous weeds," with the exception of only seven works of literature and art developed in the last three years as a result of struggling against the sinister lineup of feudal, bourgeois, and soviet revisionist art and literature.[52]

Li and his colleagues, however, were not certain whether the "revolutionary symphonic music of *Shajiabang*," listed as one of the seven proletarian works, indeed referred to their recent performance since, after many discussions by specialists on how to name the symphonic work, they had agreed to advertise it in previous performances as a "symphonic chorus," not "symphonic music."[53] Yet two months later, when Li was called back to Beijing to participate in the emerging Cultural Revolution, he did not have time to make a phone call to Jiang Qing to explain the genre confusion as he had planned to do so while in the countryside. As soon as he got off the train, Li was immediately seized by the Red Guards for interrogation as a "counterrevolutionary authority" (*fandong quanwei*) in Western music. No one could discuss, let alone clarify, anything already decided by Jiang Qing, now revered in the official press as the "flag-bearer of the revolution for literature and art" (*wenyi geming qishou*). Overnight the symphonic work became a symbol of a victory achieved in one of the most stubborn strongholds in artistic forms borrowed from the West. In historical hindsight, however, one can also argue that model theater, by definition, could not have become a model without having, as in this case, originated from a genre not conventionally believed to be so revolutionary in the first place. Without innovations using Western music, the symphonic work of *Shajiabang* would never have been born; by the same token, without model theatrical experiment, the Western symphony would not have been "saved" from extinction in China.

Similarly, the Maoist regime regarded traditional theater as another stronghold into which proletarian ideology failed to penetrate. Among more than 360 different kinds of *xiqu*, Peking opera ranked as one of the most popular and perfected artistic forms. It therefore became a frequent object of reform, as many regarded it as the least suited to depicting contemporary themes and political life in the PRC. That five of the eight best-known revolutionary model theatrical pieces are Peking operas demonstrates one of the greatest achievements of proletarian art, according to the print culture from 1966 to 1976. Of the second group of ten model works, six are Peking operas. Paradoxically, this traditional art did not seem to need reforming in the eyes of inspired foreign dramatists, who imported it to revolutionize their own theaters. As Georges Banu points out, European theater artists such as Stanislavsky, Craig, Brecht, Piscator, Tairov, and Tretiakov, who had been seeking a theatrical model at a time of artistic crisis, viewed Peking opera—as represented by Mei Lanfang's performance, which they saw in the Soviet Union in 1935—as "the crystallization of their visionary spirit."[54] Meyerhold, for instance, found in Mei Lanfang's Peking opera a replacement for the Stanislavskian memory of the actor ("I") with a memory of the stage, which focuses attention on tradition and an artistic past.[55] He wrote, "In the hour of the Russian theater's 'great turning point,' Mei Lanfang was a beacon; artists began to see that they could continue their resistance through subterfuge."[56] Ironically, in 1954 when Chinese artists studied the Stanislavsky system as the only "beacon" for all dramatic arts, even Mei Lanfang himself, although not in favor of thorough operatic reform, expressed his willingness to learn from it for possible application to Peking opera. Modern dramatic artists such as Lao She, Wu Zuguang, and Peking opera expert Zhang Geng, however, objected to such dogmatic use of the Soviet model as the only school of acting. The Soviet experts provided sound advice for ballet, Western opera, and modern drama, in which they indeed had expertise, they argued, but they did not know enough about Peking opera, whose abstract, symbolic, and expressionist acting styles would not work with the Stanislavsky method.[57] This rejection of the Soviet model, although inappropriate at the time for political reasons in 1954, would nevertheless be justified during the Cultural Revolution, when this beacon of classical Chinese art was relit to illuminate the beacon of Mao Zedong Thought, only after the operatic reform that had transformed it into a "modern" and "revolutionary" genre to battle against Soviet revisionists. It was not until post-Maoist China that Chinese dramatists could freely popularize a theatrical practice which best combines the artistic heritage of Mei Lanfang, Stanislavsky, and Brecht, first proposed by Huang Zuolin in 1962.[58]

The memory of the stage, which Banu regarded as presenting Europeans with an ideal model of theater, joined during the 1960s in China with the memory of a revolutionary past, which provided many of the central themes of model Peking opera. This reenactment of revolutionary experience, significantly, did not merely aim at Cultural Revolutionary audiences. It was believed that by acting out the roles of the revolutionary characters—that is, by creating the revolutionary other while rejecting the nonrevolutionary self—the actors would be reformed and shed their bourgeois ideology. In concentrating on every body movement and perfecting every operatic tune, the players of the model operas rechanneled their energies toward a revolutionary ideal. Through acrobatics, they achieved strict bodily control, usually to depict battle scenes; the larger purpose was to demonstrate the clash of conflicting ideologies and to testify to the "truth" that those armed with Mao Zedong Thought were the ones who eventually prevailed, both on the stage and in real life. Thus did the revolutionary heroes and heroines depicted by the players seize the theatrical space, symbolized by theatrical signs that embodied the spirit of the proletariat and its triumph over the bourgeoisie. Red flags and red stars stood for the entirely new empire of Maoist China. The revolutionary model plays' emphasis on having a vast countryside for the Communist fighters to maneuver in while plotting against their enemies in the besieged city was not accidental; it testified to the significance of the social space created by the theater, which advocated the values of the Cultural Revolution. Knowledge was being absorbed through a unique theatrical experience that itself not only resulted from imitating "real" revolutionary life, but, most important, provided millions of people with a model for more revolutionary behavior in their own "real" lives. Here was a case, then, not uncommon in those times, of life imitating art rather than the other way around.

The reform of Peking opera into a "modern" and "revolutionary" theater, however, did not begin with the Cultural Revolution. Nor could the PRC alone claim this credit. According to Zhang Geng and Huang Jusheng, Liang Qichao initiated traditional theater reform (*xiqu gailiang*)[59] in 1902, when he published three operatic texts in *New People Newspaper* (*Xinmin congbao*) while in exile in Japan. Theater reform in this context refers to romance drama (*chuanqi*), which originated from several hundred "southern-style" plays of the Ming and Qing dynasties, and "northern-style" *zaju* drama, most popular in the Yuan dynasty.[60] The rise of Peking opera did not begin until the late eighteenth century and became a target of reform with Wang Xiaonong's efforts in the late Qing period. In spite of their generic differences, however, Liang Qichao's early advocacy of theater reform resembled certain trends found in later periods. In a *chuanqi* text entitled *New Rome* (*Xin Luoma*, 1902), Liang used the voice of the dramatic character of Dante and claimed that he wrote fiction and *chuanqi* texts to raise the heroic spirit of the Chinese people to avenge their humiliation by foreigners.[61] Liang's text offered poetry, passion, and grandeur in his portrait of what he called "a founding father of a foreign country" and broke new ground in using an operatic text to advocate Chinese nationalism. Liang completed only seven plays depicting events over ten years, in spite of his original plan of a cycle of forty plays over fifty years relating the lives of three founding fathers. Although his plays revealed an unfamiliarity with theater conventions and seldom resulted in stage productions, they nevertheless became valuable texts for theater reform. Liang called for artists to act out real-life dramas in history in timely and magnificent fashion,[62] a phrase used later to describe both the Cultural Revolution and the theatrical revolution that accompanied it.

From a similar angle, Cai Yuanpei published an editorial in 1903 entitled "To Performers" (Gaoyou), in which he called on opera artists to pay more attention to state affairs and to throw themselves into opera reform. In 1904, Chen Qubing and Wang Xiaonong, himself a Peking opera scriptwriter and actor, pioneered the first theatrical journal, the *Grand Stage of the Twentieth Century* (*Ershi shiji da wutai*). Many essays published in this journal urged more respect for operatic artists, whose efforts in promoting new operas could help raise a new nationalist spirit in the Chinese nation.[63] Between 1901 and 1912, according to A Ying's A

Bibliography of Drama and Fiction in the Late Qing Dynasty (Wanqing xiqu xiaoshuo mu), as many as 150 new scripts of *chuanqi* and *zaju* drama were published in magazines and newspapers. Zhang Geng and Huang Jusheng classified them into five categories, which, in my view, surprisingly reveal some concerns similar to those of model Peking operas of the Cultural Revolution, in spite of their obvious differences. Indeed, one might even regard them as the roots of the Cultural Revolution, which pushed to the extreme those tensions between tradition and revolution already felt at the beginning of the twentieth century.

The first category, according to Zhang and Huang, dramatized the heroic deeds of national heroes in ancient times to advance a contemporary anti-Qing (anti-Manchu) movement. These heroes included Wen Tianxiang (1236–1283), a Song dynasty official who sacrificed his own life to resist the Yuan dynasty, and Zheng Chenggong (1624–1662), a Ming loyalist who bitterly resisted the Qing conqueror and recovered Taiwan from the Dutch in 1662. Although many model Peking operas depicted heroes of the immediate past, they also validated a similar myth of national heroes and heroines ready to die for the nation. Later generations eulogized them on stage as role models, whether they were ancient heroes or peers in contemporary times. This tradition continued even in post-Maoist theater. As a reaction against the Gang of Four's persecutions of PRC party leaders during the Cultural Revolution, a wave of "revolutionary leaders plays" appeared from 1978 to 1981. They reenacted episodes in the heroic lives of Communist leaders such as Zhou Enlai, Chen Yi, He Long, and many others. This theater boom spread into many other dramatic genres, such as modern drama, Peking opera, and other regional operas. One thus witnesses a continuity, at least in thematic concerns, between late Qing, Republican, Cultural Revolutionary, and post–Cultural Revolutionary theatrical activities linked to the political life of each period.

The second category depicted significant events of contemporary times, such as the "hundred days reform" *(bairi weixin)*, as seen in *The Dream of Reform (Weixin meng)* written by Mao Yuanxi Qiusheng et al., and published in installments between 1903 to 1904.[64] Most notable is a biographical play of Qiu Jin, a female revolutionary martyr executed for her anti-Qing activities in 1907. This event shocked the nation and inspired many fiction and drama writers. One play, entitled *The Injustice of Xuan-ting Kou (Xuanting yuan)*,[65] was written by Xiao Shanxiang Lingzi in 1907, only a month and a half after Qiu Jin's execution. Although it appeared sixty years earlier than its modern counterparts, this play heralded one of the creative principles of model theater: to portray "typical characters in typical circumstances" *(dianxing shijian zhong de dianxing renwu)* and to "reflect contemporary life" *(biaoxian xianshi shenghuo)*. The dramatic character of Qiu Jin could be compared, if not in concrete deeds then in spirit and stature, with Jiang Shuiying, the courageous female party secretary in a people's commune in 1960s China in *Song of the Dragon River*. Similarly, the model Peking opera *On the Docks* also portrays contemporary workers' life in Shanghai in the 1960s, with another dauntless female party secretary taking the lead. *Song of the Dragon River* and *On the Docks* formed a pair of "sister plays," in which two equally admirable heroines successfully guide their masses on the two important fronts of socialist reconstruction: agriculture and industry. Sharing a strategy of stressing class struggle, both plays manufactured dramatic antagonism, which transformed differences in personal opinions into more serious conflicts between the local and the national, and hence a life-and-death class struggle between the proletariat and their opponents. It goes without saying that this aspect marks them as radically distinct from their late Qing precursor texts.

The third category included new Peking operas that exposed foreign imperialist aggression against China, such as Russia's invasion of Heilongjiang Province in *An Un-Russian Dream (Fei xiong meng)*, the Eight Allied Armies' invasion of China in 1900 in *Wuling Spring (Wuling chun)*, and the protest against America's Chinese immigration exclusion acts in *The Spring of Overseas Chinese (Haiqiao chun)*.[66] In Hong Bingwen's *An Alarm Bell for the Yellow Race (Jing huangzhong)*, the anti-imperialist theme translates into racial conflicts between the yellow and white races. Using the metaphor of yellow and white bees fighting against each other for their own survival, the play warns yellow people that if they do not love their country and their leaders, they will forever be ruled by the white race.[67] In spite of their obvious differences in ideology and historical contexts, model Peking operas such as *Shajiabang*, *Taking Tiger Mountain by Strategy*, *The Red Lantern*, and *Fighting in the Plain* did carry out this anti-imperialist theme. They replaced European countries with the Japanese as archenemies who aimed to eliminate the Chinese nation. Concerns about racial conflict disguised themselves beneath the rhetoric of nationalism and internationalism, which was supposed to transcend ethnic differences. The Peking opera *Raid on the White Tiger Regiment*, for instance, warns Chinese people of the danger of war led by American imperialists. If the Chinese People's Volunteer Army did not fight courageously with the North Korean People's Army, the opera demonstrates, the Chinese people would suffer in the same way the Korean people had. Different from other model Peking operas that wage past revolutionary warfares, however, *Raid on the White Tiger Regiment* remains the only model opera that dramatizes a war experience of its own time. Also set in contemporary China, *Boulder Bay* portrays both military events and everyday life activities in 1963. The contemporary ballet *Son and Daughter of the Grassland*, in contrast, puts forth an ethnic minority group as a loyal other to construct a unified national identity among multiethnic groups to make the Chinese state invincible.

The fourth category covered foreign heroes and events such as the French Revolution and Louis XVI's execution in *Guillotine (Duantou tai)*, and Cuban students' struggle against Spanish colonialists in *Student Wave (Xue hai chao)*. *Resentment over the Lost Country (Wangguo hen)* portrays a heroic An Chung Keun, a Korean nationalist who in 1909 assassinated Itoh Hirobumi, the Japanese Resident-General of Korea.[68] It is interesting to note that the same story inspired an early modern drama version, *The Storms of East Asia*, as I mentioned in Chapter 1. The model Peking opera *Song of the Dragon River* seems to echo foreign hero stories by eulogizing Norman Bethume, a Canadian Communist Party member who died during the war against Japan while providing medical care to wounded Chinese soldiers. Although the model opera did not focus on Dr. Bethume, his spirit of "internationalism" and "communism" inspired other dramatic characters, especially that of the female protagonist, who used this role model of a foreign communist to educate her own villagers in a time of collective sacrifice. The staging of foreign heroes continued more rigorously in post-Maoist modern dramas, where Karl Marx conversed with a Chinese dramatist on stage about his grand theories of communism and its applicability to the twentieth century, as seen in the controversial 1983 play *The Secret History of Marx (Makesi mishi)* by Sha Yexin. Marx's love life and his friendship with Engels also became favorite topics, as is revealed in the modern drama *Marx in London Exile (Makesi liuwang Lundun;* also 1983). The same period also produced numerous plays of foreign heroes originally written by Western playwrights, such as Jules Vallés' *La Commune de Paris (Yingtao shijie)*, performed by the China Youth Art Theater in 1983.

The fifth category most resembled model theater with its advocacy of women's rights and liberation, which I will discuss at the end of this chapter. Suffice to say that, as is prevalent in all the model theater pieces, the liberation of all mankind subsumes women's liberation. This theme of women's liberation finds its earlier expression in Liu Yazi's 1904 text, *New Daughter of Songling (Songling xin nü'er)*, a remarkably well written one-act play. Depicting women's resistance to arranged marriage in his hometown, Liu designated his dramatic character, who dresses in a Western suit, to speak her mind to her audience: Asians are also people; Europeans are also people. But why does China, the great land, trample on women's rights? she asks indignantly. Chinese women are still sinking every passing day, while those white and fair foreign women enjoy equal rights with man; their names were even recorded in history, she claims. She expresses her deep admiration for Madame Roland, condemned and guillotined for her revolutionary activities during the French Revolution, and for Sophia Perovskaya, executed for her abortive attempt to assassinate Czar Alexander II.[69] Liu Yazi's championing of Chinese women's rights, although in tune with his own times, was not without a problem: it paradoxically reflected a trend not uncommon among the Chinese literati who looked to the West as the superior model for China's modernization.

Liu Yazi's reference to Sophia Perovskaya, however, echoed a popular response to her fictional biography, serialized in Liang Qichao's influential journal *New Fiction (Xin xiaoshuo)* in 1902. In the words of Mau-sang Ng, the story of Perovskaya "excited late Qing sensibilities to an overwhelming degree," and "accolades by leading litterateurs extolling her heroism and self-sacrificing spirit began to pour into the pages of the major magazines. Many saw the Russian nihilists as models of revolutionary virtue."[70] Although fictional references to Sophia Perovskaya of the same period remain well documented, such as Ding Ling's allusion in *The Diary of Miss Sophia*, the same inspiration of dramatic characters has escaped scholars' notice. In a more recent and insightful study, Hu Ying further explores the transplanted images of Sophia Perovskaya and Madame Roland, examining how these foreign female figures entered Chinese culture and were reconfigured in fiction, biography, and oral *tanci* performances in the late Qing period. Hu Ying points out that, whereas the characters "from drastically diverse cultural and historical backgrounds often appear effortlessly to share a lingua franca, be it Chinese, German, or French," they also "speak 'unnaturally,' in elegant classical Chinese." Language thus "has the inherent capacity both to absorb and to resist the foreign other. . . . The tale of the new women, then, is to a large extent a tale of translations" across cultural boundaries.[71] Like these characters,

Liu Yazi's woman character also speaks classical language in her own pro-motion of Chinese nationalism and women's concerns, thus falling into the same "processes of exoticization and domestication."[72]

Also amazing is the long list of important men of letters, such as Liang Qichao, Cai Yuanpei, and Liu Yazi, whose pioneering roles in promoting new culture and education in the late Qing period remain better known in other genres such as newspapers, fiction, poetry, and prose than do their efforts to promote theater reform. Many of their *chuanqi* and *zaju* texts, however, although ranked as "one of the greatest in Chinese literary his-tory" and "monumental in political drama" by Zheng Zhenduo, did not result in theater performance. This occurred partially because *Kunqu*, the suitable operatic genre to perform these texts, suffered a decline in popu-larity, and the few *Kunqu* troupes interested in new operas could not find patrons to sponsor performances. Published in newspapers and maga-zines, therefore, the influence of these texts was confined solely to the read-ing public, without much impact on the populace.[73] Here, theater reform in the late Qing period naturally lost ground to its modern counterparts of model theater, because the publication of each model opera in the *Red Flag (Hongqi)*, the Communist Party's key journal that everyone was sup-posed to read, did not just render a model opera an unprecedented pres-tige. Most important, the availability of written texts rapidly enabled the staging of these operas everywhere in the country, in both urban and rural areas, subsidized by the socialist state. In some cases, readings of these model texts in political study sessions, furthermore, promoted close read-ings of model operas as written texts, which mere stage performance could not sufficiently provide.

The task of transforming new operatic texts into stage performances fell on the shoulders of the reformers of Peking opera, according to Zhang Geng and Huang Jusheng. Interestingly, Shanghai, a vibrant city open to Western influence and innovative in artistic experience, became the center of theater reform. Wang Xiaonong was one practitioner of the "Shanghai school of Peking opera" *(haipai jingju)* who scripted new Peking operas that depicted contemporary state affairs. In 1908, Wang even introduced a new stage in Shanghai for producing Peking opera, using equipment and technology imported from foreign countries for stage designing and light-ing. To promote new Peking operas with contemporary themes, Wang and his cohorts successfully adapted Harriet Beecher Stowe's *Uncle Tom's Cabin* from a "new drama" *(xinju)* version, a forerunner of modern drama recently imported from the West. This episode parallels the origins of some model operas: Shanghai played an equally important part in initiating some of the model works. *Taking Tiger Mountain by Strategy*, which premiered in September 17, 1958, by the Shanghai Number One Peking Opera Troupe (Shanghai jingju yituan), had been adapted from the modern drama version of the same title performed by the Beijing People's Art Theater. The modern drama version, in turn, was based on Qu Bo's novel, entitled *Snow-Covered Forest (Linhai xueyuan)* and published in 1957. During the Great Leap Forward, when people attempted to "achieve in one day what would normally take twenty years" *(yitian dengyu ershi nian)*, artists from the Shanghai Number One Peking Opera Troupe did their share of radical theater reform by finishing the opera adaptation in ten days.[74] As rightly pointed out by Zhao Cong, Qu Bo's *Snow-Covered Forest* was an ideal candidate for opera adaptation because it imitated the popular fiction *Water Margin*, which has its own operatic repertories. Similar to *Water Margin*, in which the outlaw Song Jiang leads thirty-six good fellows to eliminate evil and corrupt officials on his way back to Liang Mountain, *Snow-Covered Forest* depicts a team of thirty-six soldiers out to capture Tiger Mountain. The dramatic characters in Qu's fiction, who are full of surprising action and fighting skills, offered rich material for acrobatic and other operatic techniques frequently used in traditional theater.[75] Several other model operas also originated from modern drama productions such as *Song of the Dragon River, Azalean Mountain*, and *Boulder Bay*.

The connection between traditional theater reform and modern drama does not stop at adaptations. Influenced by the impact of modern drama at the beginning of the twentieth century, some theater reformers in the late Qing and early Republican periods experimented with new Peking operas of contemporary costumes *(shizhuang xinxi)* in Shanghai, which was the real beginning of modern opera *(xiandai xi)*. Xu Banmei, for instance, once recalled the popularity of these operas in Shanghai. After the Wuchang Uprising against the Qing court in 1911, many audiences expressed their anger at the Qing rulers by attending these performances of Peking operas that exposed their corruption. One historian recorded as many as two hundred reformed dramas tailored to the tastes and concerns of contemporary audiences.[76] Five of these Peking operas with contemporary costume were performed in Beijing by Mei Lanfang after his two visits to Shanghai between 1913 and 1914, where he had watched modern dramas imported from the West on the new stage. One of the most popular ones, entitled *His Billows on the Sea of Sin (Niehai bolan)*, depicts a devilish Dummy Zhang, who brings an innocent poor girl to entertain strangers in his brothel. Later an upright official parades him in the street for humiliation as punishment. During the performance of this opera, Mei Lanfang noticed that many females in the audience burst into tears when the grief-stricken girl, his dramatic role, tearfully embraced her father.[77] Incidentally, Mei's inspiration by Shanghai practitioners signified a dramatic moment of competition between the Shanghai and Beijing cultures: at the moment of crisis in Peking opera, it was not Beijing but Shanghai that became the birthplace of theater reform that finally influenced Beijing culture itself, of which Peking opera stood as a pillar. The same spirit endured in the creative process of model theater, where the model Peking operas *The Red Lantern* and *Shajiabang* performed by Beijing artists benefited greatly from the original versions of Shanghai operas.

In spite of his success in theater reform, Mei Lanfang stopped performing modern operas at age twenty-five after his performance of *A Girl Kills a Snake (Tongnü zhan she)* in 1918.[78] He later claimed in his memoir that, as he grew older, it became more difficult to act the role of young ladies of modern times than ladies in the traditional repertoire, whose loose costumes and elaborate hairdos offered him more flexibility in stage movement and image makeup.[79] He also perceived an incoherence between form and content in traditional opera that made it difficult to tell contemporary stories. The symbolic and abstract acting style of traditional opera, with its painted, mask-like faces, platform shoes, and long sleeves, works well with traditional music, with slow tempo. Modern opera would, from time to time, require a much quicker pace in music, singing, and body movement. To address this situation, Mei at times felt obliged to cut certain traditional tunes and replace them with dialogue in order to more realistically portray contemporary lives.[80]

Mei's dilemma, however, seemed to be resolved by the artistic experiments of the model theater during the Cultural Revolution. Xie Boliang, for instance, believed that *Azalean Mountain, Boulder Bay,* and *Wind and Thunder of Mao Ridge (Miaoling fenglei)*, although later comers to model theater, broke new ground in opera reform by using rhymed dialogue throughout the play, an unprecedented feature. Known as "opera with rhymed dialogues" *(yunbai ju)*, these three works used poetic images, metaphors, analogies, and parables to narrow the usual gap between slow-paced sung passages *(chang)* and quick-tempoed dialogues traditionally conveyed only in spoken language *(shuobai)*. Rhymed singing passages in the traditional form could now be more naturally linked with the newly created rhymed dialogues, which, once integrated with the beat and music of the play, could in turn provide more information.[81] In some instances, model operas even used a rhymed dialogue in direct response to a rhymed sung passage preceding it. This device brought closer than before speaking *(nian)* and singing, the two distinct means of expression in traditional repertories whose incongruity had so puzzled Mei Lanfang.

Mei's desire to reform traditional opera to reflect contemporary reality, however, found a fresh expression in his new historical drama *(xinbian lishiju),* performed after Japan's invasion of China appeared imminent. His *Resisting the Jin Invaders (Kang jinbing)* and *Hatred in Life and Death (Shengsi hen),* premiered in Shanghai in 1933,[82] represented the best of this repertory, which he continued and perfected into the PRC period. Mei, of course, was not alone in this endeavor. Tian Han in 1940 also scripted *Jiang-Han Fishermen's Song (Jianghan yuge),* a new Peking opera *(xin pingju^a)* that dramatized a fishermen's uprising to defeat Jin aggressors during the Song dynasty. The same year Tian wrote *Heroic Stories of New Sons and Daughters (Xin ernü yingxiong zhuan),* which dramatizes a Ming dynasty hero fighting against foreign invaders, to inspire the Chinese audience in their efforts to resist Japanese troops. In the same fashion, Ouyang Yuqian transformed *Peach Blossom Fan (Taohua shan),* a *chuanqi* text, into a new Peking opera. He revised the image of Li Xiangjun, the female protagonist who would rather die than see her lover became a traitor. Ouyang's attempt to reform Peking opera contrasted with his earlier success of *Boulder Bay* in 1928, an innovative modern drama that had adapted traditional operatic themes and forms. In a similar fashion, CCP artists in Yan'an also experimented with traditional operatic repertories and themes of the *Water Margin (Shuihu zhuan)* stories in their productions of the new Peking opera *(xin pingju^a) Forced to Liang Mountain (Bishang Liang-shan).* Premiered on New Year's Day in 1944 by the Yan'an Peking Opera Troupe (Yan'an pingjuyuan), it was immediately hailed by Mao Zedong as the "epoch-making beginning of old theater reform" *(jiuju geming).* Mao believed that this new opera had finally reversed the history of the old theater by featuring the common people, the makers of history, on center stage.[83] PRC historians have claimed that Mao's comment marked the beginning of theater reform. As I have demonstrated, however, its inception goes back to cultural critics and theater practitioners in the late Qing period.

The dialectical relationship between form and content remains at the heart of political and artistic debates in theater reform from the late Qing, Republican, Maoist, and post-Maoist eras. Many cultural reformers took modern drama imported from the West as a remedy, if not a replacement, for traditional operas because of the former's relevance to modern life. Statistics reveal that since its start, more than eight hundred new dramas *(xinju)* were produced in twenty years, with about a hundred scripts published in newspapers and magazines, including both complete texts and outlines or fragmented scripts *(mubiaoxi).*[84] The introduction of modern drama therefore challenged and stimulated theater reform in traditional operas. In response to Hu Shi's drastic solution during the May Fourth Movement to eliminate traditional operas because of their backward and primitive elements, Zhang Geng pointed out in 1939 that, on the contrary, modern drama should learn from traditional opera the Chinese national characteristics of representing life *(huaju minzu hua)*, and that traditional opera could modernize to better answer the needs of modern audiences *(jiuju xiandai hua)*.

Although no one can predict what would have happened to traditional operatic theater in the second part of the twentieth century without the PRC, Zhang Geng was correct in claiming that old theater reform could not have succeeded in the May Fourth period and the 1930s without the radical changes that were later to occur in all aspects of society after the founding of the PRC.[85] The ideological transformation from a Confucian to a revolutionary culture and the CCP's policy of literature and art serving the interests of the socialist state provided theater with the necessary momentum for dramatic changes. To ensure an institutional structure for theater reform, Ouyang Yuqian was appointed in September 1949 as the chairman of the Theater Reform Association (Xiqu gaijin hui) under the jurisdiction of the National Association of Writers and Artists (Quanguo wenxue yishu gongzhuozhe lianhehui). The month after the establishment of the Central People's Government, the Ministry of Culture established the Bureau of Theater Reform. Although such institutional structures underwent changes in the PRC, a centralized mechanism that supervises and directs theater productions has always been part of the state apparatus, a phenomenon unique to the socialist state.

In 1951–1952, theater reform focused on revising scripts from traditional repertories, reeducating theater personnel, restructuring theater groups (including sponsoring theater troupes financially on their own, and hence struggling to survive), and reforming old theater practices such as the apprentice and "adoptive daughter" systems.[86] In November 1951, the Ministry of Culture held the First National Seminar on Traditional Theater (Quanguo xiqu gongzhuo huiyi), during which Tian Han called on theater artists to collect, preserve, and revise traditional repertories. The First National Opera Festival (Diyijie quanguo xiqu guanmo yanshu dahui), held in October 1952 in Beijing, sponsored more than ninety productions, most of which were from the original or newly revised traditional repertories, with only very few new historical and modern operas. To address this situation, Zhou Yang, in the concluding speech of the festival, urged artists to create new historical and modern operas along with their efforts to revise old repertories. To encourage this undertaking, three modern operas won awards: the north and northeast opera (pingju[a]) Child Husband (Xiao nüxu), the Shanghai opera (huju) Token of Love (Luohan qian), and the northern Jiangsu opera (huaiju) Wang Gui and Li Xiangxiang (Wang Gui he Li Xiangxiang). In contrast, only six operas from traditional repertories won awards, although most of the operas performed during the festival belonged to this category. Interestingly, all three modern operas addressed the issue of an individual's right to free love as against arranged marriages, which was guaranteed by the new marriage laws passed after the founding of the PRC. Child Husband, written by Cao Keying and premiered by the Northeast Opera Research Institute (Dongbei xiqu yanjiuyuan), for instance, depicts Yang Xiangcao, who insists on a divorce from her eleven-year-old "child husband" to marry a man of her own age. In addition to its critique of a village official who fails to support her, the opera probes into the social and economic conditions that encouraged the practice of child marriage in the rural areas, where betrothal provided extra labor for financially disadvantaged families. In a similar fashion, Token of Love, written by Zong Hua, Wen Mu, and Xing Zhi and premiered by the Shanghai People's Shanghai Opera Troupe (Shanghai renmin hujutuan), further explores a two-generational impasse created by arranged marriage. Despite the passage of many years since her arranged marriage, the mother can never forget her true love, thus subjecting herself to constant abuse by her husband. Learning from her mother's experience, the daughter becomes even more determined to fight against a proposal for an arranged marriage and subsequently marries the man of her choice. The romantic theme disappeared entirely in model operas during the Cultural Revolution, but eventually made a comeback in post-Maoist theater as a critique against the Maoist era. In all three periods, however, love stories—or the lack of them—played an essential role in providing theater reform with a unique way to attract contemporary audiences and create new plays more appropriate to the construction and reconstruction of the Chinese nation.

In the early 1950s, while attempting to promote new operas, theater artists and officials had to depend on reviving traditional repertories, which had much greater appeal to audiences than modern operas. The National Conference on Opera Scripts (Quanguo xiqu jumu gongzhuo huiyi), convened in June 1956 in Beijing by the Ministry of Culture, passed a resolution to revive traditional repertories, deemed then as lacking in diversity, vigor, and connection to contemporary life. It sent artists to different parts of China to collect scripts scattered in local villages and towns, and called on practitioners of the older generation to donate scripts. According to a 1957 report, theater workers collected as many as 51,867 scripts of different operatic genres.[87] Considering such state sponsorship, it is not surprising that, according to one estimate, the number of traditional operatic genres increased from around 100 at the beginning of the PRC to 368 by 1959. Professional operatic companies increased from around one to three thousand, thus making China "the number one theater country in human history."[88]

The poster *Performing for the Villagers (Songxi daochun)* by Ren Huaying best illustrates the momentum of such opera reform, which attempted to attract audiences of ordinary people (Fig. 18). Published in 1960, this poster depicts villagers' warm reception of a traditional opera troupe, which has just finished its play of Mu Guiying, a legendary woman warrior from the Northern Song dynasty. In the upper righthand corner of the poster, the red banner of "Mu Guiying Team" indicates that villagers had already formed their own all-women group to imitate the heroic spirit of Mu Guiying and build a new socialist countryside. A girl in the middle of the poster is carrying a water kettle with "people's commune cafeteria" inscribed on it, indicating that this scene depicts the Great Leap Forward movement, when traditional opera performers made an effort to connect their plays with contemporary life in rural China.

Modern opera productions, however, did not gain momentum until after May 1958, when the CCP held its second plenary session of the Eighth Congress, which announced the blueprint for the Great Leap Forward. To carry out this new initiative, the Ministry of Culture presided over a conference in Beijing from June 13 to July 14, 1958, to discuss how to reform traditional opera to portray contemporary life. During the conference, participants from twelve opera troupes performed their recent experiments of nine different kinds of local opera. In response to Zhou Yang's call to

FIGURE 18. Ren Huaying, *Performing for the Villagers* (People's Art Press, 1960). The University of Westminister Chinese Poster Collection.

wage "a second revolution in theater reform" to portray new characters and life in socialist China, the conference participants proposed to produce modern operas that would comprise 20 to 50 percent of their repertories within three years. The same conference also witnessed performances of the Peking operas *Capturing the Bandit Chief Zuoshandiao by Strategy* (*Zhiqin guanfei Zuoshandiao*) and *Taking Tiger Mountain by Strategy* by the Beijing Peking Opera Troupe (Beijing jingjutuan), which were forerunners of the model opera versions developed by the Shanghai Number One Peking Opera Troupe, as I mentioned earlier.

Operatic theater from traditional repertories, however, still dominated the Chinese stage from 1961 to 1963, a situation that Mao criticized as a regression to feudal and revisionist art. A momentum for theater reform gathered during the National Modern Peking Opera Festival (Quanguo jingju xiandaixi guanmo yanshu dahui) held in Beijing from June 5 to July 31, 1964, with more than five thousand theater artists, officials, and critics from eighteen provinces and autonomous regions. The festival showcased thirty-seven modern operas, four of which were selected as model operas by 1967. Four others were either promoted as the second group of model theatrical pieces or became precursor texts for their adaptations into model ballet versions in the later part of the Cultural Revolution.[89]

Although a detailed account of the entire creation process of model theater and Jiang Qing's role—or lack of it—would demand a separate study, Jiang Qing did make a few contributions to the artistic process of revising model theater, limited as they may be. She introduced the Shanghai opera *Spark in the Marshland (Ludang huozhong)*, premiered by the Shanghai People's Shanghai Opera Troupe, to the Beijing Number One Peking Opera Troupe, which revised it into the model opera *Shajiabang* by 1967. Dai Jiafang pointed out that in the film version of *The Red Detachment of Women*, it is Lianhua, a female friend, who tells Qionghua to join the Red Army after she escapes from the local despot. In the model ballet version of *The Red Detachment of Women*, Jiang Qing suggested that it fall to Hong Changqing, the male Red Army commander, to direct Qinghua (a name change from Qionghua) to join the Red Army. This change not only enhanced Hong Changqing's dramatic role in the ballet, which depends heavily on the interaction between female and male protagonists; it also eliminated one character, thus tightening the plot. Jiang Qing also came up with the idea of adapting the Peking opera *Hong Sao* into the modern ballet *Song of Nimeng Mountain*, which turned out to express human emotions more effectively through body movement than Peking opera. She also told the cast not to stretch out the plot to make it a full-fledged ballet, but to produce a shorter piece that could best tell its story in a way most appropriate to the genre.[90]

There are, of course, many more counterexamples in which Jiang Qing's suggestions resulted in less satisfactory revisions in the model theater. Some critics credited Jiang Qing with being the creator of the principle of the "three prominences" that resulted in this dogmatic formula: give prominence to positive characters among all characters, give prominence to heroic characters among positive characters; and give prominence to the main heroic character among other heroic characters. Xie Boliang, however, argued that the theories and practices of the model theater did not evolve overnight, and that Jiang Qing did not create the principle of the three prominences. Jin Shengtan, a seventeenth-century critic, already believed that *The Romance of the Western Chamber (Xixiang ji)* employed negative characters such as Zheng Heng to enhance other neutral characters. It also used characters such as Madam Cui and Faben to help create main characters; and, finally, it constructed main characters such as Zhang Sheng and Hong Niang to best portray Cui Yingying, the central character. This dramatic theory, Xie believed, could be seen as the real source of the "principle" claimed to have been invented for the model theater.[91] Xie thought that, in spite of the dogmatic nature of this principle, it actually enhanced the richness of the operatic music, which helped model theater become more popular among audiences. The three prominences of music required that one first give prominence to sung passages (chang-qiang) in the entire opera; then give prominence to three traditional Chinese musical instruments (gaohu, erhu, and yuechin) in the orchestra; and, finally, give prominence to the stringed instruments (cello, viola, violin, and double bass). Such a principle, dogmatic as it is, nevertheless was rather successful in combining the flavor of Chinese musical instruments with the richness and depth of their Western counterparts.[92]

Jiang Qing, of course, could not have played a crucial role in the entire drama of model theater without Mao's support. Indeed, despite the conventional knowledge that Mao Zedong started the public campaign against the Peking opera *Hai Rui Dismissed from Office* that triggered the Cultural Revolution in 1966, PRC drama historians have recorded Mao's personal preference for opera over modern drama. Coming from the countryside, Mao shared a passion for traditional opera with his fellow peasants. He once declared that he did not like to watch modern drama, for he himself "already acted in living modern drama every day." Watching modern drama on stage would only create more troubles for him; yet he did not oppose promoting it, as the masses, especially young people, liked it. Mao even criticized Lu Xun, his favorite revolutionary thinker, for his rejection of Chinese medicine and opera, especially Mei Lanfang's female roles. Mao regarded Peking opera as the quintessential representative of traditional operatic theaters; it would continue to exist, Mao predicted, even in the era of communism. In his later years, when traditional culture was severely criticized, Mao mandated thirty-seven traditional operas to be made into films so that they would be preserved for future generations.[93] According to one account, Mao lent personal support to the model operas: he shed tears while watching *The Red Lantern*, revised several sung passages for *Taking Tiger Mountain by Strategy*, changed the Shanghai opera *Spark in the Marshland* into *Shajiabang*, and watched six times the television broadcast of *Song of the Dragon River*.[94] Mao's passion for Peking opera seems to support the central idea of this section: that the emergence and popularity of model theater had deep roots in the traditional culture and that it cannot be viewed as a pure PRC invention.

I have so far attempted to challenge the conventional divides between the late Qing and Republican cultures from that of the PRC, between the first seventeen years of the PRC and the subsequent ten years of the Cultural Revolution, and between Cultural Revolutionary and post-Maoist art and theater. I have demonstrated that despite their obvious differences in ideology, political culture, and social and economic circumstances, cultural critics and artists from these diverse periods constantly devoted themselves to theater reform, which regarded the modernization of traditional theater as an essential part in the construction of a modern nation and Chinese identity. In the next part of this chapter, I will delineate another distinctive characteristic: the representation of heroic and liberated women in the public sphere. Model theater pushed to the extreme a displacement of family drama, which had been central in traditional operas such as *The Romance of the Western Chamber* and *The Peony Pavilion (Mudan ting)*. In the May Fourth plays, family dramas, such as those by Chen Dabei, Hong Shen, Tian Han, and Cao Yu, continued to occupy central stage as a battleground between Confucian doctrines and iconoclastic interventions. PRC theater, however, witnessed a more radical change of family drama. Lao She's *Teahouse*, for instance, explored the family story of Wang Lifa to illustrate the inevitability of socialist China as the next logical stage in Chinese history. Similarly, Yue Ye's *Joys and Sorrows (Tonggan gongku)* presented a CCP official's love triangle between his ex-wife of an arranged marriage and his present wife, married for love. Such a family drama, although intended to praise a CCP official for his attempt to appreciate rural women who gained a new life after liberation, was nevertheless criticized as a rightist play in 1958 for having tarnished the image of the party. The 1960s plays, such as *Never Forget Class Struggle (Qianwan buyao wangji)*, centered on workers' families only to ensure that the younger generation would always remember their fathers' and grandfathers' sufferings in the old society.

Continuing in this vein, model theater virtually eliminated family and love relationships. Needless to say, neither male nor female characters had family or spouses in most of the model works. Female leads dominated the stage of model theater. Thematic concerns and story lines in model theater pushed to the extreme women's role in the public domains. The theatrical conventions such as the shapely bodies of the female characters, their dramatic gestures in acting, singing, dancing, and their more-colorful-than-real-life costumes, however, imbued women with a visual power that could sometimes subvert the verbal texts to assert their separate identities, limited as they might be.

At the heart of this art form are the life stories of Chinese women, whom model theater spotlights, as institutional and ideological agents. As catalysts responsible for bringing about revolutionary changes, however, they were not portrayed as historical subjects, but rather as voiceless signifiers who spoke for the oppressed classes and their party.[95] Transformed from oppressed workers and peasants into women warriors, underground party workers, and party secretaries, these women characters were depicted as totally lacking any acquaintance with motherhood and the intimacies of family life. Thus model theater availed itself of what I have called Cultural Revolutionary feminism, which used the issue of women's exploitation for its own purposes of political unification and conformity.

In the Peking opera *Shajiabang*, for example, we learn of Sister A Qing (A Qing Sao), an underground party secretary who sent eighteen wounded Communist soldiers through enemy lines during the War of Resistance to Japan. In order to better serve as an emblem of complete devotion to the party's work, she is depicted as having no children or husband (he has left her after a quarrel). This childless, "husbandless" state affords her the luxury of playing the roles of both mother figure and female companion to the eighteen wounded soldiers, who depend on her as their local guide and underground contact—challenging functions usually assigned to male members of the party. An embodiment of the best of both male and female energies, Sister A Qing acts as the head of a newly established revolutionary family. Against the backdrop of war's harsh realities, her maternal instinct toward her "children" works in concert with her extraordinary "paternal" capabilities with respect to her mission. Her love for her children also reflects the even more glorified love of the party on the part of its dedicated soldiers. It follows that when the eighteen are trapped in the marshes, when "the sky is dark" and "a storm is brewing," they both miss the presence of Sister A Qing—the feminine ideal—and invoke the paternal guidance of the party as the absolute power. Thus Guo Jianguang, the leader of the wounded soldiers, sings: "Do not say the marshes are locked in dense mist and clouds,/Nothing can block out the radiance of . . . the red sun."[96] It might be argued that model theater has transformed domestic women into public figures whose destiny has been to erase the private history of women. These public women, however, cannot become really powerful without at the same time being domesticated by identification with "the Real," which, in Jacques Lacan's terms, must always yield to the father who, in the process of raising the party's children, evokes all that is associated with the symbolic and the imaginary.

This strange destiny of women is apparent in another model work, the Peking opera *Taking Tiger Mountain by Strategy*, in which eighteen-year-old Chang Bao disguises herself as a deaf-mute boy to protect herself from the bandit renegades who killed her mother and drove her father into the depths of the forest. On learning that the People's Liberation Army is made up of subalterns like herself, she takes up arms to join the battle against her class enemies. Her gender disguise symbolizes the fact that the old society deprived her of her womanhood. Yet although the Communist army restores her female garb to her, when she becomes a woman warrior her gender identity is once again submerged in the collective identity of the revolutionary army. She acts like a man so as to be accepted as a woman warrior. Her stage gestures and acrobatic movements are hardly distinguishable from those of the male soldiers. It is only by virtue of her red jacket that she stands out among the green army uniforms. Yet this color difference is not necessarily gender-specific, since both red stars and green uniforms are characteristic of the army and are hence male-associated in the context of the war experience.

It appears, then, that Chang Bao violates the code of gender-specific dressing and speaking, both before and after she joins the revolution. Before joining it, when she was disguised as a hunter's boy without her female voice, she was cast outside the domestic realm of womanhood by her class enemy. Once accorded a new life as a woman warrior, however, she is further distanced from womanhood by the fantasy that a new woman like herself can break away from the family structure that restricts women to their men and hence impairs women's capacity to act together with other women.[97] Although the existence of such women led the official press to assert that it was a historical fact that the revolutionary army was drawn from the people and was thus of the people and for the people, this political history concealed the discursive practice that ruthlessly erased gender difference to sacrifice female subjects to the agenda of the nation/state.

A comparison between the gender politics of contemporary China and that of early modern France is instructive in this regard. As Joan Landes notes in her study *Women and the Public Sphere: In the Age of the French Revolution*, cultural critics were so unhappy about women's participation in the salon in early modern French society, calling it the reign of women, that they declared that this exercise of female power had disarmed the patriarchal kingdom. They therefore suggested that women withdraw from the salon to reoccupy the spheres of private home and love life so that they could no longer be corrupted in the public sphere by men. This "decentralized vision of the moral regeneration of France," according to Landes, was "one in which the state would emerge stronger as the sum of its private (familial) parts, and social status by birth would be restored."[98]

In contrast to this episode in French history in which aristocratic and bourgeois women were forced to descend to the lesser role of domestic caretakers, the female characters from the working class in model theater —along with their real-life counterparts who were supposed to emulate them—ascended to and attained the much higher status of a cultural elite once they left the domestic sphere to exert female power in the public sphere as agents of the party and the state. Paradoxically, the public sphere —or the big revolutionary family to which the women were devoted—was staged in model theater to function exactly like a miniature home with its traditional structure, such as a symbolic patriarch, matriarch, and family members of all ages and both genders. The central role of the party and Chairman Mao evoked, in the words of Landes, "the king's supremacy in the grand household of the kingdom" and his power to domesticate, "even un-man, those who ought to have been his peers."[99]

An excellent example of the Cultural Revolutionary feminism we have been describing can be found in *Azalean Mountain*, a Peking opera declared by the official culture around 1973 to be a model theatrical work.[100] Ke Xiang, the female party representative, is sent out by Mao to guide the peasant self-defense corps, which badly needs party leadership after having suffered three major defeats. This female leader proves not only more than equal to the challenges she faces but also superior to both the revolutionary men in her military unit and the counterrevolutionary men her troops confront in battle. Devoted to the great man Mao, Ke Xiang removes three chief obstacles to the revolution: she defeats the Viper (Dushedan), the local despot; she turns the impetuous chief of the peasant self-defense corps, Lei Gang, into a determined member of the Communist Party; and, most significantly, she helps eliminate Wen Qijiu, the deputy peasant chief who, as the Viper's spy, attempted to lure the self-defense corps into a trap.[101]

This portrayal of a superwoman in model theater was intended to remind audiences of Mao's conception of political correctness, both in past revolutionary war experiences and in the Cultural Revolution's ongoing power struggle within the party. Thus Ke Xiang's ability to recognize Wen Qijiu's sabotage received considerable attention in the official review of the play around 1973, when the national campaign against Lin Biao's anti-party clique celebrated the revolutionary spirit known as "going against the trend" (fanchaoliu). *The Political Report of the Party's Tenth Congress*, released in August 1973, explained the importance of this phrase: Good Communist Party members, especially those in leadership positions, should have the courage to defy incorrect policymakers within the party, even when they found they were alone in going against the trend. Such fortitude would ensure that when a revisionist like Lin Biao tried to usurp the party's central leadership, he could be stopped by party members who dared to challenge his power.[102]

Since *Azalean Mountain*'s premiere coincided with the holding of the Tenth Party Congress, it was inevitable that Ke Xiang's uncovering of Wen Qijiu's plot would be lauded for demonstrating how people, though burdened by adversity, could still abide by their principles. Official reviews interpreted her conflict with Wen Qijiu as symbolizing the life-and-death struggle between the party and its traitors in the top leadership. Her story became a microcosm of the complicated and interwoven class struggles that characterized the Second Civil War period—which was the historical background of *Azalean Mountain*—and of the party's entire history.[103]

Azalean Mountain, however, merely followed the central strategy in the revisions of earlier model operas. *Shajiabang*, for instance, changed its dramatic ending of Sister A Qing pretending to help the local KMT army commander with his wedding while bringing in the disguised Guo Jianguang and his soldiers to wipe out his headquarters, as seen in the original version of the Shanghai opera. In the model-opera version, the eighteen soldiers, now recovered from their wounds, collaborated with the New Fourth Army in their victory. This revision aimed to emphasize Mao's revolutionary line that put armed struggle above underground work in the KMT-occupied areas, known as Liu Shaoqi's incorrect line. In the same fashion, Guo Jianguang assumes a more significant role, both in terms of plot structure and singing parts, than Sister A Qing, who distinguishes herself in party underground work. Similarly, in the revised version of *The Red Lantern*, Li Yuhe parallels the guerrilla fighters who succeeded on the battlefield against their enemies, thus turning the original tragic ending of Li's death into a glorious moment of armed struggle. All these changes were geared to demonstrate Mao's revolutionary truth that political power came from the barrel of a gun.

As in the case of *The White-Haired Girl* and *The Red Detachment of Women*, however, the political reading of the text could not by itself make a model play work. Other elements, such as a surrogate family structure

FIGURE 19. Ke Xiang in the model Peking opera *Azalean Mountain,* Beijing Peking Opera Troupe, 1973.

and an implicit sexual attraction, were included in *Azalean Mountain,* although the conventional gender roles of mother and lover were not.[104] In contrast to several other heroines in model plays whose husbands or lovers are never mentioned to accentuate an extremely purified revolutionary theme, Ke Xiang happens to have a husband. Still, the mere mention of the husband, who is murdered by class enemies even before the play begins, serves the same revolutionary purpose. The timely revelation of Ke Xiang's loss of her dearest one at a crucial moment of the opera helps remove doubts about her loyalty to the peasant troops, and it inspires others to avenge their class brother in the future warfare.

The missing standard kinship group is thus supplanted by a warm family atmosphere in the revolutionary army, in which Ke Xiang, a beautiful, brilliant, and loving woman, concurrently fulfills the roles of a powerful patriarch and a matriarch (Fig. 19). She can choose to play the traditional role of *yanfu* (strict father) when functioning as party secretary and conducting difficult warfare with predominantly male soldiers. Part of this persona entails teaching the soldiers to read and write (Lei Gang is her most diligent student).[105] And she can shift to the traditional role of *cimu* (loving mother) when domestic caretaking is required. She makes straw sandals for her soldiers, paying special attention to Lei Gang's needs. Lei Gang can long for her, as one does for a potential lover, when her absence and involvement in a dangerous military action makes his heart grow fonder. Her vulnerability as a woman can be capitalized upon to heighten the drama, and also to highlight her irreplaceable position in the army's power structure. In spite of her modern and revolutionary persona, however, Ke Xiang nevertheless reminds one of Song Jiang, the leader of the 108 heroes in *Water Margin*, who is rescued from the execution ground (*jiefachang*) by Cao Gai and his followers.[106] In a similar fashion, Lei Gang and his followers had rescued Ke Xiang from the execution ground with the hope of finding in her a CCP leader to change the unsuccessful course of his peasant army. Such a borrowing from a legendary fiction lent *Azalean Mountain* a helping hand in attracting contemporary audiences familiar with that tradition, even though a female protagonist challenged the very misogynist view of *Water Margin*, which depicted vicious women as the causes of some heroes' rebellious acts.[107]

Despite the absence of an explicit love story, the sexual attraction between the woman who leads and the man being led is clear to many. Even Wen Qijiu, the class enemy, comments sarcastically on the chemistry between Ke Xiang and Lei Gang while persuading Lei Gang to ignore Ke Xiang's military command: "A cloud's obstructing our chief's vision;/A giant of a man's come under the thumb of a woman."[108] Trapped in the enemy's prison as a result of having disobeyed Ke Xiang's order, Lei Gang misses her presence and wisdom and hopes that she will not, in trying to rescue him, stray into enemy territory again and risk ambush. Lei Gang's feelings for the woman party secretary obviously exceed his respect for a comrade-in-arms, which, paradoxically, could ordinarily serve to camouflage a politically incorrect sexual attraction. This situation constitutes another instance in which the revolutionary discourse of the model theater made subtle use of the traditional discourse (gendered or otherwise) it originally was designed to repudiate.[109]

Seen from this perspective, Ke Xiang's being a woman is incidental; what is not incidental is the fact that she is a leader of a military unit and a representative of "truth." In model theater, then, women became custodians of one man's wish, which in turn censored other men and women's political and moral behavior. Women stood for the party and its formidable warfare, because they could be counted on to work miracles, turning the ordinary into the good, and the good into the perfect, while exposing the bad and the backward. Nevertheless, the ploy created its own unforeseen consequences. For when women are turned into nonwomen, the revolution becomes corrupt, since it can no longer be carried through without the associated problem of inequality. When women become the private property of the party, the issue of poverty must again be deferred, because the more immediate goal of emancipation must be addressed—that is, the construction of a world in which women are liberated from their families and the whims of a male master.

The preceding analysis by no means exhausts all that can be said about women in model theater. As shown in most model works, at the same time that narratives deprived women of their gender and sexuality, theatrical representation used their bodies for the purpose of sexual titillation. Since, as Nicholas Mirzoeff remarked, "The body is involved in struggles that are political but are also inescapably issues of representation,"[110] a closer look at the body politics in model theater might help to answer such questions as "Whose body should be shown?"[111] and "Why and how should the body be shown?" It is important that all the women in model theater are positive characters—from party secretary and party representative to victim of the exploitative classes and supporter of the revolutionary war. All the negative characters—the traitor, the Japanese invader, the nationalist puppet, the landlord, and the reactionary—are men, who have been given derogatory and symbolic names such as the Viper, the Vulture (Zuoshandiao), or the Tyrant of the South (Nanbatian). They are depicted as ugly and either fat or skinny, whereas all the women characters, even the grandmothers, the mothers of revolution, are beautiful, healthy, attractive, and never overweight. Thus representation of the body "appears not as itself, but as a sign."[112] Both the perfect body and the imperfect body have become "the subject[s] of a discursive inscription."[113]

Ke Xiang, for example, demonstrates how the dominant culture has tattooed its codes on her body; her beautiful, slim, firm physique becomes a powerful metaphor for the institutional transformation of subjects. In part, this is apparent from the numerous times the stage directions direct one's attention to her body movements. On her first entrance in the second scene, when she is exhibited to the public as the captured Communist, she is described as being "in chains, her head high, strid[ing] out of the temple and turn[ing] to toss back her hair. Having crossed the threshold she halts and strikes a proud pose."[114] Upon singing her heroic line "Thrusting aside their bayonets I gaze into the distance," Ke Xiang "moves left, turns back to look into the distance, revolves, feels a wound, advances on one leg, sweeps back her hair, swings the chain at the guards, then turns to strike a pose."[115]

With another toss of her beautiful hair, she recalls the glorious past in the revolutionary base area in the Jinggang Mountains where she worked under Mao: "I see gleaming spears in the forest, red-tasseled spears. . . . / How I long . . . to leap up to the summit of the mountain!"[116] Spears and mountain summits, which some Westerners may see as phallic symbols, might suggest to the Chinese audience a romantic longing, which they also detected in Ke Xiang's profound love and manifest attachment for the great man. To emphasize her sacrifice to Mao, constant references are made to her scars, wounds, openings, ruptures, and the captivity of her body—all symbols of enslavement that, when eroticized through objectification and ennoblement, could arouse desire for possession of that body. Clearly, the representation of the body in model theater belongs to what Hortense J. Spillers would have described, had she been familiar with this Chinese context, as "a class of symbolic paradigms" that "confirm the human body as a metonymic figure for an entire repertoire of human and social arrangements."[117] What is more, model theater contributed one of the most ingenious examples of the patriarchal appropriation of women's bodies to serve as the beautiful object of gaze. The sexualizing elements of women's bodies—their hair, poses, and wounds—were cleverly employed to popularize the glorified power of the great man. Woman's bodies became a social, institutionalized language and an open space for cultural signification.

These political and sexual seductions could not be achieved without adaptations of the highly stylized formulas for body movement in Chinese operatic theater. The traditional theatrical elements such as dance and acrobatics were ingeniously reformed in model theater to distinguish social classes and opposing ideologies. For example, in the Peking opera *Shajia-*

bang, the traditional technique known as "running in a circle on the stage" was approvingly cited in the official review as having been reformed "to express quick marching that moves like swift water current or whirling wind" in the revolutionary war.[118] Even the postures of different characters became statements of truth, or confessions. As Kirk A. Denton noted, in model plays such as *Taking Tiger Mountain by Strategy*, "while positive characters are made to stand tall and erect, negative characters invariably stoop, cower and grovel to the ground."[119] Similarly, *liangxiang*, or "pose," in model operas was an eye-catching signal of the heroic, the perfect, and the proletarian.

An even more novel invention in model theater, however, was its Maoist modification of the Freudian theory of group psychology. In general, Freud viewed sexual love as inimical to the formation of groups. Sexual impulsions, according to Freud, "preserve a little of [one's] individual activity. If they become too strong they disintegrate every group formation."[120]

In direct contradiction to this theory, the ego ideal embodied in the great leader that characterized model theater had such a dynamic impact that it bound social groups together. Sexual love between individuals was effectively preserved thanks to the interplay between the revolutionary content offstage and that which was *re-presented* onstage, which appealed to the erotic imagination. Despite the fostering, in the social dramas occurring outside the theater, of a pure social revolution that discouraged sexual attraction between individuals, the dramatic representation of a woman's body and movements inside the theater served to some extent to fill the void. This minimized version of sexual love could be exploited to its fullest possible potential by theater audiences, who were free to fantasize in the dark theater; or they could allow themselves to be further seduced by the ego ideal in a forbidden, private, and necessarily one-sided love.

All of the foregoing makes it clear that the issue of gender was never taken seriously in model theater.[121] It was appropriated instead as an opportunity for ideological signification and power domination. Indeed, in model theater genders could be easily reversed. The original film version of *The Red Detachment of Women*, for example, designated Wu Qunhua as the protagonist. In the model ballet version, however, it was Hong Changqing who was promoted as the principal hero and who symbolized, above all else, the party's primacy in the army. The creation of the first male proletarian character for a Chinese ballet was acclaimed an epoch-making event in world ballet history, as it discredited Western tradition, according to which only women could fill the famous leading roles of

FIGURE 20. Model Ballet *The Red Detachment of Women*. From *Oil Paintings of the Red Detachment of Women* (Shanghai People's Press, 1972).

Sleeping Beauty, the swan, and the princess—roles that in any case were regarded as reflecting decadent bourgeois ideology.[122]

What counted, then, is not the gender of a party representative but rather the departure from the convention to prove that the proletariat was right and the bourgeoisie wrong. Yet when the official press quoted the peasant Yuan Yu-chen as testifying that the bourgeois ballets produced before the Cultural Revolution "display[ed] bare legs" and nauseated him, it is clear he did not realize that the women soldiers in *The Red Detachment of Women* also displayed bare legs; otherwise, there could not have been any ballet.[123] In this case, however, it was the female army uniform, with its short pants, that sanctioned the display of the female body (Fig. 20). This was another demonstration of model theater's blithe appropriation of a contradictory heritage, that of the old, Western, bourgeois world, which could paradoxically serve the ends of the new, Chinese, proletarian universe.

Paralleling the stories of the revolutionary women in model theater, a selective group of women at the grass-roots level of society did occupy such culturally prestigious positions as representatives of the party's congress or of the people's congress. Does this advertised sharing of political power necessarily mean there was a genuine movement toward allowing the subalterns to speak?[124] The political problems in contemporary China differed from those addressed by the Indian Subaltern Studies Group, which debated whether elite intellectuals could speak for the underclass.

In China, a sociopolitical oppressed status before 1949 was turned into a political privilege over the other classes after 1949. This novel focus blurred such troubling questions as whether there had been a substantial improvement of socioeconomic conditions. The political power of the "subalterns" was largely a fiction perpetrated by the proponents of the ruling ideology, whose aim it was to control both the previously oppressed—the subalterns—and the presently oppressed—the intellectuals and other politically discredited groups. The subalterns were in effect ruthlessly used to suppress the political underclass of intellectuals who, according to the party language current during the height of the Cultural Revolution, had to become modest pupils of the subalterns so that they might learn how to realign their stand on the side of the proletariat through a long and even painful process.[125] These demands placed on the intellectuals were intended to silence their voices and to turn their privileged knowledge into personal loss.

It must be remembered that it was the Chinese intellectuals, not the workers, peasants, and soldiers, who wrote, directed, and produced the model subaltern dramas. Under these circumstances, the already much-muted voice of the subalterns was further reduced when filtered through the voice of the intellectuals, whose sociopolitical status was among the lowest. The political exploitation experienced by the approved triad of worker, peasant, and soldier was of a quite different order than that to which the intellectuals were subjected; in the latter case, it was a question of the manipulation of their literary rather than their political power. In 1967, for instance, at the peak of the Cultural Revolution, a mass movement was initiated to re-produce model plays in amateur theaters, which were encouraged to imitate the performances of the professional model theaters. The revolutionary masses were required, for the sake of their own ideological purification, to reenact onstage their heroic selves in the struggle against their class enemies. In doing so, they had no choice but to submit to the intellectuals' treatment of their own stories, which were informed by their conceptions of the other. It was yet again a case of life imitating art instead of the other way around, in the sense that the dramatic types created for these plays by Chinese intellectuals became models for the subalterns, who were ostensibly their subject.

This ideological indoctrination on a national scale was directed simultaneously at the subaltern receivers of the instruction and its elite producers. Popular sayings during the Cultural Revolution described the reciprocal ideological reform as "acting a revolutionary character in order to become a revolutionary person" or "watching a revolutionary model play in order to become a revolutionary man or woman." In the process of playing the roles of model characters, one would experience a conflict between the true but selfish self and the untrue but heroic other, with the latter ultimately conquering the former. At the same time, any intellectual who undertook to play the heroic subaltern was powerfully and memorably affected, it was thought, through a dramatic representation that had been created by that intellectual in the first place. Two professional actors actually played their heroic model roles so well that they were crowned "model actors." Liu Qingtang, who played Hong Changqing in *The Red Detachment of Women*, became a representative in the Ninth National Congress of the CCP in April 1969 and a member of the CCP Central Committee in the Tenth National Congress in 1974. He also served as the vice-minister of the Ministry of Culture in 1975 and 1976. Yu Huiyong, whose musical scores in the model Peking opera *Azalean Mountain* won him national acclaim, was also a member of the CCP Central Committee in the Tenth National Congress and the minister of the Ministry of Culture in 1975 and 1976. Thus at least some of the actors in model theater turned out to play key roles in the political drama of the larger world and, in the process, fulfilled the early, original design of that unique art form. Not surprisingly, after Mao's death both of them were arrested as followers of the Gang of Four. Liu Qingtang was sentenced to seventeen years in prison and granted a parole for medical treatment in 1985. Yu Huiyong committed suicide on August 28, 1977, at the age of fifty-two, when he was under investigation as an accomplice of the Gang of Four.[126] It is interesting to note that even after the model theater had passed its heyday, the personal dramas of some of its key players continued to draw public attention.

It followed naturally from this emphasis on theatrical life that one would become aware of a pervasive duality in one's social behavior. During the Cultural Revolution, intellectuals were supposed to imitate their subaltern counterparts, speaking their languages, adopting their manners, wearing their clothes. Yet intellectuals could not stop being what they were. They could only impersonate their designated roles. Life became a matter of game and role playing, which can lead to a highly subversive frame of mind. Even in the recent history of China we have seen much evidence of seditious role playing, as, for example, in the political confession meeting after the 1989 Tiananmen student demonstrations, when many people were compelled to perform if they wanted to remain politically viable. Acting the "right" part—a course of action that reached its perfection with the dramatic characters in model theater—became a commonplace in contemporary China that affected everyone's behavior, both in the public and in the domestic spheres. Dramatic performance became something that Chinese people could not do without in the highly politicized—and hence, theatrical—world they inhabited.

3

Family, Village, Nation/State, and the Third World

THE IMAGINED COMMUNITIES IN MODEL THEATER

During the past two decades, modern Chinese literary studies have usually dismissed the need for any scholarly research on the revolutionary model theater. The era of model theater appears as a blank period devoid of any literary value, and Cultural Revolutionary literature—if mentioned at all—pales when compared to that of the great periods of the pre–Cultural Revolutionary and post–Cultural Revolutionary periods, presumably so rich in cultural heritage. The post-Maoist regime made this dismissal of the Cultural Revolutionary period an integral part of its four modernizations program, which was accompanied by a literary and artistic renaissance inspired partially by Western models.

In the West, cultural studies affected academia because they differed from older forms of literary criticism, which considered political implications as only peripherally relevant to the admiration of culture. In early post-Maoist China, men of letters adopted a reverse course—that is, they gave an edge to "new criticism" (to the detriment of older forms) in their attempt to marginalize a politically oriented model theater.[1] The Chinese should not be faulted for failing to follow the Western model in this regard, since, as I have pointed out elsewhere, they only turned to Western discourse to supply what they deemed lacking in a given situation at a particular moment in Chinese history. Their use of Western formalistic approaches to literary criticism can be understood as a conscious effort to debunk the Maoist ideology, which branded the notion of the aesthetic a Western idea—and hence bourgeois and reactionary. They did not realize that the proponents of certain Western discourses would have found the study of the political implications of model theater significant. The recent trends in what Simon During calls "cultural populism," for instance, serve to deepen the disenchantment with the traditional split between the popular and the elite discourses. Seen in this light, the study of model theater is worthwhile because it can be used to examine a culture of differences that prevailed in a society organized by diverse fields through which various discursive practices were inherited.[2] This theater existed as part of a cultural dynamics within a large ensemble of domination that deeply affected a nation and the everyday life of its people.[3]

Only a few scholars have attempted to redeem the study of model theater in China.[4] In his polemic 1989 essay "The Literary Spirit of the Cultural Revolution: The Triumph of Popular Idealism," Mu Gong situated the rise and fall of the model theater in the larger historical contexts of what he termed the irreconcilable differences between the elitist intellectuals and the masses. He argued that it was the Chinese intellectuals who tended to marginalize the history of the Cultural Revolution. They all (almost without exception) divided the literary history of the People's Republic of China into three periods: (1) 1949 to 1966: the seventeen years, which inherited the great tradition of the May Fourth literature; (2) 1966 to 1976: the disastrous ten years of the Cultural Revolution; and (3) 1977 to the present: the new era of post-Maoist literature that is intrinsically endowed with literary and aesthetic value.

In writing literary history in this manner, Mu Gong claimed, the Chinese intellectuals were actually rewriting their own political history. At the same time that they deplored their personal suffering during the Cultural Revolution, they only wrote about the history they chose to remember.

They often forgot that after the May Fourth Movement in 1919, it was the Chinese intellectuals themselves who had borrowed heavily from Western elitist ideas such as romanticism, utopianism, individualism, and liberalism, thereby alienating themselves from the Chinese masses. Thus, Mu Gong believed, the literary achievements of the May Fourth movement had always been looked upon with special favor in Chinese history because it represented the point in time when Chinese intellectuals first renounced the masses by importing and implementing Western concepts.

According to Mu, only Mao Zedong among notable Chinese intellectuals in the May Fourth period perceived over time the increasing alienation between the masses and the cultural elite.[5] As a promising leader of an emerging party not yet in power, Mao was bound to make his party represent the interests and ideals of the masses by persuading the intellectuals to reevaluate their goals. Only after he had successfully brought his own personal relationship to the masses into line with this philosophy did Mao himself became their "red sun"—to be lionized as the savior of the Chinese people for many years to come.[6] Seeing the masses as the driving force of the Chinese revolution, Mao shrewdly transformed Western ideals of communism and socialism into a Chinese brand of popular idealism. Thus, Mu contended, Mao's "Talk at the Yan'an Forum on Literature and Art," delivered in May 1942—in which Mao urged intellectuals to learn from the masses and to write with their interests and dreams in mind— could be viewed as a friendly warning to Chinese intellectuals, who habitually saw themselves as an elite dominating the subalterns.[7]

After 1949, however, when Chinese intellectuals finally perceived acceptance by the masses as an urgent issue, it was already too late for many of them, Mu claimed. During the numerous political movements that followed, no matter how Chinese intellectuals competed with each other in eulogizing the masses, the masses—who had meanwhile become the masters of socialist China—already possessed the political power to persecute the intellectuals.[8] It is in this situation that Mu detected the likely motivation for Mao's initiation of the Cultural Revolution: it was designed to further appease the masses, who were no longer satisfied with being mere masters in the economic and political spheres, and who now desired, above all else, to have a controlling role in the cultural and ideological spheres as well.

Mu asserted that this growing tension between the masses' demand for a popular culture and the intellectuals' belated struggle to meet that demand constitutes a fundamental dynamic in the literary history of the PRC before, during, and after the Cultural Revolution. Cultural Revolutionary literature should thus be considered a natural outgrowth of traditions that originated with the May Fourth movement. As a consequence, the usual characterization of the Cultural Revolution as a historically unprecedented disaster can only be meaningful if one is decrying the fact that never before in the history of Chinese literature had a popular form, a popular spirit, and popular taste so dominated the literary and artistic spheres in China. Yet such a triumph of the popular spirit, Mu believed, was an absolute miracle. We may have ten thousand reasons to mock it, wrote Mu; we cannot, however, deny the greatness of this miracle, which was brought about by the majority of the Chinese people with sincere hearts.[9] The culminating expression of this popular sentiment was captured in the popular songs "The East Is Red" and "The Loyalty Dance for Chairman Mao" as well as in the compositions derived from setting to music Mao's "Quotations" and classical poems during the peak of the Cultural Revolution. Some of these popular works were written by the common people themselves, who came up with their own version of literary idealism by poking fun at elitist literary traditions.

Mu maintained that with trembling hands the Cultural Revolutionary model theater was the first gift Chinese intellectuals presented to the revolutionary masses.[10] In the process of creating model theater, Chinese intellectuals reformed, among other things, the traditional genre of Peking opera, whose familiar style had helped consolidate the popular idealism of the masses. As a result, the masses became particularly attached to the formulas of the model theater: its straightforward language, easy-to-remember stage lines, and passionate dramatization of revolutionary episodes. Indeed, they indulged themselves in an operatic revolution in pursuit of a continuing revolution. Thanks to the intellectuals' creativity, the aesthetics of traditional culture was subtly combined with the new revolutionary subject matter. Paradoxically, the very act of revising traditional scripts for the model theater brought about a refinement and polishing of the popular spirit. All these historical conditions coalesced to produce what Mu termed two key elements in the literary spirit of the masses: (1) the cult of violence, or an affirmation of the historic role of the masses during the revolutionary war period; and (2) the cult of heroes and godlike figures, an unexpected by-product of European romanticism. Cultural Revolutionary literature and art should thus be seen as emanating directly from a triumphant age of popular idealism and heroism.[11]

In a dramatic reversal at the conclusion of his essay, Mu frankly admitted to resorting to pragmatism in his attempt to rescue the literary history of the Cultural Revolution. He ended by criticizing the fundamental failure of nerve on the part of Chinese intellectuals; instead of trying to please the masses, they should have confronted them and opposed their ideals, so that the "true" spirit of the intellectuals could have been established.[12] Here Mu fell into the same trap as did the Chinese intellectuals he had been describing: while seeking to redeem a literary history of the Cultural Revolution, he too remapped the past in order to honor the part of history he chose to remember. In the final analysis, his reclamation of model theater contained the contradictory purpose of recounting the sufferings of the intellectual elite, of whom he is a prominent member. His call to recover the lost spirit of the intellectuals ironically diminished the very spirit of popular idealism he had been attempting to rescue. From his elitist vantage point, he ended by looking down on the underprivileged and underrepresented subalterns, whose "literary history" he had so eloquently rewritten in the early part of his account.

Mu's treatise presented other problems as well. To begin with, it is difficult to distinguish the Chinese intellectuals from the so-called masses, whom Mu never actually defined. Was he referring to illiterate tillers of the land in the countryside who were only vaguely aware of what was happening beyond their own villages? It would be hard to imagine that these illiterate or semiliterate peasants had much to do with creating, in Mu's words, the literary spirit of the Cultural Revolution. On the other hand, might Mu have used the word "masses" to refer to those who participated in the revolutionary war and consequently became members of the party elite after 1949? And was he also including members of the younger generation whose parents were considered the oppressed classes before 1949 (thereby endowing this generation with a privileged status by virtue only of their family origin)? Yet neither group could be thought of as "the masses" in Mu's terms, since many among them enjoyed the benefits of higher education after 1949, thus themselves becoming intellectuals. Some even eventually occupied prestigious slots in the party and state power structures, which endowed them with political power.

Mu's attempt to distinguish intellectuals from the masses inevitably camouflaged the political strategy of the ruling ideologues, who had historically benefited from maneuvering people of diverse social classes and ethnic groups into opposing camps. It also served to mask the complicated, contradictory roles of Chinese intellectuals, who have traditionally survived totalitarian society by acting in both supportive and subversive roles with regard to the prevailing political agendas. (I shall address this phenomenon as manifested in the social problem plays of early post-Maoist China in Chapter 4.)

However problematic his treatise, however, Mu Gong's pioneering work helps us to take seriously the study of Cultural Revolutionary literature. Accordingly, I shall now move on to analyze the construction of a national culture and identity as they existed in the multilayered discourse of the model theater. In developing my argument, I have been intrigued by Benedict Anderson's concept that challenged the discourse of nationalism by defining the nation as an imagined political community. Every nation is *imagined*, Anderson posited, "because the members of even the smallest nation will never know most of their fellow-members, meet them, or even hear of them, yet in the minds of each lives the image of their communion."[13] Anderson's paradigm traced the roots of nationalism through an analysis of the interplay between capitalism and printing, between vernacular languages and literary languages in early modern Europe, and between official nationalism and imperialism. Notwithstanding the value of these cross-cultural and cross-historical perspectives, Anderson failed to illustrate in detail how the mechanism of the imagined community functions at the grass-roots level within a particular cultural and ideological system.

I view model theater as the ideal stage on which the ideological goals of the imagined Cultural Revolution were partially achieved through, for example, the institutions of an imagined family in *The Red Lantern*, an imagined rural community in *Song of the Dragon River*, and an imagined Third World community in *On the Docks*. All these revolutionary imaginings not only helped define the Cultural Revolution in national and international terms but at its height also were imitated, adapted, and transformed in everyday life. These big and small, familial and societal, and national and international imagined communities all came into being through the skillful manipulation of the boosters of revolutionary modern culture and not-so-revolutionary traditional culture, for the sole purpose of erecting a contemporary imperial empire of the Maoist era. My concern is to historicize studies of the model theater, whose current marginal status within Chinese literary and cultural studies paradoxically points to new avenues for research and to new approaches to popular culture and dramatic studies.

Set in the 1930s during the War of Resistance to Japan, the Peking opera *The Red Lantern* narrates the story of Li Yuhe, a poor railway worker who has adopted a mother and an orphan girl whose family members were murdered during the Peking–Hankou railway workers' strikes against a northern warlord. Li Yuhe and his adopted mother are captured, tortured, and finally executed by a Japanese police chief. Carrying out the last wishes of her father and grandmother, Li Tiemei, Li Yuhe's adopted daughter, finally succeeds in sending secret codes to the guerrillas.[14]

With this simple story line, *The Red Lantern* ingeniously evokes an imagined family, one as natural as any family that is based on biological relationships. Yet this family is also ideologically constructed to be part of the bigger family of the proletariat whose members share a common class interest in the fight against their enemies. Startling paradoxes abound in the play. On the one hand, a culturally constructed revolutionary family replaces a biological family, the better to dramatize the bitterness of the old society. On the other hand, the emotional bond between the members of the three generations of the Li family, who have lived together for the past seventeen years as a real family, is fully explored to demonstrate the "truth" that a revolutionary family is more cohesive and meaningful than a biological one, because it is formed and tempered in the storms and winds of revolutionary struggle.

This paradoxical relationship between a natural and a cultural family goes beyond the level of family structure. In almost every character and at almost every dramatic turn of the opera, one finds an interplay between these two opposing elements. The opera begins, for instance, with Li Yuhe's touching expression of fatherly love for Li Tiemei. Li Yuhe's "natural" love for his daughter acts paradoxically as a vehicle for his class consciousness as an oppressed worker. Perceiving in his growing daughter a symbolic child of the entire class of the proletariat, Li Yuhe praises Tiemei as "a good girl" who "peddles goods, collects cinders, / Carries water and chops wood. / Competent in all she does, a poor man's child."[15]

The father identifies with his daughter because of their shared class origin rather than because of blood ties. He thinks the daughter can learn to manage the house sooner than those spoiled children of the rich; she can be expected to grow up to fight for and uphold the cause of poor people. (Note how the feminine gender of the daughter is conveniently set aside by emphasizing the masculine duties she is expected to carry out, such as chopping wood.) The cultural message is nevertheless delivered in a natural way, through a father's love and pride in his beautiful daughter. Still unaware of her real identity at this early stage of the play, the daughter feels and acts just as if she were Li Yuhe's biological child and is accepted as such by the audience.

Just as he regards Tiemei as a symbolic child of the proletariat, so does Li Yuhe portray himself as a father nobler than other fathers, as befits a symbolic father of all the orphans of the oppressed class. So powerfully is the natural, class bond between father and daughter depicted that the last two lines of the above-quoted opening speech by Li Yuhe, "Different trees bear different fruits, / Different seeds grow different flowers," became catch phrases during the Cultural Revolution for many Red Guards, who vaunted their proletarian family backgrounds to gain advantage over those born into undesirable families (i.e., families of landowners, rich peasants, counterrevolutionaries, sex offenders, and rightists). Many made use of these dramatic lines to proclaim their families' revolutionary status, while many others were excluded from that special sphere by the same lines and were consigned to the opposing counterrevolutionary camp.

The image of a loving father at the beginning of scene 1 sets the tone of the play and conveys to the audience that it is about to view a family story. By contrast, scene 2 starts with the image of Grandma Li, an experienced revolutionary who is a role model for both Li Yuhe and Tiemei. In a firm voice, Grandma Li intones: "Fishermen brave the wind and waves, / Hunters fear neither tigers nor wolves; / The darkest night must end at last / In the bright blaze of revolution."[16] This blunt beginning leads to a discussion, in lighter tones, of the forthcoming visit of an uncle, who Tiemei intuitively understands is a more important member of her family:

> I've more uncles than I can count;
> They only come when there's important business.
> Though we call them relatives, we never met before—
> Still they are closer to us than our own relatives.
> Both dad and you call them our own folk;
> I can guess part of the reason why:
> They're all like my dad,
> Men with red, loyal hearts.[17]

As the rest of scene 2 unfolds, the audience learns, along with Tiemei, that her uncle is a liaison man who delivers secret codes to Li Yuhe. His revolutionary mission, however, is also depicted in family terms. After warning him that the enemy is searching for him everywhere, Li sends the liaison man off with much love and care, as if he were a family member:

"Be on guard as you go— / Mountains are high, torrents swift. / Follow small lanes and short bridges, / The quiet and safe paths." However, Li's concern has to be simultaneously expressed in terms of their shared mission: "To the revolution we offer our loyal hearts. / Shouldering the heavy task, I'll stand up to any test in the fire. / Bursting with strength, I'll be worthy of the trust of the party."[18]

The brief encounter between father and uncle and the indication of the danger involved for both constitute for Tiemei a vivid lesson in the genuine meaning of family values. In particular, entrusting the secret mission to the uncle reveals to Tiemei her father's identity as an underground worker in the Communist Party. Besides loving him as her father, Tiemei at this juncture admires Li as a zealous, revolutionary, larger-than-life fighter who seems more magnificent to her than any other parent on earth. In the process of Tiemei's learning more about her unique family, the audience was expected to be equally touched by her development from a naive child to a committed member of her own class and to absorb the same revolutionary truth that she newly discovers. It was ultimately this episode that so popularized the above-mentioned passage spoken by Tiemei during the Cultural Revolution that almost everyone who lived through the period could recognize its familiar tune. The passage was even used in an early post-Maoist film as background music to indicate that particular historical period.

Set in a gruel stall in the junk market, scene 3 extends this family drama by bringing onstage an imagined local community of people suffering in common from economic and political oppression. The place is frequented by impoverished workers whom Li Yuhe encounters and whose welfare concerns him. He is worried about Old Zhang's wound, inflicted by the "Japanese devil" who beat him up after riding in his rickshaw and not paying the fee. He listens to the complaints of fellow workers, who cannot even afford to buy moldy flour sold in the gruel stall. Superficially, these workers are unrelated, but in a larger sense their sufferings connect them to one big family of oppressed Chinese nationals whose miseries intensified after Japan's invasion of China. On this occasion, Li's speech is a catalyst, heightening the workers' awareness as it celebrates a shared Chinese identity:

So many compatriots are suffering and fuming with discontent,
Struggling under iron heels, they seethe with wrath.

Spring thunder will rumble when the time comes,
The brave Chinese people will never bow before the butcher's knife.
May our comrades come soon from the Cypress Mountains![19]

As in the earlier episodes, this nationalist discourse is once again conveyed in family metaphors. Li Yuhe and his liaison man refer to each other as *qinren*, or "relatives."[20] Tiemei and Grandma Li offer cornmeal to Huilian, their starving next-door neighbor, as they believe that "With the wall between us we're families. If we pulled it down, we'd be one." This neighborly (thus natural) love is eventually repaid by Huilian when she risks her life to help Tiemei deliver the secret codes to the Cypress Mountains, transforming her into a legitimate member of the "big revolutionary family."

The episode that most ingeniously combines familial and revolutionary elements occurs earlier in the play, at Li Yuhe's arrest by the Japanese, when Grandma Li reveals the family history to Tiemei. The story fills Tiemei with deep gratitude for the kindness of her adopted father and grandmother, whom she now appreciates all the more because they are not simply blood relations: "Granny tells a heroic and stirring episode of the revolution, / Now I know I was raised in wind and rain. / Dear granny, for all those seventeen years, / Your kindness to me has been vast as the sea."[21] This great gratitude is then immediately converted into a higher level of emotion when expressed in the form of class consciousness: "Now with high aims I see my way clear. / Blood must pay for our blood, / Successors must carry forward the cause of our [martyrdom]. / Here I raise the red lantern, let its light shine far."[22] At this point, the red lantern, a unifying symbol for underground party workers, is identified with the heroic image of Li Yuhe, an endearing father who is also a model Communist whom Tiemei aspires to emulate:

My father is as steadfast as the pine,
A Communist who fears nothing under the sun.
Following in your footsteps I shall never waver.
The red lantern we hold high, and it shines
On my father fighting those wild beasts.
Generation after generation we shall fight on,
Never leaving the field until all the wolves are killed.[23]

From this time forward, Tiemei's emotional attachment to her father increasingly intensifies through her perception of his omnipotence as a revolutionary hero. Now that her father is gone (he is being tortured by the enemies of the nation), Tiemei's heart grows tender with love for an object now beyond her reach. Upon seeing her father again for the first time since the divulgence of the real family history (in scene 8, on the execution ground), Tiemei utters, in a heartbroken voice: "Day and night I've been longing to see you again, / And now you . . . so battered and covered with blood. . . . / Dear father!"[24] When Tiemei, seizing the opportunity to impart to Li her feelings of gratitude, tearfully kneels down to reassure him that he is dearer to her than any biological father could ever be, her action once more reinforces for the audience the point that this culturally constructed family is more natural and heroic than any other comparable family related by blood. Thus well on the way to grasping the double discourse of the natural and the cultural, the audience members are in a position to appreciate Li Yuhe's assertion: "People say that family love outweighs all else, / But class love is greater yet, I know. / A proletarian fights all his life for the people's liberation." Li authenticates this apparent family legacy just before his execution by bestowing the red lantern upon Tiemei: "Making a home wherever I am, / I have lived in poverty all these years. / The red lantern is my only possession, / I entrust it to your safekeeping." Poverty—which leads to revolution—in effect becomes the family heritage, now glorified in the symbol of the lantern. The traditional practice of bequeathing a family heritage, criticized as a feudal custom during the Cultural Revolution, is ironically transformed and imbued here with a new content of passing on the revolutionary spirit. Often quoted during the Cultural Revolution, Tiemei's most popular speech refers to that paradoxical heritage:

Dad has given me a priceless treasure
To light my path forward forever.
You have given me your integrity
To help me stand firm as a rock;
You have given me your wisdom
To help me see through the enemy's wiles;
You have given me your courage
To help me fight those brutes.
This red lantern is our heirloom.
Oh dad, the treasure you leave me is so vast
That a thousand carts and ten thousand boats
Cannot hold it all.
I give you my word I will keep the lantern safe always.[25]

The seductive power of *The Red Lantern* for Cultural Revolutionary audiences resided in how its family story effectively canceled out the blood relationship commonly regarded as the foundation for all families. At the same time, it extended the hierarchical, cohesive structure that formed one big revolutionary family, a unity repeatedly depicted in other model theatrical works such as the Peking opera *Shajiabang* and *Taking Tiger Mountain by Strategy*. Once Tiemei loses her adoptive parents, after having already been deprived of her biological ones by the old society, the sharp distinctions between the family and the revolution, which can clash during the course of revolution, totally disappear on the stage of the model theater.

Although in this revolutionary drama the traditional family structure was intriguingly used as a touchstone, the ruling ideologists of Cultural Revolutionary China singled out *The Red Lantern* as a praiseworthy opera for its *rejection* of the values of the traditional culture. In the official review of the opera, the Lis were eulogized as the ideal family, bound together by the difficult course of the revolution that they traveled together. The new version of the model opera received special attention for excising the parts of the plot that in the earlier version had stressed the feudal aspects of family relations in traditional culture. One episode from the older version came in for particular comment, that in which Li Yuhe apologized to his mother before his execution for not being able to carry out his duty as a son; the line was criticized during the Cultural Revolution as an attempt to promote the traditional concept of filial loyalty to one's parents. When the new script appeared in May 1970 in the party's most authoritative magazine, *Red Flag*, this rebirth of *The Red Lantern* was viewed as a central event in the creation of a new culture under the personal leadership of Comrade Jiang Qing.[26] In post-Maoist China, however, print culture depicts Jiang Qing as having had nothing to do with *The Red Lantern*, except in usurping the credit for others' artistic creativity. She persecuted A Jia, the coauthor and director of the opera, as having sabotaged the model play.

Neither side, however, presents an all-round picture. After a lukewarm reception of the 1962 film *Successor to Revolution (Geming zihou houlai ren)*, also known as *The Record of the Red Lantern (Hongdeng zhi)*, the Kunqu opera *(kunju) Story of the Red Lantern (Hongding zhuan)*, the Shanghai opera *(huju)*, the Peking opera *The Red Lantern*, and the modern drama version *Three Generations (Sandai ren)* appeared in various parts of the country.[27] According to Xie Boliang, the Shanghai Aihua Shanghai Opera Troupe (Shanghai aihua hujutuan) contributed the most to adapting the film *The Record of the Red Lantern* to the Peking opera *The Red Lantern*. Eager to find its own niche in a competitive Shanghai theater scene, the Aihua Troupe devoted itself to making the film into a Shanghai opera. They even debated changing the title of the opera. Some considered the title *Secret Codes*, with a subtitle of "Revolutionary Detective Story," to capture more of the Shanghai audience, while others sought to retain *The Red Lantern* to preserve the theme of three generations of workers carrying out the revolution. After seven major revisions, Ling Dahe and Xia Jianqing, the talented scriptwriters, successfully expanded two scenes from the movie, the "Narrow Escape at the Gruel Stall" and "Struggling against Hatoyama at the Feast." They clarified the logic of Li Yuhe's actions and deepened his characterization.[28] Most significant, the Shanghai opera changed the ending. In the movie, Li Tiemei threw herself into a fire while holding the red lantern after the death of her family members, but the Shanghai opera concludes with her delivering the secret codes to the Communist guerrillas, thus spotlighting the central theme of "the revolution has it own successors."[29]

According to another account, Jiang Qing saw the Shanghai opera on February 22, 1963, and recommended its script to A Jia, director of the China First Peking Opera Troupe (Zhongguo jingjuyuan yituan).[30] Xie Boliang, however, did not mention Jiang Qing's role at this point but credited Weng Ouhong, the main scriptwriter, for the successful adapation of the Peking opera version (first published in 1964). Weng kept the best parts of the Shanghai opera while exploring the differences between the two. Taking advantage of the Peking opera's more elaborate performing styles and techniques, Weng presented a literary, poetic text that resulted in a more artistic performance. Unlike the Shanghai opera, which emphasized singing over speech, the Peking opera borrowed from the reciting technique *(langsong)* of the modern spoken drama. One finds the most typical example in Grandma Li's long speech narrating the revolutionary family history, known as one of the most celebrated passages in the model Peking opera for its beauty, tempo, and dramatic effects. Xie Boliang also mentioned that, even during the Cultural Revolution when Weng suffered persecution, he still periodically participated in revision discussions of *The Red Lantern*. Despite Jiang Qing's repeated interference, sources quote Weng as saying that the three key scenes ("Recounting the Family's Revolutionary History," "Struggling against Hatoyama at the Feast," and "Struggle on the Execution Ground") never "benefited from her highness's blessings."[31]

It is therefore not surprising that the Peking opera *The Red Lantern* became a national sensation during the National Peking Opera Festival in June 1964. Mao Zedong attended a performance on November 6, 1964, and reportedly shed tears over the touching story. This Peking opera soon captured major southern cities, such as Guangzhou in February 1965, and in Shanghai it had forty full-house runs in the Grand Theater (Da wutai), which had three to four thousand seats. Its success earned critical acclaim from the *Liberation Daily (Jiefang ribao)* on March 16, 1965, which praised it as "an excellent model for operatic revolution," the first reference to the notion of "model theater."[32] All these successes came about without much promotion from Jiang Qing. Her role in making the opera a model work consisted of nothing more than suggesting an adaptation from the Shanghai to the Peking opera, which consequently resulted in a crown jewel of an operatic work that was easier to popularize than its southern counterpart because of its use of a standard Mandarin dialect.

To revert to my discussion on *The Red Lantern*, in both the pre-model theater and the model theater versions, the family relationship repeated the traditional, hierarchical family structure, except that the patriarchal figure served as the head of both the household and the hierarchical party organization. To this hierarchical construct, however, was added the matriarchal figure of Grandma Li, who preserved her traditional role of the caring, loving, and sacrificing grandmother while at the same time symbolizing the nurturing images of the party and Chairman Mao, inspirational entities that had guided countless previous revolutionaries. Nonetheless, lest Grandma Li represent a threat to the male-dominated society, her subordinate status in relation to the patriarch was clearly delineated. Unlike him, she was not a party member, and her job was to help him accomplish his mission. A prototypical Communist invention, she is admirably down-to-earth, and thus is the most effective supporter of the revolution. This stock character, which pervades PRC literature, provided countless examples of revolutionary mothers and grandmothers living only to serve the predominantly male fighters of the revolution.

In many other respects, this model play seems to possess the best of the two worlds—the traditional and the revolutionary cultures. Tiemei's parents having been conveniently slaughtered by class enemies during the workers' strike, the possibility of the usual conflict between a daughter (Tiemei's mother) and a mother-in-law in a conventional Chinese family is obviated. Tiemei becomes doubly attached to Li Yuhe because he represents both a father and a mother to her. Similarly, Li Yuhe depends on the support of Grandma Li, whom he regards both as a *yanfu* (a strict father) and a *cimu* (a loving mother), the ideal complementary parental roles in traditional Chinese culture. For Li Yuhe, Grandma Li fulfills the role of respected elder. In the view of Gao Yuqian, the actress who portrayed her, she is not just a mother of an ordinary worker but also of a Communist Party member. Her love for Li Yuhe is therefore twice fortified, by motherly care and by fatherly guidance.[33] Grandma Li could remind one of those chaste widows in traditional legends who, after the untimely death of their husbands, single-handedly raised their children without any temptation to marry again. As the only male in the family, Li Yuhe, in turn, takes on the additional role of spouse to Grandma Li, for he had promised his late master, Grandma Li's deceased husband, to take care of his widow. Once again, both a conventional sexual relationship and romance are dispensed with and replaced by platonic love and companionship between two single parents from different generations. At a time when the institution of the family was such a vital tool for cultivating the mind of the proletariat, it was placed at a calculated distance, away from both the private and the public realms. As numerous couples, parents, and adolescents competed with one another in denouncing their own family members as counterrevolutionaries, the better to impress the party with their own revolutionary ardor, such imaginary family displacements portrayed on the stage echoed the chaos, betrayals, and familial disintegration that occurred during the Cultural Revolution. When the family proves incapable of protecting its members, it also fails to fulfill the central ideal of revolution, the foundation that guarantees freedom for all mankind.

Several other model-theatrical works besides *The Red Lantern* sought to salvage family ties by exploiting the role of the grandmother, typically depicted as a sage, weathered personage impervious to any sexual entanglement. Almost all the narrative forms in model theater resort to using this iconic older woman, a domestic protectress placed on this earth to be the guiding light of her children in their revolutionary careers. In the Peking opera *Shajiabang*, for instance, Granny Sha cooks meals and washes clothes for the wounded soldiers as if they were her own grandchildren. In the Peking opera *Azalean Mountain*, the term "mother" is used to refer to a sixty-year-old widow who influenced her children. Mother Du adopts Lei Gang, the peasant army leader, as her stepson after having lost her own son in the peasants' uprising. As a mother figure, Mother Du is in a better position to persuade Lei Gang to follow the party's directions, which run counter to his own impulses. To further demonstrate her support for the revolution, Mother Du sends her only grandson into the army, entrusting him to Lei Gang's care. Once again, a cultural family has been constructed upon the foundation of a natural family, the dissolution of the latter justified by the fashioning of the former.

In *Song of Nimeng Mountain*, however, it is a natural family that extends its love to a wounded soldier during the civil war in 1947. Hong Sao does not hesitate to offer her own milk after realizing that she cannot fetch water for him without risking his being discovered by the enemy. Her love for the people's army finally wins her husband's understanding for her otherwise unnatural "act of love." At the same time, it conveys the symbolic message that oppressed Chinese women willingly give their all, their milk and blood, to help give birth to a new nation. Expressing the same theme, the Peking opera *Fighting on the Plain* presents the only biological mother-daughter relationship in model theater. Before being killed by her enemies, Xiaoying's mother asks an Eight Route Army soldier to take care of Xiaoying, who should "forever follow Chaiman Mao and the Communist Party to carry to the end the revolution and war efforts against the Japanese invaders."[34] Similar to the stepfamily in *The Red Lantern*, this biological family upholds the same family values that place the revolutionary cause above the family relationship.

The influence of the wise and sustaining mother figure extended beyond the domestic sphere.[35] In the Peking opera *Raid on the White Tiger Regiment*, sixty-year-old Aunt Choe from North Korea extends invaluable aid to her children both at home and abroad during the Korean War. When Aunt Choe is murdered by the enemy, Sister Choe, her daughter-in-law, fulfills her wishes of taking over the work of assisting the war efforts of the combined troops of Chinese and North Korean soldiers against the American and South Korean troops.[36] In this imagined international community, a death in the Korean family has to be further authenticated by the memory of a death in the Chinese family. When the Chinese platoon leader Yan Weicai mourns the death of Aunt Choe, who had nursed him during his sickness, it recalls to mind his own mother, a casualty of the civil war period brought about by American soldiers: "I see Mama Choe who heroically gave her life, / And remember my own mother, killed by / The U.S.–Chiang Kai-shek gang on Mount Laoshan. /Although the two mountains are separated by sea, / Both homes are linked by cruel oppression."[37] Two otherwise unrelated family tragedies thus join to symbolize the national consciousness: "The Chinese and Korean people have suffered together, / Their class and national hatred knows no bounds. / The party leads our revolution, we vow / To give our all for mankind's liberation."[38]

The socialist imperialism implicit in Yan Weicai and his Korean counterpart's pledge to fight to defend the eastern outpost of socialism[39] is no less problematic than European imperialism, which the opera was supposedly criticizing. The author of the official review called *Raid on the White Tiger Regiment* "a brilliant song of internationalism," which was said to have inspired numerous Chinese soldiers to sacrifice their lives to defend a neighboring socialist country and to set in motion an imagined world revolution, without which a Chinese revolution could never have been completed.[40] In the brilliant blueprints drawn up for the Chinese and the world revolution, Mao's Communist Party was the dominant power, but at the same time the authority of Kim Il Sung's North Korean Labor Party was also celebrated.

The conventional family structure, although rejected by model theater as counterrevolutionary, was then exploited for its own purposes and employed again by unexpected agents. The literature of the time frequently alludes to Mao's own family as a source of strength and inspiration, depicting Jiang Qing as a great standard-bearer of the Cultural Revolution, which was guided by the shining thought of Mao Zedong. Ironically, despite being worshipped as the "empress," Jiang Qing was never referred to as "Madam Mao," or *Mao furen*, in the official press, but merely as "comrade," "comrade-in-arms," or "the most faithful student of our Chairman." As in model theater, the husband-wife relationship in Mao's own family disappeared before the eyes of the public. This not-so-subtle strategy achieved its end of consolidating the patriarchal and hierarchical system in both party and state, and the emergent lesson was that nobody, not even his own wife, could be the Great Man's equal, even if he himself said that "women can hold up half of the sky." Jiang Qing was nevertheless no ordinary woman. Imaginary national and international communities depicted in model theater conjured, in real life, a Jiang Qing who was a model woman deserving of emulation. "Each time we hail the birth of new literary creations, replete with the thought of Mao Tse-tung," the official press claimed in 1967, "we think of Comrade Chiang Ching [Jiang Qing], a splendid communist fighter who stood in the foremost ranks defending Chairman Mao's revolutionary line in literature and art, and led the revolutionary literary and art warriors in an assault against the enemy."[41] Thus a matriarch came into existence who could take her rightful place in the patriarch-headed family that surpassed all other families, as the following characteristic poem published in 1968 illustrates:

> The sky above is cloudless and blue
> As the postman smilingly enters our billet.
> A letter from home's a cheering thing,
> It's like ma was standing right here beside me.
>
> I open the letter and see the sun,
> Red and glowing, lighting up my heart,
> Ma has sent me a colored picture
> Of our dear leader, Chairman Mao.
>
> ". . . Received your letter asking for my photo,
> The whole family sat down and talked it over.
> Chairman Mao is dearer than any parent,
> Consider him to be your own pa and ma.
>
> "Chairman Mao saved us from our sea of sorrows,
> Never forget it, good child of mine.
> Neither mountains of knives nor seas of fire
> Should stop you from following Chairman Mao."
>
> I hold Chairman Mao's picture to my chest,
> Memorizing the words my ma has said.
> Chairman Mao's road is the one we're traveling,
> For ever and ever toward the sun.[42]

During the era of the Cultural Revolution, it was common practice to keep as a decoration in the home a picture of the "red sun," which replaced any family portrait. Employing the same strategy seen in *The Red Lantern*, this poem displays the traditional hierarchical structure that holds a family together and reserves for the patriarch of the national family a position of paramount power and respect. The filial narrator expresses his willingness to memorize his mother's advice to follow Chairman Mao "for ever and ever toward the sun." The dominance of the family, symbolized by the son's request for his mother's portrait, is thus skillfully preserved by fostering a fantasy that Mao is both "pa and ma."

The manipulation of Mao's image under these circumstances suggests a parallel between the sociopsychological conditions of contemporary China and those which have elsewhere given rise to fascism, as argued by

Theodor Adorno in his "Freudian Theory and the Pattern of Fascist Propaganda." In the fascist demagogue, Adorno sees at work Freud's theory of the herd instinct or group psychology, which creates "an omnipotent and unbridled father figure" so as to form an erotic tie between the master and his believers, and among believers themselves.[43] An important device of personalized fascist propaganda, according to Adorno, is the image of the great little man who embodies both omnipotence and the notion that he is just one of the common people around him. Adorno concludes that this psychological ambiguity helps to bring about "a social miracle," as the leader's image fulfills the believer's twofold wish to "submit to authority and to be the authority himself."[44] Like Adorno's depiction of fascist propaganda, which adapts the concept of love "to the abstract notion of *Germany*," Maoist model theater kept "primary libidinal energy on an unconscious level so as to divert its manifestations in a way suitable to political ends."[45] However, whereas "Hitler shunned the traditional role of the loving father and replaced it entirely by the negative one of threatening authority," as Adorno put it, the Mao-cult ideologues preserved the conventional strict father and loving mother roles, the authoritarian and nurturing elements in the traditional Chinese family, which they transposed into the perfect image of a national leader. The popular depiction of Mao as the "four greats"—the great teacher, the great leader, the great commander-in-chief, and the great helmsman—synthesized the diverse facets of the people's love mentality in Mao, promoting him as the dominator of the nation, the army, and the educational establishment.

In *The Red Lantern*, the Maoist model family found a congenial mechanism that exemplified almost all the areas of what Louis Althusser terms the "ideological state apparatus," or ISA.[46] Classic Marxist theorists exclusively emphasize repressive state apparatuses such as the government, the army, the police, the court, and the prison, but Althusser argues for the immense power of different kinds of ISAs that operate in both the public and the private spheres. *The Red Lantern*, for example, because it catalyzed the full spectrum of ISAs, made the radical Cultural Revolutionary ideology more accessible, and perhaps even temporarily acceptable, as a public discourse. To enlarge on this point, it would seem that *The Red Lantern* helped to reinforce the family ISA, the cultural ISA (literature and art), the educational ISA, and the political ISA (the party), which also partially replaced the religious ISA (since in the case of socialist China, the party discouraged church worship). On a more subtle level, even the labor-union ISA appeared in *The Red Lantern*, because the background story of the workers' strike against the warlords valorized the revolutionary heritage of the workers' union in the past. At the same time, it also explains that there is no need for workers to strike in the PRC, as they are now the masters of the socialist motherland. The National Workers Union (Quan-guo zonggonghui) thus became a highly centralized subsidiary arm of the party, without any independent status of its own. One of the few model plays allowed to be staged during this period, which later reached a much wider audience when it was filmed, televised, and broadcast in radio sta-tions throughout the nation, *The Red Lantern*, with its dynamically unfolding family story, amply utilized what Althusser called the commu-nication (i.e., press, radio, and television) ISA. A closer look detects a star-tling similarity between Althusser's concept of the ISA and Mao's theory of the Cultural Revolution, the basis for a projected "proletarian revolu-tion" in the realm of "superstructures" (including ideological spheres such as the state apparatus, education, literature, art, etc.).

Consequently, it becomes easier to understand the extraordinary impact *The Red Lantern* had on the political life of contemporary China and, by extension, the influence of Mao's theory of the Cultural Revolution on the intelligentsia in the West, both in the 1960s and at a time when Marxist and neo-Marxist theories appealed to many literary academics. Sau-ling C. Wong has argued that the introduction of Asian American studies in the late 1960s on the West Coast of America was shaped as much by interna-tional events such as the Chinese Cultural Revolution and the Maoist theory of the Third World and anticolonialism as it was by the US antiestab-lishment and anti–Vietnam War movements.[47] As a personal testimony, Jan Wong, in her autobiography *Red China Blues*, narrated in detail how a Chinese Canadian growing up in the rebellious 1960s was a "natural feminist" who believed that men exploited women, and consequently she was also a "natural Maoist" who saw the West as "a hopeless mess of racism, exploitation and shopping malls."[48] Growing up hearing her family's tales of the humiliation brought by the Chinese Exclusion Act that forbad Chinese from entering Canada, Jan Wong embraced Maoism as the prom-ising future for the oppressed both at home and abroad; in her view, "Mao was cute, a cultural icon, like Marilyn Monroe." (I was pleasantly sur-prised to read Wong's comparison of Mao to Marilyn Monroe, which I had already mentioned in my Introduction; Wong's perception as an out-sider looking at China from afar seemed to prove what I had intuitively felt.) Like many radicals of her generation, Wong read Mao, Frantz Fanon, and Betty Friedan and "*enjoyed* being alienated" (italics Wong's).[49] In her rejection of the stereotypical image of a domestic Asian Canadian woman at home, Jan Wong identified with 800 million Chinese countrymen and women and their imagined fight against US imperialist "paper tigers" in the international power struggle between socialist and capitalist countries.[50]

The subversive Maoist voice that spoke for the oppressed could find similar expression within Chinese politics long after the Cultural Revolution. Following the 1989 Tiananmen student demonstrations, the popularity of *The Red Lantern* increased dramatically. Two years later, although criticizing the opera for expressing the radical ideology of the Cultural Revolution, the *Newspaper of Literature and Art (Wenyi bao)* reported that a performance of the play in Beijing on January 1, 1991, was interrupted by enthusiastic applause forty-five times.[51] Two scenes elicited the greatest reaction. Audiences applauded ten times during act 6, in which Grandma Li describes the warlord government's bloody suppression of the striking workers, and ten times during act 8, when the Li family courageously confronts their executioners as "The Internationale" is heard in the background. The official press claimed that this warm reception—more than twenty-six years later—of a Cultural Revolutionary opera demonstrated that Chinese audiences, especially the younger generation, were beginning to appreciate plays that eulogized the revolutionary heritage and created images of the Communists serving the interests of the people.[52]

Yet in the opinion of many present at this performance, the official press had clearly been fooled. Some members of the audience registered very different reactions to the opera. The strike and execution scenes recalled the suppression of the student demonstrations and of the singing of "The Internationale" by the students in Tiananmen Square on the night of the 1989 incident before their voices were drowned out by the sounds of guns and tanks. In the 1990s, a popular opera of the 1960s would possibly evoke in the Chinese people some sympathy for and interest in a cultural past that might no longer appear as horrendous as it once had. For despite the drastic mistake that was the Cultural Revolution, many Chinese people had come to believe that Mao would never have given orders to gun down his own people. Thus the surging crowds waiting to purchase tickets for *The Red Lantern* (the scalpers' price had rocketed from six to fifty yuan) actually constituted a collective act of protest.[53] Probably with the concerns of the audiences in mind, the engineers at the radio station omitted the thunderous applause when the performance was subsequently rebroadcast.[54]

The story of the censored applause, which became widely known, testified to Chinese theater's functioning, through its negotiation and negation onstage of the official culture, as the creator of a new subculture (as such, it is largely responsible for the theater's present form). Although unknown to themselves, the audience members had created a community of their own, whose responses, in terms of the other communities both inside and outside the theater, became immensely contagious. In this instance, the imagined community was not just *imagined* by the people, or imposed by official ideology: it was already *there*, needing only to be conjured up by remembering those who had been victimized, both in the past and in the present. This situation highlights the paradoxical relationship between the imagined community in *The Red Lantern* and the real people beyond the stage who refused to forget their communal experience.[55] This imagined community can even assume international dimensions, as was made clear to me by the warm reception the local Chinese American community of Columbus, Ohio, accorded Liu Changyu on October 23, 1995, when she sang a celebrated passage from *The Red Lantern*.[56] As one of the audience members, I shared the feelings of those around me with whom I talked after the show. Although we had grown up during the traumatic times of the Cultural Revolution, we were unwilling to relinquish our memories of that extraordinary experience, which had taught us so many valuable things and given us the strength and courage to make our own way.

Theater, however, was not the only space where the memories of the Cultural Revolution lingered. Sustaining this nostalgia was also the endless reproduction of Mao memorabilia such as Mao badges, posters, portraits, statues, and quotation books that monopolized decoration and gift items in China. The reproduction of art items in the Mao cult during the Cultural Revolution had promoted sacred objects such as icons as well as aesthetic objects, both potent replacements in a society where religion and any other kind of art were deemed either Occidental, and hence decadent and bourgeois, or Oriental, and hence feudal and reactionary. What was retained in this Mao cult was the memory of the story (as Walter Benjamin put it in a different context in his "The Storyteller"), which required an afterlife and a community to listen to it. The fetishized Mao goods, which became an integral part of the political theater, contributed to a large-scale role reversal in which performers, listeners, and storytellers reproduced and received stories of the past in the often interchangeable space of the stage and real life. The lasting impact of this Mao cult could be felt even long after the Cultural Revolution was over, at the end of the

1980s and the beginning of the 1990s, in what Dai Jinhua described as a social and cultural phenomenon known as "cultural Mao Zedong." Only after the Cultural Revolution had long passed could the Mao fetish again become both the subject of endless mass reproduction and an object of aura-inspiring sentiments with an increasing power of cultural consumption. During this period of "Mao Zedong fever," compact Mao memorabilia again became popular collection items. Best-sellers of his personal anecdotes, feature films, and minitelevision series depicted Mao as the great revolutionary leader, but not without the weaknesses and sorrows of an ordinary human being. Such multiple discourses, Dai argued, both redeemed the immediate historical past and addressed the urgent need for the consumption of contemporary Chinese culture in a market economy during a period of cultural and ideological transformation. It offers us "a look back upon an age of idealism, neither without cynicism nor without sentimentality, before the great tide of pragmatism and commerce and the imminent victory of consumerism on all fronts," and "a lingering love of a nation losing divinity and prohibition, reluctant to part with a last symbol of the sacred and the taboo."[57] With the return of Maoist songs performed by popular singers and the spread of electronic music playing the familiar tunes of model theater, Chinese consumers at once affirmed and reassembled the multilayered discourse of Cultural Revolutionary theater, which, for better or worse, has already taken deep root in contemporary Chinese culture and will ultimately help to shape its course of development.

It is therefore not surprising to see a young musician incorporating Li Tiemei's popular sung passage "I Have Countless Uncles" (Wo jia de biaoshu shu bu jin) from The Red Lantern into a group of folk songs and passages from other model and traditional Peking operas mixed with rock-and-roll music. After having been broadcast as the first item for the 1986 Spring Festival Evening Show (Chunjie lianhuan wanhui), "I Have Countless Uncles" became so popular once again, both inside and outside China, that people in Hong Kong began to address guests from the mainland as "uncles." Liu Changyu, who played the role of Li Tiemei during the Cultural Revolution, now had to sing this model-opera passage after her performances of any traditional piece that had nothing to do with modern theater. The 1990s performances of the Peking operas The Red Lantern, Shajiabang, Azalean Mountain, and Taking Tiger Mountain by Strategy and the ballets The Red Detachment of Women and The White-Haired Girl became so popular that many of the productions were quickly sold out.

Some even broke the record of Peking opera production in the past decade by running a hundred shows within a given season.[58]

The Red Lantern created an imagined family. Another model play, the Peking opera Song of the Dragon River, painting on a larger canvas, created an imagined local community, one whose interests had to be sacrificed to serve the global ambitions of the party and the nation. Set in 1963 rural China, the opera depicts the dilemma of peasants from a Dragon River Brigade who must abide by the decision of the county party committee to dam the Dragon River in order to save a drought-ridden area. In so doing, the peasants are asked to flood their three hundred *mu* of rippling wheat in order to bring water onto the dry plain. When the drought worsens, the peasants have to give up another three thousand *mu* of grain fields, in addition to losing their own private lots on the riverside. The dramatic conflict develops around the collective interest of one peripheral local community, whose members have repeatedly been asked to relinquish personal aspirations and dreams for the good of the central ideal of the nation, which demands continuing sacrifices both in the past and in the future.

In rural China, where land is the peasant's lifeline and the peasant's well-being presumably always "justifies the powerholder's Mandate of Heaven," it has traditionally been almost impossible to convince peasants to give up their harvesting land.[59] Song of the Dragon River had to take pains, therefore, to make such an unusual demand credible by demonstrating that the peasants from the drought-stricken area had themselves previously come to the aid of peasants who were afflicted by a severe flood. As part of this obligatory explanation, a bitter story had to be told about the old society's ruthless exploitation of the peasants by rich landowners, which is contrasted with the loving and caring government of socialist China. Another grandmother had to be produced to testify to the superiority of the new society: during a drought-stricken year in the old society, she had "looked for water so hard her eyes went blind. After the Liberation, the doctors Chairman Mao sent cured her."[60] Having her story told by her eleven-year-old granddaughter points up the natural link between the older generation, who suffered in the past, and the younger generation, who grew up with the miseries of their elders etched into their consciousness. These two female characters on stage represent the two things Ernest Renan considers essential to the soul of a nation: "One lies in the past, one in the present. One is the possession in common of a rich legacy of memories; the other is present-day consent, the desire to live together, the will to perpetuate the value of the heritage that one has received in undivided form."[61] These two female characters, minor as they are in terms of dramatic conflict, became a crucial link between a local community and others at large who shared a common goal of striving for a better future.

To further present the need to construct a pure community by eliminating unhealthy elements, in time the peasants capture Wang Guolu, a hidden class enemy whose escape to the Dragon River Village after liberation had revived memories of his evil exploitation of the peasants in his home village. Now he is accused of attempting to sabotage construction across the Dragon River out of contempt for socialist new China. To heighten the local Chinese communities' sense of connectedness to oppressed peoples everywhere, Jiang Shuiying, the female party secretary, organizes a reading group to study Mao's essay "In Memory of Norman Bethume," which celebrates a Canadian Communist Party member who helped Chinese soldiers in the war against Japan.[62] This spirit of communism that makes a foreigner selflessly adopt the cause of the Chinese people's liberation as his own finally helps the villagers to perceive sacrificing for their own countrymen as a natural and desirable impulse. An absent white male has therefore been summoned onto the Chinese stage to further connect a local Chinese community with its class brothers and sisters of the world.

Closer to home, a local heroine, Jiang Shuiying, embodies a beautiful woman who combines the sophistication of an intellectual with the earthiness of a subaltern; her role has nothing to do with female subjectivity. In fact, in the original spoken drama version of *Song of the Dragon River* premiered by Fujian Province Drama Troupe (Fujiansheng huajutuan) in 1963, the party secretary Zheng Qiang was a male character. It was during the revision of the Peking opera version in 1966 that Jiang Qing suggested a female lead instead. The creation of a Jiang Shuiying, who shared the same last name as Jiang Qing, by the revision group showed its eagerness to please its female leader in an operatic revolution.[63] A female protagonist, however, did not change the dramatic actions originally designated for a male leader; instead, it provides Jiang Shuiying with more roles to play both as a caring mother figure and as a convincing party secretary.

The location of Jiang Shuiying's house near a road at the edge of the village of the Dragon River Brigade suggests that her own house will be the first to be flooded; as the party secretary, she is expected to make the initial sacrifice before calling on others to follow suit. The words painted on her doorway—"An Honored Family"—indicate that her husband is away serving in the army. The absent male partner both serves to accentuate her love for her country and to grant her the freedom to interact with members of her larger family, the local community. Her circumstances also give her ample opportunity to assume the role of the missing male in her own family and in the village. Filling the slot of the perfect woman character in model theater, she incorporates the unique qualities of feminine charm and masculine strength, which come into play at different moments as required by the plot. In scene 6, when Jiang undertakes the strong, almost male role of leading other men and women in the struggle to combat the drought in the fields, A Jian, a sixty-year-old male villager, undertakes the female role, performing the domestic duties of a caretaker. He brings chicken soup to Jiang, who (in his words), "sick as she is, has been standing in paddy-field water, working day and night" and "nearly keeled over in the fields."[64] This gender crossing, however, is only temporary. As with all the female characters in model theater, who are never permitted to function in a public role that does not at some point draw on their female energies, Jiang occasionally draws upon her nurturing qualities to fulfill her role as party secretary. For example, she urges the spouseless Li Zhitian, the brigade leader of Dragon River, to finish supper before rushing to his next job.

Her real task, however, consists in persuading Li to give up the land of his brigade to bring relief to the drought-stricken area. In one of the most celebrated passages of the Cultural Revolutionary period, Shuiying asks Li to look beyond the nearby mountains that block his view, in effect to recall the sufferings of the poor "brothers and sisters" living in unemancipated Third World countries:

> In the world today,
> How many slaves still in chains
> How many paupers suffer from starvation
> How many brothers take up arms
> How many sisters are exploited.
> Let us strike hard at imperialism, revisionism, and reactionaries.
> All mankind will eventually be emancipated.

In constructing an imagined international community, slaves and paupers are transported from Asia, Latin America, and Africa, and brothers and sisters are adopted, in order to justify wholesale sacrifice for ideological

PLATE 1. Liu Chengqi, *Acting Revolutionary Opera and Becoming Revolutionary People* (People's Art Press, 1975).

PLATE 2. He Shushui, *New Creations* (People's Art Press, 1975).

PLATE 3. Gu Qing, *Martial Songs Raised Our Spirit While Carrying Our Guns for the People* (Jiangxi People's Press, 1974). The University of Westminster Chinese Poster Collection.

PLATE 4. Tang Jixiang, *Red Frontline* (People's Art Press, 1975).

agendas at home. This accomplishes the shifting of a non-European racial other into the operational space of China, whose leaders were anxious to appropriate otherness for their own imperial enterprise.[65] The official historians of modern China characterize the country as a victim of Western imperialism since the time of the Opium War, yet China's own imperial yearnings have resulted in policies that appropriated otherness to justify the continuation of the Chinese Revolution. This introduction of other bodies from the Third World onto the Chinese stage valorized a socialist imperialism whose proponents used anti-European colonialism as a domestic discourse of suppression with which to combat the interests of the local communities.

The altruistic spirit advocated in this model opera was imposed on the Chinese people at a time when the populace in the vast rural areas of China—where illiteracy and poverty prevailed—desperately needed to build up its own local community. The nation's numerous ethnic minority groups were also encouraged to imitate the revolutionary characters from model theater, a theatrical form, incidentally, that was popularized mostly in the Han majority group.[66] Since the PRC's inception, the ruling ideology had been favorably disposed to acknowledge the unique histories of the numerous ethnic minority groups in China. This tendency undoubtedly accounted for the fact that most popular songs eulogizing Mao Zedong Thought during the Cultural Revolution were adaptations of folk songs of such ethnic groups as the Tibetans, the Uigurs, the Mongolians, the Koreans, and many others. This phenomenon, along with the numerous amateur productions of model-theatrical works put on by various ethnic groups in their own languages, gives the impression that racial differences were no barrier to forming one nation and one people who endured and hoped together. However, that Mao was "loved" and "worshipped" by peoples of all ethnic groups at home and abroad was a myth—a myth fabricated to facilitate the consolidation of political power.

The predominant ideology in effect located the ethnic periphery at the center of its own version of multiculturalism. The process was theatrically expressed by two popular slogans chanted on the occasion of the annual October First Tiananmen parades in commemoration of the founding of the PRC: "Long live the grand union of all the ethnic groups of the nation!" and "Long live the grand union of all peoples of the world!" Of course, both slogans are only substitutes for the most important ones: "Long live the People's Republic of China!" and "Long live Chairman Mao!" When colorfully dressed ethnic singers and dancers on the Cultural

Revolutionary Chinese stage mingled with people dressed in the costumes of black people (presumably from Africa) and other peoples of color from Asia and Latin America, Chinese audiences were expected to experience the dramatic reenactment of an ongoing world revolution characterized by a Chinese type of multiculturalism.

Song of the Dragon River used a Third World discourse as a backdrop while promoting the communist spirit in the countryside. The Peking opera *On the Docks* highlights a global discourse of world revolution in its portrayal of the working class in cosmopolitan Shanghai, the cradle of the Chinese proletariat. A different kind of model-theatrical work, *On the Docks* was lauded by Wen Jun of the official press for singing "the praises of the internationalism of the working class in China."[67] To emphasize the Third World perspective of the opera, the title of Wen Jun's article changed from "An Excellent Model of Continuing the Revolution under the Dictatorship of the Proletariat" in the original Chinese version to "An Opera about Proletarian Internationalism" in the English translation that later appeared in *Chinese Literature*, a journal targeting English-speaking readers in foreign countries, especially those from Third World countries.

Set in the Shanghai docks where imperialists used to run their businesses, the opera spotlights Fang Haizhen, a female party secretary who was brutally exploited as a child laborer before the liberation of Shanghai in 1949. Her memory of a bitter past makes her keenly cognizant of the fact that people struggling to be free "very much want the support of revolutionary people of the world."[68] Fang Haizhen and her coworkers had exposed the hidden class enemy Qian Shouwei, who was attempting to flee abroad to his imperialist masters after engaging in abortive sabotage activities. Their discovery enables the workers to complete the timely loading of a ship of rice seed for African people striving to develop their national economy so as finally to pry themselves loose from colonial exploitation. The shipment must arrive in time for sowing, and "every sack will play a part in the African people's struggle"[69] against the imperialists, who once declared that rice could not grow in Africa and Africans could solve their food problem only by importing grain.[70] Yet "our comrades," asserts Fang, went and successfully introduced the experimental cultivation of rice in two years. In the opera, the world powers' principal spheres of influence are symbolized by the opposite destinations of the Chinese ocean-going ships: Qian Shouwei's ship (known in the play as the Scandinavian ship) goes to Europe; whereas the ship Fang Haizhen protects from Qian's sabotage heads toward Africa, the jungle in the Third World where the "red sun of Mao Zedong Thought" will eventually shine.

This opera also forges a link between the suffering of the Chinese workers in the old society and that of their black brothers and sisters in present-day Africa. While educating a young longshoreman who neglects his duties, Fang refers to Qian Shouwei as paying lip service to socialism but echoing the words of his "Yankee bosses" when he [Qian] "slandered us by saying [the longshoremen] can't run the docks."[71] In 1949, American bosses pretended to comply with our order to hand over the port facilities, Fang recalls, but behind our backs they cursed us as "stinking coolies" who "wouldn't be able to manage."[72] "Never for a day do they forget this paradise now lost to them, nor abandon their dream of staging a comeback."[73] Both Qian and the imagined Yankee dreamers still "place their hopes on our next generation"[74] for realizing their fantasy of "returning one day to their old establishments."[75]

This last quotation leads to the familiar theme of the Cultural Revolution. Continuous revolution must be waged to safeguard the fruits of the past revolution. Thus was the global power struggle between East and West appropriated to uphold Mao's call never to forget class struggle, which he issued during the Tenth Plenum of the Eighth Central Committee of the Chinese Communist Party held in September 1962. That the play is set in the summer of 1963 should therefore come as no surprise. To emphasize this historic moment, the official review informed readers that a new scene showed Fang Haizhen reading a copy of the *Communiqué of the Tenth Plenary Session* and pondering its relevance to the class struggle unfolding right before her own eyes.[76] In the most popular lines of this scene, Fang Haizhen describes Shanghai port as having been linked "with every /corner of our land, and support[ing] national / construction and the people the world over."[77] This was another instance of the campaign to persuade audiences of the necessity of continuing the revolution in socialist China in order to support the Third World's revolution against imperialism and colonialism.

Furthering model theater's efforts, the official press in Cultural Revolutionary China did not fail to drive home the urgent need to transport Mao Zedong Thought onto other stages around the world. For example, on May 31, 1967, the twenty-fifth anniversary of Mao's "Talks at the Yan'an Forum on Literature and Art," a seminar on Mao's works was held by the Afro-Asian Writers' Bureau in Beijing, "headquarters of China's great proletarian Cultural Revolution." Attended by more than eighty writers from over thirty-four countries, this gathering was described as a "concrete manifestation of the fact that the whole world is entering a completely new era, an era in which Mao Tse-tung's thought is the great banner" and that "his revolutionary line and theory on literature and art are becoming a powerful ideological weapon for the revolutionary people of the world in their struggle against imperialism, revisionism and the reactionaries of all countries."[78] As is indicated by the following official report from the Chinese press, the progressive writers from Third World countries paid tribute to the Chinese imperial court by using almost the exact rhetoric heard during the Cultural Revolution:

> The seminar was pervaded by the warm love of the world's revolutionary people for Chairman Mao; it brimmed over with revolutionary solidarity and militancy. The writers and friends from many lands who eagerly entered the hall held bright red copies of Chairman Mao's precious revolutionary work, "Talks at the Yan'an Forum on Literature and Art." They gazed with boundless respect at the huge portrait of Chairman Mao, great leader of the world's revolutionary people, which hung high above the presidium; and they read aloud the quotations from Chairman Mao's works written up in Chinese, Arabic, English, and French. The meeting hall kept resounding with the cries: "Long live Chairman Mao!" "Long live the Invincible thought of Mao Zedong" and "Long live Chairman Mao! A long, long life to him!"[79]

Ironically, it appears that these writers and their friends, "fired" as they were "with strong revolutionary feeling," insisted that they must reverse the centuries-old "history by the ruling classes on both the political stage and the stage of literature and art in Asia, Africa, and the rest of the world."[80] Besides reading poems by Chairman Mao, they also recited poetry they had written "in his praise, in praise of Mao Zedong's thought and of revolution." These recitations, which "evoked storms of applause from the audience of more than a thousand Chinese and foreign friends," were followed by an even more theatrical event.[81] Presenting himself as a spokesman for the Third World, R. D. Senanayake, secretary-general of the Afro-Asian Writers' Bureau, read aloud the Message of Salute to Chairman Mao that had been unanimously adopted by the seminar and handed it over to Premier Zhou Enlai, who promised to present it to "our" great leader, Chairman Mao. Zhou, playing to the hilt his part as Mao's close comrade-in-arms, described the message as being "imbued with boundless love for Chairman Mao and hatred for the enemy" and demonstrating infinite confidence in the revolutionary cause of the whole world.[82] In conclusion, Zhou dramatically declared: "Comrades and friends, in the face of imperialism, modern revisionism, and the reactionaries of all countries, let us unite, fight together, and win victory together!"[83] In response, a different message of salute to Mao was announced as representing all writers from the Third World, which used the same radical language of the Red Guards, who had always saluted Mao as their great commander in chief:

> Chairman Mao, our great leader,
> We have witnessed the great role which your "Talks at the Yan'an Forum on Literature and Art" has played in guiding the great proletarian cultural revolution now going on in China. This earth-shaking great proletarian cultural revolution is uprooting revisionism, overthrowing reactionaries and persons in authority taking the capitalist road, thus preventing the restoration of capitalism and ensuring that socialist China, the powerful bastion of world revolution, will never change its political colour. It has made the imperialists, modern revisionists and reactionaries tremble with mortal fear. To the revolutionary peoples of Asia, Africa and the whole world, however, it is an immense source of inspiration enhancing their spirit to fight and to rebel, to smash the shackles of oppression and exploitation and win a bright future.[84]

Further proof that the dissemination of Mao Zedong Thought was stimulating political and cultural change in Third World countries was marshaled in the form of frequent, vivid accounts in the Chinese press of theatrical performances by troupes from the Third World. For example, in July and August 1967, the press reported that the visiting Somali Artists' Delegation performed on a stage set in "golden light [that] radiated from the backdrop showing a portrait of Chairman Mao, the red sun in the heart of the world's people." With surging emotion, the Somali artists, "holding copies of *Quotations from Chairman Mao Zedong* and standing before Chairman Mao's portrait," sang the Somali song "Sing the Praise of Chairman Mao" and the Chinese songs "The East Is Red," "Sailing the Seas Depends on the Helmsman," and "Long Live Chairman Mao," all of which were met by "stormy applause from the audience."[85]

The international Mao cult received additional credence as a result of the Chinese press' claim that, in 1967 alone, thirty-three different portraits of Mao were distributed all over Asia, Africa, and Latin America. Most of these depicted him reviewing "the mighty army of the cultural revolution and [showing] his wholehearted support for the revolutionary mass movement." According to the press, the portraits were supplied because revolutionary people sent thousands upon thousands of urgent telegrams, cables, and letters to Beijing, claiming that Mao's portraits would make them feel as if he were "at their side" and "fill[ing] them with strength and confidence."[86] It was also reported that, as of June 1969, there were more than 1,100 editions of Chairman Mao's works published in seventy languages in sixty countries and regions, including 52 editions of *Selected Works of Mao Zedong* translated and published in thirty-two languages in thirty-five countries.[87] It seems that the official press' construction of an imagined worldwide Maoist community in real life rendered even more credible model theater's construction of an imagined international community on the stage.

It should be noted that Africans, rather than locating universal truth in Maoist China, had sought earlier to focus on their own cultures. This was the theme, for example, of a speech given by Léopold Sédar Senghor in 1966 on "negritude," which he defined as *"the sum of the cultural values of the black world."* [88] Thus it is ironic that the African search for a national literature (which Frantz Fanon characterized as "a literature of combat, in the sense that it calls on the whole people to fight for their existence as a nation" in order to mold "the national consciousness" against colonialism) had to be viewed through the political lens of another nation that had laid claim to leadership of the Third World revolution.[89] The phenomenon of new imperialists following the old imperialists' lead in luring others to support their political and economic agendas resulted in a paradox. The sun once celebrated as never setting on the British Empire was once more celebrated, this time in the Africans' singing of the Maoist song "The East Is Red."

Before proceeding any further, it would be instructive to distinguish Eurocentrism from premodern Sinocentrism. Philip Snow, in *The Star Raft*, describes Chinese attitudes toward Africans. The Chinese were nonaggressive and uninterested in conquering land, in contrast to their European counterparts who, when they arrived in Africa decades later, "lay siege to African souls," seeking to "impose their religious conviction."[90] Snow attributes the better behavior of the Chinese to their conviction that they lived at the center of the universe and therefore had no need to conquer Africa. They regarded the journey to faraway Africa as a majestic gesture for the purpose of exchanging imperial favors for foreign "tribute."[91] Nor did the Chinese seek African gold, because China had plenty of gold and most other forms of wealth.[92] Whereas the "superior" Chinese viewed the barbarian others as unworthy of being conquered, the "superior" Europeans stayed on and ruled because of their lust for African riches.

The Maoist ideology inherited impulses both attributable to the imperial legacy of Sinocentrism and derived from the European legacy of religious imperialism. From the latter, no doubt, came the idea of converting the "heathen" mind of the African other to the "gospel" of Mao Zedong Thought. Ambitious cultural imperialism had to be backed up by an economic aid package, which in fact the Chinese delivered in the 1960s and 1970s, channeling it directly to the poor people in Africa, along with generous financial and technical support for such projects as the Tanzania-Zambia Railway. Thus, in contrast to their rich ancestors, who never made the African people beneficiaries of anything but grand and august gestures, the people of modern China, many of whom lived below the poverty line themselves, helped to reconstruct parts of an impoverished Africa. To convince the Chinese people of the necessity for such a costly sacrifice, bitterness stories about China's semicolonial past had to be told (as in the previously mentioned model play *On the Docks*), in which the African independence movements of the 1950s and 1960s against European rulers were depicted as reenactments of China's own recent past when it was victimized by Western imperialism.[93] China's imperial enterprise also represented "sweet revenge" against the Europeans, who during the colonial period in Africa began to realize that Chinese coolies were more competent and skillful at tilling the land than workers from any other country: "Only the Chinese could develop Africa"; "Chinese could show the Africans—new-caught, sullen peoples—how to work."[94] In the most unexpected and unwitting way, the modern Chinese people partially fulfilled this Western imperialist vision of China's role in Africa's development, with Mao as "the prototype of a new, evangelical variety of Chinese" missionary.[95] History in this instance provides a striking parallel. Whereas in colonial Africa the Europeans had characterized the Chinese people as model workers for Africans, in the Maoist era the image of struggling African brothers and sisters became a model for the Chinese people in furthering the Cultural Revolution. While mapping the strategies for a Third World revolution, China also saw fit to portray the African peoples as having been inspired by model theater, thus turning them into yet another type of model for the Chinese to imitate in their pursuit of world revolution.

The far-reaching effects of a global theater of the Maoist Cultural Revolution and the promotion of world revolution reached beyond Africa, as was demonstrated by the frequent performances of visiting troupes from fellow socialist countries such as Albania and Romania. For example, the Tirana amateur troupe's "With Pick in One Hand and Rifle in the Other," staged in Beijing in 1967, was taken to be living proof of Mao's revolutionary victory in literature and art in China and of "Comrade Enver Hoxha's wise leadership" in the process of further revolutionizing the entire life of Albania.[96] When the giant portraits of the two great leaders appeared onstage, with "the brilliant red flags of our two countries wav[ing] side by side," it symbolized the challenge by the two self-proclaimed leaders of the Third World countries to the imperialism of the West and the "social imperialism" of the Soviet Union. Similarly, the performance in August 1971 by the Doena Art Troupe of the Armed Forces of Romania was celebrated in the Chinese press for demonstrating the revolutionary friendship and militant unity of the two countries as well as the two parties' socialist construction and their "common struggle against imperialism and its lackeys."[97] These performances aimed to show that China, after all, was not isolated in the socialist camp.

The Chinese stage also attracted Maoist factions of a pro-Moscow Communist Party in the capitalist world. In July 1967, the Japanese Haguruma Theater, "organized by revolutionary literary and art workers, overcoming the many obstacles put in their way by the US and Japanese reactionaries and the revisionist clique of the Japanese Communist Party, finally reached Beijing, where Chairman Mao lives and where the world-shaking great Cultural Revolution was born."[98] With "boundless love for our great leader," they performed, in August, a play entitled *Advancing through the Storm*, an account of the struggle waged by the workers in the Iwaguni Bus Company under the leadership of the left wing of the Japanese Communist Party against American imperialism, Japanese monopoly capital, and the Miyamoto revisionist clique.[99] To Chinese audiences, this event offered yet another illustration of socialist China's impact on the world, resulting in the great red banner of Mao Zedong Thought being seen "flying high [even] in the heart of revolutionary people of Japan!"[100] In the troupe's other work, the five-act play *Prairie Fire*, the peasant leader Mosuke, who leads an uprising in the Chichibu Mountain area of Japan in 1884, "comes to see more clearly the necessity of organizing the people to take up arms and fight for political power" in his struggle against Shokichi, a landowner and capitalist.[101] A Chinese critic pointed out that these Japanese plays demonstrated the universality of Maoist "truth," since the comrades of the Haguruma Theater, who hailed from a foreign country, had "analyzed and portrayed this uprising in the light of Marxism-Leninism and Mao Zedong's thought."[102] As in many Chinese model plays, these Japanese plays also evoked the past to certify the "truth" of the present: "Through the fight put up by Mosuke and other members of the Party of the Poor, *Prairie Fire* expresses the great concept of the seizure of political power by force. At the same time, by exposing the renegade actions of Seiji, a 'liberal,' it directs the spear-head of its criticism against the [contemporary] Kenji Miyamoto renegade clique."[103]

I hope my study will contribute to a better understanding of what Timothy Brennan characterizes as "the nation-centeredness of the post-colonial world."[104] Whereas Brennan shows that, historically, the novel ushered in the rise of nations in the West, this study has demonstrated that, in Cultural Revolutionary China (where most novels published before the Cultural Revolution were banned along with other genres of literature), theater became an important public forum for Chinese nationalist and imperialist discourse.[105] But the state drama cannot shape a nationalist discourse of imagined communities without having recourse to the construction of gender and class. The postcolonial narration on the Chinese stage of black slave sisters needing to be rescued from colonialism helped to legitimize the Chinese patriarchal state. If Chandra Talpade Mohanty is correct in pointing out that it is in the production of a Third World difference that "western feminisms appropriate and 'colonize' the constitutive complexities which characterized the lives of women in these countries,"[106] one can argue, by the same token, that the official feminism of the Maoist state systematically appropriated the lives and interests of women both at home and abroad. Broadly defined as Third World women, these women served primarily as an ideological construct and were denied any subjectivity or personal identity. Model theater, then, became the perfect arena in which to exploit both the creative energies of the intelligentsia and the political energies of the subalterns, who were ironically reduced to the fate of "women of Africa"—that is, they were "a homogeneous sociological grouping characterized by common dependencies or powerlessness."[107]

In cross-cultural studies where global theories tend to overwhelm local contingencies, it is fruitful to discuss a domestic hegemonic discourse to locate the distribution of powers of speech and powers of control and to investigate how these and other cultural components combine to create different discourses, histories, and politics. This effort allows us to show diverse cultural systems and the common ways in which they render people silent. This study has considered the discursive strategy of model theater that can serve as the locus of serious dialogue, even within those formations that sought to exclude or marginalize it in the first place.

4

Audience, Applause, and Actor

BORDER CROSSING IN SOCIAL PROBLEM PLAYS

In the present postcolonial age, when the Eurocentric literary tradition is being challenged in the West, Chinese literature, as a specific kind of Third World literature, is becoming increasingly well known. Yet significant studies of Chinese literature, especially in the modern period, have been generally confined to fiction and, to a lesser degree, lyric poetry. The recent interest in Chinese film has turned the Western gaze to the seemingly most marketable Chinese art form. What remains least known in the West are modern Chinese plays and their political role in Chinese intellectual life.

To address this situation, I intend to argue in this chapter that, unlike other literary genres, theater operates in a public sphere where Chinese intellectuals have frequently crossed the border between the official ideology and the open, albeit limited, space permitted them by that ideology.

The border-crossing activities inherent in cross-cultural studies of the East and the West, or of traditional and modern canonicity, are easily imagined. In studies of modern Chinese drama, however, a peculiar kind of border crossing embodies an intricate play of power, stemming from the marginalized discourse against the dominant ideology.

In sharp contrast to the Cultural Revolution, when "eight hundred million Chinese people watched only eight model plays,"[1] the staging of many successful modern dramas in 1978–1979 led observers to view the period as a Chinese dramatic renaissance. In 1976, the year of Mao's death and the arrest of the Gang of Four, a number of what were then known as "social problem plays" began to appear, an apparent representation of the abundant "real-life" political dramas that had preceded them. These plays immediately attracted large audiences avid for the opportunity to choose among and enjoy a larger variety of plays. According to one report, in 1979 alone as many as sixty-two modern Chinese dramas were presented across the country to celebrate the thirtieth anniversary of the founding of the PRC. Of these, seventeen dramatized the nationwide campaign against the Gang of Four, and sixteen rehearsed the glorious lives of proletarian revolutionary leaders who had been persecuted during the Cultural Revolution.[2] Not surprisingly, when drama critics in 1982 began to notice that the theater was losing audiences to movies and television, they looked back nostalgically to this time when theater alone served as the public forum for directly addressing crucial social issues.

This brief flowering of live theater and its subsequent decline have received much attention in China. In 1987, Liu Xiaobo, a young critic then in his twenties, shocked the Chinese drama world by claiming that post–Cultural Revolutionary Chinese theater had not produced any "real" drama. Even in the so-called post-Maoist renaissance period, he argued, theater was employed exclusively as a political vehicle for reevaluating history. For example, in rejecting the experience of the Cultural Revolution, the popular anti–Gang of Four plays eulogized the values of the 1950s. When, however, the anti-rightist movement of the 1950s was repudiated as an appalling product of a radical Maoist ideology, and thus an unsuitable subject for drama, it was necessary to look further back to the war period when the Communist Party seemed closer to the people. Finally, even the war experience seemed suspect and somehow inhuman. Therefore it too was removed from consideration, and now the older values of traditional culture were approved for theatrical enactment. Governed by social and ideological criteria in this way, drama seemed a "conscious slave" to history, lacking any artistic character of its own. Liu believed that real drama had yet to emerge in modern China. Such drama, in his view, needed to be transhistorical, so that it could present a perspective uninfluenced by official history. It should be a product of the dramatist's innermost emotions and experiences as an artist, not an exegesis of the dominant ideology.[3]

Liu's remarks reflect a claim persistently advanced about modern Chinese drama. The frequency of its recurrence, however, should provoke investigation rather than, as so often, unquestioning acceptance. In his claim Liu asserted that Chinese drama failed in the decade following the end of the Cultural Revolution mainly because it could not sufficiently challenge the state power structure. From one perspective this statement is obviously true, but in this chapter I shall demonstrate that, realistically speaking, an openly antiofficial drama has never been a possibility in the tightly controlled society of modern China. In this regard, drama is significantly different from fiction and lyric poetry, which, even when officially banned, could be circulated underground and find a limited readership. In contrast, drama has always had to please both the guardians of the official ideology and the members of its audiences who, unlike the censors who control what they can see, are often attracted to the unfamiliar and the unofficial. Only by meeting these contrary demands—demands that comprise the essential features of post–Cultural Revolutionary theater—can drama in China become a public event. In order to survive in these circumstances, the best instances of post-Maoist Chinese theater almost always negotiate within a limited cultural space in the borderland between official and antiofficial discourses. Since no play can become a public event without having passed a censor, a successful post-Maoist drama usually operates within an official framework. Alternatively, to gain quick acceptance for public performance, it exhibits concern with a social problem that the authorities wish to address. As already indicated, the play must simultaneously engage the often antiofficial interests of its anticipated audiences. This border crossing between official and antiofficial discourses reenacts the peculiar cultural condition of Chinese intellectuals, whose straitened social and political circumstances are reflected in their playwriting.

Actually, recent Chinese dramas are not so unlike plays created under very different social and political conditions, as, like other dramas, they had to please their audiences even if they had censors. What makes it more difficult in the case of trying to please Chinese audiences is that it is not enough for a play to be cogent and attractive; in fact, such a straight-forwardly appealing play will have a very short life, if any. Accordingly, a play destined for success apparently had to have, beneath its official frame-work, a subtext that was both subordinate to and subversive of the primary, official text. In some cases, the two discourses have been skillfully blended and overlapped; in others, where they were diametrically opposed, they had to underscore the false coherence of the claimed "truth." Thus the seemingly irreconcilable conflict between the public and private spheres, between the official and unofficial cultures, that has epitomized life in China, could at least partially and temporarily be experienced without sham in the theater. In the darkened theater, audience members could, through laughter or applause, dismiss or even transform the message of the official ideology. Their imaginations remained free to trespass in for-bidden territories, no matter what the censor set before them. Both respon-sive to and critical of state apparatuses, at least some of the plays from post–Cultural Revolutionary theater found ways to be at once public and private, normative and subversive, official and antiofficial.

None of this is to deny the existence of censorship as an unalterable fact of life for Chinese playwrights, directors, and actors. Yet although no play was performed without the approval of the censor, once the play was mounted, the censors could not control how audiences reacted to it. Often, in the process of performance, a subtext unnoticed by or of no con-cern to the censor came to the fore. Indeed it was the critics and audiences themselves who often chose to foreground these overlooked subversive elements and thus were responsible for turning the play into a hit. In the event, a crowd's subsequent waiting overnight in front of a theater for ticket sales represented an immediate if unexpected act of subversion that did not go unremarked. Suspecting that they might contain more objec-tionable materials than they had first noticed, arts officials reread these plays with an eye to discovering the subversive elements between the offi-cially approved lines. Ironically, the news that the authorities were recon-sidering a play's orthodoxy and might ban the work served as the best promotion imaginable. Even larger crowds thronged the theater, and sales of journals or newspapers that published its text skyrocketed. By the time the censors had suppressed the play in its original form and intro-duced changes into its performance, a transformation had already taken place from theatrical event to reading activity. Because in most cases one particular play could be performed in only one or two major cities for a limited period of time even if it was favored and promoted by the official press, the actual theater audiences were easily outnumbered by readers in diverse reading communities who read the play in newspapers and journals that printed or reprinted scripts on popular demand. In the case of a controversial play that was partially prohibited from performance, such as *There Is a Small Courtyard* (*You zheyang yige xiaoyuan*, 1979), the receivers of the play predominantly consisted of readers who read the script in order to find out why it was discouraged by the official ideology.[4]

In its new incarnation, the play was now secure from any governmental prohibition and did not require the public space of the theater to be readily shared with others. The banning of the text—and the increased popularity that inevitably ensued—in effect became an essential criteria for the play's admission into a new, unofficial canon of contemporary writings. An unofficially canonized text then became part of an ironic literary history. As often seen in modern Chinese literary history, initial criticism and condemnation assured a work's official recognition by a subsequent regime and its attendant ideology. The later regime made use of the play's text and its unfortunate fate to discredit its predecessor.

Thus the history of drama in the post–Cultural Revolutionary period is inextricably bound up with political history. Often, suppression of a play was occasioned not so much by the play itself as by its reception and the possible attendant political responses. The process affected subsequent plays, so that no play was ever politically safe; embedded as it was in the history of the reception of other plays and their suppression, it was automatically suspect. To the politically astute theatergoer, the form, content, and critical fortunes of any single play could not be separated from these elements in other plays to which it seemed to allude, whether intentionally or not. Under these circumstances, reading things upside down and simultaneously backward and forward became one of the possible ways to read meaningfully and was an essential skill for political survival. In this sense, nearly everyone in contemporary China was, and still is, a profound and subtle critic. Good critics remain discreetly silent, whereas bad ones place a work in jeopardy by drawing attention to its underlying and unspeakable meanings. In the past, when those characterized as pompous critics brought the unspoken to light, the censors could do no other but impose a ban. Looking back to when such critical and censorial activity was common, one might reasonably argue that many of the social-problem plays functioned as subversive communications. As such, they operated within, outside, and in between the limited space existing between official ideology and antiofficial sentiments, which came from the heart and therefore had to remain unspoken.

Before proceeding with a detailed analysis of post-Maoist plays, a brief explanation of the methodology employed to locate antiofficial subtexts in the plays seems in order. As part of this discussion, it is fitting to examine the way in which audiences used applause to identify and approve of a subtext. However, this kind of research presents an obvious problem. In contemporary Chinese society, an antiofficial subtext would by definition not be preserved as a written document. Given the subtleties and complexities of the political situation, any kind of study that attempts to account for the undocumented and undocumentable responses from the audience is bound to elude Foucaudian historians, who are committed to documenting not the official history but rather that which is produced to counter the knowledge and power that official history embodies. To gauge the audience's reactions in the theater (as opposed to those documented in the official press, which, because of the nature of censorship in China, could not be entirely relied upon), I have resorted to whatever clues I could discover in journals and newspapers, mostly through such comments as "This play was constantly interrupted by the audience's warm applause and cheers." Above all else, however, I have drawn upon my own recollections of the performances I attended in the early post-Maoist years and upon personal interviews conducted later with theater people (whose names are omitted for obvious reasons). A textual analysis—of the plays themselves and of the criticism derived from the above-named sources—is never a sufficient method for dealing with dramatic studies, least of all when the studies have to do with China. A text is not the same as a performance, the essential component of theater. Accordingly, this study gives special attention to oral histories and undocumentable narratives, which are indispensable in reconstructing the history of contemporary Chinese theater. I offer my personal perspective and experience in theater as one eyewitness account of a period of history without in any way claiming to state an "empirical truth."

To obtain an idea of the complexity of an antiofficial subtext in an early post-Maoist drama, it is instructive to review the reception given *Winter Jasmine (Baochunhua)*. Its success, in my view, was directly attributable to its position in the narrow, limited, overlapping space between the official ideology and antiofficial discourse. Premiered in 1979 by the Liaoning

People's Art Theater (Liaoning renmin yishu juyuan), this drama skillfully exploited the official discourse about exposure of the crimes of the Gang of Four being promoted to affirm a new order in post-Maoist China.[5] In the Cultural Revolutionary period, playwrights had to draw all their revolutionary characters from the class of workers, peasants, or soldiers. *Winter Jasmine*, however, recounted the discrimination suffered by Bai Jie because of her politically incorrect family origins. Her father had been declared a counterrevolutionary for having worked for the nationalist government before 1949 and her mother a rightist for having challenged the Communist Party's radical policies in the late 1950s. The introduction of Bai Jie to the Chinese stage marked a historic occasion. Even before the Cultural Revolution, when the party's policies were less rigid and dogmatic, there had seldom been a postrevolutionary play in which the protagonist came from a questionable family background; the proscription against such a character extended to many works of literature and art. This was held to best serve the interests of the party, the working people, and the proletarian revolutionary course.

Winter Jasmine is set in the late 1970s, "when the Chinese people began their 'new Long March' " after the smashing of the Gang of Four. In a textile factory in the northeast, Li Jian, the newly appointed party secretary, decides to hold Bai Jie up to the others as a model worker, as she is the only one who has conscientiously finished her five-year quota in four years, without a single yard of defective fabric.[6] However, Wu Yiping, the deputy party secretary, argues strongly against the plan. Still under the spell of a radical class theory, Wu believes that singling out Bai Jie as a positive example for other workers to emulate would suggest a neglect of the class struggle by party leaders. She is afraid of being criticized again as a "capitalist roader," a charge leveled at her during the Cultural Revolution. Bai Jie's function in the play seems to be to repudiate Wu's dogmatic behavior, which typified earlier attitudes, and to honor those who died in labor camps and by slow torture solely for having been born into the wrong kind of family. Li Jian asks what kind of bad family influence Bai Jie could possibly have been subject to, since she was only four years old when her father died. This question became an important part of the political drama being enacted outside the theater against the Gang of Four, who were being blamed for all the bad policies during the Cultural Revolution, including discrimination against people (like Bai Jie) from so-called undesirable family backgrounds. In this regard, the play seemed to have turned into a timely celebration of the early post-Maoist regime, whose officials had originally censored, passed judgment on, and finally (not surprisingly) eagerly promoted the public performance of this play.

Yet this is certainly not the whole story. When Li Jian, arguing with Wu Yiping, contends that even Karl Marx, Friedrich Engels, Chairman Mao, and other seasoned revolutionary leaders were not all born into proletarian families, the warm applause elicited by this speech seemed to be a commentary on something transcending the mere evils of the Gang of Four.[7] In October 1979, when the play was being performed in Beijing, I witnessed this pheonomenon twice. Some of the dramatic criticism of the time referred to the audience's warm response. Shen Yi wrote: "Some of the stage lines—which seemed simple, but nevertheless reflected the reality of life—were frequently interrupted with enthusiastic applause from the audience, who, with tears in their eyes, recalled their own life experience while watching the changed fate of the dramatic characters on stage."[8] Huang Mei, a prominent drama critic, also noticed the audience's response: "I believe that this is a touching and exciting play. It is proved such by the constant applause throughout the performance—a phenomenon hardly to be found in the dramatic history of many years past."[9]

The audience response challenged the inconsistent theories of class distinctions and class struggles from the age of Mao that had not yet been rebutted during the early post-Maoist period. In late March 1979, the regime was still under the influence of Mao's anti-rightist campaign, having arrested Wei Jingsheng, a human rights activist, as a "class enemy." Criticism of this kind of theory and its attendant actions was given ammunition by the fate of Li Honglan, Li Jian's daughter, who suffered during the Cultural Revolution because of Li Jian's dismissal from the party as a renegade. It is this same Li Honglan whom Wu Yiping now wants to promote as a model worker simply because her father was recently restored to his former position as party secretary. Ironically, within a few years Li was transformed from disgraced enemy of the people to rehabilitated party secretary and extolled for his heroic acts against the evil Gang of Four. These dramatic reversals in the fortunes both of the protagonists on stage and of their counterparts in real life were seen by many audiences as grounds to protest the cruelty of an absurd social system. Moreover, the audience's enthusiastic applause after Li Jian's repudiation of Wu's party jargon represented perhaps its own loud, collective repudiation of the immediate cultural past, which for many had been fraught with painful experiences.

The theme, plot, and characterizations of *Winter Jasmine*, one of the first few dramas to reflect the feelings of the majority of individuals in early post-Maoist China, came directly from the playwright's personal contacts with textile workers in Dandong, in the province of Liaoning. It was here, says Cui Dezhi, that he met a weaver who had finished her five-year quota of work in four years without a single day's absence (in spite of a three-hour commute), but who was not qualified to attend the Municipal Model Workers Conference because of her objectionable family background. Deeply touched by the weaver's story, Cui was inspired to speak out for the millions of people in similar circumstances who had been unfairly treated. He was aware of the political danger he was courting by dealing with this sensitive issue, and friends and relatives repeatedly warned him of possible future persecution should the political winds suddenly change direction.

Cui Dezhi's courage is indeed remarkable when one considers that when he was writing the play the Party Central Committee had not yet rehabilitated people condemned as rightists in the late 1950s.[10] Not until November 1978 did the committee officially announce in *People's Daily* its decision to "uncap" all the rightists.[11] In January 1979, the party also restored citizens' rights to former landlords, rich peasants, counterrevolutionaries, and "bad" elements in the countryside.[12] Thus *Winter Jasmine* was being written at the very moment when the increasing demands for rehabilitation of rightists and counterrevolutionaries were accelerating the difficult process of change that was to result in the public announcement of a new policy. The final draft of the play was completed by March 1979, and less than two months later came the official announcement of the new policy of rehabilitation, thereby giving the play a timely official green light for public performance.

What accounts for *Winter Jasmine*'s warm reception and immediate success is the knowledge many had that the play would not have been completed and ready had it not been for the playwright's brave venture into a forbidden area at an earlier time. In a dramatic scene at the end of the play, Cui had fully imagined and explored the yet-to-be-announced new policy, and this representation onstage of an inspiring event that had come to pass in real life was taken by some audiences as an occasion for public celebration. The playwright's prediction of a radical policy change was in itself significant. When the play was performed, it served to legitimize the new political order, which immediately attempted to distance itself from the preceding order. It also celebrated the people's will, which had made these and other political changes possible in the first place. Normally, the jargon-laden text of this play would have excluded it from consideration as a serious literary work. This very language, and the way it meshed with many people's experiences, however, made the play work at this particular juncture in Chinese history and for this particular audience and their relatives and friends, who were crucially affected by the reversal of the official policies.

Some audiences for this play—a community whose shared codes of interpretation derived from their similar experiences during the Cultural Revolution—identified and approved of an emerging subtext that might have escaped the notice of the official censors. If they had noticed it, they might have used it to solidify their own post-Maoist legitimacy. Incontrovertibly, both the text and the subtext made the play a hit. It drew crowds to the theater who came to experience a political catharsis. Even people who were not usually interested in the theater came, drawn by a theatrical event that was a simultaneous commentary on the past and present political orders. Yet it is important to remember that this dramatic success could be realized only so long as the antiofficial discourse was successfully utilized as part of the predominant ideology of the post-Maoist state. In the theme of anti–Gang of Four sentiment the audience had certainly discovered an uncommon subversive dialogue, which could be given free rein in a darkened theater.

A knowledge of these circumstances makes the extraordinary popularity of *Winter Jasmine* more understandable. Immediately after the drama's premiere, both the playwright and the editorial board of *Drama Script*, which had published the text, received hundreds of letters from audiences and readers. Many of the correspondents reported that the play had moved them to tears. Some had even hand-copied the entire script so as to absorb every word. Others described their excitement at seeing an excellent play that entered a forbidden area and spoke the truth about real life.[13] Farmers from outlying regions walked dozens of miles to attend the play's premiere in the city of Shenyang.[14] Yet, for some, the expression of anger in the play was not strong enough. The well-known drama critic Huang Mei challenged the logic of the conclusion of the play, in which Bai Jie is finally permitted to attend the Municipal Model Workers Conference only after her mother has been rehabilitated. How was it, Huang asked, that Bai Jie could attend the conference if her mother was still considered an enemy of the people?[15] Thus here, cloaked as drama criticism, was a much more trenchant political critique whose target was freedom of speech in cultural and ideological matters, a subject then not publicly discussed.

In contrast to *Winter Jasmine*, which operated within the framework of the official ideology, Sha Yexin's play *If I Were for Real (Jiaru woshi zhende)* reached far beyond the space between the official ideology and its counterdiscourse.[16] It consequently set off a heated debate on the social effects of theater. Premiered in August 1979 by the Shanghai People's Art Theater (Shanghai renmin yishu juyuan), *If I Were for Real* was one of the most sophisticated dramas of early post-Maoist China. In the prologue, the playwright attempts to emphasize a close relationship between the drama on stage and the dramatic element in real life that gives birth to a theatrical event:

> Drama is based on life. Our play comes out of real-life experience; it begins with the actual conditions in which we find ourselves.
> Before the curtain goes up, then, why can we not begin this play with a depiction of the real-life situation?[17]
> Our loyal, beloved audience has poured into the theater from all directions. Naturally, they know nothing about the play they have come to see. Some are sitting in their seats leafing through the playbill they purchased, hoping to understand something of the plot before- hand. Some are crowded in the lobby, chatting with their companions, talking about the content of the play . . . smoking, eating ice cream, content and carefree, unwilling to tax their brains over anything.
> In a few moments, at the urging of a bell, the audience will file in to their seats.
> They will sit, some attentive, some casually waiting for the curtain to rise.
> Finally it's curtain time! The lights fade, the music begins, the audi- ence members' eyes are fixed on the stage. Suddenly, the music stops, the lights come on again and the voice of Miss Zhao, director of the drama troupe, is heard from behind the curtain, shouting: "Close it, close it! Wait a bit before you raise it." The main curtain, which had been raised just a crack, drops again. In a few moments Miss Zhao comes to the front of the stage.

In a very Brechtian beginning, Miss Zhao then directly addresses the members of the audience. She asks them to be a little more patient, since the players are still waiting for the arrival of several distinguished guests, Director Qian of the Political Section of the Department of Personnel and Director Sun of the Cultural Bureau of the Municipal Party Committee. They will be accompanying the most distinguished guest of all: a young man named Zhang Xiaoli. After the much delayed arrivals of these important personages, the theater manager calls for the play to begin, only to have it interrupted again by several policemen, who announce the arrest of Zhang Xiaoli. According to them, Zhang is guilty of the crime of pretending to be the son of an important party official. Before being taken away by the policemen, Zhang calls out to Zhao: "Aren't you putting on a play? Well, so am I. My play is finished now; but you can continue with yours."[18] These Brechtian "alienation effects" are intended to distance the audience from the dramatic events so as to drive home the point that everyone in contemporary China is maneuvering for political survival. With his remark, Zhang is actually challenging privileged people who use their political power to protect their vested interests. Yet, being an insignificant man without power, Zhang must cease acting in his own drama of pretending to be a powerful man before the real play can begin, in which only the privileged can act, at the expense of the marginalized people.

Blended with the Brechtian elements is the influence of the more traditional illusionist theater. Beginning with act 1, we see a series of flashbacks that subtly and gradually subvert the play's realistic mode, through which the play has tried to fool the audience. For instance, the setting of act 1 is described as the main entrance of a theater during one evening in the first half of 1979.[19] Sha Yexin, the playwright, emphasizes verisimilitude in the stage direction: "If this play is fortunate enough to be performed in a theater, then the scenery for this act would be exactly the same as the main entrance to that theater or, at least, very like it."[20] In front of this theater, Li Xiaozhang, a young man lacking any privileged family background, first gets the idea of imposture from a plot summary of Gogol's *The Inspector General* that he reads on a large poster announcing the current play. Inspired by the Russian playwright's satire, he decides he will be Zhang Xiaoli, the son of Old Zhang, a high-ranking party official in Beijing. Throughout the play, much is made of Li's imposture having been forced on him by his desperate circumstances. He has to have a powerful authority who can act as a rubber stamp for his transfer from a farm to a city job so that he and his pregnant girlfriend can be married in time.

Moreover, his so-called criminal act is depicted as merely imitative of the corrupt acts of local officials. In the second part of act 1, for instance, while waiting for an extra ticket to Gogol's play, Li Xiaozhang sees theater manager Zhao personally greeting Director Sun of the Cultural Bureau and her daughter in front of the theater. Moments later, he is refused admission by the same person because he lacks a powerful parent. Determined to beat the devil at his own game, Li, pretending to be Minister Ma, calls the theater to request a ticket for a Zhang Xiaoli, the son of his old comrade-in-arms from Beijing. The call immediately changes Li's fate. In act 2, after the performance of Gogol's play to which he had gained admission by this ruse, the manager introduces Li to many of her powerful friends, who compete with each other in trying to guess the identify of Li's father. Astutely listening to their suggestions, Li selects one of them as his true identity.

Thus the play invites us to understand that Li is no ordinary swindler. He has assumed an identity suggested to him by the local officials, who routinely jockey for power through their connections to the central power structure. Li, a very good actor, simply acts on the information freely dispensed by those in high places. He is capable of delivering convincing performances in a corrupt society in which only the untruthful can survive. It does not even occur to Li to use his new identity to secure a different job until he is asked whether he needs anything else besides a few theater tickets. In act 4, after having been invited to live with the family of Director Qian—whose husband happens to be Municipal Party Secretary Wu—Li is immediately surrounded by several people who hope to wangle some special privileges for themselves because of his close relationship to Wu. Is it any wonder, then, that Li responds indignantly when his supposed father, Old Zhang, confronts him in act 4?

OLD ZHANG: Why do you cheat others by claiming to be my son?

ZHANG XIAOLI: (*Excitedly*) Am I the only one who is cheating? No, this imposture was indeed created by all of us! Aren't those cheated by me also cheating others? Not only did they provide me with means and opportunities to cheat, but they also taught me how to cheat. I am not denying that I used your status to try to achieve my own goals. Yet it is equally undeniable that they also used my false identity to further their own personal interests, interests that were much greater in scope than my own.

OLD ZHANG: Who are these people?

ZHANG XIAOLI: *(Pulling out from his pocket some letters and reports)* This is from Theater Director Zhao, who wants a bigger apartment. This is Sun from the Cultural Bureau, who wants his son-in-law transferred from the Northeast. This is a letter from Director Qian, who wants herself and her husband "selected" to be part of a national delegation to go abroad—a letter to be presented to you in person. They all have something to ask from me, but to whom do I turn for help? They all curry favor with me, begging me to solve their problems, but who is there to solve my problem?[21]

Although these words comprise a profound social critique, perhaps the most subversive statement of the play is to be found in the epilogue, when the swindler is being tried in criminal court. In the stage directions, the playwright, Sha Yexin, stresses that in the court drama the audience plays an important role in judging whether or not the accused receives a fair trial:

Unfortunately, I've forgotten who it was that said the stage is a legislative assembly, but this stage of ours really is a court in the midst of a public trial now. As for our beloved and loyal audience, they have become the spectators at the trial. We hope that having seen the whole case with their own eyes, they'll have their own opinions about the justice of the court's decision.[22]

The following epilogue begins with the prosecutor's speech. Li Xiaozhang responds with a guilty plea, having first remarked, however, that if he had been who he claimed to be, he would have been able to achieve his goal without any legal penalties. Speaking on Li's behalf as his attorney, Old Zhang traces the roots of Li's crime to social conditions—the practice, initiated by the Gang of Four, of people benefiting from special privileges, which, according to Li's defender, destroyed China's legal system and poisoned young people's minds. Li Xiaozhang is a victim of the Gang of Four, Old Zhang argues. He also condemns the corrupt officials who, at every step of the way, helped Li with his imposture. "I'm really worried about this," he confides. "Our cadres weren't destroyed by the Gang of

Four; but they may destroy themselves if they continue to pursue these unhealthy tendencies. Take this warning, comrades," Old Zhang says, his voice reflecting his indignation. "Otherwise, some of you sitting as witnesses in this court may soon find yourselves at the mercy of the Disciplinary Court!"[23]

With this last line, delivered as the curtain fell, the play's underlying antiofficial statement finally became transparent. Blaming a swindler's crime on the Gang of Four was a clever strategy for gaining the approval of the official censors. Despite this anti–Gang of Four theme, many people in the audience could hardly have missed the blunt subtext, signaled by the constant reminders that the play is set in the dusk of the first half of 1979, more than two years after the arrest of the Gang of Four.[24] The play portrays a society rotten to its core, from deputy minister to vice premier, from bureau director to section head, from male to female officials. All the party members in the play, whether part of the dramatic action onstage or only briefly mentioned, are characterized as deceptive, snobbish, and selfish, the only exception being Old Zhang. Thus the play, by setting and plot, refers to a specific contemporary moment in the history of modern China when many Chinese people had no choice but to become involved in the political drama outside the theater. As citizens and as participants in that drama, they were being offered by this play the luxury of transforming hazardous thoughts into comfortable escape. They could be collaborators in the unrealistic dramatic events onstage and wholeheartedly surrender themselves to an imaginary movement in which the common people, with their laughter, cheers, and applause, triumphed over the official culture.

It was as if the Chinese audience members were answering the call to action issued by Augusto Boal, a Brazilian practitioner of "theater of liberation," which expects its audience to assume the protagonist's role, change the dramatic action, explore new solutions, and train themselves "for real action," thereby using the theatrical experience as a "rehearsal for the revolution."[25] Whereas Aristotelean poetics focus on dramatic characters who act and think for the spectators, and Brechtian poetics reserve the right of the spectators to think for themselves, Boal's poetics of the oppressed stressed the action and plans for social change devised by the spectators themselves.[26] However, post-Maoist theater differs from Boal's "theater of the oppressed," which could be found in "Latin American slums and rural communities from the late sixties onwards."[27] As demonstrated by *If I Were for Real*, it more closely resembles another of

Boal's theatrical constructs, "Forum Theater," which, as described by Eugène Van Erven, "involves a realistically performed scene of some form of oppression from the experience of the participants."[28] Thus Van Erven cannot claim that China, and also Vietnam, Cambodia, Laos, North Korea, Mongolia, and the Muslim nations of Asia Minor "do not do much in the way of theater of liberation."[29] As this chapter has demonstrated, China's "theater of liberation" entails a unique form of subtext, which requires an insider's knowledge and experience to detect and extract it from sometimes seemingly very official plays. To employ Van Erven's terms again, the Chinese brand of "theater of liberation" actually conjures up what Van Erven calls a "playful revolution," a theater that "many contemporary Asian theatre practitioners" have come to view "as a very attractive and effective means to attain indispensable social and political changes in their often undemocratic, corruption-ridden countries."[30] In the Chinese context, the word "playful" suggests the playfulness of the audience members as they unravel the unspoken themes of the play and, through their own dramatic action in the form of applause, tacitly agree with the real subject of a particular play.

Erving Goffman once remarked that the curtain call "wipes the make-believe away" and casts aside the characters just projected.[31] In the case of *If I Were for Real*, at the end the performers joined hands with the audience in a joint struggle against the status quo. The enthusiastic people on both sides of the stage knew to whom the curtain calls were addressed. Both sides knew, too, that the character of good Old Zhang was a formal device, a deus ex machina for resolving the conflicts that in real life found no easy resolution. That an Old Zhang did not appear until the last act in itself constituted a satiric comment on a society that had to wait around for such a miracle to happen. Furthermore, the lonely and confused Old Zhang underscored the scarcity of honest and upright officials in real life. There was in fact a historical precedent in Chinese drama for Old Zhang: the "tall, grand, and perfect" heroes and heroines—in most cases, party secretaries—of the Cultural Revolutionary model plays, dramatic characters who had alienated many audiences with their exaggerated magnanimity and absolute correctness. Now, in early post-Maoist China, when the grand characters of the proletariat were being cited as negative products of the Gang of Four–inspired ultra-left policies in literature and art, Old Zhang inspired neither admiration nor respect; indeed, he was criticized for being the least believable person in the play, a lifeless character, representing only someone's abstract concept or groundless hope.

It should be remembered, however, that Old Zhang was also a political device. The playwright, Sha Yexin, was able to point to Old Zhang in response to the charge that his play depicted a dark socialist world occupied by no one except corrupt cadres.[32] Although it was true that Old Zhang "lacked flesh and blood," Sha argued that "it was nevertheless in this character alone that the playwright's stand, viewpoint, and feelings for the party were best catalyzed."[33] This typical instance of self-defense by a playwright demonstrates the way in which authorial intention in Chinese literary and dramatic scenes may signify something entirely different from what it does in the West. At those times when they were asserting their motive for the party, writers did not expect their audiences to take their statements seriously. They were speaking only for the benefit of guardians of the status quo, so that their works would pass the muster of the official censors. The works' truly meaningful subversive voice was to be detected by and shared among astute readers and audiences who had survived the same harsh conditions lived through and depicted by the author.

This is not to deny the importance of the historical conditions that formed the backdrop for these subversive readings. As I have already noted, in early post-Maoist China the officials of the post–Cultural Revolutionary regime and the majority of Chinese readers and critics shared an interest in condemning the evils of the Gang of Four. For the officials, attacking the ousted regime helped to drive home their superiority and, they hoped, gain them popular support. Nor, in retrospect, was the subtext in these plays as subtle as I have suggested. It is therefore possible that the censors' readings might not always have been too different from those of the audience. The censors apparently chose to look the other way, as the subversive reading could be interpreted as an effective way of discrediting the Gang of Four. Similarly, Chinese readers, writers, theater producers, and theatergoers benefited from the ambiguous situation and created a critical discourse that could be simultaneously interpreted as either pro- or anti-status quo. One might thus reasonably argue that the border crossing between the official ideology and antiofficial discourse in the early post-Maoist period could not be easily identified or defined. Moreover, at that particular time, many Chinese audiences and theater people, including myself, still naively trusted the post–Cultural Revolutionary regime, which seemed to hold out the hope for a better China. As a consequence, distinguishing between official and antiofficial representations and lines of reading could become even more difficult. This fact helps to explain why some subtexts—which, to Western readers, might have appeared heavy-handed and transparent social critiques—to Chinese readers had some subtle aspects of duality that made them open to a free play of meanings. Ultimately, the political life surrounding a totalitarian regime left Chinese readers, audiences, and writers no alternative but to emphasize a sense of difference from the official culture. Yet, paradoxically, the voice of the other was skillfully expressed in a seeming voice of sameness. It echoed the official ideology while simultaneously becoming a voice of difference and dissent.

Thus the brief appearance of Old Zhang in *If I Were for Real* represented for critics an opportunity to rush to Sha's defense. They argued that the play reflected the nature of socialist China in a positive way by presenting both corrupt officials and the incorruptible Old Zhang, who finally demanded that the former be tried by the party's court.[34] How, they demanded, could anyone be blind to this fact and argue that the play exaggerated the dark side of contemporary society? Even if the charge of extreme negativism were true, Sha's defenders insisted, was it not the duty of proletarian literature and art to reveal the society's ills in order to educate the people in the ways of furthering the socialist revolution? They further claimed that the play exposed the dark age of the Gang of Four, which had left behind a host of problems for future generations to solve. As the play itself points out, it was the Gang of Four who poisoned the minds of young people and promoted the corrupt practices surrounding the dispensing of privileges.[35]

Interestingly, both those who criticized and those who defended Sha's play contributed to the complex, if contradictory, exploration of the overlapping space between official ideology and its antidiscourse. Indeed, both sides made use of the drama's time setting at two years after the arrest of the Gang of Four to advance their opposing arguments. Those who felt offended by the play insisted that it was clearly intended to denounce the China of today, after the Gang of Four. They pointed to the stage full of corrupt officials and swindlers with no sense of redemption, who would necessarily cause audience members to assume that present socialist China was indistinguishable from past China under the Gang of Four. Those who supported the play, on the other hand, insisted that the problems of crime and corruption had been inherited from and generated by the practices of the Cultural Revolution. Exposing these activities, they felt, served to illustrate the healthy state of the party, which could now criticize past wrongs and support corrective action in the present. Only a truly Marxist party, they pointed out for the benefit of the opposition, had the courage to expose its own traitors in this fashion. Disclosure of the evils of the past such as those found in Sha's play could thus only help people to appreciate the hard-earned advantages of the present regime.

Although the subversive sentiments in *If I Were for Real* were deeply felt by both sides, neither was willing to treat them openly as the real issue. The critics of the play felt that if they attempted to suppress it they would be inviting their opponents' accusation that they were following in the footsteps of the Gang of Four, which had persecuted many artists for writing anti-party plays. The memory of how Mao had used Wu Han's Beijing opera *Hai Rui Dismissed from Office* as an excuse to initiate the Cultural Revolution was still all too fresh. As for the supporters of Sha's play, they sought to "let the leopard sleep," the better to protect the play. Both sides knew all too well that the play's profundity resided in its shaking to its very foundations the image of Mao's absolute power, which, not very long ago, had been unshakable.

However, the play could not have comforted Hua Guofeng, Mao's chosen successor. In other plays of the same period, such as *When the Maple Leaves Turned Red (Fengye hongle de shihou)*, written by Jin Zhenjia and Wang Jingyu and premiered in 1977 by the China Youth Art Theater, and *Winter Jasmine*, he had been depicted as the wise leader who arrested the members of the Gang of Four to carry out Mao's deathbed wish of furthering the Chinese revolution. This approach to Hua reflected the official history in 1979. It was to be rewritten in 1981, when Hua Guofeng was eliminated as party chief for being too faithful a Maoist disciple to permit significant political changes.[36] Premiered also in 1979, however, *If I Were for Real* refrained from explicitly celebrating Hua, which might have constituted another reason for its being singled out as a target for public criticism.

In addition to its troubling plot, *If I Were for Real* provides less obvious satirical moments in which theatrical action in everyday life is depicted as a skill necessary for political survival. One such moment occurs in the prologue, when Li Xiaozhang remarks, after his arrest: "Aren't you all acting? I have just finished performing my own play. Now it is time for you to begin your show!"[37] At this juncture, Li has performed his last political act in his personal drama directed against the system. Now the play can begin and give an account, in flashbacks, of the entire sequence of his political acts. By means of the Brechtian "Verfremdung Effekt," the audience could choose to distance itself from the theatrical event and, instead, become emotionally and intellectually involved in the dramatized political event.

In act 1, when he is reproached for pretending to have an extra ticket, Li refutes the accusation: "It was only a joke. What's wrong with cheating a little bit? Isn't acting itself a kind of cheat? Aren't you fooled already if you prefer to watch a fake play in the theater when you could be watching so many real dramas around you in everyday life?"[38] That Li's imposture is inspired by the plot summary he reads on the theater poster of Gogol's *The Inspector General* only heightens the general atmosphere of cynicism. Thus we have a Russian play within a Chinese play, and both enclose the audience in a world within the play that discloses the world outside the play. The two worlds are frequently collapsed into one. As we have already seen, the stage directions specify that the doorway of the theater in act 1 should be identical to the doorway to the theater in which the present play is being performed. The actors and actresses in act 1 who are depicted waiting for extra tickets should perform in such a natural and realistic manner as to make "the members of the audience feel that they themselves were being represented onstage, or that it was indeed they up there onstage, acting themselves."[39]

Of course, both the play's critics and its advocates debated whether or not Sha's play was comparable to Gogol's satirical-allegorical phantasmagoria of tsarist Russia. Some critics asserted that Gogol's *The Inspector General* was a masterpiece of social realism, as it depicted a tsarist Russia of such unmitigated corruption that it had logically, inevitably led to the October socialist revolution. Given this view of Gogol's play, they considered it unpardonably improper to draw an analogy between tsarist Russia and socialist China.[40] Even if a swindler was to be found in our society, the play's critics argued, it would be an isolated instance whose cause would be corrected in the natural course of socialist revolution. To exaggerate certain events so as to make them appear to be omnipresent in contemporary society, they maintained, was to distort the bright reality of post–Gang of Four China.[41] One of these critics held that Sha's play was problematic because its characters and events were too close to those depicted by Gogol in nineteenth-century Russia.[42] Critics compared Sha's play unfavorably with Lao She's *Looking Westward to Chang'an (Xiwang chang'an)*, premiered by the China Youth Art Theater in 1956, which satirized the machinations of a swindler in 1950s socialist China. But Lao She, it was pointed out, had sought to differentiate his satirical play from

Gogol's. Because he loved the new socialist China, he had exerted himself to cast in a positive light both the party officials and the masses who
had taken action against the swindler and finally unmasked him. It was by
these means, one critic contended, that Lao She, apparently in contrast to
Sha, illustrated the force of justice in the revolutionary cause and created
a successful socialist satirical play.[43]

In rebuttal, Sha's supporters maintained that his critics were wrong to
focus on the uniqueness of the post–Gang of Four Chinese situation.
Similar events in different social systems could indeed be compared, they
said, especially as socialist China itself had just emerged from a feudalism
not unlike that of Russia in the tsarist period. They pointed to the most
recent remnants of that feudalism in the monarchies of the Gang of Four
and the Lin Biao anti-party cliques during the Cultural Revolution. Yet
even while defending the comparison of these two plays, the advocates of
If I Were for Real stressed that there were fundamental differences between it and Gogol's play. They pointed out that, unlike Ivan Alexandro-
vich Hlestakov, who remained at large after his imposture had been discovered, Li Xiaozhang was punished by law. Most significantly, Ivan
was not counterbalanced by an Old Zhang who, in Sha's play, was the
one who exposed the imposture. Similarly, Sha's play did not ridicule its
audiences, as did Gogol's—with good reason. Because, in Gogol's time,
audience members came from an aristocratic elite, they could be categorized as enemies of the people. Sha, on the other hand, said his defenders
loved his country and its people, and he was bent on his play helping to
bring about changes that would lead to a better and healthier society.
Therefore one would not be in the least justified in charging that Sha's
depiction of China was the same as that of the Russia of more than 143
years before.[44]

A complex, rich play of this sort that lent itself to such diverse interpretations would naturally be seen as transgressing official boundaries. No
wonder, then, that it was carefully scrutinized at an early stage by an official from the Shanghai Municipal Committee of the Chinese Communist Party. It was reported that after dress rehearsals this official, although
he encouraged the playwright, expressed the belief that the play was not
well written because it portrayed an impostor in socialist China with too
much sympathy. The official admitted that he had been "touched to
tears" during the performance, but, he declared, literature and art should
bring about "hope, courage, and strength," not "merely negative feelings."[45] He then suggested that the play be performed for restricted audi-

ences *(neibu yanchu)*, in order to solicit suggestions for improving the script before it was ready for the general public.

The history of PRC drama contains several instances of questionable plays being performed only for controlled audiences. These audiences usually consisted of officials and cadres from various levels of the party hierarchy—who were trusted not to be influenced by the play's potentially harmful content—and of critics and dramatists grasping the opportunity to get an early look before making public critiques. This event usually meant that, at a certain level of censorship, the play's political orientation had been debated. In some cases, such as Sha's play, the permission to perform for controlled audiences also indicated a compromise between those who wanted to ban the work and those who wanted to promote it. Under these special circumstances, *If I Were for Real* was allowed a short life span of forty-six performances in Shanghai, from August to November 1979, in addition to ten dress rehearsals open only to invited guests.[46]

So far, we have discussed how a subtext such as that of *If I Were for Real* could be responsible for a mixed reception. Plays that won unanimous official approval, however, did not necessarily carry a uniform, unambiguous meaning. In *Power versus Law (Quan yu fa)*, for instance, the official and antiofficial discourses were so successfully merged that celebrating the play's officially approved values simultaneously affirmed its counterdiscourse. In my view, the play's success, both with rulers of the regime and with its usually demanding audience, is attributable to its nimble negotiation of the narrow, limited, overlapping space between the official ideology and the antiofficial discourse. Set in 1978, *Power versus Law* recounts how Ding Mu, inspired by the party's campaign to reestablish legal systems after the arrest of the Gang of Four, writes a letter to the press exposing the criminal acts of Cao Da, the deputy secretary of the Municipal Party Committee who embezzled public funds to build his luxurious house. Confident that his past revolutionary record entitles him to special privileges, Cao Da threatens to arrest Ding Mu on the groundless charge that she murdered her husband during the Cultural Revolution to enhance her chances of winning another man. Under these treacherous circumstances, Luo Fang, the newly appointed secretary of the Municipal Party Committee, nevertheless wins Ding Mu's trust (Fig. 21) and encourages her to come forward. With loving support from Ding Hong, her

FIGURE 21. *Power versus Law*, premiered by the China Youth Art Theater in 1979.

daughter, and her daughter's fiancé, Ding Mu finally succeeds in exposing Cao Da.

The play, which caused a national sensation, raised the topical issue: do those in power have the right to abuse their power and take reprisal against those who challenge them?[47] Although *Power versus Law* dealt with the same themes of corruption and privilege as did *If I Were for Real*, the former play was used as a positive example with which to attack the latter. *Power versus Law* was viewed as laying bare the dark aspects of life while still providing people with hope for a bright socialist future. Where *If I Were for Real* relied on a minor character like Old Zhang, *Power versus Law* employed Luo Fang, the almost perfect new party secretary. In the words of the playwright, Luo represented the senior party officials who adhered to the party's principles and maintained revolutionary traditions after being reappointed to leading positions following the destruction of the Gang of Four.[48] This declaration of authorial intention obviously promoted the play, for it was exactly what the authorities wanted to hear.

But *Power versus Law* offered other possibilities for interpretation. Officially sanctioned critics might suggest that the play paid homage to good party officials, but other members of the audience might have focused their strong emotional responses on Cao Da, the perverse overlord whose ubiquitous real-life counterparts were far too frightening to be confronted in person. In this alternative focus, the audience's applause at the right points frequently signaled their approval and vicarious participation in the dramatic action. Consequently, a consideration of the timing of the applause throughout the play provided clues as to how it was understood by its original audiences. These acts of applause might in effect be regarded as products of a subtext of the play, one written as much by the play's viewers as by the dramatist.

My vantage point in regard to this play was influenced partly by my admiration for several cast members, as a result of which I attended more than a dozen performances by the China Youth Art Theater in Beijing between 1979 and 1980. Moreover, because Ji Shuping, my mother, played the role of Ding Mu, I could go backstage as often as I wanted to talk to cast members about the play and the reception it received in different locations. The actors were glad to give me particulars on where and how audience members applauded and shouted during the performance and what they wrote in their letters or uttered in their remarks to them about their reactions to the play. It was exhilarating for me to see another "theater" thus acting itself out, spontaneously erupting from the staged drama into postdramatic acts that the actors and actresses, in most cases, identified with and that, consequently, provoked the actors to probe deeper into the play's essence. I was also lucky, during this period, to have the thoughtful input of my mother on several nights when, after the performance, being too excited to sleep, she would sit with me under the bright moonlight in our courtyard and ponder long into the night about the meaning of the play.

As a result, I came to realize how much the story of Ding Mu and Ding Hong paralleled that of many other mothers and daughters during and after the Cultural Revolution, including our own. It was under so many bright moons earlier in the heyday of the Cultural Revolution that the loving letters exchanged between my mother (then "reforming thought" in an army camp in central Heibei) and myself (then tilling the land in the wilderness in the northeast since the age of fifteen) became an inestimable source of spiritual and emotional support. Such bonding was especially precious at a time when my father was undergoing persecution similar to that of Ding Hong's father. Such personal memories also helped me develop an understanding of how audience members related to the play's cultural "fathers"—both the ideologically correct Luo Fang and the ideologically incorrect Cao Da. I was profoundly impressed by the effect of the constant applause from members of the audience, who seldom failed to react, for instance, to the scene in which Luo Fang directly confronts Cao Da:

> LUO: Don't forget, in this city you're not the foundation but a pillar. You and I both! If we're crooked, people have the right to knock us down. The same applies to those in still higher positions, even in the Central Committee. [*Applause*] If anyone breaks the law as you have done, the people have the right to bash him down. Today (holds up the incriminating material) the people are going to bash you! [*Applause*] (act 3)[49]

The second much applauded speech followed not too long after:

> LUO: (*Beside himself*) A veteran party member? You? You're a disgrace to our party! . . . You think your past record, your present power, sets you above the law? Instead of being a servant of the people, you lord it over them. If anyone crosses you or exposes you, you frame him, convict him of crimes, eh? You've put power in place of law! Does this socialist country of ours still have feudal rule? "Nobles are exempt from punishment"—that Confucian maxim still holds, does it? No! The law doesn't just apply to the common people. [*Applause*] It doesn't make exceptions for an elite. [*Applause*] Neither your past record nor your present power can hide your crime. I warn you, we're going to have the law on you! [*Applause*] (act 3)[50]

Such eruptions of applause indicated how the audience understood the play's subtext as being subversive. The applause escaped dangerous political scrutiny. Such a response could always be explained away as the audience welcoming the correct words of the new party secretary, who represents, in the official parlance of the time, the glorious party that always "seeks truth from facts and corrects its mistakes whenever they are found."[51] Yet it was left up to audience members to applaud when and how loudly they wished, and they made the most of this outlet. Several sought out cast members, telling them: "Yes, we have seen so many party villains just like Cao Da, who should have been brought to public trial a long time ago!" Some even went so far as to also shout after the above-cited lines: "Well put! Arrest that scoundrel!" Clearly, restraint was impossible for certain members of the audience whose experiences of having been wrongly prosecuted by corrupt party officers were still all too vivid and fresh.

The tumultuous applause during and after Luo Fang's speech did not, however, necessarily signify complete endorsement of this perfect character by the audience. Just as they could respond emotionally to the criminal acts of Cao Da, so they could also (and did) react intellectually to the idealized image of Luo Fang, whose heroic stature only underscored the scarcity of his counterparts in real life. One audience member told the playwright that it was exciting to see an upright Luo Fang onstage, but that "such a Luo Fang is indeed hard to come by in real life!" Others were even more pointed in their remarks: "Have you ever found a person like Luo Fang in real life? You are truly clever. You created a Luo Fang and that gave your play a green light."[52]

Luo Fang lent himself to two different textual interpretations. For officials eager to preserve the status quo, he could be used as a cover for their faults and even help to establish their new legitimacy. For those inclined toward subversive sentiments, he bolstered their conviction that such a paragon could only be found onstage. Some audiences saw him as representing pure, absolute power. Luo Fang, after all, had to resort to his authority as the new party secretary in order to conquer the deputy party secretary, a subordinate person who became even more powerless as a result of his previous affiliation with the old regime of the Gang of Four. The wrongly accused Ding Mu would never have been rescued had she not had the good luck of meeting a Luo Fang with supreme power over her accuser.[53] Thus, a play whose theme revolved around checking power by means of the legal system was understood by many as illustrating the powerlessness of the ordinary citizen when confronted with the party apparatus. Here also was a play much touted and promoted by the purveyors of official ideology that could also be celebrated for its embedded counterdiscourse, appreciated by an audience acutely attuned to its dichotomies and ironies.

Much of the power of early post-Maoist plays derived from how they reflected (in however altered form) the political drama of everyday life. This correspondence helps to account for the popularity of these plays, but also, paradoxically, for their rapid decline. Once the political grievances they inflamed were somehow defused through theater, they lost their appeal. Within this limited period, nevertheless, drama within the four walls of the theater building continued to create and re-create political theater on the larger stage of political life. At one point, the debate about controversial plays like *If I Were for Real* became so heated that it finally caught the attention of the Party Central Committee. At the Fourth National Congress of Artists and Writers, convened in Beijing from October 31 to November 16, 1979, many delegates continued to discuss the play, along with the movie scripts *In the Archives of Society (Zai shehui de dang'an li)* and *Girl Thief (Nüzei)*.[54] Because these scripts were always lumped with Sha's play as negative examples of socialist realism and were attacked accordingly, a brief discussion of them will illuminate the subversive discourse in Sha's play.

Both of these film scripts, like Sha's play, depicted young people as victims of the Cultural Revolution. *In the Archives of Society* describes the tragic downfall of Li Lifang, a beautiful, innocent girl brutally raped by a high-ranking army official and his son. After being used as a scapegoat and dismissed from the army, Li Lifang seeks her last hope for a decent life in marriage. When her physician husband discovers on their wedding night that she is not a virgin, he expels her from the house. After also being rejected by her father for disgracing the family, Li joins a gang of delinquents and takes revenge on society by fighting, burglarizing, and killing. *Girl Thief* gave a similar account of an innocent girl reduced to becoming a professional thief after the tragic death of her mother during the Cultural Revolution.

These two film scripts were severely criticized, as had been Sha's play, for their harmful social effects, and the censors never allowed them to be made into movies in the PRC. *In the Archives of Society* was denounced for its unfair portrayal of a rapist in the People's Liberation Army. Although the rapist was identified in the film as a faithful follower of the Lin Biao anti-party clique, one critic objected that a story about a rapist in the army was still unacceptable, as it viciously attacked the socialist system, which depended on the army to safeguard its fundamental principles. The real intention of the author, this critic asserted, was to let a follower of Lin Biao represent our era, characterized by the control of a fascist, autocratic, and military system. It suggests that such a system has raped its own people and its own legal practice![55] The critic cited a recent report that the Taiwan government was preparing to produce the film, whose script they considered the best ever written by a PRC writer.[56] If our enemy views it as being to its advantage to screen this film, the critic argued, then aren't its negative social effects clear to us all?

However, those who openly supported the two film scripts and Sha's play stressed that individual writers should not be held responsible for the social effects of their work. As an example, they pointed to Lao She's play *Teahouse (Chaguan)*, which had met with widely varying receptions throughout the history of the PRC. When first performed in 1957 by the Beijing People's Art Theater to a warm reception, the content of *Teahouse* seemed incompatible with the national effort to reform private businessmen.[57] It was accordingly criticized for singing the praises of a teahouse owner whose tragic life evoked the old society, based on private ownership in an emerging capitalist economy. The second round of performances of *Teahouse*, in 1962, ran afoul of the then radical policy concerning literature and art, which could be summarized as writing about the new life of the thirteen years after liberation (*daxie shisan nian*). This policy required writers and artists to depict the life and struggle of the workers, peasants, and soldiers selflessly devoted to socialist construction and revolution. Unfortunately, Lao She's play happened to revolve around the changing historical periods in preliberation China. It was attacked, this time for a lack of enthusiasm for the new socialist China. During the Cultural Revolution, *Teahouse* was accused of being an anti-party play. Not until after the play was performed in 1979 did Lao She's defenders perceive that people had begun to appreciate its artistic value. But, tragically, the belatedly recognized "best playwright of the people" had already taken his own life thirteen years before, during the Cultural Revolution, to protest his unfair treatment and severe beating by the Red Guards. Since no one could predict, or control, the widely varying cultural conditions that governed opposing receptions of a particular work, one critic argued, the most reliable way to test its social effects was to make it available to the general public, who were the best critics. Time, history, and social practices would eventually provide the fairest judgment.[58]

The way in which this commentator assumed a distinction between the "reception" given a particular work and that given by the general public would have struck a Western reader as odd. In the critical discourse of Chinese literary and dramatic studies, however, the word "reception" usually meant—especially in early post-Maoist China—the official stamp of approval for the political content of the text, not the reception, meant in the West, by diverse reading communities and readers with changing horizons of literary expectations, as explained by Stanley Fish and Hans Robert Jauss. This difference, rather than diminishing the importance of reception study in modern China, points up its value. As this study has shown, a particular kind of reception study can account for varied interpretations of a text, including those dictated by points of view that are in opposition to the official ideology and thus would have been excluded from or maginalized by the official records, no matter how vividly they might have been inscribed in one's personal memory as a particular kind of knowledge produced by subcultures.

In the debate on the social effects of the two film scripts and Sha's play, both sides referred to another play to support their arguments. Although the play *Save Her (Jiujiu ta)* had a similar plot and theme, it had been favorably received by both the authorities and audiences. Confining its political content to the official framework of an anti–Gang of Four campaign, the play also addresses the popular concern with juvenile delinquency. Its protagonist, Li Xiaoxia, although forced to join a gang of delinquents, differs from the youthful offenders in the other scripts. On her release from detention, she is aided by a caring teacher and a loving boyfriend, who persuades her heartbroken parents to join them in helping to reform her. At the conclusion of the play, she successfully passes an entrance examination and is accepted by a college that overlooks her criminal record. The play was almost unanimously praised for having skillfully handled the delicate balance between exposing the dark aspects of society associated with the Gang of Four and singing the praises of the bright new socialist society.[59]

Some critics, however, disagreed with this assessment, pointing out that not even this safe play could guarantee that all its social effects were positive. One girl, it was reported, remained crying in her seat long after the play was over. Although her past resembled that of Li Xiaoxia, she did not enjoy the good fortune of being surrounded by loving, caring people: "Xiaoxia is saved. I want to turn over a new leaf in my life, too. But who is there to save me?" The critic suggested that this girl's distress attested to the possibility of too rosy a picture onstage leading to harmful social effects. For this girl, watching such a play was tantamount to being "thrown into a second nightmare after having been awakened from the first."[60] Delving deeper into this incident can provide us with still another example of the complexity of Chinese literary and dramatic reception studies. It appears that the first account of this girl's reaction to the play was given by Zhao Guoqing, the play's author. He used this response to illustrate how the optimistic ending of the play had awakened young people and helped their teachers and parents realize the urgent need to support and understand them.[61] The playwright's interpretation of audience response demonstrates how authorial intention can add to the enigmatic, complicated mix that makes up reception study. For not only do authors change their intentions to cope with different political climates, but their intentions may also be used by critics to discredit them.

In order to provide a forum for the ongoing discussions about the social effects of the two questionable film scripts and Sha's play, a Drama Script Seminar *(juben zuotanhui)* was sponsored by the Chinese Dramatists

Association (Zhongguo xijujia xiehui), Chinese Writers Association (Zhongguo zuojia xiehui), and Chinese Film Association (Zhongguo dianying xiehui) from January 23 to February 13 in 1980.[62] Hu Yaobang, who would become General Secretary of the Central Committee of the Chinese Communist Party two weeks later, delivered a six-hour speech expressing his views of Sha Yexin's *If I Were for Real.* It was his belief that the play did not reflect the social reality of China after the arrest of the Gang of Four.[63] Old Zhang, who seemed to be too detached from the real world, acted as if he were either an outsider or a savior of the world. Hu also felt that the playwright expressed too much sympathy for the swindler, whose existence seemed to hinge entirely on the corrupt practices of party officials. He thus asked the dramatists in the seminar how a public performance of the present version of the play might have negative effects.[64] Nothing had so clearly testified to the play's powerful subversive discourse as this event, at which a party chief felt called upon to settle the disposition of Sha Yexin's play.

Hu's intervention, and his manner in carrying it out, was actually considered a welcome change. It signaled a more relaxed atmosphere for literary and dramatic productions. Chinese artists and writers warmly applauded him when he repeatedly voiced the party's intention to cease persecuting artists and writers. "Our party will take an oath here," he vowed. "We will never impose criminal penalties on works of literature and art and never accuse writers as counterrevolutionaries for what they wrote!"[65] Hu won a reputation for his lenient treatment of intellectuals, and when he died suddenly in 1989, students demanded that he be rehabilitated in a timely fashion, which triggered the Tiananmen student movement. Again, at almost every turn of its development, theater drama in China has been intricately related to the course of political drama. In the next chapter, I will discuss these interrelationships in detail, particularly those resulting from the street theaters of Tiananmen in 1976.

Despite Hu Yaobang's intentions and their clear departure from those of his predecessors, performances of *If I Were for Real* were never resumed after this seminar, not even for controlled audiences. Hu's talk also precluded the possibility of producing the two controversial film scripts. It was only to be expected, therefore, that some critics a year later singled out the party chief's intrusive participation in the Drama Script Seminar as a main factor responsible for sluggish dramatic production. Drama, they charged, seemed to have lost its capacity to dramatize the pressing social issues of contemporary China.[66] It had increasingly moved toward the safe havens of detective and love stories, the depiction of international events, and adaptations of popular fiction. This crisis, it was felt, could be attributed to the heated discussions of negative social effects during the Drama Script Seminar. Censors now used this handy phrase to cancel questionable film scripts, which sometimes had already been put into production, such as *Grand Buildings in Their Hands (Gaolou zai tamen shouzhong)*. The censors ordered other filmmakers to make substantial cuts in their finished negatives, as happened in the production of the movie *Maple Leaves (Feng)*. All this, according to the critics, should drive home the lesson that the opinion of one party chief, or the consensus emerging from one particular seminar, should not become the guiding principles of literature and art.

The plea obviously went unheeded. In 1981 Deng Xiaoping, an even more powerful figure than Hu Yaobang, approved another censorship campaign. The target was Bai Hua's film *Bitter Love (Kulian)*, which was allowed to be shown only to controlled audiences for the sole purpose of public criticism. In this film, a counterrevolutionary artist forced into exile during the Cultural Revolution ponders the puzzling question raised by his daughter: "You are deeply in love with your country, but does this country love you?" Although *Bitter Love* depicted an intellectual's tragic experiences during the Cultural Revolution, the defenders of the official ideology believed that this patriotic story reflected hatred for the party and the socialist motherland as a whole.[67] The condemnation of this film script, along with other controversial events around the same time, finally led to the national campaign against "spiritual pollution," which occasioned a new, decisive crossing of the border by artists between the official ideology and the limited space for subversion. Consequently, potential subtexts of literature and art were ruthlessly pulled out from their contexts, analyzed, and exposed as being anti-party in nature. Official critics took to blaming the noxious influence of Western ideology. Thus ended the brief period in the very early days of post-Maoist China when, because the government needed to thoroughly repudiate the Gang of Four, the freedom of expression chronicled here briefly was tolerated. The government and the party ultimately made it clear that the makers of plays and films could never be permitted the initiative to use their work to expose the failings of the present regime and its own system of distribution of power and knowledge.

With all these seemingly immovable barriers to free expression, the residual power of the drama to convey mass sentiments against the status quo remains impressive. Indeed, it has been the concern of this chapter to demonstrate that theater, unlike other literary genres, offers continuing potential for releasing the collective energies of the Chinese people. Theater has given them the opportunity to react subversively to the predominant culture in order to position themselves against the official other, and their laughter, tears, and sorrow have made early post-Maoist theater a meaningful cultural, political experience. For these compelling reasons, we should rescue dramatic studies from the marginal position they have occupied in Chinese literature and remedy the slight they have suffered because of their so-called overt political implications. It is time finally to take seriously the cultural conditions that make non-Western theater relevant for any kind of meaningful discourse on theater practice and theory.

My effort to reconstruct this missing history, however, does not mean that post-Maoist drama did not have its own problems. In social-problem plays and movie scripts of this period, the politics of representation led to a problematic treatment of gender. Reacting against the women warriors and strong-willed party secretaries in model theater, the male authors of these early post-Maoist texts under discussion generally depicted weak women as the victimized other in their construction of a new theater. For instance, Zhou Minghua, Li Xiaozhang's pregnant fiancée in *If I Were for Real*, feels she must work as a maid for the family of a privileged official to win Li a job transfer. After Li has been brought to trial, she has a painful abortion. The woman protagonist of *In the Archives of Society* is raped and tortured and then rejected by her father and her husband. Her story is not even her own; it is narrated by a "father" figure, the upright detective. He uncovers the truth: she was forced into committing criminal acts after having been brutally raped by a high-ranking party official and his son. This discovery leads to the detective's imprisonment as an antiparty official but eventually results in his recognition as a true hero by a later regime. As so often before in theatrical history, women's woes were ingeniously converted into symbolic capital to celebrate the stature and heroic spirit of the ideologically correct fathers in their struggle against the previous regime. Reduced to their traditional roles of oppressed maid, subordinate wife, and abused daughter, women, like their sisters in the Republican period, had to wait for a male revolutionary to lead them out of the bitter sea of misery and longing. The repudiation of the previous Maoist political regime seems to have triggered a total negation of the discourse of the liberated woman. Under these circumstances, self-respect and subject identity for women were rare themes in the theater.

Thus the artist in *Bitter Love* has two women selflessly devoted to him: a poor wife, who has unswervingly supported his revolutionary and artistic career, and a rich woman from abroad, who spends her life longing for an impossible union with him. Meanwhile the artist's greatest love is reserved for his motherland, whose beauty he has dedicated himself to capturing in his artistic works. Even when he is alone and dying in the wilderness as a counterrevolutionary, he is still depicted as being full of unreciprocated longing, "a hopeless love boy" carrying on a "one-sided love affair" with his motherland.[68] To her he pledges his loyalty time and again, even at the point of his death: "It is our motherland! Our blood flows in its rivers, our childhood memories linger in its forests. On the thousand million roads and paths that crisscross the face of this land, we have walked untold millions of miles, suffered immeasurable hardships— but we have won the sacred right to say, 'I love this land, my mother-land.' "[69] In this play, women do not even expect the man they love to love them back as females. In fact, they abet him in his pursuit of his eternal love for the maternal other. In *Bitter Love*, the bodies and physical presence of women are desired and exploited by the male protagonist, who ignores their spiritual and emotional qualities. He empties women of all traits except those he finds useful and transfers those spiritual and emotional qualities onto the utopian and transcendental idea of the new nation and its ideology.

Female subjectivity is negated in a rather different way in *Winter Jasmine*. Presented as a silent, sweet, and passive daughter, Bai Jie achieves the enviable status of model worker, but this status is just another imaginary signifier that attests to male strength: it is won for her by the new party secretary Li Jian, the ousted father who had been dismissed from office during the Cultural Revolution but who has since been restored to power by the new political regime. To demonstrate Li Jian's vigor and wisdom, he is depicted as an eager "college student at the age of sixty," attentively learning the English language from a TV program.[70] At the same time that the tale of his dolorous past and his open-mindedness to foreign culture are narrated to justify his restoration as the powerful father figure, women are "sacrificed [at] the very altar which celebrates the coming of age of manhood and of fatherhood" in a new age.[71] To wit, Li Jian's wife is absent (she was beaten to death during the Cultural Revolution) while he gloriously regains his previous hold in the power structure.[72] Li Honglai, his daughter and companion in suffering during the disastrous years, is politically reeducated by her father. She, however, is deserted by her former boyfriend, who now courts Bai Jie, the new model worker. The mother of the boyfriend is portrayed as just as backward as the would-be daughter-in-law. The two join forces in attempting to persuade him to change his mind about his choice of woman, but to no avail. The triumphant homecoming of the "son" figure[73] results in his exercising his full, unhampered power to choose whatever woman he wants according to his new ideological orientation and that of his father.

Similarly, in *Power versus Law*, both Ding Mu, the persecuted mother, and Ding Hong, the vulnerable daughter, are shown as needing the strength and protection of Luo Fang, the new cultural father, and his symbolic son, Ding Hong's fiancé. Male superiority is evident in all terrains: personality, political vision, and intellectual power. The father and son have it all, whereas the mother and daughter, despite their courage, still have much to learn from the men. Even Luo Danhua, the self-righteous journalist who does not hesitate to speak her mind, must look to her father, Luo Fang, as her role model and would have had no voice or power of her own had not Luo Fang been rehabilitated as the new party secretary.

In the grand, national narrative of early post-Maoist China, women were once again deprived of their subjectivity and their right to speak for themselves. In the model theater of the past, they had at least been *signified* as a powerful other, but now, as part of the process of negating the previous political regime, they lost even this limited power. Dai Jinhua's comments about the predicament of women in fourth-generation films, which began in 1979, also apply to the dilemma of women characters on stage. In contrast to their previous roles as core signifiers for the people, the party, and the mainstream ideology, the roles of early post-Maoist women characters carried "the mission of denouncing events of history, of settling accounts against history," "of inexpressible confession," and "of historical suffering and of sacrificial offering." During this period, women characters were "accused and made to suffer, all for the sake of men's salvation and historical redemption."[74] They now appeared "in history's field of vision only to be exiled once again outside history."[75] A still more extreme form of reductionism is evident in *If I Were for Real*, whose caricatures of two corrupt, snobbish, and selfish women officials and a nagging wife are especially degrading. For the sake of the father, the silenced mother, wife, and daughter were once again relegated to their original functions of victims or vicious influences, as in the traditional, misogynist narratives of the past. The history of women's experience seems to have come full circle: from the cries for "liberating women" from the feudal yoke, first heard in the May Fourth plays, to an expression of an even more profound yearning for a second liberation of the second sex. The return of the cultural father in the new era of early post-Maoist China, however, negated the gains achieved earlier by liberated mothers and daughters of the previous regime. In rejecting theatrical tradition, post-Maoist theater paradoxically inherited the discourse of its Maoist predecessor. In both discourses women are portrayed as either strong or weak, governing or subordinated, and they are either highlighted or belittled according to the role dictated to them by the patriarchy at that historical moment. Border crossing, the subject of this chapter, is therefore limited where women are concerned by playwrights who shunned the critical issues that a sympathetic examination of gender politics generates.

5

Performing Tiananmen

FROM STREET THEATER TO THEATER
OF THE STREET

On October 1, 1949, when Mao Zedong stood up in Tiananmen Square before the eyes of the whole world and declared that the Chinese people had rallied as one proud nation, he, as a leading actor in the political drama unfolding in the young People's Republic, also inaugurated a tradition of Tiananmen street theater. Unlike the usual street theater, which is primarily countercultural, Tiananmen street theater can be understood as both celebrating and challenging the mainstream ideology in various historical and cultural contingencies.[1] It functions as a central stage on which skillful performers and indulgent audiences share an implicit mode of communication and behavior in order to applaud or challenge the status quo.

Besides the studies of Tiananmen as political theater, cultural memory, and collective identities, described in the Introduction, one needs to explore issues such as the ritualistic spectacle of parades and power, as has been done so successfully, for example, by Susan G. Davis in her study of street theater in nineteenth-century Philadelphia. Situating street theater in its appropriate social context, Davis demonstrates that such events as the Washington Centennial do not simply represent consensus and unity, but also usually express the shared strong hopes and beliefs held by members of different social, racial, and gender groups. In the context of a socialist society such as the PRC, however, the overpowering official culture can frequently submerge and appropriate characteristics of various social and ethnic groups, representing them as crucial parts of the parade ritual and then using the cheers and colorful costumes of women, children, and minority groups to affirm the values of the official culture. What both the Chinese and the Philadelphia theaters have in common is what Davis terms the "products of selectivity in transmission" in parades, which, like all other cultural forms, include "denial and forgetting" and "suppression and distortion."[2]

As part of the national public ceremonial culture, for instance, the staging and lighting of the annual National Day parades in Tiananmen Square before the Cultural Revolution were usually marked by fireworks and decorated floats reenacting the economic and political achievements of the young republic in all spheres of life and all parts of the country. Given its superabundant, exhilarating theatrical gestures, overflowing energies, and variety of dramatic modes, the revolutionary state needed a space like that of Tiananmen in which to stage its events full of grand effects and costumed actors and actresses pretending to be Tibetans, Mongolians, Koreans, Uygurs, and so on. This street theater has also incorporated the image of the Western other, in order to demonstrate the superiority of the state culture—thus the mass demonstrations in Tiananmen Square against the US missile threat to Cuba, the assassination of Dr. Martin Luther King Jr., and the US invasion of Vietnam. This kind of large-gesture revolutionary drama usually requires its participants to be competent in the performance codes, hence the familiar scenes of angry crowds shouting fiery slogans to convey their revolutionary zeal and defeat the counter-revolutionaries and imperialists.

The colorful costuming of the masses before the Cultural Revolution contrasts sharply with the dull blue-and-green clothing they wore during the Cultural Revolution, when Tiananmen Square was decorated with "oceans of red flags." The film clips of Mao, reviewing a million Red

Guards, also pose him as the producer of the majestic drama of the great revolution, proudly waving to the magnificent army of the Cultural Revolution from the balcony of the Gate of Tiananmen. These scenes of cheering and confident crowds shedding grateful tears and bursting with enthusiasm for an emerging revolution were later replaced by a street theater of darkness and disguise. The mass memorial to the late Premier Zhou Enlai on April 5, 1976, marks the first public use of street theater in the PRC period for purposes of challenging the state power, whose political surveillance on and off Tiananmen Square was mounted against its own people. At the point when the "people's policemen and women" had to disguise themselves in plain clothes in order to spy on their own people, the performing aspect of Tiananmen theater was transformed.

Taking the street theater of the April Fifth movement in 1976 as its point of departure, this chapter will delineate the intricate connections between the street theater in Tiananmen Square and what I call "the theater of the street," which reflects, on the theater stage, the essence of street theater in real life. By the theater of the street, I mean a particular group of plays that appeared in the early years of post-Maoist China, which accurately depicted factual details of the street theater in and around Tiananmen Square. This discussion of the theater of the street will then be followed by one of another form of street theater, as epitomized by the public burial in the late seventies of former revolutionary leaders and the public trial of the Gang of Four in 1980. It is well to remember that the theatrical presentations of this street theater, known as the anti–Gang of Four plays, are not merely affirmations of the early post-Maoist political regime. They are different forms of political theater that put the entire communist system on trial, as demonstrated in the public trials of Jiang Qing or Madame Mao. At many crucial junctures of the political culture, then, the theater of the street itself became a special form of street theater in which the cultural performers created their own rules for how to act and what to express in their stage lines.

A fruitful way to begin the story of the real-life Tiananmen street theater is to provide a detailed account of its representation in Zong Fuxian's *In a Land of Silence (Yuwu shengchu)*, premiered in 1978. The best example of the theater of the street, this play dramatizes the historic April Fifth movement of 1976, when tens of thousands of people gathered in Tiananmen Square to pay homage to the late Premier Zhou Enlai. As part of a street-theater audience who knew for whom the performance was intended, thousands of Chinese people posted their own poems in Tiananmen Square eulogizing Zhou, thereby acting as a moderate counterinfluence to the ultraleftists in power during the Cultural Revolution. Mindful of the potential danger in such a public display of anger, however, they attributed the poems to groups such as "Workers in the Capital City," "Premier Zhou's Children," "Three Generations of a Family," or "Sons and Daughters of the Chinese People,"[3] thereby assuring themselves of anonymity while simultaneously suggesting a silent people's revolution. It was a lyric uprising of mass proportions against the ruling ideology—a unique literary and political phenomenon unmatched by anything of the kind in any other country. Not surprisingly, the April Fifth movement was soon denounced by Gang of Four supporters as a counterrevolutionary activity. Those who copied, read aloud, or circulated Tiananmen poems were rounded up, beaten, arrested, and, in some cases, executed.

The plot of In a Land of Silence closely follows the events in Tiananmen. The play is described as taking place on "a muggy morning on a stifling day in the early summer of 1976" during "a rainy season in southern China," a setting symbolic of the contemporary political climate.[4] As the play unfolds, Ouyang Ping, a waiter in a small restaurant in suburban Beijing, visits his former girlfriend, He Yun, an officer in the Municipal Public Security Bureau. Almost nine years before, at the beginning of the Cultural Revolution, Ouyang Ping's application for party membership had been rejected because his mother was imprisoned as a traitor. Consequently, Ouyang had been obliged to break off his relationship with He Yun so that his political misfortune would not jeopardize her future. Upon their reunion years later, they are again seemingly destined to be torn apart by the ongoing political drama. Ouyang is a counterrevolutionary activist who has just fled to the city of Shanghai, and He Yun happens to be the police officer in charge of his case. He Yun realizes that the only antirevolutionary crime of which Ouyang has been accused is circulating underground copies of Tiananmen poetry. He Yun also discovers a family secret: her father, He Shifei, betrayed Ouyang's mother nine years ago. He testified to Gang of Four followers that Ouyang's mother became a traitor while in prison in 1947, when she actually had been ministering to an ill He Shifei and taking care of his entire family. At the end of the play, owing to He Shifei's second betrayal, Ouyang is finally arrested by the authorities. Everyone else in the family leaves home to carry out Ouyang's wish that they circulate Tiananmen poetry among the people. Just before the curtain falls, members of the audience see a sudden "flash of lightning" and hear "a tremendous clap of thunder," as the lone, terrified figure of He Shifei faces his own downfall: "Everyone has gone. I'm the only one left behind. How quiet it is" (act 3, 446).[5]

The element of suspense surrounding a family secret and the dramatic conclusion of the play involving a lonely, deserted patriarch remind one of Ibsen's A Doll's House and Cao Yu's Ibseneque plays, such as Thunderstorm (Leiyu). Both Ibsen's plays and Cao's imitations of them represent two major traditions that significantly influenced contemporary Chinese theater. Although In a Land of Silence revolves around the epic events that took place in and around Tiananmen Square, this does not prevent it from strictly observing the so-called Western neoclassical rule of the three unities of time, setting, and plot.[6] With three acts and six characters, the play's action is confined to nine dramatic hours, one setting (the living room of the He family), and a single plot line (the impending arrest of Ouyang Ping). When praised by such accomplished playwrights as Cao Yu and Zhao Xun for having successfully adapted Western formalist features to his requirements, however, Zong Fuxian, the worker/amateur playwright, confessed that he had never studied this particular Western technique.[7] The play had been inspired, he claimed, by his strong desire to eulogize the heroes of the April Fifth movement.[8] Responding to critics who hailed him as the first playwright to have broached a politically forbidden area, Zong confessed that he was actually a very timid person. The only reason he could have written a provocative play was that he did not realize it trod on forbidden ground. He had merely wanted to write about what he felt was a truthful, honest experience in Tiananmen Square—an objective that, he insisted, should be the essence of any playwriting.[9] Zong's statement illustrates the intimate relationship inhering between the large stage of political theater and the small stage of drama, which depend on each other for their existence, even when the connection is not consciously drawn by their willing, and sometimes unwilling, participants.

An immediate hit in early post-Maoist China, In a Land of Silence extended the excitement of the Tiananmen street-theater experience for those who had had the opportunity of participating in the real-life event. Particularly striking and evocative for this audience were the dramatic characters' reading aloud of antiofficial poetry onstage or their retelling of the life-threatening risks that were taken in circulating poetry collections from one city to another. For others who had not been there, hearing the tearful accounts of those bloody scenes helped them to fulfill a fantasy of having joined the fierce battle against the status quo—only at a safer time and remove, when the cruel realities of the political storm were replaced by a leisurely reenactment onstage. Under such circumstances, although staged with a smaller audience and in a more confined space, this theater of the street could, in the long run, by dint of numerous performances, draw a larger crowd than that of the original street-theater scene. Consequently, the theater of the street became, for some, a worthwhile substitute for what was lacking in their lives. Feeling protected in the dark theater space, audience members could choose when and where to laugh, applaud, comment, or simply remain silent as they saw fit, without having to worry about their "correct" cultural performance, unlike at other public occasions, such as political study meetings where they had no choice but to conform. The pleasure of participating in a public event that, paradoxically, guaranteed them a sense of privacy turned the theater into a welcome addition to, or temporary escape from, tedious everyday reality. What otherwise would have been a dangerous adventure in Tiananmen Square could now be imaginatively experienced, if not invented, with little risk.

In a Land of Silence was the only play to have directly re-presented the street theater of the April Fifth movement at the very moment when the post–Gang of Four authorities, headed by Party Chairman Hua Guofeng, still insisted on their own judgments in regard to counterrevolutionary activities. These judgments seemed irreversible at the time, having been rubberstamped by Mao himself, who immediately after this event appointed Hua Guofeng the first vice chairman of the Communist Party Central Committee and the premier of the State Council.[10] Thus, to have reversed these judgments would have amounted to questioning Hua Guofeng's legitimacy and that of his post–Gang of Four regime. The emotional responses to the play, however, demonstrated unequivocally that the Chinese people, although still bound to "a land of silence," demanded commitment to the pursuit of the truth. Hence this work constitutes a remarkable instance of a subversive play by virtue of the human and intellectual exhilaration it evoked. Together with other opposing forces, especially from within the party central power that backed Deng Xiaoping's comeback, this play participated in the national efforts to bring changes in the official ideology. It is indeed a play ahead of its time.

Some crucial dates in 1978 help to explicate this phenomenon. *In a Land of Silence* was premiered in Shanghai in September 1978. Its script was first published in installments in the *Wenhui Newspaper (Wenhui bao*) from October 28 to October 30 of the same year. This publication instantly transformed a theatrical event into a written text, which was read, circulated, and even hand-copied by many people with or without access to the theatrical event. Both in Beijing and in Shanghai, the play was simultaneously staged in more than forty theaters.[11] To meet the extraordinary popular demand for the play, The China Youth Art Theater in Beijing had four casts concurrently performing it in different theaters. Throughout the country, the play was also immediately adapted from its modern drama form to that of traditional theater by numerous local operas. Many of the theaters made special efforts to seek out actors and actresses previously persecuted and prohibited from performing during the Cultural Revolution. Their reappearance onstage in itself became another occasion for street theater: the celebration of their "second liberation." I remember a conversation with Lu Xi, a celebrated actress since the 1930s, who was excited about her first dramatic role since the Cultural Revolution, that of Liu Xiuying, He Shifei's wife almost driven insane by his betrayal in *In a Land of Silence*. Lu Xi put her heart and soul into creating this character on stage, as it helped her to release a sense of frustration and anger over the loss of the prime time of her career during the Cultural Revolution.[12]

The return to the stage of famous artists was paralleled by offstage activities at mass meetings and public memorials, in which distinguished dramatists and performers such as Lao She, Zhou Xinfang, Zheng Junli, and Yan Fengying, who had been hounded to death during the Cultural Revolution, were publicly rehabilitated and their ashes placed in the Babaoshan cemetery, reserved for revolutionary leaders and heroes.[13] At these street theaters, participants observed prescribed codes of performance that included the delivery of speeches by key party figures, who formally presented the official documents that reversed their previous verdicts. Established dramatists and artists enumerated the rehabilitated dramatists' and artists' past artistic achievements. Representatives of family and friends gave accounts of the victimized artists' loyalty to the party and to the late Chairman Mao before and even during their persecutions.

It was not until November 15, 1978, that the Beijing Municipal Committee of the Chinese Communist Party reversed its original verdict concerning the April Fifth movement. At the Third Plenum of the Eleventh Central Committee of the Chinese Communist Party, adjourned on December 22, 1978, it was announced that the April Fifth movement was a "revolutionary mass movement" that "had laid down the ideological foundations for the party's subsequent smashing of the Gang of Four." The Party Central Committee would repudiate all the official documents that had mistakenly denounced the movement as counterrevolutionary activity and would consider honorable all those who had sought to redress the past errors committed by the members of the Gang of Four.[14] This party gathering signified a crucial moment in early post-Maoist China when the national debate on whether or not practical experience was the only criterion for testing the validity of truth occurred. Since Hua Guofeng came to power, he and his allies had taken a hard line against any liberal expressions that might challenge Maoist doctrines. By insisting that only practical experience could prove the truthfulness of any policy or theory, members of Deng Xiaoping's camp discredited Maoist thought as the only "truth." This critical debate became the backdrop of many theatrical discussions. This larger political context was reflected in the critical debates on the plays. Those drama critics who were concerned with the negative effects of subversive plays, for instance, claimed that these unhealthy plays had aroused audiences to doubt Maoist thought. Those supporting these plays argued that they reflected people's actual experiences, and thus represented a more universal experience that questioned certain "truths" so far held as infallible. Both theater practitioners and critics, therefore, contributed to the national effort at "de-Maoization," as signified by the final reversion of the April Fifth movement verdict.

The Chinese authorities now claimed that the suppression of the April Fifth movement had been the worst crime the Gang of Four ever committed. Attributing the blame for mass murder to the Gang of Four seemed woefully belated. More than two years had passed since the Gang had vanished from the political arena. Finally, the people who had been imprisoned because of their actual or supposed participation in the April Fifth movement were finally released and granted the status of anti–Gang of Four heroes and heroines. Significantly, before the official reversal of the verdict, *In a Land of Silence* had already celebrated its own courageous characters. Heightening the paradox was the fact that the dramatizations of the underground circulation of *The Collection of Tiananmen Poetry of 1976* predated an official release and public sale of the book by a state press, with the calligraphy of the book's title that of the "wise leader" Chairman Hua Guofeng, who had become a figurehead due to his adherence to the unpopular Maoist legacy.

The subsequent national celebration of the publication of the *Collection* became another act in the official street theater, which ironically (and conveniently) affirmed the legitimacy of the post–Gang of Four regime. When the high-ranking officials from the Ministry of Culture and the National Workers Union acted out the state ritual of awarding the best-drama prize to the worker-playwright Zong Fuxian,[15] it was the new regime that occupied the center of the spectacle, basking in glory for having ended the autocratic age of the Gang of Four (presumably a real "end" after the "end" of two years before!). The continual crowds of people patiently waiting in line in front of the New China Bookstore to purchase the previously banned poetry constituted another unofficial, or perhaps even antiofficial, piece of street theater that had about it more than a suggestion of mockery at the ruling ideologues, now plainly discredited.

Thus, *In a Land of Silence* played a nuanced political role in the history of early post-Maoist China. When dramatic reality became social reality (and was directly shaped by the latter), social reality could in turn be viewed as a dramatic spectacle in which statesmen at all levels acted out their proper roles in order to consolidate the new aspects of their domination. On the basis of this episode, drama emerges as the embodiment of a publicly subversive force that appeals to mass participation. The influence of theater thus persists in domains other than the textual, the literary, and the theatrical. It can even take on the guise of cultural conspiracy—a tacit or deliberate attempt to release the voices of discontent raised against a certain faction within the political regime. As a direct consequence, the newly embraced public sentiment for individualism in society may very well generate more freedom of expression within theater itself. Accordingly, the repeated performances of *In a Land of Silence* in 1978 led to a theater boom in 1979 during which many popular plays were mounted, such as *Song of Stormy Wind (Dafengge)*, *Winter Jasmine*, *The Future Is Calling on Us (Weilai zai zhaohuan)*, and *Save Her*. This flowering of the theater paradoxically culminated in the national debate over the controversial *If I Were for Real*, a landmark play whose banning resulted, some years later, in the crisis of drama (see the discussion of this event in Chapter 4).[16] The smooth reception of *In a Land of Silence*, however, was undoubtedly attributable to its appearance at a propitious moment, when demands for reversing the verdict of the April Fifth movement were gaining momentum. To some extent, the play was a catalyst for bringing to a head a seething public and political issue. Its anti–Gang of Four story, and the manner in which it was presented, suited the moment both for its audiences and for some officials who temporarily tolerated this subversive play because it could be used to advance their interests. Other plays in the theater-of-the-street genre were not so lucky, as will be seen from considering a play with almost exactly the same theme as *In a Land of Silence*, which was nevertheless rejected by officials for its so-called dangerous political orientation.

There Is a Small Courtyard (You zheyang yige xiaoyuan) dramatizes the bloody events of the April Fifth movement through the tragic stories of three families residing in a small courtyard in the neighborhood of Tiananmen Square.[17] At the beginning of the drama, Aunt Chen is grieving because of the nine-year prison sentence given her daughter for having been a counterrevolutionary ever since the beginning of the Cultural Revolution. To make matters worse, her oldest son, who had been sent down to the countryside, has, during a long-expected homecoming in Beijing, been brutally arrested, publicly denounced, and finally sent back to the wilderness for having participated in the April Fifth movement. Already reeling from her cumulative grief and anger, Aunt Chen loses her eyesight after learning that Dujuan, her nine-year-old granddaughter, who has never seen her imprisoned mother, has been beaten to death in Tiananmen Square. Heartbroken, Aunt Chen cries out, "Why is this sky so dark?" (act 2, 147).[18]

The Du family next door fares no better. An ousted party secretary, the father has recently been criticized again for having supported Deng Xiaoping's rightist line. His wife, a famous guerrilla fighter in the revolutionary war before 1949, was tortured to death at the beginning of the Cultural Revolution. His oldest son, who raised Dujuan alone while waiting for his wife to be released from prison, has recently found Dujuan beaten to death and was himself arrested for having circulated Tiananmen poetry. He is still in prison at the end of the play, almost two years after the arrest of the Gang of Four. Meanwhile, in order to obtain a job in Beijing after college, the second son has allied himself with the authorities by turning in his friends and relatives for participating in the April Fifth movement. For years he has been haunted by what is, for him, the worst nightmare: being forced to return to the remote countryside, where one day's hard labor in the fields could only earn one a wage worth two postage stamps (act 2, 146).[19]

In spite of the second son's faults and weaknesses, he is lamented as a victim of the Cultural Revolution, in which only the ruthless could survive. All these stories strung together give the impression that there is nothing but a "dark sky" over socialist China, one critic not surprisingly complained. He feared that so many tragic, pale people onstage would promote the "current trend of wrong thinking" that questioned the fundamental principles of the party's leadership, the socialist system, the dictatorship of the proletariat, Marxism, Leninism, and Mao Zedong Thought. The play was also faulted for the implicit criticism in its dramatization of the plight of the urban educated youth who, in answering Mao's call of 1967, had settled down in the countryside, where some of them were bullied or sexually harassed by corrupt local officials. *There Is a Small Courtyard* was thus considered a failure because it merely used the April Fifth movement to express grievances and frustrations in regard to other issues.[20]

Yet for millions of urban educated youth still living in the countryside, the play's depiction of their miserable existence painfully reflected their everyday reality. In his provocative book of reportage entitled *The Dream of the Educated Youth of China*, Deng Xian, for example, recorded some of the events that took place on November 10, 1978, three days before the Beijing Municipal Party Committee's reversal of the verdict with regard to the April Fifth movement. In a remote, primitive village of Yunnan Province, an educated young woman from Shanghai died in childbirth owing to the neglect of the local doctor, who had gotten drunk during his night shift. Her lover went berserk on losing both his beloved and his firstborn to such human indifference.[21] Some months earlier, on May 1, 1978, the day when Shanghai citizens were pouring into the streets to celebrate Inter-national Labor Day, another educated youth left Shanghai, where he had been visiting his home briefly before returning to the small village in Yunnan Province. With no prospect of ever coming home again, he committed suicide at the railway tracks.[22] On October 1, 1978, when crowds in Tiananmen Square were celebrating National Day, another educated youth, who originally hailed from the city of Chengdu, hanged himself in a primitive village in Yunnan after his application to go home to take care of his dying father (his mother had also recently died) was coldly rejected by the local authorities.[23] By 1978, ten years after the initiation of the national movement that resettled educated youth in the countryside, more than 10 million of these young people remained in the countryside and saw no hope of returning to their hometowns. At a time when the nation was witnessing reversals of numerous verdicts imposed during the Cultural Revolution, the educated youth had reason to demand a similar reversal of their fate. In the ensuing years, they staged their own antiofficial street theater in the form of labor strikes in the villages, hunger strikes on railway tracks, and street demonstrations and sit-ins in Tiananmen Square. The crowning event was a mass petition meeting in Yunnan, during which ten thousand people kneeled down before the party representative from Beijing to beg the Party Central Committee to listen to their grievances. A handful of heroes and heroines, as well as traitors who caved in to pressure and temptations from the authorities, formed an inevitable part of this street theater.

The partial representation of these sensitive issues in *There Is a Small Courtyard* tested the tolerance of the officials, who felt then, in the words of Party Chairman Hua Guofeng, that the populace should still obey whatever Chairman Mao had said and ensure the continuation of whatever he had decided. It was, of course, precisely on this issue that Hua was under political attack, which eventully resulted in his ousting as party chief. By dramatizing the sorrows and dilemmas of educated youth in the countryside, the play touched on a facet of de-Maoization still too fresh and new to be openly accepted by the official censors. Thus, even defenders of the play had to argue that, although reflective of educated youth's tribulations in the countryside, these experiences did not form part of the main plot. Of the play's fourteen characters, they pointed out, only three were educated youth. Most important, the defenders further stressed, their stories should be interpreted as an exposure of the Gang of Four's sabotage of the educated youth movement, not as a criticism directed against the movement itself.[24] Typically (for contemporary Chinese politics), members of the previous regime were once again scapegoated to attest to the correctness of the policies of the current one.

However, what might truly have irritated the critics—but could not be admitted to be the real issue—was the play's eyewitness account of the innocent crowds being brutalized, the cruel clubbing, and, most of all, the children murdered in Tiananmen Square on April 5, 1976. More provocative than *In a Land of Silence*, which foregrounds what happened away from Tiananmen after the event, *There Is a Small Courtyard* plunges the audience into the midst of the events, using such visual and audio effects as white wreaths and flowers; the solemn singing of "The Internationale"; the anguished voices and weeping of the people; and the sound of the cleaning trucks that came around at midnight to attempt to wipe out the bloodstains on the ground, the tangible evidence of the carnage. Accounts of these events had already been circulating widely among the people, but the authorities repeatedly dismissed them as mere rumors spread by enemies of the people to defile the socialist system. Indeed, the play could be categorized as a reportage drama, which had, for the first time, disclosed the bloody truth about Tiananmen to the public, discrediting the distorted reporting by the official press. Moreover, it urged audiences to look beyond the particulars of individual events to their context and background, and to be critical of their historical, social, and cultural roots.

The emotional appeal of *There Is a Small Courtyard* is reinforced by its frequent allusions to other plays, which the playwright achieved through his character Madman Zheng (Zheng Jiaxin). Zheng is described as a formerly famous actor and director whose sanity finally had given way before the onslaught of brutal persecutions at the beginning of the Cultural Revolution. Throughout the play Madman Zheng moves around in his delirious world, replaying the dramatic roles that won him national recognition in the 1950s. The first that he repeatedly relives is the title role in Tian Han's *Guan Hanqing*, a play that encompasses an inner and an outer play, or a play within a play. The inner play, *Injustice to Dou'e (Dou'e yuan),*[25] was supposedly written by Guan Hanqing, the thirteenth-century Yuan dynasty playwright who depicted an innocent woman wrongly accused and executed, the victim of a false witness and a corrupt officer. The outer play, Tian Han's *Guan Hanqing*, relates how Guan Hanqing in the thirteenth century wrote his play *Injustice to Dou'e* as a criticism of the corruption of his own times, and how, as a consequence, he was imprisoned and exiled by enforcers of the ruling ideology. Tian's outer play also dramatizes the emotional response to the inner play on the part of Guan's contemporary audiences, some of whom were moved to cry out, "Death to the people's enemy!" during its performances. Confronted with the authorities' threat to ban the play, however, Guan Hanqing refused to make changes and was finally imprisoned and forced into exile. Both the inner and outer plays of *Guan Hanqing* are, of course, not just stories about a particular dramatist. They address the issues of the subversive nature of playwriting, censorship, and theater in general, with direct relevance to the numerous ways in which artistic discourse was permitted, regulated, and used by different political factors.[26]

In *There Is a Small Courtyard*, Tian Han's *Guan Hanqing* is used by Madman Zheng as a commentary on the insane world around him. In act 1, for example, when Dujuan delightedly shows her father a letter from her mother—whom she has never seen in her life—everyone on stage is in tears, for they know that the letter was written by her father in order to hide the fact of her mother's imprisonment from her. The agonizing nature of the scene is heightened by Madman Zheng's appearance and his recital, in his rich, solemn actor's voice, of Guan Hanqing's stage directions:

> ZHENG'S VOICE: The capital city of Cambaluc (present-day Peking), during the reign of Kublai Kahn, in the year A.D. 1281. A small tavern on the corner of a street close to the city gate. The street is filled by a great multitude of people watching the procession of an execution squad. Amid a flourish of trumpets, a Mongolian execution supervisor gallops past. Next come attendants beating bamboo clappers and shouting: "Pedestrians, make way, make way!" (act 1, 137)[27]

In the same way that people of contemporary China had just witnessed the murdering of innocent people in Tiananmen Square, so a great multitude of people in imperial China gathered to watch the "procession of an execution squad," whose dramatic entry, signaled by trumpets and galloping horses, reminded the crowds of the importance of such an event. The execution scene of the innocent Dou'e, where Guan Hanqing was inspired to write his thirteenth-century play, evokes the situation of Dujuan's imprisoned mother; it also foreshadows the death of Dujuan, the arrest of her father in 1976, and the murder in Tiananmen Square, to be recounted by the eyewitnesses in the course of *There Is a Small Courtyard*. And, extending beyond the context of the play, this execution scene also symbolizes the fate of dramatists throughout history, both in feudal old China and in socialist new China.

Ironically, in the late 1950s and early 1960s Tian Han's *Guan Hanqing* was hailed as one of the best socialist dramas because of its vivid exposure of a dark, feudal China. However, during the Cultural Revolution, Tian Han was accused of drawing on historical figures and legends to attack the party's policies on literature and art. The exile of Guan Hanqing, it was asserted, seemed to parallel too neatly the banishing of numerous PRC writers in the 1950s for their participation in the anti-rightist movement. In a denouement that would have seemed (outside of China) more the stuff of drama than real life, Tian Han, the foremost leftist writer before 1949 and a widely acclaimed playwright and critic after 1949, was tortured to death in prison in 1967. The execution scene from Tian Han's inner play in *There Is a Small Courtyard* thus underscores the ordeals of dramatists from different eras: the exile of Guan Hanqing in the thirteenth century and the death of Tian Han and the torture of Madman Zheng during the Cultural Revolution. The resonances are multiplied by having a Yuan play *(Injustice to Dou'e)* cast within a postliberation play *(Guan Hanqing)*, within a post–Cultural Revolutionary play *(There Is a Small Courtyard)*, all of which are simultaneously transmitted through a character who continually relives the multiple roles of playwright, actor, director, and—most tellingly—madman. All these elements point to the chaotic aspects of the Cultural Revolution and to the paradoxes inherent in the ruling ideology of early post-Maoist China. Under these circumstances, the logic activating Madman Zheng becomes clear. He identifies with Guan Hanqing, an intellectual of earlier times whose desire and efforts to rescue innocent people were frustrated by his own impotence. Hence the seemingly irrelevant lines that Madman Zheng recalls from the dramatic character he used to play in *Guang Hanqing* are actually juxtaposed to the matter in Tian Han's play: "And I? All I can do is to stand behind the crowd with folded arms and look on, restraining my indignation. This is me, the proud Guan Hanqing. How I despise myself" (act 1, line 137, *There Is a Small Courtyard*).[28] The dramatic device of Madman Zheng links a post-Maoist play to other canonical texts, both from the traditional operatic theater and from the modern spoken drama. Although Madman Zheng is himself an outsider in relation to ongoing events, his truth-saying and judicious comments highlight the harsh reality of the world around him. At given moments, Madman Zheng even emerges from his insanity. In act 2, for instance, as crowds gather in Tiananmen to commemorate Zhou Enlai, Madman Zheng describes what is happening on this April 5, 1976, as if he were directing a stage rehearsal of his own play, or his own street theater:

> ZHENG: Look! Grandmas have come with their granddaughters. The handicapped have come in wheelchairs. Soldiers from the Second Artillery Headquarters are guarding with their guns the wreaths and flowers presented to the late Premier Zhou. Look, here comes another group. . . . Look, Shulian *(Seizing the arms of his wife, facing the audience)*: The traffic has already been cut off on both ends of Chang'an Street. Workers from Radio Factory, from Shuguang Electrical Machinery Plant. . . . More than three thousand workers are marching toward us! People's policemen are giving them the green light all the way through. Old revolutionaries are saluting them with deep respect *(Tears streaming down his cheeks)*. . . . (act 2, 143–143)

The subtext is transparent: even someone who usually seems to be out of touch with reality can sense the will of the people. But, like Shakespeare's

King Lear, Madman Zheng can perceive and speak the truth only after forfeiting his sanity.

Zheng's lucidity is short-lived, however. The audience learns that his condition had deteriorated after Dujuan died in Tiananmen Square. Grief-stricken, Madman Zheng periodically confuses Dujuan with Ding Xiao-niu, a nine-year-old girl in Lao She's play, *Dragon Beard Ditch (Long-xugou)*. First premiered in 1951 by the Beijing People's Art Theater, *Dragon Beard Ditch* was regarded as one of Lao She's best plays. Indeed, it was commonly held in dramatic circles that only two genuinely good dramas came out of the PRC: *Dragon Beard Ditch* and *Teahouse*, both written by Lao She in the 1950s. The playwright said he was profoundly touched by the remaking of *Dragon Beard Ditch* by the Beijing Municipal People's Government soon after the liberation of Beijing.[29] This play dramatized the miserable life around Dragon Beard Ditch, the stinking slum street that for generations had trapped poor people in the old society. This noto-rious ditch, the setting for act 1, indeed symbolizes the old society:

> The Ditch is full of muddy, slimy water, mixed with rubbish, rags, dead cats, dead dogs and now and then dead children. The waste water from the nearby tannery and dyeworks flows into it and accumulations of nightsoil collect there to putrefy. The water in the Ditch is of various shades of red and green, and its stench makes people [quite far away feel sick]. Hence the district has earned the name of "Stinking Ditch Bank." On the two banks, closely packed together, there live labourers, handicraft workers—the multifarious toiling poor. Day in and day out, all the year round and all their lives, they struggle in this filthy environment (act 1, 7).[30]

As the play shows, it was not until the advent of the new society that the people's government was able to clear the smelly ditch and in its place build a wide road, thereby realizing the dreams of the toiling people liv-ing there. Lao She's *Dragon Beard Ditch* is thus an early example of the-ater of the street inspired by street theater.

Of more than incidental interest is the fact that Madman Zheng is depicted in *There Is a Small Courtyard* as having played a key role in Lao She's *Dragon Beard Ditch*. He performed as Madman Cheng, a folk artist who lost his sanity after being beaten by a gangster who forbade him to perform. In this way the playwright sets two madmen from two different texts to interacting with each other—Madman Zheng from the post-Maoist play *There Is a Small Courtyard* constantly relives his Madman

Cheng role from Lao She's 1950s play, which recalls for him the peak of his dramatic career. It is safe to interpret the character of Madman Cheng as having been intended by Lao She to illustrate the bitterness of the pre-1949 society, whose injustices drove men to retreat into madness; the character of Madman Zheng serves as an equally bitter satire of Maoist society, which similarly caused many honest, talented people to become insane. Madman Cheng in Lao She's *Dragon Beard Ditch* can always count on Xiaoniu, the nine-year-old girl from next door who understands him, helps him, and listens to his folk art performance. After Xiaoniu's drowning in Dragon Beard Ditch, Madman Cheng continues to talk to her as if she were still with him, oblivious to the fact that the mere mention of her name deeply saddens her mother.

After Dujuan's death In *There Is a Small Courtyard*, Madman Zheng takes to repeatedly chanting Madman Cheng's lines in memory of Xiaoniu, as if he were still living in the 1950s. In doing so, he continues to confuse the two girls' names. Dujuan from the present and Xiaoniu from his past are combined into one person, devoured by unreasonable societies. However, Madman Zheng leaves out the second part of his original lines in *Dragon Beard Ditch*, the part in which Madman Cheng celebrated Beijing after liberation:

Our city is freed, our sadness gone,
Our streets are resounding with dance and song.
But you[,] little friend, in my dreams I see;
You don't sing or dance, you don't answer me.[31]

These lines were omitted because the streets that resounded "with dance and song" right after 1949 were no longer the people's streets to celebrate. They were now stained with blood, tears, and broken dreams. How could one praise a new Beijing that persecuted its best dramatist? Some in the audience of *There Is a Small Courtyard* would remember that Lao She had committed suicide during the Cultural Revolution, a tragedy that seemed to echo the fate of Chinese artists such as Madman Cheng before liberation. Madman Cheng could at least gain a new lease on life in socialist China, but during the Cultural Revolution Lao She had to reject the new China that he had lauded in the previous decade and disown the earlier celebration of his 1950s plays. By reviving Lao She's texts and characters, *There Is A Small Courtyard* set a powerful subtext against the current reality of the new China, which was no improvement over its predecessors.

The awful, absurd nature of Lao She's death is brought home all the more when one remembers that *Dragon Beard Ditch* was warmly received by tens of thousands of people in 1951 and had "played a significant role in consolidating the newly founded people's government and in illustrating the superiority of the new socialist system." This play alone earned Lao She the title of "people's artist" from the people's government in Beijing.[32] Moreover, Lao She wrote a series of Beijing-flavored plays, a subgenre further developed in several post-Maoist plays, such as Su Shuyang's *Neighbors (Zuoling youshe)* and He Jiping's *The World's Top Restaurant (Tianxia diyilou)*. Paradoxically, another play partially belonging to this subgenre is Su Shuyang's *Taiping Lake (Taipinghu)*, which dramatized Lao She's 1966 drowning in Taiping Lake—a suicide in protest against another piece of street theater, the infamous, humiliating mass criticism of Beijing artists and physical torture by the Red Guards.

Written in 1986, on the occasion of the twentieth anniversary of Lao She's death, *Taiping Lake* depicts Lao She's last day, August 24, 1966. After having been brutally beaten by the Red Guards, Lao She wanders around Taiping Lake for a day and a night, meditating on the paradoxes of his past devotion to the party and the present anti-party charges against him. Puzzled, he engages in conversation with the living—people who still fondly remember his *Dragon Beard Ditch* and *Teahouse*—and also with the dead: his dramatic characters, such as Madman Cheng in *Dragon Beard Ditch* and Wang Lifa in *Teahouse*, the teahouse owner who committed suicide to protest the miserable old society.[33] In the course of *Taiping Lake*, scenes from both *Dragon Beard Ditch* and *Teahouse* are restaged to underscore the dramatic ironies evoked by the playwright's death in relation to the fate of his dramatic characters. When Madman Cheng from Lao She's *Dragon Beard Ditch* says, for instance, that he can only hide, as he is defenseless against others' brutality, Lao She interrupts: "Madman Cheng, you should not hide! It is not right for them to beat an honest man like you." But Madman Cheng insists that there is nothing he can do, because this is the way his character has been written for him. Lao She then promises to change his play so that the honest man will not be beaten for nothing![34]

This statement reflects Lao She's changed perspective after his persecution during the Cultural Revolution. In actuality, however, he is now powerless to change his dramatic characters, who have become monuments to a past history. And just as is it too late to rewrite his play, so it is too late to reverse that part of history in which Lao She had participated, to unknowingly maintain its facade of a happy socialist society. Lao She's plight evokes the pathos of an entire generation of Chinese intellectuals. In the words of Lao She in *Taiping Lake*, the Chinese intellectual typically "did not dare to forget to reform himself ideologically even while asleep." Lao She committed suicide in the Taiping Lake—in his own mind, the only piece of land that was still clean in China by 1966. His act serves as a satirical comment on Madman Cheng's frequently quoted prophecy in *Dragon Beard Ditch*: "There'll come a day when the Ditch won't stink, / and the water will be sweet, / Then our land will be great, the people happy, / and the world at peace."[35] The clean water of Taiping Lake thus contrasts sharply with the stinking water of Dragon Beard Ditch: Xiaoniu was at least devoured by the natural forces of a flood, but it was a political storm initiated by one man's will that drowned Lao She, her creator.

A close reading can uncover many additional political and dramatic parallels. For instance, some in the audience at *There Is a Small Courtyard* would have known that both *Guan Hanqing* and *Dragon Beard Ditch* were directed by Jiao Juyin, one of the most influential directors in the PRC. Anyone familiar with the theater scene would have realized that Madman Zheng's earlier career as a director in *There Is a Small Courtyard* alluded to Jiao Juyin, who was also persecuted during the Cultural Revolution. (When he finally died of lung cancer in 1974, Jiao Juyin was still labeled a counterrevolutionary.)[36] The combined references to Lao She and Jiao Juyin suggest, by extension, the artistic achievements of the Beijing People's Art Theater, with which both were professionally affiliated. Their lifelong devotion to this theater was responsible for the creation of its internationally known repertory, most notably including *Guan Hanqing*, *Dragon Beard Ditch*, *Peking Man (Beijing ren)*,[37] and *The Rickshaw Boy (Luotuo Xiangzi)*,[38] in all of which Madman Zheng had played the protagonist before the Cultural Revolution.[39]

Given this background, *There Is a Small Courtyard* can be read as a history of at least one theater and several generations of dramatists, and, above all, as an episode in Chinese drama that challenges the PRC founding fathers' values and actions. It also reminds one of the street theaters in the small courtyard where the artists and families of the Beijing People's Art Theater lived for decades, where many happy days were spent in the early days of the People's Republic, and where much sorrow was known during the anti-rightist movement and the Cultural Revolution. It was possible to witness similar stories in other small courtyards, such the one occupied by the members of the China Children's Art Theater, which produced *There Is a Small Courtyard* on the Beijing stage. It was undoubtedly the power of the play, both as theatrical performance and as theater of the street, that kept the officials quiescent once it had been presented to more than forty full houses and had invariably evoked warm responses from the audiences, even though these performances were not open to the public and were limited to invited guests only. When the critics finally did speak out, they focused their debate on the play's negative social effects.

Yet the playwright could not be accused of fabrication. Having grown up in a typical Beijing *tazayuanr*, or courtyard occupied by many households, in the neighborhood of Dragon Beard Ditch (the same street that Lao She depicted in his play), Li Longyun, like many young members of his generation, was sent to work on a farm for many years in the northeast wilderness.[40] His play therefore depicts the street dramas of many small courtyards with which he was intimately acquainted. His predecessor, Lao She, could never have imagined these stories when he described his authorial intentions for *Dragon Beard Ditch*: "These people, old and young, male and female, lived in the courtyard, and everything happened in the courtyard, which was like a little monument standing on the bank of the Ditch, exposing its evils" in the old society before liberation.[41]

Li Longyun evidently sought to criticize the new, rather than the old, society in his second play, *Small Well Lane* (*Xiaojing Hutong*, 1981). Very much in the tradition of Lao She's Beijing-flavored-style plays such as *Teahouse*, which depicts fifty characters from different sectors of old Beijing, this work, which encompasses the life stories of five households, contains thirteen different story lines and forty-seven old Beijing characters, including peddlers, laborers, cart drivers, maids, apprentices, fortune-tellers, prostitutes, policemen, small business owners, housewives, and concubines. Each of the five acts treats crucial events in PRC history or significant acts of street theater in the political arena. In act 1 (1949), poor people anxiously wait for Communist troops to liberate Beijing. In act 2 (1958), the radical Great Leap Forward movement arouses enthusiasm but also creates confusion and chaos among residents. In act 3 (1966), residents-turned-Red Guards search the houses of the enemies of the people, thereby further dividing their old neighbors into opposite political camps. In act 4 (1976), good and honest residents come into conflict with other residents, who are now followers of the Gang of Four. In act 5 (1980), the wrongful verdicts meted out to the play's characters are reversed, participants in the April Fifth movement are released from prison, and educated youth finally return home from the countryside. The play ends on a nostalgic note: the Small Well Lane will soon be demolished to make room for a new Beijing development project. If only, one is asked to imagine, there had lived on this special street a storyteller[42] who could have preserved for future generations (and performances) the stories of the street's inhabitants, their aspirations and tears, he might have erected a monument to the traumatic history of the PRC. Although the play's happy ending seems to celebrate the corrective power of the Communist system, the image of the oral story-teller simultaneously highlights the subversive power of oral history buried in the official written history of modern China, which transmits "truths" only from the point of view of the status quo.

To accurately depict in act 1 the street characters of Beijing, Li Long-yun read more than sixty volumes of Beijing historical records. He also delved into Ming and Qing dynasty archives, where he discovered more than ten references to the street names mentioned in the legends of "Small Well" in old Beijing.[43] Despite his faithfulness to the authentic life stories of the common people, Li Longyun at times betrayed male chauvinism, as seen in his main negative character, "Little Wife" (Xiao xifu), the vicious follower of the Gang of Four. Known only as someone's wife, and as being of "little" or shallow mind, Little Wife reminds one of the notorious Jiang Qing, considered responsible for persecuting countless innocent people. This view was popular in the early days of post-Maoist China, when Mao was still too powerful to be associated with the national tragedy of the Cultural Revolution.

As a way of further exploring this gender bias and how it was reflected in the unfolding events of street theater and the theater of the street, in the second part of this chapter I will briefly discuss a series of trial dramas that depict, directly and indirectly, Jiang Qing as the archenemy of the people. As will be seen, Jiang Qing herself tried to confute this characterization during her public trial of 1981, the site of her last performance as both a woman leader and a former actress. This image of Jiang is reflected in one of the later representations of her, in Sha Yexin's *Jiang Qing and Her Husbands (Jiang Qing he tade zhangfumen)*, which depicts her as what Tania Modleski would call "a hysterical woman, caught between two equally alienating alternatives: either identifying with the man or being an object of his desire." [44] My ultimate aim is, on the one hand, to reveal and deconstruct the familiar cultural and ideological image of Jiang Qing as the vicious public woman portrayed by the patriarchal state in a series of street-theater events. These public portrayals of Jiang are remarkable for the supposedly female traits on which they conveniently drew, such as manipulativeness and malice. On the other hand, it is equally remarkable to observe Jiang's own manipulation of Chinese feminism, which resulted in her distorted and exaggerated version of Chinese official feminism. Accordingly, I will trace her abuse of feminism from the time when she first performed the role of Nora in Ibsen's *A Doll's House* in the 1930s.

From very early on in her acting career Jiang Qing was influenced and formed by the character Nora, an imaginary, liberated other in the guise of a Western woman. One could imagine Jiang always living the life, both in public and private, of an unhappy doll imprisoned by men. It is thus possible that she envisioned herself as beset by political and personal enemies of all stripes as she navigated through her dramatic and fictional world, which required that she struggle endlessly, and fruitlessly, against numerous others. In trying to elucidate Jiang Qing's formation of her own dramatic world, I do not mean to present a more "truthful" personal history of her than that contained in the official account and in biographies popular in the 1990s. Rather, I am interested in revealing the ideological and political discourses that composed the image of the public woman, especially the one with a vital acting career both on- and offstage. Both Jiang's abuse of feminism and the equally powerful abuse of her public image perpetrated by male-dominated officialdom contributed to the perception of her as a vicious actress who had a lasting impact on the history of political theater as well as that of contemporary Chinese drama. A study of street theater and the theater of the street in early post-Maoist China would not be complete without an exploration of the complex and problematic relationships among women, theater, revolution, and history writing.

As Mao's third wife and a key personage during the Cultural Revolution, Jiang Qing has always been closely connected with the political events of Cultural Revolutionary China. It is commonly held, for instance, that Jiang played a significant role in the making of the Cultural Revolution. She is said to have used her expertise in theater to convince Mao of the hidden existence within the party of a bourgeois counterrevolutionary headquarters in literature and art directed against him. This belief led to a national campaign against the Peking Opera *Hai Rui Dismissed from Office*, premiered in 1960, which presumably alluded to Mao's dismissal of Peng Dehuai, a top party leader who had openly voiced concerns about

Mao's radical policies during the Great Leap Forward in the 1950s. The campaign mounted against this opera triggered the Cultural Revolution. In the early stages of the Cultural Revolution, Jiang's achievements in creating revolutionary model plays were said to have established her credentials as banner-holder (*qishou*) of the great proletarian Cultural Revolution in its combat against feudal, bourgeois, and revisionist *(feng-zi-xiu)* cultures.

In 1974, however, when the political campaign against the Lin Biao anti-party clique and its so-called cultural roots in Confucian ideology was going nowhere, Jiang Qing was described as having sparked yet another crusade. This one was leveled against a Shaanxi opera *(jinju)* entitled *Three Visits to Taofeng Village (Sanshang Taofeng)*, premiered in 1972, on the basis of a mere suspicion that Taofeng village referred to Taoyuan village, where Wang Guangmei, the wife of Liu Shaoqi, the former state president and central target of the Cultural Revolution, had previously stayed. The opera was thus interpreted as a malicious attempt to reverse the verdict handed to Liu Shaoqi in order to deny the fruits of the Cultural Revolution. Subsequently, the Shaanxi Opera Troupe (Shaanxi jinjutuan) was ordered to come to Beijing and perform the opera for public criticism. Deeply humiliated, the leading actress fainted onstage in the middle of the performance. This act of political theater within a staged drama followed the suicide of a drama critic who had praised the artistic achievement of the Shaanxi opera in comparison to what he called "the flat characters" of model theater.[45]

The ensuing street theater evident in the national campaign against this opera culminated in mass criticism meetings, first at the Beijing Exhibition Hall and then at the Beijing Film Studio. Three thousand people participated,[46] many of them members of the model troupes *(yangbantuan)* that had performed model plays under the guidance of Jiang. As professional actors and actresses, they were particularly skillful in articulating their outrage against this opera and, with tears streaming down their faces, in expressing their ardent love for Comrade Jiang Qing.[47] Of course, underlying this street theater was another political drama: Jiang's long-standing public attempt to oust Premier Zhou as the ultimate behind-the-scenes villain, according to the post-Maoist official account. As mass criticism escalated, the Shaanxi Opera Troupe was ordered to come to Beijing again to perform the model play *Song of the Dragon River*, with Jiang Qing as a special guest. At this performance, Jiang rudely interrupted the proceedings, ordering that the name of the female lead be changed from "Party Secretary Jiang" to "Comrade Jiang." In one gesture, she transformed the model role into the real-life supermodel heroine—herself.[48] The melodrama did not end until after another showdown with Xie Zhenhua, the first secretary of the Party Committee of Shaanxi Province, who was subjected to mass criticism for sixty days, with hundreds of thousands of innocent people being accused and criticized in the process. Xie was dismissed from office (he was rehabilitated only after the arrest of the Gang of Four) for the single crime of not having caught in time an anti-party opera.[49] It was Mao, according to the official history, who finally ended this absurd farce after Xie wrote to him for help.[50] This incident served as just one example of a familiar pattern in which "wise" Mao, in a timely fashion, corrected his wife's mistakes and rescued the country.

As the Cultural Revolution ended, the public image of Jiang Qing became increasingly negative. After the death of Zhou Enlai, when important state leaders offered condolences to his widow, Jiang became an object of hatred among the millions watching the memorial ceremonies on television. It was reported that a soldier in Shenyang grew so angry that he threw a chair at the TV set, and that a crowd in Guangzhou began to shout in unison, "Beat her up!" because she refused to take off her cap. The cap and the crimson blouse that Jiang wore on this occasion were taken as a symbolic costume that she had deliberately chosen for the purpose of making a recognizable, dramatic statement in the political power struggle.[51] In a similar dramatic performance, after Mao's death, as a million people gathered at Tiananmen Square like "a vast mute chorus for the Peking opera of the funeral," Jiang Qing acted her proper role as Mao's student and comrade-in-arms (the descriptive terms she used in her wreath inscription), walking on the stage slowly "like a lofty galleon."[52]

This proper public performance, however, did not spare Jiang from suffering the brunt of the dead leaders' body politics. For a public obsessed with the physical preservation of previous revolutionary leaders, Zhou Enlai emerged as its most popular hero because of his last wish that his ashes be scattered over the oceans, rivers, and mountains of his beloved motherland. This selfless desire to be among his own people even after his death was implicitly contrasted with the national effort to solicit designs for Mao's mausoleum so as to preserve his dead body for future generations. The symbolic "dismemberment" of Zhou's body paradoxically lent him a more majestic aura, as he could, as the popular saying went at the time, still live in one's heart, whereas Mao's memorial highlighted the decay of the body, only preventable through modern science and technology. The national celebration of the mausoleum's completion thus became another piece of official street theater, and the entombment of the previous regime's leaders was used to confirm the birth of the current regime as a legitimate successor.

The most readily seized-upon cause of this process proved to be Jiang Qing, with her living body and "evil" mind. As in the case of Marie-Antoinette, who was executed after a trial that, according to Peter Brooks, linked her crimes against the republic in the French Revolution with her "sexual immorality,"[53] the sexual relations of Jiang with her followers began to surface in popular tales as well as in some public accounts of the Cultural Revolution. Allusions to her sexual liaisons while she pursued her acting career in prerevolutionary days and to her involvement with other men during the Cultural Revolution, especially her charming companions in the performing-art circles who had helped to create model theater, were essential components of the new portrayal of Jiang as a traitor, a conspirator, and a usurper of the party's central power.[54] A woman's body was thus transformed from the desexualized comrade-in-arms of the great leader to a sexual body, re-created and rejected by a new political regime. As a consequence, Jiang's incarcerated body was celebrated at the same time as was the completion of Mao's new mausoleum, another revolutionary monument erected in Tiananmen Square. It would appear, then, that in the national consciousness the laying to permanent rest in his mausoleum of one great man signaled the punishment of his woman for being like Yang Guefei (719–756), whose feminine charm had hopelessly turned the head of an emperor, thus shattering the Tang dynasty.[55] The immortal Mao canceled out "the very idea of a 'Mrs. Mao,'"[56] who was now depicted in cartoons as a witch, with "skeletal bones" and "a siren's tail," "checking her Western costume before a stage performance."[57]

The abuse of one woman's body was juxtaposed to representations of the bodies of other women, whose vulnerability served to point out the vicious power of Jiang Qing. Zhang Zhixin, the anti–Gang of Four heroine, whose throat was cut before her execution to prevent her from shouting counterrevolutionary slogans, was elegized in poetry and drama as a tender little flower, broken by the brutality of a truthless society. Ostensibly the only woman in an entire nation who dared to resist a totalitarian regime at the cost of her marriage, child, and even her own life, Zhang Zhixin was extolled to atone for the shameful past of the majority of the Chinese people who were not able to stand up against the status quo. At least three plays celebrated her heroic life, as seen in a modern drama, a Shanghai opera *(huju)*, and a *yueju* opera, which was popular in Shanghai, Zhejiang, and Jiangsu Provinces. While one woman was conceived to be the brave and beautiful model capable of purging the national guilt, the other was pilloried as the source of evil.

The two figures of Zhang and Jiang were contrasted in the play *The Tempest in the Divine Land (Shenzhou fenglei)*, premiered in 1979.[58] Set in 1970s China, this play by Zhao Huan and Jin Jingmai centers on a pair of lovers who are imprisoned and tortured for exposing Jiang Qing and the Lin Biao anti-party cliques. In an echo of Zhang Zhixin's story, Bai Yubing, the heroine of the play, loses her sight and hearing after being severely beaten in prison. She is, however, united with her lover at the end in Tiananmen Square, where long-suffering, now jubilant crowds are parading to celebrate the defeat of the Gang of Four. However, in contrast to the real-life tragedy of Zhang Zhixin, Bai Yubing has the good fortune to be rescued by the new political regime, hailed in the play as her grand savior. Interlaced in the play, to enhance its verisimilitude, are narrated events of the Cultural Revolution, from the incident of September 13, 1971, when Lin Biao, Mao's chosen successor, died while fleeing to the Soviet Union, to October 1976, when the whole nation rejoiced over the capture of the Gang of Four. The national proclivity for rewriting political history was illustrated in this early post-Maoist play, which posited that 1976 marked the beginning of a new era and a new liberation unlike anything the Chinese people had seen since the 1949 Communist liberation. Recent history was viewed as a bitter sea of misery under a mad reign by the Gang of Four, headed by a proud, vicious woman. It was thus exhilarating for many to see Jiang Qing presented onstage as a malicious, pretentious, cruel, arrogant, bossy, moody, and suspicious woman, yet one fully aware of her physical charm.

Weng Ru, the actress who portrayed Jiang Qing, said that she wanted to show the real Jiang—namely, "a rotten movie star, a counterrevolutionary," "a female hooligan," and, above all, "a conspirator" whose dream was to be crowned as the contemporary empress.[59] Officials proclaimed themselves pleased with the recounting of the most notorious crimes committed by Jiang Qing and her followers. In act 5, for instance, Jiang visits Zhou Enlai (whom she characterizes as the "biggest Confucius of our times") in the hospital, intending to disrupt his recovery from surgery. Although Zhou Enlai is depicted as ill onstage, the critics asserted that his still glorious image inspired respect for him both as a statesman and as a national leader who understood the power of theater in contemporary China. Jin Shan, a prominent actor once imprisoned by Jiang Qing (who she feared might reveal incidents of her loose life during the 1930s), was reported as saying: "It was not until after I'd watched the performance of this play that I finally understood why during his lifetime the late premier Zhou always loved modern drama and viewed it as one of the most significant artistic genres of all." [60] This play offered another case, so prevalent in Chinese drama, of the charisma of a national father figure (Zhou Enlai) being glorified by an "emperor" of Chinese spoken drama (Jin Shan)[61] partly through the display onstage of the distasteful body of a vicious woman. Political and dramatic strategies were thus brought to bear in the patriarchal portrayal of a glaring gender difference.

While members of the Gang of Four were actual characters in *The Tempest in the Divine Land,* other plays focused on street theaters related to them. *Eventful Years (Zhengrong suiyue),* for instance, is a reportage drama that relates the intense power struggle between the Gang of Four and their political opponents.[62] Also set in autumn of 1979, the play delineates the failed attempts by the Gang's followers to sabotage the construction of a plant approved by the late premier Zhou as a key project for the Four Modernizations. Interspersed throughout this plot are political events such as Beijing citizens lining up along Chang'an Street to bid farewell to the cortege bearing Premier Zhou's body (before it was cremated); the rumors that Mao was ill and Jiang Qing was seizing state power; the sudden radio news release of Mao's death; spontaneous pledges to carry on his revolutionary course; and the celebration of the smashing of the Gang of Four under the leadership of Mao's trusted successor, Hua Guofeng. All these events were naturally conveyed from the official perspective in early post-Maoist China, with a view to justifying its political changes. Both on and off the stage, the ill-tempered Jiang Qing was once more spoken of as the ugly body most responsible for a nation's ruin; neither men nor women could be truly liberated until this destructive woman was eliminated.

These and other anti–Gang of Four plays can also be taken as courtroom dramas in which Jiang Qing was made to stand trial as a leading actress in a political theater. These "pretrial dramas" onstage preceded Jiang's public trial on November 20, 1980, when the Special Court under the Supreme People's Court started bringing to trial, in the words of the official press, "the ten principal defendants of the case of the Lin Biao and Jiang Qing cliques."[63] In fact, with Jiang Qing as the archcriminal, some staged events of the early post-Maoist era almost anticipated the wording of the indictment at the real public trial.[64] There were other parallels. For example, the persecutions related in *In a Land of Silence* and *There Is a Small Courtyard* clearly resemble the forty-seven criminal charges brought against Jiang and her followers in the public trial. In one of these, the shocking "eastern Hebei case," more than 84,000 party cadres and masses in eastern Hebei Province were framed and persecuted for having cooperated with the nationalists before liberation, and 2,954 others were persecuted to death.[65] Interestingly, Lao She's name was mentioned, in case 38 of the indictment, as one of the more than 2,600 people falsely charged and persecuted in the Ministry of Culture and units directly under it.[66] Moreover, cases 8 and 10 of the indictment charged the members of the Gang of Four with perse-cuting Zhou Enlai and accusing Deng Xiaoping of being the "chief boss" behind "the Counterrevolutionary Political Incident at Tiananmen Square" of 1976, an event dramatized in *In a Land of Silence, There Is a Small Courtyard, Small Well Lane*, and *The Tempest in the Divine Land*.[67] These correspondences demonstrate the degree to which post-Maoist theater functioned as an extended stage of the political drama, in which actors sought to play the roles that would assure their political survival.

To continue the comparison between actual and staged trials, theater audiences were expected to act as judges in the pretrial dramas. For example, *When the Maple Leaves Turned Red (Fengye hongle de shihou)*, a five-act comedy by Jin Zhenjia and Wang Jingyu, which was premiered in May 1977 by the China Youth Art Theater in Beijing, conducted an indirect trial of an evil woman character, Qin Xi, who appears to be a carbon copy of Jiang Qing. The play is set in 1976 in a highly classified scientific research institute that hires Lu Zhengrong (in spite of his background as an impostor with four previous arrests) so that he may complete his invention of the "loyalty tester." This is a machine that flashes lights after each statement made by the person being tested—white for "true," blue for "false." To guarantee the success of this project, Qin Xi, a special agent of the Gang of Four, is sent to the institute by the "four respected leaders," who believe the loyalty tester will arm the proletarian class with a powerful weapon in the ongoing class struggle against their enemies— those "capitalist roaders" who refuse to cooperate, or those who pretend to cooperate but actually harbor hatred for the four great proletarian leaders. But Feng Yuntong, the party secretary of the research institute, takes the lead in blocking this experiment by pushing through a *Wanma* 100 project, with encouragement from Premier Zhou Enlai.

A typical pretrial drama of the early post-Maoist period, *When the Maple*

Leaves Turned Red deals with a number of criminals who are being simultaneously investigated and are trotted out for the scrutiny of the audience. Preeminent among these figures is Lu Zhengrong. To expose Lu's loyalty tester as a fake, Luo Xiaoguang, an assistant researcher who had earlier been robbed by Lu Zhengrong, constructs his own "loyalty tester" and insists it be tested on Lu. Luo Xiaoguang proceeds in the same manner Lu Zhengrong used with his machine:

LUO XIAOGUANG: Now answer me: Are you loyal to your "four leaders"?

LU ZHENGRONG: Ye—yes!
    (Squawk)
LUO XIAOGUANG: Look, the white light is on. Your statement was true!

LU ZHENGRONG: See, it works well, with accuracy and efficiency. It also works on its own inventor! Gu Ailan, please record the fine result of this experiment!
LUO XIAOGUANG: Another question: How did you get arrested by the Security Bureau?
    Speak up!
LU ZHENGRONG: What? I was . . . was . . . never arrested.
    (Squawk)
LUO XIAOGUANG: Look, the blue light is on. You are a liar! Lu Zhengrong, how did you loot state-owned property—those machines?
CHEN XINHUA: Speak up!

XU HONG: How did you make up your fake personal history?
    Speak up!
LUO XIAOGUANG: Swindler! You are a swindler!
    (Lu falls to the ground, pretending to have died) (act 3, 41)[68]

Another swindler on trial in the play is Zhang Dezhi, a deputy director who followed the instructions of the Gang of Four and was a burglar during the Cultural Revolution. After being exposed by Luo Xiaoguang, Lu wants to escape before being punished by his boss. He pulls himself together, however, on recalling that his boss, Deputy Director Zhang Dezhi, also burglarized and embezzled and lied about his personal history to secure his powerful position. So Zhang is in no position to punish anyone else, Lu tells himself. Both Lu and Zhang are further contrasted with Qin Xi, who supervises the loyalty-tester experiment. At the end of the play, when Zhang Dezhi fails to reach Qin Xi's office by a direct telephone line to Beijing, many of the audience members knew they were watching a reenactment of the historic arrest of the Gang of Four, whose detention became manifest when they were no longer available to answer the phone. The exposure of Lu Zhengrong, Zhang Dezhi, and Qin Xin onstage, therefore, dramatized the arrest and subsequent trial of the Gang of Four and their followers. The word "trial" is even used in act 4 when Lu Zhengrong becomes terrified by a thunderstorm:

> LU ZHENGRONG: Look, there are lights everywhere as if it were broad daylight. Everywhere I can hear war drums shaking the earth! . . . This magnificent building can be turned, any second, into a courtroom for trial; the uniformed policemen would suddenly appear, rounding me up. Everywhere in the streets, people would shout: "Catch him! Catch him!" This is truly horrifying! (act 4, 43)

Thanks in part to a character who reminded many of Jiang Qing, this early pretrial drama became so popular that it was simultaneously performed in more than two hundred theaters around the country. It seemed as if dramatizing the "real" events in China's political life required a villainous woman character to fill the roles of laughingstock and history's ultimate victim. Remembering the iniquity of a particular woman helped people to ease painful memories of the Cultural Revolution and the parts they themselves might have played in it. So endless crowds flooded into theaters to celebrate victory over the Gang of Four and to figuratively trample its female ringleader. In the city of Chengdu alone, four theaters staged the play in the spoken-drama version in addition to three others that performed it in the local Sichuan opera style. Local audiences typically commented, "It is a great bargain to spend only forty cents for a ticket to have a good laugh in the theater for three hours!"[69] Another factor, as previously indicated, was that people reveled in the pure fun of sitting in judgment on both the dramatic characters and their real-life counterparts. Even the playwrights themselves observed, "Our socialist stage had indeed become a courtroom in which the Gang of Four was being put on trial for sentencing."[70] These historical factors help to explain why so many early post-Maoist plays dwelt on criminal acts, including those committed by young people who were simply living witnesses to the brutality of the Cultural Revolution. The actual public trial of the Gang of Four was characterized by Fox Butterfield as "almost an indictment of the entire Cultural Revolution, a period of intensified revolutionary fervor from 1966 to 1976, except that the prime actor, Mao himself, is nowhere blamed."[71]

It is the absence from all accounts of Mao as criminal that points out the absurdity of the political drama in contemporary China, which laid all blame on the head of one woman in order to protect the aura of the leader and his patriarchal, tyrannical system. Some weight should thus be given to Jiang Qing's self-defense in November 1980, in which she challenged the public trial and the forty-eight accusations leveled against her, claiming that everything she had done had Mao's approval. She seemed to see it as her mission to expose the national myth according to which she, alone the source of all evils, had brought down the empire. By insisting that Mao was behind everything she had ever done during the Cultural Revolution, she was merely underscoring the obvious fact that no one in the audience dared to articulate: no matter how skillful an actress she might have been and how artfully she had manipulated Mao, she could never have single-handedly started and sustained the Cultural Revolution for almost a decade without Mao's strong support at crucial moments. She had a point when she insisted, during the trial, that she alone should not be assigned responsibility for all the casualties of the Cultural Revolution.

In this manner did Jiang Qing redirect her trial into that of Mao. She would not allow him to rest in peace and glory while she accepted the role of scapegoat the public imposed on her. Fulfilling her destiny as a Nora-like character, Jiang asked, "Which is right—the world or I?" Neither a "political villain" nor a "political hero," Jiang believed that "she was right, and so she put the Communist system on trial."[72] Yet the question remains, to what extent did the defiant Jiang Qing really believe in the lofty ideals of the Cultural Revolution, especially at the moment when she burst out, "Glory to those innocent, imprisoned revolutionaries whose heads will be chopped off for their rebellious acts!" upon hearing her death sentence announced two years later, on January 25, 1981?[73] Or was she merely adhering to a dramatic persona? Many comments by China watchers abroad and by her biographers in China, who referred to the conscious acting aspects of her performance during the trial, seemed to incline toward the latter explanation; for example, Ross Terrill observed: "She seemed to be appearing before a crowd of millions in Tian[anmen] Square, watching for the cues, alert to each camera's position, making an appeal to some absent, suprapolitical force that could acknowledge her for what she believed herself to be."[74] Whatever her fundamental political beliefs, Jiang Qing, even after her public life had come to an end, proved consistent in scorning the traditional role of woman as housewife, deprived lover, and dutiful wife. In prison, without an audience of any kind, she often occupied her time making cloth dolls while humming to herself,[75] a habit of Nora's that she had adopted and that stayed with her for the rest of her life.[76]

At least one dramatist in contemporary China had the courage to address some of these gender-related issues. In his 1990 play *Jiang Qing and Her Husbands*, Sha Yexin begins his retelling of Jiang Qing's story when she is already in prison.[77] In the opening scene, she is bathing herself in the middle of the stage, which is illuminated by a green spotlight. Lamenting the loss of her acting career but nevertheless humming happily to herself, she acts out the opening scene of A *Doll's House*, in which Nora is waiting for Torvald to come home to celebrate Christmas. Her reliving of past glories is suddenly interrupted as she recalls being locked up in the dock during her public trial. She refuses to accept all the blame for persecuting Liu Shaoqi. How could she alone have struck down the president of the state as the number one counterrevolutionary without the passing of the party's resolution to do so by the many members of the political bureau? "I was only a dog of Mao, barking at whoever Mao wanted me to," Jiang shouted in anger.[78] From a distance, the barking of a dog is heard, which, in her childhood memories, suggests the return of her drunken father, who would brutally beat her for being a cheap girl. Next she attempts to free herself from the constraints of the courtroom dock by furiously rejecting Tang Na, her ex-husband in 1930s Shanghai, and Mao, both of whom have come forward as witnesses for her defense.[79] Neither of them, however, does she deem qualified to speak for her. She wants to tell her own story, in her own words, in order to puzzle out who is correct—the world or Jiang?

There is a blackout and the scene shifts to the 1930s, with Jiang Qing (known as Lan Ping at the time) onstage playing the role of Nora. In this play within a play, the role of Torvald is played by Mao, and Tang Na is out in the audience gazing at their performance with great interest and approbation. Tang seems to particularly enjoy the last scene, in which Nora gives her ring back to Torvald/Mao, bidding them both farewell. At this point in her life, she does not "believe in miracles any longer"—that is, that their "life together could be a real marriage" of equal partners.[80] As the door is slammed when Nora leaves behind a distressed Torvald/Mao

on the empty stage, Tang is the first to jump up from his seat to enthusiastically applaud the superb performance. In his own words, the real Nora
has been revealed, not by costumes, but by the "spiritual makeup" of the
"miracle-making" actress who identified with the dramatic character.[81]
There follows the romantic pursuit of the real-life Nora on the part of
Tang, an ardent film and drama critic who promoted Lan Ping's acting
career in Shanghai. At this point the play reverses historical events, for in
actuality Jiang Qing left Tang before she married Mao. The reversal, however, allows Tang to examine the entire scope of Jiang's life so as to demonstrate the persistence with which she pursued her independence and
freedom, even if it meant rejecting Mao, the most powerful man in China.
Although Jiang remained Mao's wife to the end, they had lived separately
for many years, and the play captures the empty nature of their relationship, devoid of spiritual and emotional ties. As for Tang Na, a bourgeois
artist in 1930s Shanghai, whom the official history associates with Jiang
Qing's earlier promiscuity and acting career, the play turns him into a
critic who wittily challenges the hypocrisy of her marriage to Mao. It was
a novelty to see a drama critic who was supposed to be ideologically
reformed and guided by the party's directives criticizing the moral values
and the emotional life of the national leader.

Throughout the rest of the play, whose time frame shifts between 1930s
Shanghai, 1940s Yan'an, and 1960s and 1970s Beijing during the Cultural
Revolution, Sha Yexin lays great emphasis on Jiang's connection with theater and drama. Through Tang's point of view, Jiang is depicted as a
courageous 1930s revolutionary[82] with a strong belief in *xinxing xiju* (new
drama), which would aid the national revolution against foreign imperialism and feudalism.[83] As someone with excellent acting instincts, Jiang
presents herself to Mao for the first time as a faithful audience member
during one of Mao's public speeches in Yan'an, asking him endless questions about the revolutionary truth that he has just been articulating so
effectively. While later living with Mao as his mistress, Jiang complains
that during her acting career she was only given such roles as the wife of a
cart driver, hunter, or other kinds of paupers. In truth, she would have
preferred to play an empress or first lady of a nation.[84]

Jiang's disillusionment in her life with Mao begins as early as the period
of passionate courting, when she is already expressing disappointment
in her new Yan'an home. It has proved to be not a paradise for love and
freedom, but rather another doll's house, even more restrictive than the
previous ones.[85] To consent to their marriage, the political bureau demands

that she be denied any political role in the party for the next thirty years, which Jiang views as an "unequal treaty," made possible only by her giving up *her* ground.[86] Her predicament as Mao's woman is stressed again in the scene set on Lu Mountain in 1959. After having been attacked for his radical policies during the Great Leap Forward, Mao has arranged to meet his second wife, He Zizhen, whom he has sought out for comfort. Their brief, touching meeting after twenty years apart is suddenly interrupted by the announcement of Jiang Qing's unexpected arrival the next day. Deeply resenting the cowardliness and selfishness displayed by Mao, who immediately asks her to leave, He Zizhen withdraws unhesitatingly, but not without a slamming of the door that echoes the conclusion of A *Doll's House*.[87]

Sha's play ends in 1976, with Jiang crying alone before Mao's dead body, her sorrow and resentment evident. She wished for many years that he would say again what he had said so tenderly and frequently in Yan'an, that he really "liked her," which was his own peasantlike way of saying he "loved her."[88] Suddenly, Mao, though on his deathbed, sits up and grants her wish. In his final talk with her, he praises her for her achievements during the Cultural Revolution, which ranked, with the defeat of the Nationalists in 1949, as the most important accomplishment of his political career. He admits that he liked her and so married her. Yet he also disliked her, and so they separated in later years. Mao confesses that he is "at least a male chauvinist, a tyrant at home" who never treated her as a really equal partner. "Our marriage has been one of inequality since its very start," Jiang responds. "I always felt that I was so much like Nora." As if tired of hearing the familiar name of a foreign woman, Mao is at once overcome with exhaustion and instantly dies, leaving the task of judging their marriage to future generations.[89]

By affirming on stage the ideological correctness of the Cultural Revolution, Mao becomes an implicit yet invaluable witness to the Jiang Qing put on trial. Mao has claimed credit and full responsibility, and Jiang is not solely to blame for the political drama of the past ten years. Most important, however, by admitting that he was a male chauvinist and dictator at home, the dramatic character of Mao permits others to imagine and to elaborate on Jiang as a woman in real life. For Chinese historians intent on hewing exclusively to whatever Mao was known to have said, the Mao in Sha's play had certainly shown them that it was possible to admit candidly that the evils ascribed to Jiang testified to Mao's corruption. In a most unexpected, dramatic fashion, a significant perspective derived from the theater of the street proved capable of reversing the verdict of the street theater in political life.

The post-Maoist stage representation of Mao and his women did not, of course, begin with Sha Yexin's play. In my introduction to *Reading the Right Text*, I discussed *Jiang Qing and Her Husbands* in the ideological context of the "revolutionary leader's play" in early post-Maoist China, demonstrating that this subgenre enjoyed popularity in the theater boom of 1978 to 1981, when the dramatic characters of CCP leaders such as He Long and Chen Yi appeared in their youthful personae during the revolutionary war period and indirectly denounced their subsequent persecution at the hands of the Gang of Four. These works included dramatizations of Mao's first wife, Yang Kaihui, as seen in a series of Yang Kaihui plays both in spoken drama and in operatic theaters.[90] They depicted Yang as the loving wife and caring mother of Mao's three young sons, who would rather die than reject Mao as her husband. Yang Kaihui became the ideal wife whom Mao had missed after his marriage to Jiang Qing. He Zizhen, Mao's second wife, appeared in at least one play, entitled *The Son of the World* (*Shijie zhizi*, 1985) and written by Zhang Guichi.[91] This play depicted the life story of Mao Anying, Mao's first son by Yang Kaihui, and his loving relationship with He Zizhen, his stepmother. While spending World War II in the Soviet Union, He Zizhen took care of Mao Anying and his brother, while Mao forgot and neglected her after his marriage to Jiang Qing. Although these plays implicitly criticized Mao's treatment of He Zizhen, they saw Mao's other women as his ideal loves and attacked Jiang Qing as a manipulative woman responsible for Mao's unhappiness and the country's disaster. Seen in this light, *Jiang Qing and Her Husbands* questioned Mao's private life and its official history by presenting Jiang Qing's relationship with Mao from her perspective. Sha Yexin could not, of course, have written this play without worrying about official censors. In my interview with him he told me that a Hong Kong actress found Jiang Qing's life story a fascinating drama and requested that he write a screenplay for her so she might play the role of Jiang Qing. This request explains the script's fluidity of time and space, which Sha believes makes it suitable for stage or movie production. Due to financial difficulties and political factors, the movie never materialized. One has to wait for an eventual premiere of this work either on screen or on stage. The circulation of this text outside of China, along with German and English translations, however, points to the importance of studying those dramas which might have a lasting impact as written texts.[92]

Eight years before the publication of *Jiang Qing and Her Husbands*, the Chinese stage saw revolutionary leader plays not just about Mao and his cohorts but also about international fathers such as Karl Marx and Friedrich Engels and their problematic relationships with their women. Although promoted in 1983 as part of the official activities to commemorate the centennial of Marx's death, two of these plays—*Marx in London Exile* (*Makesi liuwang lundun*, 1983)[93] and *The Secret History of Marx* (*Makesi mishi*, 1983)—surprisingly sparked the greatest controversy of any leader plays thus far. They were disparaged for concentrating on the daily routine and disappointments of Marx's life—his poor health, the death of his children, and the difficult period when he was writing *Das Kapital*. They also depicted his friendship with Engels, who helped tide him over with his capitalist's salary, at the expense of depicting significant events in the leader's revolutionary career. Indeed, *The Secret History of Marx*, also written by Sha Yexin, highlights the theme of Marx as an ordinary man. Upon hearing of plans for a Chinese play about him, Marx convinces a Chinese playwright visiting his grave that it be written to reveal the ordinary man rather than the saint he had become in communist hagiography. The two then agree to write the secret history of Marx's completion of *Das Kapital*—that is, the anxiety, frustration, and depression he had to overcome in order to produce his crowning intellectual achievement, a blueprint for world revolution.

The play provides Marx's own account of his daily life in May 1849, which the playwright takes down on a tape recorder, a product of modern technology bewildering to Marx. Capitalism had not expired, as he had predicted; instead, it could boast the mass manufacturing of electronic products that could be used to record the utterings of a historical figure. In addition to this subtle critique of Marx's theory, the play did not shrink from depicting how he dominated the women in his life. In the seventh act, for example, when Marx's wife notes her husband's declining health and begs him to slow down, he responds roughly, expressing regret that he married her in the first place. Seeing Marx's deplorable treatment of his wife, their housemaid intervenes:

"Enough, Karl! This is too much. How dare you to treat so cruelly a woman who has sacrificed so much for you! You can choose to escape to your work when you are frustrated. What can a woman do? She has to double her sacrifice—to copy your book day and night and to endure your misfortunes with you. She has lost three lovely children for your sake. Who else could have put up with so much as a mother and a wife? You must be out of your mind to treat her like this. And you are not going to get away with it. You have to apologize to her!" (act 7, 552)[94]

An almost identical episode occurs in *Marx in London Exile.* In this case a housemaid prepares a special dish to celebrate the silver wedding anniversary of the Marxes: a goose decorated with numerous feather pens that Mrs. Marx had used over the last decade to copy Marx's famous manuscript. The housemaid makes the offering of the dish after Marx's merciless dressing-down of his wife for having secretly borrowed money to assist German revolutionaries in exile. The scene obviously parallels that in *A Doll's House* where Nora is awakened from her dream world by Mr. Helmer's brutal accusations that she has ruined his reputation with her secret debts. Yet instead of walking out of her "doll's house" as Nora did, Marx's wife immediately forgives him, embracing him and assuring him anew of her love and understanding. The wife of the "great proletarian leader" evinces little of the spirit that animates the liberated woman from the bourgeois society which Marx critiqued. Thus Marx was simultaneously represented on the post-Maoist socialist stage as the father of the communist revolution, whose *Das Kapital* had a worldwide impact on the proletariat for many generations, and as a patriarch given to neglecting his wife so that he might arrive at his learned theories. Paradoxically, in the twentieth century Marxist theory has inspired a new generation of cultural feminists in the West to devise critiques that might have coincided with our readings of these two plays. No wonder that critics of *Marx in London Exile* claimed that the repudiation of the spirit of Marx coming from Marx the character[95] constituted a much more problematic rejection of his revolutionary principles than any emanating from his enemies' camp.

The portrayal of Marx as an irritable and self-centered man triggered a critical debate that quickly moved beyond the theater into the realm of politics and ideology. It was pointed out that *The Secret History of Marx* was *meant* to be anti-Marxist by virtue of its focus on the "private history" of "a human Marx." In other words, rendering Marx in two contradictory dimensions—the revolutionary versus the human—logically leads to the conclusion that a revolutionary is by definition not human, or that a human being cannot be a revolutionary. By limiting his portrayal of Marx to the exclusively human, wasn't the author implying that delineating Marx as a revolutionary leader could never have yielded as vivid and convincing results?[96] Arguing once more that the plays are not documentaries, Huang Wen pointed out that *The Secret History of Marx* covers eighteen years of Marx's life, from May 1849 to September 1867, when a "mature Marx had already established his entire theoretical system." For Marx, it was also a period of poverty, hardship, and exile. Yet, Huang continued, he managed along with Engels to organize the First International during this period, and he soon was recognized as the indisputable leader of the working class throughout the world. How many heroic and moving deeds Sha Yexin could have written about, had he chosen to do so! Instead, the author chose to accentuate the personality traits that Marx shared with many of us.[97] Given this emphasis, it is hardly accidental, contended another critic, that at the beginning of the play Marx prefers to receive a cigarette rather than flowers from people paying tribute at his grave. He explains: "I am a materialist. I should be presented with something materialistic." How could a revolutionary leader reject flowers from a later generation that still venerates his vision?[98] Other critics went so far as to rebuke the two plays for showcasing the trendy discontent then current among the people. How, furthermore, could Marx joke about being more productive in childbearing than in his writings? Although this line was almost always followed by audience laughter, Huang Wen maintained that the humor did not issue from Marx the character, but from the connection the audience made with contemporary China's promotion of a one-child policy to reduce rapid population growth. "What social effect would this line have had in our society had it been put forward in the name of Marxism?" Huang asked.[99] To him, the play depicted an erroneous trend in literature and art wherein humanism was championed as the overriding principle rather than Marxism.[100]

The critical debate on "humanism," of course, represented a dilemma in the transitional period between Maoist and post-Maoist discourse around 1978; although the latter attempted to discredit the former's lack of humanity during the Cultural Revolution, it depended heavily on the Marxist heritage to validate a socialist state. The staged Marx thus became an imagined leader re-created and reinterpreted according to the fancies of the critics. Marx's wife, moreover, became a pawn in the negotiation between the politics of gender and state. She therefore shared a fate similar to that of many other Chinese women characters of the same period, whose loyalty to the great men and past sufferings signified merely the beginning of a new era that would create strong and brilliant men to save mankind. Without much choice, playwrights and critics alike participated and collaborated with the ruling ideology in constructing a post-Maoist culture both within and outside theater.

In conclusion, our initial subject of Tiananmen Square can be seen as a national platform upon which numerous Chinese Noras acted out their personal street theater after having left their homes. He Yu and her mother in *In a Land of Silence* represent two generations of Chinese Noras who left a suffocating home ruled by a patriarch, only to submit to another patriarchy when they threw in their lot with the promoters of the new national campaign against the Gang of Four. In *There Is a Small Courtyard*, the sacrifice of Dujuan in the violence occurring in Tiananmen Square emphasizes the misery of her mother. She returns home after years of political imprisonment, which must have invalidated her initial departure to become involved in the struggle against the Gang of Four. The May Fourth question, "What happens to Nora after she leaves home?" has once again been negated in socialist China, where women's active, heroic public roles earn them imprisonment, persecution, and, in the end, a longing again for the peace and comfort of home. One group of women needed to be rescued by male heroes who led the struggle against the Gang of Four, as seen in the character of Bai Yubing in *The Tempest in the Divine Land*. Other women, on the contrary, were thrust into the public arena to assume sole responsibility for the disastrous politics of a past era, as witnessed in the Tiananmen street theater that drew on the reputation of the treacherous Jiang Qing and Jiang Qing-like female politicians. If the evil Jiang Qing, who had almost become a fixture of the Chinese stage, represents the obstacles and pure ill will facing a woman with the ambition and determination to go beyond traditional female roles, other heroines represented in Tiananmen street theater might also signify the futility of women's attempts to bring about the social changes that would enhance their liberation. The problems surrounding gender difference were highlighted only to testify to the malfeasance of previous leaders, the wrongheadedness of the previous ideology, and the misery these had brought down upon the people. Once women were liberated along with the entire nation, gender-based differences and injustices were once again erased from the national consciousness so as to glorify (without the slightest hint of dissent) the new political order.

6

A Stage of Their Own

FEMINISM, COUNTERVOICES, AND
THE PROBLEMATICS OF WOMEN'S THEATER

Since the beginning of modern Chinese drama, May Fourth male playwrights such as Guo Moruo, Ouyang Yuqian, and Chen Dabei, in forming a tradition to counter the Confucian ruling ideology, treated women's
liberation and equality as important political and ideological issues.[1] Female
playwrights, such as Bai Wei, depicted loving mothers and courageous
daughters waging a fierce struggle against the patriarchal society, symbolized by domineering, lustful domestic fathers or by new nationalist fathers
already corrupted by the emerging revolution.[2] The use of woman as a
metaphor for national salvation in a given political agenda was most fully
articulated in the street theater during the period of the War of Resistance
to Japan. A scene from *Put Down Your Whip (Fangxia nide bianzi)*,[3] the
period's best-known play, shows a starving daughter whipped by her help-

less, tearful father, who is fleeing from enemy-occupied territory. This image was recorded by the literary histories as having been a major source of inspiration to the Chinese people in their national struggle against foreign aggressors.[4]

In the PRC, women warriors, women party secretaries, and women model workers and peasants were continuously depicted onstage, a manifestation of the socialist-state feminism that culminated in the radical Cultural Revolutionary model theater. The concept of Chinese women's legendary equality with men was pushed to the extreme during the Cultural Revolution, as Chinese women were transformed into the liberated other in the fantasies of the ruling ideology. Early post-Maoist theater, like Chinese cinema of the same period, still presented images of abused and suffering women (as opposed to the images of men) as "merely symbols for victims caught in Chinese history." Dai Jinhua characterized these women as, ironically, victims in the campaign "for the restoration of traditional womanhood articulated by yet another kind of male-dominated culture."[5]

Despite this complex political and dramatic history, is it still possible to talk about a tradition of women's theater in modern China and, more specifically, in contemporary China, where political, economic, cultural, and ideological transformations have rendered the expressions of individual voices and their collective and community identities even more problematic and challenging? The next two chapters in this study represent, to the best of my knowledge, the first attempt to address this subject, devoting themselves as they do entirely to the study of women's theater in post-Maoist China. This chapter begins by raising the following questions: Does a women's theater exist in post-Maoist China?[6] If so, to what extent can women, given the restrictions they face in society, speak through that theater? When women finally speak in a public space such as theater, do they speak to, for, or against the official patriarchal system? Is it possible to claim that women playwrights of the post-Maoist period have contributed to the global discourse of feminist writing—writing that "has historicized and contextualized woman's absence and her enforced voicelessness" and "has literally written women into existence and given a forum to words that have gone unheard"?[7] Or is it more appropriate to say that women playwrights, much as they have tried to create a record of their existence through the stage, have articulated only a very limited message of absence and silence in a profoundly patriarchal society? Can one argue that this very voicelessness, defined by Mara L. Dukats as "suppressed history and unacknowledged agency," can be perceived as a drama of empowerment because it reveals the condition that makes its existence possible?[8] Furthermore, if we grant Nancy Fraser's concept of dominant culture as "no longer a closed and exclusive totality, but rather, a complex web of both hegemonic and counter-hegemonic forces," is it possible to argue that the marginalized woman's voice has helped shape the mainstream texts in post-Maoist theater, which is concurrently "defined and conditioned by the residual and emergent" discourse of women playwrights?[9]

There seems to be no better point of departure for effectively addressing these issues than to sort out the layers of cultural meanings and political significance contained in a trilogy of plays about women, written by Bai Fengxi in the early 1980s. One of the most important women playwrights in contemporary China writing exclusively about women's issues, Bai, through her plays, negotiated with the dominant post-Maoist culture. She redefined and reinforced it by demonstrating its critical difference from the culture of the Maoist age (as well as, where applicable, the lack of differences between the two cultures). This collaboration with the official culture lent her plays a seemingly agreeable voice and enabled her to bypass state censorship in a fashion usually denied other playwrights. By cleverly maneuvering within the confines of an ambivalent space, Bai simultaneously questioned the terms in which the post-Maoist culture had come to define itself.

In Bai's plays, both the dominant culture and the subcultures it dominated were assigned their respective dramatic roles to play on the public stage of politics. A women's community was thus forged onstage with a collective identity of its own, which, however, did not preclude it from being associated with the ongoing process of nation building in early post-Maoist China. Narratives in which women drew on their memories thus became an integral part of the official culture's master narrative, a scheme that paradoxically turned Bai's plays into a forum bringing together audiences of both genders from all walks of life.

To shed light on the cultural and ideological significance of Bai's plays, I will explore both the author's input and the collective meanings she ascribed to the men and women she presented as categories of identity in the early 1980s. I will also scrutinize the historical hindsight with which both she, the author, and I, the critic, approached and reinterpreted her texts ten years later (the summer of 1991) when I interviewed her in Beijing. Using this method, I hope to present Bai's plays in a manner that befits the historical past that produced them, a past Bai herself has characterized as "inspirational."[10]

As an activist committed to speaking for women, especially those without a voice, Bai wrote her plays to accompany her sisters "in their advance forward and [to] render a truthful account of their arduous struggle for liberation."[11] "Every day on my way to work," she said in 1980, "I was deeply disturbed by the sight of the many women of all ages" waiting at the front gate of the Fulian (the All-China Women's Federation) to express their grievances and complaints. "It was not until after I had entered this gate to interview Fulian workers and women travelers from afar that I was shocked to discover there were still dark corners in this world where so many sisters had been shut out from the brilliant sunshine of socialism." To liberate women from feudal patriarchy became for Bai an urgent task;[12] it coincided with the official agenda of debunking feudal totalitarianism, which was identified as the source of the Cultural Revolution. It is important to take note of Bai's original intentions here. Like Lizbeth Goodman, I oppose the application of Roland Barthes' concept of the death of the author to feminist theater studies; it may be particularly problematic in this context, owing to the conflict it could pose with "the tenets of feminist thought, including respect for women's voices and the questioning of academic and critical 'norms.' Feminist studies should, by definition, entail respect for the views and intentions of authors."[13]

It is therefore important to note that Bai's first play, *First Bathed in Moonlight (Mingyue chu zhao ren)*, premiered by the China Youth Art Theater in 1981, has as its protagonist Fang Ruoming, the director of the Women's Federation in a given province, a key position in the socialist state apparatus that takes care of the interests of women from all walks of life. Excited by the national call to improve people's life in the new era after the Gang of Four, Fang Ruoming devotes herself to solving marital disputes in the remote, isolated countryside, where women in poverty are sold into marriage for economic gain. Upon her first appearance onstage, Fang reflects on the significance of her job as the Fulian official: "Work concerning women is said to be exceptionally important, but actually it is treated as something insignificant; it does not get all the attention it warrants. The social milieu has been deteriorating, so problem after problem keeps cropping up. Unless we deal with the problems in real earnest, it just won't do."[14] The intention of the playwright in this case was thus expressed through the characterization of Fang Ruoming—both playwright and character were equally agitated by the still blatant exploitation of women in socialist China.[15]

This opening statement places Fang Ruoming as being in accord with the official ideology. At the same time, it sets her in direct conflict with the character of Aunt Zhang, who uses her husband's political influence to prevent her son from marrying a girl from the countryside. In act 2, when Fang Ruoming visits a mountain village to rescue a woman from an arranged marriage, she realizes, with surprise, that this woman is the very country girl Aunt Zhang had rejected as her future daughter-in-law. As a result of Zhang's interference, the girl was forced to marry a stranger, whose payment provided her mother with the necessary means to cover the expenses of her son's prospective marriage.

The resolution of this marriage situation after the appearance of a courageous Fulian official onstage can be seen, on one level, as an integral part of official feminism. In the words of Lydia H. Liu, this official feminism consists in "the emancipatory discourse of the state, which always subsumes woman under the nationalist agenda" of socialist or Maoist China.[16] The resolution can also be interpreted as a timely celebration of the official culture, which exploits women's issues for its own benefit as its own cultural capital. However, given the conditions in contemporary China, with its pervasive poverty, illiteracy, and ignorance, and with women propelled into arranged marriages and still being bought and sold like commodities, it might be simplistic and even politically irresponsible to dismiss Fulian for never being capable of representing the interests of women. As this play shows (and as numerous cases in the public records testify), Fulian, in spite of its official role of mediator—or perhaps even *because* of its power in fulfilling that function—often played a positive role in addressing women's grievances. This salutary service was observable especially in the instance of poor women, who were deprived of the economic and the political means to defend themselves. The issue of women's oppression in the countryside had been sorely neglected during the ten years of the Cultural Revolution. Consequently, addressing this issue had become an urgent matter by the early post-Maoist period. In this sense, Bai's drama reflects the continuity of social realism that she still believed in as a fundamental principle governing her playwriting.[17]

As a *zhengmian renwu* (positive character), Fang Ruoming was afforded the opportunity of allying herself with politically and economically downtrodden women. Their voices expressed concerns that temporarily overlapped with the political interests of the early post-Maoist regime, which could then congratulate itself for saving the suppressed women. The unacknowledged agency of the subaltern women was to some extent represented in Fang, the heroine approved of by the dominant culture, whose multivoiced discourse expressed both hegemonic and counterhegemonic forces. Those with a predominantly hegemonic approach to women's liberation were tolerant of occasional subversive statements that questioned the socialist system as a whole, as typified by a country woman's remark: "Socialism is as good as gold, but not [as good as] wives bought and sold."[18] The unfailing applause that greeted this utterance,[19] however, highlighted the underlying subversive discourse in the theater, where many more such polemical responses came from people on both sides of the representative frame than the author had anticipated, thus ultimately pushing the meaning of the play beyond the line of official discourse into antiofficial discourse.

The subsequent national debate on *First Bathed in Moonlight*'s political merits focused on its love triangle.[20] Thirty years before, for political reasons, Fang had left Pei Guang, her first true love, and married a "safety deposit"—a man without a questionable political background. In the course of the play, Fang realizes that her own daughter, Fang Wei, is in love with Pei Guang, her graduate-school advisor in another city. After intense soul-searching, Fang encourages her daughter to pursue her true love, in spite of her anguish at the prospect of a union between her daughter and her former love. As a gesture of reconciliation with her daughter, whom she has alienated by her initial angry response, Fang offers her the gift of her own diary, which contains these lines: "In this little book are recorded my ideals, my life and work, my successes and setbacks, my joys as well as sorrows over the last thirty-odd years. Take it, Weiwei. You should be more clearheaded and wiser than me, because time is forever advancing. . . . A page in history is now turned over. What I failed to attain you ought to achieve. You're firm about having a career. I hope you'll be firm about love too."[21]

Some prestigious drama critics condemned the presentation of such a love triangle between mother and daughter as being unacceptable by the standards of traditional Chinese ethics.[22] Others argued that an arbitrary plot had been constructed in order to demonstrate a petty bourgeois ideology that set sexual love above patriotic love for the party and the collective,[23] and that this unrealistic triangle lacked social and ideological significance.[24] Still others questioned the validity of Fang Ruoming as a positive character. While adamantly defending the rights of women in the course of mediating their problems in the countryside, she nevertheless vehemently objected when Fang Lin, her second daughter, fell in love with a plumber, the brother of the same country girl Fang had helped in act 2. How then, with such an evident double standard, could Fang be respected and regarded as a new woman of socialism? Or perhaps was Fang to be viewed as a negative character, an old, hypocritical revolutionary who was being put on display for public scrutiny? If so, what was the play really saying about the bright future of socialist China? Indeed, several Fulian officials in the city of Xi'an had been so offended by Fang's negative portrayal that they waited in front of the theater to prevent audience members from attending the play, which they considered a vicious attack against Fulian and its workers. "Comrades, please do not go to this anti-Fulian play," they implored the theatergoers, whose curiosity was naturally all the more aroused by this unusual advertisement.[25] Such an anti-Fulian event, of course, had no chance of ever being reported in the official press because of strict censorship, yet it is preserved in the memory of the playwright, who related the event to me with great enthusiasm more than a decade later. Such a street theater certainly adds to our reconstruction of a women's history through private eyes.

Once more, as has often happened in contemporary Chinese theater, controversy and critical debates proved to be the best promoters of a play. Within only a short time after the play's premiere by the China Youth Art Theater, Bai Fengxi had received more than three hundred letters. Most of them came from women, who identified themselves as the ideal spectators of the play. Jill Dolan argued that in the West every aspect of a theatrical production reflects and perpetuates the concept of the "ideal spectator," who is assumed to be "white, middle-class, heterosexual, and male,"[26] thus alienating female spectators and rendering them rebellious and unwilling participants in theater production. In contrast to Western theatrical productions, however, Bai's play can be seen as directly addressing the female members of the audience and thereby making them active agents who can readily identify with most of the female characters in the play. Because the play had an all-woman cast, a woman playwright, and a woman director, it was possible to create within the limited theater space a women's community in which female performers and spectators interacted with each other on both sides of the representational frame of the theater.

Thus, the female audience members of Bai Fengxi's play regarded themselves as insiders of the theatrical production. They differed from Dolan's description of invisible, resistant female spectators who perceive themselves as being reduced to supporting roles that facilitate the more important action of the male protagonist and who leave "the theater while the audience applauds at the curtain call and goes off to develop a theory of feminist performance criticism."[27] Not only did they applaud enthusiastically at the curtain call, but they went home and wrote their own life stories, which they sent to the playwright in demonstration of support for a theatrical production that had accurately reflected their personal experiences. Disturbed by Fang Ruoming's loveless life, one woman wrote Bai Fengxi a long letter about her own loveless marriage, which she had never disclosed before to anyone else. To extend the connection with another person—and perhaps, at this point in her life, with the only female who could really understand her predicament—this woman asked Bai to meet her at her home so that they could talk to their hearts' content like newly found sisters.

During and after the productions of the play, Bai Fengxi received numerous letters from theater audiences asking for a copy of the play so that they could study its message on the experience of women in contemporary China. Others who had not had a chance to see the play also asked for a text so that they, too, could participate in the national discussion on these issues.[28] The play had evidently initiated a collective desire to preserve women's culture, thereby setting in motion the urge to review the past and to question the complicity of the dominant culture in seeking to extinguish the private history of women. A community of readers of Bai's play was thus formed outside the theater sphere that regarded the play not only as a performance script but also as a literary, cultural, and political text.

As these readers were inspired by the text to examine the ideological structure underlying women's history, so the audience's reactions in the theater gave rise to subversive readings of the play that far exceeded the original intentions of either the playwright or the performers. The phenomenon is similar to that of Western contemporary theater, in which "the spectator becomes the active subject interpreting events and evaluating them from her or his positioned perspective."[29] As time went on, many people in the audience became increasingly impatient with the dialogue spoken by Fang Ruoming, the Fulian leader, particularly during her confrontations with Fang Lin, who upbraided her for being a hypocrite who had sacrificed love to safeguard her political career. Frequently sitting in the audience to observe the responses to her play, Bai Fengxi noticed that people never failed to applaud at the end of this statement of Fang Lin's:

LIN (*Speaking with even greater calmness and earnestness*): Mother, to all appearances you've got everything: you're in want of nothing—

neither money nor position nor family. But you and Father are a couple without love. Allow me to put it plainly: I sympathize with that uncle and with my father too; as for you, I hardly think you are a true materialist, only a[n exhibitionist]" (act 3, 159–160).

Eventually, the audiences were siding openly with Fang Lin in almost every criticism she leveled at Fang Ruoming, whose actions had never been guided by her true feelings. At the same time, Fang Ruoming's politically correct lines often drew hisses and taunts from the audience, as if she were indeed being portrayed as a negative character.[30] This unexpected outcome recast Fang Ruoming in a role that contradicted the playwright's original design and finally alienated Liu Yansheng, the actress who had striven to create onstage a new woman of socialist China. Herself an "old revolutionary" who had launched her acting career after having joined the revolution before 1949, she could not understand why audiences would mock her. Unable to tolerate what she took as a personal insult, she walked out at the height of the play's popularity, after eighty performances. But for this unforeseen development, the play could easily have run for three hundred performances with a full house. Bai Fengxi remembers the moment when she was walking past Liu's dressing table backstage and Liu suddenly called out angrily: "Xiao Bai, I will do two more performances. That's it. The role is yours to play, if you want it." This is a classic example of what can happen when, as Jill Dolan described it, "the traditional triumvirate of playwright-director-actor has been disrupted by the spectator's insertion into the paradigm as an active participant in the production of meaning."[31]

To the question why Bai Fengxi, a successful actress herself, did not take over Fang's role, Bai conceded that she should have been more courageous; after all, it was her character and her play, both of which she knew intimately. Having successfully played the title roles of *Liu Hulan*, premiered in 1956, and *Wencheng Gongzhu*, in 1960, Bai would have been a perfect replacement for Liu. Indeed, she was excited and inspired by audiences' remaking of Fang's character into one very different from her own. In my opinion, however, her decision not to assume the role constitutes a loss for contemporary Chinese theater, a missed rare opportunity for a woman playwright to have played the dramatic role she created after it had been redefined by the audience. Had she done so, her interpretation of Fang Ruoming as a "real woman" with her own strength and weaknesses would no doubt have inspired many other different readings of the play.

The result would have been a drama (in an additional sense) in which audience and performers pooled their efforts to rewrite a dramatic text and, in so doing, form an organic, working women's community. According to Bai, Liu walked out at the point when the play and the debate surrounding it were attracting national attention and the administrators at the China Youth Art Theater were intimidated by the prospect of possible official reprisals. In the face of a mounting campaign by cultural officials against the play's effects, the administrators wavered in their support. Bai subsequently learned that the Ministry of Culture had put her play on the "blacklist" of literary works denounced for being products of "spiritual pollution." A combination of personal, historical, and ideological factors in the China of the 1980s thus cut short the life of a promising women's play. Ultimately, it was the hegemonic official culture that resorted to its special sources of power and knowledge to prevent its ideology from being seriously contested.

An acquaintance with the historical framework makes it easier to understand what led to Bai's political compromise in regard to her play. As several critics have pointed out, there is a crucial difference between the original script published in the literary journal *October* and the revised text that the China Youth Art Theater used when it premiered the play in 1981. In the original script, Fang Ruoming broke up with Pei Guang because she knew that his family represented a political liability that could have cost her a successful revolutionary career (an all-too-familiar sacrifice for political officials of the People's Republic of China). In the revised text, however, the two lovers' breakup was moved back in time to the pre-1949 period and was occasioned by Fang's decision to depart for service in Yan'an, the liberated area of the Communist Party, which meant that Pei Guang was left behind to pursue his career in the nationalist-occupied area. This version of the play rendered the question of blame for the tragic outcome of the love story less controversial and less attributable to the strictures of the PRC period, when many people were constrained by political pressure to choose only politically acceptable mates. Although the playwright admits that this textual change blunted the sense of tragedy attendant on Fang Ruoming's choice, she points out that it gave the play a better chance of survival in the uncertain political climate of China in the early 1980s.[32] As Constantine Tung regretfully observed: "The playwright has created a very radical dramatic situation and her heroine is truly iconoclastic, individualist and rebellious, but Bai Fengxi stopped, hesitated and finally compromised at the very last moment of the play."[33] The depiction of a loveless family history in a public arena might have led to the recovery of a people's history (and, by extension, a women's history), but it was not to be, and thus also lost was the opportunity to challenge official history. Yet it is important to record this instance of an attempt to portray private history—a facet of life heretofore so underrepresented and, in this case, finally misrepresented on the stage—for it illuminates the various elements that were crucial to the shaping of this play.

The historical circumstances and ideological restraints operating on Bai challenged her to construct, as best she could, a play that combined the diverse and not always compatible elements of adaptation, appropriation, and contestation of the official culture, all governed by the unifying purpose of portraying a collective woman's identity within specific cultural and political contexts. In Bai's *First Bathed in Moonlight*, a microcosmic cultural history of Chinese women unfolds through the life experiences of three generations of mothers and daughters, which is remarkable for the absence of men onstage. As if to highlight the absence of men in her life, the grandmother, a successful schoolteacher who takes pride in having raised her daughter on her own, hangs her ex-husband's picture on the wall, thereby compelling this now-lonely man to see, with his own eyes, the many daily triumphs of the woman he deserted.

In this scenario of a woman onstage displaying to the audience a male body for the purpose of ridicule, the man becomes a passive beholding object and a stage prop for an active female agent who narrates, performs, and parades in front of him women's history in the making. With her solicitation of the male gaze, she asserts the gender identity of women in both the public and domestic domains and established man, the beholder, as a negative other. *First Bathed in Moonlight*, in this regard, evokes the history play of British feminist theater in the 1970s, which "targeted the ways in which the official English history had ignored women altogether."[34] The play is also provocative for the contrast it draws between the grandmother's personal history, characterized by its fulfillment without benefit of a man, and the problematic story of her daughter. The latter's tragic love story serves to scrutinize the official history of the PRC, which ignored men as well as women. One is consequently led to ask: which generation was better off, that of the grandmother or of the mother?

The cultural significance inherent in the grandmother's display of the insensate, thus "dead," body of the absent man was not universally recognized, particularly not among drama critics who required that a play adhere to the standard aesthetic values. One such critic, Gao Jinxian, regarded the episode as forming part of a ridiculous plot. It was truly an original approach to have her ex-husband's picture presented on an altar all these years after he had deserted her, he commented sarcastically.[35] Gao's formalistic judgment echoed other literary and drama critics, whose ostensible aesthetic considerations masked a political motive. As Gao demonstrated in his own review,[36] these critics were intent on denouncing the play for having traced the root of a human tragedy to the suppressive socialist society. (The advancement of ideological and political positions under the guise of discussions of aesthetics is a tactic fully explored in Chapter 8, on experimental theater.) It is also possible that the play's insolent display of the "dead" body of the man disturbed the drama critic, who felt uncomfortable confronting the working out onstage of a version of body politics from the woman's vantage point.

It is not sufficient, however, to dwell on the lonely, passive body of the male, for this image forms only part of the story. An all-woman cast in itself does not prevent emotional and spiritual longings for ideal men by different generations of women. On the contrary, the absent men, as described by their lovers, seem all the more desirable precisely because of their invisibility. For instance, Pei Guang, from his description, comes off as the quintessential good man, one who combines the best values from at least three patriarchal traditions in China. First, Fang Wei portrays him as a Confucian man of wisdom, learning, and culture, "with an inexhaustible wellspring of knowledge." Second, he seems to possess the spirit of the May Fourth romantic man, who is as magnificent as "a statue of marble" and thus captures the hearts of women from two different generations. (It is therefore not surprising that Fang Wei, once deprived of the right to love, "will be pining for him forever" and will "never be able to forget him for a single moment.")[37] In addition, Pei is depicted as a Maoist model of selflessness, since he "doesn't care for ease and comfort or personal gains and losses"; he is so nobleminded that being with him makes one "feel edified."[38] All these patriarchal values are employed to support the Four Modernizations promoted in early post-Maoist ideology. Pei Guang is characterized, finally, as a new man of science, from whom Fang Wei, a graduate student, has learned what constitutes dedication to science.[39]

If Pei Guang can be viewed, looking through the eyes of the older generation residing in urban China, as a new prototype for a cultural "father" figure, Fan Xi, Fang Lin's boyfriend, might be regarded as a new prototype for a cultural "son" figure from the country. Similarly idealized by the women's evocations without himself ever appearing onstage, Fan Xi also has attributes that derive from the "best" patriarchal traditions. In pursuing a romance with a subaltern, Fang Lin seems to have rejected the social convention dictating that one sets about to choose a mate as if one were shopping for a commodity of equal value to oneself. Nevertheless, the two lovers cannot be united unless they follow the mandate of the post-Maoist cultural "father" figure, whose new policy of Four Modernizations made provisions for their union. The policy makers recognized that China could not leave backwardness behind without reorganizing its higher-educational institutions. As a result, Fang Lin's status was improved because of her position as a college teacher of the English language. At the same time, the mesmerizing power of the English language has to be linked to the desires of individuals at home so that it will not be rejected as an instrument of cultural imperialism. Fang Lin's lover must be a local plumber, a member of the working class in the university environment. He must come from the countryside, the rural base cultivated by the partisans of revolutionary idealism. He must be spoken of as a former army recruit, for then he will reflect the noblest aspects of the national consciousness. Although as a worker/peasant/soldier he has a perfect body that calls to mind the glorious feats of proletarian vigor, he is described as being strikingly different from his rustic brothers and sisters. He has to have a perfect mind, whose command of classic learning encompasses the entire world, and, to participate in intellectual discourse with him, his girlfriend must join him in reading his favorite classical texts. Moreover, to satisfy a woman's predilection for the pleasurable, he also has to have the charisma of a gentleman. He has to be described as "cultivated"[40] by his lover and as "very quiet and courteous, a most likable chap,"[41] by Fang Ruoming, his mother-in-law-to-be, who finally accepts him because of his gentility. His romantic temperament, fully evident in expressions of his genuine love, has to be paradoxically combined with his "earnest attitude toward life" and "his industry at work,"[42] all quintessential traits of the Maoist man.

A good son and model citizen, Pei Guang promises to be an ideal father and husband. He gently steers Fang Lin away from her public role as rebellious daughter and into the private spheres of womanhood, wifehood, and motherhood. His acceptance into her mother's household—devoid of father and grandfather—symbolizes the return of the patriarch. With this construct, the playwright can once again depict family love as encompassing a public, "universal" love for the nation and state. Yet all this takes place without the physical presence of the lover onstage. Apparently, a public discourse on the significance of this absent figure is more powerful than seeing him in the flesh would be. One might even posit that the idealistic portrayal of these perfect men made it impossible to present them onstage. Imagine, for example, a Pei Guang, supposedly in his fifties but looking as if he were Fang Wei's age, or a Fan Xi, a familiar, well-known type of subaltern but having an unusual air of gentility. In my interview with her, Bai Fengxi herself admitted that the love affair between Fan Xi and Fang Lin was so idealistic as to be impractical. "In real life, I would never advise my own daughter to marry a man who came from the country-side," she said. "I picked a doctor as a good match for my daughter, since I strongly believe that she could only get along with someone who has the same intellectual family background as she does."[43]

In 1991, Bai Fengxi and I also recalled my part in helping her to create the subaltern man and woman onstage as a result of who we were in early post-Maoist China. After graduating from college in 1977, I became a teacher of English at the Beijing Institute of Foreign Languages, my alma mater. Bai Fengxi, a friend and colleague of my mother from the China Youth Art Theater, interviewed me in 1980. I was considered a new type of enlightened woman who possessed the "hot skills" of English language and knowledge about the West, but who remembered her past as a worker/peasant/soldier/college student (gong-nong-bing xueyuan) who owed her higher education to the egalitarian policies of the Cultural Revolution.[44] Fang Lin's characterization, as Bai repeatedly assured me, was partially modeled on my experience. Indeed, Song Jie, the actress who played Fang Lin, interviewed me several times, learned a few English phrases from me, such as "generation gap," and even visited my young colleagues at the Beijing Institute of Foreign Languages to "delve into life"—to familiarize herself with the life and manner of a college English teacher so she could present a "true-to-life" character. Engaged to a man from a peasant background, I also provided Bai Fengxi with a "real-life" story to be transformed into a dramatized version of the unlikely romance between Fang Lin and Fan Xi. This relating of personal history is meant to convey this transitional era's excitements and confusions. This sense of liberation from the past is reflected in the attraction to the image of English teacher, which ran somewhat counter to the continuing cele-brations of subaltern prototypes, still found in early post-Maoist stage characters. Bai Fengxi, the playwright, and Song Jie, the actress, believed that my story represented a new generation of intellectual women who were bound to be different from Maoist women but were nevertheless still trapped by the very Maoist values that made these women attractive in the first place.

Despite being an all-woman drama, *First Bathed in Moonlight* seems to undermine rather than bolster feminist concerns. Because of the absence of both the cultural "father" and obedient "son" figures, one feels all the more keenly their central place in the lives of the women. It seems that Bai Fengxi unknowingly thwarted her intention of highlighting and supporting women's rights in China and created instead a new patriarch to replace the old one. Like the fathers and sons before them, these absent fathers and sons again dominate the mothers and daughters; the latter succumb to the intense desire for the perfect man. The grandmother has encouraged this desire, despite her ex-husband's rejection of her. This affirmation of convention is reinforced by Fan Wei's reconciliation with her mother, whose "many fine qualities" (e.g., integrity, earnestness, and the spirit of self-sacrifice for the good of all) are singled out for admiration at the end of the play.[45] In the final analysis, the socialist new women and men of Maoist China join hands with the matriarchs and patriarchs of traditional society in celebrating the official culture, which allows only limited, paradoxical voices of women to be heard.

In contrast with her first play, which emphasizes political agendas of early post-Maoist China as a particular rostrum for voicing women's concerns, Bai Fengxi's second play, *An Old Friend Comes at a Stormy Time (Fengyu guren lai)*, premiered by the China Youth Art Theater in 1983, minimizes the public sphere to stress women's lives at home. Indeed, in this play Bai seems to be more interested than before in the various, often conflicting voices in the drama that lies behind the characters onstage and in the places that license the speeches of those characters. One way of interpreting the play is to view it as a forum for the multiple voices and ambiguous positions of women who, with their polyphonic worldviews, argue for their distinct versions of truth without a closure.

As a sequel to her first play, Bai's *An Old Friend* seems at first sight to have also challenged the patriarchal culture and its underlying myth of the irreconcilable conflict experienced by women trying both to have a career and fulfill their family roles. This polarity is emphasized by the drama's portrayal of two mothers: Mo Jin, a mother who has willingly given up her career for what she calls the peace and harmony of her family; and Xia Zhixian, a successful gynecologist who had to leave her husband in order to free herself from heavy family duties. Although former class-mates in college, the two mothers represent two diametrically opposed views of women's place in society. The recent marriage of Xia Zhixian's daughter, Peng Yin'ger, and Mo Jin's son, Cheng Kang, further intensifies the differences between the two mothers-in-law. Both offspring are promising mathematicians. Cheng Kang ranks second in a graduate school entrance examination, below only his wife Peng Yin'ger, who is therefore chosen to enroll in a European graduate school.

Mo Jin believes in the old Chinese saying that "for a woman lack of talent equals virtue," and she persuades Cheng Kang to ask Peng Yin'ger to relinquish her opportunity for him. He argues that a Chinese family with a Ph.D. husband is more acceptable, and hence more harmonious, than a family with a Ph.D. wife, especially if the degree is to be obtained from abroad. Enraged by Cheng Kang's patriarchal attitude, Yin'ger decides to end a marriage that will stunt her intellectual growth. She goes home to seek support from her mother, whose own life has consisted of struggles against the patriarchy. Much to her disappointment, however, her mother also advises her to forgo her opportunity. In her view, a woman must sacrifice for the sake of family harmony. It now occurs to Yin'ger that perhaps her mother's ideas are colored by her lonely, single existence; she has been unable to make a successful career a substitute for a happy family life and is regretful, as advancing age precludes the other choice. Yet hearing Mo Jin attack Yin'ger for her selfishness in neglecting her familial duties, Xia Zhixian surprises her daughter by reversing her opinion and encouraging her to go abroad. A woman is not a moon, Xia tells her daughter. She does not need to depend on another's light to glow. She urges her daughter to pursue her dream and to radiate her own light. [46] According to Bai Fengxi, this line was so instrumental in raising the consciousness of Chinese women in the general public that many female students subsequently used it as the title for their baccalaureate and master's theses on feminist issues. [47]

In *An Old Friend,* Bai denounces the traditional role of women for the way it limits their creativity to the domestic sphere only. In rejecting her husband, who wants only a gentle wife, not a successful doctor, Xia Zhixian recovers her feminine individuality, which was previously precluded by a father-dominated society. [48] The intellectual fulfillment of woman is very well captured by Xia Zhixian's profession: she is a gynecologist, the "mother" of all mothers, whose obstetric work in the delivery room has saved the lives of numerous mothers and babies. This metaphor contains, in the words of Linda Gordon, "a celebration of women's unique and superior qualities with . . . an emphasis on mothering as both source and ultimate expression of these qualities."[49] In this sense, the form of individual accomplishment behind the character of Xia Zhixian also transcends the limited voices of certain feminists who, in their efforts to disrupt the established gender hierarchy, affirm the superiority of women's minds over their bodies. In her performance in the delivery room, however, Xia Zhixian proves that she excels in both biological reproduction and intellectual creation—she is a master of both worlds.

Xia Zhixian's proficiency in the delivery room offers both a compensation for her meager family life and a disturbing source of regret. In fact, satisfaction and regret are so closely intertwined that they at once affirm and challenge Xia Zhixian's feminist stand against the demand that women restrict themselves to a domestic role. Here, then, is a genuine dialogic voice raised against what would otherwise be a feminist and, hence, monologic play. Indeed, many voices in the play are opposed to the just-described feminist discourse. Mo Jin, the conservative mother, makes a long-distance telephone call to Peng Lun, Xia Zhixian's ex-husband, and asks him to rush home to resolve the family crisis by persuading his daughter to yield. Having been a victim of his ex-wife's career-oriented life, Mo Jin argues, Peng Lun is the person who might best be expected to prevent history from repeating itself. To everyone's surprise, however, when Peng Lun and Xia Zhixian meet again for the first time in twenty years, Peng apologizes to Xia for not having supported her in her career, and he urges his daughter to learn from her mother and firmly pursue her own dreams. Furthermore, Cheng Kang's father also makes a telephone call in which he sternly tells his wife, Mo Jin, that her attitude toward Yin'ger is entirely wrong: "Please tell Comrade Peng Lun I'll come to see him shortly and that I want to drink a toast together with him to Yin'ger's forthcoming trip abroad."[50]

This unexpected dramatic moment turns on a very "feminist" voice for women's fulfillment being celebrated by two fathers who, according to one feminist perspective, have deprived women of the economic and political means to achieve independence. At this moment, then, Bai's play could not be characterized as feminist, as it portrays women's liberation as requiring confirmation by the patriarchal fathers. It is important to note here that Mo Jin's husband, a high-ranking party official who represents power in the play, can with one phone call resolve any problem. In an echo of the device Bai used in *First Bathed in Moonlight*, his voice is rendered all the more powerful because of his absence. He is the only person in the play without any real name except for "Old Cheng" and never appears on the stage. But he does not need to. His amplified voice on the telephone functions as a deus ex machina in the play. Thus Bai's play can be read, at least at this juncture, as a political repositioning in the post-Maoist era, in which feminist concerns are used merely to celebrate Deng Xiaoping's political domination. Bolstering this reading are the play's constant allusions to the Four Modernizations and the overseas study program, which Deng promoted. The play's feminist outlook obviously cannot be compared with that of mainstream Western feminism, which does not adequately address the fate of women living in a socialist society. Feminist discourse in these environments is always in danger of being appropriated by the ruling ideology. To borrow Karl Mannheim's distinction between utopia and ideology, we might say that Xia Zhixian entrusts herself to the utopia of women's liberation only to be betrayed by the ruling ideology, which appropriates women's issues in the interest of political repression.

The cultural father's last word is further negotiated by another voice. Hearing her husband criticizing her attitude, Mo Jin breaks down and protests: "Don't forget that I sacrificed my earlier career to guarantee your success today. Deep inside, don't I know that people respect Xia Zhixian for her achievements, whereas they respect me for being your wife? If I had her accomplishment, I'd rather not be your 'esteemed' wife!"[51] This statement again points up the predicament of women. If the depiction of Xia Zhixian's lonely personal life can be seen as a patriarchal commentary on professional women, then Old Cheng's criticism of Mo Jin can equally be regarded as a rejection of women's familial role. In either case, women are placed in an untenable situation. Not only is it "natural" for father to demand that mother give up her career, as happened to Xia Zhixian, but, after he himself has benefited from the sacrifice, he can then turn around and belittle it for being "culturally" wrong, as happened to Mo Jin.

Mo Jin at this point serves as another dramatic voice that makes a multileveled representation of life. On one level, the play asks whether women can have both a successful career and a happy domestic life. A persistent voice suggests that it is possible and ideal for a woman to strive for and attain both. The story of Xia Zhixian and her daughter, Peng Yin'ger, seems to hold the promise of a better future for a younger generation that benefits from its parents' mistakes. Yet, on closer examination, the play's multiple voices are equally convincing in suggesting that a society's unreasonable demands in regard to women's professional and domestic roles make it impossible for any woman to be content with either role. Xia Zhixian's life demonstrates that a professional woman will inevitably fail in her role as mother and wife, whereas Mo Jin's experience proves that a devoted domestic woman will also be unacceptable to the males of the patriarchal culture. The predicament causes Mo Jin to protest against the sexist society that glorifies fathers, who demand the impossible from women, making both their leaving and staying home impossible. Rather than being directed against patriarchal values, Mo Jin's personal, limited protest is leveled at the male betrayal of the social contract whereby women sacrifice in return for male recognition. She thus vents the frustration of one who, having been content enough to live in reflected glory, experiences a keen sense of injury when that side benefit is no longer forthcoming. By insisting that men fulfill their obligations in the social contract, she at least unmasks their hypocrisy and prevents male chauvinists from posing as feminists. Her insistence is fueled by a longing for male affirmation, which alone gives meaning to her sacrifice.

On another level, Mo Jin's voice also casts doubt on the authority of the Western discourse whose invention of women's liberation has offered no better solution to the problem of the restrictions of women than to the predicament faced by males. Xia Zhixian is an Ibsenesque heroine who, in the 1980s, still fails to answer the question of what happens to Nora after she leaves home. The painful irony is that rather than, by her own example, holding out the promise of a better future, Xia Zhixian passes on to her daughter a myth of women's liberation. Indeed, her daughter's prospect for happiness is in greater doubt than was her mother's, since her intellectual promise is as yet unfulfilled and, in contrast with her mother, her career orientation (mathematician) is far removed from the sphere of domesticity. In this regard, Mo Jin's voice contrasts with and perhaps even negates those of many other mothers and daughters who still entertain illusions about women's liberation and the Western institutions that gave birth to it, such as the Western education for which Yin'ger yearns. In one dramatic moment, Mo Jin rejects two cultural fathers—a domestic one and a foreign one—who presumably could never be wrong in delineating the rules for women's behavior. She is consequently one of the play's most important characters, and although we would have least expected it of her, she resists (for reasons the significance of which she does not know or understand) any single version of truth, knowledge, and power, thereby in effect resisting a final solution to all the dramatic conflicts involved. Constantine Tung correctly observed that "Mo Jin's anger and sorrow reveal the dilemma and burden of a woman in modern times."[52]

The above analysis demonstrates that Bai Fengxi's *An Old Friend Comes at a Stormy Time* presents a multiplicity of roles and voices, both feminine and masculine, radical and conservative, authoritative and individualistic. This multiplicity does not destroy drama, as Bakhtin claimed, but rather strengthens the dialectical force of the genre.[53] In the context of women's theater in post-Maoist China, these different voices among the women characters themselves can stimulate immediate and creative responses from participating theater audiences. Furthermore, the meanings of a drama can be best expressed through the often contradictory or multiple visions of author, director, and audience, all of whom contribute to its final revelation of undetermined and undeterminable meanings. Although Bai intended in *An Old Friend* to create "equally good characters on stage without a clear demarcation between the 'right' and the 'wrong,' " she was pleasantly surprised by audiences' negative response to Mo Jin. They were unfailingly disgusted by the voice of Mo Jin as a *guan taitai*, or "Madam Official," who, in Yin'ger's words, is depicted as a "good-for-nothing living in clover by virtue of her husband's power and position, and lording it over others by virtue of his authority."[54] Indeed, according to Bai Fengxi,[55] the following lines spoken by Peng Yin'ger were greeted by audience applause that lasted as long as three minutes:

> If her husband is an official, then she's the official in control of that official. If he has hundreds of thousands of men under his command, then she has under her command a man in command of hundreds of thousands. She runs everything—not only things she is entitled to run, but also those she has no right to run. (*Pause.*) Such women should ask themselves just how much good they do for the people (act 3, 70).

The audience in this instance was not reacting to the gender issues that were usually prominent in Bai's plays. Rather, what was being evoked were their frustrating personal experiences in the highly bureaucratic, corrupt society of early post-Maoist China, when party officials became the easy targets of the public's ridicule and contempt. Male and female spectators in this instance transcended their gender differences and reacted equally strongly to the quoted statements.[56] The "fundamental feminist notion," advocated in the West, that the personal is political became relevant at this particular moment of contemporary Chinese theater because it explained the reception of this Chinese women's play, which envisions, among other things, "several interconnected sets of social relations — relations of work, of class, of race, and of sex/gender."[57] The class-inspired grievances against the privileged few, to which audience members gave voice, did not always strike drama critics in the same fashion. According to Bai Fengxi, they were more apt to perceive the character of Mo Jin as a woman victimized by the male-dominated society precisely because she had faithfully followed its rules. Once again, the dialogical and polyphonic voices were being further polarized by the different reading habits and performance receptions of diverse audiences, thus making a definitive interpretation for an interesting and paradoxical women's play impossible.

The third work in Bai Fengxi's trilogy of women's plays, entitled *Where Is Longing in Autumn (Buzhi qiusi zai shuijia)*, premiered by the China Youth Art Theater in 1986, was considered by drama critics to be deficient because it lacked a linear plot or a main character that could capture the interest of the audience.[58] According to Bai Fengxi, however, during a seminar on the play attended by drama critics and playwrights, Zhang Xian, then a graduate student, argued to the contrary. He believed that the play represented a big leap forward from Bai's two earlier plays precisely because it deviated from a plot-centered structure. Instead, its series of scattered points of interest constituted a new structure that required more depth in characterization and more mature dramatic techniques than those employed in the two other plays.

Notwithstanding this issue of dramatic structure, it is instructive to investigate why this play became a hit at a particular historical juncture when the private voices of women were being submerged in and sacrificed to the new romantic image of the nation, which struggled to compete with the powerful, modern West. The rise of a market economy introduced people to the prospect of striking it rich, an utterly unimaginable possibility in the most recent past. The turbulent efforts to foreground women's liberation and equality issues became intricately interlaced with the new problems in a nation that had suddenly developed a desire to become part of the modern world, which, as Hannah Arendt puts it, is "that curiously hybrid realm where private interests assume public significance."[59] Whatever women's voices one could find in this particular play were thus uneasily and uncertainly subsumed within the voice of the nation and state, which thereby gained in ambiguity. As a consequence of this endeavor, it appears fruitful to try to get a sense of the nation as it was viewed by women playwrights and, conversely, to investigate women's culture within the historical and cultural contexts that evoked its unique voices.

Bai Fengxi herself best characterized the unique voices of these women in the China of 1986. The play, she said, faithfully records the thoughts of a perplexed author who is dedicated to writing about a group of perplexed women in a rather perplexing new era of historical transformation.[60] The confusion and sense of loss brought on by the new era and the nostalgia for an irretrievable past are most associated with the character Su Zhong-yuan, whose anxieties in the rapidly modernizing world are exacerbated by challenges from her three children. She is annoyed by Ye Wei, her only son, who has failed his college entrance examinations three times but who prides himself on conducting business deals in five-star hotels and restaurants and is entirely wrapped up in his new dream of becoming a millionaire. Worse still, he falls in love with a fashion model, one of a group who were despised by some for doing the least reputable work possible and likened to prostitutes in the mid-1980s.

In sharp contrast is Ye Fei, Su's "scholarly" daughter. She has a master's degree in computer science. Without the approval of the authorities, she moonlights as a private consultant for computer software companies. Her decision to work in a free-enterprise environment truly bothers her mother, who still believes in the stability represented by a dependable "rice bowl" from the government. Moreover, as the only married offspring, she shocks her mother by divorcing her husband without a solid reason, while making all kinds of male friends in order to live by her motto: "Read ten thousand volumes, travel ten thousand miles, and get acquainted with outstanding people from all over the world."[61] Intent on her ideals of cultivating and perfecting the self, Ye Fei does not worry about how she is being judged by people. Her depiction calls into question, among other things, the Chinese feminine ideal, in which an educated woman is supposed to be happier in a domestic sphere than her more traditional counterpart, deprived of education. Ye Fei declares that she is purposely rejecting fulfilling the multiple roles expected of her—good wife, good mother, good daughter, good daughter-in-law, and good worker—because they would prevent her from undertaking the only role she cares to play: someone who is good to herself.[62]

Throughout the play, Ye Fei's efforts to walk out on her marriage are paralleled by her mother's attempts to find a marriage partner for Ye Yun, her younger daughter. Although an equally successful scholar, Ye Yun is devalued in the eyes of the society, which questions her mental state solely because she is a spinster in her mid-thirties. Harassed by a pushy mother who wants above all to see a speedy marriage take place, Ye Yun wonders why people are more tolerant of a couple who have married without love than they are of a single woman who has opted for an independent, meaningful life on her own.[63] The play ends with no closure and no resolution for a mother's anguish. However, it does demonstrate, through the mother's reflections, some understanding and acceptance of a widening generation gap in an increasingly perplexing universe:

SU: I may be getting on in years, but, you know, I do try hard to be abreast of the times. (*Taking Ye Yun's hand.*) Yet, for the life of me, I can't keep up with you children. (*As if to herself.*) Looks like the older generation cannot fully understand the ways of the younger generation, nor the younger generation the ways of the older generation. But whether we elderlies [*sic*] can be reconciled to your ways matters less and less, while life will go on without your having to be reconciled to our ways. (*A glance at Ye Fei.*) Well, since life holds so many unknown factors, go ahead and explore them for yourselves (act 4, 286).

The seemingly irreconcilable dramatic conflicts between mother and daughters suggest the moral conscience and tribulations of the nation as it emerges from familiar paths and speeds up its efforts toward modernization and commercialization. They also serve to explicate the feminine conscience of a group of highly educated women who are repositioning themselves, however tentatively, between a private space of their own and a public space that paradoxically both limits that private space and approves of it. The emergence and growing awareness of this double consciousness explains why in 1987 and 1988, when few new plays lasted for more than a dozen performances, *Where Is Longing in Autumn* played to a full house for more than a hundred performances.[64] The much criticized images of fashion models, millionaires, divorcees, and single women at that time—now quite conventional in China—accounted for the popularity of the play, which connected the audience members with very current subjects that were much on their minds.

Many women wrote to Bai Fengxi expressing their sympathies with the characters, their reflections, and their appreciation of the play. One woman said she believed the play had indeed given her a second life; it had provided her with "spiritual food to live on" in an indifferent and hostile society in which she felt increasingly isolated as a single woman. At one point, she was even suspected by her sister-in-law and her own mother of having had an affair with her brother purely because she did not appear to have a strong desire to be married. Alienated both from society and from her own family, she had even written letters to Fulian for help, without obtaining much useful response. This play, however, saved her from utter despair. "I can be understood after all," she wrote. "I should therefore be strong and go on exploring my own dreams with self-respect and self-confidence."[65] Many other women made similarly intense personal and emotional connections with the work. In fact, so warmly received was this play by people from all walks of life that the editors of *October*, in an unprecedented action, published a separate volume of the script immediately after the play's initial publication, in response to numerous requests from readers all over the country.[66]

A discussion of Bai's trilogy of women's plays would be incomplete without touching on the importance in them of mother-daughter bonding. According to Meng Yue and Dai Jinhua, this theme can be traced back to May Fourth women playwrights such as Bai Wei and her play *Breaking Out of Ghost Pagoda (Dachu youlingta)*, one of the earliest examples of women's theater.[67] The play, Meng and Dai point out, portrays an unprecedented loving relationship between mother and daughter. Their amity contrasts with the antagonistic father-son relationship in *Diary of a Madman* by Lu Xun, in which, at the turn of the century, a May Fourth "son" figure rejects Chinese fathers while identifying with the ideal fathers of the West. Because history belongs to fathers, not mothers,[68] Meng and Dai contended, daughters in the May Fourth literary tradition tended to identify with weak mothers who had historically been victimized by fathers. In the process, the daughters retrieved their mother's stories, thereby forming a women's collective experience that had been buried in history."[69]

Bai Fengxi's trilogy both continues the historical tradition delineated by Meng and Dai and violates it. Almost all the mothers in the plays tend to be loving and understanding despite their initial differences with their daughters. In each play, one detects a similar progression toward the realization of ideal mothers while the daughters draw strength from them in constructing their subject position as women. On the other hand, a suppressive, almost dictatorial strain is discernible in almost all the mothers' authoritative voices.[70] Given the absence of the fathers, both on and off the stage, the mother's rule over the daughters' lives at a certain point reminds one of the power of a father figure. Whereas Fang Rouming adopts a hypocritical attitude toward Fang Lin's unsuitable lover, Xia Zhixian demands that Yin'ger abandon her career to help her husband. Similarly, Su Zhongyuan pursues aggressive matchmaking on behalf of one daughter while resisting the other daughter's decision to obtain a divorce. Their harsh behavior evoke the role of father as found in such Republican-era works as *Thunderstorm* by Cao Yu.[71]

These mothers sometimes act as surrogate fathers who are attempting to control rebellious daughters and their values. In the PRC, the party and Chairman Mao were conventionally endowed with the loving, feminine, and thus all-encompassing and overpowering image of the mother. In this culture, the ruling ideology appropriated the mother-daughter relationship as a signifier of a new national identity. In this regard, the Chinese tradition also echoes twentieth-century Arabic literary tradition, which depicts woman as a "historical metaphor," "most commonly represented through the allegory of mother/earth/country," in which there is a "reinscription of ancient Middle Eastern mythology."[72]

Bai Fengxi's trilogy acts as a forum by and for highly educated women who had the luxury of dwelling on women's issues in salons or in their comfortable homes. This feature can also be found in many other works of women's literature in the PRC period as well as the May Fourth and the traditional periods. These literary daughters and mothers in urban China have no particular connection with female factory workers or peasants, and cannot express the voices of those mothers and daughters who bear the suppressive brunt of tradition in the vast countryside. A woman from the country *was* represented onstage in the first play, but only to demonstrate the political correctness of the Fulian official and to celebrate the liberating power of elitist, privileged women with a better education and higher social position. In this case, it is the elite woman, not the powerful father, who acts as deus ex machina to magically dissolve a poor woman's arranged marriage. Elite women in Bai's second and third plays possess the scientific knowledge and intellectual power to help in China's modernization and Westernization. In the process, their work widens the gap between rich and poor as well as the class distinction between literary daughters and illiterate mothers. In discussing the making of women's history, therefore, one risks forgetting the complexity of the subalterns' political histories and the need for their own version of women's liberation.

Contemporary women writers—and the characters of mothers and daughters that they created—used their writing and rewriting of each other's tales as symbolic and cultural capital whereby they advanced their own literary and political status in their respective spaces. Consequently, for all these reasons, and despite Bai Fengxi's sincere efforts to speak for women, her trilogy of women's plays could never be considered genuine "alternative" feminist theater (characterized by Goodman as "in essence counter-cultural," or against "mainstreaming").[73] To point out the historical limitations of women's theater, however, is not to discredit its crucial assault on the predominant patriarchal ideology. It is rather to remind women writers and critics (myself included) of these limitations, so that we may become increasingly reflective about and critical of our own work. In this spirit, we can do most justice to Bai's trilogy of women's plays and the challenging forum they create for exploring the unanswered questions posed by women's theater in contemporary China.

7

From Discontented Mother
to Woman Warrior

BODY POLITICS IN POST-MAOIST THEATER

In her insightful essay on women and Chinese cinema, Dai Jinhua narrates what she calls the plight of Hua Mulan,[1] the legendary woman warrior who won military battles on behalf of her aged father. According to Dai, one sees in this story of Hua Mulan the gender predicament of contemporary women, who can become heroes only through adopting the role of a man, "a most important mirror image."[2] Such a discourse of women finds its best expression in the literary history of 1949 to 1976. During this period, the chronicle of woman as the liberated other was replaced by that of the suffering masses. Once women had given their heart and soul to their savior's glorious socialist project, their stories of a bitter past were immediately forgotten.[3] As a result, they worked under a "double load of duties and playing two gender roles: the traditional female and the new masculine warrior."[4] The disappearance of woman warriors after 1976 in post-Maoist China, however, represents for Dai a "retrogressive movement of Chinese history," in which images of abused and suffering women were once again differentiated from those of men and were subsequently presented as "merely symbols for victims caught in Chinese history: women were now the ironic victims for the restoration of traditional womanhood articulated by yet another kind of male-dominated culture."[5]

Interestingly, however, Chinese women in the theater of the late 1980s did not suffer the same historical regression. Women playwrights such as Zhang Lili, who were fascinated by the military theme *(junshi ticai)* and contemporary army plays, produced works containing the image of woman warrior in post-Maoist China. Making use of national allegories, national-identity themes, and the national discourse of post-Maoist China, these plays paradoxically revived, if they did not actually empower, the seemingly old-fashioned figure. These women characters in post-Maoist theater nevertheless did not merely duplicate the liberated women in Maoist literature, who "fell quietly outside history's field of vision as a collective female body."[6] They fundamentally challenged the plight of Hua Mulan and attempted to reclaim, as far as possible, female identity within the limited space of the People's Liberation Army, the most male-dominated and restrictive domain in the public arena.

We may turn, for example, to Zhang Lili's play *Green Barracks (Lüse yingdi)*, published in 1990 during the rapid introduction of capitalism and commercialism into contemporary China. As opposed to other plays of the same period, which usually depict the changing mentality of the Chinese people, this play *seems* to embrace an earlier tradition in PRC literature, known as the military theme, in its presentation of the training of women soldiers in the predominantly male People's Liberation Army. *Green Barracks* treats its subject differently than do conventional army plays. In the latter, soldiers usually train in remote areas, away from urban centers. The women soldiers in *Green Barracks*, in contrast, are stationed near a "special economic zone" *(jingji tequ)*. This expression refers to an economic "oasis" that allows for the full play of capitalism in what is still officially represented as socialist China. At first glance, this play seems to fit almost perfectly into the official ideology of post-Maoist China, which, while admitting that economic reform and development were very much needed to improve the quality of people's lives in general, still expected them to adhere to socialist and communist values through personal sacrifice and devotion to nationalist and socialist ideals.

Woman soldiers, therefore, are celebrated in this play for their idealism and nationalism, and for their willingness to abandon fashionable careers as models and company spokeswomen to become soldiers defending the motherland.[7] The company is led by two experienced women commanders who gave up their family roles as mothers and wives to answer the call to duty. Two recruits are Fang Xiaoshi, an elegant city girl who loves music and poetry, and Tian Xiangxiang, a country girl who longs to become the wife of an imaginary millionaire husband. A different character is Liu Mei, who has served in the army for a few years and is now eager to emigrate to a foreign country with her fiancé. Through rigorous military training and personal sacrifice on the part of the two company commanders, the recruits are finally transformed into crack troops, as able and tough as their male counterparts. A few years later, at the end of the play, Fang Xiaoshi returns as the new political instructor of the company to carry on the demanding task of her predecessors. She will be training a new group of recruits who have the same aspirations she had when she first came into the army, and who are similarly unaware and unprepared for the arduous military training in store for them.

This post-Maoist play seems to conform to at least three previous traditions of representing women. First, the story of women warriors echoes traditional literary and operatic representations of Hua Mulan. Whereas the Mulan tale celebrates the honor of one woman's father, *Green Barracks* commemorates the collective spirit of a group of women devoting themselves to the ideals of the "territorial integrity" (*lingtu wanzheng*) and national unity of the motherland in an equally patriarchal society, contemporary China. The honor of one woman's father in the traditional tale is instantly transformed into that of the collective body of all fathers of the symbolic order. Second, the spirit of the woman warrior recalls the dramatic canon of the May Fourth period, typified by the woman playwright Bai Wei's play *Breaking Out of Ghost Pagoda*. However, whereas Bai's play depicts the disintegration of one patriarchal family in which a daughter dies in the arms of her mother after attempting to flee her father's sexual oppression, *Green Barracks* portrays a group of women who reject family life entirely for a higher realm of spiritual pursuits and moral obligations. Third, *Green Barracks* appears to draw most directly from the Maoist representation of liberated, revolutionary women, as Dai Jinhua puts it, "women disguised as men," who "have to dissolve their female subjectivity and grow up in a large collectivity as 'women heroes.' "[8] In particular, *Green Barracks* seems to have duplicated the familiar story of *The Red Detachment of*

Women, in which a women's military unit fights local despots on Hainan Island during the second revolutionary war period. Unlike its precursor, however, *Green Barracks* is preoccupied with the urgent need to preserve the revolutionary tradition of women in a period of moral crisis, instigated by a surging commercialism.

In my introduction to *Reading the Right Texts*, I situated *Green Barracks* in the historical context of the soldier play, from the Red Army drama through the PRC liberation army plays to model theater and post-Maoist transfigurations. In particular, I compared the model ballet *The Red Detachment of Women* to *Green Barracks* in terms of their common depiction of an all-women soldier's company with only one male protagonist. Despite their different explorations of the colors red and green, of androgyny and cross-dressing, both works expressed a prevalent, unequal gender relationship. *Green Barracks*, however, did present a group of post-Maoist women bewildered by past expectations of their revolutionary roles and the new demands for women to return home and pursue their individual happiness.

With those historical contexts in mind, I will examine the various ways in which *Green Barracks*, as a social and cultural text, illustrates how the process of creating disciplined soldiers desexualizes and defeminizes female bodies. I emphasize the problem of femininity within the context of military training, a process of public transformation from female agency to revolutionary (and hence, by definition, male-like) soldiers. (By "female agency" I mean "the capacity, condition, or state of acting or of exerting power" as a female subject.)[9] How is it that the woman soldier, rather than female agency, is celebrated? What is exemplified by the preference of a woman soldier's body over her female agency? To what extent have female bodies been politicized and displayed in contemporary China?[10] What bodies in particular evoke cultural suspicion, scrutiny, desire, controversy, and repression in the course of the country's political struggles and within its national and international agendas?[11] Why does this play celebrate defeminization, which is juxtaposed with great anxiety to the female roles of mother, girlfriend, fiancée, and the female ideal of the womanly, the beautiful, the domestic, and the faithful to the home? I argue that these seemingly contrasting, paradoxical depictions of women highlight gender politics in contemporary Chinese society, which has pronounced female bodies to be crucially different from male bodies. These paradoxical depictions will eventually help to explain the final return of women warriors in the post-Maoist period, when one might have expected their combative spirit in defense of the motherland to be rejected. In fact, that spirit has had to be endorsed as one way of recovering female individuality, which is in danger of being lost in a rapidly changing society.

At the outset of the play, the emphasis is on the fragile, delicate female bodies of the new recruits, who must first be transformed so that they will look and act like male soldiers. Thus, in act 1, Lu Xiaoyun, the political instructor of the company, undertakes the difficult task of convincing the new soldiers to cut their hair short. "It is obviously true that all of you love your hair," Lu says, "yet your hair is no longer a personal matter once you become a soldier. The army demands uniformity and discipline, which make no exception for your hair. Our first task today is to cut your hair short!" Despite their screams and tears, the new recruits must accept this painful symbolic initiation into the army through a crucial step of defeminization. The process becomes tougher and more immediate in act 2, which focuses on the training ground, where the new recruits from the women's unit are ordered to compete with the men's unit. Functioning as part of the subtext, the stage directions draw readers' attention to the changed bodies of the female soldiers: with their short hair, they now appear to be more alert and energetic. Even their army uniforms seem to fit them better, now that their "slender legs are wrapped tightly in army trousers."[12]

This is the first—and what is to be a typical—moment in the play in which women soldiers are celebrated at the expense of their female agencies and female bodies. The exultation, however, has to be interrogated before more facets of female agency are unequivocally removed from female bodies. Later in the same act, the harsh and strict physical training finally takes its toll, despite the new soldiers' efforts to keep up. Fang Xiao-shi is so exhausted that she can no longer move her legs. As punishment, she is ordered to stand alone in the fields under the burning sun and not permitted any food or water. At this moment onstage we see a desolate, lonely, and tortured body separated from other bodies, those of her female companions, who are longing for her return. In other words, we see a fragile body on public display as a critique of the gendered body, inadequate in comparison with the so-called ideal (and hence, honorable) body of the male. Of course, what is essentially being conveyed through the image of this female body is the female agency resisting a culture that demands the transformation of the feminine into the disciplined masculine.

The highlighting of Fang's body reminds one of what Foucault describes, in his *Discipline and Punishment*, as the politicization of docile bodies.

Foucault argues that, beginning in the early seventeenth century, the image of the soldier became that of someone who could be affirmed from a distance: he owns certain signs—typical signs of his strength and courage.[13] This "bodily rhetoric of honor" in the "ideal figure of the soldier," according to Foucault, can be recognized through his movements, his strength, his courage, and his manner."[14] For Foucault, then, in the course of human history the body had become the object of compelling investments; the body imposed on itself "constraints, prohibitions, or obligations."[15] The classical age, Foucault further argues, had treated the body as "object and target of power," to be manipulated, shaped, trained by the dominate culture.[16] Docile bodies, Foucault observes, were connected by methods of discipline that "became general formulas of domination."[17] It was discipline that "produce[d] subjected and practiced bodies, 'docile bodies,' " which were made more obedient as they became more useful.[18]

In spite of his insights, Foucault fails to discuss gender politics as reflected in representations of bodily differences. As *Green Barracks* testifies, the ideal, time-honored body of male soldiers was the basis of institutional formulas of domination employed to discipline subjected and manipulated female bodies.[19] In addition, a male agency had to be created to further silence female agency. The central story of Fang Xiaoshi, a lover of music and literature (her name literally means "a little bit of poetry"), demonstrates this point. More than anyone else in the play, Fang personifies an overflowing of female energy that hinders the mastery of military maneuvers confronting the new soldiers. Paradoxically, it is Sima Changjiang, the only male character in the play, who is presented as being most comfortable with Fang's female energy. When Fang, as punishment, must stand alone, Sima comforts her, bringing her chewing gum, water, and food, and patiently listening to her complaints about her ruthless women commanders.

In act 4, when Fang runs away from the barracks into the forest, Sima again tracks her down, keeps her company, and appreciates her musical and poetic talents, as if Fang and he were soulmates. Like a tender and caring mother, Sima helps Fang put on her army uniform and reassures her that not everyone is good soldier material but that she can succeed, since she is an intelligent, aspiring individual, different from the women around her. Having gently imposed the army uniform (designed specifically for a male body) on Fang, Sima convinces her that, unlike the other recruits, she will be able to function as an outstanding soldier. Fang thus loses her female agency. First, a male agent affirms the physical difference between the two genders and favors the male as the superior and stronger one; second, he claims that one female body is different from and superior to others. Flattered and comforted by Sima's confirmation that she is different from other women, Fang is now determined to persist and become the unique soldier Sima expects her to be. To be a good soldier is to emulate Sima, the male ideal of excellence. It is significant that this decisive act of disciplining Fang's female form into a docile body of the honorable soldier is not carried out by her women commanders, who act like exemplary male soldiers, but by Sima, the only male agent, who paradoxically acts like a woman. In this sense, this modern play resembles the premodern tales in *Liaozhai's Records of the Strange (Liaozhai zhiyi)*, in which, in the words of Judith Zeitlin, "masculinity has thus become reevaluated as an essentially *moral* quality, one that women, as well as men, can achieve through self-cultivation and right conduct."[20]

Fang Xiaoshi is not the only woman soldier to come under the spell of Sima's magical power. On several occasions elsewhere in the play he is described as the party representative of the women's company. He takes over the educational and ideological function of role model in a much more effective, soothing manner than the women commanders. Indeed, because he works as a technician who teaches women soldiers their signal communication skills, he has the best opportunity to play the role of inspiring teacher. Through his patience during their technical examinations, he helps them graduate from his training class. To help them relax after the hard trials of the day, he organizes a night outing into the city, where they wear their colorful civilian clothes and enjoy being women again for the first time since entering the army. When he is reprimanded by the company commander for this lapse in discipline, Sima shoulders the entire blame to protect the frightened women soldiers.

In all these instances, Sima provides the women soldiers with motherly energies and protection to help them make sense of a confusing and chaotic experience. He can even be seen as a symbolic link between the "green barracks," where most of the women are not allowed to be different, and city life, where most of the women originally came from and to which they long to return. In fact, the patient, caring, tender, and soft Sima contrasts clearly with the two women commanders, who are tough, demanding, and strict stereotypes of male characteristics. These characters have already lost their female agency, and their female bodies are now respected as embodiments of masculinity. This state of affairs leaves a gap for Sima to fill in his role as a surrogate "female" agent who makes spiritual and emotional connections with his female counterparts.[21] In doing so, he reshapes them into their culturally expected roles and consequently disciplines them into docile bodies that will abide by the necessary constraints, prohibitions, or obligations.

Yet Sima has other facets. Along with his female qualities we are also constantly reminded of his masculinity. He is a dashing, well-educated, and gorgeous man who has charmed almost all the women soldiers who have crossed his path. Although Fang Xiaoshi has made pronounced strides toward being transformed into a more mature masculine soldier, she has gradually fallen in love with Sima, who seems to possess the best of the two gender worlds. Hopelessly in love, she is enchanted by her daily contact with him as a spiritual guide. She longs for his masculine body yet is pessimistic about her chances of fulfilling her desire, as the army strictly forbids men and women to have love affairs. She can only kiss his military uniform, drying in the open grounds surrounding the barracks. This expression of emotion is seen by Liu Mei, a jealous competitor for Sima's love, who reports it to the company commander, thus bringing about a confrontation between Fang Xiaoshi and Liu Mei.

Heartbroken and lovesick, Fang decides to enroll in the army academy. She believes that after graduation in three years she will return as an army officer and have the right to pursue her love. Her confrontation with Liu Mei represents another test of Fang's will to resist her desire to love and to be loved, because Liu Mei believes that wearing an army uniform is not as important as preserving a woman's right to love. The army is not the right sphere for women, Liu Mei argues. It is not even a suitable place for human beings if it does not allow an eighteen-year-old girl to fall in love. Had she been in love like Fang, she would have pursued the object of her love at all costs. With some hesitation, Fang reaffirms her choice of a military career: "I like being a soldier. Everyone has her way of living. For me, life as a soldier is a fairly good choice."[22] In her last effort to assert—in order to finally relinquish—her wish for the freedom to love, Fang declares her desire for Sima to Jiang Hua, the company commander: "I am a human being. How can I not think about [the man I love]? Do you know how hard I have tried to suppress my passion in order to be worthy of this army uniform! I would have done anything to win his love had I not been wearing this uniform—it should have been within my natural right to love."[23]

In view of Fang's conscious efforts to combat her natural desires, the most ironic twist in the play is Sima's rejection of her love. Indeed, throughout the play, Sima, without being fully aware of it, has been in love with

Bai Yu, the most beautiful woman in the company. Her extraordinary beauty, according to Sima, is especially brought out by her army uniform. Bai Yu is also presented as a strong, mature soldier, with the requisite masculinity and discipline. Perhaps what makes Bai Yu even more desirable to Sima is her refusal to accept his love because she believes a devoted soldier should never fall in love with a particular man. Her paramount concerns are her military career and the "family" placed in her care in the women soldiers' company. She is a devoted wife to her unit and a dutiful daughter to her motherland.

Thus Bai Yu follows the tradition of selflessness and sacrifice. Earlier models in the play include the company commander, who lost her only son to illness while she took care of the "children" in her company, and the political instructor, who passed up several opportunities to be released from the army and lost her husband to a fashionable woman. However, in a critical sense, Bai Yu differs from the two women commanders in being the only one who combines the "abundance and richness" of a woman with the "brilliance and spiritedness of a man."[24] In her capacity as platoon leader, ranked between immature new recruits and mature and desexualized women commanders, Bai Yu perhaps represents a fluid, transitory space between femininity and masculinity. Sima thus loves both the beauty of her body and, supposedly, the brilliance of her mind. In Bai Yu, we see the concept of the ideal woman soldier, whose female agency has long been drained out of her yet whose body still retains sex appeal. In this way, the female body becomes a signifier for the masculine and the ideal.

What Sima loves is the idea of loving. He does not know whether or not the object of his love truly exists. He does not realize that the Bai Yu he sees now will eventually vanish in the course of her career (as in the case of the company commander), sacrificed to the love of her company. Nor is he aware that the ex-husband of the political instructor now devalues the very same qualities— the brilliance and spiritedness of a man —that he once admired in his wife during the earlier years of their romance, when they both worked in the army. The play seems to suggest that, even if love had a chance to develop between Bai Yu and Sima, he might still end up leaving her after they reenter the modern civilian world, for the modern world is full of temptations and far removed from the army. The world represented in the play as a "green barrack" is free of the characteristic corruption of urban areas and commercial culture.

In her competition with Bai Yu, Fang Xiaoshi loses for two reasons that commonly confront women in a patriarchal society: she is not as beautiful as the other woman and has to wage an intense inner struggle to resist her own desire to be finally accepted as a good soldier on the society's patriarchal terms. Furthermore, upon her return in the last act as a model woman soldier, she has to be even more noble and selfless. In a conversation with Bai Yu, she claims to already have a boyfriend, whom she met in the academy. This new situation clears the way for the love affair to develop between Sima and Bai Yu, who have been promoted to higher ranks and now have a right to fall in love. Yet in spite of Fang's sacrifice, Bai Yu still insists that her home will be the army and that she will never fall in love with anyone. This stance of Bai Yu, cast by the play as a celebration of a woman's devotion to the motherland, totally rejects womanhood, motherhood, domesticity, and attachment to the home hearth. In the final analysis, even Sima himself is drained of both his female and male agencies. Consequently he represents neither male nor female energy, but rather the host for confused identities of both genders. What started out as a play emphasizing the differences between male and female bodies appears to have canceled out those very differences. This is a distinctly different state of affairs from that depicted by the Ming and Qing accounts of gender transgressions described in physical and biological terms. In these accounts, the "metamorphosis of women into men now becomes a matter for rejoicing, whereas men who become women are at best tolerated, if not punished, by the authorities."[25] In the contemporary play, however, both male and female gender transformations, which are conveyed in symbolic and metaphorical terms, are equally accepted, manipulated, publicized, and politicized by the cultural authorities to enhance their own political agenda.

One can nevertheless still argue that *Green Barracks*, intended by the playwright as a celebration of the equality of men and women in socialist China, has portrayed women's pain, anxiety, and frustration in the process of trying to be equal. The triumph of the male spirit as symbolized at the end of the play suggests that even when women are finally accepted as equals, they are still different. After all, they come from an unusual female unit in a predominantly male-oriented army. Since this deviation from the norm merely confirms the legitimacy of the norm, it becomes difficult to read the play as a celebration of the liberation of the women. In this sense, *Green Barracks* can still be viewed as belonging to the canon of woman warrior texts. Its crucial difference from its precursors resides in the playwright's efforts to break away from old patterns and dramatize female identity in the most strictly controlled domain, the People's Liberation Army.

By examining the issue of body politics in the play, one can perceive that gender and sexual differences are urgent concerns in the devising of new national characteristics in contemporary China. These characteristics are much more fluid and flexible than before. Both ideal male and ideal female images were drawn from stereotypes in traditional culture and revolutionary culture. On the other hand, they are also reconfigured for the agenda of creating a new national identity in post-Maoist China. In Sima, the ideal man, and Bai Yu, the ideal woman, we see an ingenious remaking of two people into figures who at once embody their own binary oppositions and reject those very oppositions at different moments. This discussion of the representations of female bodies (and, in contrast, of male bodies) in a military unit can help us examine a dominant culture's suspicions, longings, controversies, and strategies for repression during a period of political struggle.

Where did this fascination with women warriors in 1990 China come from? As Dai Jinhua pointed out, women warriors had already disappeared from major films and works of fiction. I believe that these characters were recovered by women playwrights who felt deeply the loss of self-esteem and identity experienced by women during the economic reforms. In the early post-Maoist period, when women playwrights, confronted with the swift expansion of the new forms of social organization, capitalism, and urbanization, initially attempted to reclaim the private and familial domains as a means of forging individual connections to the social and public spheres, they met with disappointing results. Zhang Lili's earlier dramatic works, for instance, show a clear trajectory from the depiction of a frustrated wife in her 1984 play *Unequal Formula of Life (Rensheng budeng-shi)*, to a discontented mother in her 1986 play *Mother, You Were Young Once Before (Mama, ni ye ceng nianqing)*, to women in supporting and subjugated roles in another 1986 play, *Homecoming (Gui qu lai)*, and finally to the portrayal of competitive warriors in *Green Barracks* of 1990. In Zhang's last play, she reclaimed the public domain as a legitimate sphere for women's display of their talents and subjectivity. I argue that this historical retrogression from discontented mother to vibrant woman warrior illustrates the process by which contemporary Chinese women refuse to be signified as negative reference points from which to ground male positivity. Once again they long to be able to "hold up half of the sky" and to be equal to their male counterparts, both at home and in the public sphere.

Nonetheless, the return of the woman warrior does not constitute a mere repetition of the Maoist style of representing women who were in actuality subordinated to the male-dominated party and socialist agenda. Their reappearance on the stage was intended to reconstruct women's subjectivity and sexuality to decentralize the male-centered discourse on modernity. The military theme enacted on a public stage thrust women onto a new battlefield for the purpose of reclaiming the neglected personal and political aspects of their lives. The playwright thus provided a non-Western example of what Elizabeth Weed terms the "reversal of the political/personal hierarchy by feminism," which "means that the political is already marked by, constituted by the personal, and most important, it means that both terms are displaced."[26]

It is instructive to examine Zhang Lili's first play, *Unequal Formula of Life*, which garnered considerable critical acclaim for the first female amateur dramatist. Zhang wrote it after having typed many scripts for a theater group in the city of Guangzhou,[27] and it created an uncommon stir at its first performance. Authoritative drama critics such as Yu Qiuyu interpreted it as successfully questioning increasingly cynical views toward the social institution of marriage at a time of deteriorating moral values, thereby triggering a heated debate in the journal *Chinese Women (Zhongguo funü)*.[28] In the larger scheme of things, however, the play reflects the dissatisfaction of women with their newly found "happiness" at home after years of being compelled to fulfill the demanding roles of liberated women during the Maoist period. During the early post-Maoist period, many Chinese women retreated to the home front where their role was reduced to that of performing chores inside their homes. Ye Zi, Zhang's protagonist in *Unequal Formula of Life*, feels suffocated by her obedient husband, whose highest aspiration in life is to be her slave, as if she were his master.[29] Having assumed the reverse gender role of homemaker, the man of the house thoroughly enjoys meticulously performing household chores.

Feeling restless at home despite (or more possibly because of) the fact that she is adored by a perfect husband who seems to combine masculine charm and feminine sweetness, Ye Zi longs for an unavailable other. This other man she imagines on a remote island devoting his life to a military career at the expense of his marriage, which is on the verge of breaking up because his wife refuses to give up the comforts of city life. Ye Zi dreams of joining such a man in a simple home on a remote island where she can pursue her career as a doctor in a military unit. Zhang Lili's play thus dramatizes a significant historical regression in the role of women. First, the drive in the post-Maoist period to achieve economic success and material comfort seems to have lured women back to the home. Women thereafter have no choice but to relive their earlier predicament as domesticated mothers and daughters, as depicted in the May Fourth literature. In many works in this literature, women characters seeking their own identity feel compelled to flee their homes to escape the autocratic ways of their fathers.

Second, Ye Zi's rejection of her domestic role and appreciative husband evokes the parting between Lin Daojing, a college student who leaves home to join the Communist revolution, and Yu Yongze, the attentive husband who exerts himself to keep his wife inside the "doll house." This well-known scene in both the novel and the 1959 film *The Song of Youth* (*Qingchun zhige*), masterpieces in the PRC literary canon, characterizes the predicament of the Chinese Nora, whose strivings "became the antithesis of traditional feminine ideas" and who longed for a place in the public arena, away from her oppressive home.[30] Despite the different circumstances, Ye Zi's yearning for the idealistic military commander echoes Lin Daojing's attachment to Lu Jiachuan, a Communist martyr who initiated her into her revolutionary career. The different ideological climates of the pre-1949 period and post-Maoist China do not prevent the women of both generations from harboring the same need to break away in pursuit of personal freedom and spiritual fulfillment. Paradoxically, by rejecting a comfortable home, Ye Zi, the idealistic 1980s woman in China, helps to advance and glorify the Chinese nationalist agenda, whose spirit is captured in the familiar exhortation that all must contribute to the defense of the motherland. In the process, she abets the patriarchal domination of women, who are once more reduced to the status of deprived, though liberated, others.

Unequal Formula of Life, however, does not merely duplicate the earlier traditions. After trying to win over her ideal lover, Ye Zi eventually rejects him as a hypocrite who dares not pursue true love and seek a divorce for fear of unfavorable public opinion and damage to his military career. She thus discards both a modern man, devoid of male chauvinism, and a traditional man whose male chauvinism is discernible in his devotion to the patriarchal tradition. In this regard, Ye Zi outdoes her counterparts in the PRC literature, refusing both the traditional role of Qin Xianglian, deserted by her husband, and that of Hua Mulan, who faces the predicament of having to carry a double load of duties, that of "the traditional female and the new masculine warrior."[31]

Ye Zi is more fortunate than these women because she has the luxury of rejecting her weak husband. Through her own travails, she proves that home alone, even when it has a room of her own and a loving husband, can never become a truly fulfilling space for a woman deprived of opportunities in the public sphere. Her rejection of both men calls into question the values of a society that defines the various roles of women in terms of how they best promote the interests of its male members. The question nevertheless remains: if Ye Zi's ideal lover had the courage to end his marriage, would she then have lived out her dream of having both a happy home and a satisfying career on that remote island?

Upon close scrutiny, it seems that Ye Zi, despite her awareness of the problematic patriarchal culture, is much more committed to the socialist doctrine of self-sacrifice in the interests of the nation than to any particular man. She can question her lover's wish to conform but cannot change the just cause that earns a male conformist's devotion. She can reject her husband's disinterestedness in pursuing a public career, but not her own desire to be an integral part of the national effort toward building a better and stronger socialist country. The feminization of her husband, on the other hand, can be seen as passive-aggressive resistance on his part to a culture's call to collective action, which she and her lover paradoxically embrace.

This play offers another instance in which the concerns of Chinese women playwrights for female agency are corrupted and appropriated by the 1980s post-Maoist discourse, which pretended to be vitally different from its Maoist predecessor. The voices of female subjectivity were never truly articulated as a resistance to the predominant ideology. The women's seemingly diverse voices can be seen as having "[slipped] into a simple pluralism which, while replacing assimilation as an ideal, nonetheless keeps power relations intact and simply inflects the many within the paradigm of the one."[32] In post-Maoist theater, the "paradigm of the one" is usually too quickly embedded in the women's "new" voice, which falls under the "category of woman" but does not deviate from the official experience of women.[33]

Zhang Lili seems to take the debate further from the vantage point of the mainstream stage when she opens her play with a Brechtian "alienation effect." "Dear friends," says Ye Zi, addressing her audience, "how I hope to benefit from your correct—or relatively correct—answer to my dilemma, after you hear about my story!" Her need for others to approve of her decision to leave her husband recalls Lu Xun's question in 1923: "What happens after Nora leaves home?" This question resonates in a Chinese society in which, at a later date, women's lack of economic freedom was deemed a factor that might impel them to return to their homes.[34] It also evokes Nora's own desire to find out "which is right—the world or I?"[35] Raising such a question at the beginning of the play imparts a sobering, self-conscious, and reflective tone to Ye Zi, who is distinguished from the Chinese Noras of earlier times by her economic freedom. At the play's conclusion, Ye Zi, having made known her story, poses some questions to her lover in a soliloquy: "How are you doing since we parted? How is your life? You are such a perfect soldier, with your devotion to your idealism, beliefs, and dreams. You have also succumbed to worldly views. How I long to find out what you think of my divorce. Can you tell me if there are still shining spirits ahead that would guide me through a lifelong journey?"[36] This passionate longing of Ye Zi for another man, for the "masculine ideal," makes the already limited feminist scope of the play even more questionable and problematic. In this sense, she may be worse off than previous Chinese Noras, who were at least free from illusion in regard to other men. Ye Zi thus becomes at most a reluctant Nora, or a Nora who, despite her seeming rejection of her ideal man, leaves one home while dreaming of another.

While Zhang Lili's first play investigates a woman's private role in the home, her second play, *Mother, You Were Once Young Before*, goes further, probing into the social, ideological, and psychological makeup of a discontented mother. Shu Chang, once an eminent ballet dancer in her youth in the 1950s, is now only occasionally remembered by those close to her as a pure, white, beautiful swan who once shone in the spotlight. The collective memory of the culture and society at large, however, no longer recalls her glamorous past. When she was young, beautiful, and famous, she was admired and pursued by two handsome, talented poets. One wrote heroic poetry about conquests and honor for the official culture; the other, passionate and tender love poetry that he dedicated to Shu Chang and their pure love. Numerous awards and high prestige were the enviable lot of the first poet, along with a life of privilege and comfort. The poet of private love, however, having been condemned as a rightist for failing to concentrate his energies on enhancing the political correctness of the party, was exiled to a remote region. Sha Sha, the younger son of the Shu family, describes the private poet's five collections of love poetry as beauti-fully melancholy and sentimental. It evokes more aesthetic feeling than the poetry written by his "old father." Whenever the official radio an-nounces that the latter has won another national award, the gushing na-tionalistic feelings expressed in his poems embarrass the son at school among his peers.[37] On several occasions, Sha Sha alludes to the charac-terization of his father as the dutiful son of the culture, bought by and sold wholesale to the nation, whose guardians erase private memories to consolidate all that pertains to the public and the collective. Unhappily married to the public poet for years, Shu Chang is torn when the private poet, her true love, returns from exile after the death of Mao.

As one of many good-hearted public men, Sha Jishi, the father, is liberal-minded about ending a marriage that was never meant to be. The play captures the historic moment when some of Sha Jishi's countrymen are reflecting on a national past full of mistakes, and when Sha Jishi also rejects past representations of his poetic oeuvre as a signifier of nationalism. In an honest talk with his son, Sha Jishi admits that his wife never loved him and that only a historical misunderstanding provided him with a situ-ation in which he loved her.[38] When Shu Chang asked a girlfriend to deliver an invitation to Bi Lei, the private poet, it was mistakenly handed to Sha Jishi, who responded by finding his way to her dark apartment. Too ashamed to admit her unintended intimacy with Sha Jishi, Shu Chang never had the courage to correct this mistake. "Historical misunderstand-ing" also refers to numerous political movements such as the anti-rightist campaign, which removed talented writers such as Bi Lei from society and deprived them of the ability to pursue their happiness. Now, in the 1980s, with public history being rewritten in China, Sha Jishi is inclined to accept reality and to rewrite the family history as well. He leaves his home and invites his wife's lover to move in so that the two can create a new his-tory comprised of love and tenderness.

Since such a scheme would make Shu Chang feel twice cheated, she demurs. To scuttle her past would be to reject her public life and a once successful career, forever associated in her mind with the power and attractions of youth. Nor can she let go of her family, which, however broken, affords her a sense of unity and connection to her two sons. Al-though never a warm place, her house has been home to her for the past thirty years, and without it she would feel desolate and utterly alone. She has to push aside the tenderness of her lover, or the real happiness she has known at home, in order not to lose all trace of what the larger culture inscribed on her body and in her heart. To forget is to forgive the culture's cruel characterization of woman as discontented and problematic while serving as the sexual provider, homemaker, and state builder. To forget is to foster the national amnesia that neglects the role of woman as a constructor of her identity and cannot easily be altered and adjusted with each new regime. Shu Chang, unwilling to overlook how she has been treated in the past, confronts Sha Jishi about his poetry award money. Rumor claims that the money has gone into renting another apartment where Sha Jishi entertains other, younger women.

Having thus refused to allow her family to treat her as an old, unhappy woman, Shu Chang is similarly unwilling to forgive the patriarchal order. History must be constantly re-created and relived in order to be remembered by a subject, a family, and a nation. By choosing not to forget, she manages to regain some sense of living again, however partially, in that memory of the contrasting space of the stage where the past was evoked by a present performance. By not letting go of her past, she holds on to that limited public and private space which the culture allowed her to bask in for a short period of time. It is for her dancer's body rather than a mother's mind that she longs to be remembered. As Jiwei Ci observes, "if the body has been the site of taming, it has also been the locus of resistance. For the body is forever sensitive to pain, and pain dictates its own laws of memory and forgetfulness."[39] Shu Chang's body thus incorporates both a cultural and a personal signifier, for even though, as Ci points out, the "body does not know what is moral . . . it knows what is not. Every brainwashing is a denial of the body, an attempt to make one believe the opposite of what the body says. But the body has its own way of fighting back. Its silence is merely a sign that it does not find the pain intolerable."[40] It fights back against the charisma of the national leader who "promises these pleasures and much more, and on that promise has rested the leader's ability to undertake and the people's willingness to submit to the remaking of Chinese memory."[41] By refusing to forgive, Shu Chang bears witness to her powerlessness when she had to submit to disrespect and dismemberment.

This couple's contradictory views toward history are also reflected in the conflicting attitudes of their two sons. Sha Sha, the younger, resents his parents' hypocrisy and cowardliness, especially his mother's desperate attempt to hold on to a broken family. Consequently, he fails his college entrance examination, disappointing his mother's high hopes for him, because he cannot compose an essay entitled "My Family." "I was totally confused by the title, not knowing how to write . . . ," he explains. "No one in the family understands me, nor do I understand any one of them. I could not write about the warmth and love of my family. I had no choice but to hand in an empty sheet of paper."[42] As an agent of change, Sha Sha does not want his mother to be chained to the past; she ought to repudiate her rejection by choosing to live this present life fully, while planning for tomorrow. He urges her to change her life, to follow her heart and pursue her true love in the same spirit that he has cherished Bi Mengyang, the lovely daughter of his mother's lover. According to Shu Chang, Bi Mengyang is better off, psychologically and emotionally, because although she grew up with only one parent, she benefited from a much more honest and healthy environment than his own. In spite of his apparent courage in facing reality, Sha Sha's rejection of the past actually represents his unique way of rejecting adulthood. He frequents the "Disneyland of the Orient," which, in his mind, is an ideal place for adults to visit, because their existence is so lifeless that they need, more than children, a playful paradise to help open them up to a blissful world.[43] All this boyishness indicates the impossibility and impracticability of forgiveness. Only children, in other words, can be cheated into forgetting, while adults know better and can never afford to overlook the past.

Sha Yang, Sha Sha's older brother, does not understand Sha Sha's desire for change nor their mother's dilemma. Sha Yang is a victim of the culture's emphasis on a man's career at the expense of his happiness in love. Many years before, his mother had forced him to leave his girlfriend because she feared that a love affair would divert his attention from his college education. Having turned himself into his mother's ideal son, Sha Yang becomes a successful businessman who, as a developer of five-star hotels, is equipped to profit from the economic boom. Like his father, he works indefatigably to realize the new national agenda while appearing to have lost all enthusiasm for pursuing any love interests. However, once having become his father's son (both his poetic father whose poetry helps write the official history and his cultural father who rewards such devotion to the nation), he can no longer understand his mother's sorrows and suffering. He perceives his own honor as being implicated in the issue of his family's unity and regards his mother as shameful when he surprises her in the act of kissing her lover in his own home. In this respect, he is different from his father, who has seen fit to go on with his life. Sha Yang, meanwhile, prevails on his father to come back home with him, in the hope that his parents may yet achieve a reconciliation. Unable to face the harsh reality, he remains in this sense his mother's son, for they are both equally trapped by the past. He differs from his younger brother, too, who is cynical about educational and professional choices but steadfast about his choice in love.

The conflicts between mother and sons strongly echo Cao Yu's *Thunderstorm*, a canonical play of the Republican period.[44] In this play, a Phaedra-like mother is tortured by her love-hate relationships with her two sons. While the younger one of natural birth is naive, vibrant, idealistic, and future-oriented, the older one, a stepson, is moody, cynical, and past-oriented. The mother makes advances to the elder son, who rejects her after falling in love with a maid. Zhang's play, of course, drops the incest originally present in Cao Yu's play. This plot structure makes Zhang's play into a surprisingly critical rendering of the predicament of post-Maoist Chinese women, who, even after many years of being eulogized as the "iron women holding up half of the sky," are as doomed as the women who lived in the remote past of Republican China. These former iron women are more discontented than their Republican counterparts, because their experience in public and professional life has made their homecoming and imprisonment in the home all the more intolerable to them.

Just as the women in Republican China sought a way out of their meaningless homes, so did their descendants in post-Maoist China who have to break out of their doll's houses to discover for themselves, once again, which was right—the world or themselves. This seemingly perennial question undoubtedly accounts for Zhang Lili's fourth play, *Homecoming*. The May Fourth women detected the opportunities inherent in the nationalist or communist revolution for releasing their energies and reclaiming their identities, and the post-Maoist women depicted on the stage similarly seemed to need a larger cause to lure them out of the home. *Homecoming* is set during the 1980 China-Vietnam border war, when both men and women were called on to prepare to make limitless sacrifices. As men become once more the living national emblems of bravery and selflessness, women, in spite of their desire to move beyond their houses, cannot resist the country's call to traditional, dutiful roles as sacrificing lovers, wives, and mothers. They leave their private domains only to be sent home again, but this time to a new "home" established close to the enemy line. In this fashion, they too can partake of the glory meted out to men, the heroes devoted to the territorial integrity of the nation.

This history's reclaiming of women as "imaginary signifiers" is especially evident at the play's end, when a military unit finally wins a grueling battle after having lost its valuable members to the enemy attack. A diverse group of "virtuous" women then travels far from their hometowns to console the survivors of the war. One of the survivors is Gao Liangzi. At the beginning of the battle Gao faked an injury for fear of dying in the war, which to him meant losing his beautiful fiancée, Jie Zi. Touched by the heroic deeds of his fellow soldiers, however, Gao throws himself into battle, from which he emerges a wounded hero. He has lost a leg and wants to end his engagement to Jie Zi so as not to become a lifelong burden to her, but Jie Zi proves herself equal to the role of virtuous woman. She travels thousands of miles to join Gao and take care of him for the rest of his life.

Li Xiaomei appears to represent an intended contrast to this pure but illiterate country girl. An intelligent, successful journalist from the city, she had for years pleaded with her husband, Jiang Nan, to quit the army as a condition for her staying in their marriage. As an army unit political instructor, however, Jiang Nan takes pride in caring for his "children," especially the new recruits, who "had just left their own mothers."[45] After learning that he has lost his "children" in the war, Xiaomei, despite her ambivalence about her marriage, does not hesitate to uproot herself from the city and to establish their new home at the frontier, where she adopts children orphaned by the war. This twist constitutes an interesting reworking of the "revolutionary family theme" from the prototype *The Red Lantern*, in which two generations of workers adopt an orphan girl to form a revolutionary family. In *The Red Lantern*, both the father and the grandmother are seasoned supporters of CCP revolution from the outset of the play, whereas in Zhang's *Homecoming* the woman is transformed from a discontented wife before the war to a fulfilled mother after it. The symbolic signifier of adoption in forming a family and a nation takes on much more complexity in Zhang's play than it did in its precursor from the Cultural Revolution, since it happens in post-Maoist China after doubts about Maoist idealism had already returned public women to their homes in the first place. Their return to the battlefield to adopt orphans in contemporary China reflects both the discontinuity and continuity of revolutionary themes in the PRC theater.

By the end of the play, Li Xiaomei is expressing her desire to confess, not to God, but to those "martyrs who were never given enough time to play their roles as fathers and mothers to their own children." She thereby renounces her former dream of having her own home to embrace a stepfamily in the unlikeliest place—a military unit at the frontier.[46] She also has to give up her established career as a journalist in order to become a mother to the children of martyrs. Similarly, Yan Yan, whose most creative efforts lie in narrating beautiful stories to children, has to renounce her calling as a teacher of preschool. She now joins her fiancé, the platoon leader Wen Bing, at the front line to establish their home with a disabled soldier, whom they will care for as if he were a member of their family. These three very different women acting out a trilogy of homecoming became symbols of the ideal mother who, according to Virginia Woolf in a different context, is "intensely sympathetic, immensely charming, utterly unselfish," someone who "sacrificed herself daily" and "was so constituted that she never had a mind or a wish of her own."[47] One wonders, however, if this depiction of idealistic motherhood in the Chinese context merely repeats the images of nurturing women in the model theater, which, as noted before, emptied women's personal life to construct a new cultural myth to underpin the post-Maoist political regime.

In Zhang Lili's *Homecoming*, the women, in their supporting roles, are portrayed in such uniformly traditional ways. The male soldiers, however, look distinctively different from most war heroes in the PRC. *Homecoming* questions both the Maoist and the post-Maoist perspectives in its characterization of Tao Qi, a new recruit who was a millionaire in a big city. Unlike the Maoist soldier, who was usually depicted as being tall, grand, and perfect, Tao Qi is a little man with carnal appetites who wants to release his sexual energies before a battle. Yet this unfit soldier is celebrated as a hero who dies on the battlefield. Upon being elevated to the status of martyr, he is shown not as a conventional exemplar of nobility, selflessness, and devotion to his motherland, but rather as a man suffering from a fundamental sense of the meaninglessness of life. He chooses to die while protecting Xi Shi, whose girlfriend he had stolen. He had been torn between a new girl from the countryside and his former girlfriend from the city, who had betrayed him by her intimacy with a rich businessman from Hong Kong. Finding it impossible to choose between them, Tao Qi had resorted to death as a much simpler solution. Indeed, the play is permeated by this character's complete sense of despair, especially with his mother, who deserted him when he was very young to stay married to a wealthy man in Canada.

Through Tao Qi's story, the play bitterly criticizes the post-Maoist pursuit of economic success. Abandoning his previous career as a successful entrepreneur, Tao Qi pursues death after having been rejected by the two people who should have loved him the most, his mother and his first girlfriend. In the military unit, where he throws in his lot with other poor fellow soldiers, Tao Qi finds a warm home that money could not buy.[48] He was very touched by the unique qualities of the ordinary and, in some cases, poor people he met in the army, which seemed to him like a haven in an increasingly complex modern world. "I have seen through it all," Tao Qi said. "Who doesn't know how difficult it is to live in this present world! Yet what *is* most difficult? It is loving and sacrificing yourself for others at the very moment when you yourself are having a difficult time."[49] Although he had been resentful of the military unit's strict discipline, he had come to realize that he did not want to be anywhere else, since "it is still the army that has gathered most of the good people left in this world."[50]

In celebrating the army as a "sweet, sweet home," Tao Qi invokes the PRC literature that favored a big, revolutionary family at the expense of a private one. The canonical texts of the PRC period leave their mark when Tao Qi has somehow to be redeemed as a real hero at the end of play, as the survivors pay tribute to him at his grave. Appearing as a phantom, Tao Qi tells his commanders that he would have wished to be a better soldier if he had been given a second chance to live. He regrets rejecting his mother, who had begged for his forgiveness just before his death. Never having had a chance to love and be loved by his mother, he now wishes that he could have called out to her for the first time in his life. He also now understands why "mother" is always used as a metaphor for his home country: "Now I came to realize that 'motherland' means my own mother. . . . At the very moment when I was torn away from my mother-land—which I had defended with my own blood—I felt as if I had also lost my mother."[51]

When the mother and the land become one, the lost self is finally trans-formed into a national hero. His death nevertheless challenges a system that wastes precious and innocent lives. That Tao Qi adopts a phantom's persona to visit the platoon leader Wen Bing, who desires to come to know him once again as a good soldier, emboldens one to go beyond Tao Qi's seemingly affirmative words about the motherland.[52] The living must ele-vate the dead so that they can erase their emotional turmoil and guilt at having survived a bloody war. And what could be a greater reward for the dead than the kind of public recognition bestowed on Tao Qi for having been a true hero along party lines? Nor is Tao Qi the phantom respon-sible for being viewed differently from Tao Qi the soldier. The phantom is called upon and spoken to by the other, the living one, who has the full power of imagining and reconfiguring who the dead—and hence, the idealized—Tao Qi should be. In this period, the national drama that glorified nationalist discourse, assuming that it was still recognized as such by audiences and reviewers, would not have made too much sense had it not been contested by the fate of the individual. Thus the touching utterances of individuals as they express their human needs and bodily desires make for remarkable personal stories. The playwright could be seen as trying to hew to the boundaries of official censorship in regard to Tao Qi, but one would still have difficulty passing him off as a real hero, although this seeming antihero possesses, at bottom, a shining character. Tao Qi touches the audience's heart, and in so doing he makes the play work. His tribulations raise questions about the human predicament and about the paradoxical demands of the ruling ideologies of different historical periods.

At the very end of the play, at the graveyard the women speak for male soldiers who are no longer there. Yan Yan announces: "You have always considered yourselves very ordinary people. But Yan Yan will not forget you. The motherland and the people will not forget you. We will always remember: upon the towering and lofty banner of the Republic is marked in boiling blood your youthful heart; in the vast land of the Republic are engraved your deep and profound emotions! Please accept our salute—to the soldiers of the Republic!"[53] Although this conclusion echoes plays from the Maoist period celebrating the state and the new nation, it can also be viewed subversively. The red color of the national flag is painted with the warm blood of the youth whose deaths help to make sense out of what the republic truly represents. The vast republic cannot possibly manage to raise and protect its sons and daughters. Who is to blame for the demise of the brightest and the most beautiful among us?

This problematic view of history lends meaning to the words of Su Shu, another bright soldier who died in the war. As he addresses his surviving fellow soldiers through the voice of a phantom, he expresses no disappointment at having lost the chance to fulfill his ambition of becoming a writer. (His motivation in joining the army had been to gain firsthand experience so he might write about the lives of soldiers.) "Writers are not necessarily any smarter," Su Shu now tells his comrades-in-arms. "The kind of soldiers they usually depict in literature do not always measure up to the soldiers I have come to know."[54] He would have liked to write about real soldiers such as Tao Qi, Gao Liangzi, and Wen Bing, but wonders if the soldiers in his own writing "could have really been understood by those still living in this world."[55] With these words, Su Shu casts doubt upon literary and historical writings of contemporary China, suggesting that true-to-life soldiers are yet to be found in PRC literature. The unhappy, unfulfilled male characters in *Homecoming* dramatically foreground the even weaker voices of the female characters. This state of affairs might very well account for the progression to Zhang Lili's next and last play, *Green Barracks*, in which the women warriors return to take center stage, as discussed at the beginning of this chapter.

As one might anticipate, the preoccupation of Zhang Lili and other women playwrights with women's public roles incurs some risks. The writer's imagination could be overpowered by the symbolic order established by the father in the society, leading her to create women characters who are neither inside nor outside of national discourse, neither known or unknown as creative individuals. Women playwrights themselves can, willy-nilly, cast their women characters as representing darkness and chaos, viewing them as a destructive force of the social order. This outcome is exemplified by *Fission (Liebian)*, a 1985 play by Xu Yan, which presented an ugly mother and wife.[56] Rarely did the post-1949 stage see such a figure, who was at odds with the predominant female images of earth mother, maternal power, and historical narrator found in PRC literature. In his 1937 play *The Wilderness (Yuanye)*, Cao Yu created a malicious Mother Jiao, whose instincts to protect her passive son drove her to abuse her daughter-in-law. She has been interpreted as a "remnant of the cultural past and present, an exemplar of Chinese superstition and backwardness."[57] Yet mothers cannot be equated with mothers-in-law, especially in a traditional society where the patrilocal and patriarchal family structure often made the mother-in-law–daughter-in-law relationship one of considerable tension and enmity. Xu Yan's ugly wife and mother is not born out of an oppressive family structure and marks a departure from Republican and Maoist conventions.

Taking place during the economic reforms, *Fission* features Yi Beilin, a popular and successful director of an industrial district in a major city. A modern entrepreneur, he rejects bureaucracy, bribery, and blackmail and promotes free elections, even at a time when the chief competitor for his public office seems to have the best chance of defeating him.[58] As a skillful diplomat and shrewd businessman, he has won the respect of his business associates from the capitalist West. Although he easily captures the hearts of blond ladies from the West, Yi above all else is a principled party secretary in the Maoist tradition. He promotes his daughter to the position of deputy editor-in-chief of a major newspaper only after she has proved her own righteousness by proposing to expose her father's weakness and mistakes during the election season. In doing so, he renders himself vulnerable in two ways. First, political opponents can use this promotion of a family member in the forthcoming election to accuse him of corruption. Second, appointing someone to a top journalistic position who reveals his problems puts his election campaign on the defensive. Yet this "perfect" father, who represents the masculine ideal of the post-Maoist regime, can do such remarkable things.

The playwright sets off this idealistic image of the symbolic and cultural father by providing its negative counterpart, Lu Shijie, Yi Beilin's wife. She is depicted as selfish, manipulative, cruel, and perhaps most important, unattractive. An active force in politics, she uses her influence as "first lady" to order newspaper editors to reject articles that might damage her husband's chance to be elected.[59] This devotion forms a striking contrast with her behavior during the Cultural Revolution. Then, she exposed her husband's anti-party crimes to the authorities, pushing him to the edge of the abyss when he most needed understanding and support from his family. Nor could she forgive Xia Yu, a film director, who rescued Yi Beilin from severe beatings by the Red Guards one rainy night and comforted him with her love after he had been betrayed by his wife. Lu Shijie forced Xia Yu to take a job in a remote region and promise never to come back. Having driven one woman thousands of miles away, Lu keeps close to her another woman who, like Xia Yu, has devoted her life to Yi Beilin. Unlike Xia Yu, she has been deprived of the opportunity of telling him about her sacrifice. This other woman is Ku Jie, which means "bitter elder sister," a name she herself adopted to replace her original name, Tian Jie, which means "sweet elder sister." The name change occurred many years earlier, after her wedding night, when she waited in vain for Yi Beilin to come and take off her wedding scarf, as required by tradition. Only later was she told that he had run away from the arranged marriage in protest against this traditional institution. As for Ku Jie, however, once she had been promised to a man, she was forever committed to securing his happiness. Several years later, she tracked him down and told Lu Shijie the story in exchange for merely being allowed to work in the house as a maid and take care of Yi's daily needs. At the juncture when the play takes up her story, she is too old to continue working in Lu's household and plans to move back to her hometown. She is heartbroken again when Lu Shijie prevents her from revealing her true identity to Yi Beilin, her only wish after thirty years of sacrifice.

The play takes its most dramatic turn when Yi Beilin, learning about Lu Shijie's abuse of Ku Jie, decides to confront a blackmail scheme by revealing his true feelings for Xia Yu in an open debate with his political opponent. This removal of a mask in public provides the audience with a rare instance on the contemporary Chinese stage in which an extramarital affair is treated as a poetic transgression of ethical and ideological boundaries. Significantly, a supreme affirmation of this act comes from a woman, a girlfriend of Yi Beilin's daughter. Confessing that she now respects Yi Beilin much more than before for being a real man, she indicates just how courageous his act was: "In China, there is no blunder that is so grave as an extramarital affair, which can arouse more indignation in people than any other 'crime.' . . . Whether or not they really are against it, they all act as if they were saints or Virgin Marys in competing with each other to denounce such a 'stupid mistake.' "[60]

This modeling of Yi Beilin as a truly "heroic" man sets him apart from his predecessors in contemporary Chinese drama who had to resist emotional intimacy and even physical attraction to women in order to prove their integrity as Maoist men. The deviation is unheard of even in portrayals of post-Maoist public men, who can rebel against the ideological dictates of the previous regime but not against the marital institution, which, in many instances, protects loveless marriages. In this play, a "fission" occurs between the image of the public man and that of the private man. This fission is accomplished by abandoning the mask of the perfect public man—in Yi Beilin's case, by openly admitting that his marriage has failed and declaring his true love. Through this act Yi becomes truly responsible to the public, and honest in his private life. The home is where one would expect that one could talk about the politically forbidden, and where honesty and love could prevail. In truth, however, the home is often a place where one must hide one's feelings so as not to be betrayed by those who know one best, as happened in many "happy families" during the Cultural Revolution.

When Yi Beilin leaves home, accompanied by his two children, who have taken his side and rejected their mother, we see for the first time in modern Chinese dramatic history that an undesirable mother is left alone onstage, deserted and devastated. This is a striking reversal of the celebrated last scene in Cao Yu's *Thunderstorm*, which finds the father alone onstage after his children, wife, and ex-lover have either been killed, gone insane, or departed forever. The early post-Maoist play *In a Land of Silence* by Zong Fuxian, known as the best, most successful imitation of the father-text *Thunderstorm* (in the Bloomian sense of the word), is another model from which *Homecoming* departs. Zong's play ends with a disgraced father abandoned onstage by his children and wife, who can no longer tolerate his betrayals of family and friends during and immediately after the Cultural Revolution.

How, then, are we to explain a woman playwright breaking ranks with male counterparts and presenting a destructive woman? One might argue that even a woman playwright known for treating women's issues and subjectivity in her plays does not work without the residual influence of traditional misogyny.[61] Indeed, the fate of a wife abandoned after her husband's departure from their house reverses numerous stories of Noras since the May Fourth movement who chose to leave their "doll's houses" in search of happiness and independence. An even worse status is conferred on a woman who chose to manage the home for her man for years and is then cast off; her status is diminished from that of a hostess to that of an outcast, and she is scarcely better off than a lover or a maid. When, as happens in *Fission*, a lover from the film industry is elevated to the status of new hostess of a powerful household (Yi Beilin and Xia Yu will wed after he wins the elections) and, by virtue of her special history, shares the glamorous spotlight with the elite of high society, where does that leave a mother? Does she not once again become the madwoman in the attic — invisible, of no consequence?

Indeed, Lu Shijie is worse off than a domestic woman, who, though she may never venture out of her house, is at least spared being condemned in public as someone who is crazy and an evil strategist or manipulator. It is assumed by all that she has only herself to blame for her disgrace and downfall — after all, was she not granted a public role but then brought down and disqualified by her lack of virtue? If all this is allowed, does it still justify her present abject state, in which she might even envy Ku Jie, whose lifelong sacrifice is finally rewarded by Li Beilin's recognition of her? Li Beilin's limited power to recall is a telling endorsement of the culture's traditions and the father's amnesia. His belated gratitude toward Ku Jie paradoxically leads to the banishment of another woman, and the less-than-subtle readmission of all those traditional images of woman as passive sexual object, devoted mate, and dutiful server. As for the warrior's spirit, it is found here in the form of a vicious monster that highlights women's failure as public figures and, in the final analysis, legitimizes male

power and the new social order enshrining it. So this play does not capi-
talize on the woman warrior myth that elsewhere has served as a source of
hope for women. The woman warrior remains a useful myth, but a myth
nevertheless. One can perhaps argue that this woman playwright does not
necessarily write with women's interests at heart; she merely celebrates
the new cultural father who is dedicated to accumulating spiritual and
material wealth for the new nation, even if in that process the interests of
the mother are sacrificed.

Yet I favor another argument to make sense of this problematic treatment of women. In contemporary Chinese society, this atypical representation of women as the source of evil might be interpreted as an ingenious
challenging of the Maoist revolutionary discourse of women. As "signifiers for the suffering masses," degendered "iron maidens," and liberated
warriors,[62] women in these guises were used to strengthen the subalterns'
interest in the revolutionary cause. The images of women in the early post-
Maoist period fared no better, as this study has demonstrated. Xu Yan's
play put this "perfect" image of women on trial for the first time by plac-
ing women on the same footing as men. If women can hold up half of the
sky, as Mao once claimed, they must also take half of the blame for human
weakness and imperfection. Far from always being earth mothers and supportive sisters, women can be just as vicious as men. Only after women
have finally been taken down from their pedestals and stripped of their
mythical and ideological trappings can their femininity, individuality, and
humanity be expressed. Thus, although *Fission* may not appear to be a
woman's play, one can interpret it as an implicit critique of the plight of
Chinese women. From this perspective, the lonely woman onstage can become as charged and striking an image as the madwoman in the attic. The
fate of Chinese women, as shown in this play, is hopelessly confined by
the very system that has promised them half of the sky. The predominant
culture has turned women's bodies into lonely, unpleasant, and desperate
resisters of male desire and into ugly, spiteful figures for men and women
to reject.

Given the foregoing, can one really argue that feminist theater exists in
post-Maoist China? A working definition might be Lizbeth Goodman's
notion of a theater that "aims to achieve [a] positive re-evaluation of
women's roles and/or to effect social change, and which is informed in
the project by broadly feminist ideas."[63] When Zhang Lili's four plays are

read chronologically, her attempts to reappraise women's diverse roles in a rapidly changing society are clearly related to the central concern of bringing about changes in women's experience. Animated by their own ideas of what it meant to be a woman in contemporary China, these playwrights could define feminist theater in China as a cultural phenomenon interpreted by and for Chinese women.

The dramatic line of development from the heroic women in Zhang Lili's plays to the shrewish women in Xu Yan's play can be viewed as a consequence of the process of women's self-reevaluation and as a modern parallel to the relationship, described by Judith Zeitlin, between the heroic and shrewish women in Chinese traditional fiction. Whereas the heroic woman, with her "degree of personal integrity and morality [that is] considered highly untypical of her sex," presents "no threat to the greater social order," "the shrew is a justification for and a vindication of the most misogynist views of women. She may be dominant, but she is not in the least masculine. She does not behave like a man, for her misrule embodies an exaggeration and intensification of all the worst and quintessentially feminine traits in Chinese thinking. She is not so much *un*feminine as *hyper*feminine."[64] In traditional fiction, the interaction flows only between the reader, the text, and the author. A more complex, dynamic interaction occurs on the Chinese stage because of the impact of diverse interpretations and perceptions of producers, directors, performers, readers, and audiences. All of these elements may affect the play and contribute additional, meaningful ways of examining Chinese women and contemporary Chinese culture in general.

8

A Stage in Search of a Tradition

THE DYNAMICS OF FORM AND CONTENT
IN POST-MAOIST THEATER

Since its inception, modern Chinese drama has been inseparable from the May Fourth movement and its anti-imperialist and antitraditionalist agenda. During its history, however, this anti-imperialist thrust has in many instances led to a paradox, as the antitraditional aspect of modern Chinese drama undermines its anti-imperialist dimension.[1] The best example of this contradiction can be found in the well-known appearance of Hu Shi's *The Main Event of One's Life*, in which he imitated Ibsen's *A Doll's House*. Hu sought to introduce Western dramatic form as an alternative to the traditional operatic theater, viewed at the time as "a dehumanized literature." Hu chose a Western form of drama to express the thematic concerns of May Fourth intellectuals, whose very antitraditional position found its best target in the old form of operatic theater. A similar history seems to have repeated itself in early post-Maoist China, when Chinese playwrights turned to Western dramatic forms, such as epic and absurdist theater, to revive the stagnant theater dominated by the Maoist doctrine of socialist-realism with its emphasis on "healthy" or "ideologically correct" themes.

To further explore the dynamics of form and content, this chapter will focus on a group of plays in early post-Maoist theater that are known for their formalistic features. In fact, critics claimed it was primarily for their innovative formalist features that these plays won approval. While this claim remains true, the "aesthetic" aspects in many instances cannot survive or become culturally meaningful without also being personal and political. This is not to say that aesthetic or highly literary and dramatic forms are not appreciated on the Chinese stage, or that in early post-Maoist China they were always deemed secondary to political and thematic concerns. Rather, it means that the so-called aesthetic considerations in contemporary Chinese drama can only take hold when incorporated with political considerations. In a censored society, these considerations are also profoundly and inevitably personal. Because they were inseparable from their historical and political contexts, dramatic styles and techniques were never treated merely as formalistic categories. They reflected the dramatists' visions of the world, their positions vis-à-vis the characters they depicted and the audience they were trying to attract, the state ideology they appropriated or manipulated in presenting their ideas, and the collective consciousness that had given rise to theatrical space as a relatively coherent imagined community. These contexts will be viewed as meeting grounds for the dialectics of form and content, and the dichotomies of private and public, traditional and modern, and East and West. In the course of discussing these dichotomies, I will also treat gender politics in contemporary Chinese theater, where the representations of women characters further complicate the relationships between those dichotomies.

Hu Shi's *The Main Event of One's Life* adopted from Western theater not only the spoken form but also illusionist theater, otherwise known as proscenium theater. As the Greek word *proskēnion* indicates (*pro*, before; *skēnē*, tent), proscenium theater is oriented toward the invisible (fourth) wall between audience and players, which helps to create the illusion of a representative stage. What is enacted beyond the wall is supposed to represent real life and events, whose verisimilitude is supposed to be so convincing as to be unquestioned by audiences, according to Richard Southern,[2] although most realistic theater compromised with illusionist theater. This illusionist theater, which reached its apex in nineteenth-century realistic and naturalist theater as represented by Ibsen, Chekhov, and Strindberg, became the predominant dramatic genre in modern China and was promoted in the PRC as the form most closely conforming to the Maoist theory of literature.

The *Sitanni tixi* (Stanislavsky method), based on a theory of acting developed and practiced by the Russian Konstantin Stanislavsky, further helped to establish illusionist theater on the Chinese stage. Stanislavsky's emphasis on a completely realistic performance, achieved through voice and body training, re-creation of the dramatic situation in terms of the actors' own personal impressions and memories, and total identification with the situations and characters of the plays, was freely adopted and absorbed into Chinese theatrical practice in order to represent socialist China. As was pointed out by Liu Housheng, one of the most respected drama theoreticians and critics of his time, during the seventeen years between 1949 and 1966 fully 99 percent of dramatic productions exhibited a marked influence of the Stanislavsky method, whereas only 1 percent consisted of Brechtian theater, as represented by a total of three productions: *Eight Red Flags Fluttering against the Wind (Bamian hongqi yingfeng piao)* in 1958, *Mother Courage (Dadan mama he tade haizimen)* in 1959, and *Braving the Torrent (Jiliu yongjin)* in 1963.

Modernist theater is a newcomer to the Chinese stage. As a result, a play whose structure depended on or was inspired by a modernist experiment became popular for its daring characteristics. Chinese dramatists' and critics' support for modernist theater in the early and mid-1980s reflected, more than anything else, their wish to figure in the arena of world theater. Responding to the politicized literary and artistic scene of previous decades, some dramatists and critics assumed that some aspects of world theater were "superior" in terms of their "aesthetic" and formalist features. This hankering for artistic values was strengthened by the appalling experiences of socialist China. Thirty years of isolation had caused the Chinese to fall drastically behind the rest of the world, and they feared they might never catch up. It thus became incumbent on Chinese dramatists to produce modernist plays for approving audiences in order to enter the world community and never again leave it. The first experiments with Western modernist theater, which foreshadowed experimental movements in other genres such as fiction and film, underscore the necessity for studies of contemporary Chinese drama. They demonstrate both the potential for and limitations of a cross-cultural transformation, for to please and entertain Chinese audiences, the early experimental theater was restricted by the very political and cultural conditions that had compelled dramatists to introduce Western movements into China in the first place.

For example, so-called absurdist plays such as *Bus Stop (Chezhan)*, premiered in 1983, and *WM* in 1985, despite their apparent use of absurdist theatrical elements from the West, in essence constituted political and ideological reactions to the traumatic years of the Cultural Revolution. Gerenue Barmé was correct in contrasting the waiting for a bus that never comes in *Bus Stop* with the plot of Beckett's *Waiting for Godot*:

> They are left waiting, certainly, but they have an aspired direction; their dilemma is far from being either existential or absurd. It is rather one of strategy and means—when and how they should move on. There is never any real doubt that they can and must go towards the city. Gao [Xingjian's] work does not aim at forcing the audience to confront the half-realized fears and anxieties of the human mind. Rather his positivistic view of contemporary Chinese society has a definite moral undertone: unite and work together, but be careful not to neglect the importance and value of the individual.[3]

In a similar fashion, *Hot Currents Outside the House (Wuwai you reliu)*, premiered in 1980 and which Tian Xuxiu claimed was "the first absurdist play" in contemporary China, shared very few characteristics with its Western counterparts.[4] Set in early post-Maoist China, when Maoist values were being challenged by materialist pursuits, the play relates the machinations of an orphaned brother and sister who try to avoid sharing their rooms with their other brother during his visit. Since their parents' death, this brother had been taking care of them, using all the money he saved while working as a farmer. While plotting how to keep him out of their separate, warm rooms, the siblings are constantly visited by their brother's spirit, which recounts his struggles to build a village in the harsh wilderness near the Soviet border. The play concludes with the radio news that their brother has been found frozen to death after having spent the night trying to protect a bag of wheat seeds for his villagers. Ashamed of their selfishness, the brother and sister begin to realize what they have lost and initiate a search for their brother, who, they believe, is everywhere, even perhaps among the audience, whence they have just heard him calling them. The moralistic tone of the play clearly marks it as belonging to the realist tradition, and its commemoration of the brave life of an educated youth in the countryside affirms the Maoist ideals of the Cultural Revolution. In fact, nowhere in the play can one detect any of the essential characteristics of absurdist theater: metaphysical anguish over the absurdity of the human condition, rage against the futility of civilization, or a depiction of senseless human activity in which nothing really happens or matters.

Nevertheless, Chinese critics still hailed *Hot Currents* as being modernistic. They asserted that it merely differed from the Western version of absurdism, typified by cynicism and "a sense of despair in passive waiting." This first Chinese attempt at absurdist theater, on the other hand, was content to apply the genre's formalistic features, with which it conveyed a "positive" sense of "fear in expectation."[5] This interpretation typified the dynamic relationship between form and content as seen by critics and dramatists, for whom the aesthetic and formalistic features of Chinese theater had to be clothed in a "politically correct" ideology. Although eager to see Western techniques employed in dramatic productions, Chinese dramatists and critics felt obliged to describe the Western other as a "passive," pessimistic entity in order to make room for the creation of an "active," optimistic Chinese self. Perhaps this derived partially from the desire of Chinese artists to adopt Western forms to Chinese content; or perhaps Chinese artists hoped by using this approach to evade the censorship system in early post-Maoist China—in a discourse on literature and art informed by political considerations, one had to beat the devil at his own game. Talking about theater in ideological terms disarmed protests against formalistic and artistic experiments that might later land a play in a political debate.

In terms of its formalistic features, *Hot Currents* reminds one not so much of the modernist theater as of Thornton Wilder's *Our Town*. It evokes Wilder's sense of timelessness, which in *Hot Currents* is achieved by the older brother moving freely in time and space between past and present, life and death, and various geographical locales. Eschewing the Aristotelian concept of drama, with its requirement of a definite beginning and end, both *Our Town* and *Hot Currents* opt for a sense of the totality of time—the beginning of the country (in the former) and of the family (in the latter)—an affirmation of collective and cultural values, and nostalgic longing for an idealized past. Both plays belong to a theatrical tradition that delivers a view, not just a representation, of life.

But though Wilder was personally inspired by the nonillusionist tradition of operatic Chinese theater, as both Chinese and American critics have claimed, contemporary Chinese dramatists such as Wei Minglun, in attempting to reform the Chinese theatrical tradition, were inspired by what they understood as the absurdist tradition. Wei surprised Chinese dramatic circles in 1986 with his daring experimental play *Pan Jinlian*, which he described as "absurd theater in the *chuanju* (Sichuan opera) style" *(huangdan chuanju)*. Its "absurdity," Wei Minglun insisted, resided only in its "absurdist form," used by the playwright to invite characters from different countries and historical periods to comment on the tragic story of Pan Jinlian, one of the most "notorious" female characters in Chinese literature.[6] Wei's ultimate goal suited the kinds of themes that were at home in the realist tradition, such as the liberation of women from the cultural past by "exploring the close relationships between human beings and society and between historical discourse and contemporary reality." By his own admission, he was quite aware that his concept of "absurdity" might have nothing to do with that defined by his Western counterparts, who nevertheless had no exclusive right to "invent the word 'absurd.' "[7] One might argue that an understanding of the word used in theatrical absurdism makes it imperative that the play show the absurdity of human experience. Wei nevertheless bypassed this issue by asserting his Chinese way of defining terms originating in the West.

As one Chinese dramatist noted, *Pan Jinlian* is a play about one woman in conflict with five men: (1) Zhang Dahu, the rich man who forces her into an arranged marriage after she refuses to become his concubine; (2) Wu Dalang, the poor, short, ugly man Pan must marry; (3) Ximen Qing, the dashing, vicious playboy who has a fleeting affair with Pan and enters into a plot with her to kill her husband; (4) Wu Song, the he-man tiger killer who responds to Pan's flattery by killing her to avenge the murder of his brother, Wu Dalang; and (5) Shi Nai'an, author of *Water Margin*, whose patriarchal position is exposed and challenged by various fictional and historical characters from several canonical works, from both the Chinese and Western literary traditions.[8] Unlike the traditional tales *Water Margin* and *Golden Lotus (Jinpingmei)*, from which the above-mentioned plot line was initially drawn, the *chuanju Pan Jinlian* critically comments on their works' misogyny by pitting its female protagonist against the fifth man.

Tolstoy's heroine Anna Karenina, for instance, appears onstage to lament Pan Jinlian's suffocating marriage when Pan is frustrated by her husband's lack of courage in defending himself when he was teased and mocked by others.[9] Anna Karenina also intervenes at a crucial point to advise Pan to commit suicide, as she did, instead of murdering her husband.[10] Lü Shasha, a character from the contemporary novel *No. 5 Garden Street*

(*Huayuanjie wuhao*), becomes involved in a discussion with Pan Jinlian and Anna Karenina about the social contract whereby unhappy marriages are perpetuated in both Russia and China and in traditional and modern societies. Unlike Pan, who lived in a traditional society that did not easily let her out of her marriage, Lü Shasha feels fortunate to be living in contemporary China where she can obtain a divorce from her insane husband.

Other historical figures are summoned onto the stage to help find a solution for Pan's dilemma. Wu Zetian, the Tang dynasty empress who reigned from 690 to 705, is outraged by the unjust patriarchal society in which emperors enjoy "three thousand concubines" while producing a legal discourse that makes it possible to treat Wu Song as a hero for killing Pan Jinlian. Wu Zetian orders Tang Cheng, "an official of the seventh rank" (*qipin zhimaguan*), to help clear Pan. Known as one of the most incorruptible officials in Chinese history, he saved countless wrongly accused people from unjust punishment and death. Nevertheless, he is unable to find any article in the thousand-year-old Chinese laws that can gain Pan a pardon for the "sinful" act of having revealed her love to her brother-in-law.[11] This episode, widely considered to contain some of the most thought-provoking moments in the work, points up "the inevitable fate of women in a feudal society."[12] The opera thus finds fault with the entire patriarchal system, which, although it admits its own corruption (by creating the myth of this particular *qingguan*, or upright official), still discriminates against women.

This meditation on the condition of women in China's past is juxtaposed to women's present prospects through the comments of a contemporary female judge. She points out that, although Pan today could have left an unhappy marriage, this does not guarantee that a woman like her would find happiness, as statistics show that 30 percent of marriages in contemporary China are still arranged.[13] The mere appearance of a female judge, which might at first be taken as a sign of triumphant feminism, should actually be small comfort. As the judge warns, no real solutions have emerged to solidify women's rights in the post-Maoist society. Other fictional characters such as Jia Baoyu, the quintessential lover from *The Dream of the Red Chamber* (*Hongloumeng*), also drop by to speak on Pan Jinlian's behalf. Had Pan been a part of his fictional world, Jia believes, her beauty would have been praised, and the valor she displayed in struggling to secure her own happiness would have won admiration.[14]

This international intervention to the fate of Pan Jinlian was premiered by the Sichuan Opera Troupe of Zigong City (*Zigongshi chuanjutuan*) on October 8, 1985, and was enthusiastically received by audiences in Chengdu, Beijing, Shanghai, and Hong Kong. College students without any prior exposure to *chuanju* tradition were said to be "electrified" by its shocking message, and it inspired numerous productions in other genres, such as modern drama and local operas popular in Shanxi Province and Shanghai.[15] At one point, fifty theaters in twenty cities were performing the work. Numerous articles about it appeared in 130 newspapers and journals, 10 of which dedicated special columns to the continuous discussion of the controversy sparked by the play.

Some people adamantly opposed the staging of *Pan Jinlian*. They were disturbed by its "unhealthy" theme and, pointing to a growing divorce rate in China, feared it might encourage extramarital affairs. One critic cited his personal experience in a Chinese prison, where he had learned that 60 to 70 percent of female criminals were adulterous murderers, and that 90 percent of them came from the countryside. A play justifying adultery, he claimed, could only make the situation worse. He noted, furthermore, that *Pan Jinlian* reflected the vulgar, shallow mentality of city dwellers keen on "following the fashion" in divorce trends without taking the trouble to explore the "objective social reality" and "historical circumstances" that had brought about tragic events.[16] Despite this critic's claims, he exhibited not so much his concern for the women in rural China as his "moral" stance toward divorce among city dwellers, since in contemporary China city people still comprise most of theater audiences. In addition, the link between the work and more divorces seemed to be an issue only among a small group of theatergoers and critics, and so the play could not be said to significantly affect women's rights in the countryside. It is more to the point to note that the voices of subalterns were being appropriated to air the interests of intellectuals, and that rural Chinese women were being used to advance the various ideological and political agendas of the urban elite.

What, on the other hand, caused audiences to welcome *Pan Jinlian* with open arms? Why did audiences previously uninterested in *chuanju* suddenly become "mesmerized" by *Pan Jinlian*?[17] One answer emerges: the success of *Pan Jinlian* signaled a way out of the current crisis in drama. Instead of casting contemporary stories in traditional theatrical forms, such as *chuanju*, one could, in order to appeal to contemporary audiences, draw on and rewrite stories from traditional repertoires.[18] For what had captured the attention of contemporary audiences in this case was the author's daring reversal of the verdicts in criminal cases of literary history, which traditionally had been characterized by biases against women.

This point of view was vigorously advanced by Hu Bangwei, a scholar of traditional fiction. Hu argued that although *Water Margin* was the first significant work of fiction to recount the struggles of peasant heroes against the corrupt imperial court, its depiction of women typified the misogynistic views found in traditional Chinese literature. In rewriting the literary history of China from a feminist point of view, Hu asserted that the majority of literary works since the Qing dynasty (1644–1911) were least successful in one respect: the representation of women. Even the literary and dramatic works of the Tang (618–907), Song (960–1279), and Yuan (1279–1368) dynasties, though replete with spectacularly attractive and brilliant women characters, could not be said to have endowed them with personalities and emotions of any noteworthy depth. In most cases, the most interesting female characters were the stereotypical prostitutes with hearts of gold.[19] Especially faulted were the fictional works of the Ming (1368–1644) and Qing (1644–1911) dynasties, such as *Three Kingdoms (Sanguo yanyi)*, in which not even a single female character displayed strength or any other admirable qualities that male characters displayed in abundance. Thus *Water Margin*, which inherited this misogynistic legacy, had Wu Song make his "heroic" but illogical choice of joining the rebels against the imperial court to expiate his "crime" of murdering Pan Jinlian, when the latter had been a victim of the very feudal system he was supposed to combat.[20]

The prejudice against women in traditional fiction seems to have been allowed to exist side by side with the class-based assumption in Communist historiography against the imperial elite, which was said to have exploited and oppressed the peasant class. However, a participant in the peasant uprising was just as eager as his oppressor to maintain the inferior status of the second sex. Wu Song and others like him might attack the corrupt imperial regime, but they would never question the patriarchal system that guaranteed them their "rightful" male privileges. The literary history of China also did its part to support the system by creating mythical and national heroes who thrived at the expense of female members of the society.

Interestingly, in his critique of the misogynist discourse in traditional fiction, Hu provided directions for the rewriting and reappraisal of the history of drama, a marginalized genre in Chinese literary studies, at least in the West. Yuan dynasty drama, in his view, was one of the few traditional genres to create exceptional, "bright-colored and distinctive female characters made of flesh and bone."[21] Hu's archaeological endeavors (in the Foucaultian sense) directed at recovering the history of drama were joyfully shared by Wei Minglun, who wrote an essay stating his authorial intention of challenging the patriarchal aspects of *Water Margin* in the *chuanju Pan Jinlian*.

To achieve his purpose, Wei conducted a dialogue with Ouyang Yuqian, who wrote a modern drama version of *Pan Jinlian* in 1928.[22] The latter playwright had been criticized for presenting a heroic Pan, because he had been influenced by the "sex-driven Freudian theory," a product of the "petty bourgeoisie."[23] Wei lauded the May Fourth spirit that Ouyang exhibited in creating an "antifeudal" heroine who remained controversial sixty years after her initial appearance. Ouyang's daring in reversing the verdict that had traditionally been meted out to the condemned female character contrasted sharply with her treatment in *Water Margin*, which adheres to the Confucian doctrine that admonished the novel's readers: "women and people of low birth are very hard to deal with" (*wei nüren yu xiaoren nan yang ye*).[24] Of the 108 "heroic rebels" in *Water Margin*, only three are women. Almost all the other women characters are portrayed as evil, lustful women murdered by their men. Their men escape to the Liang Mountains, where they evidently metamorphose into a group of "good and brave men" (*haohan*) committed to restoring moral government. In other words, these men could apparently not have become heroes without the provocation of female villains. (For example, Shi Xiu murders Pan Qiaoyun; Song Jiang murders Yan Xijiao; Lu Junyi murders Jia Shi; Shi Jin murders Li Ruilan; and Lei Heng beats Bai Xiuying to death.) Only one good woman can be found in this work. Significantly named Zhen Niang (chaste woman), she is lauded for her devotion and obedience to her husband, Lin Chong, a "Liang Mountain" hero. Her virtue is used to set off numerous "vicious" women such as Pan Jinlian, who violate the Confucian ethical code of *sangang* (the three cardinal orders whereby a ruler guides his subject, a father his son, and a husband his wife) and *wuchang* (the five constant virtues of benevolence, righteousness, propriety, wisdom, and fidelity).[25]

Wei Minglun insisted that one cannot accept later critics' excuse of the fictional writer's "historical limitations" to condone these misogynist attitudes. Dramatists such as Guan Hanqing, Wang Shifu, and Tang Xianzu, who created vivid, courageous female characters, would have depicted Pan

Jinlian very differently.[26] Redeeming certain dramatic works as feminism-conscious texts, however, does not undo the misogyny found in traditional theater, which filled its repertoire with plays adapted from traditional fiction such as *Water Margin*. Most middle-aged audiences had been exposed to this kind of bias since their childhood. A recent informal survey found that many hardly reacted (they felt "numbed," they said) to a television drama entitled *Wu Song*, which rehearsed the familiar tale of "Wu Song heroically killing his evil sister-in-law to avenge his brother." Consequently, many spectators were shocked by Wei Minglun's unconventional *chuanju*.[27] But this response only demonstrated how much work was needed to combat the "feudal" ideology still rampant in socialist China and to reclaim the theatrical space that had been and was still supporting the male-dominated ideology.

Thus we see that the furious debate arising from the staging of the *chuanju Pan Jinlian* revolved around its theme and "social function," not its vaunted formalist innovations. Even the few formalist debates that did take place were disguised in ideological discourse. One critic, for instance, pointed out that *Pan Jinlian* had dismantled the traditional theatrical form that usually separated *honglian* (the red-faced character of loyalty) from *heilian* (the black-faced character of treachery). For the first time in Chinese theatrical history, *Pan Jinlian* deconstructed this one-dimensional structure by introducing a character with a complex personality that could no longer be classified as either positive or negative.[28] This formalist innovation could not have been achieved had the author not boldly related the opera to the contemporary issues of women's suppression and liberation. The well-known literary critic Liu Bingyan was undoubtedly commenting on this phenomenon in his observation on contemporary critics. While many of them, he felt, were trapped in their lofty pursuit of "a pure literature and art" that ignored social reality, Chinese audiences, spectators, and readers "made their own choice"; that is, they embraced the previously neglected theatrical form with its scandalous twist on a traditional tale, obviously preferring it over more popular genres and media, such as television, film, fiction, and other trendy modernist plays, which displayed little or no concern with social and ideological issues.[29] These different perceptions of the function of art explain the diametrically opposed formalistic views of this *chuanju* either as "a monumental work" that revived a theater in crisis or as a "disaster" that "violated the long tradition of the *chuanju*" by artificially blending elements of the foreign and the Chinese, the modern and the ancient.[30] In the PRC, where many regard gender politics as primarily "gender trouble," any modernist attempts in literature and art to grapple with the relevant issues are generally considered to be of secondary importance. Such bold forays remain possible only in the imaginations of the "elitist" artists, whose formalistic concerns may sometimes be appreciated by the mass audience but are unlikely to be seen by them as having much to do with their own concerns.

The same argument is applicable to epic theater, another tradition in search of a stage in contemporary China. Some Chinese dramatists were fascinated by Brecht's advocacy of a socially engaged theater that emphasizes sociology, ideology, semiology, and morality. They discovered that the Brechtian belief in the possibility of effecting social change through epic theater matched almost perfectly how audiences in the Maoist tradition were encouraged to ponder the historical process critically through dramatic representations of the "typical" and the "progressive." This explains the successful Chinese production, in 1979, of Brecht's *Life of Galileo*, which, as I have pointed out elsewhere, invited the audience to relate Galileo's misfortunes to their own experiences during the Cultural Revolution.[31] That approach ran counter to the intended Brechtian "alienation effect," designed to distance the audience from the staged events; it also departed from the original intention of the producers, who planned to experiment with a "faithful" Brechtian production. The blending of Brechtian theater with socialist-realist theater can also be seen, to great advantage, in Liu Shugang's 1985 play, *The Dead Visiting the Living* (*Yige sizhe dui shengzhe de fangwen*).[32] Based on the lives of the national heroes An Ke and Cao Zhengxian, the play recounts the murder of Ye Xiaoxiao by two thieves on a bus as the other passengers look on passively. Throughout the rest of the play, the dead Xiaoxiao comes back to visit the living, to confront the indifferent passengers and to commune with his two best childhood friends: Tang Tiantian, the woman he loved, and Liu Feng, his adversary in work and love. Despite the claims of critics that this play aptly combined socialist-realist, Western absurdist, and symbolist techniques, what really makes it an interesting, successful piece of experimental theater are its Brechtian "alienation effect" and its echoes of Greek tragedy obtained by the use of masks and a chorus. Drawing on Brecht's concept of an episodic plot with epic overtones that can effectively address social concerns, *The Dead Visiting the Living* consistently "alienates" its audiences from the immediate events by connecting the past with the present, the dead with the living, and the actors with the audience.

The audience, as observers, is supposed to find rational alternatives to the dramatic action.

The enduring attraction of Brechtian theater to address realistic concerns of modern China received further demonstration in the 1986 successful production of *The Nirvana of Gou'er Ye (Gou'er Ye niepan)*, which explored the sorrows of peasants.[33] Celebrated as the ultimate achievement of a Chinese search for a Brechtian theater,[34] the play won acclaim from drama critics for its combination of different schools of modernism — such as "alienation effects," expressionism, symbolism — with the Beijing-flavored plays perfected by the Beijing People's Art Theater. All these Western modernistic devices, some critics pointed out, were fully explored to serve the ultimate goal of realist theater, which still dominates contemporary China. This play broke with the image of happy peasants forever grateful to Mao for emancipating them from the old society, as portrayed on the Maoist stage. Instead, the work recounts the broken dream of a Gou'er Ye, who in 1980 still lives in his own world as he tills his private land without realizing the tremendous changes that have occurred in his village since the Land Reform of the early 1950s.

As was typical of the stories of many peasants, Gou'er Ye feels extremely blessed when he is allotted three acres of land and the arch over the gateway from the property of Qi Yongnian, the detested village landowner. Unlike characters in other Maoist stories, however, Gou'er Ye does not embrace the collective movement of the early 1950s, in which peasants were persuaded to give their newly acquired land to the state. As an atypical character, Guo'er Ye declares: "I don't want meetings, I don't want glory. I want my land, my horse, and my cart."[35] He goes insane when his dream of owning his own land is suddenly shattered.

During the more than thirty years of madness that follow, Gou'er Ye lives in his dream world, in which he feeds his own horses and tills his own land — all of which now in reality belong to the collective. In his world of fury and hallucination, he constantly talks to the ghost of Qi Yongnian, the former landowner who was beaten to death during the Cultural Revolution by the Red Guards, imagining himself as owning more land and horses than Qi Yongnian had ever dreamt of in the old days. Gou'er Ye has a paradoxical relationship with Qi. On the one hand, Gou'er Ye feels politically superior to Qi, since the latter had been declared a "class enemy of the people." On the other hand, however, Gou'er Ye still pursues the same dream as Qi to become one of the wealthiest landowners in his region. Even more paradoxically, although he found it hard to accept his son's decision to marry Qi's daughter, which could have had political repercussions, he protected her as if she were his own daughter. This attitude becomes especially quizzical when authorities single her out as the only "criminal" in the family responsible for Gou'er Ye's abnormal behavior because her father was a rich landowner before liberation. This in-law relationship symbolizes, to a large extent, the intricate connections between the former poor peasant and former landowner, who still share many things in common despite the Maoist ideology that separates them as political and economic opposites.

As an exact duplicate of Qi, Gou'er Ye piously believes that land is the most important thing: "with land, you own everything; without land, you lose everything." Land is even more important than having a wife. For example, to harvest Qi Yongnian's crops after the latter has fled their war-stricken village, Gou'er Ye neglects his first wife, who then falls victim to bandits. During his days of madness, he can recognize his own land and animals but not his second wife. He eventually loses her to Li Wanjiang, the team leader who had sought to persuade him to give up his private land so that the whole village could enter overnight "the stage of communism." The same Li Wanjiang, during the era of economic reform in the 1980s, informs Gou'er Ye that he can now own his own land and horses, which cures him of his insanity. The restored Gou'er Ye, however, can never comprehend what happened in the previous thirty years, nor does he care to find out. However, to clear the ground for his son's marble factory, the arch over the gateway given him during land reform—the symbol of his replacing Qi Yongnian—is condemned to destruction. Gou'er Ye burns down the arch and leaves home to search for his own paradise, where he will be left alone to dream without intrusion from the outside world of chaos and disillusionment.

The play's denouement reveals the meaning of the title, *The Nirvana of Gou'er Ye*. If "nirvana" means a state of absolute blessedness or freedom from the pain and changes of the external world, then the private history of Gou'er Ye is unique. As an insane man, he is able to act as his true self: the authorities left him alone to till his land far away from the village and did not persecute him as an ideological threat to the revolutionary norms of the village. Gou'er Ye's two silent withdrawals to the wilderness can be seen as a ritual spectacle, or a staged event, in which flight from society's norms grants one liberty in paradise. One can perhaps even argue that Gou'er Ye suggests a countermemory of the collective rural community.

His insanity allows him to live outside history, sparing him the suffering of major historical events such as the Cultural Revolution and the difficult transition in the 1980s, when peasants dreamed of owning their land and managing their factories. Yet when one looks at the desolate life of many unemployed workers and bankrupt factory owners, one cannot but wonder if the peasant's new dreams can easily come to pass in a highly competitive semimarket economy. Gou'er Ye's story therefore effectively erases the official history of the PRC that glorified the liberated peasants and even casts doubt on the supposedly bountiful future promised by the post-Maoist regime.

Having lived for many years in rural China where he learned about peasants, the playwright Jin Yun (Liu Jinyun) illustrates the paradoxical burdens of the Chinese intellectual. In his attempt to speak out for the peasants, most of whom are still illiterate and lack the capacity to argue for themselves, he gave the lie to the Maoist claim that workers and peasants were history's decisive force. On the other hand, however, blessed with the knowledge of power, Jin Yun demonstrated his own superiority as a member of the Chinese intellectual elite. Intellectuals had been treated as outcasts until they had supposedly cast off their bourgeois ideology and adopted that of the proletariat from whom, as shown in this play, they have nothing to learn. It is therefore significant to note Jin Yun's declared "authorial intention"; he did not merely want to denounce the "ultraleftist" party politics of the Maoist age. Instead, he mocked the conservative, arrogant, and vengeful characteristics of the "petty peasants" (*xiaonong yishi*) and their contradictory honest, kindhearted, ignorant, and superstitious natures.[36] Other critics supported Jin's claim, pointing out that his play did not result simply from living in rural China for a couple of years to "delve into life"; it drew from nearly thirty years of reflection to express his deepest emotions.[37] Others, however, challenged the realist nature of Jin's play, which they felt did not move beyond early post-Maoist "scar literature." Gao Jian, a renowned drama critic, criticized the "imposed structure" of the play, which reduced the complexity of rural life to a simplified dramatic conflict between peasants and their land and lacked understanding of the complicated personalities of Chinese peasants as individual human beings. Gao claimed that Chinese playwrights enjoyed a unique advantage because they had been encouraged to live among the common people and acquire firsthand materials to create vivid dramatic characters and intriguing plots. The experience, however, led them to employ dramatic characters and conflicts to explain abstract ideas and principles without enough artistic investment.[38] Maoist and post-Maoist theater, Gao implied, differed only in that the former glorified the peasants while the latter exposed the absurdity of this glorification.

Many other critics, however, seemed to agree on the formalistic innovations of *The Nirvana of Gou'er Ye*. Divided into sixteen episodes, the play follows the "stream of conciousness" of Gou'er Ye in a reversed time sequence from present to past. The Brechtian conception of "alienation effects" comes into play when Gou'er Ye's son, standing in contemporary time, comments on the stupidity of his father who burst into tears at his own father's graveyard and lamented the loss of their land in the 1950s. The audience was therefore encouraged to think for itself—it had the guidance of the son's commentary on the events instead of merely following the thoughts and actions of Gou'er Ye.[39] Others suggested that the play recalled expressionist techniques from Arthur Miller's *The Death of a Salesman*. Gou'er Ye's conversations with the ghost of Qi Yongnian recall scenes when Willy Loman's past talks with his brother Ben, which intersected with the present action of the play. The best review of the play, however, was reserved for the stage performance of Lin Liankun, a well-known actor from the Beijing People's Art Theater specializing in acting roles from Beijing-flavored plays. His Gou'er Ye drifted convincingly in and out of insanity and evolved from an ambitious young man to a crushed old codger. Critics agreed that Lin's contribution made *The Nirvana of Gou'er Ye* an artistic whole and helped to continue the Beijing-styled plays inherited from earlier dramatists such as Lao She and Jiao Juyin.

The formalistic features of *The Nirvana of Gou'er Ye* bear the imprint of one other theatrical tradition in search of the Chinese stage: the suggestive theater, as reflected in the bare stage and a certain fluidity of time and space. As I have pointed out elsewhere, the idea of suggestive theater was promoted by the Chinese director Huang Zuolin, who envisioned the ideal Chinese theater of the future as a combination of three divergent views, those of Stanislavsky, Brecht, and Mei Lanfang, the quintessential *xiqu* actor.[40] For Huang, the three approaches differed in an essential way. "Stanislavsky believed in the 'fourth wall,'" Brecht wanted to abolish it, while for Mei Lanfang the wall had never existed, because Chinese theater had always been so highly conventionalized that it had never set out to create an illusion of real life. Huang Zuolin concluded that "realism is the keynote for Western art" and "suggestiveness" the keynote for Chinese art.

Huang Zuolin himself produced a piece of suggestive theater, *China Dream (Zhongguo meng)*, written by William Huizhu Sun and Faye Chunfang Fei. It illustrates his notion that the ideal Chinese theater should be characterized by a combination of the "four inner characteristics" (the "suggestiveness" of life, movement, language, and decor) with the "four outer characteristics" (fluidity, plasticity, a sculptural quality, and conventionality).[41] As befits a prime example of "suggestive theater," *China Dream* constantly shifts among diverse temporal and geographical spaces, such as China and the United States, the past and the present, the city and the countryside, and the worlds of dream and reality. At the point when Mingming, a successful businesswoman living in America, has fallen in love with John Hodges, a scholar of Chinese philosophy, the scene instantly switches back to many years earlier, during the Cultural Revolution when she was working with her first love in the remote countryside. The two young lovers in this scene play their parts on a bare stage consisting only of a drawn circle at the center and communicate mostly through dance, mime, and body contact and movement, without resorting to much conventional dialogue. The play in fact is a showcase for acting techniques from traditional opera and modern drama, as well as from the song-dance drama *(gewuju)*. By using one actor to play six different roles—American lover and Chinese lover, restaurant chef, waiter, journalist, Mingming's grandfather—the play achieves an unusual degree of theatrical fluidity and continuity that contributes to the imaginative flow.

The critics applauded the play's theatrical achievements, but, not surprisingly, they reproached the playwright for advocating a "superficial" cross-cultural understanding between two entirely different cultures and ideologies. For instance, Zhang Geng, a leading drama critic, claimed that what was in some respects an enchanting story of an American scholar of Chinese philosophy falling in love with a Chinese woman actually is devoid of lasting appeal, as the American's emotions are based on a shallow understanding of Chinese culture. Similarly, Mingming's love for John is based on the cursory favorable impression she has formed of American culture. The story might interest an audience curious about cross-cultural experiences, but it could hardly be said to explore in depth the dramatic characters and the cross-cultural theme.[42] Gao Jian, another major critic of Chinese drama, asserted that the play exhibits a kind of radicalism, for a confused, frustrated Chinese woman regains her confidence and self-esteem only through affirmation from an American lover;

her self-image seems to veer from one pole to the other, influenced first by the "rejection of white men" in general and then by the "affirmation of a white man" in particular. When confronted with the harsh realities of racial discrimination and financial difficulties, she comes off no better than a "spiritual beggar," for she does not strive to be self-reliant and independent.[43]

Yet the charges that *China Dream* was essentially an expression of "Orientalism" (on the part of John, in his imaging of the feminine Asian other) and "Occidentalism" (on the part of Mingming, in her construction of the idealistic Western other) can—and should—be considered problematic in view of the political circumstances surrounding the production of the drama. As explained by Faye Chunfang Fei, one of the play's coauthors, Huang Zuolin had originally planned to end the play when a breach develops between the two lovers after John rejects Mingming's proposal that he give up his legal practice to devote himself to his research on Taoism. For political reasons, this ending, which questions the sincerity of John's enthusiasm for Chinese culture, had to be changed later in favor of an ending stressing harmony between the two cultures. According to Fei, not long after the 1989 Tiananmen demonstrations, when the state apparatus was launching another political campaign of "antibourgeois liberation," a play that concluded with the promotion of "Chinese culture, especially by an American, seemed a reasonable choice, and this strategy did work."[44] Censors approved the work, allowing for its production and favorable reception in Beijing and Shanghai.

The critic Gao Jian's charge that *China Dream* suffered from an Orientalist tendency (although he did not actually use the term "Orientalist") in fact reflected the official Occidentalism, which served the state in its efforts to suppress its own people by portraying the West as a negative other in order to support Chinese nationalism. After the play had passed the censors and had become available for audiences to interpret freely, it still appeared, to some, to express an antiofficial Occidentalism, that gave Chi-nese dramatists an opportunity to use the image of the Western other for political liberation and self-definition. In this light, Mingming's flashback to her experience during the Cultural Revolution might be regarded as a pointed critique of the totalitarian Maoist system. Her love for a Western man, moreover, might be understood as a rejection of her contemporary life in socialist China. Both the Chinese woman's and the Western man's longing for the ancient beauty and harmony of traditional Chinese society, expressed in their love of Taoist philosophy or Mingming's questioning of rural modernization policies, might be viewed as another imagining of the other (in this case, the ancient Chinese other). It also contrasts sharply with the goals of modernization, globalization, and self-colonization, all of which the Chinese government has been trying to promote since the beginning of the "reform era."

The use of an ancient other to voice concerns over present times also figures in *Sangshuping Chronicles (Sangshuping jishi)*, written by Chen Zidu, Yang Jian, and Zhu Xiaoping, a play known in Chinese dramatic circles as a successful experimentation with Greek theater. Based on Zhu Xiaoping's series of novels about Sangshuping, a small, isolated village in the northwestern part of China, it presents the sorrows, tragedies, and less dramatic events in the daily lives of the villagers. These people, the play shows, inhabit a place where, despite all that has happened elsewhere in the world, ignorance, illiteracy, sexual suppression, primitive ways, and a brutal patriarchal structure have remained unchanged for thousands of years. The sense of futility aroused by any attempt to bring about change is communicated by the bare, revolving stage, which alternately displays the various geographical features characteristic of the "yellow earth plateau": uphill, downhill, and the cave houses in between. This landscape full of deep valleys and steep hills is the result of a thousand-year-old soil erosion and the consequent brutally harsh living conditions.

As the drama critic Qu Liuyi remarked, the revolving stage, with its many aspects of the landscape revealed from many different angles, does more than expand the usual theatrical space. It provides a continuously moving performance space upon which singing and dancing chorus members can portray villagers harvesting wheat or participating in local rituals, such as begging the "dragon of the rain" to fall on the neighboring village while they, the villagers of Sangshuping, hasten to harvest the wheat in time. The revolving stage thus functions as a "genre painting" of local customs and daily life in the village.[45] It also helps to illustrate the relative insignificance of individuals caught in the flow of time, since no matter how meaningful their personal experiences may appear to be, they are only passengers occupying a brief moment on an empty stage, whose lives will most likely make no impression on the course of history.

Time and space, the play implies, become meaningful only insofar as one is willing to hold on to memories of the historical past with the aid of such human feelings as hope and anguish. For example, in one scene, a woman is stripped naked by her insane husband in front of the villagers, who further surround and insult her, as if watching a caged animal. However, as the teasing crowd disperses, still mocking and laughing, one sees a piece of marble representing the statue of a goddess standing in the woman's place, while the woman herself disappears into the singing chorus, who now meditate on the fate of an innocent girl who has drowned in the flowing river of history, but has left behind a frozen image in an infertile land inhabited by impotent men.

The work draws on the literary and dramatic trend known as "meditation on the historical and cultural past" *(lishi wenhua fansi)*. According to its directors, it attempts to present a "living fossil" to symbolize the cultural and historical sentiments of the past five thousand years, as a way of calling for real change in contemporary China. This appeal is conveyed by stressing the changeless nature of the village. Li Jindou, a Communist production team leader, seems no different from the local despots depicted in pre-1949 literature. At once a slave to his immediate superior and a tyrant to the villagers, he rules as patriarch of his clan, persecuting and imprisoning Wang Zhike because he is an outsider with a different surname. Nowhere in the play is there any hint of the familiar story from classic socialist literature of people who were living in poverty before 1949 waiting to be liberated by Communist saviors. The drama imparts the message that the "sea of bitterness and misery of the poor people before liberation" is evident in the very landscape of contemporary China, and will only grow worse with the unfolding events of the Cultural Revolution. This message receives reinforcement from the play's setting in 1968–1969 and its demonstration of constant suffering during that period.

The setting used as a backdrop for the Cultural Revolution, while continuing to underscore the passage of time, indicates the importance of periodization in Communist historiography. No one can openly insist that socialism after 1949 effected absolutely no changes, even in this poor village. Nevertheless, it is legitimate to suggest the unparalleled disasters and terrors of the Cultural Revolution from 1966 to 1976, the only period in postliberation China that could thus be publicly criticized. Although *Sangshuping Chronicles* could consequently be presented to the official censors as a celebration of a "second liberation" brought about by the current political regime, it nonetheless left audiences much scope for interpreting it in any way they chose. Punctuating the play from beginning to end, the chorus' song, with its ambiguous blend of acclamation and questioning of China's five-thousand-year history (including that of the PRC), certainly leaves the impression that China still needs enlightenment and liberation.

What could the play have to say to any of the women in the audience who might be aware of feminist issues? In *China Dream*, Mingming, toward the ironic end of the play, turns the tables on the Western man, forcing him (and the audience) to "wipe out that condescending smile and complacency to see the rift in their own lives between dream and reality, between idealism and pragmatism."[46] In *Sangshuping Chronicles*, however, the power relationship between men and women is very different. The work highlights the fact that women's miseries did not abate with the triumph of the Communist Party in 1949, despite what many texts of PRC literature would have us believe. Entirely isolated from the outside world, villagers, as they have done for the past thousands of years, still arrange marriages for their children. A twelve-year-old girl is sold into marriage in exchange for a wife for her insane brother, who subsequently abuses and drives the wife to suicide. An eighteen-year-old widow throws herself into a well in protest against Li Jindou, her father-in-law, who forced her to marry his second son. Since Li Jindou is the only patriarch, embodying all possible power as tribal chief and Maoist production team leader, the women in *Sangshuping Chronicles* never even begin to imagine they could be liberated from the patriarchal tradition. Their indifference to time and change is symptomatic of their willingness to be buried by history. By committing suicide, they erase the memory of their own suffering from the mind of the nation that helped their persecutors to thrive. Only when the new nation feels the need to meditate on its heritage does it consent to notice the suffering its gender politics have caused women. The silent, powerless women of this play thus paradoxically reveal more about women's conditions in contemporary China than the plays about their "liberated" sisters who had once walked out of their homes and villages only to be suppressed again by another subsequent patriarchal ideology.

Despite Chinese dramatists' extensive efforts to introduce various forms of experimental theater, the majority of the repertoire in post-Maoist China remained within the confines of the illusionist tradition. Most of the social-problem plays discussed in Chapters 4 and 5, for instance, belong to this tradition, with the exception of the Brechtian-like *If I Were for Real*. Most of the Tiananmen street plays considered in Chapter 5 also attempted to create "the fourth wall"—a favorite term with Chinese dramatists and critics from the traditional school, who regarded the illusionist tradition as one of the quintessential features of the Western dramatic genre. Again, the sole exceptions were a Brechtian-like play, *Jiang Qing and Her Husbands* (which also has features of illusionist theater), and *There Is a Small Courtyard*, a play growing out of the indigenous theater tradition and known as a "Beijing-flavored play" *(jingwei'er xi)*,[47] despite its illusionist dimensions. Furthermore, almost all the plays from the realist schools examined in Chapters 6 and 7 written by women playwrights, especially Bai Fengxi's women trilogy, drew predominantly from the illusionist tradition. Even in the mid-1980s, when experimental theater seemed for a brief time to have taken over the Chinese stage, illusionist theater retained its appeal for Chinese dramatists and audiences. Its enduring attraction is attested to by the successful production of *Black Stones (Heise de shitou)*. As a critical response to the glorious portrayal of the proletariat in Maoist China, *Black Stones*, premiered by the Daqing City Theatre (Daqingshi huanjutuan) in 1987, depicts the grave hardships of petroleum workers, no longer portrayed as proud masters of socialist China. Despite the negative treatment of the workers' lives, however, *Black Stones* was unanimously applauded by the state apparatus and audiences. Reportedly, the play was such a hit in the northeastern city of Daqing that it was immediately invited to come to Beijing. The Chinese Dramatic Art Research Association and the editorial board of *Drama Script* journal held a joint seven-hour seminar on *Black Stones* on December 6, 1987, which was attended by more than thirty key officials and drama experts. After the seminar, Cao Yu, the honorary president of the Chinese Dramatic Art Research Association, presented the association's Best Playwright Award to Yang Limin, and the Best Acting Award to the company, Daqing Theatre.[48] The play and its successful run were widely hailed for providing the first ten-year period of dramatic experiment in the post-Maoist era with its crowning achievement.

It is easier to understand the impact of *Black Stones* if one is aware of the preceding PRC literary tradition, which stressed the heroic spirit of the working class. Many Chinese people in the early 1960s were familiar with the stories of legendary petroleum workers who forged China's first proletarian industry in the wilderness known as Daqing. The plot of a popular 1975 movie *The Pioneers* (*Chuangye*; script by Zhang Tianmin) is based on the biography of Wang Jinxi, a national hero whose exploration team achieved such feats that they served as an inspiration for the nation. In theater, many remember the production of *The Rising Sun* (*Chusheng de taiyang*, 1966). Performed in 1966 by an amateur cast of workers and their spouses from Daqing, it vividly conveyed how the spouses "hold up half of the sky," as Mao expected them to. The wives opened up virgin land so it would grow grain and vegetables to support the petroleum project during the difficult early years.[49] The national media extensively covered the restaging of this play as further testimony to the crimes of the Gang of Four.

Also revealed at this time was the untold story of the couple Sun Weishi and Jin Shan, a renowned director and actor, respectively, of the China Youth Art Theater. They had settled in the wilderness of Daqing from 1964 to 1966 and "delved into life" as ordinary workers while writing and helping the local people to produce *The Rising Sun*. The performances of the play in Beijing in March 1966, on the eve of the Cultural Revolution, were warmly received by professional dramatists and critics, and highly praised by Premier Zhou Enlai as the first play to dramatize the lives of Daqing workers.[50] During the Cultural Revolution, however, Jin Shan was imprisoned for seven and half years and his wife, Sun Weishi, was tortured to death in 1968 after a seven-month imprisonment. Sun was frequently cited after the Cultural Revolution as a martyr who had been persecuted by Jiang Qing. Jiang apparently was annoyed by Sun's unwillingness to convert *Azalean Mountain*, a modern drama performed by the China Youth Art Theater, into a model play. She supposedly had to choose Peking opera as the "experimental field" for her "dramatic revolution" at least in part because Sun did not comply with her persistent requests for a "modern dramatic revolution." Sun had been born "red," as the orphan of revolutionary martyrs. She enjoyed the title of "first proletarian director," having been trained in the Soviet Union during World War II and maturing in the "rich soil of the socialist motherland." However, she died "black," with such deadly labels as "counterrevolutionary" and "spy for Soviet revisionists." This type of live political theater inevitably called for a restaging of *The Rising Sun* as a move in the ongoing national drama waged against the Gang of Four. While the enduring spirit of Daqing people was being captured on the Beijing stage, the performance simultaneously gave a belated salute to the talented and innocent artists who had died for their revolutionary art. Ironically, the image of women in socialist theater—both the "heroic" spouses of workers onstage and their ardent imitators in real life—were products, as well as victims, of Maoist official feminism, which manipulated the agenda of women's liberation for the construction and consolidation of political power.

Set against this horizon of literary expectations, *Black Stones* astonished post-Maoist audiences with its bleak description of workers—little men who fared no better than their "liberated" female others—and their frustrations in the "most barbarous" wilderness.[51] Indeed, the very image of the color black in the title of the play contrasts sharply with that of red in *Red Storm* and *The Red Lantern*, allusions to revolutionary zeal and heroic heritage. Nowhere could one find the familiar characters who had battled nature and class enemies with their determined spouses by their side. With an episodic structure that has no central plot, *Black Stones* acts out the daily fatigue of workers as permanent mimesis of a troubling industrializing world no different from that of the capitalist societies. Set in a messy camp cabin that is the workers' temporary home, the play begins with a frustrated young man urinating through the window, and another struggling with his muddy boots after his return from the chilling night shift. One hears the sad reading of a tender letter from the wife of Veteran, an oil-rig builder who nine years before left behind his wife in his remote hometown because he had no idea how to deal with the red tape that would have approved her transfer. Some women take for granted their right to be united with their husbands, but this wife says in her letter that she has no unrealistic dreams of their being together. She only wishes that during his next homecoming he might stay with her a few more days so they could try to have a baby, who would keep her company in the lonely years to come. This depiction of a traditional timid and docile Chinese woman calls to attention the qualities of numerous women and men who did not feel entitled to the fulfillment of their most basic human needs.

It should be noted that although the play is set in contemporary times, Veteran is depicted as a typical model worker of the 1960s—disciplined, diligent, and uncomplaining. He seldom speaks and is only half literate. The audience learns of his pain only indirectly, when fellow workers grab his letter and read it aloud. We realize that if it were up to him he would not choose to tell his story, and his destiny seems to be that his voice will be heard only faintly. However, as the play progresses, and his wife's paperwork becomes halted again after having been approved sixteen times by different levels of authorities, Veteran sees that he has no alternative but to attempt to bribe the officials. Wu Xue, a prestigious dramatist and high-ranking official in the Art Bureau of Ministry of Culture, reported that during performances the words "sixteen stamps" elicited warm applause from the audience, many of whom seemed to identify with Veteran's frustrating dealings with a corrupt bureaucracy.[52] Veteran's basic honesty is highlighted in ironic fashion, when he spends the greater part of a day wandering fruitlessly around the administrative building, not knowing which door to enter to deliver his gifts. At a subsequent meeting called to criticize his unlawful act, he apologizes wholeheartedly for his "terribly shameful" behavior, in which he failed to live up to the expectations of the party. Although a victim of the system, he still is loyal to it, blaming himself for letting it down and not even contemplating that it might have disappointed him. This story, of course, typifies that of many nameless veterans who fought in the war for the CCP and were later sent to reclaim the virgin land in the remote northeast. Like Veteran in the play, many of these men volunteered to relocate to the wilderness without knowing what was in store for them and what they stood to lose. In a sense this drama about Veteran is a cultural monument, which embodies grief, loss, or obligation.

To drive home what Maoist history meant for the proletariat, *Black Stones* has another character, a Captain Qin, who personifies the revolutionary heritage that Daqing workers helped to create in the 1960s. For him, opposing this heritage would discredit his lifelong sacrifices and his stories of a glorious past. When, after a week of hard labor far from the amenities of civilization, the young workers request permission to go to the village for a look at some women, Captain Qin worries that this may damage the unblemished reputation of the petroleum team. In the dogmatic style typical of his generation, he reminds them of the pioneering days. Workers vowed then they would not visit their families for three years, not date for five years, and not marry for eight years, so that they might drill all the petroleum they possibly could for the country.

Clinging to his heritage allows Captain Qin to make sense of his past. He is prepared to die, forever faithful, at his post rather than ever violate his tradition. And yet he does have a moment of doubt, during which he apologizes to the young workers for not giving their reasonable demands due consideration. "Ah, human beings!" he exclaims at that point. "Some things they can't get straight even after a lifetime."[53] After he dies, the young workers mourn this father figure. Belatedly identifying with him, they commemorate him most meaningfully, perhaps, by erecting a national monument to the veteran workers, the most underrepresented members of the proletariat, who "came to us right out of history."[54] The literal meaning of the word *Daqing* is "grand celebration," but in this instance its use has the dramatic irony of connoting the end of a tradition. For this type of play to be accepted on a still socialist stage in 1987 and to bypass censorship required the help of a character, Lin Jian, the new secretary of the Party Committee of the Exploration Corporation. He represents the party's new policy in post-Maoist China of seeing to workers' welfare, which the previous regime had neglected, and his ploy of living and working among the workers without revealing his identity until the end suggests what they might hope for from the next generation of leadership. This device of creating a new party secretary to protect a play from being branded harmful to the regime in power was employed in several post-Maoist plays.

Nevertheless, certain aspects of *Black Stones* remained controversial, such as the death of Captain Qin, which seemed to question the making of the socialist man. Deeply stirred, one critic insisted that history was not always made by the wise and clever man; it was the seemingly confused who always pushed history forward. Clearly this remark referred ironically to Mao's famous assertion, "People, and people only, are the driving force of history." From this perspective, the "tragic sublimity" in the death of Qin, if any, would suggest Arthur Miller's definition of tragedy, which "brings us not only sadness, sympathy, identification and even fear; [but] also, unlike pathos, brings us knowledge or enlightenment." It shows us what life could have been through Qin's acknowledgment of having "missed accomplishing his joy."[55]

It is fitting to recall here that, in the 1960s, Chinese theatrical discourse denied any need for scripting tragedy. "Positive drama" (*zhengju*, close to tragicomedy) and comedy, argued the drama critics, would eventually replace tragedy, which had little place on the socialist stage, since the dramatic conflicts of characters merely reflected the different opinions of people without opposing class interests. Tragedy was required only for plays depicting the deadly class struggle between workers and their oppressors before Liberation, when revolutionary setbacks could give temporary victory to the reactionaries and result in the tragic death of the proletarian heroes. During the post-Maoist theater debate, however, some critics rescued tragedy by pointing out that it was a legitimate form for current plays, which were now allowed to focus on the tragic flaws of individuals without referring to society as the cause of their fall.[56] To validate post-Maoist ideology, tragedy was also permitted to depict the Chinese people's struggles against the Gang of Four or other Maoist radicals who, for a limited period of time, caused tragedy to overtake socialist China.

Black Stones seems to straddle this duality with great effectiveness. On the one hand, Captain Qin's death occasions tragic sublimity; on the other, it is blamed on the residual Gang of Four radical ideology, which ignored proletarian interests, a situation that Lin, as the new party leader, promises to redress. As we have seen, Lin does not reveal himself until very late in the play, when his official status is needed to authorize a helicopter to save Captain Qin. This type of official character holds out the promise of a new, more responsive regime and revalidates the idea of the "savior of the people" embodied in the old socialist system. In this case, however, the savior might have arrived too late. Not only had the audience already been exposed to Veteran's and Captain's disillusioning stories, but they were also likely to sympathize with Jubilee, another "little man," who appears even more marginalized than his peers. An orphan of a veteran roughneck killed in an accident in the 1960s, Jubilee thinks of the team as his home. Returning from a dangerous journey and in search of cigarettes and wine for his fellow workers, Jubilee cannot believe his ears when he learns that Blackie, his master and trusted friend, has killed his pet, an injured wild goose Jubilee rescued. Blackie had gone after the animal in a fit of rage after being criticized by the authorities for loving Phoenix, a married woman from the nearby town. Knowing these circumstances, however, does not console Jubilee, who cries out in anguish, "Why on earth can't you let live a little thing like this!" It is at this point that the meaning of the name "Jubilee" comes into full play: literally defined as "little celebration," the word pays tribute to numerous little men like Jubilee whose sacrifices and sorrow must be remembered. It also questions the reason for the "grand celebration" of Daqing, which, after years of "painstaking and arduous effort," is still a godforsaken wilderness.

The play does not end with Lin's revelation, nor with Captain's Qin's death. Rather, it concludes with a denouement that leaves one uncertain as to what will happen to Blackie and his lover, Phoenix, who has just joined him after having murdered her brutal husband. The team has left for a new construction site with the new party secretary in the lead, and Blackie and Phoenix are left alone on stage. Their embracing bodies appear deserted and vulnerable, as an insignificant couple barely surviving at society's margins. Although the invention of the Lin character prevented the play from being attacked as an unhealthy tragedy, some audience members might ask who is to blame for these tragic events that occur, not just on stage, not just before the smashing of the Gang of Four, but now, every day?

Thus protected by ambiguities and a double discourse, this desolate play was received as one of the most successful works of the post-Maoist theater. Some critics remarked that after many years of "putting up" with modernistic experiments full of distasteful sexuality, pop music, and exotic plots, it was comforting to see "a final return to serious realism, the most vital tradition in contemporary theater." Kang Hongxin further argued that *Black Stones* courageously depicted life without glossing over reality. It frankly represented the dark world of those workers who had received very little from the state in return for their hard labor. With vivid, "true-to-life characters" who displayed human weaknesses and desires rather than being idealistic proletariats, Kang claimed the play called for economic reforms throughout the country.[57] He maintained that realistic tradition should probe deeply into the human soul, its discontent and despair. Yang Limin seconded Kang's view by eulogizing Shakespeare as a giant of realistic art, whose Shylock in *The Merchant of Venice* has been mistakenly represented throughout dramatic history as a clown, a villain, a persecuted Jew, a grand tragic hero, or even a noble patriot. These one-dimensional depictions, he claimed, ignored the charm of Shylock as someone who possesses the natural desires of a human being, whether they be beautiful or evil.[58]

Other critics considered *Black Stones* the first realistic drama to meditate on human history "through a particular angle of sexuality." For them the play allegorized the painful historical process whereby human beings were transformed from images of "machinelike" "stone men" without natural desires to images of "real men" liberated from the burden of medieval "asceticism."[59] Furthermore, unlike other social-problem plays, such as *If I Were for Real*, whose characters were created to address specific social ills, *Black Stones* focused on the emotions of individuals while disregarding the imperatives of indoctrination. Citing Karl Marx's idea that liberating the German nation would liberate mankind, one critic asserted that it could be adapted to this Chinese play, which demonstrates that to liberate mankind it is necessary to liberate each individual human being. In its attention to the individual, *Black Stones* was unique; it courageously dealt with previously forbidden areas of behavior—presenting a worker urinating onstage, for example—and thereby signaling a newly awakened consciousness that no human activity was shameful.[60] To reconcile this attitude with the Maoist theory of literature, the critic contended that real drama must, first of all, "penetrate deep into the human soul while at the same time dissecting the history of mankind, which is a history of a changing process of human nature."

Beside its strong ties to the precepts of illusionist theater, *Black Stones* has also (to a lesser degree) inherited some peculiarities of indigenous theater, which draws on local dialects and idioms of northeastern China in order to vividly and faithfully portray the life and personalities of people from a particular geographical region. Along with Zhang Mingyuan's plays such as *Wild Grass (Yecao,* 1995), Yang Limin's *Black Stone* represents one of the best repertories of "Northeastern-flavored drama" *(Dongbei xiju).*[61] Indeed, to a large extent, the indigenous theater is also illusionist and can even be argued to be a subgenre of the illusionist tradition developed from regional cultures. The most influential indigenous theater is best represented by Beijing-flavored plays, which can be traced back to Lao She's texts, such as *Dragon Beard Ditch* and *Teahouse* (see Chapter 5). The genre was further developed in Li Longyun's *There Is a Small Courtyard* and *Small Well Lane.* A crowning achievement of this genre can be found in the successful performance of *The World's Top Restaurant,* written by He Jiping, a woman playwright who researched the past of its real-life counterpart. Premiered in 1988 and set in Beijing between 1917 and 1928, the play dramatizes the rise and fall of the Beijing Roast Duck Restaurant from its golden age to its final days of destruction by two young owners who for years lived off the restaurant, neglecting it.

Despite being rooted in old Beijing, the play's dramatic structure fits Bernard Beckerman's structural analysis of drama as temporal art rather than as an artistic form composed of plot and character. For example, it can be segmented into three "units of time," each of which consists of steps that build resistance and lead to confrontation. Each act contains the following sequence, originally described by Beckerman: (1) "a precipitating context" that points to the direction of the impending action; (2) "a project" that focuses on the energies of each performer; (3) "a building up to the crux"; and (4) a subsequent "relaxation" of dramatic tension.[62]

The first act, for instance, is devoted to the crisis brought on by the death of the father. While on his deathbed, he calls not for a physician but for the immediate hiring of the outsider Lu Mengshi as the new manager instead of his two sons, who had broken his heart by their lack of interest in the business. The second act is further subdivided into two scenes, each with its own crux and relaxation pattern. The first scene is set three years later in a period of great financial hardship, when Lu Mengshi cleverly fends off creditors and troublemakers as he expands his business by constructing a new building. In the second scene, Lu tricks the two sons into giving up their remaining interest in the business' management so that he might, by dint of his efficient management and creative abilities, restore the restaurant to its former greatness. Eight years have elapsed between act 1 and act 3, in the course of which the restaurant has become known as "the best one under heaven." To audiences' great dismay, however, the two heartless sons suddenly return to reclaim the fruits of Lu's hard work and vision. Following these three sets of resistances and confrontations, which build toward a climax, an epilogue finally "relaxes" and brings all the "units of time" together, when Lu, after his departure, has a couplet sent to the restaurant. Asking "Who is the owner and who is the guest?" the couplet concludes the play with a suspenseful climax that has both the characters and the audience pondering the meaning of this message.[63] In effect, it is the guests, the outsiders, who have shown themselves to be the genuine owners of the restaurant; those who were the owners in name actually were the outsiders.

Although Chinese critics did not reveal a familiarity with Beckerman's dramatic theory, some of them shared his orientation to treating theater not as literary text but as a performed art. The reception of *The World's Top Restaurant* centered around the performing aspects of the play as done by the Beijing People's Art Theater, known as the only institution capable of producing real Beijing-flavored plays. Much credit was given to the directors and actors for their "second creation" (*erdu chuangzhuo*), which turned the script into a theatrical event bursting with vivid and diverse Beijing characters from more than seventy years ago. Without the older generation of directors and actors, who had spent years learning the dialect, mannerisms, customs, body movements, and life-styles of old Beijing natives, one critic pointed out, no one could have been able to enjoy a first-rate Beijing-style play.[64] Reportedly, the directors attended every performance to test the "authenticity" of the play in front of the Beijing audience and, depending on its effect, to modify the next performance.[65] This helps to explain the enthusiastic applause of audiences at the points when the actors demonstrated a particularly superb piece of acting. Examples included scenes when Chang Gui, a devoted waiter, chanted an elaborate menu for the distinguished guests,[66] or when the servant of the restaurant's owner, without uttering a word, bowed and scraped to win his master's favor.[67] All these factors contributed to making *The World's Top Restaurant* an unusually popular play, as demonstrated by the continuing strong ticket sales after more than fifty-eight performances in only two months.[68] This achievement marked a record during the lean years of Chinese theater when critics were discussing little except how to solve "the drama crisis."

In addition, the play (as was customary with contemporary Chinese theater of different traditions and schools) offered an occasion for the playwright and critics to compete in pointing out the social significance of realist-indigenous theater, of which Beijing-flavored plays represented the best examples. Several critics have remarked that the play's popularity can be most meaningfully explained by its meeting "the literary expectations"[69] of at least four different kinds of Beijing audiences: (1) popular audiences who enjoy watching exciting scenes of hustle and bustle in an old restaurant, which they had not personally experienced; (2) the specific community of Beijing residents still "addicted to" and fascinated by Beijing roast duck cuisine, which remains one of the biggest attractions of Beijing culture; (3) intellectuals and scholars, to whom the play offers the opportunity to ponder the aesthetic and philosophical questions of Chinese tradition via a theatrical representation of its cuisine subculture; (4) entrepreneurs, who could ruminate on the regional characteristics of the Beijing people and their presumed capacity for overcoming their jealousy and narrow-mindedness to succeed in a highly competitive global society.[70] Because of the play's appealing formalistic features and cultural and ideological components, the drama critics accurately characterized it as "suitable both for old and young" (laoshao jieyi) and "enjoyable both for the popular folk and the elite" (yasu gongshang).[71]

The play's devotion to conveying realistic detail was brought home when an audience member apparently forgot that he was watching a drama, not real life. A self-proclaimed old resident of Beijing and fan of Beijing drama, he pointed out mistakes in some of the menu items and the order of their presentation at a banquet and questioned if a particular Beijing opera star mentioned in the play was enjoying popularity at the time. This gentleman argued that, had more accurate data been used, The World's Top Restaurant would have been better able to communicate what the "real people" and "real events" of the historical period between 1917 to 1928 had been like. Then the play could have come closer to matching the best drama of the genre, Lao She's masterpiece, Teahouse.[72] Other critics judged The World's Top Restaurant as inferior to Teahouse on another score, because the former's time span of 1917 to 1928 was not regarded as being as instructive as that of Teahouse. Teahouse set its first act in 1898 (the end of the reform movement), its second act in 1918 (the transitional period between the Qing dynasty and Republican China), and its third act in 1945 (after the defeat of the Japanese). Consequently, *Teahouse* was perceived as indicating the historical necessity of the decline of the previous political regimes. In *The World's Top Restaurant*, however, the rise and fall of a particular business seems isolated from and irrelevant to the direction of historical events;[73] it could even be associated with an unhealthy nostalgic longing for the past at a time of economic and political reform.[74] Other critics took issue with this view and insisted that, precisely because of its historical neutrality, *The World's Top Restaurant* surpassed its precursor text. Its lasting appeal, they claimed, was attributable to its being a dramatic entity with its own internal conflicts and logic, thus avoiding the danger of contamination by political and ideological contingencies and interpretations.[75] In effect, the play was accorded the typical treatment meted out to contemporary Chinese drama: no matter how salient the aesthetic values of a particular play in the eyes of one group of critics, other critics, whose educational and personal experiences dictated a different approach, inevitably would look at it as a forum for political and ideological views.

He Jiping, the playwright, however, did not allow others to determine the play's interpretation. She provided her own explanation for what she called its "universal appeal." While spending two years and a half "delving into life" in a Beijing roast duck restaurant, she had been deeply touched by the intelligence and dedication of the managers, chefs, and waiters, who had been unjustifiably looked down upon as being on the lowest rung of the social ladder. Part of her original intention had been to set history straight by demonstrating that the rich, the leisured, and so-called cultivated elite class excelled only at eating, drinking, and playing around. The hardworking common folk were the creators of Chinese culinary art, which, in her view, should be deemed a form of high art on a par with classical music, poetry, and painting. From the art of Chinese cuisine, which consisted in the artist/cook mixing five tastes—sour, sweet, bitter, spicy, and salty—she extrapolated the underlying theme of the play: the unfair treatment of the common people, whose lives were also made up of the same "five ingredients." By asking at the end of the play, "Who is the owner and who is the guest?" she felt she was restoring the status of the "guests" to that of the "owners," or "the makers of history."[76]

In providing an account of commoners, however, He Jiping overlooked an essential facet of such an examination: the fate of women. The only woman character in an otherwise all-male cast, Yu Chu was depicted as a beautiful, intelligent prostitute. She was devoted to Lu Mengshi, the ambitious married manager, and used her considerable feminine charms to help him realize *his* ambition of creating the best restaurant under heaven. At the end of the play, when Lu returns to his wife and child in the country after having been fired by the owners, Yu Chu seems never to have expected him to act differently. Perhaps Yu Chu's story would have been more unpalatable to feminist-minded spectators had they also kept in mind the way the female characters not seen on the stage were portrayed. Although he had described his wife as ugly, Lu had not deserted her, as she had been able to give birth to a son who could inherit his property. With an effective homemaker at home in the peaceful countryside and a self-less, loving mistress helping him run his business in the problematic city, Lu Mengshi seemed to have provided himself with the best possible arrangement the patriarchal society could offer.

He Jiping, a Chinese woman playwright, has repeated Linda Loman's remark about her husband Willy in Arthur Miller's *Death of a Salesman:* "So attention must be paid." Unfortunately, according to Gayle Austin, Miller's play only "paid attention to Willy and to his trouble," with no one asking, "But what about Linda?"[77] Similarly, in this Chinese play, men's ordeals and suffering are seriously depicted, while the other gender is reduced to the single body of a "well-known" prostitute whose occupation is most closely associated with the notion of women as commodities. For Yu Chu's portrait, the playwright combined the traditional images of *xiaji*—the "chivalrous prostitute" willing to forgo her personal needs for her true love while using her body and mind in negotiations with other men—and the "earth mother," associated with endurance and forgiveness. The depiction left intact the impression that women were the ultimate outsiders, despite the playwright's scheme to turn "guests" into "owners." Women's losses, loneliness, and longings received no attention, and the Chinese critics commented that Yu Chu's sorrow as a woman should have been explored with more depth and emotion.[78]

In my view, any discussion of the formalistic and thematic features of Beijing-flavored theater must include gender politics. In laying claim to representing "true-to-life" Beijing characters, playwrights like Lao She and He Jiping seemed inevitably to re-create the age-old patriarchal world of old Beijing, populated by male characters such as warlords, eunuchs, imperial guards, pimps, wrestlers, waiters, chefs, diehards from the last dynasty, and teahouse and restaurant owners. Female characters were left with little space in which to act and react, and only roles for marginalized characters such as plot brewers were available to them.

This perspective could help account for the persistent presence of the minor character of prostitute or housewife in Lao She's *Teahouse*, the precursor text. In this play, Dingbao, another stereotypical "whore with a heart of gold," is a prostitute/waitress who has been compelled to take up this work because of life's hardships.[79] Just as Austin faults *Death of a Salesman*, "among the half-dozen most lauded plays in the canon, and the most imitated," for the way it "cuts women's experience out of consideration for 'serious drama,' "[80] so should *Teahouse* and *The World's Top Restaurant*, by virtue of their central positions in the Chinese dramatic canon, be faulted for unquestioningly reflecting and thereby accentuating the patriarchal world of old Beijing.[81] Moreover, although we find father-son relationships in *The World's Top Restaurant* and mother-son and father-son relationships in *Teahouse*, these well-received Beijing-flavored plays contain no mother-daughter relationships, echoing what Austin terms "the lack of mother-daughter engagement of any kind in the American dramatic canon."[82] The high canonical status of these two Chinese plays was therefore achieved at the expense of the representation of women.

Whereas *The World's Top Restaurant* ponders Chinese culture by recapturing its indigenous past, Guo Shixing's *Birdman (Niaoren)*, another well-received Beijing-flavored play, premiered by the Beijing People's Art Theater in 1992, meditates on the question of Chinese identity and national characters in post-Maoist China. It features dramatic conflicts between a Chinese man, a Chinese-American man, and an American-educated Chinese man in 1990s Beijing, with its old traditions responding to the challenges of contemporary times.[83] The three-act play takes place on a stage "in the process of being built into a huge bird cage, which includes even a portion of the audience's seats," and revolves around a group of bird-loving men in the city of Beijing who spend all of their leisure time raising, examining, and talking about birds. Fascinated by this cultural phenomenon, Dr. Ding Baoluo (Paul Ding), a Chinese-American psychiatrist, establishes a Birdman Psychiatric Center. Ding hopes to restore the mental health of the birdmen by retrieving their deeply buried memories of traumatic childhood experiences. In this way he hopes to use his Western-acquired knowledge of psychoanalysis to fulfill his lifelong wish of serving his motherland.

Ding's subsequent experience proves frustrating and confusing, however, for he does not always comprehend the literary and dramatic allusions that sprinkle his patients' talk under hypnosis. Nor can he share their amusement when they summon from their subconscious the names of local theaters, restaurants, movie stars, and fictional characters that would be known to Chinese people whose lives were affected by identical cultural and political events in the PRC. Never purely "personal" (a key word in psychoanalysis), these memories are in fact almost always political and collective. Ding's most embarrassing moments occur in act 3 when San Ye (The Third Master), a retired Peking opera star, easily masters Ding's psychiatric tricks by rescripting, directing, and acting out a familiar scene from a Peking opera that cleverly puts Ding himself on trial, forcing him to admit that he himself was afflicted with the psychological problems he had earlier attributed to his patients. (One of these problems was that he had been a "Peeping Tom" as a little boy, an impulse that had later developed into a desire to prey on women.)

Ding's passionate need to treat others is driven by a narcissistic desire to project his own past experience and psychological difficulties onto his patients. His insight into the problems of others reflects an instinct to imagine dramatic events and characters that he can turn into a staged play, with him as producer and director. He is nevertheless shown to be no smarter than his "patient"—the retired Peking opera star—who surpasses him in staging an even more exciting play. Ding must consequently admit that he has become "addicted" to psychoanalysis. For him, analyzing a person offers the same gratification as reading an intriguing book. The more he reads, the more creative he becomes in imagining the subject's experiences and conjuring up his mental problems. He seems to have derived inordinate pleasure from constructing these fictional worlds while claiming that he was simply reporting the "truth." But, back in China, as he attempts to cure Chinese patients, Ding is lured into reliving his early memories of growing up as a Chinese American, and his "patient" examines, questions, and challenges these memories. It is indeed his experience in a Chinese bird-loving community that helps him retrieve these early memories of himself when he was a young member of a minority group and always figuratively "peeping into" the forbidden mainstream windows of a racist, predominantly white America.

The play's boundaries between bird and human being—and their complex realms of confinement and freedom—can be read symbolically as an in-between space of hybridity, ethnicity, and cultural diversity in which immigrants cannot be understood without considering their interactions with their counterparts in the country of the other. And, in this play, diversity and difference are examined not on the other side of the ocean in the "melting pot" of America, but instead right in the middle of a bird market in the center of Beijing. It turns out that the impact of Ding Baoluo's experiences in America is partially neutralized because of his contact with the birdmen in his "root" country. Ding's efforts to aid the birdmen to lay aside their painful early memories in China paradoxically helps him to resolve the conflicts inherent in his own childhood.

Ding Baoluo is not the only character to acquire self-knowledge in the course of the play. In spite of San Ye's skeptical attitude toward psychoanalysis, it is clear that he is deeply affected by Ding's probing of his identification with his bird. In one respect, he learns that when old age and declining status at the Peking opera deprived him of his former special identity, he compensated for lost glories by worshipping his bird, which could still sing beautifully when bidden to do so. "Playing with the bird means entertaining yourself; the bird singing perfectly reminds you of past years when you yourself could sing magnificently," Ding convinces San Ye.[84] San Ye's total immersion in the bird thus reflects his despair at his impotence, his lack of confidence, and his loneliness and nostalgia for the past; he worries that he would never be able to train the next generation of actors, even if he were to devote all his time and energy to ensuring that his artistic skills were passed down to them. San Ye's apprehensions appear justified after he discovers a talented young man from the country who cannot understand why thirteen hours of training a day to become an opera star would give him a better future than his modest dream of remaining a "country bumpkin" and enjoying life taking care of his pigs.[85] The process of trying to create a next generation of stars proves Ding right: San Ye's vision of reviving Peking opera is nothing but a fantasy. Ultimately, only the world of birds can provide him with a lingering sense of belonging to a world of art and beauty.

Ding's pseudoscience does confer one benefit on San Ye. In the effort to expose Ding, in his "swan-song" performance, though no cleverer than the other birdmen, San Ye temporarily regains something of his previous power and heroic stature. In this role, he plays the wise, incorruptible Judge Bao, who punishes and sentences Ding, the confused pseudoscientist. He also condemns a Dr. Chen, a Chinese bird expert with a Western degree who has killed the last surviving bird of an endangered species so as to preserve it as a specimen for public display. This Western-educated Chinese scientist had gained recognition as a global scientist and was revered by members of the world community dedicated to protecting animal rights. But now his punishment is coupled with the deportation of Charlie (Cha Li), an American bird expert who had once awarded Dr. Chen a medal for scientific achievement. This sarcastic commentary on hypocritical scholars—the Chinese man who had sought Western approbation and his American patron—reflects a loss of identity that rendered Chinese economically and culturally vulnerable to imperialist powers. Empowered as a judge in an imperial court, San Ye is in a position to reaffirm the Chinese national character, which has about it a "birdlike" quality. As another bird lover puts it, the Chinese national character bears similarities to the personality of a lark, which, "once born in the sand, never leaves the sand." Like this bird, "we would never go abroad no matter how wonderful a foreign country is; we can never tear ourselves away from our humble dwellings."[86] San Ye's triumphant conquering of others in this inner play, moreover, supports what he perceives as the magic power of the operatic theater, whose artistic spirit he has mastered as the national treasure, and which, it is felt, will somehow survive its apparent crisis and decline.

One feature that distinguishes *Birdmen* from its precursor texts in Beijing-flavored theater is its setting on a street corner of Beijing, which in the 1990s has lost its old charm and atmosphere. The Pepsi-Cola sign (*baishi kele*) at the back of the stage and the references to a company's bankruptcy delineate a commercialized China whose new economic order is dominated by foreign capital. The current Western presence is juxtaposed to collective memories of a semicolonial past, heard in the birdmen's random comparisons between the Birdman Psychiatric Center and foreign concessions (*zujie*) at the beginning of the twentieth century. The center also makes the birdmen think of stories they have heard about American medical experiments with x-rays; these were said to have killed innocent Chinese people in Xiehe Hospital, established with funds from the humiliating Boxer indemnity imposed in 1900 by foreign nations after their attack on Beijing (known in Chinese history as *genzi peikuan*). The Chinese American's use of Freudian psychoanalysis to demonstrate that Chinese birdmen have psychological problems appears as cultural domination in a new guise, outstripping in insolence former economic domination.

The birdmen's resistance to this latest cultural influence supplies much of the play's dramatic conflict and accounts for much of its charm. The audience's laughter is usually evoked by the clash of opposing discourses (local/foreign, regional/global, empirical/scientific, traditional/modern, and personal/collective). Other national identities and misidentities also come into play, with amusing results. Audiences applauded and laughed repeatedly, for instance, when a birdman calls Charlie, the American man, *taijun*, a familiar, respectful form of address used for Japanese invaders during World War II.[87] Whether foreigners were from America or Japan, from East or West, they were seen as just outsiders bearing no possible relation to Chinese people. On another occasion during the play within the play, San Ye, as Judge Bao, advises a Chinese interpreter not to marry Charlie, as foreigners are not known for their constancy. Yet upon being told by the Chinese woman that she herself did not plan to remain married to Charlie forever, San Ye switches to another persona, that of the streetwise contemporary Chinese man. The latter advises her to follow the ancient Chinese practice of "staying married even to a cock" *(jiaji suiji)* and "staying married even to a bird" *(jianiao suiniao)*. The audience erupted into laughter at the second, newly coined proverb in the context of this bird play, and at the humor produced by the contradictory voices of San Ye, who seemed to step in and out of the role of Judge Bao at will.

The prominent place of Peking opera in the inner play within an outer play served to deplore its decline and lent the entire play a resonance unmatched by other Beijing-flavored modern dramas. Lin Liankun, the actor who played San Ye, gave a masterful performance as both the die-hard Peking opera star in the outer play, performed in the style of modern drama, and as Judge Bao in the inner play, performed in the Peking opera style. His great range of body movements, singing, and acting, which he used to shuttle between the two dramatic genres, contributed enormously to the spectacular performance aspects of the play, whose visual, auditory, and sensual richness can be better experienced in the actual space of the theater. More than any other Beijing-flavored drama, *Birdman* needs to be seen on the stage if one is to appreciate the beauty and depth of the diverse acting styles and local color, as well as the magnificent display of conventions from both modern drama and traditional theater. Playing with birds suggests the desire of Beijing citizens to play with dramatic repertory, as exemplified by the character of Pangzi (Fat Man). Obsessed with theater stars and a theatrical career that has never materialized, he still longs to become San Ye's apprentice so he can master the art of Peking opera. The portrayal of this common man of Beijing—rustic, unsophisticated, yet passionate about theater—is a critique of the other elitist characters of old Beijing. Their love of the local culture reflects both strength (the attachment to their cultural heritage) and weakness (the reluctance to move on to and welcome new facets of a modernized cosmopolitan city).

This play about a Beijing bird culture also resembles its precursor texts such as *Teahouse* and *The World's Top Restaurant* in its marginalization of women's experience. Among the fifteen named and many other unnamed characters who appear onstage, there are only two women: Xiao Xia, a country bumpkin who, after begging everyone to hire her as a maid, is employed by Ding Baoluo to take care of his patients; and Luo Man (literally, "Romance"), Charlie's interpreter, whose knowledge of the English language and shapely figure provide her with assets she can exchange for an American "green card." These two women represent polar opposites of stereotypical female characterization: rustic/sophisticated, rural/urban, illiterate/educated, and China-rooted/West-oriented, with apparently no possibility of compromise. With only this dichotomy to contemplate, a feminist critic or spectator might ponder a subversive reading of the following concluding scene by choosing not to be part of this world.

At dusk, as the setting sun can be seen amid brushes and trees in the bird market, Ding Baoluo, after having watched a wonderful performance of Peking opera, celebrates a successful day of therapeutic treatment. When everyone else is gone, however, he examines and then drops heavily on a table the gavel (*jingtang mu*) that Judge Bao had used earlier to scare him with; Ding is frustrated by his defeat at the hands of his Chinese counterpart, who mocked his Western knowledge and theories. The last word of the play, however, is uttered by a bankrupt company manager who has just begun to be absorbed by bird raising, after having been disillusioned in his hopes of achieving material success. As the curtain is about to come down, he has just finished examining his newly acquired prize possessions but then realizes that the birds refuse to fly out toward freedom when the door is opened for them. With the entire stage (the previously described enormous cage) bathed in the orange light of the setting sun, the play concludes, inviting the audience—feminist or otherwise—to consider human bondage of all kinds. This human bondage had previously also been symbolized by a chain that handcuffed San Ye, who used it to train his new opera apprentice, to Pangzi, who feels attached to it because it is the only way he can feel connected to San Ye. Handcuffed to the same chain is Ding Baoluo when he is condemned as a criminal by Judge Bao/San Ye. Thus, what had originally been offered up as indigenous theater with a Beijing flavor at this point emerges as a play influenced by such Western influences as that of the absurdist theater, a play abounding with images and symbols that communicate the perplexity and anxiety of human existence surrounded by an indecipherable cosmos. *Birdmen*'s modernistic tone—for which it is indebted to the modern literary revolution brought about by Yeats, Lawrence, Joyce, Eliot, Proust, Valéry, Mann, Rilke, and Kafka—is far from accidental. The play deals with the profound cultural shock produced by social, economic, ideological, and international conflicts, and by the threat of rupture from a familiar path. At the end of such a play, one might imagine some feminist critics or spectators going home and celebrating their exclusion from this gloomy world of patriarchs and patriots. They might actually prefer their marginal lives as a way of setting themselves off from the mainstream male-dominated society.

My study of the Chinese stage in early post-Maoist China reminds me of Luigi Pirandello's play *Six Characters in Search of an Author*, in which a stage director is persuaded by six characters to turn their complicated life stories into a play. In trying to carry out this plan, however, the stage director finds himself at a loss as to how to conclude the play. His refusal to continue writing the script in accordance with his characters' demands recalls the frustration that has led Chinese dramatists and critics to alternatively accept and reject the various Western theatrical traditions, which have, like Pirandello's characters, often seemed to insist on being copied exactly on the Chinese stage. However, when Chinese dramatists seek out an author—as one would seek God or a father figure embodied in Western theatrical traditions—to validate their own formalist innovations, they often hesitate, finding themselves at the last moment compelled by their own intense experiences to return to their own agenda of cultural rejuvenation and political liberation. Thus Chinese dramatists, selecting from among diverse formalistic traditions from both East and West, have created a "melting pot" of their own. With multiple options to explore, Chinese theater can now be more effective than ever, as it inquires into the crisis of a culture, the beginnings of modernity, the erosion of the collective, and the power of the father. The need no longer exists to search for an author. There are many authors, all of them present in the audience, waiting for their compelling experiences to be represented on the stage, which, fortunately, has already been enriched by, but not confined to, the several traditions I have here described.

APPENDIX

A Selected List of Plays from the Republican to the PRC Periods in English Translation

This list does not include abridged translations, excerpts from plays, or some earlier translations. In some cases, more than one citation of the same title is given for the readers' convenience. Although the list focuses on modern spoken drama, selected Peking operas, ballet and folk-opera scripts, and Yuan dramas relevant to this study are also included. Plays from Taiwan and Hong Kong are not listed here as they go beyond the coverage of this study.

Bai, Fengxi 白峰溪. *First Bathed in Moonlight* (*Mingyue chuzhao ren* 明月初照人). Translated by Guan Yuehua. In Bai Fengxi, *The Women Trilogy*, 104–203. Beijing: Panda, 1991.

———. *Once Loved and in a Storm Returning* (*Fengyu guren lai* 风雨故人来). Translated by Guan Yuehua. In Bai Fengxi, *The Women Trilogy*, 9–103. [Also Translated as *Friend on a Rainy Day* by Diana B. Kingsbury, in her comp. and trans., *I Wish I Were a Wolf: The New Voice in Chinese Women's Literature*, 64–122. Beijing: New World Press, 1994.]

———. *Say, Who Like Me Is Prey to Fond Regret?* (*Buzhi qiusi zai shui jia* 不知秋思在谁家). Translated by Guan Yuehua. In Bai Fengxi, *The Women Trilogy*, 204–287. [Also in Chinese Literature 2 (1990): 70–127.]

Boulder Bay (*Panshiwan* 磐石湾). Script produced by the Shanghai Peking Opera Troupe, written by A Jian (Ah Chien 阿坚). *Chinese Literature* 4 (1976): 55–122.

Cao, Yu 曹禺. *Bright Skies* (*Minglang de tian* 明亮的天). Translated by Chang Peichi. Beijing: Foreign Languages Press, 1960.

——. *The Consort of Peace* (*Wang Zhaojun* 王昭君). Translated by Monica Lai. Hong Kong: Kelly & Walsh, 1980.

——. *Peking Man* (*Beijing ren* 北京人). Translated by Leslie Nai-Kwai Lo, with Don Cohn and Michelle Vosper. New York: Columbia University Press, 1986.

——. *Sunrise* (*Richu* 日出). Translated by A. C. Barnes. Beijing: Foreign Languages Press, 1960.

——. *Thunderstorm* (*Leiyu* 雷雨). Translated by Wang Tso-liang and A. C. Barnes. Beijing: Foreign Languages Press, 1958.

——. *The Wilderness* (*Yuanye* 原野). Translated by Christopher C. Rand and Joseph S. M. Lau. Hong Kong: Hong Kong University Press, 1980.

Chen, Baichen (Chen Pai-ch'en) 陈白尘. *Men and Women in Wild Times* (*Luanshi nannü* 乱世男女). Translated by Edward M. Gunn. In Edward M. Gunn, ed., *Twentieth-Century Chinese Drama*, 126–173.

Chen, Qitong (Chen chi-tung) 陈其通. *The Long March* (*Wanshui qianshan* 万水千山). Beijing: Foreign Languages Press, 1956.

Chen, Xiaomei, ed. and intro. *Reading the Right Text: An Anthology of Contemporary Chinese Drama*. Honolulu: University of Hawai'i Press (forthcoming).

Chen, Zidu 陈子度, et al. *Sangshuping Chronicles* (*Sangshuping jishi* 桑树坪纪事). Translated by Cai Rong. In Haiping Yan, ed., *Theater and Society*, 189–261. Armonk, N.Y.: M. E. Sharpe, 1998.

Cheung, Martha P. Y., and Jane C. C. Lai, eds. *An Oxford Anthology of Contemporary Chinese Drama*. Hong Kong: Oxford University Press, 1997.

Ding, Xilin (Ting Hsi-lin) 丁西林. *Oppression* (*Yapo* 压迫). Translated by Joseph Lau. In Edward M. Gunn, ed., *Twentieth-Century Chinese Drama*, 41–51. [Also in *Renditions* 4 (Autumn 1974): 117–124; and translated as *The Oppressed*, in Ku Tsung-ni, ed., *Modern Chinese Plays*, 55–74.]

Duan, Chengbin (Tuan, Cheng-pin) 段承滨, and Du Shijun (Tu Shih-tsun) 杜士俊. *Taming the Dragon and the Tiger* (*Xianglong fuhu* 降龙伏虎). Translated by A. C. Barnes. Beijing: Foreign Language Press, 1961.

Ebon, Martin, ed. *Five Chinese Communist Plays*. New York: The John Day Co., 1975.

Fighting on the Plain (*Pingyuan zhuozhan* 平原作战). July 1973 script of the China Peking Opera Troupe 中国京剧团集体创作, written by Zhang Yongmei (Chang Yung-mei) et al. 张永枚执笔. *Chinese Literature* 5 (1974): 3–54.

Gao, Xingjian 高行健. *Alarm Signal* (*Juedui xinhao* 绝对信号). Translated by Shiao-Ling S. Yu. In Shiao-Ling S. Yu, ed., *Chinese Drama after the Cultural Revolution*, 159–232.

——. *Between Life and Death* (*Shengsi jie* 生死界). In Gao Xingjian, *The Other Shore: Plays by Gao Xingjian*, 45–79. Translated by Gilbert C. F. Fong. Hong Kong: The Chinese University Press, 1999.

——. *Bus Stop* (*Chezhan* 车站). Translated by Kimberly Besio. In Haiping Yan, ed., *Theater and Society*, 3–59. [Also translated as *The Bus Stop* by Shiao-Ling

S. Yu, in Shiao-Ling S. Yu, ed., *Chinese Drama after the Cultural Revolution*, 233–289.]

——. *Dialogue and Rebuttal* (*Duihua yu fanjie* 对话与反诘). In Gao Xingjian, *The Other Shore*, 81–135.

——. *Nocturnal Wanderer* (*Yeyou shen* 夜游神). In Gao Xingjian, *The Other Shore*, 137–190.

——. *The Other Shore* (*Bi'an* 彼岸). Translated by Jo Riley. In Cheung and Lai, eds., *An Oxford Anthology of Contemporary Chinese Drama*, 1–44.

——. *The Other Shore: Plays by Gao Xingjian*. Translated by Gilbert C. F. Fong. Hong Kong: The Chinese University Press, 1999.

——. *Weekend Quartet* (*Zhoumo sichong zou* 周末四重奏). In Gao Xingjian, *The Other Shore*, 191–253.

——. *Wild Man* (*Yeren* 野人). Translated, introduced, and annotated by Bruno Boubicek. *Asian Theater Journal* 7.2 (1990): 195–249.

Guan, Hanqing (Kuan Han-ching 关汉卿). *Selected Plays of Kuan Han-Ching*. Translated by Yang Hsien-yi and Gladys Yang. Beijing: Foreign Languages Press, 1958.

——. *Snow in Midsummer* (*Dou'e yuan* 窦娥冤). Translated by Yang Hsien-yi and Gladys Yang. In Walter J. Meserve and Ruth I. Meserve, eds., *Modern Drama from Communist China*, 16–37. New York: New York University Press, 1970.

Gunn, Edward M., ed. *Twentieth-Century Chinese Drama: An Anthology*. Bloomington: Indiana University Press, 1983.

Guo Moruo 郭沫若. *Cai Wenji* 蔡文姬. Translated by Feng Fumin and Bonnie S. McDougall. In Guo Moruo, *Selected Works of Guo Moruo: Five Historical Plays*, 315–406. Beijing: Foreign Languages Press, 1984.

——. *Qu Yuan* 屈原. Translated by Yang Hsien-yi and Gladys Yang. In Guo Moruo, *Selected Works of Guo Moruo*, 87–191.

——. *Selected Works of Guo Moruo: Five Historical Plays*. Beijing: Foreign Languages Press, 1984.

——. *The Tiger Tally* (*Hufu* 虎符). Translated by Feng Fumin and Bonnie S. McDougall. In Guo Moruo, *Selected Works of Guo Moruo*, 193–313.

——. *Twin Flower* (*Tangdi zhihua* 棠棣之花). Translated by Feng Fumin and Bonnie S. McDougall. In Guo Moruo, *Selected Works of Guo Moruo*, 1–86.

——. *Wu Zetian* 武则天. Translated by Feng Fumin and Bonnie S. McDougall. In Guo Moruo, *Selected Works of Guo Moruo*, 407–521.

Guo, Shixing 过士行. *Birdmen* (*Niaoren* 鸟人). Translated by Jane C. C. Lai. In Martha P. Y. Cheung and Jane C. C. Lai, eds., *An Oxford Anthology of Contemporay Chinese Drama*, 295–350.

He, Jingzhi 贺敬之, with Ding Yi 丁毅. *The White-Haired Girl* (*Baimao nü* 白毛女). Translated by Hsien-yi Yang and Gladys Yang. Beijing: Foreign Languages Press, 1954. [Also in Walter J. Meserve and Ruth I. Meserve, eds., *Modern Drama from Communist China*, 105–180; and in Martin Ebon, ed., *Five Chinese Communist Plays*, 27–117.]

He, Jiping 何冀平. *The First House of Beijing Duck* (*Tianxia diyilou* 天下第一楼). Translated by Hsiao-Ling S. Yu. In Shiao-Ling S. Yu, ed., *Chinese Drama after the Cultural Revolution*, 423–484. [Also translated by Edward M. Gunn as *The World's Top Restaurant*. In Xiaomei Chen, ed., *Reading the Right Text*].

Hong Shen (Hung Shen) 洪深. *Yama Chao.* (*Zhao Yanwang* 赵阎王). Translated by Carolyn T. Brown. In Edward M. Gunn, ed., *Twentieth-Century Chinese Drama*, 10–51.

Hu, Ke 胡可. *Locust Tree Village* (*Huaishuzhuang* 槐树庄). Beijing: Foreign Languages Press, 1961.

——. *Steeled in Battles* (*Zai zhandou le chengzhang* 在战斗里成长). Translated by Tang Sheng. Beijing: Foreign Languages Press, 1955.

Hu, Shi (Hu Shih) 胡适. *The Greatest Event in Life* (*Zhongshen dashi* 终身大事). Translated by Edward M. Gunn. In Edward M. Gunn, ed., *Twentieth-Century Chinese Drama*, 1–9. [Also in A. E. Zucker, ed., *The Chinese Theater*, 119–128. Boston: Little, Brown, 1925.]

Jin Jian (Chin Chien) 金剑. *Chao Hsiao-lan* 赵小兰. Translated by Chang Su-chu. In *The Women's Representative*, 5–43. Beijing: Foreign Languages Press, 1956.

Jin, Shan 金山. *Red Storm* (*Hongse fengbao* 红色风暴). Beijing: Foreign Languages Press, 1965.

Jin, Yun 锦云. *Uncle Doggie's Nirvana* (*Gou'er Ye niepan* 狗儿爷涅盘). Translated by Ying Ruocheng. In Martha P. Y. Cheung and Jane C. C. Lai, eds., *An Oxford Anthology of Contemporary Chinese Drama*, 89–147. [Also translated as *The Nirvana of Grandpa Doggie*, in Shiao-Ling S. Yu, ed., *Chinese Drama after the Cultural Revolution*, 349–422.]

Ku, Tsung-ni 顾宗沂, ed., and trans. *Modern Chinese Plays*. Shanghai: Commercial Press, 1941.

Lao, She 老舍. *Dragon Beard Ditch* (*Longxugou* 龙须沟). Translated by Liao Hung-ying. Beijing: Foreign Languages Press, 1956. [Also in Walter J. Meserve and Ruth I. Meserve, eds., *Modern Drama from Communist China*, 43–104.]

——. *The Rickshaw Boy.* (*Luotuo Xiangzi* 骆驼祥子) Adapted by Mei Ch'ien (Mei Qian 梅阡). Translated by Richard F. S. Yang and Herbert M. Stahl. New York: Selected Academic Readings, 1964.

——. *Teahouse* (*Chaguan* 茶馆). Translated by John Howard-Gibbon. Beijing: Foreign Languages Press, 1980. [Also translated as *Tea House*, *Chinese Literature* 6 (1980): 16–91.]

Li, Huang, et al. 李恍. *War Drums on the Equator* (*Chidao zangu* 赤道战鼓). Beijing: Foreign Languages Press, 1966. [Also in *Chinese Literature* 7 (1965): 3–72.]

Li, Jianwu (Li Chien-wu) 李健吾. *Springtime* (*Qingchun* 青春). Translated by David Pollard. In Edward M. Gunn, ed., *Twentieth-Century Chinese Drama*, 174–227.

Li, Zhihua (Li Chih-hua) 李之华. *Struggle against Counter-Struggle* (*Fan fanbai douzheng* 反翻把斗争). Beijing: Cultural Press, 1950.

Liang, Bingkun 梁秉坤. *Who's the Strongest of Us All?* (*Shuishi qiangzhe* 谁是

强者). Translated by Shun Cheng. In Martha P. Y. Cheung and Jane C. C. Lai, eds., *An Oxford Anthology of Contemporary Chinese Drama*, 3–88.

Liu, Shugang 刘树纲. *The Dead Visiting the Living* (*Yige sizhe dui shengzhe de fangwen* 一个死者对生着的访问). Translated by Charles Qianzhi Wu. In Xiaomei Chen, ed., *Reading the Right Text*.

Lu, Xun 鲁迅. *The Passer-by* (*Guoke* 过客). Translated by Yang Hsien-yi and Gladys Yang. In Lu Xun, *The Selected Works of Lu Hsun*, 1: 332–338. Beijing: Foreign Languages Press, 1956. [Also in Walter J. Meserve and Ruth I. Meserve, eds., *Modern Drama from Communist China*, 38–42.]

Ma, Zhongjun 马中骏. *The Legend of Old Bawdy Town* (*Laofengliuzhen* 老风流镇). Translated by Janice Wickeri. In Martha P. Y. Cheung and Lai Jane C. C., eds., *An Oxford Anthology of Contemporary Chinese Drama*, 185–261.

Meserve, Walter J., and Ruth I. Meserve, eds. *Modern Drama from Communist China*. New York: New York University Press, 1970.

Mitchell, John, ed. *The Red Pear Garden: Three Dramas of Revolutionary China*. Boston: David R. Godine, 1973.

On the Docks (*Haigang* 海港). Revised by the "On the Docks" Group of the Shanghai Peking Opera Troupe (Shanghai jingjutuan *Haigang* juzu jiti gaibian 上海京剧团《海港》剧组集体改编). Beijing: Foreign Languages Press, 1973. [Also in *Chinese Literature* 5 (1972): 52–98.]

The Orphan Chao (*Zhaoshi gu'er* 赵氏孤儿). Translated by Ian McLanchlan and Stephene Wong. *Eastern Horizon* 3 (January 1964): 46–54; (February 1964): 40–53; and (March 1964): 48–57.

Ouyang Yuqian (Ou-yang Yu-ch'ien) 欧阳玉倩. *P'an Chin-lien* 潘金莲. Translated by Catherine Swatek. In Edward M. Gunn, ed., *Twentieth-Century Chinese Drama*, 52–75.

Peking People's Art Theater. *Between Husband and Wife* (*Fuqi zhijian* 夫妻之间). Translated by Sidney Shapiro. In *The Women's Representative*, 95–119. [Also in *China Reconstructed* (Supplement) 6 (1953).]

Raid on the White Tiger Regiment (*Qixi Baihutuan* 奇袭白虎团). By the Shandong Provincial Peking Opera Troupe (Shandongsheng jingjutuan 山东省京剧团). Beijing: Foreign Languages Press, 1972. [Also in *Chinese Literature* 3 (1973): 3–48; earlier version, Beijing: Afro-Asian Writers Bureau, 1967; and in *Chinese Literature* 5 (1965): 3–48.]

The Red Detachment of Women (*Hongse niangzijun* 红色娘子军). Revised collectively by the China Ballet Troupe. *Chinese Literature* 1 (1971): 2–80.

The Red Lantern (*Hongdeng ji* 红灯记). Revised collectively by the China Peking Opera Troupe (Zhongguo jingjutuan jiti gaibian 中国京剧团集体改编). Translated by Foreign Languages Press. Beijing: Foreign Languages Press, 1972. [Also in *Chinese Literature* 8 (1970): 8–52. An earlier version translated by Yang Hsien-yi and Gladys Yang, script by Weng Ouhong 翁偶虹 and A Jia 阿甲, *Chinese Literature* (May 1965): 3–48; in Walter J. Meserve and Ruth I. Meserve, eds., *Modern Drama from Communist China*, 328–368; also in Lois Wheeler Snow, *China on Stage: An American Actress in the People's Republic*, 257–303. New York: Random House, 1972.]

Ren, Deyao (Jen Teh-yao) 任德耀. *Magic Aster* (*Malanhua* 马兰花). Translated by William C. White. Beijing: Foreign Languages Press, 1965. [Also in Walter J. Meserve and Ruth I. Meserve, eds., *Modern Drama from Communist China*, 181–218.]

Sha, Seh 莎色, et al. *Letters from the South* (*Nanfang laixin* 南方来信). Translated by Sidney Shapiro. *Chinese Literature* 3 (1966): 3–64. [Also in Walter J. Meserve and Ruth I. Meserve, eds., *Modern Drama from Communist China* 279–327.]

Sha, Yexin 沙叶新. *If I Were for Real* (*Jiaru woshi zhende* 假如我是真的). Translated by Lee Yee. In Lee Yee, ed., *The New Realism: Writings from China after the Cultural Revolution*, 262–322. New York: Hippocrene Books, 1983.

———. *Jiang Qing and Her Husbands* (*Jiang Qing he tade zhangfumen* 江青和她的丈夫们). Translated by Kirk A. Denton. In Xiaomei Chen, ed., *Reading the Right Text*.

Shajiabang (*Shachiapang*) 沙家浜. Revised collectively by the Peking Opera Troupe of Beijing (Beijing jingjutuan jiti gaibian 北京京剧团集体改编). Beijing: Foreign Languages Press, 1972. [Also in *Chinese Literature* 11 (1967): 3–53; in Snow Lois Wheeler, *China on Stage*, 127–190; an earlier version was translated as *Spark Amidst the Reeds* (*Ludang huozhong* 芦荡火种) by Wang Tseng-chi 汪曾琪 et al., *Chinese Literature* 9 (1964): 3–63.]

Shen, Ximeng (Shen Hsi-meng) 沈西蒙, et al. *On Guard beneath Neon Lights* (*Nihongdeng xia de shaobing* 霓虹灯下的哨兵). Beijing: Foreign Languages Press, 1966.

Snow, Lois Wheeler. *China on Stage: An American Actress in the People's Republic*. New York: Random House, 1972.

Song of the Dragon River (*Longjiang song* 龙江颂). Collectively revised by Song of the Dragon River Group of Shanghai (Shanghai shi *Longjiang song* juzu jiti gaibian 上海市《龙江颂》剧组集体改编). Beijing: Foreign Languages Press, 1972. [Also in *Chinese Literature* 7 (1972): 3–52.]

Sun, Weishi 孙维世. *A New Dawn* (*Chusheng de taiyang* 初升的太阳). *Chinese Literature* 10 (1977): 3–83.

Sun, Yu 孙竽. *The Women's Representative* (*Funü daibiao* 妇女代表). Translated by Tang Sheng. In *The Women's Representative*, 44–94. [Also in Walter J. Meserve and Ruth I. Meserve, eds., *Modern Drama from Communist China*, 181–218.]

Taking Tiger Mountain by Strategy (*Zhiqu Weihushan* 智取威虎山). Collectively revised by the *Taking Tiger Mountain by Strategy* Group of Shanghai Peking Opera Troupe (Shanghai jingjutuan *Zhiqu Weihushan* juzu jiti gaibian 上海京剧团《智取威虎山》剧组集体改编. Beijing: Foreign Languages Press, 1971. [Earlier version translated as *Taking the Bandits' Stronghold* (Beijing: Foreign Languages Press, 1968); also in *Chinese Literature* 8 (1967): 129–181; also translated by Richard E. Strassberg, in John Mitchell, ed., *The Red Pear Garden*, 203–285; also in Lois Wheeler Snow, *China on Stage*, 40–98; and in Martin Ebon, *Five Chinese Communist Plays*, 155–210.]

Tian, Han (T'ien Han) 田汉. *Kuan Han-ch'ing* 关汉卿. Translated by Foreign Languages Press, 1961. [Also in Edward M. Gunn, ed., *Twentieth-Century Chinese Drama*, 324–380.]

———. *The Night a Tiger Was Captured* (*Huohu zhiye* 获虎之夜). Translated and introduced by Randy Barbara Kaplan. *Asian Theatre Journal*. 2:1 (1994): 1–34.

———. *One Evening in Soochow* (*Suzhou yehua* 苏州夜话). Translated by Tsung-ni Ku. In Tsung-ni Ku, ed., *Modern Chinese Plays*, 2–22.

———. *A West Lake Tragedy* (*Hu shang de beiju* 湖上的悲剧). Translated by Tsung-ni Ku. In Tsung-ni Ku, ed., *Modern Chinese Plays*, 93–117.

———. *The White Snake* (*Baishe zhuan* 白蛇传). Translated by Yang Hsien-yi and Gladys Yang. Beijing: Foreign Languages Press, 1957. [Also in John Mitchell, ed., *The Red Pear Garden*, 49–120.]

Tsogtnarin (Chaoketunaren) 超克图纳仁. *Golden Eagle* (*Jinying* 金鹰). Beijing: Foreign Languages Press, 1961.

Wang, Peigong 王培公, and Wang Gui 王贵. *WM* (*Women* 我们). Translated by Thomas Moran. In Haiping Yan, ed., *Theater and Society*, 60–122. [Also in Shiao-Ling S. Yu, ed., *Chinese Drama after the Cultural Revolution*, 291–348.]

Wang, Shuyuan 王树元, et al. *Azalean Mountain* (*Dujuanshan* 杜鹃山). *Chinese Literature* 1 (1974): 3–68. [Also in Martin Ebon, ed., *Five Chinese Communist Plays*, 263–328.]

Wei, Minglun 魏明伦. *Pan Jinlian* 潘金莲. Translated by David Williams, with the assistance of Xiaoxia Williams. In Haiping Yan, ed., *Theater and Society*, 123–188. [Also translated as *Pan Jinlian: The Story of One Woman and Four Men* by Shiao-Ling S. Yu, in *Asian Theatre Journal* 10.1 (1993): 1–48; also in Shiao-Ling S. Yu, ed., *Chinese Drama of the Cultural Revolution*, 97–158.]

The Women's Representative 妇女代表. Beijing: Foreign Languages Press, 1956.

Wu, Han 吴晗. *Hai Rui Dismissed from Office* (*Hai Rui baguan* 海瑞罢官). Translated by C. C. Huang. Honolulu: University Press of Hawai'i, 1972.

Wu, Yuxiao (Wu Yu-hsiao) 武玉笑. *Young Folk in a Remote Region* (*Yuanfang qingnian* 远方青年). Translated by Chang Su. *Chinese Literature* 11 (1964): 3–79. [Also published as *Young Folk in a Remote Region*, Beijing: n.p., 1964.]

Xia, Yan (Hsia Yen) 夏衍. *Under Shanghai Eaves* (*Shanghai wuyan xia* 上海屋檐下). Translated by George Hayden. In Edward M. Gunn, ed., *Twentieth-Century Chinese Drama*, 76–125.

Xing, Yixun 刑益勋. *Power versus Law* (*Quan yu fa* 权与法). *Chinese Literature* 6 (1980): 31–91.

Xiong, Fuxi (Hsiung Fu-hsi) 熊佛西. *The Artist* (*Yishujia* 艺术家). Translated by Tsung-ni Ku. In Tsung-ni Ku, ed., *Modern Chinese Plays*, 119–137.

———. *The Drunkard* (*Zui le* 醉了). Translated by Tsung-ni Ku. In Tsung-ni Ku, ed., *Modern Chinese Plays*, 75–89.

Xu, Pinli 徐频莉. *Old Forest* (*Laolin* 老林). Translated by Martha P. Y. Cheung and Jane C. C. Lai. In Martha P. Y. Cheung and Jane C. C. Lai, eds., *An Oxford Anthology of Contemporary Chinese Drama*, 263–294.

Yan, Haiping, ed. and intro. *Theater and Society: An Anthology of Contemporary Chinese Drama*. Armonk, N.Y.: M. E. Sharpe, 1998.

Yang, Chiang 杨泽. *Windswept Blossoms* (*Fengxu* 风絮). Translated by Edward M. Gunn. In Edward M. Gunn, ed., *Twentieth-Century Chinese Drama*, 228–275.

Yang, Limin 杨利民. *Black Stones* (*Heise de shitou* 黑色的石头). Translated by Timothy C. Wong. In Xiaomei Chen, ed., *Reading the Right Text*.

Yang, Lufang (Yang Lu-fang) 杨履方. *Cuckoo Sings Again* (*Buguniao you jiao le* 布谷鸟又叫了). Translated by Daniel Talmadge and Edward M. Gunn. In Edward M. Gunn, ed., *Twentieth-Century Chinese Drama*, 276–323.

Yang, Qian. *Hope* (*Xiwang* 希望). Translated and introduced by Mary Ann O'Donnell. *Asian Theatre Journal* 17. 1 (2000): 34–50.

Yao, Cunming (Yao Chung-ming) 姚春明, et al. *Comrade, You've Taken the Wrong Path* (*Tongzhi, ni zoucuo le lu* 同志，你走错了路). Translated by A. M. Condron. Beijing: Foreign Languages Press, 1962.

Yu, Shang-yuan 余上沅. *The Mutiny* (*Bingbian* 兵变). Translated by Tsung-ni Ku. In Tsung-ni Ku, ed., *Modern Chinese Plays*, 23–53.

Yu, Shiao-Ling S., ed., trans., and intro. *Chinese Drama after the Cultural Revolution, 1979–1989: An Anthology*. New York: The Edwin Mellon Press, 1996.

Yuan, Changying 袁昌英. *Southeast Flies the Peacock* (*Kongque dongnan fei* 孔雀东南飞). Translated by Amy D. Dooling and Kristina M. Torgeson. In Amy D. Dooling and Kristina M. Torgeson, eds., *Writing Women in Modern China: An Anthology of Women's Literature from the Early Twentieth Century*, 209–252. New York: Columbia University Press, 1998.

Zhang, Lili 张莉莉. *Green Barracks* (*Lüse yingdi*, 绿色营地). Translated by Yuanxi Ma. In Xiaomei Chen, ed., *Reading the Right Text*.

Zhang, Mingyuan 张明媛. *Wild Grass* (*Yecao* 野草). Translated by Philip F. Williams. In Xiaomei Chen, ed., *Reading the Right Text*.

Zong, Fuxian (Tsung Fu-hsien) 宗福先. *In a Land of Silence* (*Yuwu sheng-chu* 于无声处). Translated by Shu-ying Tsau. In Edward M. Gunn, ed., *Twentieth-Century Chinese Drama*, 409–443.

Zhou, Weibo (Chou Wei-po) 周惟波, Deng Yangsheng (Tung Yang-sheng) 董阳声, and Ye Xiaonan (Yeh Hsiao-nan) 叶小楠. *The Artillery Commander's Son* (*Paobing siling de erzhi* 炮兵司令的儿子). Translated by Stanley Dubinsky and Edward M. Gunn. In Edward M. Gunn, ed., *Twentieth-Century Chinese Drama*, 448–467.

NOTES

Prologue

1. Throughout this study, I have used expressions inherent in Maoist discourse, such as "ex-slaves," "feudal society," "bumper harvest," and "socialist new China," in order to give general readers a taste of Maoist discourse in the PRC culture. I hope students and scholars who are familiar with that discourse can easily identify their Chinese counterparts. In the rest of this study, I consistently use these PRC terms without using quotation marks, to avoid confusion with cited materials and maintain the flow of language for stylistic reasons.

2. In the 1963 season, *Wish You Health (Zhuni jiankang)* was performed most often, with 190 shows. The lowest record goes to *Seizing the Power (Duoyin)*, staged least often, with only 25 performances. Although both plays shared the common theme of "never forget class struggle" with *Young Folk in a Remote Region* as part of a CCP ideological campaign at that time, the latter was popular thanks to a distinguished cast and an "exotic" Moslem ethnic culture. This and other statistics in the rest of this study are the results of research done in the library of the China Youth Art Theater.

3. For an English translation, see Wu Yuxiao, *Young Folk in a Remote Region.*

4. Ronald Harwood, *All the World's a Stage*, 7.

5. *Iron Transportation Troops* was premiered in 1953 by the China Youth Art Theater. A second run in 1958 showed its important status in the theater repertoire. The drama script by Huang Ti was published in *Juben* 10 (1953): 28–75. There

is no major difference between the published and performed scripts. I was deeply impressed by the beautiful calligraphy and intense labor that went into the performed script, which was hand-copied in fountain pen with black ink. It is also amazing to see other precious documents, such as rehearsal notes taken by the director and theater manager, local and national reactions to the play, CCP leaders' critiques of the play, and cast members' reactions to these critiques. Similar documents for all other plays performed by the theater since 1949 also survived the Cultural Revolution, a period when many precious documents were lost.

6. *Iron Transportation Troops*, script of the China Youth Art Theater's production, 51.

7. In Chinese culture, "uncle" is used to show children's respect for males of an older generation. It does not necessarily mean that they are relatives.

8. Chen Yongjing, my father, was Director of Stage Designers (Wutai meishu dui) for the China Youth Art Theater until the start of the Cultural Revolution. He designed stage settings and costumes for eleven plays from 1950 to 1964. For a biographical account and theoretical analysis of his artistic achievements, see Cai Tiliang, "Xinchao qifu yi quanquan" (Surging thoughts and emotions with a sincere heart).

9. *The Inspector General* was performed in 1952. It was part of the cultural events in Beijing, promoted by the Ministry of Culture, to commemorate the hundredth anniversary of the death of the Russian playwright Nikolai Gogol (1809–1852).

10. *Uncle Vanya* was performed in 1954. It was part of the cultural events in Beijing commemorating the fiftieth anniversary of the death of Anton Chekhov (1860–1904).

11. *A Doll's House* was performed in 1956 to commemorate the fiftieth anniversary of the death of Henrik Ibsen (1828–1906).

12. The 1959 premiere of *Love and Intrigue* was part of the national events in honor of the two hundredth anniversary of the birth of Friedrich Schiller (1759–1895).

13. *Shakuntala*, premiered in 1957, was attributed to Kalidasa (373?–415?), the most celebrated Indian dramatist of the Sanskrit stage.

14. The renowned role of Bao'er, played by Jin Shan, was accompanied by an equally renowned director, Sun Weishi, the first artistic director and the first PRC expert in Konstantin Stanislavsky. As the adopted daughter of Premier Zhou Enlai, Sun had been privileged to have an opportunity to study in the USSR, where she received a degree in acting and directing from the Moscow Drama College in 1946. See Xian Jihua and Zhao Yunsheng, eds., *Huaju huangdi Jin Shan zhuan* (The biography of Jin Shan: The emperor of drama), 199–200.

15. For an insightful study of a typical play of this category, see Xiaobing Tang, "The Lyrical Age and Its Discontents: On the Staging of Socialist New China in *The Young Generation*," in his *Chinese Modern*, 163–195. Interestingly, by 1964, when fifty-eight theater groups had performed *The Young Generation* in twenty-

seven cities, as Tang has pointed out, the China Youth Art Theater did not participate in this national fever.

16. Among nine plays, one was a "history play," *The Death of Li Xiucheng (Li
Xiucheng zhi si)*, written by Yang Hansheng. The other was a "revolutionary history play," *Azalean Mountain (Dujuanshan)*, written by Wang Shuyuan. Nine plays
in a single year was almost a record high in contrast to three in 1950, two in 1951,
one in 1952, two in 1953, five in 1954, three in 1955, six in 1956, seven in 1957, nine
in 1958, seven in 1959, six in 1960, one in 1961, three in 1962, ten in 1963, four in
1964, one in 1965, two in 1966, one in 1972, four in 1975, one in 1976, five in 1977,
three in 1978, six in 1979, five in 1980, four in 1981, four in 1982, five in 1983, nine
in 1984, five in 1985, three in 1986, three in 1987, three in 1988, two in 1989, one in
1990, three in 1991, three in 1992, three in 1993, two in 1994, two in 1995, two in
1996, three in 1997, and two in 1998.

17. Wang Bing adapted *Guess Who's Coming to Dinner*, in which he played the
lead character. Directed by Chen Rong, it premiered in Beijing in 1980.

18. The People's Art Theater (Beijing renmin yishu juyuan), for instance, was under
the municipal administration of Beijing. So was the China Experimental Theater
(Zhongyang shiyan huajuyuan).

19. The May Fourth was an intellectual and literary movement initially triggered
by the student demonstration in Tiananmen Square on May 4, 1919, to protest the
terms of the Treaty of Versailles. I adopt Kirk Denton's periodization of the May
Fourth movement as extending from 1915 to 1922, which he defines as "a broad
cultural revolution characterized principally by radical anti-traditionalism." (See
Denton, *Modern Chinese Literary Thought*, 113.) PRC literary historians claim
that the May Fourth drama started in 1917 at the end of the Republican Revolution with Hu Shi's critique against traditional operatic theater in *New Youth (Xin
qingnian)*. They believe that it ended in 1927 after the coup of the Nationalist Party
against the Communist Party, when dramatists were debating the "national drama
movement" *(guoju yundong)*. This is a standard periodization in the PRC, which
is sometimes applied to other literary genres. See Ge Yihong et al., eds., *Zhongguo
huaju tongshi* (A history of modern Chinese drama).

20. For a survey of the history of the China Youth Art Theater, see *The China Youth
Art Theater* (n.d.), a photo album of its stage performances over thirty years.

21. These statistics include close to 200 multi-act plays and seventy one-act plays
produced from 1949 to 1999, the year in which the China Youth Art Theater celebrated its fifieth anniversary, as indicated in its photo album. I am grateful for a
list provided by Wu Qing of the China Youth Art Theater library.

22. For a survey of worker, peasant, and soldier plays in the PRC and their historical roots, see Xiaomei Chen, Introduction, *Reading the Right Text: An Anthology of Contemporary Chinese Drama*.

23. After Jin Shan finished writing the script of *Red Storm*, he traveled to Tianjin to read it to the cast, which was then performing Tian Han's *The Journey of Beautiful Ladies (Liren xing)*. The legend goes that the cast was so excited by the script that they asked to rehearse it at night after performing *The Journey* during the day. Within only seventy-two hours, they succeeded in putting together a dress rehearsal. Premiered in Tianjin in 1958, the play was an immediate hit, with 273 performances to follow in Beijing and other cities. In was restaged in 1991 in celebration of the seventieth anniversary of the founding of the CCP. Although Wang Futang was praised for his successful performance of Shi Yang in a style close to Jin Shan, the reception was lukewarm at best. I attended one of the performances in 1991, which had about thirty people in the audience. I was still touched by the persistence and devotion of the cast, who performed as if it were a full house. Some members of the younger generation saw it as an opportunity to stage a signature piece of the theater and had given up profitable movie and television drama roles to participate.

24. *The Leopard Bay Battle* was written by Ma Jixing and first appeared in *Drama Script* 5 (1964): 51–97. The restaging of the play by the China Youth Art Theater in 1977 resulted in a record two hundred performances.

Chapter One: Introduction

1. One of the earliest seeds of modern Chinese drama can be traced back to 1866 when the Amateur Dramatic Club of Shanghai (Shanghai xiren yeyu jutuan) was established by foreign residents who built a Lyceum theater for their own entertainment. This was the first time Zheng Zhengjiu and Xu Banmei, two pioneers in modern Chinese drama, first encountered Western dramatic forms. Hu Shi's play *The Main Event of One's Life*, written in 1919, was the first original dramatic script by a Chinese playwright. The earlier productions by the Spring Willow Society, Alexandre Dumas fils' *Camille (Chahua nü)* in February 1907 (two acts only) and *The Black Slave Cries Out to Heaven* in June 1907 in Tokyo, were adaptations from foreign scripts, not original scripts by Chinese playwrights.

2. For selected studies in modern and contemporary Chinese theater, see Hua-yuan Li Mowry, *Yang-pan hsi—New Theater in China*; Colin Mackerras, *The Chinese Theatre in Modern Times*; Roger Howard, *Contemporary Chinese Theatre*; Edward Gunn, "Shanghai's 'Orphan Island' and the Development of Modern Drama" and *Unwelcome Muse*; Chang-tai Hung, "Female Symbols of Resistance in Chinese Wartime Spoken Drama"; Bernd Eberstein, ed., *A Selective Guide to Chinese Literature, 1900–1949*; Rudolf Wagner, *The Contemporary Chinese Historical Drama*; Haiping Yan, "Male Ideology and Female Identity: Images of Women in Four Modern Chinese Historical Plays"; Katherine Hui-ling Chou, "Staging Revolution: Actresses, Realism, and the New Woman Movement in Chinese Spoken Drama and Film, 1919–1949"; and Chang-tai Hung, "*Spoken Drama*."

3. For a survey of literary historiography and canon formation in modern Chinese literature from the 1920s to 1980, see Yingjin Zhang, "The Institutionalization of Modern Literary History in China, 1922–1980."

4. C. T. Hsia, *A History of Modern Chinese Fiction*, 3d ed., xlvi. For a critical debate on Hsia's paradigm and its relationship to various issues in the study of modern Chinese literature, see Perry Link, "Ideology and Theory in the Study of Modern Chinese Literature"; Kang Liu, "Politics, Critical Paradigms"; Michael S. Duke, "Thoughts on Politics and Critical Paradigms in Modern Chinese Literature Studies"; and Longxi Zhang, "Out of the Cultural Ghetto."

5. There have been successful tours of modern Chinese drama, such as Lao She's *Teahouse (Chaguan)*, which was received favorably in Germany, France, Switzerland, Japan, Canada, and Hong Kong in the 1980s. Such cases, however, are rare in drama history.

6. Since the 1980s, many drama productions, especially those in urban centers such as Beijing and Shanghai, were recorded on videotape. Unlike film, however, which can be distributed through the commercial market, drama videotapes are not as accessible to the public, although major drama performances sometimes are broadcast on local and national television networks.

7. Martin W. Huang, book review, *The Columbia Anthology of Modern Chinese Literature*, 1989. One noticeable exception is *The Literature of China in the Twentieth Century* by Bonnie S. McDougall and Kim Louice, which covers poetry, fiction, and drama from 1900 to 1989.

8. See Jeffrey C. Kinkley, ed., *After Mao: Chinese Literature and Society* (1978–1981).

9. One might point out here the already marginalized position of East-West comparative studies in the history of comparative literature, which, to a large degree, can be characterized as Eurocentric. Seen in this context, the greater attention paid to traditional Chinese theater than to modern drama does not imply that older forms have received considerable interest of any scale.

10. See, for example, Owen Aldridge's chapter, "Voltaire and the Mirage of China," in his *The Reemergence of World Literature*, 141–166, and Leonard Cabell Pronko, *Theater East and West*. The erudite study by Tao-Ching Hsu, *The Chinese Conception of the Theater*, is an exception.

11. See, for example, Elisabeth Eide, *China's Ibsen*.

12. Lan Fan, *Zhongguo xiju bijiao lungao* (A comparative study of Chinese and Western theaters), 53.

13. Ibid., 62.

14. Ibid., 204–205.

15. Hong Shen, "Daoyan (Introduction)," 74.

16. Ibid., 74–75.

17. *Peer Gynt* was translated by Xiao Qian and performed by the Central Drama College in Beijing from 1984 to 1985. Although both the translator and the director attempted an original Norwegian production, Chinese audiences in many cases reacted in Chinese terms, viewing the play as a way of relating to people's experiences during the Cultural Revolution.

18. C. Clifford Flanigan, "Comparative Literature and the Study of Medieval Drama," 96, 58.

19. Ibid., 58.

20. Ibid., 60.

21. Ibid., 60–61.

22. Ibid., 97.

23. Chen Baichen and Dong Jian, *Zhongguo xiandai xiju shigao* (A draft history of modern Chinese drama), 456–457.

24. See Zhang Zhong et al., *Dangdai wenxue gaiguan* (A survey of contemporary literature), 239.

25. Gao Wensheng, *Zhongguo dangdai xiju wenxue shi* (A history of the dramatic literature of contemporary China), 43–44.

26. Dai Jinhua, *Dianying lilun yu piping shouce* (A handbook of film theory and criticism), 5.

27. For selective studies on the Cultural Revolution in English, see Adrian Hsia, *The Chinese Cultural Revolution*; Richard H. Solomon, with the collaboration of Talbott W. Huey, *A Revolution Is Not a Dinner Party*; Andrew Hall Wedeman, *The East Wind Subsides: Chinese Foreign Policy and the Origins of the Cultural Revolution*; Ellen Judd, "Prescriptive Dramatic Theory of the Cultural Revolution"; Michael Schoenhals, ed., *China's Cultural Revolution, 1966–1969: Not a Dinner Party*; Roderick MacFarquhar, *The Origins of the Cultural Revolution*; William A. Joseph, Christine P. W. Wong, and David Zweig, eds., *New Perspectives on the Cultural Revolution*.

28. Zhang Zhizhong, "Lishi zhi mi he qingchun zhi wu" (The mystery of history and the mistakes of youth), 65.

29. Some examples are: Fulang Lo, *Morning Breeze: A True Story of China's Cultural Revolution*; Xiao Di Zhu, *Thirty Years in a Red House: A Memoir of Childhood and Youth in Communist China*; Xiguang Yang and Susan McFadden, *Captive Spirits: Prisoners of the Cultural Revolution*. Examples of Chinese American women's experiences include Jan Wong, *Red China Blues*, and James R. Ross, *Caught in a Tornado: A Chinese American Woman Survives the Cultural Revolution*. In this section on the representation of the Cultural Revolution, I focus on

the popular book market without including a large body of Western scholarship, which belongs in a separate study.

30. A different version of this idea was first delivered as a conference paper entitled "Time, Money, and Work: The Flow of Transnational Cultural Capital in the Making of Neo-American Nationalism in Chinese American Women Writers' Autobiography," at the Thirty-Second American Studies Association of Korea International Seminar in October 1997, Seoul, Korea. This short conference paper was published in *Journal of American Studies* 29.2 (1997): 414–421. For a more recent study on the construction of the English-language Cultural Revolution memoir "as an affirmation of a superior Western way of life," see Peter Zarrow, "Meanings of China's Cultural Revolution: Memoirs of Exile."

31. Nien Cheng, *Life and Death in Shanghai*, ix.

32. Ibid., 6.

33. Ibid., 365.

34. Ibid., 539.

35. Ibid., 538.

36. Sidonie Smith and Julia Watson, "Introduction: De/Colonization and the Politics of Discourse in Women's Autobiographical Practices," xix. Their "Introduction" helps outline the complexity and problems of reading Chinese women's autobiographies as colonial interventions or reaffirmations in a transnational context, in contrast to the practice of the diverse cultures of others covered in this anthology.

37. Chandra T. Mohanty and Satya P. Mohanty, "Contradictions of Colonialism," *Women's Review of Books* 7 (1990): 19; cited by Smith and Watson, xix.

38. Cheng Nien, *Life and Death in Shanghai*, 6.

39. Anchee Min, *Red Azalea*, 70.

40. Ibid., 71.

41. See the reviews excerpted on the cover of *Red Azalea*.

42. Anchee Min's lecture, entitled "Living in a World Turned Upside Down: The Story of a Young Woman Coming of Age during the Chinese Cultural Revolution," was delivered on Nov. 1, 1996, in the Ohio Statehouse Atrium, Columbus, Ohio. It was part of the Ruth Shuman McLean Lectureship Series sponsored by the Church United in Memory of McLean, who "saw the lectureship as an opportunity for central Ohioans to hear from women whose works and lives were examples of a quest for wholeness and hope" (Program Note).

43. Guanlong Gao, *The Attic: Memoir of a Chinese Landlord's Son*, 3, 4–5.

44. Gong Xiaoxia's book review of *Scarlet Memorial* has already pinpointed this problem.

45. "Joint-venture business" refers to companies and factories in the PRC that are cosponsored by Chinese and foreign investors.

46. Ronald Harwood, *Taking Sides*, 18.

47. For a typical introduction to these works in the English language, which was aimed at promoting the Cultural Revolution and its model theater to a readership outside of China, see "Magnificent Ode to the Worker, Peasant, and Soldier Heroes." For different accounts of how many model theaters were promoted, see Chapter 2, n. 11.

48. Anchee Min, *Red Azalea*, 3.

49. Ibid., 11.

50. Ibid., 61.

51. Ibid., 81–82.

52. Ibid., 17.

53. The word "poster" is used here a bit loosely. In the context of my discussion, I include both *xuanchuanhua* (propaganda posters), which were originally intended as such, and paintings of various styles, such as the ones in discussion here. Some of these were later printed in large quantities as prints to be sold in bookstores and functioned in a similar way as the *xuanchuanhua* in the private and public space.

54. According to Julia F. Andrews, *nianhua* painting "can be applied to almost any picture sold at the end of the Chinese Lunar year, when the populace traditionally cleans house and replaces worn-out images of folk deities and decorations." See Andrews, *Painters and Politics in the People's Republic of China, 1949–1979*, 59.

55. It is interesting to note the implicit gender politics here. It was said in the print culture at that time that in the process of creating revolutionary model ballet, Hong Changqing, the party representative to the Detachment of Women, was made the lead protagonist in order to highlight the party's leadership in the revolutionary war. This step was seen as a key victory in reforming the bourgeois form of Western ballet, which always assigned central roles to soft and weak female leads and only supporting roles to male characters. See, for example, Hong Changying, "Xiongwei zhuangmei, guangcai zhaoren," 31. Such privileging of male over female leads found its expression in the size of the oil paintings: the very first one of Wu Qinghua was among the smallest, whereas the one depicting Hong Changqing guiding her to the liberated areas was the largest. The latter image was also one of the most popular, since it stressed the significance of the party in its role of educating and emancipating subaltern women.

56. See Preface to *Youhua Hongse Niangzijun* (Oil paintings of *The Red Detachment of Women*).

57. "Qianyan."

58. Ban Wang, *The Sublime Figure of History*, 208–209. Chapter 6, "The Cultural Revolution: A Terrible Beauty Is Born," has an insightful discussion on the theatri-

cality of the Cultural Revolutionary period. For a fuller account of my own *xuan-chuandui* experience, see Xiaomei Chen, "From 'Lighthouse' to the Northeast Wilderness."

59. Chen Kaige's *Farewell My Concubine* received unprecedented critical and popular success, according to Pauline Chen. It won the prize for Best Foreign Film from Los Angeles and New York film critic circles, among others. (See Pauline Chen, review of *Farewell My Concubine*). Not surprisingly, it was regarded "not so much about China's bloody 20th-century history as it is about show business." Gong Li was viewed as having "the toughness and the fashion flair of your basic Hollywood heroine of the '30s." See Tom Gliatto's review. The film was also lauded by Western film critics as belonging to a familiar epic tradition, "lying somewhere between *Gone with the Wind* and Bertolucci's *The Last Emperor*." See Jonathan Romney's review.

60. In Peking opera, actors can specialize in acting female roles. Mei Lanfang, the most famous Peking opera actor, is a case in point.

61. I am grateful to Patricia Sieber, who talked to me about the possible reading of traitors in this film.

62. This is a typical post-Maoist phrase in official print culture to describe the dark nature of the Cultural Revolution and to separate the post-Maoist regime as completely different from its predecessor.

63. Jan Wong, "Lunch with Jan Wong."

64. David Strand, "Civil Society and Public Sphere in Modern Chinese History," 63.

65. Frank N. Pieke, *The Ordinary and the Extraordinary*, 238.

66. Ibid., 239.

67. Ibid., 224.

68. Joseph W. Esherick and Jeffrey N. Wasserstrom, "Acting Out Democracy: Political Theater in Modern China," 839.

69. Ibid., 841.

70. Ibid., 842.

71. Linda Hershkovitz, "Tiananmen Square and the Politics of Place," 400.

72. Ibid., 395.

73. Ibid., cited by Hershkovitz from D. Cosgrove and P. Jackson, "New Directions in Cultural Geography," *Area* 19 (1987):95–101.

74. Hershkovitz, 55.

75. Hong Wu, "Tiananmen Square: A Political History of Monuments," 85.

76. Richard Schechner, *The Future of Ritual*, 55.

77. Ibid., 58.

78. Wen Fu, *Tiananmen jianzheng lu* (A witness history of Tiananmen), 1:97–98.

79. Wen Fu, 2:535–536.

80. Ban Wang's *The Sublime Figure of History* gives a brief but thoughtful account of the Tiananmen mass spectacles and other political rituals such as propaganda skits during the Cultural Revolution, 197–207.

81. For an account of Mao's eight reviews of the Red Guards and other key events of the Cultural Revolution, see Yan Jiaqi and Gao Gao, *Zhongguo wenge shinian shi* (A history of the ten-year Chinese Cultural Revolution), 88–90.

82. Wen Fu, 2:792.

83. Harriet Evans and Stephanie Donald, "Introduction," *Picturing Power in the People's Republic of China*, 2. For a study of Mao posters, see Robert Benewick, "Icons of Power: Mao Zedong and the Cultural Revolution." For a pioneering work on Red Guard artists and their representations of Mao, see Julia Andrews, *Painters and Politics in the People's Republic of China*, 1949–1979, 319–349.

84. A reprint of this poster can be found in my "Growing up with Posters in the Maoist Era," in Evans and Donald, eds., *Picturing Power*, 101–122, 116, fig. 6.5; For an oil painting with the same theme, see Julia Andrews, *Painters and Politics in the People's Republic of China*, 1949–1979, plate 10.

85. Robert A. Pois, "The National Socialist Volksgemeinschaft Fantasy and the Drama of National Rebirth."

86. Ibid., 22.

87. Ibid., 18.

88. Ibid., 22.

89. Mao Zedong, *Quotations from Chairman Mao Tsetung*, 300. I am not equating workers/peasants/soldiers with storm troopers, but pointing out the parallel relationship between theater and radical political action.

90. Referring to this poster, Craig Clunas pointed out that it "depicts the kind of scene in which a work like this was ostensibly created. When I visited Huxian on 1 August 1975 my enthusiasm for this work, recorded in my notebook at the time, was fulsome to the point of severe embarrassment today: 'This stuff is just the antidote to most Chinese art. When you see what the peasants are actually painting, your faith revives.'" He later realized that these so-called peasant painters were indeed "extensively supported in their work by rusticated professional artists" (Clunas, "Souvenirs of Beijing," 53). For a reprint of this poster, see plate 1 in Evans and Donald, eds., *Picturing Power*; L17 in the University of Westminster's collection, originally released in Shanghai, 1974.

91. Pois, "The Nationalist Socialist Volksgemeinschaft Fantasy," 24.

92. Ibid.

93. Ibid.

94. Ibid., 27.

95. Ibid.

96. This and other popular Maoist songs were later adapted to rock and roll in post-Maoist China, when popular culture combined Western "fashion" with Maoist ideology to appeal to both the younger generation and older one that lived through the Maoist era.

97. For a detailed study of the relationship between Chinese historical drama and political events in PRC China, see Rudolf G. Wagner, *The Contemporary Chinese Historical Drama*. Wagner's study focuses on the adaptation and reform of traditional Chinese operatic theater and their political implications. Similar cases can indeed be found in modern Chinese drama.

98. Glen W. Gadberry, "Introduction: The Year of Power—1933," 1–15, 4.

99. Pois, 18.

100. Ibid.

101. This extreme version of class theory developed during the Cultural Revolution was actually called "blood theory" *(xuetong lun)*. It divided people into "five red categories" and "five black categories" according to what their parents did before 1949. The red category includes people whose parents were workers, poor and lower-middle-class peasants, CCP martyrs during the war period and CCP officials, and city dwellers of the poor class. The black category refers to those whose parents were landowners, rich peasants, counterrevolutionaries, bad elements, and "rightists." In this theory, "blood" indicates class status, which is based on the socio-political background of different groups. Although the same class theory was applied to ethnic-minority groups during the Cultural Revolution, one could also argue that the revolution was mostly triggered and promoted by the predominant Han people in the ruling ideology and was imposed on societies mostly inhabited by ethnic minority groups.

102. Ron Engle, "Theatre in Detmold 1933–1939: A Case Study of Provincial Theatre during the Nazi Prewar Era," 39.

103. Rufus J. Cadigan, "Eberhard Wolfgang Möller: Politically Correct Playwright of the Third Reich," 72.

104. Engle, 39.

105. Ibid., 41.

106. Pois, 19.

107. Jonathan M. Weiss, *French-Canadian Theater*, 1.

108. Ibid.

109. Ibid., 2.

110. Ibid.

111. It was in this theater that a few Chinese men of letters, such as Zheng Zheng-qiu and Xu Banmei, later were initiated into Western dramatic forms. See Ge Yihong, ed., *Zhongguo huaju tongshi*, 7.

112. Some drama histories have traced the first piece of modern Chinese drama ever produced on stage to the February adaptation of Dumas fils' *La Dame aux Camélias* in the same year (1907) by the same group of overseas students in Japan, known as the Spring Willow Society. Since only two acts of this French play were performed, the full-fledged dramatic adaptation of Harriet Beecher Stowe's novel *Uncle Tom's Cabin* should, in my view, be considered as the first performance of modern Chinese drama, whereas Hu Shi, *The Main Event of One's Life*, is the first original Chinese original script.

113. Chen Baichen and Dong Jian pointed out that it was not accidental that the Spring Willow Society chose to perform this particular play as its first production. They were especially attracted to the play's thematic concern of racial oppression. For the same reason, Lin Shu's original translation was also a "hit" with its readers. Chen and Dong, *Zhongguo xiandai xiju shigao*, 49.

114. Ge Yihong, 20.

115. Ibid. See Chapter 2 for a Peking opera version of the same story.

116. John Conteh-Morgan, *Theatre and Drama in Francophone Africa*, 49.

117. Ge Yihong, 7–10.

118. Conteh-Morgan, 50.

119. Ibid., 67.

120. Ibid., 70–71.

121. *War Drums on the Equator*, written by Li Huang, Zhang Fengyi, Lin Yinwu, and Zhu Zuyi, dramatized African people's resistance to US intervention in the Congo. It was premiered by the Drama Troupe of the Political Department of the Navy in the People's Liberation Army (Zhongguo renmin jiefangjun haijun zhengzhibu huajutuan) in February 1965 and was celebrated as the first modern drama to depict Africans. It was later adapted into several regional operatic theaters, such as *huju* (Shanghai opera), *pingju*[b] (North and Northeast local opera), and *chuanju* (Sichuan opera), *caichaxi* (the *Caicha* opera of Jiangxi Province). For an English translation of the modern drama version, see Li Huang et al., *War Drums on the Equator*. The Chinese script of *Chidao Zhangu* was published by *Zhongguo xiju chubanshe* (Beijing, 1965).

122. Frank Dikötter, *The Discourse of Race in Modern China*, 192. Dikötter also recorded: "In an often quoted speech, delivered in 1963, Mao claimed that 'in Africa, in Asia, in every part of the world there is racism; in reality, racial problems are class problems.' The race problem had become a class problem" (192).

123. Gao Wensheng, ed., *Zhongguo dangdai xiju wenxue shi*, 172.

124. This play was written by Wu Baixin, a native Hezhe, and was premiered by Harbin Theater in 1962.

125. Written by Tian Han in 1960, *Princess Wencheng* was premiered by the China Youth Art Theater in 1960. The story's latest appearance can be seen in a 2000 television drama directed by woman director Cai Xiaoqing under the same title. It was reported that Cai had watched the China Youth Art Theater's production in her youth and had ever since cherished the desire to direct her own version of *Princess Wencheng*. See Liu Jun, "Sanshi nian qingxi *Wencheng Gongzhu*."

126. Gao Wensheng, 182–183.

127. Sue-Ellen Case, *Feminism and Theatre*, 16.

128. Ibid., 17.

129. All three of these plays were written by Gao Xingjian and directed by Lin Zhaohua. Both *The Bus Stop* and *The Alarm Signal* were received as the first works to introduce elements of the Theater of the Absurd to a Chinese audience. For an early study of *The Bus Stop* in English, see Geremie Barmé, "A Touch of the Absurd: Introducing Gao Xingjian, and His Play 'The Bus Stop.'" English translations of *The Bus Stop* can be found in Haiping Yan, ed., *Theater and Society*, 3–59. For an English translation of *Wildman*, see Gao Xingjian, *Wild Man*.

130. Sue-Ellen Case critiqued the pitfalls of Western feminist studies of Shakespearean plays as confined to "reading within the text rather than within the practice." See her *Feminism and Theatre*, 25. My chapter on post-Maoist women's theater also reads the text within the practice of women's lives, by interviewing women theater practitioners in and out of theater.

Chapter Two: Operatic Revolutions

1. Dai Jiafang, *Yangbanxi de fengfeng yuyu* (The wind and rain of revolutionary model theater), 267.

2. Ibid., 275.

3. The report did not specify the university.

4. "Yindao daxuesheng zoujin jingju" (Introducing Peking opera to university students).

5. Peter Edgerly Firchow, *The Death of the German Cousin*, 10.

6. For a historical survey of the major events of the Cultural Revolution, see Yan Jiaqi and Gao Gao, *Zhongguo wenge shinian shi* (A history of the ten-year Chinese Cultural Revolution), especially 441–448, for an account of the model theater and its significance in the Cultural Revolution.

7. The revised version of *Shajiabang* was first published in *Hongqi* (Red flag), the most authoritative party journal, 6 (1970): 8–39. An English translation can be found in *Chinese Literature* 11 (1970): 3–62. Other newspapers and journals that published model play versions of various Peking operas include *Guangming ribao* (Guangming daily), *Jiefang ribao* (Liberation daily), and *Wenhuibao* (Wenhui newspaper). *Jiefangjun bao* (Liberation Army daily) published only one model opera entitled *Raid on the White Tiger Regiment* in 1972.

8. For the Chinese script of *The Red Detachment of Women*, see *Hongqi* 7 (1970): 35–65.

9. An English translation of *Taking Tiger Mountain by Strategy* can be found in *Chinese Literature* 8 (1967): 129–181. The July 1970 script, or the revised model-play version, can be found in *Geming yangbanxi juben huibian* (The collection of revolutionary model plays) (Beijing: Remin chubanshe, 1974), 1:7–73.

10. The revised model-play version of *Raid on the White Tiger Regiment* can be found in *Hongqi* 11 (1972): 26–54. For an English translation, see *Chinese Literature* 3 (1973): 3–54.

11. This account of Dai Jiafang differs from that of Xie Boliang. Xie Boliang believed the first eight model works were officially declared such in the editorial of *Renmin ribao* (People's daily) entitled "Geming wenyi de youxiu yangban" (Excellent models for revolutionary art), May 31, 1967. Seven years later, in 1974, Renmin wenxue chubanshe published *Geming yangbanxi juben huibian* (An anthology of revolutionary model theatrical works), which added four more works to the rank of model theater: the Peking operas *Song of the Dragon River*, *The Red Detachment of Women*, *Fighting in the Plain*, and *Azalean Mountain*. Before and after the appearances of these operas, Xie pointed out, the revolutionary symphonic work *Taking Tiger Mountain by Strategy* and modern ballets *Song of Nimeng Mountain* and *Son and Daughter of the Grassland* were also reviewed as model works, thus adding to a total of fifteen. If one omits works that bear the same titles but overlap with other genres, the total is thirteen, nine of which are Peking operas. Since the 1974 anthology of twelve model works was published as volume one, it was expected that other model works would be designated as such at a later point. In 1976, the Peking opera *Boulder Bay* and articles promoting model works appeared in the journal *Renmin wenxue* (People's literature). In the same year, the Peking opera *Wind and Thunder of Mao Ridge (Miaoling fenglei)* was published as a separate edition. These two and several other new model works would have been officially declared as such if the Gang of Four had not been ousted in 1976. See Xie Boliang, *Zhongguo dangdai xiqu wenxue shi* (A history of contemporary Chinese operatic theaters), 247. Dai Jiafang, on the other hand, pointed out that *Boulder Bay*, together with the second group of ten, was personally ap-

proved by Jiang Qing as a model work. Dai also believed that *Wind and Thunder of Mao Ridge* belonged to the third group that never materialized as model works. See Dai Jiafang, *Yangbanxi de fengfeng yuyu*, 229.

12. The ballet version of *Song of Nimeng Mountain* was adapted from a Peking opera version entitled *Hong Sao*, first performed by the Liubo City Peking Opera Troupe (Liuboshi jingjutuan) and the Qingdao Peking Opera Troupe (Qingdaoshi jingjutuan) during the National Festival of Peking Opera on Contemporary Themes, held in Beijing from June 5 to July 31, 1964. See *Hong Sao* (Beijing: Zhongguo xiju chubanshe, 1965). The opera version was adapted from Zhi Xia's fiction of the same title. Mao Zedong, Zhu De, and Yang Shangkun watched the Peking opera in August 12, 1964, and received its crew with warm praises. Premiered in 1972, the ballet version of *Song of Nimeng Mountain* was made into a film version of the same title, completed in 1973 and released in 1975.

13. *Hongyun Hills*, a model Peking opera version of *Song of Nimeng Mountain*, was premiered in April 1976 by the Shandong Peking Opera Troupe (Shandong jingjutuan). See Dai Jiafang, *Yangbanxi*, 220–224.

14. The script of the Peking opera *The Red Detachment of Women* can be found in April 1972 in *Hongqi*. It was released as a movie two months later.

15. *Boulder Bay* was adapted from *The Great Wall in the Southern Sea (Nanhai changcheng)*, a modern drama premiered in 1964 by the Soldiers Theater of the Guangzhou Military Unit (Guangzhou budui zhanshi huajutuan) and scripted by Zhao Huan. Produced by the Shanghai Peking Opera Troupe, it was approved as a model work in 1975, and a movie version was released in 1976. *Boulder Bay* is the only model work that has a love story, although the dramatic conflict of the couple focuses on whether their "small family" is more important than the "big revolutionary family."

16. Precursor texts of the Peking opera *The Red Lantern* include the film *Successor (Ziyou hou lai ren)* by the Changchun Film Studio in 1962 and the Peking opera *Successor to Revolution* by the Harbin Peking Opera Troupe (Harbin jingjutuan), among others.

17. A "model peasant" or "model worker" in socialist China is an honorable title usually awarded to an exemplary person whose extraordinary contribution to his or her community is pointed to as an example for others to imitate.

18. "Comments on the Ballet *The White-Haired Girl*." I have changed the original spelling of the names to the pinyin system to be consistent with the rest of this study.

19. Ibid.

20. Such bitter stories found their best example in the group sculptures of *The Rent-Collecting Courtyard (Shouzuyuan)*, which presented real-life figures of poor peasants paying their rent to Liu Wencai, a rich landlord in Sichuan Province. Visiting such popular art exhibitions became part of political education during

the height of the Cultural Revolution. For figures and a description of *The Rent-Collecting Courtyard* exhibition in English, see "We Must Revolutionize Our Thinking and Then Revolutionize Sculpture." For sample poems and afterthoughts written by visitors to the exhibition, see "Appraisals of 'Compound Where Rent Was Collected.'" For a Chinese version, see Cai Ruohong, "Mao Zedong wenyi sixiang de shengli" (The victory of Mao Zedong thought).

21. Ling Kuei-ming (Ling Guiming), "Taking up Arms," 106.

22. Ibid., 107.

23. Jiwei Ci, *Dialectic of the Chinese Revolution*, 82.

24. The opera was collectively written by the Yan'an Lu Xun Literature and Art Academy, with He Jingzhi, Ding Yi, and Wang Bin as scriptwriters and Ma Ke, Zhang Lu, and Huo Wei as composers. The first edition of the opera was published by Yan'an xinhua shudian in June 1946. For an English translation, see He Jingzhi, Ding Yi, and Ma Ke, *The White-Haired Girl*, trans. Gladys Yang and Yang Hsien-yi.

25. For a detailed account of how the opera came into being, see He Jingzhi, "*Bai-maonü* de chuangzuo yu yanshu" (The writing and performance of *The White-Haired Girl*), which first appeared as the preface to the second edition of *The White-Haired Girl* published by Zhangjiakou xinhua shudian in 1946 and was later collected in He Jingzhi, *He Jingzhi quanji* (Complete works of He Jingzhi).

26. He Jingzi, "Xin geju *Baimaonü*" (New folk opera *The White-Haired Girl*), 291.

27. Yu Lu-yuan, "The Revolutionary Ballet '*The White-Haired Girl*,'" 121–122.

28. For a typical post-Cultural Revolutionary article on the Gang of Four in relation to the opera, see Lin Zhihao, "Pipan 'Sirenbang' fadong de weigong geju *Baimaonü* de miulun" (Criticizing the Gang of Four's condemnation of the folk opera *The White-Haired Girl*). See also Yan Entu, "Renmin de yishu renmin ai" (People love people's art).

29. Meng Yue, "*Baimaonü* yu Yan'an wenxue de lishi fuzai xing" (*The White-Haired Girl* and the political complexities of Yan'an literature), 172. See also Meng, "Female Images and National Myth."

30. Meng Yue, "*Baimaonü* yu Yan'an wenxue," 173–174.

31. Ibid., 175.

32. Ibid., 178.

33. Ibid., 179.

34. Ibid., 180.

35. Ibid., 181–182.

36. Ibid., 183–184.

37. Ibid., 187.

38. For an account of how the Beijing Dance School Experimental Ballet started to adapt *The Red Detachment of Women* from film to ballet in 1963, see Dai Jaifang, *Yangbanxi de fengfeng yuyu*, 93–101. The May 1970 script of the model ballet version, collectively revised by the China Ballet Troupe, can be found in *Geming yangbanxi juben huibian* (Selected works of model theater), 1:207–277.

39. According to an article published in *Renmin ribao* on April 28, 1962, the first film award since 1949 known as "bai hua jiang" (one-hundred-flower award) was initiated by the firm journal *Dazhong dianying* (Popular film), which received 117,939 ballots from the audience members. *The Red Detachment of Women* received four out of the total of fourteen awards. See *Hongse Niangzijun*, 465.

40. Wu Qunhua—a traditional female name, with *qun* meaning "beautiful jade" and *hua* meaning "flower"—was the original name in the film version; it was later changed to Wu Qinghua in the model ballet version. In this case, with *qing* meaning "clean and pure" and *hua* (with a different intonation and character) meaning "China," the revolutionary overtone of the new name in the model ballet version was clear to most of the audience. For a study on the "naming" of Chinese names from antiquity to the present and from traditional practice to the Maoist variations (for example, the persecution of people with the politically incorrect names during the Cultural Revolution), see Viviane Alleton, *Les Chinois et la passion des noms*. For a book review in English, see Susan D. Blum, review of *Les Chinois et la passion des noms*.

41. Liang Xin, "Renwu, qingjie, aiqing ji qitai" (Character, plot, love, and other issues), 242.

42. Ibid., 248.

43. Zhu Xijuan, "Cong nünu dao zhanshi" (From slave girl to warrior), 315.

44. See Hans Robert Jauss, *Toward an Aesthetic of Reception*.

45. Ge Yihong et al., eds., *Zhongguo huaju tongshi* (A history of modern Chinese drama), 32.

46. Jin Chongji, ed., *Zhou Enlai zhuan* (A biography of Zhou Enlai), 1:21. *A Silver Dollar* premiered on October 9, 1915, on the occasion of celebrating the eleventh anniversary of the founding of Nankai School. The drama script, written by the Nankai New Drama Troupe (Nankai xinjutuan), can be found in Zhang Geng and Huang Jusheng, eds., *Zhongguo jindai wenxue daxi (1840–1919)* (A treasury of modern Chinese literature), 913–974.

47. Dai Jiafang, *Yangbanxi de fengfeng yuyu*, 97.

48. Ibid., 94–101.

49. Ibid., 106.

50. Ibid., 111.

51. For a brief summary of the forum and its historical context, see Jonathan D. Spence, *The Search for Modern China*, 603.

52. For the Chinese source, see "Lin Biao Tongzhi weituo Jiang Qing Tongzhi."

53. Dai Jiafang, *Yangbanxi de fengfeng yuyu*, 119–200.

54. Georges Banu "Mei Lanfang: A Case against and a Model for the Occidental Stage," 153–154.

55. Ibid., 155.

56. Ibid., 158.

57. Zhao Cong, *Zhongguo dalu de xiqu gaige* (Opera reform in the Mainland), 76–80.

58. For Huang Zuolin's theory, see Xiaomei Chen, *Occidentalism*, 130–132.

59. Wang Guowei once defined *xiqu* as the genre that uses singing and dancing to act out a story. See Wang Guowei, *Xiqu lunwen ji*, 201. The term *xiqu*, translated as "dramatic arias written for the stage" by Dale Johnson, includes more than 360 different kinds of operatic genres that use singing, speaking, acting, and acrobatics, whereas *xiju* (drama) may refer to both operatic and spoken dramas. Dale Johnson, "Ch'ü," in William H. Nienhauser, ed. and comp., *The Indiana Companion to Traditional Chinese Literature*, 349–352, 351. The Chinese word *gailiang* (improvement) is different from *gaige* (reform), which was later used as the standard expression for reformation in theater. Although *gailiang* suggests a milder effort than *gaige*, I use "theater reform" to refer to both because I think that they are very similar in spirit. The later term of "opera revolution" *(jingju geming)* used during the Cultural Revolution suggested a much more radical reform than its predecessors.

60. Cyril Birch, "Ch'uan-ch'i," in William H. Nienhauser, ed. and comp., *The Indiana Companion*, 353–356, 353.

61. Liang Qichao, *Xin Luoma*, in Zhang Geng and Huang Jusheng, eds., *Zhongguo jindai wenxue daxi*, 1:325.

62. Ibid., 1:324–325.

63. Zhang Geng and Huang Jusheng, "Daoyan" (Introduction), 7.

64. Mao Yuanxi Qiusheng et al., *Weixin meng* (The dream of reform), in Zhang Geng and Huang Jusheng, 1:356–381.

65. Xuanting Kou in Shaoxing, Zhijiang Province, was where Qiu Jin was executed. The dramatic text of *Xuanting yuan* by Xiao Shanxiang Lingzi can be found in Zhang Geng and Huang Jusheng, eds., *Zhongguo jindai wenxue daxi*, 1:505–545.

66. Zhang Geng and Huang Jusheng, "Daoyan," 8.

67. Yang Shixiang, *Zhongguo xiqu jian shi* (A brief history of Chinese traditional operas), 404.

68. Ibid., 405–406.

69. Liu Yazi, *Songling xin nü'er* (The new daughters of Songling), in Zhang Geng and Huang Jusheng, eds., 1:546–548.

70. Mau-sang Ng, *The Russian Hero in Modern Chinese Fiction*, 12–13.

71. Hu Ying, *Tales of Translation*, 11–12.

72. Ibid., 10.

73. Zhang Geng and Huang Jusheng, "Daoyan," 8–9.

74. Xie Boliang, *Zhongguo dangdai xiqu wenxue shi* (A history of contemporary Chinese operatic theaters), 183–184.

75. Zhao Cong, *Zhongguo dalu de xiqu gaige*, 175. Robert E. Hegel also pointed out the adaptations of earlier literature such as *Water Margin* and *Romance of the Three Kingdoms* in Qu Bo's novel *Snow-Covered Forest*, a precursor text for the model Peking opera *Taking Tiger Mountain by Strategy*. According to Hegel, in the model opera, "realism disappears; so, too, does all visible trace of Qu Bo's debt to *Water Margin*, leaving only an unconvincing paragon of socialist virtue." See his "Making the Past Serve the Present in Fiction and Drama: From the Yan'an Forum to the Cultural Revolution," 221.

76. Wan Qingrong, "Lun zichan jieji xiqu gailiang yundong de meixue sixiang" (On the aesthetics of the bourgeois drama reform), 382.

77. Su Yi, *Jingju erbai nian gaiguan* (A two-hundred-year history of Peking opera), 390.

78. Wang Changfa and Liu Hua, "Mei Lanfang nianpu jianbiao" (A chronology of Mei Lanfang's life), 191.

79. Mei Lanfang, "Buzai paiyan shizhuang xi" (Why I stopped performing Peking operas with contemporary costumes), 172.

80. Ibid., 172–173.

81. Xie Boliang, *Zhongguo dangdai xiqu wenxue shi*, 241–245.

82. Wang Changfa and Liu Hua, "Mei Lanfang nianpu jianbiao," 193.

83. Lan Hai, *Zhongguo kangzhan wenyi shi*, 260–261. For an insightful study of Mei Lanfang's early career and the image building of Mei as an icon for Chinese national culture, see Joshan Goldstein, "Mei Lanfang and the Nationalization of Peking Opera, 1912–1930."

84. Zhang Geng and Huang Jusheng, "Daoyan," 15.

85. Xi Mingzhen, "Xiju shi, lun de jianshe zhe" (An architect of opera history and theory), 10.

86. Zhao Cong, *Zhongguo dalu de xiqu gaige*, 55–59.

87. Ibid., 59–60.

88. Xie Boliang, *Zhongguo dangdai xiqu wenxue shi*, 160.

89. During the 1964 modern opera festival, the Peking operas *The Red Lantern*, *Spark in the Marshland* (later revised as *Shajiabang*), *Taking Tiger Mountain by Strategy*, and *Raid on the White Tiger Regiment* were selected by the festival as "excellent plays" and became model operas by 1967, the last two being premiered as early as 1958 and 1957 respectively. *Azalean Mountain* and the Peking opera version of *The Red Detachment of Women* were later named as the second group of ten more model theatrical works, together with the ballet versions of the Peking operas known in this modern opera festival as *Hong Sao* and *Son and Daughter of the Grassland (Caoyuan yingxiong xiao jiemei)*.

90. Dai Jiafang, *Yangbanxi de fengfeng yuyu*, 217–218.

91. Xie Boliang, *Zhongguo dangdai xiqu wenxue shi*, 260–261. Xie did not elaborate on whether Jiang Qing, who first mentioned the importance of giving prominence to main, heroic characters in 1964, or Yu Huiyong, who theorized the "three prominences" in 1968, were actually aware of Jin Shengtan's theory. Even though one cannot establish a direct influence, it is still helpful to point out that this theory was not a new invention during the Cultural Revolution.

92. Ibid., 259–260.

93. Ibid., 155–156.

94. Ibid., 160.

95. For selected studies on the problematic relationship between women and revolution in socialist China, see Kam Louie, "Love Stories: The Meaning of Love and Marriage in China"; Tani E. Barlow, "Theorizing Woman: *Funü, Guojia, Jiating* (Chinese Women, Chinese State, Chinese Family)"; Lydia H. Liu, "Invention and Intervention: The Making of a Female Tradition in Modern Chinese Literature"; Tonglin Lu, ed., *Gender and Sexuality in Twentieth-Century Chinese Literature*; Xiaomei Chen, "Reading Mother's Tale—Reconstructing Women's Space in Amy Tan and Zhang Jie"; Christina K. Gilmartin et al., eds., *Engendering China: Women, Culture, and the State*; Harriet Evans, *Women and Sexuality in China*; Ravni Thakur, *Rewriting Gender: Reading Contemporary Chinese Women*; and Mayfair Mei-hui Yang, ed. and intro., *Spaces of Their Own: Women's Public Sphere in Transnational China*.

96. The May 1979 script of the revolutionary model Peking opera version of *Shajiabang* can be found in *Hongqi* 6 (1970): 8–39. Quotations are from the English translation entitled *Shachiapang*, collectively revised by the Peking Opera Troupe, in *Chinese Literature* 11 (1970): 3– 62, 34. The model opera was adapted from the

Peking opera *Spark in the Marshland* by Wang Zengqi, Yang Yumin, Xiao Jia, and Xue Enhuo. The Peking opera *Spark in the Marshland* was further adapted from the *huju* (Shanghai opera) of the same title, collectively written and performed by the Shanghai People's Shanghai Opera Troupe, with Wen Mu as scriptwriter. For a study on the adaptation of the model Peking opera to a Cantonese opera *Sagabong* with a focus on the musical elements, see Bell Yung, "Model Opera as Model: From *Shajiabang* to *Sagabong*." For a study of music in the Peking opera *Taking Tiger Mountain by Strategy*, see Barbara Mittler, " 'Mit Geschick den Tigerberg erobern' Zur Interpretation einer Multiplen Quelle" (Taking *Tiger Mountain by Strategy*: On interpreting a multiple source). For an informative study of the neglected field of Chinese music and politics, see Barbara Mittler, *Dangerous Tunes: The Politics of Chinese Music in Hong Kong, Taiwan, and the People's Republic of China since 1949* (Wiesbaden: Harrassowitz, 1997).

97. Joan B. Landes, *Women and the Public Sphere*, 31.

98. Ibid., 27.

99. Ibid., 21.

100. For a sample article in English that introduces new model works around 1973, see Chang Yung-mei, "Create More Typical Proletarian Heroes."

101. For a brief account of the play in English, see also Colin MacKerras, *The Chinese Theater in Modern Times*, 210.

102. "The Political Report of the Chinese Communist Party's Tenth Congress" was delivered by Zhou Enlai in August 24, 1973, and published in *Hongqi* 9 (1973): 5–17.

103. He Kongzhou, "Yiqu dangde lingdao de zhuangli songge" (A magnificent song of the party's leadership), 50.

104. The modern revolutionary Peking opera *Azalean Mountain* was adapted from the modern drama version of the same title and premiered by Shanghai Youth Art Theater (Shanghai qingnian yishu juyuan) in 1963, with Wang Shuyuan as the scriptwriter.

105. The examples are cited from the English translation of *Azalean Mountain* published in *Chinese Literature* 1 (1974): 3–69, 29. The Chinese text of the model play, known as the September 1973 script, was written by Wang Shuyuan et al. and published in *Hongqi* 10 (1973): 46–83.

106. Xie Boliang also pointed out this similarity. See Xie, *Zhongguo dangdai xiqu wenxue shi*, 238.

107. A typical example can be found in the story of Wu Song, whose brother Wu Da was killed by his adulteress wife Pan Jinlian. To avenge his brother's death, Wu Song killed Pan Jinlian. He had no choice but to join the Liang Mountain heroes against the imperial court.

108. Wang Shuyuan, *Azalean Mountain*, 33.

109. Colin MacKerras pointed out that Ke Xiang stands for "a new type of heroine. In earlier model dramas there were runaway slave-girls who joined the revolution, or female party secretaries in a commune or city organization, but until September 1973 the heroic guerrillas, or military party leaders, were all men. The significance of the fact [Ke Xiang] is a woman is accentuated by the scene in which [Wen Qijiu] suggests to [Lei Gang] that he has lost his power of judgment through being too much under the thumb of a woman. This no doubt reflects the problem of equality between the sexes, which still exists in China today, even after twenty-five years of Communist government." See MacKerras, *The Chinese Theatre*, 210.

110. Nicholas Mirzoeff, *Bodyscape*, 7.

111. Ibid.

112. Ibid., 3.

113. Ibid.

114. Wang Shuyuan et al., *Azalean Mountain*, 12.

115. Ibid., 13.

116. Ibid.

117. Hortense J. Spillers, "Mama's Baby, Papa's Maybe: An American Grammar Book," 66.

118. "Striving to Portray the Proletarian Heroes of People's War," 69.

119. Kirk A. Denton, "Model Drama as Myth: A Semiotic Analysis of *Taking Tiger Mountain by Strategy*," 127.

120. Sigmund Freud, *Group Psychology and the Analysis of the Ego*, 72–73.

121. Despite her interesting readings of women characters in model theater, I disagree with Bai Di's argument that "model theater is in its cultural essence feminist," which "lies in its systematic construction of heroic women's images against the background of CCP history, and of their strategic appropriation of class and political identities in order to escape from subordinate gender identities." See her "A Feminist Brave New World: The Cultural Revolution Model Theater Revisited," 5.

122. Yu Xiao and Cheng Bo, "Renlei jiefang wo jiefang" (The liberation of mankind means my own liberation), 64.

123. "Revolutionary Literature and Art Must Serve the Workers, Peasants, and Soldiers," 130.

124. My use of the term "subaltern" differs from its use by the Indian subaltern studies scholars who attempted to recover the common people's voices in the historical writings of colonial authorities and Indian nationalist elites (see Gayatri Chakravorty Spivak, "Can the Subaltern Speak?"). For an insightful critique of the implication of subaltern studies in a Chinese context, see Gail Hershatter,

"The Subaltern Talks Back: Reflections on Subaltern Theory and Chinese History." Hershatter analyzed the relational nature of subalternity in Chinese history where local contexts and multiple political subjectivities are crucial to understanding subaltern-speak. In my use of the word "subaltern" in the rest of this study, I am aware of the various and complex meanings in different contexts. The PRC official discourse, for instance, designated workers, peasants, soldiers, and other working people as subalterns due to their economically oppressed position before 1949. They became "liberated subalterns" after 1949, which in official language translates into contented citizens and even happy "masters" of socialist China. While their liberated status in most instances served to celebrate the necessity of a socialist China and did not necessarily grant them real political and intellectual power, it is also true that on limited occasions they could affect other people's lives. One example is the movement to send down educated youth from the city to the countryside during the Cultural Revolution. They were expected to follow the example of the local peasants who, on certain occasions, had the power to decide if they were "reformed" enough to qualify for studying in a city college. When I use the term "subaltern women," therefore, I may be referring to their supposedly oppressed status before 1949 in the PRC official vocabulary; I may also be alluding to the so-called image of liberated women in the PRC period, when they were expected to hold up half of the sky. In reality, however, they may still have remained as subaltern as their counterparts before 1949 thanks to their insufficient educational background and lack of power in political life and gender politics.

125. "Remould World Outlook," 7. This is an English translation of an editorial published jointly by the *People's Daily*, *Red Flag*, and *Liberation Army Daily*, known as "liangbao yikan shelun" (an editorial by two newspapers and one journal), an avenue of periodic new policy declarations by the official culture during the Cultural Revolution. For important studies on the complex roles of Chinese intellectuals in modern and contemporary China, see Merle Goldman, *China's Intellectuals: Advise and Dissent*, *Sowing the Seeds of Democracy in China*; Merle Goldman, ed., with Timothy Cheek and Coral Lee Hamrin, *China's Intellectuals and the State*; and Jerome B. Grieder, *China's Intellectuals and the State in Modern China*.

126. Dai Jiafang, *Yangbanxi de fengfeng yuyu*, 258–262, 234. For an informative essay on Yu Huiyong's artistic and political career, see Richard Kraus, "Arts Policies of the Cultural Revolution: The Rise and Fall of Culture Minister Yu Huiyong." For a study of the social and political roles of writers and performing artists in the PRC from 1949 to 1979, see Bonnie S. McDougall, "Writers and Performers, Their Works, and Their Audiences in the First Three Decades."

Chapter Three: Family, Village, Nation/State, and the Third World

1. Simon During, "Introduction," *The Cultural Studies Reader*, 2. During talked about the characteristics of early cultural studies in Great Britain in the 1950s,

which historically paralleled the Great Leap Forward movement in China, a period when the dominated, or the "subaltern" working class—to use Antonio Gramsci's term—were mobilized to participate in the high wave of Chinese socialism. At a time when "culture was thought about less as an expression of local communal lives linked to class identity and more as an apparatus within a large system of domination" in Britain, China, in contrast, was on its way to building a local, regional, and national identity as a purely proletarian state where class distinctions would override every other factor of social life (During, 5).

2. Ibid., 22.

3. Ibid., 5.

4. The exceptions were in the late 1990s, when Xie Boliang and Dai Jiafang's studies reflected a trend to consider model theater in the context of *xiqu* history and the biographies of Cultural Revolutionary political figures. Dai's study spins off from his early work on the biography of Yu Huiyong. In the 1980s, another attempt to legitimize model theater is also worth noting. Arguing against a simple dismissal of the Cultural Revolutionary period as nothing but political maneuvering of literature and art, Pan Kaixiong and He Zhaojun proposed that Cultural Revolutionary literature be contextualized within the larger framework of the literary tradition of the PRC, which had indeed paved the way for its consequent emergence. According to them, PRC literature and Cultural Revolutionary literature share at least three similarities. First, both periods followed the practice of *zhuti xianxing* (concept first), which urged writers to conceptualize the themes of their creative writing by bearing in mind the priorities of the party's political agendas and the social problems thereby identified while participating in the mass movements themselves. Second, literatures in both periods privileged stories of workers, peasants, and soldiers at the expense of other politically disadvantaged social groups. Third, both emphasized the creation of "typical characters in typical situations," which culminated in the stereotypes of characters known as *gao-da-quan* (the grand, the tall, and the perfect) in model theater. Because both "shared the same kind of literary spirit," Cultural Revolutionary literature should at least be considered as "significant" as PRC literature, and hence "not be excluded from serious research." See Pan Kaixiong and He Shaojun, "Wenge wenxue" (Cultural-Revolutionary literature), 166.

5. Mu Gong, "Wenge de wenxue jingshen" (The literary spirit of the Cultural Revolution), 168.

6. Ibid.

7. Ibid. For an English translation of Mao's Yan'an talk, see Mao Zedong, *"Talks at the Yan'an Conference on Literature and Art."*

8. Mu Gong, "Wenge de wenxue jingshen," 169.

9. Ibid.

10. Ibid., 171.

11. Ibid., 172–173.

12. Ibid., 173.

13. Benedict Anderson, *Imagined Communities*, 15.

14. For an early account of the play and its performance in English, see Lois Wheeler Snow, *China on Stage*, 241–255.

15. The model-play version of the opera, known as the May script of *The Red Lantern*, collectively revised by the China Peking Opera Troupe (Zhongguo jingjutuan), can be found in *Hongqi* (1970), 23–46. The English translations are cited from *The Red Lantern*, in *Chinese Literature* 8 (1970): 8–52.

16. Ibid., 12.

17. Ibid., 12–13.

18. Ibid., 14.

19. Ibid., 16.

20. In the English translation of *The Red Lantern*, *qinren* is rendered as "comrades" for its metaphorical meanings. *Qinren*, however, usually refers to one's parents, spouse, children, and other members of the family.

21. *The Red Lantern*, 30.

22. Ibid.

23. Ibid.

24. Ibid., 45.

25. Ibid., 46.

26. For a detailed account of how the revision of the play was a process of class struggle between Mao's revolutionary line and Liu Shaoqi's revisionist line as carried out by his agents, such as Lu Dingyi, Chou Yang, Lin Mohan, Xia Yan, and A Jia in the circle of literature and art, see Zhongguo jingjutuan *Hongdeng ji juzu* (*The Red Lantern* cast at China Peking Opera Troupe), "Wei suzao wuchan jieji."

27. Dai Jiafang, *Yangbanxi de fengfeng yuyu* (The wind and rain of revolutionary model theater), 42.

28. Xie Boliang, *Zhongguo dandai xiqu wenxue shi* (A history of contemporary Chinese operatic theaters), 194–195.

29. Ibid., 196.

30. Dai Jiafang, *Yangbanxi de fengfeng yuyu*, 23, 42.

31. Xie Boliang, *Zhongguo dandai xiqu wenxue shi*, 197–202.

32. Dai Jiafang, *Yangbanxi de fengfeng yuyu*, 23–25.

33. Gao Yuqian. "Nuli suzao geming muqin de xingxiang" (Strive to create an image of a revolutionary mother) 229–247.

34. Zhang Yongmei, *Fighting on the Plain*, 572. English translation mine. For an English translation, see *Fighting on the Plain, Chinese Literature* 5 (1974): 3–54.

35. For a historical account of the narrative of mother in the Republican period, see Sally Taylor Liebermann, *The Mother and Narrative Politics in Modern China*.

36. The September 1972 script of *Raid on the White Tiger Regiment* can be found in *Hongqi* 11 (1972): 26–54. For an English translation, see *Chinese Literature* 3 (1973): 3–54.

37. Quotations are from *Raid on the White Tiger Regiment*, 23.

38. Ibid.

39. Ibid., 33.

40. To further attest that such a story of an international community really took place in history, *Hongqi* published an article written by Yang Yucai, a combat hero of the Chinese People's Volunteers who fought in the Korean War. His article claimed that *Raid on the White Tiger Regiment* was indeed based on the actual exploits of his scout platoon. With regard to the authenticity of the mother figure in the play, Yang used these words to testify to the opera's true-to-life-nature: "Old Aunt Choi in the opera epitomizes all the revolutionary people of Korea. I once had to go out on a mission in a snowstorm. After trekking all day through snow a yard deep, my clothes soaked with snow and sweat were frozen stiff. When I reached a gully, I suddenly collapsed from cold and hunger, unable to go another step. It was Aunt Choi who found me and took me home. My padded uniform and padded boots were frozen and wouldn't come off. Aunt Choi thawed my bootlaces with her breath and then pulled off my boots. Next, she melted the ice on my buttons with her lips and took off my uniform. She saved my life and helped me rejoin my unit. Aunt Choi's husband, son and daughter-in-law had all been killed by the US invaders, leaving her only a young grand-daughter. She looked on us Volunteers as her own people and sheltered us at the risk of her own life. At the sight of the enemy she burned with hatred. If she had met a US devil in the mountains, she would have killed him ruthlessly with her bare hands. Aunt Choi in the opera represents countless old aunties among the revolutionary Korean people. To win the war, they gave their last ounce of strength." See Yang Yucai, "*Qixi Baihutuan* shi yichu." The quotation is from an English translation of this article entitled "An Opera Embodying Mao Zedong's Thought." It is interesting to note that the opera was first performed by the Chinese People's Volunteer Army in 1957 in Korea at Zhou Enlai's suggestion to use a traditional art to reflect the heroic spirit of the Chinese and North Korean soldiers.

41. Wen Wei-ching, "The Course of a Militant Struggle," 97.

42. Yang Chih-an, "Chairman Mao Is Dearer Than Any Parent," 58–59.

43. Theodor W. Adorno, "Freudian Theory and the Pattern of Fascist Propaganda," 124–125.

44. Ibid., 127.

45. Ibid., 123.

46. Louis Althusser, "Ideology and Ideological State Apparatuses," 141–148.

47. Sau-ling C. Wong, "Denationalization Reconsidered," 3.

48. Jan Wong, *Red China Blues*, 12–13.

49. Ibid., 15.

50. Ibid., 13.

51. Jin Qiu, "Ji *Hongdeng ji* re" (The popularity of *The Red Lantern*).

52. Ibid.

53. Ibid.

54. My friends in China conveyed this information to me. Even if it was circulated through "rumor mills," it is important to note that political rumors are sources of information in a highly censored society. A typical example can be found in the case of the widely circulated rumor about the arrest of the Gang of Four before the official press had a chance to announce it publicly.

55. For a cross-reference, see Anderson, *Imagined Communities*, 33. Commenting on the Filipino writer's depiction of the national movement, Anderson remarks: "It should suffice to note that right from the start the image (wholly new to Filipino writing) of a dinner-party being discussed by hundreds of unnamed people, who do not know each other, in quite different quarters of Manila, in a particular month of a particular decade, immediately conjures up the imagined community" (7).

56. To a full house at Capital University, Columbus, Ohio, this performance was sponsored by the Ministry of Culture of China as an act of participation in the international activities celebrating the fiftieth anniversary of the end of World War II. The same year, on November 1, I also attended the Central Ballet of China's performance of the "revolutionary model ballet" *The Red Detachment of Women* in the Ohio Theater, Columbus, which was a smashing success and elicited a warm response, especially from local Chinese communities. The Chinese revolutionary ballet, of course, had to be prefaced by a Western piece, *Giselle*, to demonstrate that the supreme ballet style and skill shown in the following piece were equal to those of any first-rate ballet troupe in the world.

57. Dai Jinhua, "Redemption and Consumption: Depicting Culture in the 1990s," 127, 129.

58. Dai Jiafang, *Yangbanxi de fengfeng yuyu*, 1–4.

59. Helen F. Siu, comp. and intro., *Furrows: Peasants, Intellectuals, and the State*, 12.

60. The January 1972 script of the model-theater version of *Song of the Dragon River* was first published in *Hongqi* 3 (1972): 36–62. Citations are from the English translation in *Chinese Literature* 7 (1972): 3–52, 25.

61. Ernest Renan, "What Is a Nation?" 19.

62. *Song of the Dragon River*, 34.

63. Dai Jiafang, *Yangbanxi de fengfeng yuyu*, 191–192. For more information on the revision process of the play, see Dai Jiafang, 191–196.

64. *Song of the Dragon River*, 31.

65. Karen Pinkus, who has also considered (although from a different vantage point) the issue of treating black people as a racial other, analyzes the representation and manipulation of black bodies in fascist advertising and popular culture in Italy in the 1930s, when Italy was trying to catch up with other European colonial powers in the effort to appropriate the last few pieces of territory available in Africa. She demonstrates that the perceived relationships between race, gender, and class, as filtered through the construction and consumption of the image of the black body, played a crucial role in the formation of the national conscience for an entire generation of Italians. See Pinkus, *Bodily Regimes*, 24.

66. For a recent study of ethnic groups in China, see Stevan Harrell, ed., *Cultural Encounters on China's Ethnic Frontiers*. For a study of racial prejudice and racial difference in China, see Frank Dikötter, *The Discourse of Race in Modern China*.

67. Wen Jun, "Wuchanjieji zhuanzheng xia jixu geming de guanghui dianxing" (An excellent model of carrying out the continued revolution under the dictatorship of the proletariat), 49.

68. Ibid.

69. Quoted from the English translation *of On the Docks* (January 1972 script), published in *Chinese Literature* 5 (1972): 52–98, 57. For the original Chinese text of the January 1972 script, see *Haigang, Hongqi* 2 (1972): 22–48.

70. *On the Docks*, 61.

71. Ibid., 91.

72. Ibid.

73. Ibid., 92.

74. Ibid.

75. Ibid., 91.

76. Wen Jun, "Wuchanjieji zhuanzheng xia," 50.

77. *On the Docks*, 72.

78. "Seminar Sponsored by the Afro-Asian Writers' Bureau," 49.

79. Ibid.

80. Ibid., 54.

81. Ibid.

82. Zhou Enlai has been credited, in contemporary Chinese political and diplomatic history, as the architect of the Sino-African relationship. Philip Brown, for instance, notes Zhou's concrete contribution to building up the bond between the Chinese people and their African brothers and sisters. During his 1963 visit to African countries, Zhou Enlai argued that "China and Africa were brought together . . . by their common experience of oppression at the hands of the colonial Europeans. In the Sudan he hit on a convenient symbol, the Victorian general Charles George Gordon, who had started his career by helping to suppress the 'Taiping' rebellion of Chinese peasants against alien Manchu rule and ended it as the victim of an African uprising, speared by the Mahdi's dervishes in the governor's palace at Khartoum. The Sudanese people, said Zhou, had 'finally punished' General Gordon." See Philip Snow, *The Star Raft*, 75.

83. "Seminar Sponsored by the Afro-Asian Writers' Bureau," 55.

84. "Seminar Held by the Executive Secretariat of the Afro-Asian Writers' Bureau," 63. For other documents of the seminar in English, see "Speech by Sudanese Delegate—Abmed Mohamed Kheir," "Let the Great Red Banner of Mao Tse-tung's Thought Fly All over the World," and "Stride Forward along Chairman Mao's Revolutionary Line on Literature and Art."

85. "Performance by Somali Artists' Delegation."

86. "Chairman Mao's Portraits Distributed All Over the World," 132–133.

87. "World's Revolutionary People Enthusiastically Translate and Publish Chairman Mao's Works," 154.

88. Léopold Sédar Senghor, "Negritude," 28; italics in original.

89. Frantz Fanon, "On National Culture," 47. For an anthology that provides historical contexts for Léopold Sédar Senghor's and Frantz Fanon's works, see Diana Brydon, ed., *Postcolonialism: Critical Concepts in Literary and Cultural Studies*.

90. Philip Snow, *The Star Raft*, 29.

91. Ibid., 30.

92. Ibid.

93. Ibid., 70.

94. Ibid., 46.

95. Philip Snow recounts an interesting episode with regard to the image of the Chinese as missionary: "The portrait of a 'Young Chinese Missionary'—gaunt, inspired, in a scholar's long gown—is said to have hung for some years in the Vatican

before it was discovered to be a representation of the youthful Mao Zedong pacing the hills of his native province of Hunan. The Vatican was mortified, and the portrait was removed. But perhaps the cardinals had not really blundered. Mao was the prototype of a new, evangelical variety of Chinese. After twelve years of war, first against the Japanese invaders and then against the American-backed Nationalist regime of Chiang Kai-shek, Mao and his Communist Party finally won control of China in 1949. It was a victory, in their eyes, not so much for Communism as for China itself. 'The Chinese people have stood up,' Mao assured his followers: 'from now on no one will insult us again.' The Chinese Communists exulted in the certainty that they had put an end to China's century of humiliation at the hands of foreign powers. In driving foreign influence forcibly from its territory, China, they maintained, had set an example which other subjugated nations should and would follow. They were fired by a missionary urge to spread the news" (69).

96. "Revolutionary Songs and Dances, Militant Friendship,"103.

97. Hu Wen, "Militant Songs and Dances from Romania," 92.

98. Hsiang-tung Chou, "Let the Flames of Revolution Burn More Fiercely!" 107.

99. Ibid.

100. Ibid., 111.

101. Ibid., 109–108.

102. Ibid., 108.

103. Ibid., 109.

104. Timothy Brennan, "The National Longing for Form," 47.

105. Ibid., 49. For a study of fictional works created during the Cultural Revolution and an annotated bibliography of these works, see Lan Yang, *Chinese Fiction of the Cultural Revolution*.

106. Chandra Talpade Mohanty, "Under Western Eyes," 54.

107. Ibid., 59.

Chapter Four: Audience, Applause, and Actor

1. This was a popular saying among the Chinese people during and after the Cultural Revolution.

2. Wu Xue, "Xu" (Introduction), 1.

3. Liu Xiaobo, "Shinian huaju guanzhao" (A survey of the dramatic production of the last ten years).

4. For a survey of the historical context of Li Longyun's *There Is a Small Court-yard* and other plays, see Haiping Yan, "Theater and Society: An Introduction to Contemporary Chinese Drama," in her *Theater and Society*, ix–xlvi.

5. For a plot summary and a brief review of the play in English, see Bian Hu, "*Winter Jasmine*: A New Play."

6. Cui Dezhi, *Baochunhua*, 10. Translations mine.

7. This and other subsequent information on audience response are recounted according to my recollection.

8. Shen Yi, "Xin changzheng lushang de baochunhua" (A winter jasmine on the road of a new long march), 49.

9. Huang Mei, "Guanyu *Baochunhua* de yifengxin" (A letter concerning *Winter Jasmine*), 47.

10. Cui Dezhi, "Ganyu shenghuo, chuangzuo caiyou chulu" (Delving into life is the only way out for literary creation), 4. For another account of the writing process of the play, see Cui Dezhi, "Tan *Baochunhua* de xiezuo" (On the writing of *Winter Jasmine*).

11. "Yixiang zhongda de wuchuan jieji zhengce" (A significant proletarian policy), 1.

12. See "Shiying qingkuang bianhua de yixiang zhongda juece" (A significant decision to adjust to a new situation).

13. Yan Guoyuan, "Laigao laixin zhaideng" (Letters to the editor), 93.

14. Shen Yi, "Xin changzheng lushang de baochunhua," 51.

15. Huang Mei, "Guanyu *Baochunhua* de yifengxin," 48.

16. The Chinese text can be found in Sha Yexin, *Yesu, Kunzi, pitoushi Lienong* (Jesus, Confucius, and the Beatle Lennon), 3–79; for an English translation, see Sha Yexin, *If I Were for Real*, 261–322.

17. The translation is from Lee Yee's *New Realism*, 262. When there was a discrepancy between the Chinese text and Yee's translation, I translated the missing lines. The translation of this paragraph is mine, as it is absent from Yee's translation.

18. Sha, *If I Were for Real*, 264.

19. Ibid.

20. Ibid.

21. The translations are mine, based on the script in Sha Yexin's *Yesu, Kunzi, pitoushi Lienong*, 69.

22. Sha, *If I Were for Real*, 319.

23. Ibid., 322.

24. Ibid., 264.

25. Augusto Boal, *Theatre of the Oppressed*, 122.

26. Ibid., 122.

27. Eugène Van Erven, *The Playful Revolution*, 16. For a brief account of Boal's theory and practice of theater of the oppressed in connection with what Van Erven terms the "theater of liberation" in Asia, see 14–19.

28. Ibid., 17.

29. Ibid.

30. Ibid., xiii.

31. Erving Goffman, *Frame Analysis*, 131–132.

32. For a survey article summarizing the critical debate on the social effects of *If I Were for Real* and other controversial scripts, see "Guanyu *Zai shehui de dang'an li*" (Debate on *In the Archives of Society* and other works). For an article in English on the debate, see Hu Fu, "Controversial Plays."

33. Sha Yexin, "Guanyu *Jiaru woshi zhende*" (Concerning *If I Were for Real*), 42.

34. Qu Liuyi, "Yishu shi zhen-shan-mei de jiejing" (Art is a crystallization of the truthful, the good, and the beautiful).

35. For typical arguments along these lines, see Sha Yexin, "Guanyu *Jiaru woshi zhende*," 41–42.

36. Hua Guofeng was officially replaced by Hu Yaobang as the chairman of the Central Committee of the Chinese Communist Party in the Sixth Plenum of the Eleventh Party Congress, held June 27–29, 1981, in Beijing. See "Zhongguo Gong-chandang di shiyijie zhongyang weiyuanhui diliuci quanti huiyi gongbao" (Communiqué of the Sixth Plenum of the Eleventh Central Committee of the Chinese Communist Party).

37. Sha, *If I Were for Real*, 6. Translations mine.

38. Ibid., 9. Translations mine.

39. Ibid., 7. Translations mine.

40. Yuan Shaojie, "Cong sange pianziju de bijiao zhong kan fengciju de chuang-zuo" (On the dramatic creation of satirical plays through a comparative study of three swindler plays), 24.

41. Ibid., 25.

42. Bai Hui, "Chongti wangshi lun shifei" (Recounting the past events in order to judge who is right), 4.

43. Yuan Shaojie, "Cong sange pianziju de bijiao zhong kan fengciju de chuang-zuo," 26. Lao She's *Looking Westward to Chang'an* was written in 1955. The script

first appeared in *Renmin wenxue* (People's literature), January 1956, and was later published as a separate play by Beijing zuojia chubanshe, 1956.

44. Li Geng, "Dui juben *Jiaru woshi zhende* de yijian" (A reading of the drama script *If I Were for Real*), 7–8.

45. Zheng Huaizhi. "Guanyu *Jiaju* yanshu yihon de yixie qingkuang" (Some facts concerning what happened after the performance of *If I Were for Real*), 3.

46. Ibid. For an official account of how the play was not banned, see Liu Jin, "Yiduan chahua—guanyu *pianzi* de xiugai wenti" (An explanation—concerning the revision of *If I Were for Real*).

47. For a typical review of the play, see Lin Kehuan, "Zhandou de yishu—ping huaju *Quan yu fa*" (Military art—*Power versus Law*).

48. Xing Yixun, "*Quan yu fa* chuangzuo mantan" (On writing *Power versus Law*), 55.

49. The script of this play was first published in *Juben* 10 (1979): 2–33. The English translations are from Xing Yixun, *Power versus Law*, 80.

50. Xing Yixun, *Power versus Law*, 81.

51. Quoted from "Zhongguo Gongchandang di shiyijie zhongyang weiyuanhui diwuci quanti huiyi gongbao" (Communiqué of the Fifth Plenum of the Eleventh Central Committee of the Chinese Communist Party), adopted on February 29, 1980. This is a typical official statement justifying the party's decision to rehabilitate Liu Shaoqi, former vice-chairman of the Central Committee of the Chinese Communist Party, then president of the People's Republic of China, who was persecuted to death during the Cultural Revolution—a central item on the agenda of this plenum. (An English translation of this communiqué can be found in the *Beijing Review*, March 10, 1980, 7–10.) The release of the communiqué can also be viewed as an expression of the immediate cultural and ideological context of *Power versus Law*, which, according to its playwright, was intended to respond to this call of the party to redress the large number of frame-ups and falsely prosecuted cases left over from history.

52. Xing Yixun, "*Quan yu fa* chuangzuo mantan," 56.

53. Ibid.

54. For plot summaries, reviews, and critical discussions of these three scripts in English, see Hu Fu, "Controversial Plays," *Chinese Literature* 8 (1980): 16–19.

55. Mo Yan, "Chifa de gaojian—ping *Zai shehui de dang'an li*" (A belated article—on *In the Archives of Society*), 34.

56. Ibid., 33.

57. An English translation of *Teahouse* can be found in *Chinese Literature*, June 1980, 16–91. For a brief account in English of the fate of *Teahouse* in the history of the PRC, see Ruocheng Ying, "Lao She and His 'Teahouse.' "

58. Wang Xingzhi, "Guanyu shehui xiaoguo de sikao" (Some thoughts on social effects), 94–96.

59. Du Gao, "Huaju chuangzuo pengbo fazhan de liunian" (On the most booming six years of dramatic creation, 1976–1982), 86.

60. Wang Xingzhi, "Guanyu shehui xiaoguo de sikao," 94.

61. Zhao Guoqing, "*Jiujiu ta* chuangzuo zhong de yixie xiangfa" (Some thoughts during the writing of *Save Her*), 81.

62. For an account of this event, see Huang Weijun, "Guanche baijia zhengming fangzhen de chenggong shijian" (A successful practice of carrying out the policy of letting a hundred schools of thought contend), 11.

63. Hu Yaobang was elected a member of the Standing Committee of the Political Bureau and the party's general secretary during the Fifth Plenum of the Eleventh Central Committee of the CCP, held in Beijing, February 23–29, 1980. Hu became chairman of the CCP during the Sixth Plenum in June of 1981.

64. Hu Yaobang, "Zai juben chuangzuo zuotanhui shang de jianghua" (Talk on the seminar of dramatic scripts), 15.

65. Ibid., 18.

66. Xie Junhua, "Zongjie jingyan lizhi gaige" (Learning from past experiences for a better reform), 58–59.

67. "Sixiang jiben yuanze burong weifan" (Four fundamental principles should not be violated).

68. Bai Hua's *Bitter Love* was first published in *Shiyue* (October), 3 (1979): 140–171, 248. An English translation of the movie script can be found in Hua Bai, *Unrequited Love*, 21–95; citations are from this translation, 56. The movie script of *In the Archives of Society*, written by Wang Jing, was first published in *Dianying chuangzuo* (Film script) 10 (1979): 22–43. An English translation by Ellen Klempner can be found in Lee Yee, ed., *The New Realism*, 102–141. The movie script *Woman Thief*, written by Li Kewei, was first published in *Dianying chuangzuo* 11 (1979): 30–50. Unlike *In the Archives of Society* and *Woman Thief*, which were banned from being made into films, *Bitter Love* was indeed shown for a brief period of time to a limited audience, for the purpose of being criticized as a negative example of "spiritual pollution." For a more detailed study of the critical debate on Bai Hua, see Merle Goldman, "The Campaign against Bai Hua and Other Writers," in her *Sowing the Seeds of Democ-racy in China*, 88–112.

69. Bai Hua, *Unrequited Love*, 95.

70. Cui Dezhi, *Baochunhua* (Winter jasmine), 3.

71. Dai Jinhua, *Jingcheng tuwei* (Breaking the mimetic mirror), 34.

72. Cui Dezhi, *Baochunhua*, 4.

73. Ibid.

74. Dai Jinhua, "Invisible Women," 265.

75. Ibid.

Chapter Five: Performing Tiananmen

1. Eugène Van Erven has described the theater of liberation movement in the Philippines, which politicized and mobilized the masses to overthrow Marcos' dictatorship, and *Madang* (open-square) theater in South Korea, which transformed spectators into slogan-chanting political demonstrators. As the rest of this chapter will show, due to its strict censorship system, the antimainstream function in Chinese street theater is much more subtle and at times even overlaps with the mainstream discourse in order to more effectively subvert it. It is not entirely true, however, as Van Erven claimed, that Chinese theater artists "do not do much in the way of theater of liberation." See his *Playful Revolution*, xv.

2. Susan G. Davis, *Parades and Power*, 17.

3. For detailed accounts of the poetry of the 1976 Tiananmen movement, see Yuan Ying, "Minxin—du *Tiananmen shichao*" (The will of the people—readings from *Collections of Tiananmen Poetry*).

4. All the quotations from this play are cited from Zong Fuxian (Tsung Fu-hsien), *In a Land of Silence*, in Edward M. Gunn, ed., *Twentieth-Century Chinese Drama*, 409–447. The spellings of characters' names were changed to be consistent with pinyin. The original Chinese text, entitled *Yuwu shengchu*, was first published in *Renmin xiju* (People's drama) 12 (1978): 48–76. This was the actual script for its premiere by the Amateur Theater of Shanghai Workers Cultural Club (Shanghaishi gongren wenhuagong yeyu huajutuan) in November 1978.

5. Zong Fuxian, *In a Land of Silence*, 446.

6. In the West, the famous neoclassic theories of the "three unities" were never universally accepted, with many critics debating across generations whether or not Aristotle's idea of tragedy being kept "within a single circuit of the sun, or something near that" means from "sunrise to sunset rather than a 24-hour day," as advocated by Francesco Robortello during the Italian Renaissance. See Marvin Carlson, *Theories of the Theatre*, 38–40. The quotation is from Robortello, *Librum Aristotelis de arte poetica explicationes*, 1: 368; cited by Carlson, 39–40. Chinese dramatic critics and scholars, however, frequently attribute such a concept to Aristotle and view it as one of the most important features of the heritage of Western drama, and hence an important criterion for judging formalistic features of Chinese dramatic texts.

7. Cao Yu, Zhao Xun, and Zong Fuxian, "*Yuwu shengchu* sanren tan" (Three dramatists on *In a Land of Silence*), 18.

8. Zong Fuxian, *"Yuwu shengchu, Xue zongshi rede* chuangzuo tan" (How I wrote *In a Land of Silence* and *Blood Is Always Hot*), 46.

9. Zong Fuxian, "Wode qian bansheng" (My autobiography), 24.

10. For an official account of this event, see "Tiananmen guangchang shijian shuoming le shenme?" (What did the Tiananmen incident tell us?).

11. See "Huang Zuolin yu Meiguo liuxuesheng de tanhua" (Huang Zuolin's interview with American student Elizabeth Bernard), 4.

12. For a biography of Lu Xi, see Xie Bo, "Lu Xi zhuan."

13. With more than seven hundred participants, the ceremony to place the ashes of Lao She was held on June 3, 1978, presided over by Wu De, then the director of the Beijing Revolutionary Committee (Beijingshi gemin weiyuanhui). The same ceremony was held for Zhou Xinfang, a leading Peking opera actor who was persecuted to death on March 8, 1975, for having played the title role in *Hai Rui Criticizing the Emperor (Hai Rui shangshu)*, on August 16, 1978, in Shanghai, presided over by Wang Yiping, party secretary of the Shanghai Municipal Party Committee; for Zheng Junli, a well-known dramatist, film actor, and director, persecuted to death on April 23, 1969, in Shanghai; for Yan Fengying, a leading actress in the Anhui opera *(huangmei xi)*, persecuted to death in April 1968, in Anhui Province on August 21, 1978. Dates are listed in *Zhongguo xiju shinian taishiji,* (The chronicle of Chinese dramatic events over ten years), 6–7.

14. See "Zhongguo Gongchandang di shiyijie zhongyang weiyuanhui disanci quanti huiyi gongbao" (Communiqué of the Fifth Plenum of the Eleventh Central Committee of the Chinese Communist Party).

15. The ceremony held by the National Workers Union to award the "best-drama" prize to Zong Fuxian was held on December 28, 1978, in Beijing. See *Zhongguo xiju shinian taishiji*, 10.

16. *Song of Stormy Wind* by Chen Baichen was first published in *Juben* (Drama script) 1 (1979): 48–96. The revised version of *The Future Is Calling for Us* by Zhao Xinxiong was published in *Juben* 8 (1979): 2–34; *Save Her*, by Zhao Guoqing, was first published in *Xinyuan* (New garden) 3 (1979), 4–43.

17. The play was written by Li Longyun in March 1979, first published in *Heilongjiang xiju* (Heilongjiang drama) 2 (1979), and later reprinted in *Xinhua yuebao, wenzhaiban* (Xinhua monthly journal [Selections in the humanities]) 9 (1979): 134–157. The play was premiered in April 1979 by the China Children's Art Theater (Zhongguo ertong yishu juyuan). English translations are mine, based on the script from *Xinhua yuebao*.

18. Li Longyun, *There Is a Small Courtyard*, 147.

19. Ibid., 146.

20. See Shi Ding, "Jie lingtang, kuqihuang de beiju" (A tragedy of making use of the memorial hall to cry over one's own grievances). See also Nie Haifeng, "Sisuo, dan bie wangdiao xinnian" (Think deeply but do not lose faith).

21. Deng Xian, *Zhongguo zhiqing meng* (The dream of the educated youth of China), 4–15.

22. Ibid., 16–17.

23. Ibid., 16–19.

24. See Wang Zheng, "Juzuojia de jianxin he pipingjia de gunzi" (The playwright's hardship versus the critic's club), 8.

25. For an English translation, see Guan Hanqing (Kuan Han-ch'ing), *Injustice to Tou O: A Study and Translation*.

26. The original Chinese text of *Guan Hanqing* was first published in *Juben* 5 (1958): 2–33 and was later collected in *Zhongguo lishiju xuan* (A selected collection of Chinese history plays) (Hong Kong: Shanghai Book Co., 1961). For a detailed study of this play in English, see Rudolf G. Wagner, "A Guide for the Perplexed and a Call to the Wavering: Tian Han's *Guan Hanqing* (1958) and the New Historical Drama," in his *The Contemporary Chinese Historical Drama*, 1–79. Commenting on the significance of *Guan Hanqing*, Wagner believes that it is "a historical play about a playwright writing a historical play," and that it is a "guide for the perplexed" to "educate the knowing in the secrets of reading historical plays, and as such it is at the same time" "preface to the 'new historical plays' of the coming years" (2). By writing this historical drama, "Tian Han defined the present *ipso facto* as a time of crisis calling for this genre, and he initiated both his colleagues and the public in the arts of crafting and deciphering such texts" (3).

27. The English translations are quoted from *Kuan Han-ch'ing* [Guan Hanqing], in Edward Gunn, ed., *Twentieth-Century Chinese Drama*, 325. The romanization of Chinese names has been changed to the pinyin system.

28. This is a direct quotation from Tian Han, *Guan Hanqing*. English translations are cited from *Kuan Han-ch'ing*, in Gunn, 334.

29. Lao She (Lao Sheh), "How I Wrote *Dragon Beard Ditch*," 93.

30. Lao She, *Dragon Beard Ditch*, 7. Written in July 1950, it first appeared in *Beijing wenyi* (Beijing literature and art) in the September to November issues of 1950; it was published as a single play by Beijing dazhong chubanshe in 1951 and later collected in his *Lao She wenji* (Collected works of Lao She) (Beijing: Renmin wenxue chubanshe, 1987), 11:99–166.

31. See act 2, scene 1 of *Dragon Beard Ditch* and act 3 of *There Is a Small Courtyard*.

32. Ke Ying, "Renmin yishujia Lao She" (Lao She: Artist of the people), 76.

33. Lao She's *Teahouse* first appeared in *Shouhuo* (Harvest) (July 1957), and was later published as a single play (Beijing: Zhongguo xiju chunbanshe, 1988). It was later collected in *Lao She wenji*, 11:360–427. An English translation can be found in *Chinese Literature* 6 (1980): 16–93, along with a brief introduction to the history and reception of the play by Ying Ruocheng entitled "Lao She and His 'Teahouse' " and an essay written by Lao She himself in 1958 entitled "In Reply to Some Questions about 'Teahouse.' "

34. See part 1 of *Taiping Lake*, first published in *Xin juzuo* (New drama script) 5 (1986). English translation mine. This play was premiered in January 1988 by the Beijing People's Art Theater, after fourteen revisions of the script by the playwright himself. Despite much publicity, however, the reviews were far from favorable: the play disappointed the audience because its innovative form—which switched between past and present and between the living and the dead—seemed to undercut the potential power of drama, which demands action and thought, not just new techniques. For a sample review in this vein, see Dou Xiaohong, "*Taipinghu* de yihan" (The disappointment of *Taiping Lake*), and Zhang Donggang, "Xiju bu jinjin zuowei xingshi" (Drama is not just about form).

35. Lao She, "How I Wrote *Dragon Beard Ditch*," 94.

36. For an informative biography and summary of Jiao Juying's dramatic achievements, see Jiang Rui, "Jiao Juyin de yishu daolu."

37. For an English translation, see Cao Yu, *Peking Man*.

38. For an English translation, see Lao She, *The Rickshaw Boy*.

39. Li Longyun, *There Is a Small Courtyard*, act 1, 137.

40. See Dong Jian, "Cong *Xiaoyuan* dao *Xiaojing*" (From *A Small Courtyard* to *Small Well*), 29.

41. Lao She, "How I Wrote *Dragon Beard Ditch*," 97.

42. Li Longyun, *Small Well Lane*, 77, 178. The script was first published in *Juben* 5 (1981): 36–76. According to Chen Baichen, a prominent playwright and Li's graduate advisor when Li was studying as an M.A. student at the Chinese Department of Nanjing University, this play was premiered by the Beijing People's Art Theater in July 1983, but was permitted only three performances for controlled audiences because of its questionable "political healthiness" and was not allowed to be performed for the general public until January 1985. The republication of its script in *Zhongshan* (Bell Mountain) literary magazine in February 1984 was considered a symbolic victory for those dramatists and critics who had lobbied through various channels for its acceptance by the official censors. See Chen Baichen, "Guanyu *Xiaojing Hutong* de tongxin" (Correspondence with Li Longyun on *Small Well Lane*), 79. As one present at one of these later performances, I sensed the audience members' enthusiasm for this play, intensified by an angry sentiment that such a sensational play had had to wait for so long to be allowed to appear before the general public.

43. Wen Guangli, "Du *Xiaojing Hutong*" (Afterthoughts on *Small Well Lane*), 77.

44. Tania Modleski, "Time and Desire in the Woman's Film," 537.

45. For a full account of this event and others surrounding it, see Lin Qingshan, *Jiang Qing chenfu lu* (The rise and fall of Jiang Qing), 2:637–655. Although Lin claimed that his work was "biographical literature" in his "Postscript," he assured his readers that he had spent ten years interviewing people directly involved with the life of Jiang Qing and collecting published records and unpublished materials in order to write these two volumes. As a further footnote to the theme of this chapter on street theater, it is important to observe that Lin himself was a target of public criticism for his controversial essay on philosophical issues in 1964, which provoked more than five hundred articles nationwide attacking his "anti-party" point of view. "Before the curtain call of this act," Lin recalled, "the curtain for another act—that of the Cultural Revolution—was already being drawn." Lin Qingshan, "Postscript," 2:787–788, 787.

46. Lin Qingshan, 2:643, 645.

47. Ibid., 643.

48. Ibid., 650.

49. Ibid., 654.

50. Ibid.

51. For these and other incidents surrounding Zhou's death, see Ross Terrill, *The White-Boned Demon*, 358–359.

52. Ibid., 368. For another biography of Jiang Qing, based on her personal interviews with her, see Roxanne Witke, *Comrade Chiang Ch'ing*. For an insider's view of Mao's private life written by his personal physician, see Li Zhisui, *The Private Life of Chairman Mao*.

53. Peter Brooks, "Melodrama, Body, Revolution," 13.

54. See, for instance, Yan Jiaqi and Gao Gao, *Zhongguo wenge shinian shi* (A history of the ten-year Chinese Cultural Revolution), 445. In this book, Yan and Gao state that Jiang Qing "developed out-of-the-ordinary relationships" *(fazhan le bu xunchang de guanxi)* with Yu Huiyong, the composer of the Peking opera *Taking Tiger Mountain by Strategy*, with Hao Liang, the leading actor who played Li Yuhe in the Peking opera *The Red Lantern*, and with Liu Qingtang, the male lead who played Hong Changqing in the ballet version of *The Red Detachment of Women*.

55. Yang Guifei's real name was Yang Yuhuan. "Guifei" means "the highest-ranking concubine in the imperial court."

56. Terrill, *The White-Boned Demon*, 373.

57. Ibid., 372.

58. The Chinese script of *The Tempest in the Divine Land*, by Zhao Huan and Jin Jingmai, can be found in *Juben* 11 (1979): 4–37. It was premiered in 1979 by the Soldiers Theater of the Guangzhou Military Unit.

59. Weng Ru, "Wo yan Jiang Qing" (My creation of the dramatic role of Jiang Qing), 8.

60. Jin Shan, "Xikan zhuo Jiang Qing" (Watching with delight Jiang Qing's arrest on stage), 8.

61. Due to his extraordinary success as a movie and stage actor, Jin Shan was nicknamed the "emperor of spoken drama," as evidenced by the title of his biography, *Huaju huangdi Jin Shan zhuan* (The biography of Jin Shan, the emperor of spoken drama), by Xian Jihua and Zhao Yunsheng.

62. The Chinese script of *Eventful Years*, written by Gu Erxin and Fang Hong-you, can be found in *Renmin xiju* 1 (1978): 49–82.

63. See "The Trial of Lin-Jiang Cliques Begins."

64. For the full text of the indictment in Chinese, see "Zhonghua Renmin Gong-heguo zuigao renmin jianchayuan tebie jianchating qisushu" (Indictment of the Special Procuratorate of the Special Court under the Supreme People's Court in the People's Republic of China), *Renmin ribao* Nov. 21, 1990, 1–3. For an English translation, see "Indictment of the Special Procuratorate," *Beijing Review* 23.48 (December 1, 1980): 9–28.

65. "Indictment of the Special Procuratorate," 19.

66. Ibid., 22.

67. Ibid., 13–14.

68. The Chinese script of *When the Maple Leaves Turned Red* was first published in *Renmin xiju* 6 (1977): 22–50. English translations are mine.

69. See Wu Xue's speech at the drama seminar on *When the Maple Leaves Turned Red*, sponsored by the journal *Renmin xiju*, in "Fenghong jijie hua fengju" (Discussing a maple play in the maple season), 68–69.

70. See Jin Zhenjia and Wang Jingyu, "Tan *Fengye hongle de shihou* de chuang-zuo he yanchu" (On the writing and performance of *When the Maple Leaves Turned Red*), 36, 40.

71. Fox Butterfield, " 'Gang of 4' and 6 Other Ex-Leaders Go on Trial," A12.

72. Terrill, *The White-Boned Demon*, 390–391.

73. Lin Qingshan, *Jiang Qing chenfu lu* (The rise and fall of Jiang Qing), 1:11.

74. Terrill, *The White-Boned Demon*, 15.

75. Ibid., 392. According to Terrill, Jiang Qing requested Peng Zhen that she be allowed to make cloth dolls in order to avoid the compulsory manual labor otherwise imposed on all political prisoners.

76. Ibid., 68.

77. For an English translation by Kirk A. Denton, see Sha Yexin, *Jiang Qing and Her Husbands*.

78. Sha Yexin, *Jiang Qing he tade zhangfumen* (Jiang Qing and her husbands), 9–10. I thank Edward Gunn for providing a copy of this play. All the quotations of the play are from the same text. Translations are mine.

79. In Sha's play, Tang Na is identified as Jiang's second husband, and Mao the third. See Sha Yexin, *Jiang Qing he tade zhangfumen*, 11–12. This differs from Lin Qingshan's account in *Jiang Qing chenfulu*, which describes Jiang as having been married to Pei Minglun, her first husband, to Yu Qiwei, her second husband, and to Tang Na, her third husband, before marrying Mao, her fourth husband. See Lin Qingshan, 1:28, 53, 177–178.

80. Sha Yexin, *Jiang Qing he tade zhangfumen*, 16. The Chinese stage lines here are direct translations from Ibsen's text. See Henrik Ibsen, *A Doll's House*, 232.

81. Sha Yexin, *Jiang Qing he tade zhangfumen*, 20.

82. Ibid., 27.

83. Ibid., 29.

84. Ibid., 41.

85. Ibid., 75.

86. Ibid., 78–79.

87. Ibid., 93.

88. Ibid., 115.

89. Ibid., 121.

90. The modern drama *Yang Kaihui* was written by Qiao Yu, Shu Yuan, and Li Zibo and was premiered by the Teacher's Theatre of Central Drama College (Zhongyang xiju xueyuan jiaoshi yanchutuan) in 1978. The script was first published *Renmin xiju* 7 (1978): 49–89.

91. Zhang Guichi's *The Son of the World* was published in *Juben* 11 (1985): 3–33.

92. For a German translation of Sha Yexin's play and a critical study, see Natascha Vittinghoff, *Geschichte der Partei entwunden — eine semiotische Analyse des Dramas Jiang Qing und ihre Ehemänner von Sha Yexin* (1991) (History, recovered from the grip of the party—a semiotical analysis of *Jiang Qing and her husbands* by Sha Yexin) (Bochum: Projekt Verlag, 1995). I thank Barbara Mittler and Martin Gieselmann for this information.

93. The Chinese script of Zhao Huan's *Marx in London Exile* can be found in Zhongguo xiju chubanshe, ed., *You zhenyi de huaju juben xuanji* (Selected controversial plays) (Beijing: Zhongguo xiju chubanshe, 1986), 1:105–203.

94. Sha Yexin, *The Secret History of Marx*, in Zhongguo xiju chubanshe, ed., *You zhenyi de huaju juben xuanji*, 1:463–560. The script was first published in *Shiyue* 3 (1983): 4–37.

95. See Yang Bing, "Liange xie Makesi de xi gei women shenme jingyan jiaoxun? (What can we learn from the two plays on Marx?)," in Zhongguo xiju chubanshe bianjibu, ed., *You zhenyie de huaju juben xuanji*, 1:227–245, 231.

96. Huang Wen, "Tan 'Zuowei rende Makesi' " (On "Marx as a human being"), in Zhongguo xiju chubanshe bianjibu, ed., *You zhenyie de huaju juben xuanji*, 1:561–567.

97. Ibid., 562.

98. Yang Bing, "Liange xie Makesi de xi gei women shenme jingyan jiaoxun?" 230.

99. Huang Wen, "Tan 'Zuowei rende Makesi,' " 563.

100. Ibid., 564.

Chapter Six: A Stage of Their Own

1. An earlier version of this chapter was published in the *Journal of Asian Studies* 56.1 (February 1997): 3–25. I thank the *JAS* editorial board and two reviewers for their helpful and insightful comments, especially the careful and detailed suggestions for revision by the editorial board. My thanks also to audiences and colleagues at National Normal University, Taipei, where an early draft was presented in 1996.

2. See, for example, Bai Wei's 1928 play, *Breaking Out of Ghost Pagoda* (*Dachu youlingta*). For an insightful analysis of Bai's play with feminist critique, see Meng Yue and Dai Jinhua, *Fuchu lishi dibiao*, 161–164.

3. This play, written by Chen Liting in 1931, was first performed on National Day of the same year by leftist dramatists and actors such as Zhang Min and others. During its numerous performances by many different progressive groups, the play underwent many revisions and was finally published in written form in 1936 in *Guide to Everyday Life* (*Shenghuo zhishi*), 2:9.

4. A classic account of the reception of this play by literary and dramatic historians in the People's Republic of China can be found Ge Yihong, ed., *Zhongguo huaju tongshi* (A history of modern Chinese drama), 203.

5. Dai Jinhua, "Invisible Women," 259.

6. What I mean by "women's theater" is close to Lizbeth Goodman's definition of "feminist theatre as a form of cultural representation made by women, which is informed by the situated perspectives of its makers, its performer, its spectators and its critics," a theater "which aims to achieve positive re-evaluation of women's roles and/or to effect social change, and which is informed . . . by broadly feminist ideas." See Lizbeth Goodman, *Contemporary Feminist Theatres*, 36–37. It is important to point out that when I interviewed Bai Fengxi in 1991 she asked me to explain to her why her plays were popularly received in the West as feminist and to what extent her works were feminist according to Western theories. She was happy to learn about the connections between her concerns about women's issues in China with those in the West. This episode shows that Western feminist theories were not irrelevant to the creation of her plays and can provide interesting perspectives for their reception and interpretation.

7. Mara L. Dukats, "The Hybrid Terrain of Literary Imagination," 51.

8. Ibid., 60.

9. Ibid., 53, cited in Nancy Fraser and Sandra Lee Bartky, "Introduction," in Fraser and Bartky, eds., *Revaluing French Feminism*, 1–24.

10. Interview with Bai Fengxi, August 1991, Beijing.

11. Bai Fengxi, "Preface," *The Women Trilogy*, 7.

12. Interview with Bai Fengxi, August 1991, Beijing.

13. Lizbeth Goodman, *Contemporary Feminist Theatres*, 20. In the same paragraph, Goodman also confirms the possible use of Roland Barthes' concept of the theory of spectatorship: "When the intentions of authors are considered as they have been in this study, the concept of 'the death of the author' must be questioned. Yet the concept does have important implications for theories of spectatorship, which inform the study of feminist theatre" (20).

14. Bai Fengxi, *First Bathed in Moonlight*, 109. For Chinese texts of the trilogy, see Bai Fengxi, *Bai Fengxi juzuo xuan* (Selected plays of Bai Fengxi).

15. Interview with Bai Fengxi, August 1991, Beijing.

16. Lydia H. Liu, "Invention and Intervention," 196.

17. During my interview with Bai Fengxi, she explained to me that all three of her women's plays were critiqued by established drama critics as mere products of socialist realism, which was then considered to be old-fashioned in comparison with other, more popular experimental dramas influenced by Western traditions. Yet she persistently pursued the aesthetic beauty of this tradition, which, in her view, was more appropriate for expressing the subtlety and nuances of female experiences and emotions than those dramatic techniques offered by other Western traditions such as modernism and experimental theater.

18. Bai Fengxi, *First Bathed in Moonlight*, 130. Quotations cited hereafter are from Guan Yuehua's translation in Bai Fengxi, *The Women Trilogy*, 104–203.

19. Interview with Bai Fengxi, August 1991, Beijing.

20. For important essays on this controversy, see Wang Chunyuan, "Ba mei daidao shenghuo zhong lai" (A play that has brought beauty into life), 7–10, and Du Gao, "Ping *Mingyue chu zao ren*" (On the mother-daughter love triangle in *First Bathed in Moonlight*), 18–19.

21. Bai Fengxi, *First Bathed in Moonlight*, 198.

22. Gao Jinxian, "Yichu buhe qingli de aiqingxi" (A play on love without much logic), 2.

23. Chen Guang, "Ping huaju *Mingyue chu zhao ren*" (On *First Bathed in Moonlight*), 41–42. Xu A'li also argued that the love triangle involving mother and daughter is too "strange and unrealistic" to have any "artistic typicality" in representing reality, as required by Marxist aesthetics. See Xu A'li, "Buneng wei qi er qi," 3.

24. Chen Guang "Ping huaju *Mingyue chu zhao ren*," 42.

25. Interview with Bai Fengxi, August 1991, Beijing. According to Bai, this incident occurred at the performance of the play by the Xi'an Drama Troupe in the city of Xi'an.

26. Jill Dolan, *The Feminist Spectator as Critic*, 1.

27. Ibid., 2–3.

28. Interview with Bai Fengxi, August 1991, Beijing.

29. Goodman, *Contemporary Feminist Theatres*, 21.

30. Interview with Bai Fengxi, August 1991, Beijing.

31. Jill Dolan, "In Defense of the Discourse," 59.

32. Interview with Bai Fengxi, August 1991, Beijing.

33. Constantine Tung, "Tensions of Reconciliation," 247.

34. Meenakshi Ponnuswami, "Feminist History in Contemporary British Theatre," 291.

35. Gao Jinxian, "Yichu buhe qingli de aiqingxi," 2.

36. Ibid.

37. Bai Fengxi, *First Bathed in Moonlight*, 175–176.

38. Ibid., 175.

39. Ibid.

40. Ibid., 155.

41. Ibid., 190

42. Ibid., 155.

43. Interview with Bai Fengxi, August 1991, Beijing.

44. From 1971 to 1976, some universities and colleges were reopened to students recruited from workers, peasants, and soldiers. A large portion were selected upon the recommendations of local people from the educated youth who had worked among them during the Cultural Revolution. It was not until 1977, after the death of Mao, that college entrance examinations were reinstated as a precondition for college admission.

45. Bai Fengxi, *First Bathed in Moonlight*, 198–199.

46. Bai Fengxi, *Once Loved and in a Storm Returning*, 75. The script of this play was first published in *Shiyue* (October 1983): 38–69, 5. I use Constantine Tung's translation of the title, *An Old Friend Comes at a Stormy Time*, when discussing the play in the text. Translations are cited from Guan Yuehua's translation in Bai Fengxi, *The Women Trilogy*, 9–103.

47. Interview with Bai Fengxi, August 1991, Beijing.

48. Linda Gordon, "What's New in Women's History," 27.

49. Ibid.

50. Bai Fengxi, *Once Loved and in a Storm Returning*, 99.

51. Ibid., 158.

52. Tung, "Tensions of Reconciliation," 245.

53. Mikhail Mikhailovich Bakhtin has been celebrated as a leading player in the polyphony of contemporary literary criticism. His conception of novelization, with its emphasis on a spontaneous existence and the interaction of a multiplicity of meanings, voices, and languages, has with good reason captured the "dialogic imagination" of twentieth-century philosophers, historians, and literary critics. Recently, however, much scholarly work has been done to expand his theory beyond its original concern with narrative form. Critics of lyric poetry, for example, have demonstrated that dialogic discourse also exists in lyric poetry, which very much goes against Bakhtin's original claim that lyric poetry, a traditionally high genre, is mainly characterized by monologic discourse, with its single-voicedness and close-endedness. Likewise, efforts have also been made in the field of narrative studies to show that some novelistic discourses have "monologic" characteristics that Bakhtin claimed belonged only to the genres of the epic and the lyric.

Perhaps there is good reason for Bakhtin's neglect of the drama, for considered in light of the major premises of his scheme, it turns out to be perhaps the most problematic of all major genres. On its surface, drama is "dialogic," being characterized by a dialogue in which different characters speak spontaneously in their own voices, arguing for their own versions of truth, attempting to win the approval and sympathy of their fellow characters and, at the same time, of the audience. At first consideration, then, drama is obviously dialogic and polyphonic in Bakhtin's sense of these terms. Yet the opposite case can also be made, and this led Bakhtin, surprisingly, to consign drama to the realm of the monologic; for despite the presence of dialogue, drama is usually marked by its monologic structure and worldview. See Bakhtin, Problems of Dostoevsky's Poetics, trans. Caryle Emerson (Minneapolis: University of Minnesota Press, 1984), 17. Since Aristotle, drama has traditionally been regarded as an imitation of a single action, with agents who are necessarily either good or bad. Because this line of "primary distinction" between virtue and vice is one that divides the whole of mankind, as Aristotle claims, drama can be regarded as a fundamentally monologic discourse that expresses a mono-lithic worldview without a multiplicity of voices and meanings.

Imported almost entirely as a Western form, modern Chinese spoken drama seems equally to bear a budding polyphonic motif that develops into a plurality of fully valid melodies within the limits of a single composition. The very notion of the "dialogic imagination," for example, has great value in interpreting, or perhaps reinterpreting, Bai Fengxi's women's theater in the post-Maoist era. From my anal-ysis of Bai's text it is easy to see that drama is by its very nature dialogic, since it by definition requires the immediacy of a creative and participating audience in the theater. It can thus be regarded as an even more dialogic and polyphonic genre than the novel, which is complete with a mere interaction between a text and a single reader. Because it is a more collective genre, the meanings of a drama can only be expressed by the often contradictory or multiple visions of author, director, and audience, all of whom must contribute to its realization. Drama can thus be regarded as the most open-ended, polyphonic, and problematic of all the genres. To overlook this polyphony, to accept Bakhtin's faulty analysis in this regard, is to perpetuate the subordinate place to which drama has been relegated in the present state of studies of modern Chinese literature. Such a situation, monologic in a double sense, calls out for an immediate corrective of the dialogic definition that Bakhtin taught so well.

54. Bai Fengxi, *Once Loved and in a Storm Returning*, 70.

55. Interview with Bai Fengxi, August 1991, Beijing.

56. Interview with Bai Fengxi, August 1991, Beijing.

57. The complete quote from Teresa de Lauretis reads: "It is no longer possible to maintain that there are two spheres of social reality: the private, domestic sphere of the family, sexuality, and affectivity, and the public sphere of work and pro-ductivity. . . . Instead, we can envision several interconnected sets of social relations —relations of work, of class, of race, and of sex/gender." See de Lauretis, *Technol-ogies of Gender*, 8–9.

58. Interview with Bai Fengxi, August 1991, Beijing.

59. Hannah Arendt, *The Human Condition*, 33–35.

60. Interview with Bai Fengxi, August 1991, Beijing.

61. Bai Fengxi, *Say, Who Like Me Is Prey to Fond Regret*, 222. I have translated the title of this play as *Where Is Longing in Autumn*.

62. Ibid., 199.

63. Ibid., 214.

64. Interview with Bai Fengxi, August 1991, Beijing.

65. Ibid.

66. Ibid.

67. For accounts of mother-daughter discourse in some contemporary writings, see Xiaomei Chen, "Reading Mother's Tale," and Sally Liebermann, *The Mother and Narrative Politics*.

68. Meng Yue and Dai Jinhua, *Fuchu lishi dibiao* (Emerging from the surface of history), 17.

69. Ibid., 18.

70. I agree with Constantine Tung's comment that in Bai's plays "the mothers are all authoritarian, strong-willed, domineering and, sometimes, oppressive, and it is the mother, not the father, who is facing the younger generation's rebellious challenge." See Tung, 239.

71. For an English translation of Cao Yu's *Thunderstorm*, see Cao Yu (Ts'ao Yu), *Thunderstorm*.

72. Mona Fayad, "Reinscribing Identity," 148.

73. Goodman, *Contemporary Feminist Theatres*, 27. Goodman's comments on the "counter-cultural" element of British feminist theater are worth quoting as a useful comparison to the Chinese scene in question: "For the most part, however, feminist theatre is still largely 'alternative.' Only a major structural change in all theatre could transfer feminist theatre as genre into the mainstream, for the emphasis on collective and non-hierarchical ways of working which are intrinsic to feminist theatre mitigate against 'mainstreaming.' Indeed, most schools of feminism are opposed in theory, and most feminist theatres in practice, to the concept of 'mainstreaming.' In any case, canonization and mainstream production of feminist theatre are both rare" (27).

Chapter Seven: From Discontented Mother to Woman Warrior

1. A small part of the first section of this chapter was presented at a conference on "China's Perception of Peace, War and the World: A Multidisciplinary Symposium," Vienna, Austria, 1996. It was included in a conference proceeding, Gerd Kaminisky, Barbara Kreissl, and Constantine Tung, eds., *China's Perception of Peace, War and the World* (Vienna: Schriftenreihe der Landesverteidigungsakademie, 1997), 160–167.

2. Dai Jinhua, "Invisible Women," 258. Judith T. Zeitlin discusses the gender transformations of women warriors, grotesque women, and shrewish women as reflected in Pu Songling's *Liaozhai zhiyi* (Liaozhai's records of the strange). Among the stories of what she calls "the heroic cross-dressers of the romantic traditions," she lists "the famous woman-warrior Mulan, who was immortalized in two separate anonymous ballads *(yuefu)*, one dated possibly as early as the Southern Dynasties, another dated to the Tang. Out of deep filial piety, Mulan donned male clothing and joined the army in her aged father's place. After a spectacular military career, she returned home and voluntarily resumed a female identity. The eponymous heroine of the Tang tale "Xie Xiao'e" is another famous case. Xiao'e disguised herself as a man for several years in order to avenge the murders of her father and husband. After accomplishing her mission, she shaved her head and became a nun. The author, Li Gongzuo (ca. 770–850), does not censor her for violating gender norms; on the contrary, he is explicit about having recorded the tale "to commemorate her extraordinary *female* virtue." Zeitlin, *Historian of the Strange*, 118. See also Joseph R. Allen, "Dressing and Undressing the Chinese Woman Warrior."

3. Ibid., 257–258.

4. Ibid., 259.

5. Ibid.

6. Ibid., 256.

7. From a cross-cultural perspective, one might recall Sue-Ellen Case's study of the image of women warriors as a political invention in ancient Greek public life. With the rise of the polis (city-state), new cultural institutions such as architecture, religions, and myths—"theatre being only one among several"—"became allied with the suppression of women by creating the new gender role of 'Woman,' which served to privilege the masculine gender and oppress the feminine one. At best, the new cultural categories of gender were constructed as categories of difference and polarity. 'Woman' appeared as the opposite of man. This move can best be seen in the new myths and associated architectural descriptions of the Amazons, which conflate female gender with the image of the outsider and with characteristics typical of the male. The Amazons, dangerous but defeated, reverse the 'natural' gender roles. They are warriors who force man to do 'women's' work, such as child-rearing, while the women go off to war. . . . The new architecture of the Acropolis, the civic center of Athens, displays the downfall of the Amazons and the rise of Athena. Central to the new political order, then, is the fall of these women who would defy correct gender associations, and the rise of a woman who would enforce the new image of 'Woman' in the *polis*. This demise of the old images of women and the rise of Athena are central themes in the *Oresteia*." *Feminism and Theatre*, 9–10.

8. Dai Jinhua, "Invisible Women," 263.

9. *Webster's Third New International Dictionary* (1992), s.v. "agency."

10. Charlotte Furth states: "Gendered bodies are understood through culturally specific repertories of gestures and emotions which assign significance to acts and define objects of desire at the level of the erotic; as well as by codes of the masculine and feminine at the level of psychic experience and personal identity. This way of thinking has intersected with feminist analysis of gender as socially constructed through kinship, religion and other roles, and feminist rejection of 'biology' as natural basis of gender distinctions. Accordingly, sex, referring to physical characteristics and biological capabilities, is distinguished from gender, which represents the cultural and social meaning attached to sexed bodies. The 'sexual' becomes that aspect of gender which deals with culturally constructed biological and erotic meanings." Furth, "Androgynous Males and Deficient Females," 1–2.

11. I am grateful to Jennifer Terry, whose graduate course on body politics at Ohio State University helped me think about these issues in the Chinese context.

12. All quotations of the play are from Zhang Lili, *Green Barracks*, in her *Zhang Lili juzhuo xuan* (Selected plays of Zhang Lili), 271. Translations are mine. This play was first written in 1990 and later published in *Xin juzuo* (New drama script) 3 (1992). An English translation by Yuanxi Ma can be found in Xiaomei Chen, ed., *Reading the Right Text*.

13. Michel Foucault, *Discipline and Punish*, 179.

14. Ibid.

15. Ibid., 180.

16. Ibid.

17. Ibid.

18. Ibid., 181–182.

19. *Green Barracks*, along with its many other precursor women warrior texts, provides a modern illustration of what Charlotte Furth describes in Ming and Qing anecdotes of female transformation into males, which were "marked by a total suppression of the sexual in favor of the social" ("Androgynous Males and Deficient Females," 18). Whereas Furth's discussion focuses on the physical and biological transformation from female to male and from male to female, the play under discussion illustrates the symbolic and metaphorical transformation from female to male-like warriors, and from male to female-like caretakers, as shown in the following discussion of Sima Changjiang. I see, however, the same kind of thematic and theoretical concerns, or what Furth terms the "clues to the meaning of female and male as biological and social categories" (1).

20. Zeitlin, *Historian of the Strange*, 127.

21. For a reference on "the practice of cross-gender casting in dramatic scenes of love and desire," see Sue-Ellen Case's discussion of Shakespeare's use of triple-gender crossing and sexuality in his five comedies *Two Gentlemen of Verona*, *The Merchant of Venice*, *As You Like It*, *Twelfth Night*, and *Cymbeline*, in which

"leading 'female' characters pretend to be male." Within this practice, Case argues, "The celibacy of the stage was maintained by omitting the presence of the female body and by representing physical sexuality in the language" (*Feminism and Theatre*, 22).

22. Zhang Lili, *Green Barracks*, 303.

23. Ibid., 319.

24. Ibid., 267.

25. Zeitlin, *Historian of the Strange*, 108. Zeitlin also quotes from Amboise Paré, a French physician of the sixteenth century, to gain a cross-cultural perspective on gender transgression: "Paré contends that shifts in gender are exclusively one-way; it is possible only for women to become men, not the reverse: 'We therefore never find in any true story that any man ever became a woman, because Nature tends always toward that which is most perfect, and not, on the contrary, to perform in such a way that what is perfect should become imperfect' " (Zeitlin, 108). Once again, we see in this Chinese play a deviation from Western norms. Zeitlin's chapter "Dislocations in Gender" also provides an informative discussion on the historiographic and romantic traditions of female and male cross-dressers in the Ming and Qing literatures. For the original quote, see Paré, *Des Monstres et Prodiges*, 30.

26. Elizabeth Weed, "Introduction: Terms of Reference," xv.

27. Yu Qiuyu, "*Xu*" (Introduction), 1.

28. Ibid., 4.

29. All quotations of this play are from Zhang Lili, *Unequal Formula of Life*, in her *Zhang Lili juzuo xuan* (Selected plays of Zhang Lili), 227. Translations are mine. This play was first written in January 1984 and later published in *Xin juzuo* 3 (1985): 19–35.

30. Eide, *China's Ibsen*, 102. Eide's study offers a historical survey of the Chinese reception of Ibsen and Nora in modern Chinese literature and literary criticism. See especially part 2 on "Feminism" and part 3 on "Literature and Criticism," 71–147.

31. Dai Jinhua, "Invisible Women," 259.

32. Weed, "Introduction," xviii.

33. Ibid.

34. Lu Xun, "Nuola zou hou zenyang" (What happened after Nora left home), 1218–1222. This essay was originally presented as a talk at the Peking Women's Normal College, Dec. 26, 1923.

35. Ibsen, *A Doll's House*, 229.

36. Zhang Lili, *Unequal Formula of Life*, 260–261.

37. All quotations of this play are from Zhang Lili, *Mother, You Were Young Once Before*, in her *Zhang Lili juzhuo xuan*, 6, 19. Translations are mine. This play was written in October 1986 and first published in *Xin juzuo* 5 (1988).

38. Zhang Lili, *Mother, You Were Young Once Before*, 13.

39. Jiwei Ci, *Dialectic of the Chinese Revolution*, 97.

40. Ibid.

41. Ibid., 98.

42. Zhang Lili, *Mother, You Were Young Once Before*, 25.

43. Ibid., 45.

44. Cao Yu's *Thunderstorm* was first published in *Wenxue jikan* (Literature quarterly) in July 1934 and was later published as a separate volume with the same title (Shanghai: Shanghai Wenhua shenghuo chubanshe, 1947). For an English translation by Wang Tso-liang and A. C. Barnes, see Cao Yu, *Thunderstorm*.

45. Play quotations are from Zhang Lili, *Homecoming*, in her *Zhang Lili juzhuo xuan*, 108. Translations are mine. This play was first written in March 1986 and later published in *Juben* 4 (1987): 4–35 as *Xueran de fengcai*.

46. Zhang Lili, *Homecoming*, 133.

47. Virginia Woolf, "Professions for Women," 237.

48. Zhang Lili, *Homecoming*, 125.

49. Ibid., 114.

50. Ibid.

51. Ibid., 126.

52. Ibid., 125.

53. Ibid., 134.

54. Ibid., 127.

55. Ibid.

56. I emphasize the word "ugly" while describing this kind of mother, who is "vicious," manipulative, and "evil" in spirit. In plays from the Maoist period, there are instances of "politically incorrect" mothers who are reformed ideologically, such as Wu Yiping in *Winter Jasmine*, discussed in Chapter 4. Even the three corrupt women officials in *If I Were for Real* are portrayed as "misled" characters under the influence of the Gang of the Four, thus needing ideological reeducation by an ideal father, such as Old Zhang. They are not presented as vicious and evil like the mother in *Fission*. See Chapter 4 for a discussion of *If I Were for Real*.

57. Christopher C. Rand, "Introduction," in Cao Yu, *The Wilderness*, trans. Rand and Joseph S. M. Lau, vii–vl, xxxv.

58. Xu Yan's *Fission* was published in *Juben* 10 (1985): 6–25 and premiered by the Guangzhou Drama Troupe (Guangzhou huajutuan). Quotations of this play are cited from Xu Yan's *E, nürenmen* (Oh, Women), 125–192. Translations are mine.

59. Ibid., 138.

60. Ibid., 185.

61. Xu Yan has written at least two other major plays about women's issues. In her *Oh, Women* (published in *Shiyue* 6 [1987]: 175–197, revised in 1989, and premiered by Guangzhou huajutuan), Xu Yan portrayed a series of woman characters ranging from deputy mayor, architect, film star, and feminist advocate. Through their unhappy and failed relationships with men, they constantly ask questions about women and society, women and tradition, and women and independence. One character finds in the weakness of women themselves the perpetuation of traditional values against women. "What is women's right? What is women's liberation? What runs through our blood is an inferiority complex within ourselves that has taken root there for thousands of years. The real enemies of women are indeed women themselves. It will not be until women have finally conquered their own sense of inferiority that they will finally be able to stand on the same level as men" (see Xu Yan, *E, nürenmen*, 71; translations are mine). In another intriguing plot in this play, a woman deputy mayor wants to go to see a controversial play, but is advised not to do so because she will be surrounded by people from the news media right after the theater production; whatever she says about the play will thus be quoted as official support for it (Xu Yan, *E, nürenmen*, 54). Here we see a reenactment of real-life experience onstage, which tremendously affects how theater events are produced and received in contemporary China. In another play entitled *I Am the Sun (Woshi taiyang)*, Xu Yan depicts a group of rock-and-roll singers who believe that art is the most important thing and does not shine without the true love of a woman; both art and woman transcend the worldly, the hypocritical, the ugly, and the political. However, while some women are portrayed as the inspirations of art and music in the new era, another woman (a wife) from one's past has to be presented as short and unattractive to justify a man's right to love other women whenever he sees fit. The short and unattractive woman is thus used as a metaphor wielded against past political history and ideological agendas. In these representations of women, only a certain kind of woman is celebrated, whereas others are degraded. The script of *I Am the Sun* can be found in Xu Yan, *E, nürenmen*, 75–124. This play was first published in *Juben* 5 (1989): 2–17 and premiered by Guangzhou huajutuan.

62. Dai Jinhua, "Invisible Women," 264, 263.

63. Lizbeth Goodman, *Contemporary Feminist Theatres*, 36–37.

64. Zeitlin, *Historian of the Strange*, 130.

Chapter Eight: A Stage in Search of a Tradition

1. A shorter and earlier version of this chapter appeared in *Asian Theater Journal* 18.2 (2000): 200–221. I thank Samuel Leiter, the editor, and two reviewers for their helpful comments.

2. In the history of Western dramatic theory, the first reference to the proscenium theater, or the illusionist theater, can be traced back to Denis Diderot, who stated in 1758: "Whether you write or act, think no more of the audience than if it had never existed. Imagine a huge wall across the front of the stage, separating you from the audience, and behave exactly as if the curtain had never risen" (Denis Diderot, "On Dramatic Poetry." 251). For discussions on the proscenium or illusionist theatre, see Richard Southern, *The Seven Ages of the Theatre*, 179, 240–260, and Oscar Brockett, *History of the Theatre*, 145–147.

3. Geremie Barmé, "A Touch of the Absurd." For a critical study in English, see William Tay, "Avant-garde Theater in Post-Maoist China," and Haiping Yan, "Introduction" to her *Theater and Society*, ix–xlvi. English translations of *Bus Stop* by Kimberly Besio and by Shiao-Ling Yu can be found in Yan, ibid., and Shiao-Ling Yu, *Chinese Drama after the Cultural Revolution*. For a critical study of Gao Xingjian in English, see Kwok-kam Tam, ed., *Gao Xingjian the Soul Searcher: Critical Perspectives on His Works* (Hong Kong: The Chinese University Press, 2001).

4. Tian Xuxiu, ed., *Duoshengbu de juchang* (Multivoiced theater), 30.

5. Ibid., 6.

6. Wei Minglun, "Wo zuozhe feichang 'huangdan' de meng" (I have a very "absurd" dream), 78.

7. Ibid., 79.

8. Fang Qun, "Wuge nanren yigen shengzi" (Five men with one rope), 151–152.

9. Originally published in 1986 in *Xiju yu dianying* (Drama and film), the revised and most recent version of Wei Minglun's *Pan Jinlian* was collected in Wei, *Pan Jinlian*. The following page numbers refer to this edition, 28–29. Translations by David Williams and by Shiao-Ling Yu can be found in Haiping Yan, ed., *Theater and Society*, and Shiao-Ling Yu, ed., *Chinese Drama*.

10. Wei Minglun, *Pan Jinlian*, 62–63.

11. Ibid., 46.

12. Hu Bangwei, "Duiyu lishi he xianshi de shenchen fansi" (Deep reflections on the historical past and contemporary reality), 134.

13. Wei Minglum, *Pan Jinlian*, 58.

14. Ibid., 17.

15. A modern drama version entitled *One Woman and Four Men (Yinü sinan)* was performed in Hong Kong in 1988, with a cast including actors and actresses from Hong Kong, Guangzhou, Shanghai, Sichuan Province, and the United States. An "absurdist Shaanxi opera" *(Qinqiang huangdan ju)* of *Pan Jinlian* was staged by No. 1 Shaanxi Opera Troupe of Xi'an city in July 1986, and by the Shaanxi Opera Troupe of Wulumuqi city in Xinjiang Autonomous Region in the same year. A Shanghai opera *(kunqu)* version was adapted in 1987 in Shanghai by the Shanghai Opera Troupe.

16. Zhang Yihe, "Chuanju *Pan Jinlian* de shiwu yu qushi" (The problem and tendency in *Pan Jinlian*), 162–163.

17. Liu Bingyan, "Guanyu chuanju *Pan Jinlian* he ta yinqi de yindian lianxiang" (On the Sichuan opera *Pan Jinlian* and afterthoughts inspired by it), 86.

18. Ibid.

19. Hu Bangwei, "Duiyu lishi he xianshi de shenchen fansi," 127.

20. Ibid., 128–130.

21. Ibid., 128.

22. An English translation of Ouyang Yuqian's *Pan Jinlian* by Catherine Swatek can be found in Edward M. Gunn, ed., *Twentieth-Century Chinese Drama*, 52–75.

23. Wei Minglun, "Wo zuozhe feichang 'huangdan' de meng," 72–74.

24. Ibid., 71.

25. Ibid.

26. Ibid., 72.

27. Liu Bingyan, "Cixiang fengjian youling de lijian" (A sharp sword against the ghost of feudalism), 90.

28. Zhang Yunchu, "Pan Jinlian xingge lun" (On the personality of Pan Jinlian), 103.

29. Liu Bingyan, "Cixiang fengjian youling de lijian," 93.

30. Huang Shang, "Guanyu Pan Jinlian" (On Pan Jinlian), 97.

31. Xiaomei Chen, *Occidentalism*, 61–67.

32. Liu Shugang's *The Dead Visiting the Living* was first premiered by the China Central Experimental Theatre on June 16, 1985, with Tian Chengren and Wu Xiaojiang as codirectors. Translations are mine. For a more elaborate reading of the play and an English translation by Charles Qianzhi Wu, see Xiaomei Chen, ed., *Reading the Right Text*.

33. *The Nirvana of Gou'er Ye* was written by Jin Yun (Liu Jinyun) and premiered by the Beijing People's Art Theater in 1986. For an English translation of this play, see "Uncle Doggie's Nirvana," translated by Ying Ruocheng, in Martha P. Y. Cheung and Jane C. C. Lai, eds., *An Oxford Anthology of Contemporary Chinese Drama*, 89–147. The Chinese text was published in *Juben* 6 (1986): 4–30.

34. Xiao Ding, "Huaju *Gou'er Ye Niepan* fanying qianglie" (Enthuastic reception of the modern drama *The Nirvana of Gou'er Ye*), 78.

35. *Uncle Doggie's Nirvana*, 115.

36. Xiao Ding. "Huaju *Gou'er Ye Niepan* fanying qianglie" (Enthusiastic reception of the modern drama *The Nirvana of Gou'er Ye*), 78.

37. Quoted from a speech given by Wang Hongtao, published in an article entitled "*Gou'er Ye niepan* wu ren tan" (Five critics on *The Nirvana of Gou'er Ye*), 18.

38. Gao Jian, "Ping 'yongsu shehuixue — shehui xue — shenmei xiju' de sanjieti yanjin moshi" (On the theory of "three-level progression" in Chinese theater from mediocre sociology, to sociology, and to aesthetic theater), 5.

39. Quoted from a speech given by Xu Xiaozhong, recorded in "*Gou'er Ye niepan* wu ren tan," 10.

40. Xiaomei Chen, *Occidentalism*, 130–133.

41. *China Dream* was coauthored by William Huizhu Sun and Faye Chunfang Fei, and codirected by Huang Zhuolin, Chen Tijiang, and Hu Xuehua. It was premiered by the Shanghai People's Theater in July 1987, and was followed by three performances in Beijing in September 1987, during the China Drama Festival. I am grateful to its two authors for providing me with the drama scripts of different versions and other information on its performance and reception. For an informative study of the play, see Claire Conceison, "Between Orient and Occident."

42. Yu Yilin, "Duju meilide xieyi xiyu" (A suggestive play with its own charm), 15.

43. Gao Jian, "*Zhongguo meng* — qite de meng" (*China Dream* — a unique dream), 5.

44. Faye Chunfang Fei, *Huang Zuolin: China's Men of the Theatre*, 156.

45. Qu Liuyi, "Xibu huangtu gaoyuan de huhuan" (The calling of the yellow earth plateau), 5.

46. I am grateful to Faye Chunfang Fei, coauthor of the play, for clarifying this point in her private communication.

47. In Chapter 5, I discussed other plays related to Tiananmen street plays. *Dragon Beard Ditch* can be seen as being situated between illusionist theater, with its emphasis on representations of real life, and indigenous theater, with its use of Beijing dialect, mannerisms, and other regional characteristics. According to Chinese drama critics, *Taiping Lake* was not a very successful attempt at combining

indigenous theater with illusionist theater, which constantly shifts between the living and the dead, past and present, and different geographical locales without any coherent artistic unity.

48. Mei Zi, "Zhongguo huaju yishu yanjuihui wei *Heise de shitou* banfa jiangzhuang" (China Dramatic Art Research Association awarded a prize for *Black Stones*), in *Huaju yishu yanjiu: Heise de shitou zhuanji* (Dramatic art research: A special issue on *Black Stones*), edited by Zhongguo huaju yishu yanjiuhui (The Research Institute of Chinese Modern Dramatic Art), 228. According to Mei, another seminar on the performing art of *Black Stones* was jointly held by the Arts Bureau of Ministry of Culture (Wenhuabu yishuju), China Dramatists Association (Zhongguo xijujia xiehui), *Drama Journal (Xijubao)*, and Central Drama College.

49. *The Rising Sun* was performed by the Amateur Drama Troupe of Daqing Workers and Spouses (Daqing zhigong jiashu jieyu yanchudui) in 1966. For an English translation, see *A New Dawn*, a play produced collectively by Daqing workers and housewives, script written by Sun Weishi, *Chinese Literature* 10 (1977): 3–83.

50. Xian Jihuan and Zhao Yunsheng, *Huaju huangdi Jin Shan zhuan* (A biography of Jin Shan, the emperor of modern Chinese drama), 260–261.

51. Act 1, 4. The quotations are from the Chinese script of *Black Stones* published in *Juben* 2 (1988): 4–25, 36. English translations are mine.

52. "*Hese de shitou* zai Jing yanshu zuotanhui zhaiyao" (Excerpts from Beijing seminar on the performing art of *Black Stones*), in *Huaju yishu yanjiu*, 106.

53. Yang Limin, *Black Stones*, 24.

54. Ibid. An English translation of *Black Stones* by Timothy C. Wong can be found in Xiaomei Chen, ed., *Reading the Right Text*.

55. Arthur Miller, *The Theater Essays of Arthur Miller*, 11; cited by Marvin Carlson, *Theories of the Theatre*, 405.

56. Gao Wensheng, *Zhongguo dangdai xiju wenxueshi* (A history of the dramatic literature of contemporary China), 334–339.

57. Kang Hongxing, "Xianshi zhuyi buduan shenghua de youyi chengguo" (Another achievement in the development of realism), in *Huaju yishu yanjiu*, 138–140.

58. Yang Limin, "Zai shidai mianqian de fansi" (Meditation on our times), in *Huaju yishu yanjiu*, 6–7.

59. Wu Ge, "Zaodong de shitou, duoqing de shitou" (Restless and affectionate stones), in *Huaju yishu yanjiu*, 50–52.

60. "*Heise de shitou* sanren tan" (Three critics on *Black Stones*), in *Huaju yishu yanjiu*, 76–77.

61. For a discussion and an English version of Zhang Mingyuan's *Wild Grass* translated by Philip F. Williams, see Xiaomei Chen, ed., *Reading the Right Text*.

62. Bernard Beckerman, *Dynamics of Drama*, 44–128.

63. He Jiping, *The World's Top Restaurant*. Page numbers refer to the Chinese text, *Tianxia diyilou*, published in *Shiyue* 3 (October 1988): 47–75. An English translation, *The First House of Beijing Duck* by Shiao-Ling S. Yu, can be found in Shiao-Ling S. Yu, ed., *Chinese Drama after the Cultural Revolution*, 423–484. Another translation, entitled *The World's Top Restaurant* by Edward M. Gunn, can be found in Xiaomei Chen, ed., *Reading the Right Text*.

64. Zhang Ziyang, in "*Tianxia diyilou* bian" (Debate on *The World's Top Restaurant*), *Zhongguo xiju* (Chinese drama) 10–12. This is a report by a journalist from *Chinese Drama* on a seminar on *The World's Top Restaurant* attended by alumni of the China Central Drama School.

65. Gu Wei, "*Tianxia diyilou* de qian he hou" (Before and after the production of *The World's Top Restaurant*), 53. As codirector of the play (together with Xia Chun), Gu summarizes how, after earlier setbacks in Beijing-style plays such as *Taiping Lake (Taipinghu)* and *The Stone-Tablet Carrier (Beibeiren)* at the beginning of 1988, the Beijing People's Art Theater was determined to make *The World's Top Restaurant* a smashing success. At a difficult time when more than 130 people had already retired and when the budget was substantially cut due to "theater management reform" *(juyuan tizhi gaige)*, the two directors successfully experimented with a "two-cast system" *(shuang zu zhi)*, in which a senior cast rotated regularly with a junior cast to give the latter more practice on stage. In order to portray old Beijing characters realistically, they read history books and visited chefs and waiters in both the old and the new Quanjude Beijing roast duck restaurants in order to gain firsthand experience of the play's setting. They also enforced a new "bonus system" that rewarded devoted actors and actresses. This sense of running theater as a business, according to Gu, contributed to the success of the production. This report demonstrates Chinese dramatists' persistent efforts to promote theater in a difficult time of economic reform.

66. According to Hu Jinzhao, the famous actor, Lin Liankun's skill in chanting the menu while playing Chang Gui elicited applause unprecedented in the history of Chinese theater. See Hu Jinzhao, "Wei *Tianxia dililou* qiuci" (On the defects of *The World's Top Restaurant*), 33. The videotape of one production also recorded the same warm responses from the audience.

67. I recorded the audience applause live in the videotape made by Beijing dianshitai (Beijing Television Station) in November 1988 and thank Edward Gunn for kindly lending me his tape.

68. Gu Wei, "*Tianxia diyilou* de qian he hou," 54.

69. This phase *qidai shiye* is a Chinese translation of "horizons of literary expectations" in Hans Robert Jauss's *Toward an Aesthetic of Reception*.

70. Dong Naibin, "Wei wu qiong er jiu yu chu" (The more one ponders, the richer the meaning of the play), 14–15.

71. Ibid., 14.

72. Hu Jinzhao, "Wei *Tianxia dililou* qiuci, 33.

73. Dou Xiaohong's speech was recorded in *"Tianxia diyilou* bian," 11.

74. Qu liuyi, *"Tianxia diyilou* de lishi wenhua yishi" (Historical-cultural conscious-ness in *The World's Top Restaurant*), 4. While commenting favorably on what he calls the "historical-cultural consciousness" in the play, Qu rebuts others' claim that it worships too much the old culture, which is unhealthy in developing a "contemporary spirit" in order to move beyond tradition.

75. Zhang Ziyang, in *"Tianxia diyilou* bian," 10. See also Tian Geng and Wu Ling-hua, "Shuishi zhuren shuishi ke" (Who is the guest and who is the owner?), 7–8.

76. He Jiping, *"Tianxia diyilou* xiezuo zhaji" (Afterthoughts on writing *The World's Top Restaurant*), 42–43.

77. Gayle Austin, *Feminist Theories for Dramatic Criticism*, 1.

78. Zou Ting, "Nongdan yiren jian gongli" (Dramatic depth through a balanced depiction), 51.

79. Such an old trope as "the whore with a heart of gold" in modern drama can also be seen in Cao Yu's *Sunrise* (*Richu*, 1935), a "masterpiece" of illusion-ist theater. In this play, the "good-heartedness" of Chen Bailu, an upper-class courtesan, is demonstrated in her persistent attempt to rescue a teenage prosti-tute of the lower class. See Cao Yu, *Richu* (Beijing: Zhongguo xiju chubanshe, 1957), and Tsao Yu, *Sunrise*, trans. A. C. Barnes (Beijing: Foreign Language Press, 1960).

80. Austin Gayle, *Feminist Theories for Dramatic Criticism*, 50.

81. A distinction, however, should be made between *Teahouse* and *The World's Top Restaurant*, which depict the Beijing life-style before 1949, and Li Longyun's imi-tation of Lao She's Beijing-flavored plays, such as *There Is a Small Courtyard* and *Small Well Lane*, which depict events and experiences after 1949. The more bal-anced representations of men and women in Li's plays nevertheless fit almost per-fectly into the construction of women's experience in post-1949 China, which advocates gender equality as an important goal of socialist revolution.

82. Gayle Austin, 51.

83. Although this chapter is organized by discussions on the different styles of theater, I also attempt, at the same time, to give a sense of the chronological de-velopment of events. Those interested in the highlights of theater between the 1988 play *The World's Top Restaurant* and the 1992 play *Birdman* can refer to an informative article on theater events from 1990 to 1991 by Claire Conceison, "The Main Melody Campaign in Chinese Spoken Drama."

84. Quotations are from the Chinese script of *Birdman* by Guo Shixing, pub-lished in *Xin juzuo* (New drama script) 3 (1993): 3–21, 15. Translations are mine.

An English translation of the play entitled *Birdman* by Jane C. C. Lai can be found in Cheung and Lai, eds., *An Oxford Anthology of Contemporary Chinese Drama*, 295–350. For an insightful study in English, see Claire Conceison, "The Occidental Other on the Chinese Stage."

85. Guo Shixing, *Birdman*, 17.

86. Ibid., 4.

87. Ibid., 7. I thank Edward Gunn for providing me with a videotape of *Birdman's* performance by the Beijing People's Art Theater, jointly made by Beijing Television Station and Beijing People's Art Theater in May 1993. My observations on the audience's laughter were based on my viewing of this videotape, recorded live with a theater audience.

GLOSSARY

Chinese characters for authors and titles listed in the Bibliography and Appendix are not repeated here.

A Jia 阿甲
A Jianbo 阿坚伯
A Qing Sao 阿庆嫂
A Ying 阿英
An Ke 安坷
Baguo Lianjun 八国联军
Bai Fengxi 白峰溪
Bai Hua 白桦
Bai hua jiang 白花奖
Bai Jie 白洁
Bai Maonü 白毛女
Bai Wei 白薇
Bai Xiuying 白秀英
Bai Yu 白羽
Bai Yubing 白玉冰
bairi weixin 百日维新
baishi kele 百事可乐
Bali shengmuyuan 巴黎圣母院
Bamian hongqi yingfeng piao 八面红
　旗迎风飘
Ban da lian ke (Bandarenko) 班达连柯

Banhu 板胡
Baochunhua 报春花
Bao'er Kechajin (Pavel Korchaghin)
　保尔·柯察金
Baotong 报童
Baoziwan zhandou 豹子湾战斗
Bawang bieji 霸王别姬
bei huan li he 悲欢离合
Beibeiren 背碑人
Beidahuang 北大荒
Beijing dianshitai 北京电视台
Beijing geming weiyuanhui 北京革命
　委员会
Beijing jingjutuan 北京京剧团
Beijing qingnianhui 北京青年会
Beijing ren 北京人
Beijing renmin yishu juyuan 北京人
　民艺术剧院
Beijing wudao xuexiao shiyan
　baleiwutuan 北京舞蹈学校实验芭
　蕾舞团

benkan jizhe 本刊记者

Bi Lei 毕磊

Bi Mengyang 毕梦扬

bianlian 变脸

biaoxian xianshi shenghuo 表现现实
生活

bingtuan zhanshi 兵团战士

Bishang Liangshan 逼上梁山

Buyi 布依

Cai Yuanpei 蔡元培

caichaxi 采茶戏

Caiyicai, shuilai chi wancan 猜一猜，
谁来吃晚餐

Cao Da 曹达

Cao Keying 曹克英

Cao Yu 曹禺

Cao Zhenxian 曹振贤

Caoyuan ernü 草原儿女

Caoyuan yingxiong xiao jiemei 草原
英雄小姐妹

Cha Li 查理

Chaguan 茶馆

Chahua nü 茶花女

Chang 唱

Chang Bao 常宝

Chang Gui 常贵

Chang zhi shangge gei dang ting
唱支山歌给党听

changqiang 唱腔

Changqing zhilu 常青指路

Chao Gai 晁盖

Chen Bailu 陈白露

Chen Dabei 陈大悲

Chen Kaige 陈凯歌

Chen Liting 陈鲤庭

Chen Qubing 陈去病

Chen Yi chushan 陈毅出山

Chen Yi shizhang 陈毅市长

Chen Yong 陈颙

Chen Yongjing 陈永倞

Cheng Dieyi 程蝶一

Cheng Kang 程康

Chengdu 成都

Chezhan 车站

Chidao zhangu 赤道战鼓

Chuang Guandong 闯关东

Chuangye 创业

chuangzuo zu 创作组

chuanju 川剧

chuanqi 传奇

chuanxi 川戏

Chun zhi ge 春之歌

Chunjie lianhuan wanhui 春节联欢
晚会

Chunliu she 春柳社

Chusheng de taiyang 初升的太阳

Chuxin 出新

Ci Jiwei 慈济伟

cimu 慈母

cunzhang 村长

Da wutai 大舞台

Dachu youlingta 打出幽灵塔

Dachun 大春

Dadan mama he tade haizimen 大胆
妈妈和她的孩子们

Dadui de yewan 大队的夜晚

Dafengge 大风歌

Dahong denglong gaogao gua 大红灯
笼高高挂

Dai 傣

Daqingshi huajutuan 大庆市话剧团

daxie shisan nian 大写十三年

dianxing shijian zhong de dianxing
renwu 典型事件中的典型人物

Didao zhan 地道战

Dihou wugong dui 敌后武工队

Dilei zhan 地雷战

Ding Bao 丁宝

Ding Baoluo 丁保罗

Ding Hong 丁红

Ding Mu 丁牧

Ding Shande 丁善德

Ding Xiaoniu 丁小妞

Ding Yi 丁毅

Ding Yong 丁勇

Diyijie quanguo xiqu guanmo yanchu
dahui 第一界全国戏曲观摩演出
大会

Dong Naibin 董乃斌

Dongbei xiju 东北戏剧

Dongbei xiqu yanjiuyuan 东北戏曲研究院

Dongjin, dongjin 东进,东进

Dongya fengyun 东亚风云

Dou'e yuan 窦娥冤

Du Shijun 杜士俊

Duan Chengbin 段承滨

Duan Xiaolou 段小楼

Duantou tai 断头台

Dujuan 杜鹃

Dujuanshan 杜鹃山

Duoyin 夺印

Dushedan 毒蛇胆

erdu chuangzuo 二度创作

erhu 二胡

Erqin 二琴

Ershi shiji da wutai 二十世纪大舞台

fan "Sirenbang" xiju 反"四人帮"戏剧

Fan Xi 范喜

Fanchaoliu 反潮流

fandong quanwei 反动权威

Fang Haizhen 方海珍

Fang Hongyou 方洪友

Fang Lin 方琳

Fang Ruoming 方若明

Fang Wei 方纬

Fang Xiaoshi 方小诗

Fang Zhenzhu 方珍珠

Fangxia nide bianzi 放下你的鞭子

Fei Chunfang 费春放

Fei xiong meng 非熊梦

Feijialuo de hunyin 费加罗的婚姻

Feng 枫

Feng Yuntong 冯云彤

feng-zi-xiu 封、资、修

Fulian 妇联

Furongzhen 芙蓉镇

gangqin banchang 钢琴伴唱

gangqin xiezou qu 钢琴协奏曲

Gangtie shi zenyang liancheng de 钢铁是怎样练成的

Gao Liangzi 高粱子

Gao Xingjian 高行健

gao-da-quan 高大全

gaohu 高胡

Gaojiasuo huilanji 高加索灰阑记

Gaolou zai tamen shouzhong 高楼在他们手中

Gaoyou 告优

geju 歌剧

geming jiaoxiang yinyue 革命交响音乐

geming xiandai jingju 革命现代京剧

geming xiandai wuju 革命现代舞剧

geming yangbanxi 革命样板戏

Geming ziyou houlairen 革命自有后来人

gengzi peikuan 庚子赔款

gewuju 歌舞剧

gong-nong-bing xiju 工农兵戏剧

gong-nong-bing xueyuan 工农兵学员

Gu Ailan 顾爱兰

Gu Erxin 顾尔镡

Gu Qing 谷青

guan taitai 官太太

Guangzhou budui zhanshi huajutuan 广州部队战士话剧团

Guo Jianguang 郭建光

Guojia da juyuan 国家大剧院

Guojia juyuan 国家剧院

guoju yundong 国剧运动

Harbin jingjutuan 哈尔滨京剧团

haipai jingju 海派京剧

Haiqiao chun 海侨春

Hao Liang 浩亮

Hao Wei 好为

Haohan 好汉

He Jiping 何冀平

He Long 贺龙

He Luting 贺绿汀

He Shifei 何是非

He Shushui 何叔水

He Yun 何芸

He Zizhen 何子珍

heilian 黑脸

Heinu yutianlu 黑奴吁天录

Heiye manman lu changchang 黑夜漫漫路长长

Hezheren de hunli 赫哲人的婚礼

Hong Bingwen 洪炳文
Hong Changqing 洪常青
Hong gaoliang 红高粱
Hong Sao 红嫂
Hong Shen 洪深
Hongdeng zhuan 红灯传
Honghu 洪湖
Hongjun zhanshi xiangnian Mao Zhuxi 红军战士想念毛主席
honglian 红脸
Hongloumeng 红楼梦
Hongse de zhendi 红色的阵地
hongweibing wuhui 红卫兵无悔
Hongyungang 红云岗
Hu Xin'an 胡辛安
Hua Guofeng 华国锋
Hua Mulai 花木兰
Huafang guniang 花房姑娘
huaiju 淮剧
huaju 话剧
huaju minzu hua 话剧民族化
Huang Jusheng 黄菊盛
Huang Shiren 黄世仁
Huang Zi 黄自
Huang Zuolin 黄佐临
huangdan chuanju 荒诞川剧
Huanghe 黄河
Huayuanjie wuhao 花园街五号
huju 沪剧
Huo Wei 霍维
huobao ju 活报剧
Ji Junxiang 纪君祥
Ji Shuping 冀淑平
Jia Baoyu 贾宝玉
Jia Hongyuan 贾鸿源
Jia li tuo po (Kalidasa) 迦利陀婆
Jia Shi 贾氏
jiaji suiji, jianiao suiniao 嫁鸡随鸡，嫁鸟随鸟
Jialilue zhuan 伽里略传
Jiang Hua 江华
Jiang Nan 江南
Jiang Qing 江青
Jiang Shuiying 江水英
Jiang Wen 姜文

Jiang Zemin 江泽民
Jianghan yuge 江汉渔歌
Jiao Juyin 焦菊隐
jiefachang 劫法场
Jie Zi 秸子
Jiliu yongjin 激流勇进
Jin Chongji 金冲及
Jin Qiu 金丘
Jin Shengtan 金圣叹
Jin Zhenjia 金振家
Jing huangzhong 警黄钟
jingji tequ 经济特区
jingju 京剧
jingtang mu 惊堂木
jingwei'er xi 京味儿戏
Jinhua tuan 进化团
jinju 晋剧
Jinpingmei 金瓶梅
Jiujiu ta 救救她
jiuju geming 旧剧革命
jiuju xiandai hua 旧剧现代化
jiuxi 旧戏
juben zuotanhui 剧本座谈会
Judou 菊豆
Juedui xinhao 绝对信号
junshi ticai 军事题材
Juxian 菊仙
juyuan tizhi gaige 剧院体制改革
Kang jinbing 抗金兵
Ke Qingshi 柯庆施
Ke Xiang 柯湘
Ku Jie 苦姐
Kulian 苦恋
kunju 昆剧
Lanxin xiyuan 蓝心戏院
Lao Si 老四
laoshao jieyi 老少皆益
Lei Gang 雷刚
Lei Heng 雷横
Lei Ping 雷平
Leiyu 雷雨
Li Chang 李畅
Li Delun 李德伦
Li Gongzuo 李公佐
Li Honglan 李红兰

Li Huang 李恍

Li Huanzhi 李焕之

Li Jian 李键

Li Kewei 李克威

Li Lifang 李丽芳

Li Ruilan 李瑞兰

Li Shuangshuang 李双双

Li Shuangshuang xiaozhuan 李双双小传

Li Tiemei 李铁梅

Li Wanjiang 李万江

Li Xiangjun 李香君

Li Xiaomei 李晓梅

Li Xiaoxia 李晓霞

Li Xiaozhang 李小璋

Li Xifan 李希凡

Li Xiucheng zhi si 李秀成之死

Li Yuhe 李玉和

Li Zhitian 李志田

Li Zhun 李准

Li Zibo 郦子柏

liangbao yikan shelun 两报一刊社论

liangxiang 亮相

lianhuanhua 连环画

Liao Chengzhi 廖成志

Liaoning renmin yishu juyuan 辽宁人民艺术剧院

Liaozhai zhiyi 聊斋志异

Liebian 裂变

Lin Biao 林彪

Lin Chong 林冲

Lin Daojing 林道静

Lin Jian 林坚

Lin Kehuan 林克欢

Lin Liankun 林连昆

Lin Mohan 林默涵

Lin Shu 林纾

Lin Zhaohua 林兆华

Ling Dake 凌大可

Ling Guiming (Ling Kuei-ming) 凌桂明

Lingtu wanzheng 领土完整

Linhai xueyuan 林海雪原

Liren xing 丽人行

lishi wenhua fansi 历史文化反思

lishiju 历史剧

Liu Changyu 刘长瑜

Liu Chengqi 刘称奇

Liu Feng 柳风

Liu Housheng 刘厚生

Liu Hulian 刘胡兰

Liu Lianying 刘莲英

Liu Mei 柳眉

Liu Qingtang 刘庆棠

Liu Shaoqi 刘少奇

Liu Wencai 刘文彩

Liu Xiuying 刘秀英

Liu Yansheng 刘燕生

Liuboshi jingjutuan 溜博市京剧团

Lu Dingyi 陆定一

Lu Jiachuan 卢家川

Lu Jingruo 陆镜若

Lu Junyi 卢俊义

Lu Mengshi 卢孟实

Lu Shijie 鲁是洁

Lu Xi 路曦

Lu Xiaoyun 鲁小云

Lu Xun 鲁迅

Lu Zhengrong 陆峥嵘

Ludang huozhong 芦荡火种

Lugouqiao 芦沟桥

Luo Danhuan 罗丹华

Luo Fang 罗放

Luo Man 罗漫

Luo Xiaoguang 罗晓光

Luohan qian 罗汉钱

Luotuo Xiangzi 骆驼祥子

Lü Shasha 吕莎莎

Lüse yingde 绿色营地

Ma Ke 马可

Ma Sicong 马思聪

Ma Zhongjun 马中骏

Makesi liuwang lundun 马克思流亡伦敦

Makesi mishi 马克思秘史

Mao Yuanxi Qiusheng 茂苑惜秋生

Mao Zedong Sixiang xuanchuandui 毛泽东思想宣传队

Mei Lanfang 梅兰芳

Meng Yue 孟悦

Miaoling fenglei 苗岭风雷
Ming Ming 明明
Mo Jin 莫瑾
Mu Guiying 穆桂英
mubiaoxi 幕表戏
Nanbatian 南霸天
Nanhai changcheng 南海长城
Nankai xinjutuan 南开新剧团
Nanning 南宁
neibu yanchu 内部演出
nian 念
nianhua 年画
Niaoren 鸟人
Nie Er 聂耳
Niehai bolan 孽海波澜
Nimeng song 沂蒙颂
nongmin qiyejia 农民企业家
Nuola 娜拉
Nüzei 女贼
Ouyang Ping 欧阳平
Ouyang Yuqian 欧阳玉倩
Pan Jinlian 潘金莲
Pan Qiaoyun 潘巧云
Pangzi 胖子
Panshiwan 磐石湾
pantu, tewu, neijian 叛徒,特务,内奸
Pei Guang 裴光
Peng Dehuai 彭德怀
Peng Lun 彭仑
Peng Yin'ger 彭银鸽
Peng Zhen 彭真
Pi'er jinte 皮尔·金特
pingju 平剧[a], 评剧[b]
Pingyuan youji dui 平原游击队
Pingyuan zuozhan 平原作战
Pu Songling 蒲松龄
Qi Yongnian 祁永年
Qian Haoliang 钱浩梁
Qian Shouwei 钱守维
Qiao Yu 乔羽
qidai shiye 期待视野
Qin Xianglian 秦香莲
Qin Xin 秦昕
Qinchai dachen 钦差大臣
qingchun wuhui 青春无悔

Qingchun zhige 青春之歌
Qingdaoshi jingjutuan 青岛市京剧团
qingguan 清官
Qinqiang huangdan ju 秦腔荒诞剧
Qiongren de haizi zao dang jia 穷人的孩子早当家
qipin zhimaguan 七品芝麻官
qishou 旗手
Qiu Jin 秋瑾
Quanguo jingju xiandaixi guanmo yanchu dahui 全国京剧现代戏观摩演出大会
Quanguo meishu zuopin zhanlanhui 全国美术作品展览会
Quanguo wenxue yishu gongzuozhe lianhehui 全国文学艺术工作者联合会
Quanguo xiqu gongzuo huiyi 全国戏曲工作会议
Quanguo xiqu jumu gongzuo huiyi 全国戏曲剧目工作会议
Quanguo zonggonghui 全国总工会
Quanjude 全聚德
quyi 曲艺
Rang shehui zhuyi xin wenyi zhanling yiqie wutai 让社会主义新文艺占领一切舞台
Ren Huaying 任华英
ru lü lin 入绿林
Sandai ren 三代人
sangang wuchang 三纲五常
Sanguo yanyi 三国演义
Sanjiao qian geju 三角钱歌剧
Sanmao 三毛
Sanming, sangao 三名,三高
Sanshang Taofeng 三上桃峰
Sanye 三爷
Sanzimei dengdai Geduo 三姊妹等待戈多
Sha Jishi 沙基石
Sha Sha 沙沙
Sha Yang 沙扬
Shaanxi jinjutuan 陕西晋剧团
Shagong daluo (Shakuntala) 莎恭达罗

Shandong jingjutuan 山东京剧团

Shanghai aihua hujutuan 上海爱华沪剧团

Shanghai jingju yituan 上海京剧一团

Shanghai renmin hujutuan 上海人民沪剧团

Shanghai renmin yishu juyuan 上海人民艺术剧院

Shanghai wudao xuexiao 上海舞蹈学校

Shanghai xiju xueyuan xiju yanjiusuo 上海戏剧学院戏剧研究所

Shanghai xiren yeyu jutuan 上海戏人业余剧团

Shanghai zhichun 上海之春

Shanghaishi gongren wenhuagong yeyu huajutuan 上海市工人文化宫业余话剧团

shaoshu minzu xiju 少数民族戏剧

Shengsi hen 生死恨

Shenyang 沈阳

Shenzhou fenglei 神州风雷

Shi Huifang 史慧芳

Shi Jin 史进

Shi Nai'an 施耐庵

Shi Xiu 石秀

Shi Yongkang 施咏康

Shijie zhizi 世界之子

shishi qiushi 实事求是

shizhuang xinxi 时装新戏

Shouzuyuan 收租院

Shu Chang 舒畅

Shu Yuan 树元

shuangzu zhi 双组制

Shuihu zhuan 水浒传

shuishi zhuren shuishi ke 谁是主人谁是客

shuobai 说白

Sima Changjiang 司马长江

Sitanni tixi 斯坦尼体系

siwu yundong 四五运动

Song Jiang 宋江

Song Jie 宋洁

Songling xin nü'er 松陵新女儿

Song xi dao cun 送戏到村

Su Shu 苏书

Su Shuyang 苏叔阳

Su Zhongyuan 苏重远

Sun Weishi 孙维世

taijun 太君

Taipinghu 太平湖

Tang Cheng 唐成

Tang Jixiang 汤集祥

Tang Na 唐纳

Tang Tiantian 唐恬恬

Tang Xianzhu 汤显祖

Tao Qi 陶其

Taohua shan 桃花扇

Taoyuan 桃园

teyue pinglun yuan 特约评论员

Tian Chengren 田成任

Tian Han 田汉

Tian Jie 甜姐

Tian Xiangxiang 田香香

Tianmei 甜妹

Tiedao youji dui 铁道游击队

Tong 侗

Tongnü zhan she 童女战蛇

tongsu wenhua 通俗文化

Wang Bin 王滨

Wang Dachun 王大春

Wang Guangmei 王光美

Wang Gui he Li Xiangxiang 王贵和李香香

Wang Guolu 王国碌

Wang Jing 王靖

Wang Liping 王力萍

Wang Shifu 王实甫

Wang Xiaonong 汪笑侬

Wang Zengqi 汪曾祺

Wangguo hen 亡国恨

Wanniya jiujiu 万尼亚舅舅

Wanqing xiqu xiaoshuo mu 晚清戏曲小说目

Wei Minglun 魏明伦

wei nüren yu xiaoren nan yang ye 惟女人与小人难养也

Weilai zai zhaohuan 未来在召唤

Weixin meng 维新梦

Wen Bin 文斌

Wen Mu 文牧
Wen Qijiu 温其九
Wen Tianxiang 文天祥
Wencheng Gongzhu 文成公主
Wenhuashi de xin jiemu 文化室的新
　节目
wenyi geming qishou 文艺革命旗手
Wo jia de biaoshu shu bu jin 我家的
　表叔数不尽
Woshi taiyang 我是太阳
Wu Baixin 乌白辛
Wu Dalang 武大郎
Wu De 吴德
Wu Han 吴晗
Wu Peifu 吴佩浮
Wu Qinghua 吴清华
Wu Qionghua 吴琼花
Wu Song 武松
Wu Xiaojiang 吴晓江
Wu Yiping 吴一萍
Wu Zetian 武则天
Wuhan junqu huajutuan 武汉军区话
　剧团
wuju 舞剧
Wuling chun 武陵春
Wutai meishu dui 舞台美术队
Wuwai you reliu 屋外有热流
Xi Mingzhen 席明真
Xi Shi 细石
Xia Chun 夏淳
Xia Jianqing 夏剑青
Xia Yan 夏衍
Xia Yu 夏雨
Xia Zhixian 夏之娴
Xiaji 侠妓
Xi'an 西安
Xian Xinghai 冼星海
xiandai xi 现代戏
Xiao Jia 肖甲
Xiao nüxu 小女婿
Xiao Qi 萧琦
Xiao Qian 萧乾
Xiao Xia 小霞
Xiao xifu 小媳妇
Xiao Yingzi 小英子

Xiaojinzhuang 小靳庄
Xiaonong yishi 小农意识
Xie Junhua 谢俊华
Xie Xiao'e 谢小娥
Xie Zhenhua 谢振华
Xiehe yiyuan 协和医院
Xi'er 喜儿
xiju weiji 戏剧危机
Xile (Schiller) 席勒
Ximen qing 西门庆
xin de zhengzhi quanwei 新的政治
　权威
Xin ernü yingxiong zhuan 新女儿英
　雄传
Xin Luoma 新罗马
xin pingju 新平剧[a]，新评剧[b]
xin wenhua 新文化
xinbian lishiju 新编历史剧
Xing Zhi 辛之
xinju 新剧
xinxi 新戏
xinxing xiju 新兴戏剧
Xiong Fuxi 熊佛西
xiqu 戏曲
Xiqu gaijin hui 戏曲改进会
xiqu gailiang 戏曲改良
Xiwang Chang'an 西望长安
Xixiangji 西厢记
Xu Banmei 徐半梅
Xu Xiaozhong 徐晓钟
Xuanting yuan 轩亭怨
Xue Enhou 薛恩厚
Xue hai chao 学海潮
Xuesuo yi 血蓑衣
xuetong lun 血统论
Yan geming xi, zuo geming ren 演革
　命戏，做革命人
Yan Weicai 严伟才
Yan Yan 燕燕
Yan Xijiao 阎惜娇
Yan'an 延安
Yan'an pingjuyuan 延安平剧院
Yan'an qingnian yishu juyuan 延安青
　年艺术剧院
yanfu 严父

Yang Bailao 杨白老
Yang Guifei 杨贵妃
Yang Kaihui 杨开慧
Yang Shangkun 杨尚昆
Yang Xiangcao 杨香草
Yang Yucai 扬玉才
Yang Yuhuan 杨玉环
Yang Yumin 杨毓珉
Yang Zirong 杨子荣
yangbantuan 样板团
yasu gongshang 雅俗共赏
Ye Fei 叶绯
Ye Wei 叶维
Ye Xiaoxiao 叶肖肖
Ye Yun 叶纭
Ye Zi 叶子
Yecao 野草
Yi Beilin 易北林
yi ku si tian 忆苦思甜
Yidai yinghao 一代英豪
Yimeng song 沂蒙颂
Yingtao shijie 樱桃时节
Yinmou yu aiqing 阴谋与爱情
yinshi wenhua 饮食文化
yitian dengyu ershi nian 一天等于二十年
Yiyuan qian 一元钱
Youhua Hongse Niangzijun 油画《红色娘子军》
Yu Chu 玉雏
Yu Daiqin 于黛琴
Yu Huiyong 于会泳
Yu Luoke 遇罗克
Yu Shangyuan 余上沅
Yu Yongze 余永择
yuefu 乐府
yueju 越剧
yueqin 月琴
yunbai ju 韵白剧
Zai shehui de dang'an li 在社会的档案里
zaju 杂剧
Zhang Dahu 张大户
Zhang Dezhi 张得志
Zhang Geng 张庚

Zhang Guichi 张贵驰
Zhang He 张贺
Zhang Jiaxin 张家新
Zhang Lu 张鲁
Zhang Min 章泯
Zhang Xian 张贤
Zhang Xiaoli 张小理
Zhang Zhixin 张志新
Zhange gu douzhi, kangqiang wei renmin 战歌鼓斗志,扛枪为人民
Zhao Cong 赵聪
Zhao Huan 赵寰
Zhao Taimou 赵态侔
Zhao Xun 赵寻
Zhaoshi gu'er 赵氏孤儿
Zhen Niang 贞娘
Zheng Chenggong 郑成功
Zheng Heng 郑恒
Zheng Jiaxin 郑家新
Zheng Qiang 郑强
Zheng Yi 郑义
Zheng Zhenduo 郑振铎
Zheng Zhengqiu 郑正秋
zhengju 正剧
zhengmian renwu 正面人物
Zhengrong suiyue 峥嵘岁月
zhenjie 贞节
Zhi Xia 知侠
zhijing xin 致敬信
Zhiqin guanfei Zuoshandiao 智擒惯匪座山雕
Zhiqu Weihushan 智取威虎山
Zhongguo dianying xiehui 中国电影协会
Zhongguo ertong yishu juyuan 中国儿童艺术剧院
Zhongguo huajutuan 中国话剧团
Zhongguo jingjuyuan yituan 中国京剧院一团
Zhongguo meng 中国梦
Zhongguo qingnian yishu juyuan 中国青年艺术剧院
Zhongguo renmin jiefangjun haijun zhengzhibu huajutuan 中国人民解放军海军政治部话剧团

Zhongguo xijujia xiehui 中国戏剧家协会

Zhongguo yishu yanjiuyuan huaju yanjiusuo 中国艺术研究院话剧研究所

Zhongguo zuojia xiehui 中国作家协会

zhongjian renwu 中间人物

zhongjun 忠君

Zhongshen dashi 终身大事

Zhongyang shiyan huajuyuan 中央实验话剧院

Zhongyang xiju xueyuan jiaoshi yanchutuan 中央戏剧学院教师演出团

Zhongyang yuetuan 中央乐团

Zhou Lai 周来

Zhou Minghua 周明华

Zhou Yang 周扬

Zhou Zhentian 周振天

Zhu De 朱德

Zhu Zuyi 朱祖贻

Zhuang 壮

Zhuanzhe 转折

Zhuni jiankang 祝你健康

Zigongshi chuanjutuan 自贡市川剧团

Ziyou hou lai ren 自有后来人

Zong Hua 宗华

zujie 租界

Zuolin-youshe 左邻右舍

Zuoshandiao 座山雕

BIBLIOGRAPHY

This bibliography includes journal articles, published drama scripts, and book titles cited in the text and notes. Only one English translation of any particular work is listed. Other translations of the same title can be found in the Appendix.

Adorno, Theodor W. "Freudian Theory and the Pattern of Fascist Propaganda." In Andrew Arato and Eike Gebhardt, eds., *The Essential Frankfurt School Reader*, 118–137. New York: Continuum, 1995.

Adorno, Theodor W., and Max Horkheimer. "The Cultural Industry: Enlightenment as Mass Deception." In Simon During, ed., *The Cultural Studies Reader*, 29–43. London: Routledge, 1993.

Aldridge, A. Owen. *The Reemergence of World Literature*. Newark: University of Delaware Press, 1986.

Allen, Joseph R. "Dressing and Undressing the Chinese Woman Warrior." *Positions* 4.2 (1996): 343–379.

Alleton, Viviane. *Les Chinois et la passion des noms* (The Chinese and their passion for names). Paris: Aubier, 1993.

Althusser, Louis. "Ideology and Ideological State Apparatuses." In his *Lenin and Philosophy and Other Essays*, trans. B. Brewster, 127–186. New York: Monthly Review, 1971.

"An Opera Embodying Mao Zedong's Thought." *Chinese Literature* 10 (1967): 59–64.

Anderson, Benedict. *Imagined Communities: Reflections on the Origin and Spread of Nationalism*. London and New York: Verso, 1983.

Andrews, Julia F. *Painters and Politics in the People's Republic of China, 1949–1979*. Berkeley: University of California Press, 1994.

"Appraisals of 'Compound Where Rent Was Collected.'" *Chinese Literature* 4 (1967): 111–121.

Arendt, Hannah. *The Human Condition*. Chicago: Chicago University Press, 1958.

Austin, Gayle. *Feminist Theories for Dramatic Criticism*. Ann Arbor: The University of Michigan Press, 1990.

Bai, Di. "A Feminist Brave New World: The Cultural Revolution Model Theater Revisited." Ph.D. diss., Ohio State University, 1997.

Bai Fengxi 白峰溪. *Buzhi qiusi zai shui jia* 不知秋思在谁家 (Where is longing in autumn?). In her *Bai Fengxi juzuo xuan* 白峰溪剧作选 (Selected plays of Bai Fengxi), 161–237. Beijing: Zhongguo xiju chubanshe, 1988.

———. *Fengyu guren lai* 风雨故人来 (An old friend comes at a stormy time). In her *Bai Fengxi juzuo xuan*, 83–160. Beijing: Zhongguo xiju chubanshe, 1988.

———. *First Bathed in Moonlight*. In her *The Women Trilogy*. Translated by Guan Yuehua. 104–203. Beijing: Chinese Literature Press, 1991.

———. *Mingyue chu zhao ren* 明月初照人 (First bathed in moonlight). In her *Bai Fengxi juzuo xuan*, 1–81.

———. *Once Loved and in a Storm Returning (An old friend comes at a stormy time)*. In her *The Women Trilogy*, 9–103.

———. "Preface." In her *The Women Trilogy*, 7–8.

———. *Say, Who Like Me Is Prey to Fond Regret* (Where is longing in autumn?). In her *The Women Trilogy*, 204–287. Beijing: Chinese Literature Press, 1991.

———. *The Women Trilogy*. Translated by Guan Yuehua. Beijing: Chinese Literature Press, 1991.

Bai, Hua 白桦. *Unrequited Love: With Related Introduction Materials*. Edited by T. C. Chang, S. Y. Chen, and Y. T. Lin, 21–95. China Study Series No. 3. Taibei: Institute of Current China Studies, 1981.

Bai Hui 白慧. "Chongti wangshi lun shifei" 重提往事论是非 (Recounting the past events in order to judge who is right). *Shanghai xiju* 上海戏剧 (Shanghai drama) 1 (1980): 2–5.

Banu, Georges. "Mei Lanfang: A Case against and a Model for the Occidental Stage." Translated by Ella L. Wiswell and June V. Gibson. *Asian Theatre Journal* 3.2 (1986): 153–178.

Barlow, Tani E. "Theorizing Woman: *Funü, Guojia, Jiating*" (Chinese women, Chinese state, Chinese family). *Gender* 10 (1991): 132–160.

Barmé, Geremie. "A Touch of the Absurd—Introducing Gao Xingjian, and His Play 'The *Bus Stop*.'" *Renditions* 19/20 (1983): 373–377.

Barreca, Regina. *Perfect Husbands*. New York: Doubleday, 1993.

Beckerman, Bernard. *Dynamics of Drama*. New York: Drama Book Specialists, 1979.

Benewick, Robert. "Icons of Power: Mao Zedong and the Cultural Revolution." In Harriet Evans and Stephanie Donald, eds., *Picturing Power in the People's Republic of China*, 123–137. Lanham, Md.: Rowman & Littlefield, 1999.

Benjamin, Walter. "The Storyteller." In his *Illuminations*, trans. Hannah Arendt, ed. and intro. Harry Zohn, 83–109. New York: Schocken Books, 1968.

Blum, Susan D. Review of *Les Chinois et la passion des noms*, by Viviane Alleton. *The Journal of Asian Studies* 54.4 (1995): 1089–1090.

Boal, Augusto. *Theatre of the Oppressed*. London: Pluto Press, 1979.

Boschetto-Sandoval, Sandra Maria. "The Monsters of Her Mind: Reading[Wise] in Amanda Labarca Hubertson's 'Defenseless.'" *College Literature* 22.1 (1995): 119–130, 125.

Boulder Bay. Script produced by the Shanghai Peking Opera Troupe in May 1975. Written by Ah Chien. *Chinese Literature* 4 (1976): 55–122.

Brennan, Timothy. "The National Longing for Form." In Homi K. Bhabha, ed., *Nation and Narration*, 44–70. London: Routledge, 1990.

Brockett, Oscar. *History of the Theatre*. Boston: Allyn & Bacon, 1968.

Brooks, Peter. "Melodrama, Body, Revolution." In Jacky Bratton, Jim Cook, and Christine Gledhill, eds., *Melodrama*, 11–24. London: British Film Institute, 1994.

Brydon, Diana, ed. *Postcolonialism: Critical Concepts in Literary and Cultural Studies*. 5 vols. London: Routledge, 2000.

Butterfield, Fox. "'Gang of 4' and 6 Other Ex-Leaders Go on Trial in China after a Delay." *New York Times*, Nov. 21, 1980 (late ed.), A1, A12.

Cadigan, Rufus J. "Eberhard Wolfgang Möller: Politically Correct Playwright of the Third Reich." In Glen W. Gadberry, ed., *Theatre in the Third Reich: The Prewar Years*, 65–74. Westport, Conn.: Greenwood Press, 1995.

Cai Ruohong 蔡若虹. "Mao Zedong wenyi sixiang de shengli" 毛泽东文艺思想的胜利 (The victory of Mao Zedong Thought). *Hongqi* 红旗 *(Red Flag)* 3 (1966): 26–33.

Cai Tiliang 蔡体良. "Xinchao qifu yi quanquan" 新潮起伏意拳拳 (Surging thoughts and emotions with a sincere heart). *Qingyi* 青艺 *(Journal of the China Youth Art Theater)* 58.2 (1994): 31–36.

Cao Yu (Ts'ao Yü). *Leiyu* 雷雨 (Thunderstorm). Shanghai: Wenhua shenghuo chubanshe, 1936.

——. *Peking Man*. Translated by Leslie Nai-Kwai Lo with Don Cohn and Michelle Vosper. New York: Columbia University Press, 1986.

——. *Thunderstorm*. Translated by Wang Tso-liang and A. C. Barnes. Beijing: Foreign Languages Press, 1958.

——. *The Wilderness*. Translated by Christopher C. Rand and Joseph S. M. Lau. Hong Kong: Hong Kong University Press, 1980.

Cao Yu, Zhao Xun 赵寻, and Zong Fuxian 宗福先. "Yuwu shengchu sanren tan" 《于无声处》三人谈 (Three dramatists on *In a Land of Silence*). *Renmin xiju* 人民戏剧 (People's drama) 1 (1979): 16–20.

Carlson, Marvin. *Theories of the Theatre*. Ithaca, N.Y.: Cornell University Press, 1984.

Case, Sue-Ellen. *Feminism and Theatre*. New York: Methuen, 1988.

"Chairman Mao's Portraits Distributed All Over the World." *Chinese Literature* 11 (1967): 132–134.

Chang, Yung-mei. "Create More Typical Proletarian Heroes." *Chinese Literature* 5 (1974): 102–107.

Chen Baichen 陈白尘. *Dafengge* 大风歌 (*Song of stormy wind*). *Juben* 剧本 (Drama script) 1 (1979): 48–96.

———. "Guanyu *Xiaojing Hutong* de tongxin" 关于《小井胡同》的通信 (Correspondence on *Small Well Lane*). *Juben* 1 (1985): 79–85.

Chen Baichen and Dong Jian 董健. *Zhongguo xiandai xiju shigao* 中国现代戏剧史稿 (A draft history of modern Chinese drama). Beijing: Zhongguo xiju chubanshe, 1989.

Chen Gang 陈刚. "Ping huaju *Mingyue chu zhao ren*" 评话剧《明月初照人》 (On first bathed in moonlight). *Juben* 12 (1981): 40–42.

Chen, Pauline. Review of *Farewell My Concubine* by Chen Kaige. *Film Comment* 30.2 (March-April 1994): 85, 3.

Chen, Xiaomei. "From 'Lighthouse' to the Northeast Wilderness: Growing Up among Ordinary Stars in Maoist China." In Xueping Zhong, Wang Zheng, and Bai Di, eds., *Some of Us: Chinese Women Growing Up in the Mao Era*, 53–76. Piscataway, N.J.: Rutgers University Press, 2001.

———. "Growing Up with Posters in the Maoist Era." In Harriet Evans and Stephanie Donald, eds., *Picturing Power in the People's Republic of China*, 101–122.

———. "Modern Chinese Spoken Drama." In Victor H. Mair, ed., *The Columbia History of Chinese Literature*, 848–877. New York: Columbia University Press, 2001.

———. *Occidentalism: A Theory of Counter-Discourse in Post-Mao China*. New York: Oxford University Press, 1995.

———. "Reading Mother's Tale—Reconstructing Women's Space in Amy Tan and Zhang Jie." *Chinese Literature: Essays, Articles, and Reviews* 16 (1994): 111–132.

———. "Time, Money, and Work: The Flow of Transnational Cultural Capital in the Making of Neo-American Nationalism in Chinese American Women Writers' Autobiography." *Journal of American Studies* 29.2 (1997): 414–421.

———, ed. and intro. *Reading the Right Text: An Anthology of Contemporary Chinese Drama*. Honolulu: University of Hawai'i Press, forthcoming.

Chen, Zidu 陈子度, Yang Jian 杨健, and Zhu Xiaoping 朱晓平. *Sangshuping Chronicles*. Translated by Cai Rong. In Haiping Yan, ed., *Theater and Society: Anthology of Contemporary Chinese Drama*, 189–261. Armonk, N.Y.: M. E. Sharpe, 1998.

———. *Sangshuping jishi* 桑树坪纪事 (Sangshuping chronicles). *Juben* 4 (1988): 4–28.

Cheng, Nien. *Life and Death in Shanghai*. New York: Grove Press, 1986.

Cheung, Martha P. Y., and Jane C. C. Lai, eds. *An Oxford Anthology of Contemporary Chinese Drama*. Hong Kong: Oxford University Press, 1997.

The China Youth Art Theater (1949–1999). A photo album. Beijing: N.P., 1999.

"China's Great Revolutionary Army of Literature and Art Advances Victoriously in the Direction Indicated by Chairman Mao—Literature and Art Workers Hold Rally in Peking for Great Proletariat Cultural Revolution." *Chinese Literature* 2 (1967): 3–17.

Chou, Hsiang-tung. "Let the Flames of Revolution Burn More Fiercely!" *Chinese Literature* 12 (1967): 107–111.

Chou, Katherine Hui-ling. "Staging Revolution: Actresses, Realism, and the New Woman Movement in Chinese Spoken Drama and Film, 1919–1949." Ph.D. diss., New York University, 1997.

Chow, Rey. *Primitive Passions*. New York: Columbia University Press, 1995.

Ci, Jiwei. *Dialectic of the Chinese Revolution*. Stanford, Calif.: Stanford University Press, 1994.

Clunas, Craig. "Souvenirs of Beijing." In Harriet Evans and Stephanie Donald, eds., *Picturing Power in the People's Republic of China*, 47–61.

"Comments on the Ballet *The White-Haired Girl*." *Chinese Literature* 8 (1966): 133–140.

Conceison, Claire. "Between Orient and Occident: The Intercultural Spoken Other in *China Dream*." *Theatre Insight* 10.1 (1999): 14–26.

———. "The Main Melody Campaign in Chinese Spoken Drama." *Asian Theater Journal* 11.2 (1994): 190–212.

———. "The Occidental Other on the Chinese Stage: Cultural Cross-Examination in Guo Shixing's *Bird Men*." *Asian Theater Journal* 15.1 (1998): 87–101.

Conteh-Morgan, John. *Theatre and Drama in Francophone Africa*. Cambridge, Mass.: Cambridge University Press, 1994.

Cui Dezhi 崔德志. *Baochunhua* 报春花 (Winter jasmine). *Juben* 4 (1979): 2–40.

———. "Ganyu shenghuo, chuangzuo caiyou chulu" 干预生活，创作才有出路 (Delving into life is the only way out for literary creation). *Renmin xiju* 11 (1979): 3–4.

———. "Tan *Baochunhua* de xiezuo" 谈《报春花》的写作 (On the writing of *Winter Jasmine*). *Juben* 6 (1979): 24–27.

Dai Jiafang 戴嘉枋. *Yangbanxi de fengfeng yuyu* 样板戏的风风雨雨 (The wind and rain of revolutionary model theater). Beijing: Zhishi chubanshe, 1995.

Dai Jinhua 戴锦华. *Dianying lilun yu piping shouce* 电影理论与批评手册 (A handbook of film theory and criticism). Beijing: Kexue jishu wenxian chubanshe, 1993.

———. "Invisible Women: Contemporary Chinese Cinema and Women's Film." Translated by Mayfair Yang. *Positions* 3.1 (1995): 255–280.

———. *Jingcheng tuwei* 镜城突围 (Breaking the mimetic mirror). Beijing: Zoujia chubanshe, 1995.

———. "Redemption and Consumption: Depicting Culture in the 1990s." Translated by Edward M. Gunn. *Positions* 4.1 (1996): 127–143.

Davis, Natalie Zemon. "City Women and Religious Change." In her *Society and Culture in Early Modern France*, 65–96. Stanford, Calif.: Stanford University Press, 1975.

Davis, Susan G. *Parades and Power: Street Theatre in Nineteenth-Century Philadelphia*. Philadelphia: Temple University Press, 1986.

Deng Xian 邓贤. *Zhongguo zhiqing meng* 中国知青梦 (The dream of the educated youth of China). Beijing: Renmin wenxue chubanshe, 1973.

Denton, Kirk A. "Model Drama as Myth: A Semiotic Analysis of *Taking Tiger Mountain by Strategy*." In Constantine Tung and MacKerras Colin, eds., *Drama in the People's Republic of China*, 119–136. Albany: State University of New York Press, 1987.

———, ed. *Modern Chinese Literary Thought*. Stanford, Calif.: Stanford University Press, 1996.

Deviji, Faisal Fatehali. "Hindu/Muslim/Indian." *Public Culture* 5.1 (1992): 1–18.

Diderot, Denis. "On Dramatic Poetry." In Barrett H. Clark, ed., *European Theories of the Drama*, 237–251. Revised by Henry Popkin. New York: Crown Publishers, 1965.

Dikötter, Frank. *The Discourse of Race in Modern China*. Stanford, Calif.: Stanford University Press, 1992.

Dolan, Jill. *The Feminist Spectator as Critic*. Ann Arbor, Mich.: UMI Research Press, 1988.

———. "In Defense of the Discourse: Materialist Feminism, Postmodernism, Poststructuralism . . . and Theory." *The Drama Review* 33.3 (Fall 1989): 58–71.

Dong Jian 董健. Cong *Xiaoyuan dao Xiaojing* 从《小院》到《小井》(From *A Small Courtyard to Small Well*). *Nanjing Daxue xuebao* 南京大学学报 (Nanjing University academic journal) 4 (1981): 29–36.

Dong Naibin 董乃斌. "*Wei wu qiong er jiu yu chu*" 味无穷而炙愈出 (The more one ponders, the richer the meaning of the play), *Zhongguo xiju* 中国戏剧 (Chinese drama) 8: 1988, 14–15.

Dou Xiaohong 窦晓红. "*Taipinghu de yihan*" 《太平湖》的遗憾 (The disappointment of *Taiping Lake*). *Wenyibao* 文艺报 (*Literary Gazette*) 11 (March 19, 1988): 5.

Du Gao 杜高. "Huaju chuangzuo pengbo fazhan de liunian" 话剧创作蓬勃发展的六年 (On the most booming six years of dramatic creation, 1976–1982). *Juben* 10 (1984): 80–86.

———. "Ping *Mingyue chu zao ren* de munü aiqing jiuge" 评《明月出照人》的母女爱情纠葛 (On the mother-daughter love triangle in *First Bathed in Moonlight*). *Renmin xiju* 12 (1981): 18–19.

Dukats, Mara L. "The Hybrid Terrain of Literary Imagination: Maryse Condés's *Black Witch of Salem*, Nathaniel Hawthorne's Hester Prynne, and Aimé Césaire's Heroic Poetic Voice." *College Literature* (special issue on *Third World Women's Inscriptions*) 22.1 (1995): 51–61.

Duke, Michael S. "Thoughts on Politics and Critical Paradigms in Modern Chinese Literary Studies." *Modern China* 19.1 (1993): 41–70.

During, Simon. "Introduction." *The Cultural Studies Reader*, 1–25. London: Routledge, 1993.

Eberstein, Bernd, ed. *A Selective Guide to Chinese Literature, 1900–1949*. Vol. 4, *The Drama*. Leiden: E. J. Brill, 1990.

Eide, Elisabeth. *China's Ibsen*. London: Curzon Press, 1987.

Engle, Ron. "Theatre in Detmold 1933–1939: A Case Study of Provincial Theatre during the Nazi Prewar Era." In Glen W. Gadberry, ed., *Theatre in the Third Reich: The Prewar Years*, 33–45. Westport, Conn.: Greenwood Press, 1995.

Esherick, Joseph W., and Jeffrey N. Wasserstrom. "Acting Out Democracy: Political Theater in Modern China." *The Journal of Asian Studies* 49.4 (1990): 835–865.

Evans, Harriet. *Women and Sexuality in China*. New York: Continuum, 1997.

Evans, Harriet, and Stephanie Donald. "Introduction." In Harriet Evans and Stephanie Donald, eds., *Picturing Power in the People's Republic of China*. Lanham, Md.: Rowman & Littlefield, 1999.

Fang Qun 方群. "Wuge nanren yigen shengzi" 五个男人一根绳子 (Five men with one rope). In Wei Minglun, *Pan Jinlian: Juben he Juping*, 151–152. Beijing: Sanlian shudian, 1988.

Fanon, Frantz. "On National Culture." In Patrick Williams and Laura Chrisman, eds., *Colonial Discourse and Post-Colonial Theory*, 36–52. New York: Columbia University Press, 1994.

——. *The Wretched of the Earth*. Translated by Constance Farrington. Harmondsworth, UK: Penguin, 1967.

Fayad, Mona. "Reinscribing Identity: Nation and Community in Arab Women's Writing." *College Literature* 22.1 (1995): 147–160.

Fei, Faye Chunfang. "*Huang Zuolin: China's Man of the Theatre*." Ph.D. diss., City University of New York, 1991.

Feilla, Cecilia. "Regarding Women: The Politics of Beholding in Rousseau's 'Letter to M. d'Alembert on the Theatre'." *Women and Performance* 7.1 (1994): 3–18, 4.

Fenan, Ernest. "What Is a Nation?" In Homi K. Bhabha, ed., *Nation and Narration*, 8–22. New York: Routledge, 1990.

"Fenghong jijie hua *feng* ju" 枫红季节话《枫》剧 (Discussing a maple play in the maple season). *Renmin xiju* 11 (1977): 66–72.

Ferguson, Priscilla Parkhurst. *Paris as Revolution: Writing the 19th-Century City*. Berkeley: University of California Press, 1994.

Fighting on the Plain. July 1973 script of the China Peking Opera Troupe. Written by Chang Yung-mei and others. *Chinese Literature* 5 (1974): 3–54.

Firchow, Peter Edgerly. *The Death of the German Cousin*. Lewisburg, Pa.: Bucknell University Press, 1986.

Flanigan, C. Clifford. "Comparative Literature and the Study of Medieval Drama." *Yearbook of Comparative and General Literatures* 35 (1986): 56–97.

Foucault, Michel. *Discipline and Punish: The Birth of the Prison*. Translated by Alan Sheridan. New York: Vintage/Random House, 1979.

Fraser, Nancy. "Introduction." In Nancy Fraser and Sandra Lee Bartky, eds., *Revaluing French Feminism: Critical Essays on Difference, Agency, and Culture*, 1–24. Bloomington: Indiana University Press, 1992.

Freud, Sigmund. *Group Psychology and the Analysis of the Ego*. Translated and edited by James Strachey. New York: Norton, 1959.

Fu, Hu. "Controversial Plays." *Chinese Literature* 8 (1980): 116–119.

Furth, Charlotte. "Androgynous Males and Deficient Females: Biology and Gender Boundaries in Sixteenth- and Seventeenth-Century China." *Late Imperial China* 9.2 (1988): 1–25.

Gadberry, Glen W. "Introduction: The Year of Power—1933." In Glen W. Gadberry, ed., *Theatre in the Third Reich: The Prewar Years*, 1–15. Westport, Conn.: Greenwood Press, 1995.

Gao, Guanlong. *The Attic: Memoir of a Chinese Landlord's Son*. Berkeley: University of California Press, 1996.

Gao Jian 高鉴. "Ping 'yongsu shehuixue—shehuixue—shenmei xiju' de sanjieti yanjin moshi" 评庸俗社会学, 社会学, 审美戏剧的三阶梯衍进模式 (On the theory of "three-level progression" in Chinese theater from mediocre sociology, to sociology, and to aesthetic theater). *Wenyibao* 6 (Feb. 7, 1987): 5.

———. "Zhongguo meng—qite de meng" 《中国梦》: 奇特的梦 (China Dream—a unique dream). *Wenyibao*, Oct. 10, 1987, 5.

Gao Jinxian 高进贤. "Yichu buhe qingli de aiqingxi" 一出不合情理的爱情戏 (A play on love without much logic). *Beijing xijubao* 北京戏剧报 (Beijing drama newspaper) 48 (1982): 2.

Gao Wensheng, 高文升 ed. *Zhongguo dangdai xiju wenxue shi* 中国当代戏剧文学史 (A history of the dramatic literature of contemporary China). Nanning: Guangxi renmin chubanshe, 1990.

Gao Xingjian 高行健. *Chezhan* 车站 (Bus stop). *Shiyue* 十月 (October) 3 (1983): 119–138.

———. *Bus Stop*. Translated by Kimberly Besio. In Haiping Yan, ed., *Theater and Society: Anthology of Contemporary Chinese Drama*, 3–59.

———. *Wild Man*. Translated, introduced, and annotated by Bruno Boubicek. *Asian Theater Journal* 7.2 (1990): 195–249.

Gao Yuqian 高玉倩. "Nuli suzao geming muqin de xingxiang" 努力塑造革命母亲的形象 (Strive to create an image of a revolutionary mother). In Zhongguo xijujia xiehui 中国戏剧家协会 (China Dramatist Association), ed., *Jingju Hongdeng ji pinglun ji* 京剧红灯记评论集 (Collection of essays on Peking Opera *The Red Lantern*), 229–247. Beijing: Zhongguo xijujia chubanshe, 1965.

Ge Yihong 葛一虹 et al., eds. *Zhongguo huaju tongshi* 中国话剧通史 (A history of modern Chinese drama). Beijing: Wenhua yishu cubanshe, 1990.

Geertz, Clifford. *The Interpretation of Cultures*. New York: Basic Books, 1973.

Geming xiangbanxi juben huibian 革命样板戏剧本汇编 (Selected works of model theater). Beijing: Renmin wenxue chubanshe, 1974. Vol. 1.

Gilmartin, Christina K., et al., eds. *Engendering China: Women, Culture, and the State*. Cambridge, Mass.: Harvard University Press, 1994.

Gliatto, Tom. Review of *Farewell My Concubine* by Chen Kaige. *People Weekly* 40.2 (January 17, 1994): 15:2.

Goffman, Erving. *Frame Analysis: An Essay on the Organization of Experience*. Boston: Northeastern University Press, 1973.

Goldman, Merle. *China's Intellectuals: Advise and Dissent*. Cambridge, Mass.: Harvard University Press, 1981.

———. *Sowing the Seeds of Democracy in China: Political Reform in the Deng Xiaoping Era*. Cambridge, Mass.: Harvard University Press, 1994.

———, ed., with Timothy Cheek and Carol Lee Hamrin. *China's Intellectuals* and the State: In Search of a New Relationship. Cambridge, Mass.: Harvard University Press, 1987.

Goldstein, Joshua. "Mei Lanfang and the Nationalization of Peking Opera, 1912–1930." Positions 7.2 (1999): 377–420.

Gong, Xiaoxia. Review of Scarlet Memorial by Gao Guanlong. The China Journal 37 (January 1997): 164–166.

Goodman, Lizbeth. Contemporary Feminist Theatres. London: Routledge, 1993.

Gordon, Linda. "What's New in Women's History." In Teresa de Lauetis, ed., Feminist Studies/Critical Studies, 20–30. Bloomington: Indiana University Press, 1986.

"Gou'er Ye niepan wu ren tan" 《狗儿爷涅盘》五人谈 (Five critics on The Nirvana of Gou'er Ye). Xiju pinglun 戏剧评论 (Drama Review) 1 (1987): 8–18.

Greenblatt, Stephen. Marvelous Possessions. Chicago: University of Chicago Press, 1991.

——. Shakespearean Negotiations. Berkeley: University of California Press, 1988.

Grieder, Jerome B. China's Intellectuals and the State in Modern China: A Narrative History. New York: The Free Press, 1981.

Gu Erxin 顾尔镡 and Fang Hongyou 方洪友. Zhengrong suiyue 峥嵘岁月 (The eventful years). Renmin xiju 1 (1978): 49–82.

Gu Wei 顾威. "Tianxia diyilou de qian he hou" 《天下第一楼》的前和后 (Before and after the production of The World's Top Restaurant). Xiju yanjiu 戏剧研究 (Drama studies) 2 (1989): 53–54.

Guan Hanqing (Kuan Han-Ch'ing) 关汉卿. Injustice to Tou O: A Study and Translation. Translated by Shih Chung-wen. Cambridge: Cambridge University Press, 1972.

"Guanyu Zai shehui de dang'an li deng zuopin de zhengming" 关于《在社会的档案里》等作品的争鸣 (Debate on In the Archives of Society and other works). Wenyibao 9 (1980): 38–41.

Gunn, Edward M. "Shanghai's 'Orphan Island' and the Development of Modern Drama." In Bonnie McDougall, ed., Popular Chinese Literature and Performing Arts in the People's Republic of China, 1949–1979, 36–53. Berkeley: University of California Press, 1984.

——. Unwelcome Muse: Chinese Literature in Shanghai and Peking, 1937–1945. New York: Columbia University Press, 1980.

——, ed. Twentieth-Century Chinese Drama. Bloomington: Indiana University Press, 1983.

Guo Shixing 过市行. Birdmen. Translated by Jane C. C. Lai. In Martha P. Y. Cheung and Jane C. C. Lai, eds., An Oxford Anthology of Contemporary Chinese Drama, 295–350.

——. Niaoren 鸟人 (Birdmen). Xin juzuo 新剧作 (New drama script) 3 (1993): 3–21.

Haigang 海港 (On the docks). Shanghai jingjutuan Haigang juzu 上海京剧团

《海港》剧组 (The production crew of *On the Docks* in the Shanghai Peking Opera Troupe). *Hongqi* (Red flag) 2 (1972): 22–48.

Harrell, Stevan, ed. *Cultural Encounters on China's Ethnic Frontiers*. Seattle: University of Washington Press, 1995.

Harwood, Ronald. *All The World's a Stage*. London: Secker & Warburg, 1984.

———. *Taking Sides*. London: Faber & Faber, 1995.

He Jingzhi 贺敬之. "Baimaonü de chuangzuo yu yanchu"《白毛女》的创作与演出 (The writing and performance of *The White-Haired Girl*). In his *He Jingzhi quanji* 贺敬之全集 (Complete works of He Jingzhi), ed. Wang Zongfa 王宗法 and Zhang Qiyou 张器有, 30–38. Nanjing: Jiangsu renmin chubanshe, 1982.

———. *He Jingzhi quanji* 贺敬之全集 (Complete works of He Jingzhi). Edited by Wang Zongfa and Zhang Qiyou. Nanjing: Jiangsu renmin chubanshe, 1982.

———. "Xin geju *Baimaonü*" 新歌剧《白毛女》(New folk opera *The White-Haired Girl*). In his *He Jingzhi quanji*, 286–292. Nanjing: Jiangsu renmin chubanshe, 1982.

He Jingzhi, Ding Yi 丁毅, and Ma Ke 马可. *Baimaonü* 白毛女 (The white-haired girl). Shanghai: Xinhua shudian, 1949.

———. *The White-Haired Girl*. Translated by Gladys Yang and Yang Hsien-yi. Beijing: Beijing waiwen chubanshe, 1954.

He Jiping 何冀平. *The First House of Beijing Duck*. Translated by Shiao-Ling S. Yu. In Shiao-Ling S. Yu, ed., *Chinese Drama after the Cultural Revolution, 1979–1989*, 423–484. Lewiston, N.Y.: The Edwin Mellen Press, 1996.

———. *Tianxia diyilou* 天下第一楼 (The world's top restaurant). *Shiyue* 3 (1988): 47–75.

———. "Tianxia diyilou xiezuo zhaji"《天下第一楼》写作扎记 (Afterthoughts on writing *The World's Top Restaurant*). *Zhongguo xiju* 中国戏剧 (Chinese drama) 9 (1988): 42–43.

———. *The World's Top Restaurant*. Translated by Edward M. Gunn. In Xiaomei Chen, ed., *Reading the Right Text: An Anthology of Contemporary Chinese Drama*.

He Kongzhou 何孔周. "Yiqu dangde lingdao de zhuangli songge" 一曲党的领导的壮丽颂歌 (A magnificent song of the party's leadership). In *Geming xiandai jingju Dujuanshan pinglun ji* 革命现代京剧《杜鹃山》评论集 (A collection of essays on the revolutionary model Peking opera *Azalea Mountains*), 50–55. Beijing: Beijing renmin chubanshe, 1974.

Hegel, Robert E. "Making the Past Serve the Present in Fiction and Drama: From the Yan'an Forum to the Cultural Revolution." In Bonnie S. McDougall, ed., *Popular Chinese Literature and Performing Arts in the People's Republic of China, 1949–1979*, 197–223. Berkeley: University of California Press, 1984.

"Heise de shitou sanren tan"《黑色的石头》三人谈 (Three critics on *Black Stones*), in *Huaju yishu yanjiu: Heise de shitou zhuanji*, 175–184.

"Heise de shitou zai Jing yanchu zuotanhui zhaiyao"《黑色的石头》在京演出

座谈会摘要 (Extracts from the seminar on the Beijing performance of *Black Stones*), in *Huaju yishu yanjiu: Heise de shitou zhuanji*, 96–112.

Hershatter, Gail. "The Subaltern Talks Back: Reflections on Subaltern Theory and Chinese History." *Positions* 1.1 (1993): 103–130.

Hershkovitz, Linda. "Tiananmen Square and the Politics of Place." *Political Geography* 12.5 (1993): 395–420.

Hong Changying. "Xiongwei zhuangmei, guangcai zhaoren" 雄伟壮美, 光彩照人 (The magnificent and brilliant ballet performance). In *Zan Hongse Niangzijun* 赞《红色娘子军》 (On *The Red Detachment of Women*), 29–37. Guangzhou: Guangdong remin chubanshe, 1970.

Hong Shen 洪深. "Daoyan" 导言 (Introduction). In Hong Shen, ed., *Zhongguo xin wenxue daxi, xiju ji*, 中国新文学大系, 戏剧集 (Compendium of new Chinese literature, drama volume). Shanghai: Liangyou, 1935.

Hongse Niangzijun 红色娘子军 (The red detachment of women). Zhongguo wujutuan jiti gaibian 中国舞剧团集体改编 (Collectively revised by China Ballet Troupe). In *Geming yangbanxi juben huibian* 革命样板戏剧本汇编 (A collection of revolutionary model plays), 1: 207–277.

"*Hongse Niangzijun* huo zuijia gushipian jiang"《红色娘子军》获最佳故事片奖 (*The Red Detachment of Women* won the best movie award). In *Hongse Niangzijun: cong junben dao dianying*《红色娘子军》: 从剧本到电影 (*The Red Detachment of Women*: From script to film). Beijing: Zhongguo dianying chubanshe, 1964.

Howard, Roger. *Contemporary Chinese Theatre*. London: Heinemann, 1978.

Hsia, Adrian. *The Chinese Cultural Revolution*. Translated by Gerald Onn. New York: McCraw-Hill, 1972.

Hsia, C. T. *A History of Modern Chinese Fiction*. 3d ed. Bloomington, Ind.: Yale University Press, 1999.

Hsu, Tao-Ching. *The Chinese Conception of the Theater*. Seattle: University of Washington Press, 1985.

Hu Bangwei 胡邦炜. "Duiyu lishi he xianshi de shenchen fansi" 对於历史和现实的深沉反思 (Deep reflections on the historical past and contemporary reality). In Wei Minglun, *Pan Jinlian: Juben he juping* 剧本和剧评, 124–136.

Hu, Bian. "*Winter Jasmine*: A New Play." *Chinese Literature* 10 (1980): 121–123.

Hu Jinzhao 胡金兆. "Wei *Tianxia dililou* qiuci" 为《天下第一楼》求疵 (On the problems of *The World's Top Restaurant*). *Zhongguo xiju* 8 (1988): 33.

Hu, Wen. "Militant Songs and Dances from Romania." *Chinese Literature* 1 (1972): 89–92.

Hu Yaobang 胡耀邦. "Zai juben chuangzuo zuotanhui shang de jianghua" 在剧本创作座谈会上的讲话 (Talk on the seminar of dramatic scripts). *Wenyibao* 1 (1981): 2–20.

Hu, Ying. *Tales of Translation: Composing the New Woman in China, 1899–1918*. Stanford, Calif.: Stanford University Press, 2000.

Huaju yishu yanjiu: Heise de shitou zhuanji 话剧艺术研究:《黑色的石头》专辑 (Dramatic art research: A special issue on *Black Stones*). Edited by Zhongguo huaju yishu yanjiuhui 中国话剧艺术研究会编 (The Research

Institute of Modern Chinese Dramatic Art). Beijing: Zhongguo huaju yishu yanjiuhui, 1988.

Huang, Martin W. Review of *Columbia Anthology of Modern Chinese Literature*, ed. Joseph S. M. Lau and Howard Goldblatt (New York: Columbia University Press). *The Journal of Asian Studies* 54.4 (1995): 1089–1090.

Huang Mei 荒煤. "Guanyu *Baochunhua* de yifengxin" 关于《报春花》的一封信 (A letter concerning *Winter Jasmine*). *Juben* 11 (1979): 47.

Huang Shang 黄裳. "Guanyu *Pan Jinlian*" 关于潘金莲 (On *Pan Jinlian*). In Wei Minglun, *Pan Jinlian: Juben he juping*, 97–99.

Huang Ti 黄梯. *Gangtie yunshubing* 钢铁运输兵 (Iron transportation troops). Shanghai: Xin wenyi chubanshe, 1954.

Huang Weijun 黄维钧. "Guanche baijia zhengming fangzhen de chenggong shijian" 贯彻百家争鸣方针的成功实践 (A successful practice of carrying out the policy of letting a hundred schools of thought contend). *Renmin xiju* 3.4 (1980): 6, 11.

Huang Wen 黄汶. "Tan 'Zuowei rende Makesi'" 谈 "作为人的马克思" (On "Marx as a human being"). In Zhongguo xiju chubanshe bianjibu, ed., *You zhenyie de huaju juben xuanji*, 561–567.

"Huang Zuolin yu Meiguo liuxuesheng de tanhua" 黄佐临与美国留学生的谈话 (Huang Zuolin's interview with American student Elizabeth Bernard). *Xiju yishu—hu* 戏剧艺术—沪 (Dramatic art—Shanghai) 4 (1983): 1–6.

Hung, Chang-tai. "Female Symbols of Resistance in Chinese Wartime Spoken Drama." *Modern China* 15 (April 1989): 149–177.

———. "Spoken Dramas." In his *War and Popular Culture: Resistance in Modern China, 1937–1945*, 49–92. Berkeley: University of California Press, 1994.

Ibsen, Henrik. *A Doll's House*. In *A Doll's House and Other Plays*. Translated by Peter Watts. 145–232. Harmondsworth, UK: Penguin, 1965.

"Indictment of the Special Procuratorate." *Beijing Review* 23.48 (Dec. 1, 1980): 9–28.

Jauss, Hans Robert. *Toward an Aesthetic of Reception*. Translated by Timothy Bahti, introduced by Paul de Man. Minneapolis: University of Minnesota Press, 1982.

Jiang Rui 蒋瑞. "Jiao Juyin de yishu daolu" 焦菊隐的艺术道路 (The artist journey of Jiao Juyin). In Zhongguo yishu yanjiuyuan huaju yanjiusuo 中国艺术研究院话剧研究所 (The Institute of Modern Chinese Drama in the Chinese Academy of Art), ed., *Zhongguo huaju yishujia zhuan* 中国话剧艺术家传 (Biographies of modern Chinese dramatists), 2: 303–336. 6 vols. Beijing: Wenhua yishu chubanshe, 1986.

Jin Chongji 金冲及, ed. *Zhou Enlai zhuan* 周恩来传 (A biography of Zhou Enlai). 2 vols. Beijing: Zhongyang wenxian chubanshe, 1998.

Jin Qiu 金丘. "Ji *Hongdeng ji* re" 记《红灯记》热 (The popularity of *The Red Lantern*). *Wenyi bao* 3 (Jan. 19, 1991): 4.

Jin Shan 金山. "Xikan zhuo Jiang Qing" 喜看捉江青 (Watching with delight Jiang Qing's arrest on stage). *Renmin xiju* 11 (1979): 8–10.

Jin Yun 锦云. *Uncle Doggie's Nirvana* 狗儿爷涅盘 (*Gou'er Ye niepan*). Translated by Ying Ruocheng. In Martha P. Y. Cheung and Jane C. C. Lai, eds., *An Oxford Anthology of Contemporary Chinese Drama*, 89–147.

Jin Zhenjia 金振家 and Wang Jingyu 王景愚. *Fengye hongle de shihou* 枫叶红了的时候 (When the maple leaves turned red). *Renmin xiju* 6 (1977): 22–50.

———. "Tan *Fengye hongle de shihou* de chuangzuo he yanchu" 谈《枫叶红了的时候》的创作和演出 (On the writing and performance of *When the Maple Leaves Turned Red*). *Renmin xiju* 7 (1978): 37–40.

Joseph, William A., Christine P. W. Wong, and David Zweig, eds. *New Perspectives on the Cultural Revolution*. Cambridge, Mass.: Council on East Asian Studies, Harvard University, 1991.

Judd, Ellen R. "Prescriptive Dramatic Theory of the Cultural Revolution." In Constantine Tung and Colin MacKerras, eds., *Drama in the People's Republic of China*, 94–118. Albany: State University Press of New York, 1989.

Kang Hongxing 康洪兴. "Xianshi zhuyi buduan shenghua de youyi chengguo" 现实主义不断升华的又一成果 (Another achievement in the development of realism). In *Huaju yishu yanjiu: Heise de shitou zhuanji*, 138–140.

Ke Ying 克莹. "Renmin yishujia Lao She" 人民艺术家老舍 (Lao She: Artist of the people). In Zhongguo yishu yanjiuyuan huaju yanjiusuo 中国艺术研究院话剧研究所 (The Institute of Modern Chinese Drama in the Chinese Academy of Art), ed., *Zhongguo huaju yishujia zhuan* 中国话剧艺术家传 (Biographies of modern Chinese dramatists), 2: 50–95. 6 vols. Beijing: Wenhua yishu chubanshe, 1986.

Kinkley, Jeffrey C., ed. *After Mao: Chinese Literature and Society (1978–1981)*. Cambridge, Mass.: Council on East Asian Studies, Harvard University, 1985.

Kraus, Richard. "Arts Policies of the Cultural Revolution: The Rise and Fall of Culture Minister Yu Huiyong." In William A. Joseph, Christine P. W. Wong, and David Zweig, eds., *New Perspectives on the Cultural Revolution*, 219–241. Cambridge, Mass.: Council on East Asian Studies, Harvard University, 1991.

Lan Fan 蓝凡. *Zhongguo xiju bijiao lungao* 中国戏剧比较论稿 (A comparative study of Chinese and Western theaters). Shanghai: Xuelin chubanshe, 1992.

Lan Hai 蓝海. *Zhongguo kangzhan wenyi shi* 中国抗战文艺史 (A history of literature and art during the War of Resistance to Japan). Jinan: Shandong wenyi chubanshe, 1984.

Landes, Joan B. *Women and the Public Sphere: In the Age of the French Revolution*. Ithaca, N.Y.: Cornell University Press, 1988.

Lao She (Lao Sheh) 老舍. *Chaguan* 茶馆 (Teahouse). In his *Lao She wenji* 老舍文集 (Collected works of Lao She), 11: 360–427. 16 vols. Beijing: Renmin wenxue chubanshe, 1987.

———. *Dragon Beard Ditch* 龙须沟 (*Longxugou*). Translated by Liao Hung-ying. Beijing: Foreign Languages Press, 1956.

———. "How I Wrote *Dragon Beard Ditch*." In his *Dragon Beard Ditch*, trans. Liao Hung-ying, 93–97. Beijing: Foreign Languages Press, 1956.

———. *Longxugou* 龙须沟 (Dragon Beard Ditch). In his *Lao She wenji* (Collected works of Lao She), 11: 99–166. 16 vols. Beijing: Renmin wenxue chubanshe, 1987.

———. *The Rickshaw Boy*. Adapted by Mei Ch'ien (Mei Qian) 梅阡. Translated by Richard F. S. Yang and Herbert M. Stahl. New York: Selected Academic Readings, 1964.

———. "Teahouse." *Chinese Literature* 6 (1980): 16–93.

Lauretis, Teresa de. *Technologies of Gender: Essays on Theory, Film, and Fiction*. Bloomington: Indiana University Press, 1987.

"Let the Great Red Banner of Mao Zedong's Thought Fly All Over the World" (Speech by Indonesian delegate F. L. Risakotta). *Chinese Literature* 9 (1967): 83–93.

Li Geng 李庚. "Dui juben *Jiaru woshi zhende* de yijian" 对剧本《假如我是真的》的意见 (A reading of the drama script *If I Were for Real*). *Renmin xiju* 3 (1980): 7–8.

Li Huang 李恍, et al. *Chidao zhangu* 赤道战鼓 (War drums on the equator). Beijing: Zhongguo xiju chubanshe, 1965.

———. *War Drums on the Equator*. Beijing: Foreign Languages Press, 1966.

Li Ke 里克. "Ta ouge nüxing de zunyan" 她讴歌女性的尊严 (She sings a song of woman's dignity). *Xijubao* 戏剧报 (Drama journal) 4 (1984): 48–49.

Li Longyun 李龙云. "*Xiaojing Hutong*" 小井胡同 (Small Well Lane). *Zhongshan* 钟山 (Bell Mountain) 2 (1984): 178–236, 77.

———. *You zheyang yige xiaoyuan* 有这样一个小院 (There is a small courtyard). *Xinhua yuebao, wenzhaiban* 新华月报文摘版 (Xinhua monthly journal [Selections in the humanities]) 9 (1979): 134–157.

Li, Zhisui. *The Private Life of Chairman Mao*. Translated by Tai Hung-chao. New York: Random House, 1994.

Liang Qichao 梁启超. *Xin Luoma* 新罗马 (New Rome). In Zhang Geng and Huang Jusheng, eds., *Zhongguo jindai wenxue daxi*, 1:324–355.

Liang Xin 梁信. *Hongse Niangzijun: Cong junben dao dianying*《红色娘子军》: 从剧本到电影 (The Red Detachment of Women: From script to film). Beijing: Zhongguo dianying chubanshe, 1964.

———. "Renwu, qingjie, aiqing ji qita" 人物, 情节, 爱情及其他 (Character, plot, love, and other issues). In his *Hongse Niangzijun: Cong junben dao dianying*, 228–250.

Liebermann, Sally Taylor. *The Mother and Narrative Politics in Modern China*. Charlottesville and London: University of Virginia Press, 1998.

"Lin Biao Tongzhi weituo Jiang Qing Tongzhi zhaokai de budui wenyi gongzuo zuotanhui jiyao" 林彪同志委托江青同志召开的部队文艺工作座谈会纪要 (The report of the forum on cultural work in the PLA presided over by Comrade Jiang Qing on behalf of Comrade Lin Biao). *Renmin ribao* 人民日报 (People's daily), May 29, 1967.

Lin Kehuan 林克欢 "Zhandou de yishu—Ping huaju *Quan yu fa*" 战斗的艺术: 评话剧《权与法》(Military art—on drama *Power versus Law*). *Remin yishu* 人民艺术 (People's art) 1 (1980): 28–29.

Lin Qingshan 林青山. *Jiang Qing chenfu lu* 江青沉浮录 (The rise and fall of Jiang Qing). 2 vols. Beijing: Zhongguo xinwen chubanshe and Guangzhou wenhua chubanshe, 1988.

Lin Zhihao 林志浩. "Pipan 'Sirenbang' fadong de weigong geju *Baimaonü* de miulun" 批判 "四人帮" 发动的围攻歌剧《白毛女》的谬论 (Criticizing the Gang of Four's condemnation of the folk opera *The White-Haired Girl*). In He Jingzhi, *He Jingzhi quanji*, ed. Wang Zongfa and Zhang Qiyou, 256–276. Nanjing: Jiangsu renmin chubanshe, 1982.

Ling, Kuei-ming. "Taking Up Arms." *Chinese Literature* 7 (1972): 106–108.

Link, Perry. "Ideology and Theory in the Study of Modern Chinese Literature." *Modern China* 19.1 (1993): 4–12.

Liu Bingyan 刘宾雁. "Cixiang fengjian youling de lijian" 刺向封建幽灵的利剑 (A sharp sword against the ghost of feudalism). In Wei Minglun, *Pan Jinlian: Juben he juping*, 89–93.

——. "Guanyu chuanju *Pan Jinlian* he ta yinqi de yidian lianxiang" 关于川剧《潘金莲》和它引起的一点联想 (On the Sichuan opera *Pan Jinlian* and afterthoughts inspired by it). In Wei Minglun, *Pan Jinlian: Juben he juping*, 82–88.

Liu Jin 刘金. "Yiduan chahua—guanyu *pianzi* de xiugai wenti)" 一段插话：关于《骗子》的修改问题 (An interjection—concerning the revision of *If I Were for Real*). *Wenyibao* 2 (1981): 38–39.

Liu Jun 刘军. "Sanshi nian qingxi *Wencheng Gongzhu*" 三十年情系《文成公主》(Thirty years' attachment to *Princess Wencheng*). *Dazhong dianying* 大众电影 (*Popular Film*) 7 (2000): 9–10.

Liu, Kang, "Politics, Critical Paradigms." *Modern China* 19.1 (1993): 13–40.

Liu, Lydia H. "Invention and Intervention: The Making of a Female Tradition in Modern Chinese Literature." In Ellen Widmer and David Der-wei Wang, eds., *From May Fourth to June Fourth*, 194–220. Cambridge, Mass.: Harvard University Press, 1993.

Liu Shugang 刘树纲. *The Dead Visiting the Living*. Translated by Charles Qianzhi Wu. In Xiaomei Chen, ed., *Reading the Right Text: An Anthology of Contemporary Chinese Drama*.

——. "Yige sizhe dui shengzhe de fangwen" 一个死者对生者的访问 (The dead visiting the living). *Juben* 5 (1985): 8–37.

Liu Xiaobo 刘晓波. "Shinian huaju guanzhao" 十年话剧观照 (A survey of the dramatic production of the last ten years). *Xijubao* 1 (1987): 9–11.

Liu Yazi 柳亚子. *Songling xin nü'er* 松陵新女儿 (The new daughters of Songling). In Zhang Geng and Huang Jusheng, eds., *Zhongguo jindai wenxue daxi*, 1:546–548.

Lo, Fulang. *Morning Breeze: A True Story of China's Cultural Revolution*. San Francisco: China Books & Periodicals, 1989.

Longjiang song 龙江颂 (Song of the Dragon River). Shanghaishi *Longjiang song* juzu jiti gaibian 上海市《龙江颂》剧组集体改编 (Collectively revised by the production crew of *The Song of the Dragon River* of Shanghai). *Hongqi* 3 (1972): 36–62.

Louie, Kam. "Love Stories: The Meaning of Love and Marriage in China." In Jeffrey C. Kinkley, ed., *After Mao: Chinese Literature and Society, 1978–1981*, 61–87. Cambridge, Mass.: Harvard University Press, 1985.

Lu, Tonglin, ed. *Gender and Sexuality in Twentieth-Century Chinese Literature.* Albany: State University of New York Press, 1993.

Lu Xun 鲁迅. "Nuola zou hou zenyang" 娜拉走后怎样 (What happened after Nora left home). *Funü zazhi* 妇女杂志 (Women's journal) 10.8 (1924): 1218–1222.

MacFarquhar, Roderick. *The Origins of the Cultural Revolution.* 3 vols. New York: Columbia University Press, 1974–1997.

MacKerras, Colin. *The Chinese Theatre in Modern Times: From 1840 to the Present Day.* Amherst: University of Massachusetts Press, 1975.

"Magnificent Ode to the Worker, Peasant, and Soldier Heroes." *Chinese Literature* 12 (1968): 107–116.

Mannheim, Karl. *Ideology and Utopia: An Introduction to the Sociology of Knowledge.* Translated by Louis Wirth and Edward Shils. New York: Harcourt Brace Jovanovich, 1936.

Mao Yuanxi Qiusheng 茂苑惜秋生 et al. *Weixin meng* 维新梦 (The dream of reform). In Zhang Geng and Huang Jusheng, eds., *Zhongguo jindai wenxue daxi,* 1:356–381.

Mao, Zedong. *Quotations from Chairman Mao Tsetung.* Beijing: Foreign Language Press, 1972.

———. *"Talks at the Yan'an Conference on Literature and Art": A Translation of the 1943 Text with Commentary* by Bonnie S. McDougall. Ann Arbor: University of Michigan, Center for Chinese Studies, 1980.

McDougall, Bonnie S. "Writers and Performers, Their Works, and Their Audiences in the First Three Decades." In Bonnie S. McDougall, ed., *Popular Chinese Literature and Performing Arts in the People's Republic of China, 1949–1979,* 269–304. Berkeley: University of California Press, 1984.

McDougall, Bonnie S., and Kam Louie. *The Literature of China in the Twentieth Century.* New York: Columbia University Press, 1997.

Mei Lanfang 梅兰芳. "Buzai paiyan shizhuang xi" 不再排演时装戏 (Why I stopped performing Peking operas with contemporary costumes). In his *Wutai shenghuo sishi nian* 舞台生活四十年 (Forty years on stage), 3:172–177. 3 vols. N.p. Tianxing chubanshe, 1964.

Mei Zi 梅子. "Zhongguo huaju yishu yanjiuhui wei *Heise de Shitou* banfa jiangzhuang" 中国话剧艺术研究会为《黑色的石头》颁发奖状 (China Dramatic Art Research Association awarded a prize for *Black Stones.* In *Huaju yishu yanjiu: Heise de shitou zhuanji,* 228.

Meng Yue 孟悦. "*Baimaonü* yu Yan'an wenxue de lishi fuza xing (*The White-Haired Girl* and the political complexities of Yan'an literature). *Jintian* 今天 (Today) 1 (1993): 171–188.

———. "Female Images and National Myth." In Tani E. Barlow, ed., *Gender Politics in Modern China,* 118–136. Durham, N.C.: Duke University Press, 1993.

Meng Yue and Dai Jinhua 戴锦华. *Fuchu lishi dibiao* 浮出历史地表 (Emerging from the surface of history). Zhengzhou: Henan renmin chubanshe, 1989.

Miller, Arthur. *The Theater Essays of Arthur Miller.* Edited and introduced by Robert A. Martin. New York: Viking Press, 1978.

Min, Anchee. "Living in a World Turned Upside Down: The Story of a Young Woman Coming of Age during the Chinese Cultural Revolution." Ohio Statehouse Atrium, Columbus, Ohio, Nov. 1, 1996.

———. *Red Azalea*. New York: Berkley Books, 1995.

Mirzoeff, Nicholas. *Bodyscape*. London: Routledge, 1995.

Mittler, Barbara. *Dangerous Tunes: The Politics of Chinese Music in Hong Kong, Taiwan, and the People's Republic of China since 1949*. Wiesbaden: Harrassowitz, 1997.

———. "'Mit Geschick den Tigerberg erobern' Zur Interpretation einer Multiplen Quelle" (*Taking Tiger Mountain by Strategy*: On interpreting a multiple source. In Andreas Eckert and Gesine Kruger, eds., *Lesarten eines globalen Prozesses: Quellen und Interpretationen zur Geschichte der europaeischen Expansion* (Readings of a global process: The history of the European expansion in sources and interpretations). Hamburg: Lit, 1998. 35–51.

Mo Yan 漠雁. "Chifa de gaojian—ping *Zai shehui de dang'an li*" 迟发的稿件—评《在社会的档案裏》(A belated article—on *In the Archives of Society*). *Wenyibao* 9 (1980): 33–37.

Modleski, Tania. "Time and Desire in the Woman's Film." In Gerald Mast, Marshall Cohen, and Leo Braudy, eds., *Film Theory and Criticism*, 536–548. 4th ed. New York: Oxford University Press, 1992.

Mohanty, Chandra Talpade. "Under Western Eyes: Feminist Scholarship and Colonial Discourses." In Chandra Talpade Mohanty, Ann Russo, and Lourdes Torres, eds., *Third World Women and the Politics of Feminism*, 51–80. Bloomington: Indiana University Press, 1991.

Moi, Toril. *Sexual/Textual Politics*. London: Routledge, 1985.

Mowry, Hua-yuan Li. *Yang-pan hsi—New Theater in China*. Berkeley: Center for Chinese Studies, University of California, 1973.

Mu Gong 木公. "Wenge de wenxue jingshen—minzhong lixiang de huihuang shengli" 文革的文学精神—民众理想的辉煌胜利 (The literary spirit of the Cultural Revolution—the triumph of popular idealism). *Zhongshan* 2 (1989): 167–173.

Ng, Mau-sang. *The Russian Hero in Modern Chinese Fiction*. Hong Kong: The Chinese University Press of Hong Kong, 1988.

Nie Haifeng 聂海风. "Sisuo, dan bie wangdiao xinnian" 思索: 但别忘掉信念 (Think deeply but do not lose faith). *Renmin xiju* 9 (1979): 10–11.

Nienhauser, William H., ed. and comp. *The Indiana Companion to Traditional Chinese Literature*. Bloomington: Indiana University Press, 1986.

Okihiro, Gary. "Is Yellow Black or White?" *Margins and Mainstreams: Asians in American History and Culture*, 31–61. Seattle: University of Washington Press, 1994.

On the Docks. On the Docks Group of the Peking Opera Troupe of Shanghai. *Chinese Literature* 5 (1972): 52–98.

Ouyang Yuqian. "*Pan Jinlian*." Translated by Catherine Swatek. In Edward M. Gunn, ed., *Twentieth-Century Chinese Drama*, 52–75. Bloomington: Indiana University Press, 1983.

Pan Kaixiong 潘凯雄 and He Shaojun 贺绍俊. "Wenge wenxue: Yiduan zhide chongxin yanjiu de wenxue shi" 文革文学: 一段值得重新研究的文学史 (Cultural Revolutionary literature: A literary history deserving research once again). *Zhongshan* 2 (1989): 164–166.

Paré, Amboise. *Des Monstres et Prodiges.* Edited by Jean Céard. Geneva: Librairie Droze, 1971.

"Performance by Somali Artists' Delegation." *Chinese Literature* 11 (1967): 137.

Pieke, Frank N. *The Ordinary and the Extraordinary.* London: Kegan Paul International, 1996.

Pinkus, Karen. *Bodily Regimes.* Minneapolis: University of Minnesota Press, 1995.

Pois, Robert A. "The National Socialist Volksgemeinschaft Fantasy and the Drama of National Rebirth." In Glen W. Gadberry, ed., *Theatre in the Third Reich: The Prewar Years,* 17–31. Westport, Conn.: Greenwood Press, 1995.

Ponnuswami, Meenakshi. "Feminist History in Contemporary British Theatre." *Women and Performance* 7.2–8.1 (1995): 287–311.

Pronko, Leonard Cabell. *Theater East and West.* Berkeley: University of California Press, 1967.

"Qianyan" 前言 (Preface). *Qingzhu Zhonghua Renmin Gongheguo chengli ershiwu zhounian quanguo meishu zuopin zhanlan zuopin xuanji* 庆祝中华人民共和国成立二十五周年全国美术作品展览作品选集 (Selected works from the National Art Exhibition in celebration of the 25th anniversary of the founding of the PRC). Beijing: Renmin meishu chubanshe, 1974.

Qixi Baihutuan. 奇袭白虎团 (Raid on the White Tiger Regiment). Shandong sheng jingjutuan 山东省京剧团 (Shangdong Provincial Peking Opera Troupe). *Hongqi* 11 (1972): 26–54.

Qu Liuyi 曲六乙. "Tianxia dililou de lishi wenhua yishi" 《天下第一楼》的历史文化意识 (Historical-cultural consciousness in *The World's Top Restaurant*). *Xiju pinglun (jing)* 戏剧评论—京 (Drama review—Beijing) 5 (1988): 4–5.

———. "Xibu huangtu gaoyuan de huhuan" 西部黄土高原的呼唤 (The calling of the yellow earth plateau). *Xijubao* 3 (1988): 4–5.

———. "Yishu shi zhen-shan-mei de jiejing" 艺术是真善美的结晶 (Art is a crystallization of the truthful, the good, and the beautiful). *Wenyibao* 4 (1980): 49–53.

Raid on the White Tiger Regiment. Shandong Provincial Peking Opera Troupe. *Chinese Literature* 3 (1973): 3–54.

The Red Detachment of Women. Revised collectively by the China Ballet Troupe. *Chinese Literature* 1 (1971): 2–80.

The Red Lantern. Collectively revised by the China Peking Opera Troupe. *Chinese Literature* 8 (1970): 8–52.

"Remould World Outlook." *Chinese Literature* 8 (1970): 3–7.

Renan, Ernest. "What Is a Nation?" Translated by Martin Thom. In Homi K. Bhabha, ed., *Nation and Narration,* 8–22. London: Routledge, 1990.

"Revolutionary Literature and Art Must Serve the Workers, Peasants, and Soldiers." *Chinese Literature* 7/8 (1968): 127–138.

"Revolutionary Songs and Dances, Militant Friendship." *Chinese Literature* 12 (1967): 102–106.

Robortello, Francesco. *In librum Aristotelis de arte poetica explicationes.* Translated by Bernard Weinberg. In his *A History of Literary Criticism in the Italian Renaissance.* 2 vols. Chicago: University of Chicago Press, 1961.

Romney, Jonathan. Review of *Farewell My Concubine* by Chen Kaige. *New Statesman and Society* 7.284 (January 7, 1994): 33, 2.

Ross, James R. *Caught in a Tornado: A Chinese American Woman Survives the Cultural Revolution.* Boston: Northeastern University Press, 1994.

Schechner, Richard. *The Future of Ritual.* London: Routledge, 1993.

Schnapp, Jeffrey T. "Border Crossings: Italian/German Peregrinations of the Theater of Totality." *Critical Inquiry* 21 (1994): 80–114.

Schoenhals, Michael, ed. *China's Cultural Revolution, 1966–1969: Not a Dinner Party.* Armonk, N.Y.: M. E. Sharpe, 1996.

"Seminar Held by the Executive Secretariat of the Afro-Asian Writers' Bureau to Commemorate the 25th Anniversary of Chairman Mao's *Talks at the Yan'an Forum on Literature and Art,* 'Message of Salute to Chairman Mao'," June 5, 1967, Beijing. *Chinese Literature* 9 (1967): 60–65.

"Seminar Sponsored by the Afro-Asian Writers' Bureau to Commemorate the 25th Anniversary of Chairman Mao's 'Talks'" *Chinese Literature* 9 (1967): 48–56.

Senghor, Léopold Sédar. "Negritude: A Humanism of the Twentieth Century." In Patrik Williams and Laura Chrisman, eds., *Colonial Discourse and Post-Colonial Theory,* 27–35. New York: Columbia University Press, 1994.

Sha Yexin. 沙叶新 "Guanyu *Jiaru woshi zhende*" 关于《假如我是真的》 (Concerning *If I Were for Real*). *Shanghai xiju* 6 (1980): 39–42.

———. *If I Were for Real.* Translated by Lee Yee. In Lee Yee, ed., *The New Realism: Writings from China after the Cultural Revolution,* 261–322. New York: Hippocrene Books, 1983.

———. *Jiang Qing and Her Husbands.* Translated by Kirk A. Denton. In Xiaomei Chen, ed., *Reading the Right Text: An Anthology of Contemporary Chinese Drama.*

———. *Jiang Qing he tade zhangfumen* 江青和她的丈夫们 (Jiang Qing and her husbands). Hong Kong: Fanrong chubanshe, 1991.

———. *Jiaru woshi zhende* 假如我是真的 (If I were for real). In his *Yesu, Kongzi, pitoushi Lienong,* 3–79.

———. *Yesu, Kongzi, pitoushi Lienong* 耶稣・孔子・披头士列侬 (Jesus, Confucius, and Lennon). Shanghai: Shanghai wenyi chubanshe, 1989.

Shachiapang. Collectively revised by the Beijing Opera Troupe. *Chinese Literature* 11 (1970): 3–62.

Shajiabang 沙家浜. Beijing jingjutuan jiti gaibian 北京京剧团集体改编 (Collectively revised by Peking Opera Troupe). *Hongqi* 6 (1970): 8–39.

Shen Yi 沈毅. "Xin changzheng lushang de baochunhua" 新长征路上的报春花 (A winter jasmine on the road of a new Long March). *Juben* 7 (1979): 49–51.

Shi Ding 石丁. "Jie lingtang, kuqihuang de beiju" "借灵堂, 哭凄惶" 的悲剧 (A tragedy of making use of the memorial hall to cry over one's own griev-ances). *Renmin xiju* 6 (1979): 26–28.

"Shiying qingkuang bianhua de yixiang zhongda juece" 适应情况变化的一项 重大决策 (A significant decision to adjust to a new situation). *Renmin ribao*, January 29, 1979.

Shram, Stuart R. *The Thoughts of Chairman Mao Tse-Tung*. London: Library 33 Limited, 1967.

Sinfield, Alan. "Royal Shakespeare: Theatre and the Making of Ideology." In Jonathan Dollimore and Alan Sinfield, eds., *Political Shakespeare*, 158–181. Ithaca, N.Y.: Cornell University Press, 1985.

Siu, Helen F., comp. and intro. *Furrows: Peasants, Intellectuals, and the State*. Stanford, Calif.: Stanford University Press, 1990.

"Sixiang jiben yuanze burong weifan" 四项基本原则不容违反 (Four funda-mental principles should not be violated). *Jiefangjun bao* 解放军报 (Libera-tion army daily) April 20, 1981.

Smith, Sidonie, and Julia Watson. "Introduction: De/Colonization and the Politics of Discourse in Women's Autobiographical Practices." In Sidonie Smith and Julia Watson, eds., *De/Colonizing the Subject*. Minneapolis: University of Minnesota Press, 1992.

Snow, Lois Wheeler. *China on Stage*. New York: Random House, 1972.

Snow, Philip. *The Star Raft: China's Encounter with Africa*. London: Weiden-feld and Nicolson, 1988.

Solomon, Richard H., with the collaboration of Talbott W. Huey. *A Revolution Is Not a Dinner Party*. Garden City, N.Y.: Anchor Press, 1975.

Southern, Richard. *The Seven Ages of the Theatre*. New York: Hill and Wang, 1961.

"Speech by Sudanese Delegate—Abmed Mohamed Kheir." *Chinese Literature* 9 (1967): 73–81.

Spence, Jonathan. *The Search for Modern China*. New York: Norton, 1990.

Spillers, Hortense J. "Mama's Baby, Papa's Maybe: An American Grammar Book." *Diacritics* 17.2 (1987): 65–81.

Spivak, Gayatri Chakravorty. "Can the Subaltern Speak?" In Cary Nelson and Lawrence Crossberg, eds., *Marxism and the Interpretation of Culture*, 271–311. Chicago: University of Illinois Press, 1988.

———. "The Rani of Sirmur." In Francis Barker, Peter Hulme, Margaret Iversen, and Diane Loxley, eds., *Europe and Its Others*. Vol. 1, *Proceedings of the Essex Sociology of Literature Conference*. Colchester: University of Essex, 1984.

Strand, David. "Civil Society and Public Sphere in Modern Chinese History." In Roger V. Des Forges, Luo Ning, and Wu Yen-Bo, eds., *Chinese Democracy and the Crisis of 1989*, 53–85. Albany: State University of New York Press, 1993.

"Stride Forward along Chairman Mao's Revolutionary Line on Literature and Art" (Speech by Chinese delegate Chi Pen-yu). *Chinese Literature* 9 (1967): 94–112.

"Striving to Portray the Proletarian Heroes of People's War." *Chinese Literature* 11 (1970): 63–75.

Su Yi 苏移. *Jingju erbai nian gaiguan* 京剧二百年概观 (A two-hundred-year history of Peking opera). Beijing: Beijing yanshan chubanshe, 1989.

"*Taking Tiger Mountain by Strategy*." *Chinese Literature* 8 (1967): 129–181.

Tanaka, Stefan. *Japan's Orient*. Berkeley: University of California Press, 1993.

Tang, Xiaobing. "The Lyrical Age and Its Discontents: On the Staging of Socialist New China in *The Young Generation*." In his *Chinese Modern*, 163–195. Durham: Duke University Press, 2000.

Tay, William. "Avant-Garde Theater in Post-Maoist China: *The Bus Stop* by Gao Xingjian." In Howard Goldblatt, ed., *Worlds Apart: Recent Chinese Writing and Its Audiences*, 111–118. Armonk, N.Y.: M. E. Sharpe, 1990.

Tennenhouse, Leonard. "Strategies of State and Political Plays: *A Midsummer Night's Dream, Henry IV, Henry V, Henry VIII*." In Jonathan Dollimore and Alan Sinfield, eds., *Political Shakespeare*, 109–126. Ithaca, N.Y.: Cornell University Press, 1985.

Terrill, Ross. *The White-Boned Demon*. New York: William Morrow and Company, 1984.

Thakur, Ravni. *Rewriting Gender: Reading Contemporary Chinese Women*. London: Zed Books, 1997.

Tian Geng 田耕 and Wu Linghua 吴令华. "Shuishi zuren shuishi ke" 谁是主人谁是客 (Who is the guest and who is the owner?). *Xiju pinglu (jing)* 5 (1988): 7–8.

Tian Han 田汉. "*Guan Hanqing*" 关汉卿. In *Zhongguo lishiju xuan* 中国历史剧选 (A selected collection of Chinese history plays). Hong Kong: Shanghai Book Co., 1961.

———. "*Kuan Han-ch'ing*" [Guan Hanqing]. Translated by Foreign Languages Press. In Edward M. Gunn, *Twentieth-Century Chinese Drama*, 324–380. Bloomington: Indiana University Press, 1983.

Tian Xuxiu 田旭修, ed., intro., and selection. *Duoshengbu de juchang* 多声部的剧场 (Multivoiced theater). Shijiazhuang: Huacheng wenyi chubanshe, 1988.

"Tiananmen guangchang shijian shuoming le shenme?" 天安门广场事件说明了什麼? (What did the Tiananmen incident tell us?). Editorial. *Renmin ribao*, April 18, 1976.

"*Tianxia Diyilou bian*"《天下第一楼》辨 (Debate on *The World's Top Restaurant*). *Zhongguo xiju* 中国戏剧 (Chinese drama) 11 (1988): 10–12.

"Trial of Lin-Jiang Cliques Begins." *Beijing Review* 23.48 (Dec.1, 1980): 3–4.

Tung, Constantine. "Tensions of Reconciliation: Individualistic Rebels and Social Harmony in Bai Fengxi's Plays." In Constantine Tung and Colin MacKerras, eds., *Drama in the People's Republic of China*, 233–253. Albany: State University of New York Press, 1987.

Van Erven, Eugène. *The Playful Revolution*. Bloomington: Indiana University Press, 1992.

Wagner, Rudolf G. *The Contemporary Chinese Historical Drama*. Berkeley: University of California Press, 1990.

Wan Qingrong 万庆荣. "Lun zichan jieji xiqu gailiang yundong de meixue sixiang" 论资产阶级戏曲改良运动的美学思想 (On the aesthetics of the bourgeois drama reform). In Zhongguo yishu yanjiuyuan yanjiusheng bu 中国艺术研究院研究生部 (Graduate program in the Chinese Academy of Art), ed., *Zhongguo yishu yanjiuyuan shoujie yanjiusheng shuoshi xuewei lunwen ji, xiqu juan* 中国艺术研究院首届研究生硕士学位论文集, 戏曲卷 (Selected essays of M.A. theses of the first-year graduate students of Chinese Academy of Art, opera vol.), 373–400. Beijing: Wenhua yishu chubanshe, 1985.

Wang, Ban. *The Sublime Figure of History.* Stanford, Calif.: Stanford University Press, 1997.

Wang Changfa 王长发 and Liu Hua 刘华. "Mei Lanfang nianpu jianbiao" 梅兰芳年谱简表 (A chronology of Mei Lanfang's life). In Zhou Jichang 周姬昌, *Mei Lanfang yu Zhongguo wenhua* 梅兰芳与中国文化 (Mei Lanfang and Chinese culture), 189–198. Wuhan: Wuhan Daxue chubanshe, 1994.

Wang Chunyuan 王春元. "Ba mei daidao shenghuo zhong lai" 把美带到生活中来 (A play that has brought beauty into life). *Renmin xiju* 11 (1981): 7–10.

Wang Guowei 王国维. *Xiqu lunwen ji* 戏曲论文集 (Selected essays on Chinese traditional opera). Beijing: Zhongguo xiju chubanshe, 1957.

Wang Peigong 王培公. WM 我们 (We). *Juben* 9 (1985): 6–33.

——. WM. Translated by Thomas Moran. In Haiping Yan, ed., *Theater and Society: An Anthology of Contemporary Chinese Drama*, 60–122.

Wang, Ping. *Foreign Devil.* Minneapolis: Coffee House Press, 1996.

Wang, Shuyuan 王树元, et al. *Azalean Mountain.* Peking opera. *Chinese Literature* 1 (1974): 3–69.

——. *Dujuanshan* 杜鹃山 (Azalean Mountain). Peking opera. *Hongqi* 10 (1973): 46–83.

Wang Xingzhi 王行之. "Guanyu shehui xiaoguo de sikao" 关于社会效果的思考 (Some thoughts on social effects). *Juben* 3 (1980): 93–96.

Wang Zengqi 汪曾祺, Yang Yumin 杨毓珉, Xiao Jia 肖甲, and Xue Enhuo 薛恩厚. *Ludang huozhong* 芦荡火种 (Spark in the marshland). Peking opera. Beijing: Zhongguo xiju chubanshe, 1964.

Wang Zheng 王正. "Juzuojia de jianxin he pipingjia de gunzi" 剧作家的艰辛和批评家的棒子 (The playwright's hardship versus the critic's club). *Renmin xiju* 9 (1979): 7–10.

"We Must Revolutionize Our Thinking and Then Revolutionize Sculpture." *Chinese Literature* 4 (1967): 97–110.

Wedeman, Andrew Hall. *The East Wind Subsides: Chinese Foreign Policy and the Origins of the Cultural Revolution.* Washington, D.C.: Washington Institute Press, 1987.

Weed, Elizabeth. "Introduction: Terms of Reference." In her ed., *Coming to Terms: Feminism, Theory, Politics*, ix–xxxi. New York: Routledge, 1989.

Wei Minglun 魏明伦. *Pan Jinlian: The History of a Fallen Woman.* Translated by David Williams with the assistance of Xiaxia Williams. In Haiping Yan, ed., *Theater and Society: An Anthology of Contemporary Chinese Drama*, 123–188.

———. *Pan Jinlian: Juben he juping* 潘金莲：剧本和剧评 (*Pan Jinlian*: Script and criticism). Beijing: Sanlian shudian, 1988.

———. "Wo zuozhe feichang 'huangdan' de meng" 我做着非常"荒诞"的梦 (I have a very "absurd" dream). In his *Pan Jinlian: juben he Juping*, 70–81.

Weiss, Jonathan M. *French-Canadian Theater*. Boston: Twayne Publishers, 1986.

Wen Fu 文夫. *Tiananmen jianzheng lu* 天安门见证录 (A witness history of Tiananmen). 3 vols. Beijing: Zhongguo yanshi chubanshe, 1998.

Wen Guangli 温广鲤. "Du *Xiaojing Hutong*" 读《小井胡同》 (Afterthoughts on *Small Well Lane*). *Juben* 5 (1981): 77.

Wen Jun 闻军. "Wuchanjieji zhuanzheng xia jixu geming de guanghui dianxing" 无产阶级专政下继续革命的光辉典型 (An excellent model of carrying out the continued revolution under the dictatorship of the proletariat). *Hongqi* 2 (1972): 49–53.

Wen Mu 文牧. *Ludang huozhong* 芦荡火种 (Spark in the marshland). Shanghai opera. Shanghaishi renmin hujutuan jiti gaibian 上海市人民沪剧团集体改编 (Collectively revised by the Shanghai People's Shanghai Opera Troupe). Shanghai: Shanghai wenhai chubanshe, 1964.

Wen, Wei-ching, "The Course of a Militant Struggle." *Chinese Literature* 12 (1968): 97–106.

Weng Ru 翁如. "Wo yan Jiang Qing" 我演江青 (My creation of the dramatic character of Jiang Qing). *Xiju yu dianying* 戏剧与电影 (Drama and film) 2 (1981): 8–9.

Williams, Atrik, and Laura Chrisman. "Introduction." *Colonial Discourse and Post-Colonial Theory*, 1–20. New York: Columbia University Press, 1994.

Witke, Roxane. *Comrade Chiang Ch'ing*. Boston: Little, Brown & Company, 1977.

Wong, Jan. "Lunch with Jan Wong." *Globe and Mail*, Saturday, February 12, 2000.

———. *Red China Blues*. Toronto: Doubleday, 1997.

Wong, Sau-ling C. "Denationalization Reconsidered: Asian American Cultural Criticism at a Theoretical Crossroads." *Amerasia Journal* 21.1 and 2 (1995): 1–27.

Woolf, Virginia. "Professions for Women." In her *The Death of the Moth and Other Essays*. Reprint 1984. San Diego: Harcourt Brace Jovanovich, 1942.

"The World's Revolutionary People Enthusiastically Translate and Publish Chairman Mao's Works." *Chinese Literature* 11–12 (1969): 154–156.

Wu Ge 吴戈. "Zaodong de shitou, duoqing de shitou" 燥动的石头，多情的石头 (Restless and affectionate stones). *In Huaju yishu yanjiu: Heise de shitou zhuanji*, 50–52.

Wu Han. *Hai Rui Dismissed from Office* 海瑞罢官 (*Hai Rui baguan*). Translated by C. C. Huang. Honolulu: University Press of Hawai'i, 1972.

Wu, Hong. "Tiananmen Square: A Political History of Monuments." *Representations* 35 (1991): 84–117.

Wu Xue 吴雪. "Xu" 序 (Introduction). Qingzhu Zhonghua Renmin Gongheguo chengli sanshi zhounian xianli yanchu huo chuangzuo yidengjiang juben xuanji 庆祝中华人民共和国成立三十周年献礼演出获创作一等奖剧本选集 (Selected first-prize plays from the PRC thirtieth-anniversary drama festival). 1: 1–9. 3 vols. Chengdu: Sichuan Renmin hubanshe, 1980.

Wu Yuxiao (Wu Yu-hsiao) 武玉笑. *Young Folk in a Remote Region*. Translated by Chang Su. *Chinese Literature* 11 (1964): 3–79.

———. *Yuanfang qingnian* 远方青年 (Young folk in a remote region). Beijing: Zhongguo xiju chubanshe, 1964.

Xi Mingzhen 席明真. "Xiju shi, lun de jianshe zhe" 戏曲史, 论的建设者 (An architect of opera history and theory). In *Zhang Geng A Jia xueshu taolun wenji* 张庚阿甲学术讨论文集 (A collection of critical essays on Zhang Geng's and A Jia's achievements), 8–14. Beijing: Zhongguo xiju chubanshe, 1992.

Xian Jihua 冼济华 and Zhao Yunsheng 赵云生, eds. *Huaju huangdi Jin Shan zhuan* 话剧皇帝金山传 (The biography of Jin Shan: The emperor of drama). Beijing: Zhongguo wenlian chuban gongsi, 1987.

Xiao Ding 肖丁. "Huaju *Gou'er Ye Niepan* fanying qianglie 话剧《狗儿爷涅盘》反应强烈 (Enthuastic reception of the modern drama *The Nirvana of Gou'er Ye*). *Zhuopin yu zhenming* 作品与争鸣 (Literary work and debate) 8 (1987): 78–79.

Xiao Shanxiang Lingzi 萧山湘灵子. *Xuanting yuan* 轩亭冤 (The injustice of Xuanting). In Zhang Geng and Huang Jusheng eds., *Zhongguo jindai wenxue daxi, xijuji.* 1:505–545.

Xie Bo 解波. "Lu Xi zhuan." 路曦传. In Li Hui 李辉 et al., eds., *Zhongguo xiandai xiju dianying yishujia zhuan* 中国现代戏剧电影艺术家传 (Biographies of modern Chinese drama and film artists). 1: 66–83. 2 vols. Nanchang: Jiangxi renmen chubanshe, 1984.

Xie Boliang 谢柏梁. *Zhongguo dangdai xiqu wenxue shi* 中国当代戏曲文学史 (A history of contemporary Chinese operatic theaters). Beijing: Zhongguo shehui kexue chubanshe, 1995.

Xie Junhua 谢俊华. "Zongjie jingyan lizhi gaige" 总结经验立志改革 (Learning from past experiences to promote reform). *Yalujiang* 鸭绿江 (Yalu River) 1 (1981): 58–60, 31.

Xing Yixun 刑益勋. *Power versus Law. Chinese Literature* 6 (1980): 31–91.

———. "Quan yu fa" 权与法. *Juben* 10 (1979): 2–33.

———. "Quan yu fa chuangzuo mantan" 《权与法》创作漫谈 (On writing *Power versus Law*). *Juben* 2 (1980): 55–58.

Xu A'li 徐阿李. "Buneng wei qi er qi" 不能为奇而奇 (One should not try to be "innovative" for the sake of innovation). *Beijing ribao* 北京日报 (Beijing daily). Dec. 6, 1981.

Xu Yan 许雁. *E, nürenmen* 哦, 女人们 (Oh, women). Guangzhou: Huacheng chubanshe, 1990.

———. *Liebian* 裂变 (Fission). In Xu Yan, *E, nürenmen*, 125–192.

———. *Woshi taiyang* 我是太阳 (I am the sun). In Xu Yan, *E, nürenmen*, 75–124.

Yan Entu 严恩图. "Renmin de yishu renmin ai" 人民的艺术人民爱 (People love people's art). In He Jingzhi, *He Jingzhi quanji*, 277–285.

Yan Guoyuan 晏国元. "Laigao laixin zhaideng" 来稿来信摘登 (Letters to the editor). *Juben* 7 (1979): 93.

Yan, Haiping. "Male Ideology and Female Identity: Images of Women in Four Modern Chinese Historical Plays." In Helene Keyssar, ed., *Feminist Theater and Theory*. New York: St. Martin's Press, 1996.

———, ed. and intro. *Theater and Society: An Anthology of Contemporary Chinese Drama*. Armonk, N.Y.: M. E. Sharpe, 1998.

Yan Jiaqi 严家其 and Gao Gao 高皋. *Zhongguo wenge shinian shi* 中国文革十年史 (A history of the ten-year Chinese Cultural Revolution). Hong Kong: Xianggang Dagonbao she, 1986.

Yang Bing 杨炳. "Liange xie Makesi de xi gei women shenme jingyan jiaoxun?" 两个写马克思的戏给我们什么经验教训 (What can we learn from the two plays on Marx?). In Zhongguo xiju chubanshe bianjibu, ed., *You zhengyi de huaju juben xuanji*, 1:227–245.

Yang, Chih-an. "Chairman Mao Is Dearer Than Any Parent." *Chinese Literature* 9: (1968): 58–59.

Yang, Lan. *Chinese Fiction of the Cultural Revolution*. Hong Kong: Hong Kong University Press, 1998.

Yang Limin 杨利民. *Heise de shitou* 黑色的石头 (Black stones). *Juben* 2 (1988): 4–25.

———. *Black Stones*. Translated by Timothy C. Wong. In Xiaomei Chen, ed., *Reading the Right Text*.

———. "Zai shidai mianqian de fansi" 在时代面前的反思 (Meditation on our times). In *Huaju yishu yanjiu: Heise de shitou zhuanji*, 1–8.

Yang, Mayfair Mei-hui, ed. and intro. *Spaces of Their Own: Women's Public Sphere in Transnational China*. Minneapolis: University of Minnesota Press, 1999.

Yang Shixiang 扬世祥. *Zhongguo xiqu jian shi* 中国戏曲简史 (A brief history of Chinese traditional operas). Beijing: Wenhua yishu chubanshe, 1989.

Yang, Xiguang, and Susan McFadden. *Captive Spirits: Prisoners of the Cultural Revolution*. Hong Kong: Oxford University Press, 1997.

Yang Yucai 扬玉才. "*Qixi Baihutuan* shi yichu tixian le Mao Zedong sixiang de haoxi" 奇袭白虎团是一出体现了毛泽东思想的好戏 (*Raid on the White Tiger Regiment* embodies Mao Zedong Thought). *Hongqi* 9 (1967): 38–41.

Yao Wenyuan 姚文元. "Ping *Hai Rui Baiguan*" 评《海瑞罢官》(On *Hai Rui Dismissed from Office*). *Wenhuibao* 文汇报 (Wenhui newspaper), Nov. 10, 1965.

Yee, Lee, ed., *The New Realism: Writings from China after the Cultural Revolution*. New York: Hippocrene Books, 1983.

"Yindao daxuesheng zoujin jingju" 引导大学生走进京剧 (Introducing Peking opera to university students). *Xiju dianyingbao, Liyuan zhoukan* 戏剧电影报 梨园周刊 (Drama and film by-weekly, Peach Garden weekly) 9 (1999). (Electronic edition, www.chinacue.cn.net).

Ying, Ruocheng. "Lao She and His '*Tea House.*'" *Chinese Literature* 6 (1983): 3–11.

"Yixiang zhongda de wuchuan jieji zhengce" 一项重大的无产阶级政策 (A significant proletarian policy). *Renmin ribao*, Nov. 17, 1978.

Youhua Hongse Niangzijun 油画《红色娘子军》 (Oil paintings of *The Red Detachment of Women*). Shanghai: Shanghai renmin chubanshe, 1972.

Yu, Lu-yuan. "The Revolutionary Ballet '*The White-Haired Girl.*'" *Chinese Literature* 9 (1968): 58–59.

Yu Qiuyu 余秋雨. "Xu" 序 (Introduction). In Zhang Lili, *Zhang Lili juzuo xuan* 张莉莉剧作选 (Selected plays of Zhang Lili), 3–7. Beijing: Zhongguo xiju chubanshe, 1992.

Yu, Shiao-Ling S., ed. and intro. *Chinese Drama after the Cultural Revolution, 1979–1989.* Lewiston, N.Y.: The Edwin Mellen Press, 1996.

Yu Xiao 宇晓 and Cheng Bo 程波. "Renlei jiefang wo jiefang" 人类解放我解放 (The liberation of mankind means my own liberation). In *Jingtian dongde de weida geming chuangju* 惊天动地的伟大革命创举 (An earth-shaking great revolutionary event), 54–67. Hong Kong: Sanlian, 1970.

Yu Yilin 余义林. "Duju meilide xieyi xiju" 独具魅力的写意戏剧 (A suggestive play with its own charm). *Xijubao* 11 (1987): 15–16.

Yuan Shaojie 袁少杰. "Cong sange pianziju de bijiao zhong kan fengciju de chuangzuo" 从三个骗子剧的比较中看讽刺剧的创作 (On the dramatic creation of satirical plays through a comparative study of three swindler plays). *Dandong shizhuan xuebao* 丹东师专学报 (The academic journal of Dandong Normal Institute) 1 (1982): 22–32.

Yuan Ying 袁鹰. "Minxin—du *Tiananmen shichao*" 民心: 读天安门诗抄 (The will of the people—readings from *Collections of Tiananmen Poetry*). *Shanghai wenyi* 上海文艺 (Shanghai literature and art) 12 (1978): 91–93.

Yue, Ming-Bao. "Gendering the Origins of Modern Chinese Fiction." In Tonglin Lu, ed., *Gender and Sexuality in Twentieth-Century Chinese Literature and Society*, 47–65. Albany: State University of New York Press, 1993.

Yung, Bell. "Model Opera as Model: From *Shajiabang* to *Sagabong*." In Bonnie S. McDougall, ed., *Popular Chinese Literature and Performing Arts in the People's Republic of China, 1949–1979*, 144–164. Berkeley: University of California Press, 1984.

Zarrow, Peter. "Meaning of China's Cultural Revolution: Memoirs of Exile." *Positions* 7.1 (1999): 165–191.

Zeitlin, Judith T. *Historian of the Strange*. Stanford, Calif.: Stanford University Press, 1993.

Zhang Donggang 张东钢. "Xiju bu jinjin zuowei xingshi" 戏剧不仅仅作为形式 (Drama is not just about form). *Shanghai xiju* 6 (1988): 34–35.

Zhang Geng 张庚 and Huang Jusheng 黄菊盛. "Daoyan" 导言 (Introduction). In Zhang Geng and Huang Jusheng, eds., *Zhongguo jindai wenxue daxi*, 1:1–20.

——, eds. *Zhongguo jindai wenxue daxi (1840–1919) xijuji*, 中国近代文学大系, 戏剧集 (A treasury of modern Chinese literature, 5th division: *Drama*), 2 vols. Shanghai: Shanghai shudian, 1995.

Zhang Lili 张莉莉. *Green Barracks*. Translated by Yuanxi Ma. In Xiaomei Chen, ed., *Reading the Right Text: An Anthology of Contemporary Chinese Drama*.

——. *Gui qu lai* 归去来 (Homecoming). In her *Zhang Lili juzuo xuan*, 61–134.

——. *Lüsi yingdi* 绿色营地 (Green barracks). In her *Zhang Lili juzuo xuan*, 263–327.

——. *Mama, ni ye ceng nianqing* 妈妈，你也曾年轻 (Mother, you were young once before). In her *Zhang Lili juzuo xuan*, 3–60.

——. *Rensheng budengshi* 人生不等式 (Unequal formula of life). In her *Zhang Lili juzuo xuan*, 215–261.

——. *Zhang Lili juzuo xuan* 张莉莉剧作选 (Selected plays of Zhang Lili). Beijing: Zhongguo xiju chubanshe, 1992.

Zhang, Longxi. "Out of the Cultural Ghetto." *Modern China* 19.1 (1993): 71–101.

Zhang Yihe 章饴和. "Chuanju *Pan Jinlian* de shiwu yu qushi" 关于川剧《潘金莲》的失误与趋势 (The problem and tendency in *Pan Jinlian*). In Wei Minglun, *Pan Jinlian: Juben he juping*, 156–164.

Zhang, Yingjin. "The Institutionalization of Modern Chinese Literary History in China, 1922–1980." *Modern China* 20.3 (1994): 347–377.

Zhang Yongmei 张永枚. *Pingyuan zuozhan* 平原作战 *Geming yangbanxi juben huibian* 革命样板戏剧本汇编 (An anthology of revolutionary model plays), 1: 539–602. Beijing: Renmin wenxue chubanshe, 1974.

Zhang Yunchu 张云初. "Pan Jinlian xingge lun" 潘金莲性格论 (On the personality of Pan Jinlian). In Wei Minglun, *Pan Jinlian: Juben he juping*, 100–112.

Zhang Zhizhong 张志忠. "Lishi zhi mi he qingchun zhi wu" 历史之谜和青春之误 (The mystery of history and the mistakes of youth). *Zhongguo yanjiu yuekan* 中国研究月刊 (A monthly journal of SINICA research), August 1996, 64–70.

Zhang Zhong 张钟 et al. *Dangdai wenxue gaiguan* 当代文学概观 (A survey of contemporary literature). Beijing: Beijing Daxue chubanshe, 1980.

Zhao Cong 赵聪. *Zhongguo dalu de xiqu gaige* 中国大陆的戏曲改革 (Opera reform in the mainland). Hong Kong: Xianggang Zhongwen Daxue chubanshe, 1968.

Zhao Guoqing 赵国庆. "*Jiujiu ta* chuangzuo zhong de yixie xiangfa"《救救他》创作中的一些想法 (Some thoughts during the writing of *Save Her*). *Juben* 1 (1980): 79–83.

Zhao Huan 赵寰 and Jin Jingmai 金敬迈. "Shenzhou fenglei" 神州风雷 (The tempest in the divine land). *Juben* 11 (1979): 4–37.

Zhao Xinxiong 赵梓雄. "Weilai zai zhaohuan" 未来在召唤 (The future is calling on us). *Juben* 8 (1979): 2–34.

Zheng Huaizhi 郑怀之. "Guanyu *Jiaru* yanchu yihou de yixie qingkuang" 关于《假如》演出以后的一些情况 (Some facts concerning what happened after the performance of *If I Were for Real*). *Wenhuibao*, Feb. 23, 1981.

Zhiqu Weihushan 智取威虎山. Shanghai jingjutuan *Zhiqu Weihushan* juzu jiti gaibian 上海京剧团《智取威虎山》剧组集体改编 (Collectively revised by the production crew of *Taking Tiger Mountain by Strategy* of the Shanghai Peking Opera Troupe). In *Geming yangbanxi juben huibian* 革命样板戏剧本汇编 (A collection of revolutionary model plays). 1: 7–73. Beijing: Renmin chubanshe, 1974.

"Zhongguo Gongchandang di shiyijie zhongyang weiyuanhui diliuci quanti huiyi gongbao" 中国共产党第十一届中央委员会第六次全体会议公报 (Communiqué of the Sixth Plenum of the Eleventh Central Committee of the Chinese Communist Party). *Renmin ribao*, June 30, 1981.

"Zhongguo Gongchandang di shiyijie zhongyang weiyuanhui disanci quanti huiyi gongbao" 中国共产党第十一届中央委员会第三次全体会议公报 (Communiqué of the Third Plenum of the Eleventh Central Committee of the Chinese Communist Party). *Renmin ribao*, Dec. 24, 1978.

"Zhongguo Gongchandang di shiyijie zhongyang weiyuanhui diwuci quanti huiyi gongbao" 中国共产党第十一届中央委员会第五次全体会议公报 (Communiqué of the Fifth Plenum of the Eleventh Central Committee of the Chinese Communist Party). *Renmin ribao*, March 1, 1980.

Zhongguo jingjutuan *Hongdeng ji* juzu 中国京剧团《红灯记》剧组 (The *Red Lantern* cast at China Peking Opera Troupe). "Wei suzao wuchan jieji de yingxiong dianxing er douzheng" 为塑造无产阶级的英雄典型而斗争 (Strive for the creation of proletarian model heroes). *Hongqi* 5 (1970): 47–56.

Zhongguo jingjutuan jiti gaibian 中国京剧团集体改编 (Collectively revised by the China Peking Opera Troupe). *Hongdeng ji* 红灯记 (The red lantern). *Hongqi* 8 (1970): 8–43.

Zhongguo xiju chubanshe bianjibu, ed. 中国戏剧出版社编缉部 *You zhengyi de huaju juben xuanji* 有争议的话剧剧本选集 (Selected controversial plays). 2 vols. Beijing: Zhongguo xiju chubanshe, 1986.

Zhongguo xiju shinian tashiji 中国戏剧十年大事记, 1976–1986 (The chronicle of Chinese dramatic events over ten years). *Xijujia tongxin zengkan* 戏剧家通信增刊 (A special edition of correspondence for dramatists). Beijing: *Zhongguo xiju nianjian* bianjibu, 1986.

Zhonghua Renmin Gongheguo zuigao renmin jianchayuan tebie jianchating qisushu 中华人民共和国最高人民检察院特别检察厅起诉书(Indictment of the Special Procurate of the Special Court under the Supreme People's Court in the People's Republic of China). *Renmin ribao*, Nov. 21, 1990.

Zhou Enlai. 周恩来 "Zhongguo Gongchandang dishici quanguo daibiao dahui shang de zhengzhi baogao" 中国共产党第十次全国代表大会上的政治报告 (Political report of the Chinese Communist Party's Tenth Congress). *Hongqi* 9 (1973): 5–17.

Zhu, Xiao Di. *Thirty Years in a Red House: A Memoir of Childhood and Youth in Communist China*. Amherst: University of Massachusetts Press, 1998.

Zhu Xijuan 祝希娟. "Cong nünu dao zhanshi" 从女奴到战士 (From slave girl to warrior). In Liang Xin, *Hongse Niangzijun: Cong junben dao dianying*, 305–319. Beijing: Zhongguo dianying chubanshe, 1964.

Zong Fuxian 宗福先 (Tsung Fu-hsien). *In a Land of Silence*, trans. Shu-ying Tsau. In Edward M. Gunn, ed., *Twentieth-Century Chinese Drama*, 409–443. Bloomington: Indiana University Press, 1983.

———. "Wode qian bansheng" 我的前半生 (My autobiography). *Shanghai xiju* 1 (1987): 23–24.

——. *Yuwu shengchu* 于无声处 (In a land of silence). *Renmin xiju* 12 (1978): 48–76.

——. "*Yuwu shengchu, Xue zongshi rede* chuangzuo tan"《于无声处》《血总是热的》创作谈 (How I wrote *In a Land of Silence* and *Blood Is Always Hot*). *Jiangsu xiju* 江苏戏剧 (Jiangsu drama) 7 (1984): 45–48.

Zou Ting 邹霆. "Nongdan yiren jian gongli" 浓淡宜人见功力 (Dramatic depth through a balanced depiction.) *Xiju yanjiu* 2 (1989): 50–52.

INDEX

Page numbers in *italic* refer to illustrations.

Save Her (*Jiujiu ta*), 187, 203, 374n. 16; *Small Well Lane* (*Xiaojing Hutong*), 214–215, 319, 376n. 42; *The Tempest in the Divine Land* (*Shenzhou fenglei*), 220–221, 233; as theater of the street, 56. See also *If I Were for Real* (*Jiaru woshi zhende*); *There Is a Small Courtyard* (*You zheyang yige xiaoyuan*); *Winter Jasmine* (*Baochunhua*)

anti imperialism, 63, 95–96, 148–150, 291. *See also* Eight Allied Armies (*Baguo Lianjun*)

Anti-Rightist campaign, 160, 166, 167

applause. *See* audience applause

April Fifth (1976) movement (*siwu yundong*), 49, 56, 197–198; Deng Xiaoping and, 222; official view of, 201–202; plays about, 197, 198–201, 204–205, 206–211. *See also* anti-Gang of Four plays

Arabic literature, 259

Arendt, Hannah, 255

Armed Working Team behind the Enemy's Lines, An (*Dihou wugong dui*), 77

art: Communist Party policies, 102, 188; in Cultural Revolution, 37–38, 90; exhibitions, 34, 38, 353n. 20; Maoist view of, 58, 80. *See also* paintings; posters

"Art comes from a life of struggle; the working people are the master," 57

artists: relationships with workers, 57

Attic: The Memoir of a Chinese Landlord's Son, The (Gao), 29–30

audience applause: approval conveyed by, 182–183, 242–243, 254, 315; censorship of, 143–144; comments of critics, 166; as signal of subversive understanding, 143–144, 164, 240

audiences: controlled, 180, 189; for experimental theater, 67; ideal spectator, 241; playwrights' interpretations of responses, 187; of post-

Maoist theater, 24, 25, 161–162; required attendance of model works, 33; roles, 25, 173; types, in Beijing, 321; women in, 241–242

Austin, Gayle, 323, 324

Austria, 32, 51–52

Azalean Mountain (*Dujuanshan*), 99, 111–116; heroine, 111, 113, *113*, 114–116; Jiang Qing and spoken drama version, 313; music scores, 120; performances, 112, 145; portrayals of women, 137–138; rhymed dialogue, 100; subject, 76

Baguo Lianjun. *See* Eight Allied Armies

Bai ethnic group, 63

Bai Fengxi: acting career, 243–244; feminism of works, 381n. 6; *First Bathed in Moonlight* (*Mingyue chu zhao ren*), 238–249, 258–259; intentions, 238; interview of author, 248; mother-daughter relationships in plays, 258–259; *An Old Friend Comes at a Stormy Time* (*Fengyu guren lai*), 249–255, 258–259; *Where is Longing in Autumn* (*Buzhi qiusi zai shui jia*), 255–259; women trilogy, 14, 237, 260, 312, 381n. 17

Bai Hua, 189

Bai Wei, 258, 263

Baimao nü. *See* White-Haired Girl, The

Bakhtin, Mikhail, 254, 383–384n. 53

Bali shengmuyuan. *See* Hunchback of Notre Dame, The

ballet: Western traditions, 85–86, 117–118. *See also* model ballets

Banu, Georges, 91, 92

Baochunhua. *See* Winter Jasmine

Baoziwan zhandou. *See* Leopard Boy Battle, The

Barmé, Gerenue, 294

Barthes, Roland, 238, 381n. 13

Bawang beiji. *See* Farewell My Concubine

histories of, 82; literature and art policies, 102, 188; plays about leaders, 94, 229–232; relations with United States, 52; Shanghai Municipal Party Committee, 87, 179–180; treatment of intellectuals, 188; view of April Fifth movement, 201–202

Chinese Dramatic Art Research Association, 312

Chinese Dramatists Association (Zhongguo xijujia xiehui), 187–188

Chinese Film Association (Zhongguo dianying xiehui), 188

Chinese Literature, 150

Chinese Women (*Zhonguo funü*), 272

Chinese Writers Association (Zhongguo zuojia xiehui), 188

Chuangye. See Pioneers, The

chuanju. See Sichuan opera

chuanqi. See romance drama

Chunliu she. *See* Spring Willow Society

Chusheng de taiyang. See Rising Sun, The

Chuxin. See New Creations

Ci, Jiwei, 80, 277

Civil War, 76

class struggle: Cultural Revolution theory, 59, 349n. 101; Maoist view of, 2, 7–8, 78, 151, 166; old society blamed for current problems, 78–80, 299; reflected in drama, 2, 7–8; themes of model works, 87, 95, 112

classes: blood theory (*xuetong lun*), 349n. 101; theatrical portrayals, 62. See also *Winter Jasmine* (*Baochunhua*)

classical music. *See* model symphonic works; symphonic works

Clinton, Bill, 31, 50–51

Collection of Tiananmen Poetry of 1976, The, 202–203

Columbus, Ohio, 144, 365n. 56

Commune de Paris, La (*Yingtao shijie*): Vallés, 96

Communist Party, Chinese. *See* Chinese Communist Party

Communist Party, Japanese, 156

composers, 89, 120

Confucianism, 300

Conteh-Morgan, John, 62–63

corruption, 183, 254, 314–315

Cui Dezhi, 167

cultural Mao Zedong, 145

Cultural Revolution: author's experiences, 13–14, 31–32, 35–36, 37, 40–46, 55–56, 71, 182; best-sellers published in West, 26–31; educated youth sent to countryside, 43–46, 204, 205–206; effects on actors and theater people, 13–14, 134, 201, 207–209, 213, 313; films set during, 46–47, 184–185, 186–188, 189; initiation, 58, 125, 177, 216–217; Mao's support of, 225; Mao's theory of, 142; mass criticism meetings, 217; memories of, 26, 32, 33, 144, 145; official accounts of, 53; plays set during, 160, 204–205, 220–221, 310; political theater, 47, 48, 53; purposes, 125; scholarship on, 26; street theater, 196–197, 217. *See also* model theater (*geming yangbanxi*); Red Guards

cultural studies, 123–124

Dachu youlingta. See Breaking out of Ghost Pagoda

Dadui de yewan. See Evening at the Production Brigade, An

Dai ethnic group, 63

Dai Jiafang, 89, 106, 362n. 4

Dai Jinhua, 24, 145, 192, 236, 258, 261–262, 263, 271

dancers: bodies of, 37, 118; in model works, 79–80; in Western ballet, 117–118

Daqing, 312–313, 314–319

Daqing City Theatre (Daqingshi huanjutuan), 312

Davis, Susan G., 196

meng), 307–309, 311; *The Dead Visiting the Living (Yige sizhe dui shengzhe de fangwen)*, 302–303; *Hot Currents Outside the House (Wuwai you reliu)*, 294–295; *The Nirvana of Gou'er Ye (Gou'er Ye niepan)*, 303–306; *Pan Jinlian*, 296–299, 300, 301; *Sangshuping Chronicles (Sangshuping jishi)*, 309–311; *Three Sisters Waiting for Godot (San zimei dengdai gedou)*, 66–67

families: effects of Cultural Revolution, 137; importance of background, 130, 165, 167, 349n. 101; nation as, 140, 141; revolutionary, 280, 282. *See also* grandmothers; mothers

family dramas: eliminated from model theater, 108–109; portrayals in model theater, 137, 138; in PRC period, 108; surrogate families in model works, 112–114, 129–131, 133, 134, 136, 138, 280; traditional operas, 108

Fang Zhenzhu (Lao), 9

Fangxia nide bianzi. See *Put Down Your Whip*

Fanon, Frantz, 154

Farewell My Concubine (Bawang beiji): film, 46–47, 347n. 59; Peking opera, 46–47

fascism, 140–141, 366n. 65

Fei, Faye Chunfang, 307

Fei xiong meng. See *Un-Russian Dream, An*

Feijialou de hunyin. See *Marriage of Figaro, The*

feminism: criticism of literary portrayals of women, 299; cultural, 231; Cultural Revolutionary, 109, 111, 236; of female playwrights, 235; Jiang Qing's abuse of, 216; of May Fourth movement, 96–98, 193, 235; official Chinese, 158, 236, 239, 314; in post-Maoist theater, 311; repudiation of,

190–191; in socialist societies, 252; theater studies, 238

feminist theater: British, 245, 385n. 73; characteristics, 260, 288, 381n. 6; in post-Maoist China, 288–289; scholarship on, 65. *See also* women's theater

Fengye hongle de shihou. See *When the Maple Leaves Turned Red*

Fengyu guren lai. See *Old Friend Comes at a Stormy Time, An*

Fighting in the Plain (Pingyuan zuozhan), 77, 95, 138

films: censorship, 185, 189; condemned during Cultural Revolution, 77; on national heroes, 312–313; peasant stories, 12; political influences, 84; portrayals of women, 190–191; scholarship on, 18–19; set during Cultural Revolution, 46–47, 184–185, 186–188, 189; shown during Cultural Revolution, 77; stars, 68; of traditional opera performances, 107

First Bathed in Moonlight (Mingyue chu zhao ren): absence of men, 245, 246–248, 249; audience responses, 240, 241–244; Bai, 238–249; blacklisting of, 244; characters, 238–241; debate on, 240–241, 244; mother-daughter relationship, 258–259; performances, 238; publication, 244; revised version, 244–245; subversive readings, 240, 242–244

Fish, Stanley, 186

Fission (Liebian): Xu, 284–286, 287–288, 289

Flanigan, Clifford C., 22–23

folk dramas, 63

folk opera (*geju*), 80. See also *White-Haired Girl, The (Baimao nü)*

Forced to Liang Mountain (Bishang Liangshan), 101

Forster, Friedrich, 59

Forum Theater, 174

Foucault, Michel, 265–266

Four Modernizations program, 123, 246, 247, 252

Fourth National Congress of Artists and Writers, 184–185

France: armed forces in China, 51–52, 95; colonies in Africa, 62–63; gender politics, 110–111; medieval drama, 23; Revolution, 219

Fraser, Nancy, 237

Freud, Sigmund, 117, 141

Fujian Province Drama Troupe (Fujiansheng huajutuan), 147

Fulian (All-China Women's Federation), 238, 239, 241, 258

Furongzhen. See *Small Town of Furong, The*

Gadberry, Glen W., 59

Gang of Four: arrests of followers, 120; crimes of, 165, 202, 222; criticism of, 172, 175–176, 179, 189; fall of, 81, 221, 313; trials, 222, 224–225. See also anti-Gang of Four plays; Jiang Qing

Gangtie shi zhenyang liancheng de. See *How Steel Is Made*

Gangtie yunshubing. See *Iron Transportation Troops*

Gao, Guanlong, 29–30

Gao Jian, 305, 307–308

Gao Jinxian, 245–246

Gao Xingjian: *The Alarm Signal* (*Juedui xinhao*), 66, 351n. 129; *Bus Stop* (*Chezhan*), 66, 294, 351n. 129; *Wildman* (*Yeren*), 66, 67

Gao Yuqian, 137

geju. See folk opera

geming xiandai wuju. See model ballets

geming yangbanxi. See model theater

Geming zihou houlai ren. See *Successor to Revolution*

gender politics: Chinese views of, 302; comparison of China and France, 110–111; patriarchy, 246–247, 251–252, 299, 311, 323; in PRC, 311. See also feminism; men; women

gender transgressions, 388n. 25

Germany: armed forces in China, 51–52, 95; medieval drama, 23; street theater in Nazi period, 56–58; theater, 5, 59–60. See also Brecht, Bertolt

Girl from a Green House, A (*Huafang guniang*), 69

Girl Kills a Snake, A (*Tongnü zhan she*), 100

Girl Thief (*Nüzei*), 185, 186–188

Goebbels, Joseph, 57, 60

Goffman, Erving, 174

Gogol, Nikolai: *The Inspector General*, 5, 170–172, 178–179

gong-nong-bing xiju. See worker, peasant, and soldier plays

Goodman, Lizbeth, 238, 260, 288

Gordon, Linda, 251

Gou'er Ye niepan. See *Nirvana of Gou'er Ye, The*

Grand Stage of the Twentieth Century, The (*Ershi shiji da wutai*), 93

grandmothers, portrayals of: in model theater, 136, 137–138, 146; in women's theater, 245–246

Great Britain. See Britain

Great Leap Forward, 12, 84, 99, 104, 217

Great Proletarian Cultural Revolution. See Cultural Revolution

Great Wall, 14

Greece: theater, 302, 309; women warriors in ancient, 386n. 7

Green Barracks (*Lüse yingdi*): Zhang, 262–270, 271, 284

group psychology, 117, 141

Gu Qing, 35–36, *Plate* 3

Gu Wei, 395n. 65

Guan Hanqing, 300

Guan Hanqing (Tian), 207–209, 213, 375n. 26

Guerrillas in the Plain, The (*Pingyuan youji dui*), 77

Guess Who's Coming to Dinner (*Caiyicai, shuilai chi wancan*), 8

Gui qu lai. See Homecoming
Guillotine (Duantou tai), 96
Guo Moruo, 235
Guo Shixing: Birdman (Niaoren), 324–330
Guojia dajuyuan. See National Grand Theater
guoju yundong. See national drama movement

Haguruma Theater, 156–157
Hai Rui Dismissed from Office (Hairui baguan): Wu, 58, 107, 177, 216–217
Haigang. See On the Docks
Haiqiao chun. See Spring of Overseas Chinese, The
Han people, 3, 64, 149
Hao Liang. See Qian Haoliang
Harwood, Ronald, 3, 32
Hatred in Life and Death (Shengsi hen): Mei, 101
He Jingzhi, 80. See also White-Haired Girl, The (Baimao nü)
He Jiping: The World's Top Restaurant (Tianxia diyilou), 212, 319–323, 324, 395n. 65
He Long, 94, 229
He Luding, 89
He Shushui, 35, 36, 38, Plate 2
He Zhaojun, 362n. 4
He Zizhen, 228, 229
Hebei Province, 222
Heilongjiang Province, 95
Heinu yutianlu. See Black Slave Cries Out to Heaven, The
Heise de shitou. See Black Stones
Heiye manman lu changchang. See Long Journey into Endless Night
heroes and heroines: foreign, 96; in model works, 94, 95, 174; national, 7, 94, 312–313; revolutionary, 34. See also revolutionary leader plays
Heroic Stories of New Sons and Daughters (Xin ernü yingxiong zhuan): Tian, 101

Hershkovitz, Linda, 50
Hezhe ethnic group, 63
Hezheren de hunli. See Marriage of the Hezhe People, The
His Billows on the Sea of Sin (Niehai bolan), 99–100
Hitler, Adolf, 32, 57, 58, 59, 141
Homecoming (Gui qu lai): Zhang, 271, 279–284
Hong Bingwen, 95
Hong gaoliang. See Red Sorghum
Hong Kong, 52, 145
Hong Sao, 106, 353n. 12
Hong Shen, 19, 108
Hongdeng ji. See Red Lantern, The
Hongdeng zhi. See Record of the Red Lantern, The
Hongdeng zhuan. See Story of the Red Lantern
Hongloumeng. See Dream of the Red Chamber, The
Hongqi. See Red Flag
Hongse de zendi. See Red Frontline
Hongse fengbao. See Red Storm
Hongse niangzijun. See Red Detachment of Women, The
Hongyun Hills (Hongyungang), 77
Hot Currents Outside the House (Wuwai you reliu), 294–295
How Steel Is Made (Gangtie shi zhenyang liancheng de), 7, 7
Hoxha, Enver, 156
Hsia, C. T., 18
Hu Bangwei, 299–300
Hu Shi, 102; The Main Event of One's Life (Zhongshen dashi), 291, 292–293
Hu Yaobang, 188, 370n. 36, 372n. 63
Hu Ying, 97
Hua Guofeng, 177, 200, 202, 206, 221, 370n. 36
Hua Mulan, 261–262, 263, 274, 386n. 2
Huafang guniang. See Girl from a Green House, A
huaiju. See northern Jiangsu opera
huaju. See modern Chinese drama

Huang Jusheng, 93, 94, 98
Huang Mei, 166, 168–169
Huang Shiren, 80
Huang Wen, 232
Huang Zi, 89
Huang Zuolin, 92, 306–307, 308
Huanghe. See Yellow River (Huanghe) piano concerto
Huayuanjie wuhao. See No. 5 Garden Street
huju. See Shanghai opera
human rights, 30–31
Hunchback of Notre Dame, The (Bali shengmuyuan), 85
Huo Wei, 89

I Am the Sun (Woshi taiyang), 390n. 61
Ibsen, Henrik, 5, 6, 22, 293; *Peer Gynt*, 22, 344n. 17. See also *Doll's House, A*
ideal spectator, 241
ideological state apparatuses (ISAs), 141–142
If I Were for Real (Jiaru woshi zhende): alienation effects, 170, 177–178; debate on, 176–177, 178, 179, 181, 184–185, 186–188, 203; official scrutiny of, 179–180; performances, 180; portrayals of women, 190, 192; satirical elements, 177–178; Sha, 169–173; subversive subtext, 172–173, 174–175
illusionist theater, 292–293, 306, 311–312, 319, 391n. 2
imagined communities, 128, 144, 148–150, 154, 157
imperialism: Chinese, 155, 157; European, 62–63, 95, 154, 155; Japanese, 62, 95, 96; Western, in China, 51–52, 155, 327. *See also* anti-imperialism
In a Land of Silence (Yuwu shengchu): Zong, 197, 198–201, 202, 203–204, 222, 233, 287
In the Archives of Society (Zai shehui de dang'an li), 184–185, 186–188, 190, 372n. 68

Indian Subaltern Studies Group, 118, 360n. 124
indigenous theater, 63, 319, 321, 393–394n. 47. *See also* Beijing-flavored plays; Northeastern-flavored drama (*Dongbei xiju*)
Injustice of Xuanting Kou, The (Xuanting yuan): Xiao, 94–95
Inspector General, The (Qinchai dachen): Gogol, 5, 170–172, 178–179
intellectuals: literary histories of China, 124–125; persecution in Cultural Revolution, 119, 120, 189, 201, 212, 213; political roles, 127; relationship with masses, 125, 127, 259; roles in model theater, 119, 120, 126, 158; treatment by Communist Party, 188; Western, 142; women, 248–249, 256–258, 259. *See also* May Fourth movement
Iron Transportation Troops (Gangtie yunshubing), 3–5, 4, 339–340n. 5
ISAs. *See* ideological state apparatuses
Italy: armed forces in China, 51–52, 95; fascism, 366n. 65
Itoh Hirobumi, 62, 96

Japan: armed forces in China, 51–52, 95; Chinese students in, 61, 350n. 112; foreign plays performed in, 61, 350n. 112; imperialism, 62, 95, 96; theatrical troupes, 156–157. *See also* War of Resistance to Japan
Japanese Communist Party, 156
Jauss, Hans Robert, 85, 186
Ji Junxiang, 20
Ji Shuping, 68, 71; experiences in Cultural Revolution, 41, 182; performances, 1–3, 5–6, 5, 6, 182; Xinjiang tour, 2
Jialilue zhuan. See Life of Galileo, The
Jiang Qing: abuse of feminism, 216; acting career, 216, 219, 227; criticism of, 81, 86, 215, 229; cultural workers' forum, 90; death sentence, 225; fall

Ma Sichong, 89

Main Event of One's Life, The (Zhong-shen dashi): Hu, 291, 292–293

Makesi liuwang Lundun. See *Marx in London Exile*

Makesi mishi. See *Secret History of Marx, The*

Mama, ni ye ceng nianqing. See *Mother, You Were Young Once Before*

Mannheim, Karl, 252

Mao Anying, 229

Mao cult, 144–145, 152–154

Mao Yuanxi Qiusheng, 94

Mao Zedong: on artists' roles, 57; attack on *Hai Rui Dismissed from Office*, 58, 107, 177; on class struggle, 2, 7, 151; criticism of traditional opera, 105; Cultural Revolution theory, 142; death, 221; depicted in plays, 226–229; founding of PRC, 52–53; "In Memory of Norman Bethume," 147; interest in traditional opera, 107; lack of blame for Cultural Revolution, 225; mausoleum plans, 218–219; in May Fourth period, 125; motives for Cultural Revolution, 125; on new Peking opera, 101; performances attended, 80, 86, 88, 107, 136; popular images, 141; popular song in praise of, 44, 58; portraits of, 367–368n. 95; on poverty, 78; public image, 143; published works, 82, 154; on racism, 351n. 122; relationship with He Zizhen, 228–229; relationship with Jiang Qing, 139, 218, 227–228; relationship with Yang Kaihui, 229; reviews of Red Guards, 53, 54–55, 196–197; similarities to Hitler, 58; sun as symbol for, 34, 81, 125, 140; support of Cultural Revolution, 225; support of model theater, 59, 107; swim across Yangtze River, 55; "Talks at the Yan'an Forum on Lit-

erature and Art," 38, 58–59, 80, 125, 151–152, 153

Marie-Antoinette, Queen of France, 219

Marriage of Figaro, The (Feijialou de hunyin), 1–2

Marriage of the Hezhe People, The (Hezheren de hunli), 63

marriages, arranged, 103, 239, 285, 311

Martial Songs Raised Our Spirit While Carrying Our Guns for the People (Zhange gu douzhi, kangqiang wei renmin), 35–36, *Plate 3*

Marx in London Exile (Makesi liuwang Lundun), 96, 230, 231

Marx, Karl, 96, 230–232, 318

May Fourth movement: demonstrations, 49, 341n. 19; feminism, 96–98, 193, 235; influence on Cultural Revolutionary literature, 126; influence on PRC culture, 82; literature, 273; opposition to traditional opera, 17, 102, 291; period, 341n. 19; plays, 8, 108, 291–292, 300; playwrights, 235, 258, 263; promotion of modern drama, 17; relationship to masses, 125; similarities to post-Maoist theater, 291–292; Western influences, 82, 97, 125; women playwrights, 258, 263

meditation on the historical or cultural past (*lishi wenhua fansi*), 310

Mei Lanfang, 91, 92, 99–100, 101, 107, 306

men: absence from plays, 245, 246–248, 249, 258; domestic role, 272; ideal images, 271; masculinity, 267, 268; patriarchy, 246–247, 251–252, 299, 311, 323; roles in post-Maoist China, 286

Meng Yue, 82–83, 84, 258

Merchant of Venice, The (Shakespeare), 318

Miaoling fenglei. See *Wind and Thunder of Mao Ridge*

military theme (*junshi ticai*) plays, 262. *See also* soldier plays

Miller, Arthur, 306, 316, 323

Min, Anchee, 28–29, 33–34

Mingyue chu zhao ren. See *First Bathed in Moonlight*

Ministry of Culture: authority over China Youth Art Theater, 8; Bureau of Theater Reform, 102; financing of theaters, 68; officials during Cultural Revolution, 73; persecution during Cultural Revolution, 222; theater blacklist, 244; theater reforms in 1950s, 103, 104–105

Mirzoeff, Nicholas, 115

missionary schools, 62

model actors, 120

model ballets (*geming xiandai wuju*): costumes, 118; dancers, 79–80; development of Chinese style, 87; female characters, 346n. 55; *Son and Daughter of the Grassland (Caoyuan ernü)*, 77–78, 96; *Song of Nimeng Mountain (Nimeng song)*, 76–77, 106, 138; use of form, 85–86; Western influences, 48, 85; women's bodies, 118. See also *Red Detachment of Women, The (Hongse niangzijun)*; *White-Haired Girl, The (Baimao nü)*

Model Opera for Children, 38–40, 39

model symphonic works: piano accompaniment to *The Red Lantern*, 77; *Shajiabang*, 76, 89, 90–91; Western influences, 48; *Yellow River (Huanghe)*, 77

model theater (*geming yangbanxi*): actors, 73–74, 120, 145; amateur performances, 32, 40, 45–46, 98, 119–120, 149; body movement, 116–117; children's performances, 38–40, 42; comparison to Nazi theater, 59, 60; concept of, 136; diverse cultural traditions in, 82, 84, 86–87; film adaptations, 89; functions, 78, 81–82;

heroes and heroines, 174; influence on politics, 74; lack of scholarship on, 25–26, 123; list of works, 33, 75, 76–78, 91, 352n. 11; Mao's support of, 59, 107; mass publication, 98, 134; performances, 33; performances in 1990s, 143–144, 145–146; performances in ethnic languages, 149; performances in United States, 144, 365n. 56; political messages, 37, 78–80, 81–82, 95, 112, 128; as political theater, 48–49; popularity, 126; principles, 95; relationships to posters and performances, 33–34, 37, 40; required attendance, 33; revisions of works, 81, 82, 83, 112; revolutionary experience represented in, 75–76, 77–78, 81–82, 92–93, 111–112; role models, 40; roots in traditional theater, 107; scholarship on, 124, 362n. 4; similarities to early twentieth-century works, 94–99; three prominences principle, 106–107, 358n. 91; traditional and Western forms, 48, 82; value of studying, 124; views of in post-Maoist China, 74, 123, 124; Western elements, 88–89, 91. *See also* Jiang Qing, roles in model theater; Peking opera model works

model troupes (*yangbantuan*), 217

modern Chinese drama (*huaju*): American students of, 71; anti-Gang of Four plays, 160; anti-imperialism, 291; canon, 62; challenges of writing, 19, 22; comparisons to traditional theater, 21; contradictions in, 291; early twentieth-century, 61–62, 101; foreign influences, 342n. 1; foreign performances, 343n. 5; history, 17, 60–62, 342n. 1; illusionist theater, 293; of late 1970s, 160; Mao's view of, 107; model works adapted from, 99; political aspects, 23, 61–62; in PRC period, 20; in Republican period, 85;

scholarship on, 18–20, 22, 23–24; social-problem plays, 160, 163–164, 190–193, 311; themes, 61; Western influences, 17, 21–22, 62, 291, 292–294, 342n. 1. *See also* post-Maoist theater

modern opera (*xiandai xi*), 99, 103, 104–105, 358n. 89

modernist theater, 293–294, 330

Modleski, Tania, 215

Mohanty, Chandra Talpade, 157–158

Möller, Eberhard Wolfgang, 59–60

Monroe, Marilyn, 142

Mother, You Were Young Once Before (*Mama, ni ye ceng nianqing*): Zhang, 271, 275–279

mothers: adopted children, 280–281; association with motherland and Mao, 259, 282; conflicts with sons, 278–279; ideal, 281; portrayals in model theater, 136, 137–138; relationships with daughters, 138, 258–259, 324; symbolism, 140, 259

Mu Gong, 124–128

Mulan. *See* Hua Mulan

multiculturalism, 149. *See also* ethnic minorities in China

music. *See* songs; symphonic works

musical instruments, 107

Nanjing: modern drama performances, 61–62

National Art Exhibition (Quanguo meishu zuopin zhanlanhui), 34, 38

National Association of Writers and Artists (Quanguo wenxue yishu gongzhuozhe lianhehui), 102

National Conference on Opera Scripts (Quanguo xiqu jumu gongzhuo huiyi), 104

national drama movement (*guoju yundong*), 22

National Grand Theater (Guojia dajuyuan), 67–68, 69

national identity: depicted in ballets, 96; expressed in plays, 131–132, 324, 327; ideal images, 271; role of theater, 10, 62, 64

National Modern Peking Opera Festival (Quanguo jingju xiandaixi guanmo yanshu dahui), 105

National Theater of Norway, 6

national theaters: creation of, 60. *See also* China Youth Art Theater

National Workers Union (Quanguo zonggonghui), 142, 203

nationalism: ceremonies, 53, 149, 196, 205; in Europe, 128; expressed in plays, 4–5, 93, 95–96, 157; imagined communities and, 128; parades, 196; roots of, 128

negritude, 154

Neighbors (*Zuoling youshe*): Su, 212

Never Forget Class Struggle (*Qianwan buyao wangji*), 108

New Creations (*Chuxin*), 35, 36, 38, Plate 2

New Daughter of Songling (*Songling xin nü'er*): Liu, 97–98

new drama (*xinju*), 102

New Ensembles from the Cultural Club, The (*Wenhuashi de xin jiemu*): Wang, 42, 43

New Fiction (*Xin xiaoshuo*), 97

new historical drama (*xinbian lishiju*), 101

New Rome (*Xin Luoma*): Liang, 93

Newspaper of Literature and Art (*Wenyi bao*), 143

Ng, Mau-sang, 97

nianhua-style paintings, 34, 35, 40

Niaoren. See *Birdman*

Nie Er, 89

Niehai bolan. See *His Billows on the Sea of Sin*

Nimeng song. See *Song of Nimeng Mountain*

Nirvana of Gou'er Ye, The (*Gou'er Ye niepan*): Jin, 303–306

Quanguo xiqu jumu gongzhuo huiyi.
See National Conference on Opera
Scripts
Quanguo zonggonghui. *See* National
Workers' Union
Quebec theater, 60

racial groups: discrimination, 61, 142;
Mao on racism, 351n. 122; Nazi
views, 59; theatrical portrayals, 61,
62, 95. *See also* ethnic minorities in
China
Raid on the White Tiger Regiment
(*Qixi Baihutuan*), 38, 76, 95–96,
138–139, 364n. 40, *Plate 4*
Railroad Guerrilla, The (*Tiedao youji
dui*), 77
*Rang shehui zhiyi xin wenyi zhanling
yiqie wutai. See* "Let Socialist New
Arts Occupy All Stages"
realistic theater, 292, 303
reception study, 186, 187
Record of the Red Lantern, The
(*Hongdeng zhi*), 134–135
Red Azalea (Min), 28–29, 33–34
Red Detachment of Women, The
(*Hongse niangzijun*) ballet: appeal
of, 86–87; characters, 117, 346n. 55,
355n. 40; comparison to *Green
Barracks*, 263–264; development of,
86, 88; film, 35, 84–85, 106, 117,
355n. 40; oil paintings of, 36, 36, 37–
38, 118, 346n. 55; performances, 86,
145, 365n. 56; photographs, 36; revisions, 86; scenes depicted in posters,
35; subject, 76
Red Detachment of Women, The
(*Hongse niangzijun*) Peking opera,
77
Red Flag (*Hongqi*), 98, 134
Red Frontline (*Hongse de zendi*), 38,
Plate 4
Red Guards: family backgrounds, 130,
349n. 101; memoirs, 26, 33; persecution of artists, 212; reviews in Tianan-

men Square, 53, 54–55, 196–197;
violence, 31–32, 47–48
Red Lantern, The (*Hongdeng ji*): actors,
73–74; amateur performances, 34;
anti-imperialism, 95; audience
responses, 134; comparison with
Black Stones, 314; development, 134–
135; gender in, 129; ideological state
apparatuses depicted in, 141–142;
Mao's reaction to, 107; music, 145;
performances, 143–144, 145; piano
accompaniment, 77; plot, 76, 128–
133; political impact, 142; political
messages, 141–142; popularity in post-
Maoist China, 143; posters related to,
34–35, 38, *Plate 1, Plate 4*; revised
version, 112, 134; Shanghai opera version, 100; subversive readings, 143–
144; success, 136; surrogate family,
129–131, 133, 134, 136, 280; traditional
and revolutionary cultures in, 136–
137; women portrayed in, 136
Red Sorghum (*Hong gaoliang*), 68
Red Storm (*Hongse fengbao*): Jin, 11, 11,
314, 342n. 23
Ren Huaying, 104, 105
Renan, Ernest, 146–147
*Rensheng budengshi. See Unequal For-
mula of Life*
Rent-Collecting Courtyard, The
(*Shouzu yuan*), 353n. 20
Republican China: modern drama in,
21–22, 85; Peking opera, 99–100;
women in, 279. *See also* May Fourth
movement
Republican Revolution (1911), 61–62
Resentment over the Lost Country
(*Wangguo hen*), 96
Resisting the Jin Invaders (*Kang jin-
bing*): Mei, 101
revolution: experiences dramatized
in model works, 75–76, 77–78, 81–
82, 92–93, 111–112; relationship to
theater, 48–49
revolutionary leader plays, 94, 229–232

revolutionary model theater. *See* model theater (*geming yangbanxi*)

Rising Sun, The (*Chusheng de taiyang*), 313

romance drama (*chuanqi*), 93–95, 98, 101

Romance of the Western Chamber, The (*Xixiang ji*), 106, 108

romance themes: absence from model theater, 108–109; in model works, 85, 116; in post-Maoist theater, 103–104; in PRC theater, 108

Romania, 156

Russia: armed forces in China, 51–52, 95; theater, 5, 7, 91, 91–92, 293. *See also* Chekhov, Anton; Gogol, Nikolai; Soviet Union

San zimei dengdai gedou. See Three Sisters Waiting for Godot

Sandai ren. See Three Generations

Sangshuping Chronicles (*Sangshuping jishi*), 309–311

Sanguo yanyi. See Three Kingdoms

Sanjiao qian geju. See Threepenny Opera, The

Sanshang Taofeng. See Three Visits to Taofeng Village

Save Her (*Jiujiu ta*), 187, 203, 374n. 16

Scarlet Memorial (Zheng), 30, 31

Schechner, Richard, 50

Schiller, Friedrich von, 5, 60

schools, missionary, 62

Secret History of Marx, The (*Makesi mishi*): Sha, 96, 230–232

Senanayake, R. D., 152

Senghor, Léopold Sédar, 154

sexual relationships: extramarital affairs, 298; in model theater works, 114–115, 117

Sha Yexin, 169; *Jiang Qing and Her Husbands* (*Jiang Qing he tade zhangfumen*), 215, 226–229, 312; *Secret History of Marx, The* (*Makesi mishi*), 96, 230–232. See also *If I Were for Real* (*Jiaru woshi zhende*)

Shaanxi opera (*jinju*), 217

Shaanxi Opera Troupe (Shaanxi jinjutuan), 217

Shajiabang (Peking opera): anti-imperialism, 95; body movement, 116–117; children's performances, 39; development, 106, 107; Mao's involvement, 107; performances, 74, 90, 145; portrayals of women, 109, 137; revisions, 112; subject, 75

Shajiabang (Shanghai opera), 100

Shajiabang (symphonic work), 76, 89, 90–91

Shakespeare, William, 318

Shanghai: Cultural Revolution in, 27–28; model works performed in, 99, 136; *On the Docks* (*Haigang*), 76, 95, 150–151; Peking opera in, 100; rivalry with Beijing, 100; theater in early twentieth century, 98; theaters, 60, 342n. 1

Shanghai Aihua Shanghai Opera Troupe (Shanghai aihua hujutuan), 134

Shanghai Dance School (Shanghai wudao xuexiao), 87

Shanghai Municipal Party Committee, 87, 179–180

Shanghai Number One Peking Opera Troupe (Shanghai jingju yituan), 99

Shanghai opera (*huju*), 100, 103, 106, 134, 135

Shanghai People's Art Theater (Shanghai renmin yishu juyuan), 169

Shanghai People's Shanghai Opera Troupe (Shanghai renmin hujutuan), 103, 106

shaoshu minzu xiju. See ethnic minority plays

Shen Yi, 166

Shengsi hen. See Hatred in Life and Death

Strand, David, 49

street theater: in Beijing courtyards, 213–214; comparative studies, 56–57; in Cultural Revolution, 196–197, 217; in Nazi Germany, 56–58; official, 195, 202–203; parades, 196; performance codes, 196; in Philadelphia, 196; protests, 195, 205–206; in wartime, 235–236; women's roles, 233. *See also* political theater; theater of the street; Tiananmen Square

Strindberg, August, 293

Student Wave (Xue hai chao), 96

Su Shuyang, 212–213

subalterns: portrayals in model theater, 158; relationship with intellectuals, 125, 127, 259; status in PRC, 118–119, 360–361n. 124; women as, 239, 259

Successor to Revolution (Geming zihou houlai ren), 134–135

suggestive theater, 306–309

Sun Weishi, 313, 340n. 14

Sun, William Huizhu, 307

"Swimming across the Ten-thousand-mile Yangtze River," 56

swimming contests, 55–56

symphonic works: Chinese composers, 89; uses in Nazi Germany, 58; Western, 89–90. *See also* model symphonic works

Taiping Lake (Taipinghu): Su, 212–213, 376n. 34, 393–394n. 47

Taking Sides (Harwood), 32

Taking Tiger Mountain by Strategy (Zhiqu Weihushan): anti-imperialism, 95; body movement, 117; Mao's revisions, 107; modern drama version, 99; performances, 99, 105, 145; portrayals of women, 109–110; posters related to, 38–39, 39; source, 99, 357n. 75; subject, 76

"Talks at the Yan'an Forum on Literature and Art" (Mao), 38, 58–59, 80, 125, 151–152, 153

Tang Jixiang, 38, *Plate 4*

Tang Na, 226–227, 379n. 79

Tang Xianzu, 300

Taohua shan. See Peach Blossom Fan

teachers, English-language, 247, 248

Teahouse (Chaguan): changing views of, 185–186; comparison to *The World's Top Restaurant*, 321–322; female characters, 324; foreign performances, 343n. 5; Lao, 212, 214, 319; theme, 108

television, 69–70, 107, 301

Tempest in the Divine Land, The (Shenzhou fenglei), 220–221, 233

Terrill, Ross, 225–226

theater: border-crossing in, 159–160, 161, 175; in early twentieth century, 93–95, 96–98; history of, 299–300; number of openings, 341n. 16; reform attempts, 101–102, 105, 107–108; reforms in 1950s, 102–103, 104–105; reforms in PRC, 102; relationship to real life, 169, 184, 188; relationship to revolution, 48–49. *See also* audiences; modern Chinese drama (*huaju*); post-Maoist theater

theater of liberation, 173, 174

theater of the street: anti-Gang of Four plays, 56; audiences' views of, 200; debates, 203; depictions of April Fifth 1976 events, 56, 197, 198–201, 204–205, 206–211; illusionist, 311–312; importance, 203–204; meaning of term, 197; political context, 202. *See also* political theater; street theater

Theater Reform Association (Xiqu gaijin hui), 102

There Is a Small Courtyard (You zheyang yige xiaoyuan), 204–205, 206–211; allusions to other plays, 207–211, 213–214; Beijing-flavored play style, 312, 319; political allusions, 222; portrayals of women, 233; publication of text, 163

Third World: as community, 148–150; national liberation movements, 63, 150–154, 155–156; theatrical troupes, 153; women, 157–158; writers from, 152–153

Thomas Paine (Johst), 60

Three Generations (*Sandai ren*), 134

Three Kingdoms (*Sanguo yanyi*), 299

three prominences principle, 106–107, 358n. 91

Three Sisters, The (Chekhov), 66

Three Sisters Waiting for Godot (*San zimei dengdai gedou*): Lin, 66–67

Three Visits to Taofeng Village (*Sanshang Taofeng*), 217

Threepenny Opera, The (*Sanjiao qian geju*): Brecht, 70

Thunderstorm (*Leiyu*): Cao, 199, 259, 279, 286–287

Tian Han, 101, 103, 108, 208; *Guan Hanqing*, 207–209, 213, 375n. 26

Tian Xuxiu, 294

Tiananmen Square: founding of PRC, 52–53, 195; May Fourth demonstrations, 49, 341n. 19; National Day observances, 53, 149, 196, 205; plans for National Grand Theater, 67–68, 69; plays set in, 220–221; poetry posted in, 198, 199, 202–203; political geography, 50; political theater in, 49–50, 195, 196; protests, 206; reviews of Red Guards, 53, 54–55, 196–197; scholarship on, 51–55; street theater, 196–197, 233; student demonstrations (1989), 49–50, 120, 188; visits of American presidents, 51; Zhou's funeral, 218. *See also* April Fifth (1976) movement

Tianjin, 85

Tianxia diyilou. See World's Top Restaurant, The

Tibetans: theater, 63–64

Tiedao youji dui. See Railroad Guerrilla, The

Token of Love (*Luohan qian*), 103

Tokyo: Chinese student performances, 61, 350n. 112

Tolstoy, Leo, 296

Tong ethnic group, 63

Tonggan gongku. See Joys and Sorrows

Tongnü zhan she. See Girl Kills a Snake, A

traditional opera (*xiqu*): body movement, 116–117; comparison to Western theater, 21; conventions used to interpret political events, 49; family dramas, 108; filmed, 107; genres, 104; journals, 93; Kunqu opera (*kunju*), 98, 134; Maoist view of, 91, 105, 107; meaning of term, 356n. 59; opposition of May Fourth intellectuals, 17, 102, 291; performances, 104, 105; popularity, 104; portrayals of women, 301; reforms, 93–95, 101–102, 103, 104–105, 126; regional, 103; scholarship on, 20, 21; Sichuan opera (*chuanju*), 87, 224, 296. *See also* Peking opera (*jingju*); Shanghai opera (*huju*)

tragedy, 316

Tung, Constantine, 244–245, 254

Tunnel War (*Didao zhan*), 77

Uncle Doggie's Nirvana. See Nirvana of Gou'er Ye, The (*Gou'er Ye niepan*)

Uncle Tom's Cabin (Stowe), 61, 98

Uncle Vanya (*Wanniya jiujiu*): Chekhov, 5, 6

Unequal Formula of Life (*Rensheng budengshi*): Zhang, 271, 272–275

United States: armed forces in China, 51–52, 95; Asian American studies, 142; books on Cultural Revolution, 27; Chinese Americans, 144, 324–325; Chinese immigrant exclusion acts, 95; Chinese immigrants, 61; drama, 8, 62, 306, 323, 324; ethnic

responses, 79, 87; ballet, 83, 87, 88; criticism of, 80–81; film, 83; folk opera version, 80, 81, 82–83, 354n. 24; folktale, 80, 82; history, 80, 81; performances, 87–88, 145; plot, 76, 80; political messages, 79–80, 81; posters related to, 40, 41; revisions, 83; themes, 87

Wild Grass (Yecao): Zhang, 319

Wilder, Thornton, 295

Wilderness, The (Yuanye): Cao, 284

Wildman (Yeren): Gao, 66, 67

Wind and Thunder of Mao Ridge (Miaoling fenglei), 100

Winter Jasmine (Baochunhua), 164–169; audience responses, 166, 167–168; performances, 164–165, 203; plot, 165; political message, 177; portrayals of women, 191–192; subversive subtexts, 168; success, 164, 168, 203

Witness History of Tiananmen, A (Wen), 51–53

WM, 294

women: audience members, 241–242; autobiographies, 28; in era of economic change, 255–258, 271; ideal images, 271, 281, 288; intellectuals, 248–249, 256–258, 259; literary characters, 273–274, 289, 299–301; Mao's view of roles, 313; Marx and, 230–231, 232; in patriarchal society, 297; in Republican period, 279; roles in French public sphere, 110–111; roles in post-Maoist China, 262, 272, 273, 274, 279, 289; roles in Western ballets, 117–118; single, 257–258; soldiers, 110, 262–270; status in PRC, 118–119, 233, 239, 311; theatrical directors, 70; in Third World, 157–158; traditional representations, 281; traditional roles, 250–251, 261–262, 264, 314; voicelessness, 236. See also bodies, women's; mothers

women playwrights: illusionist plays, 312; May Fourth, 258, 263; in post-Maoist China, 262, 271; preoccupation with women's public roles, 284; roles, 65. See also Bai Fengxi; He Jiping; Zhang Lili

women warriors: ancient Greek, 386n. 7; Green Barracks (Lüse yingdi), 262–270; Hua Mulan, 261–262, 263, 274, 386n. 2; interest in, 271–272; in model works, 109, 110, 115–116; traditional representations, 261, 263, 270–271. See also Azalean Mountain (Dujuanshan); Red Detachment of Women, The (Hongse niangzijun)

women's liberation: Maoist view of, 263–264; themes in early twentieth-century plays, 96–98, 193; themes of model works, 96–97, 115; themes of post-Maoist plays, 296, 301; Western discourse, 253. See also feminism

women's portrayals in model theater, 108–110; in ballets, 117–118, 346n. 55; bodies, 108, 115–116, 117, 118; equality, 236; gender roles, 114, 129; mothers and grandmothers, 136, 137–138, 146; perfection, 148; roles in public sphere, 108, 109, 111, 236; as symbols, 117–118, 136, 146–147; theatrical conventions, 108; Third World women, 157–158; traditional roles, 136; as warriors, 109, 110, 115–116

women's portrayals in theater: anti-Gang of Four heroines, 219–220, 233; in Beijing-flavored plays, 322–324, 329, 396n. 81; destructive, ugly characters, 284–286, 287, 289; in military, 262–270, 272; mother-daughter relationships, 258–259, 324; in post-Maoist theater, 190–193, 236, 250–251, 288; in socialist theater, 313–314; in social-problem plays, 190–193; in traditional opera, 301; traditional roles, 190–191; in United States, 324;

as victimized other, 190; wives of workers, 313, 314

women's theater: absence of men, 245, 246–248, 249, 258; audience responses, 254; death of the author, 238; domestic life, 249, 252–253; grandmothers, 245–246; issues, 236–237; limitations, 260; May Fourth period, 258; post-Maoist, 236–237; use of term, 381n. 6. *See also* Bai Fengxi; feminist theater

Wong, Jan, 47, 142–143

Wong, Sau-ling C., 142

Woolf, Virginia, 281

worker, peasant, and soldier plays (*gong-nong-bing xiju*), 11–13, 108, 314–319. *See also* peasant plays; soldier plays

worker plays: *Black Stones (Heise de shitou)*, 312–313, 314–319; *Never Forget Class Struggle (Qianwan buyao wangji)*, 108; *On the Docks (Haigang)*, 76, 95, 150–151; *Red Storm (Hongse fengbao)*, 11, 11, 314, 342n. 23; *The Rising Sun (Chusheng de taiyang)*, 313. See also *Red Lantern, The (Hongdeng ji)*; *Winter Jasmine (Baochunhua)*

workers: family backgrounds, 167; internationalism, 150–151; labor unions, 141–142, 203; model, 353n. 17; national heroes, 312–313; petroleum industry, 312–313, 314–319; relationships with artists, 57

World War II. *See* War of Resistance to Japan

World's Top Restaurant, The (Tianxia diyilou): He, 212, 319–323, 324, 395n. 65

Woshi taiyang. See I Am the Sun

Wu Han: *Hai Rui Dismissed from Office (Hairui baguan)*, 58, 107, 177, 216–217

Wu Hong, 50

Wu Song, 301

Wu Xue, 314–315

Wu Yuxiao, 2–3

Wu Zuguang, 91–92

Wu'er Kaixi, 49–50

Wuling Spring (Wuling chun), 95

Wuwai you reliu. See Hot Currents Outside the House

Xia Chun, 395n. 65

Xia Jianqing, 135

Xian Xinghai, 89

xiandai xi. See modern opera

Xiao nüxu. See Child Husband

Xiao Qian, 22, 344n. 17

Xiao Shanxiang Lingxi, 94–95

Xiaojing Hutong. See Small Well Lane

Xie Boliang, 100, 106–107, 134, 135, 362n. 4

Xie Zhenhua, 218

Xin ernü yingxiong zhuan. See Heroic Stories of New Sons and Daughters

Xin Luoma. See New Rome

Xin xiaoshuo. See New Fiction

xinbian lishiju. See new historical drama

Xing Zhi, 103

Xinjiang Uighur Autonomous Region, 2–3

xinju. See new drama

xiqu. See traditional opera

Xiqu gaijin hui. See Theater Reform Association

Xiwang chang'an. See Looking Westward to Chang'an

Xixiang ji. See Romance of the Western Chamber, The

Xu Banmei, 99, 342n. 1

Xu Yan: *Fission (Liebian)*, 284–286, 287–288, 289; *Oh, Women*, 390n. 61

xuanchuandui. See propaganda teams

Xuanting yuan. See Injustice of Xuanting Kou, The

Xue hai chao. See Student Wave

ABOUT THE AUTHOR

Xiaomei Chen received her doctorate in comparative literature from Indiana University. Her publications include *Occidentalism: A Theory of Counter-Discourse in Post-Mao China* (Oxford University Press, 1995; revised second edition, Rowman & Littlefield, forthcoming) and *Reading the Right Text: An Anthology of Contemporary Chinese Drama* (University of Hawai'i Press, forthcoming). She is currently associate professor of Chinese and comparative literature at Ohio State University.